D0223520

FEMINIST THEORY READER

Feminist Theory Reader is an ideal reader for courses in gender and women's studies, and social theory more generally. The third edition updates the collection of important classical and contemporary works of feminist theory within a multiracial transnational framework. This edition includes 16 new essays; the editors have organized the readings into four sections.

Section I—Theorizing Feminist Times and Spaces—REVISED SECTION

Classical conversations and debates about gender, difference, and women's experiences are juxtaposed with essays that challenge the prevailing representation of feminism as waves. It includes both documents-of-the-moment and alternative genealogies of feminist theory.

Section II—Theorizing Intersecting Identities

Readings theorize the intersections of gender with class, race, nation, religion, ethnicity, globalization, and sexuality. It includes readings that investigate social processes of gender identity formation and first person essays by feminist scholars reflecting on the complex identities they negotiate in professional and personal lives.

Section III—Theorizing Feminist Knowledge and Agency

Epistemological conversations between standpoint and poststructural theories that debate the grounds of feminist knowledge-building and gender identity formation in social experience and discourse.

Section IV—Imagine Otherwise—NEW SECTION

Readings present new tools for building effective knowledge for social justice in a world of asymmetrical relational differences. Topics include bodies, emotions, identity, difference, connection, and transnational social justice.

Introductory essays by the editors placed at the beginning of each of the four major sections lay out the framework that brings the readings together, and provide historical and intellectual context of the readings.

Carole R. McCann is Director and Professor of Gender and Women's Studies and an affiliate faculty member of the Language, Literacy, and Culture Graduate Program at the University of Maryland, Baltimore County (UMBC). Her research expertise includes, feminist science studies, twentieth century history of birth control, eugenics, and population, and feminist theory. Her publications include *Birth control Politics in the United States, 1916–1945* (Cornell University Press, 1994, 1999). She is currently working on a book manuscript about masculinities in mid-century population sciences.

Seung-kyung Kim is Director and Associate Professor and Chair of Women's Studies at the University of Maryland College Park. Her research expertise includes gender and labor politics, Ethnography, Feminist Theory, and Women in East Asia and Asian America. The author of numerous articles and book chapters, her publications include *Class Struggle or Family Struggle? Lives of Women Factory Workers in South Korea* (Cambridge University Press, 1997, 2009); *South Korean Feminists Bargain: Progressive Presidencies and the Women's Movement, 1998–2007* (forthcoming, Routledge). She is currently working on a book manuscript, *Global Citizens in the Making? Transnational Migration and Education in Kirogi Families.*

FEMINIST
LOCAL AND GLOBAL
THEORY
PERSPECTIVES
READER

THIRD EDITION

Edited by

CAROLE R. McCANN AND SEUNG-KYUNG KIM

LIBRARY
ANTIOCH UNIVERSITY
LOS ANGELES

Routledge
Taylor & Francis Group

NEW YORK AND LONDON

First published 2013
by Routledge
711 Third Avenue, New York, NY 10017

Simultaneously published in the UK
by Routledge
2 Park Square, Milton Park, Abingdon, Oxon OX14 4RN

Routledge is an imprint of the Taylor & Francis Group, an informa business

© 2013 Taylor & Francis

The right of the editors to be identified as the authors of the
editorial material, and of the authors for their individual chapters,
has been asserted in accordance with sections 77 and 78 of the
Copyright, Designs and Patents Act 1988.

All rights reserved. No part of this book may be reprinted or reproduced
or utilised in any form or by any electronic, mechanical, or other means,
now known or hereafter invented, including photocopying and recording,
or in any information storage or retrieval system, without permission in
writing from the publishers.

Trademark notice: Product or corporate names may be trademarks or
registered trademarks, and are used only for identification and
explanation without intent to infringe.

Library of Congress Cataloging in Publication Data
    Feminist theory reader : local and global perspectives /
    Edited by Carole R. McCann and Seung-Kyung Kim.—Third Edition.
    pages cm
    Includes bibliographical references and index
    1. Feminist Theory. I. McCann Carole R. (Carole Ruth), 1955–
    II. Kim, Seung-Kyung, 1954–
    HQ1190.F46346 2013
    305.4201—dc23
    2012032636

ISBN: 978–0–415–52101–7 (hbk)
ISBN: 978–0–415–52102–4 (pbk)
ISBN: 978–0–203–59831–3 (ebk)

Typeset in Minion
by Swales & Willis Ltd, Exeter, Devon

Printed and bound in the United States of America by Sheridan Books, Inc. (a Sheridan Group Company).

CONTENTS

PREFACE TO THE THIRD EDITION

In the introduction to the first edition of *Feminist Theory Reader*, we expressed our hope that it would challenge readers, as we challenged ourselves, to rethink the complex meanings of difference outside of contemporary Western feminist contexts. The second edition extended that challenge, encouraging readers to rethink the numerous ways in which gender, sexuality, race, ethnicity, class, religion, and nationality are reconfigured by emerging global–local configurations of power. The third edition assembles readings that rethink feminist times and spaces by challenging the prevailing representation of feminist movements as waves.

In this third edition, Section I has been reorganized to include both historical accounts and documents-of-the-moment that archive the ideas and emotions of the mid- and late-twentieth-century feminisms. Together these reading enrich our understanding of the many histories of feminist theory. In addition, a new Section IV, Imagine Otherwise, draws on recent efforts to move beyond the debates between postmodern and standpoint theories towards frameworks that build on the strengths of each perspective. These frameworks renew discussion of the grounds for feminist solidarity, and they reassert the social group women, however unstable, as the agent of feminist politics. In particular, the section includes feminist analyses of emotions, bodies, and affect. The new edition endeavors to continue to expand the diverse voices of transnational feminist scholars throughout.

Introductory essays by the editors placed at the beginning of each of the four major sections lay out the framework that brings the readings together, provide historical and intellectual context for the readings, and, where appropriate, point to critical additional readings not included here. Five core theoretical concepts—gender, difference, women's experiences, the personal is political, and intersectionality—anchor the anthology's organizational framework. The introductory essay for Section I provides a detailed discussion of these concepts.

Other than those changes, the *Reader* retains the same structure as the second edition. Section II, Theorizing Intersecting Identities, examines macro-level processes that configure intersections of gender, race, class, geographic/national, and/or sexual differences. Readings alternatively focus attention on the material and discursive processes connecting capitalism, patriarchy, heteronormativity, Orientalism, and globalization. In addition, it presents personal narratives that reflect on the subjective experiences of intersecting social processes. The readings delineate the complex politics of shifting locations and blurred boundaries, and they illuminate the tensions pervading experiences of intersecting identities, and border-crossings.

Section III presents two key feminist theoretical currents: standpoint theories and poststructuralist theories. Readings make the demanding concepts used in these theories more accessible for students by introducing concepts and frameworks, particularly the concepts of the disciplined body, Orientalism, the nation, and heteronormativity.

The new edition includes 16 new readings. The editors have provided test questions, which instructors can request from textbooksonline@taylorandfrancis.com.

ACKNOWLEDGMENTS FOR THE THIRD EDITION

We were first inspired to compile a feminist theory reader in 1995 through a Ford Foundation's Summer Institute on Women and Gender in an Era of Global Change, a faculty development seminar offered by the Curriculum Transformation Project at the University of Maryland, College Park, where we first met. Both of us have taught theories of feminism courses for many years. In many ways, our development as feminist scholars, teachers, and as editors of this volume has moved as U.S. women's studies has moved. We belong to the generation who lived through the 1970s women's movements in Korea and the United States, and who received graduate training in Women's Studies in the U.S. in the 1980s. Through our training and subsequent teaching experiences in the 1990s, we became convinced that "women's studies core curricula that remain exclusively oriented to U.S. content and Western feminist perspectives no longer meet the standards of scholarly rigor and political relevance that define our field" (McDermott 1998: 88). We each decided to participate in the faculty development seminar as a way to begin to incorporate into our courses "the experiences, voices, and strategies for change of women around the world" (Rosenfelt 1998: 4).

While revising our courses, we often complained about the difficulty we had in locating a suitable upper-level feminist theory anthology. This difficulty prompted us to develop our own selection of readings, and our feminist theory courses became the experimental sites where we tried, revised, and retired various collections of articles. In addition, the process of our collaborative work shaped the final form of this reader in a very fundamental way. Over the several years of reading and teaching, we engaged in an extended dialogue that we found to be incredibly valuable. Through our own efforts to construct and update a coherent textbook of feminist theory without losing the particularity of different locations and opportunities for creating feminist theory, we constructed a strong personal friendship and a professional association that has greatly enriched our other scholarship and our teaching. Our ongoing collaboration embodies the kind of dialogue often recommended as a productive way to build effective feminist knowledge and alliances between women of the global north and south in an era of ever expanding globalization (Taylor 1993). This collaboration has continued to be very rewarding for both of us as we worked on each subsequent edition.

Many individuals have aided our collaboration through the years. First and foremost, we thank the students in our feminist theory classes. As with the first and second editions, we tried out several combinations of articles in our classrooms before deciding on the revisions to the third edition. Through the years, sometimes complaining and sometimes enjoying the endless readings we required them to do, students have been very generous in sharing their thoughts. Their insights, critiques, and suggestions have been invaluable in making this reader more accessible.

We thank Debby Rosenfelt, Director of Curriculum Transformation Project and Summer Institute at the University of Maryland, College Park, who provided an opportunity for us to meet and work together. Debby has been supportive of our project throughout the past seventeen years and her continuous words of encouragement have meant a lot to us. We also thank our colleagues in the Department of Women's Studies at the University of Maryland College Park and Gender and Women's Studies Program at the University of Maryland, Baltimore County (UMBC) for the vibrant intellectual communities that sustain our work: Amy Bhatt, Jessica Berman, Elsa Barkley Brown, Lynn Bolles, Bonnie Dill, Kate Drabinski, Katie King, Jason Loviglio, Viviana MacManus, Christine Mallinson, Jeffrey McCune, Pat McDermott, Claire Moses, Tara Rodgers, Michelle Rowley, Catherine Schuler, Orianne Smith, Ashwini Tambe, Elle Trusz, and Ruth Zambrana.

We are grateful to our editor, Steven Rutter for recognizing the value of this anthology and for his continuing support throughout the long process of preparing the current edition. Steve arranged for several reviewers to provide their assessments of the *Reader*. We would like to thank Alejandra Elenes, Arizona State University; Audrey Bilger, Claremont Mckenna College; Mimi Marinucci, Eastern Washington University; Angela Hubler, Kansas State University; Kimberly Williams, Mount Royal University; Althea L. Tait, Old Dominion University; Janet Lee, Oregon State University; Angelique Nixon, University of Connecticut; and Emily Noelle Ignacio, University of Washington for the time and attention they gave to their thoughtful reviews. We have benefited tremendously from their insightful suggestions and incorporated many into the current edition. In addition, we thank all the women's studies professors and students at conferences who have offered us their appraisal of the anthology's strengths and weaknesses. We greatly appreciate this feedback. It is always useful to hear comments and suggestions from those who use the anthology in classrooms because our goal is to compile a useful pedagogical resource.

We have been very lucky to have the assistance of graduate students to help us the with manuscript preparation. In particular, we are indebted to Emek Ergun for her tireless efforts in support of this project. Jeannette Soon and Carissa Liro-Hudson also provided timely assistance with in the final weeks of revision. Their work has made this process much easier.

Lastly, we would like to thank our families for their support and assistance: Carole thanks Mel and Rustin. Seung-kyung thanks John, Anna, and Ellen.

FEMINIST THEORY: LOCAL AND GLOBAL PERSPECTIVES

In its most general sense, the word "feminism" refers to political activism by women on behalf of women. The term originated in France in the 1880s. It combines the French word for woman, "femme," with the suffix meaning political position, "ism," and was used in that time and place to refer to those who defended the cause of women (Cott 1986b; Moses 1998a). Widely used in the U.S. women's movements beginning in the 1970s, it indicated opposition to women's subordinate social positions, spiritual authority, political rights, and/or economic opportunities. However, beyond that general description, the meaning of feminism has never been historically stable or fixed (Delmar 1986; Moses 1998a). For all its ambiguity and limitations, the term nonetheless signals an emancipatory politics on behalf of women. It contends that the prevailing unjust conditions under which women live must be changed. Moreover, it assumes that a group of historical agents—women—will take action to change them.

Feminist theories, like other political philosophies, provide intellectual tools by which historical agents can examine the injustices they confront and build arguments to support their particular demands for change. Feminist theories apply their tools to building knowledge of women's oppression.[1] That knowledge is intended to inform strategies for resisting subordination and improving women's lives. Feminist theories ask questions, including: How do structures of gender difference subordinate women as women? How can we understand the ways in which specific events result from gender oppression, rather than unique individual misfortune? How can we be sure that we have clear understandings of oppressive situations? How is women's subordination as women connected to related oppressions based on race, ethnicity, nationality, class, and sexuality? How can women resist subordination? What kinds of changes are needed?

Answers to these kinds of questions make assumptions about who "we" are, how and why things got to be the way they are, and what changes may be needed. In other words, answers to these questions rest on some notion of ontology (theories of being and reality), epistemology (theories of how knowledge is produced), and politics (relations and practices of power). The last term is, perhaps, the most important purpose of feminist theory: to inform effective politics. A central principle of feminist theory is that theory should be accountable to politics. It should make sense of women's situations and point to effective strategies for change.[2]

This anthology assembles readings that present key aspects of the conversations and debates[3] within multiracial and transnational U.S. feminisms, and places those local conversations and debates within a global perspective. As Amrita Basu observes in the article included here, the term "global … may connote the breadth and universality that is often associated with Western feminism." On the other hand, as she notes, the term "local … can connote the supposed particularism, provincialism and primordialism of the Third World." Instead, she offers a more specific definition, which we follow. We use the term "local" to refer to "indigenous and regional" feminist theories and movements, in whatever region they arise. We use the term "global" to refer to theories and movements that emerge within "transnational" locations and discourses (Basu Reading 6). In juxtaposing feminist voices from the United States, Europe, Latin America, Asia, Africa, and Australia, we highlight the complex relationships of local and global feminist theories to transnational women's and gender movements. Transnational refers to the literal movement of people, ideas, and resources across national boundaries. At the same time, when used to refer to persons, it evokes the processes and experiences of crossing geopolitical borders and identity boundaries. Such crossings have both physical and psychological implications, as migrants live their lives both here and there, physically separated from but often in frequent contact with kin, community, and culture (Parreñas Reading 20). Many of the authors included here are transnational in both their personal and professional identities.

The global feminisms Basu identifies emerge from the linkages, networks, and alliances between a diverse array of organizations, movements, and issue-based campaigns that have developed within global civil society. In the context of the four conferences on women convened by the United Nations since 1975, international political leaders and non-governmental women's groups from around the world have articulated international law concerning women's rights, have struggled over the terms of international women's activism, and have developed enduring linkages and alliances. Transnational feminist organizations, movements, and campaigns are firmly grounded in the rights articulated in the 1979 Convention on the Elimination of All Forms of Discrimination Against Women.[4] But the new space of feminist agency and transnational women's movements created within global civil society is not one in which all women are suddenly equal nor one in which all women have the same concerns. Global civil society reverberates with historical power relations of race, colonialism, class, and gender. These shifting sites of power continue to shape the possibilities and limitations for feminist politics even as new forms of domination emerge with new forms of globalization. Thus, the relationships of local and global, even the meaning and use of these words, arise in historically specific contexts (Grewal and Kaplan 1994).

In the ten years since the first edition of *Feminist Theory Reader*, unrelenting globalization has come to frame the local and the global in new and expanding ways.[5] Globalization (discussed in greater depth in Section II: Introduction) refers to the "social, economic, cultural, and demographic processes that take place within nations but also transcend them" (Parreñas Reading 20). Although globalization began to intensify during the last two decades of the twentieth century, since 2001 we have witnessed evergreater speed and reach of communications, surveillance, and financial technologies.

Economic, political, cultural, technological, and demographic exchanges around the world deny the possibility of isolated local spaces. Thus, neither the local nor the global are pure, homogeneous, or mutually exclusive sites for either feminist interventions or the workings of global capitalism. The realities and practices of global–local inter-sections are instead fraught with contradictions and dislocations configured in and through messy and multidirectional global cultural flows (Appadurai 1996).

The feminist conversations and debates we present here are anchored by five theo-retical concepts—gender, difference, women's experiences, the personal is political, and intersectionality—which have been integral to late twentieth and early twenty-first-century feminisms and to the field of women's and gender studies (Grant 1993). These five concepts and tracing the tensions between them in feminist dialogues and debates provide a useful heuristic device for learning feminist theory. However, there is and can be no one theory of gender subordination or one strategy for change because women live in so many different social, economic, cultural, and political circum-stances. Nor has the development of feminist theory been linear or unidirectional. No final answers have emerged. Thus, the readings brought together here do not present a single homogenous story. We do not claim that this collection of essays speaks "for everybody, to everybody, or about everything" (Young 1990: 13). There are interrup-tions, overlaps, disagreements, disjunctures, and contradictions among the essays. The feminist identities articulated within this anthology also shift and change with these interruptions, overlaps, disjunctures, and contradictions. As Judith Butler has noted elsewhere, "Gender identities emerge, … shift, and vary so that different identifica-tions come into play depending upon the availability of legitimating cultural norms and opportunities" (Butler 1990b: 331).

Yet much useful knowledge is generated through recurring themes and difficult dialogues[6] about what feminism is and can be; about how to do feminist theory; about which theories adequately explain women's status in different social groups and his-torical locations; and about which theories offer the best strategies for changing gender relations. We believe, taken together, the essays effectively represent the multivocal feminist theory of this historical moment, as well as the multiple and shifting sites of feminist identities. We hope the resonance and discord among the multiple voices and perspectives in this collection of essays will push readers to examine their own assump-tions, the explanatory power and limits of the theories, and the relationships between feminist theories and practices. We end the anthology with readings that point to the new directions of feminist theory that have emerged from previous strands of conver-sation and debate between postmodern and standpoint theorists, and between queer[7] and feminist theorists even as they take up longstanding and recurring themes—bodies and emotions—central to feminist discourses.

In assembling the readings, our guiding principle has been to make the theoretical foundations of U.S. women's studies intelligible to contemporary students by includ-ing a mixture of old and new material, which represent pivotal moments of intellectual insight. In particular, we reframe the discussion of feminist theory by balancing the writings of women of color—representing numerous ethnic identities and postcolonial locations—with those of Western women and white women. The *Reader* also does not focus narrowly on gender. Instead, it examines both systems of gender, and systems of difference and domination that intersect with gender to shape women's situations and women's identities (Collins Reading 37). Yet, because even the word "feminism" is not used throughout the world, our framing of the feminist conversations risks (re)imposing Western categories and chronology on transnational women's movements and gender politics.

Realizing how easy it is to slip into a U.S.-centric view of the world, we begin with readings that both present the conventional periodization of "the first and second waves" of feminism and destabilize that rendering of feminist pasts. In addition, we do not simply add a section about global feminism. Nor do we provide readings that either exoticize Third World women or portray them as homogeneous victims of global capitalism and local patriarchal culture. Instead, we incorporate global perspectives throughout the anthology in order continually to challenge Western hegemonic concepts and categories. In addition, we do not merely incorporate the challenges made by women of color and women of the global south to themes and agendas defined by white and Western feminists. We include conversations among women of color about issues of gender, race, colonialism, and sexuality and conversations within local U.S. feminism informed by insights generated by women of color and women of the global south. Appropriate labels for regions of the post-colonial world are always imprecise. Although the geographic terminology of global north and global south does not adequately convey the political configuration of the world, we use it as the best approximation available. We also include poetic voices to highlight the importance of poetry as a form of feminist theorizing worldwide. Thus we have tried to "incorporate ideas that have been developed by emergent and post-colonial feminists in a way that centralize their theoretical perspectives in U.S. classrooms, rather than just using their experience to illustrate predefined Western feminist theories" (McDermott 1998: 90).

In the years since the first edition of the *Feminist Theory Reader* was published, transnational and global perspectives on feminist theory has been widely recognized as a significant and important strand of feminist theory and politics. This recognition coincided with the dramatic increase in scholarship building on what Chandra Talpade Mohanty terms comparative feminist analysis (Mohanty Reading 48). Comparative feminist analysis seeks to break the binary positioning of local/global through comparison of contextualized and historicized investigations of women and gender processes in different social and geopolitical locations. In so doing, it builds a fuller understanding of the myriad ways in which gender, sexuality, ethnicity, class, and nationality are produced under global–local configurations of power. Throughout the *Reader*, we hope to challenge readers, as we challenged ourselves "to rethink the complex meanings of 'difference' in contexts outside of … Western feminism" (Rosenfelt 1998: 6). In so doing, we hope to move closer to "a curriculum that illuminates the multiple levels … at work in globalization and tracks the power of its political logic as it crosses international boundaries" (Mohanty 1996, as cited in McDermott 1998: 95). In addition, even as the concept of gender grounds feminist theorizing in a number of feminist spaces, the meanings of sex, gender, and sexuality have been contested and reconfigured through ongoing dialogues with lesbians, transgender scholars, and queer theorists. Discussions about how gender difference is related to and different from that based on sexual orientation, sexuality, and gender identity have stimulated much theorizing about how sex, gender, and sexuality might be connected and/or disconnected in theory and practice. Strands of these conversations appear throughout all the sections of the *Reader*.

We also gave a lot of thought to how to locate the voices of feminists that rely on white, northern, middle-class, and/or heterosexual experiences as *the* experience of gender subordination. Some readings, especially early ones, construct and recapitulate this experience as the experience of 'women in general,' which we seek to destabilize. We disrupt the logic of the hegemonic feminist subject by situating her within conversations that include many voices inside and outside the U.S., and that analyze gender in the context of race, nationality, class, and sexuality (Sandoval 1990). We locate theories based upon white, middle-class, heterosexual northern women's lives as another variety of local feminist theory and practice, which has dominated feminist discourse because of unearned privileges of race, nation, class, and sexuality. We think it is better to retain these historical artifacts and encourage students to re-examine that privileged, particular, local experience of gender. In so doing, we take "the task of unmasking privilege seriously by trying to locate the places it finds a home, rather than simply noting that it must be at work." In her cogent analysis of who the "we" is in Simone de Beauvoir's *The Second Sex*, Elizabeth Spelman argues that "we honor her work by asking how such privilege functions in her own thinking" (1988: 77; see also Taylor 1993).

The Feminist Theory *Reader* has four sections, each of which begins with an introductory essay by the editors that lays out the framework that brings the readings together, locates the historical context of the readings, and, where appropriate, points to critical additional readings not included here. The introductory essay for Section I includes an in depth discussion of the five core concepts used to organize the reader. Those concepts do not represent the only threads of conversation between the readings. Themes of identity, autonomy, and belonging also resonate across them. In addition, readings provide students with a solid introduction to concepts and frameworks from other fields that have been so central to feminist theorizing, particularly the work of Karl Marx, Michel Foucault, Edward Said, and Antonio Gramsci. We hope that the plethora of themes and issues within the readings will generate wide-ranging discussion in the classroom.

Section I: Theorizing Feminist Times and Spaces takes up and destabilizes the conventional narrative of feminist pasts captured by the wave metaphor. Readings include both third person scholarly accounts and documents-of-the-moment that archive the ideas and emotions of the mid- and late-twentieth-century feminisms. The third person analyses question the value of existing narratives and offer stories that complicate our understanding of feminist times and spaces. Documents-of-the-moment illuminate difficult conversations about the social causes and consequences of gender subordination and women's personal experiences as a basis for building feminist knowledge. In particular, they include voices of feminists of color who challenge the narrow focus on sex difference and argue that any adequate theory of gender oppression must take account of the intersecting systems of difference and domination in which people live their lives. These readings illuminate the exclusions constructed by the initial definitions of U.S.

feminist theory's core concepts. They point to the false universalism and essentialism of those concepts and examine systematic differences among women. The section includes voices representing feminist poetry, black, Chicana, lesbian, transgender, transnational, radical, and liberal feminism, and global reproductive rights activism.

Section II: Theorizing Intersecting Identities includes readings that theorize the ways in which gender is continually reconfigured by complex and multiple global processes. The readings in the first subsection present feminist theoretical efforts to elaborate the structural intersections of gender with multiple dimensions of oppression, including class, race, ethnicity nationality, religion, and sexuality. Like a kaleidoscope in which a jumble of objects are refracted through a prism in constantly shifting patterns, the readings offer a shifting prism of difference, through which to examine the mobile and multiple configurations of domination in women's and men's lives. They also unsettle the notion that race, nation, class, sexuality, or gender can be treated as fixed, essential, or separable categories. The second subsection includes first person accounts of the tensions pervading experiences of intersecting identities. The readings present self-reflexive narratives about identity, the terms of belonging to community, and the challenges of boundary-crossing. They delineate the complex politics of location in feminist theory (Mani Reading 41; Kaplan and Grewal 1994; Rich 2001). The readings offer students of diverse backgrounds models for how to negotiate the conflicts and contests that comprise feminist activism in an era of perpetual war, economic collapse, and globalization.

Section III: Theorizing Feminist Knowledge and Agency, presents two central solutions offered by feminist theorists for constructing grounds for feminist politics: feminist standpoints theory and poststructural analyses of gendered discourse, power, and performativity. The readings build on insights generated by conversations represented in Section II. Standpoint theories argue that women's social location is a resource for the construction of a uniquely feminist perspective on social reality, which, in turn, can ground feminist political struggles for change. Taken together, the included selections lead students to consider that there might be a multiplicity of feminist standpoints. Poststructural feminisms focus on operations of power in any/every articulation of a feminist subjectivity, suggesting that any assertion of a stable gender identity or stable unity among women involves an exclusion of some kind. The basic concepts of poststructuralist theory, including the relationship of language and subjectivity, and of discourse and power, are presented along with selections that raise questions about the essentializing, disciplining, and normalizing functions of the concepts, "woman," "sex," "gender," and "experience." Through the essays, students will begin to see the normative functions of discourse and a feminist critique of identity politics.

Section IV Imagine Otherwise draws readings from recent efforts to move beyond the debates between postmodern and standpoint theories towards frameworks that build on the strengths of each perspective. These readings point in new directions to tentative resolutions of how to think/act to change gender relations. In discussions ranging from intensive economic globalization and the politics of emotion to queer theory and Chicana feminism, the readings reposition women's lives and everyday experiences as a central focus of feminist theorizing and they reassert the social group women, however unstable, as the agent of feminist politics. On one hand, the readings illustrate how poststructural theories of discourse and power have reshaped feminist social theory. On the other hand, readings also illustrate the new materialism evident in poststructural feminist theories, which responds to critiques that it gives too much attention to texts at the expense of embodiment. In particular, the section includes feminist analyses of emotions, bodies, and affect.

* * *

As a group, the voices, concepts, and analyses brought together within the *Reader* provide frameworks for understanding feminist politics across national boundaries and the social processes that shape relational differences of gender and its intersections with race, ethnicity, nation, class, and sexuality. They advocate an open and flexible intellectual posture, urging students to question what they 'know' about the past, and to develop a habit of asking what else is going on here. While conveying a sense of hopefulness, the readings do not offer easy answers. They do offer useful guidance on how to think about and enact feminist strategies for change in our local situation and within a transnational world, encouraging all of us to reflect on the shifting identities and asymmetries of power we must negotiate in this time of perpetual war, economic collapse, and increasing nationalist fervor.

Notes

1. For definitions of oppression see Marilyn Frye (1983) who defines oppression as constraints on and limitations of life options because of one's identity as a member of a subordinated group. See also Iris Marion Young (1990) who identifies five forms of oppression: exploitation, marginalization, powerlessness, cultural imperialism, and violence.
2. How well this relationship between theory and political practice has developed is itself an issue of debate by scholars and activists alike.
3. The sense of conversations we intend here is informed by Katie King's definitions. She distinguishes between conversations and debates; the former involves "political contours," the latter "theoretical contents." She also describes conversations not as a single thing in which we all share but as ongoing, overlapping, and shifting. See King 1994: xi, 56, and 87.
4. More than 100 nations have signed the Convention, but the United States is not one of them.
5. As publishing has become more global, we met with problems securing permission to publish some classic articles worldwide and in electronic form.
6. This phrase is taken from Johnnella Butler's work. See for example, Johnnella Butler and John Walter 1991.
7. Queer refers to spaces and identities outside of heteronormativity. See Walters Reading 43.

SECTION I

THEORIZING FEMINIST TIMES AND SPACES

INTRODUCTION

Throughout the world in the 1960s and 1970s, women's challenges to their subordinate status seemed to explode in struggles involving issues of equal rights, social conventions of femininity and heterosexuality, reproductive self-determination, violence, poverty, anti-racism, and anti-colonialism, among others. While very visible, this period was not unique. At earlier points in modern history, women's movements in many locations across the world allied with nationalist, anti-colonial liberation movements, and labor activism to promote changes in women's social status and political rights. In this section, we assemble a group of readings that encourage readers to question what they know about past feminist movements. Picking up "different strands running in tandem," the readings tell different stories that elaborate the myriad connections and conversations that comprise contemporary feminist theory (Barkley Brown 1992). While destabilizing the conventional representation of feminist genealogies (first, second, third waves), we also contextualize the feminist theoretical conversations and debates through a genealogy of core feminist concepts.

The readings in the Feminist Movements subsection urge readers to rethink feminist times and spaces by challenging the prevailing representation of feminist movements as waves. Certainly, women's movements have varied in intensity throughout the modern era, as exemplified by the eagerness with which women in different times and places adopt or reject the label, feminist (Moses 1998a). In the mid-twentieth century, North American feminists used the metaphor of 'waves' to describe patterns of 'ebb' and 'flow' in feminist activism. They labeled the myriad women's movements of the mid-nineteenth and early twentieth centuries the 'first wave of feminism.' They labeled themselves the 'second wave.'[1] As histories often do, this description of the past validated the present. Arguing that the first wave subsided before the work of women's liberation was complete, these self-named second wave feminists took up the fight "to end male supremacy" (Bunch Reading 15)

While the wave metaphor may have had strategic value in the 1970s, the following readings suggest that it is of limited usefulness as a tool for explaining various coalescences and fractures in feminist movements. As a framework for telling feminist histories, the wave metaphor obscures more than it illuminates. As historian Elsa Barkley Brown has argued, "history is everyone talking at once, multiple rhythms being played simultaneously." Therefore stories of women's lives and social movements are simultaneous, multiple, and connected. However, both formal scholarship and movement histories, tend "to isolate one conversation," often as if it took place against a backdrop of silence. "The trick," she argues, is to contextualize that conversation, "making evident its dialogue with so many others" (1992: 297). The multiple stories, conversations, debates, and dialogues of feminist times and spaces are complexly related, and, because they are enmeshed in the hierarchies of differences that organize the world, they are asymmetrical. The conventional accounts of highs and lows of feminist waves configure a story that honors the lives and activities of white, middle-class, heterosexual women in the global north, and overlooks the activities of women situated otherwise. Thus, for instance, the period described as the low point of feminist activism between 1920 and 1960 saw continuous efforts by working-class union women to secure workplace justice (Cobble 2005). Moreover, the conventional narratives represent the activities of women situated otherwise as "different from" and "later than." Such accounts ignore that, from the outset, relational differences and dialogues configure all knowledge, including feminist theories. The readings in this section recommend that we develop the habit of asking what else was/is going on whenever we engage accounts of women's and social justice movements.

Feminist Movements

To invoke alternative images and metaphors of women's activism, we start this section with a poem by Yosano Akiko (1878–1942) who is internationally recognized as one of the leading poets and writers of early modern Japan. The poem (Reading 1) appeared in the 1911 inaugural volume of Seitō (Bluestockings), the first Japanese feminist literary journal. In this poem, Yosano compares the creativity and vitality of women to dormant volcanoes. Drawing from the natural landscape of Japan, composed of mountains that were once blazing volcanoes, Yosano uses this imagery as a metaphor to characterize the situation of women. She suggests that the creative energy of women, like fire of dormant volcanoes, has not been extinguished. It is gathering momentum to explode and women's inner genius will shake the entire land.

Following the suggestion by Elsa Barkley Brown to make connections between the numerous stories and conversations of the past, Nancy Hewitt rethinks the history of "first wave" feminism by "re-embedding the Seneca Falls Convention in the world of 1848" (Reading 2). In so doing, she situates the emblematic founding moment of "first wave feminism" within the wider context of social justice movements around the globe that year. Her essay demonstrates that the angle from which we access the past shapes the stories we come to know. By shifting away from the conversations and connections available from the point of view of Elizabeth Cady Stanton, the most prominent white middle-class woman in official histories of the nineteenth-century women's movement, Hewitt illuminates the myriad of other connections between Seneca Falls and the people and movements surrounding it. She reminds readers that 1848 was an eventful year. Slavery was abolished in the West Indies, the signing of the Treaty of Guadalupe Hidalgo ended the Mexican-American war, the *Communist Manifesto* was published, and revolutions occurred in France and Germany. She also reminds us that Seneca Falls was located in what had been the Iroquois nation, and that women's claims for justice were closely connected to the American abolitionist movement. Finally, she reminds us that the women and men in attendance at the convention came from and brought with them a myriad of connections and perspectives on women's condition.

In the mid-twentieth century, Simone de Beauvoir (Reading 3) published her highly influential treatise, *The Second Sex.* In it, de Beauvoir articulates key arguments about the condition of women that would be taken up by feminists in the 1970s. Rejecting biological determinism and the "eternal feminine," De Beauvoir starts from the premise that "one is not born a woman," but becomes one, and asks then "what is a woman?"[2] She argues that while men define themselves as the exemplary case of humanity, they define women in terms of their difference from men. "He is the subject … she is the other." That definition marks women by what they lack. Moreover, she argues, "she appears to him as a sexual being. For him she is sex—absolute sex, no less." It is not surprising therefore, that "knowledge" about "women's nature," often sexualized, justifies their subordination. Thus, de Beauvoir concludes, women must address for ourselves "… how the fact of being women will affect our lives. What opportunities precisely have been given us and what withheld? What fate awaits our younger sisters, and what directions should they take?" (Reading 3) An exhaustive philosophical treatise on the condition of women, feminist scholars have returned repeatedly to de Beauvoir's work.[3]

Linda Nicholson (Reading 4) asks if any aspect of the wave metaphor is still useful. In answering that question, she summarizes the activity around gender that occurred in the U.S. between the passage of women's suffrage and the emergence of the "second wave" as well as elaborating on the commonly used terms, liberal, radical,[4] and socialist feminist. She concludes that while the metaphor had strategic historical value, it should be discarded because it does not adequately capture the "different kinds of activism around gender" in U.S. history. It gives the false impression that a single feminism lies beneath the peaks and valleys of feminist waves. Furthermore, it cannot usefully account for the uneven outcomes of feminist activisms, some of which succeeded and some of which did not. She would reserve use of the metaphor to describe periods, when feminist claims resonate with "the felt needs of ordinary women and men," mobilizing "large numbers of people in very public, noisy, and challenging ways" (Reading 4). However, she urges readers not to overlook the quieter work required to institutionalize social change.

Becky Thompson (Reading 5) contests what she calls the "hegemonic feminism" that organizes most conventional accounts of "second wave" feminism. She tells an alternative history focused on the rise of multiracial feminism. In particular, she contests those scholars who conclude that radical feminism subsided by the early 1970s. This assessment, she argues, limits our understanding of feminist activism to the narrow conjuncture of the new left and women's liberation movements. It also limits our understanding of radical to anti-patriarchal activism. One can only read the 1970s and 1980s as a period of dissipated feminist activism if one discounts the spaces in which women of color and anti-racist white women struggled to build a movement to end multiple forms of domination. To the contrary, she argues, the 1970s and 1980s saw the rise of multiracial feminism. It was a period in which "issues that had divided many of the movement's constituencies … were put on the table" (Barbara Smith cited in Thompson Reading 5). Once on the table, multiracial women's groups engaged in difficult dialogues required to be accountable across difference. Thompson chronicles the key scholars, organizations, and events in multiracial feminisms, contextualizing the key concepts that multiracial feminist theory generated, such as interlocking oppressions, the politics of location, and coalition politics.

Amrita Basu (Reading 6) discusses a vitally important strand running in tandem with, but independent from, U.S. women's movements. Her account focuses on the women activists who came together around the U.N. "Decade for Women" to articulate an international women's rights agenda at the four international conferences on women between 1975 and 1995. Basu's analysis illuminates the sites of coalescence and conflict between women of the global north and global south. Her account of this history indexes the asymmetries of power and perspective that shaped global feminist networks from early "bitter contestation" in the period from 1975 to 1985 to the contemporary coalitions formed in the period from 1985 to 1995. She highlights struggles over the priorities and terms of international women's activism, noting the women of the global north tend to favor issues involving personal freedoms while women of the global south prioritize economic issues of poverty and development. She makes clear that women of the global south set their own agenda, and were not "waiting for" U.S. women to lead them. Basu argues that with all the differences, what women have in common are political goals, defined in specific historical times and places. She suggests that greater attention to the geopolitics that shape both contentious issues and common goals will enable feminist networks to flourish in the current climate of intensified globalization. Although the geographic terminology of global north and global south does not adequately convey the political configuration of the world, following Basu's example we use it as the best approximation available.

Asking if feminist waves are transatlantic, Michelle Rowley (Reading 7) critiques the pedagogical reliance on feminist waves from the perspective of transnational feminists teaching in U.S. women's studies classrooms. While the wave metaphor should be discarded, she argues, genealogies are nonetheless important. Drawing on the poetic voice of Etheridge Knight, an Afro-Caribbean poet, Rowley reminds us that our relational connections, past, present, and future, make us who we are and who we may become. She offers Knight's evocative phrase, "whereabouts unknown," to posit a new method for composing feminist genealogies, one that recognizes, "the importance of unexpected, diverse, and surprising beginnings." The wave metaphor, she notes, "frames" the "whereabouts" that "are already known." In its place, she offers the term, "politics and conditions of emergence," which allows us to "place emphasis on the power dynamics and context that lead to specific feminist issues and responses coming into full force." In other words, Rowley advocates that we investigate the "whereabouts" of what is "unknown" in order to elaborate the there and then of the conditions spurring feminist action (Reading 7).

Local Identities and Politics

The readings in second subsection provide a number of additional entry points into feminist debates of the 1970s and 1980s. Some are third person accounts; some are documents-of- the-moment that archive strands of conversation within feminist theory.

The language and the emotions indexed in the readings speak to both universal claims made in the voice of normative feminist subject as well as the counter claims of those excluded from it. Together these readings endorse Rowley's recommendation that we examine the conditions of emergence within the local feminist times and spaces to which they refer. Likewise, we encourage readers to ask what else was going on, what else informed these local identities and politics.

The readings represent only a very small number of those that might have been chosen. We selected them because they offer insight into the five concepts with which, we believe, students can gain an understanding of contemporary feminist theory. Those concepts are gender, difference, women's experiences, the personal is political, and intersectionality. In the remainder of this chapter, we introduce the readings in the Local Identities and Politics subsection by way of an intellectual genealogy of those core concepts. Not intended to be definitive or exhaustive, it locates the following readings in their time and place, situating them in the relational differences, the asymmetrical connections, and ongoing contentions archived within them.

GENDER—Even as women moved into new areas of public life across the globe in the twentieth century, Western social scientists amassed evidence that they said demonstrated the natural basis of sex differences (Delphy 1993; Stern 2005; Meyerowitz 2002). Anglophone feminists developed the concept of gender to counter the claim that biology is destiny.[5] As case in point, Ann Oakley's, 1972 book, *Sex, Gender, and Society*, offers a meticulous critique of data about sex differences, arguing that whatever small differences exist are exaggerated by the methods used to measure them. Height is a classic example. On average, men are taller than women are. However, the range of difference within each group is greater than the differences between them. The comparison by average height obscures similarities and exaggerates differences to the benefit of men. Concurring with de Beauvoir, Oakley notes, women's differences from men are construed as inferiority. In contrast to "natural" sex differences, Oakley defines masculinity and femininity as the products of the gendered social process of learning and internalizing behaviors, roles, and personality traits deemed appropriate to each sex. She concludes that the resulting gender types overstate the otherwise minimal biological sex differences. Minimal biological sex differences are completely obscured by social practices (and prejudice). Besides, modern technology and contraception made those differences irrelevant. She concludes that "man-made" interpretations of sex differences secure male dominance and women's devaluation, which amounts to injustice.

Oakley bolsters her argument that gender is socially determined with anthropological evidence of cultural variations in the activities and personality characteristics associated with men and women in "other cultures."[6] Another example of this common strategy in early feminist theories of gender appears in Gayle Rubin's influential 1975 essay, "The Traffic in Women: Notes on the Political Economy of Sex." Like Oakley, Rubin describes the cultural processes of gender, the sex/gender system, as that which takes the raw material of human babies/bodies and produces gender-differentiated beings with complementary skills and personalities. When properly coupled, gendered beings produce the basic social unit—the family. The sex/gender system subordinates women by positioning them as the objects exchanged by men to create family and community. Rubin's careful explication of the sex/gender system is peppered with references to "exotic"[7] gender and sexual practices in the global south taken from anthropology.[8] These examples augment her argument that gender is differentiated everywhere, but not always in the same way.

Multiracial and transnational feminists have critiqued this argumentation strategy, pointing out that it distorts their heritage as it constructs "other" women as "decorations" for the political struggles and theorizing of Western white women (Lorde 1981: 96).[9] Such references to other cultures index the diversity of gender and demonstrate that male domination is universal. The implication is that, even though the details may differ, all women are subjected to the same underlying patriarchal gender system. "To imply," however, as Audre Lorde notes, "that all women suffer the same oppression simply because they are women, is to lose sight of the many varied tools of patriarchy" (95). Moreover, these appropriative uses of the global south are emblematic of Orientalist discourses, as Edward Said has demonstrated (Said 1978). Following Said, Orientalist discourses constructed by colonial regimes and ordinary travelogues created an imaginative geography—"the East," "the Orient" and "the West," "the Occident." Often in racialized terms, Orientalist discourse sets up the binary opposition of primitive and civilized, through which "the West" understands itself as superior in all things. The contrast represents the (white) West as more progressive, more advanced, and thus world leaders. Transnational feminists have shown that although Said may have overlooked it, inasmuch Orientalist discourse casts "other" women either as exotic and/or as sexually victimized in contrast to Western women, gender is central to Orientalism (Mohanty 1991b; Abu-Lughod Reading 21). Western feminist theories participate in Orientalist discourses when they pluck examples of women's oppression elsewhere to support their own arguments, and when they presume to say what the most important issues for all women. Such Orientalist arguments and postures raise particular dilemmas in organizing around gender and sexuality within transnational communities of color around the world. Amrita Basu notes that the 1980 U.N. Conference erupted in controversy over just such issues (Reading 6; see also Rao 1991).

Another important strand of feminist theorizing about gender surfaces in Rubin's essay: She credits the sex/gender system with cultural construction of sexuality as well gender. This observation points to critiques lesbian feminist would make about the heteronormative assumptions underlying initial feminist theories of gender. For instance, Shulamith Firestone's (Reading 14) discussion of "the culture of romance" assumes that desire is heterosexual. What counts as erotic is the coupling of masculine male bodies with feminine female bodies. Thus, while her argument elaborates de Beauvoir's observation that men sexualize women, it ignores the specifically heterosexual components of the culture of romance, thus reiterating heterosexist reasoning. So, do lesbians fit into the category of women, into the category of feminist? Charlotte Bunch's essay (Reading 15) addresses such questions as she challenges reflexive heterosexism and homophobia in mid-twentieth-century women's movements. Her argument situates lesbianism as a political and sexual identity. A "woman-identified" political separatism, she asserts, offers the best means of overthrowing patriarchy because "lesbianism threatens male-supremacy at its core." Clearly angered by the exclusion of lesbians from feminist organizations, Bunch's argument is audacious in a historical period of enormous stigma attached to lesbianism, and one frequently hurled at feminists as anti-male.

In the 1990s, queer theory contested feminist accounts of gender, suggesting that if the cultural processes configure gender and compulsory heterosexual couplings, more is going on here than feminists have accounted for. Dialogue between queer theorists and feminist theorists has generated feminist theories of heteronormativity and the cultural configuration of heterosexuality, and it continues to inform accounts of the relationship between gender, male dominance, and heteronormativity. That is, does the gender system primarily serve systems of male dominance, resulting in the subordination and devaluation of women? Alternatively, does it primarily serve heteronormativity, resulting in exclusion of queer sexualities, genders, bodies, and identities? Does gender then serve the ends of heteronormativity?

In addition, critiques by queer and transgender theorists unsettled the feminist assumption that biological sex is pre-social. They theorize a far more complex and contingent relationship between bodies, sexes, sexualities, and genders, arguing that culture configures sexed bodies as well as genders (Butler 1990 and Delphy 1992). Leslie Feinberg's essay (Reading 17) is an early example of a feminist/transgender political treatise that challenges the binary opposition of men and women. Feinberg defines gender as "self-expression, not anatomy." Ze[10] challenges the automatic linkage of body type and gender identity. Instead, ze argues, within the history of gender oppressions, non-normative (queer) configurations of bodies and gender identities have been subject to severe repression. However, ze notes that transphobia has its own specific dynamics, which are detailed in the essay.

Recent feminist scholarship has, in response, returned to the relationship between biology and culture to consider how much of what we call anatomical sex difference is shaped by culture and to critique the gender binary (the binary opposition of sexes, sexualities, and genders) that prevails in most social, including feminist, theory.[11]

As this brief summary suggests, the fundamental feminist concept, gender, ignited an explosion of scholarship but it does not have a single or uncontested definition. Sometimes gender refers to characteristics of individuals; the meanings of sex differences ingrained on bodies, minds, and identities. Sometimes it refers to the processes by which sex difference was struggled over, enacted in cultural practices, and inscribed in and deployed by social institutions (schools, courts, hospitals, and the media). Sometimes, gender refers to culturally prescribed performances in everyday activities and expressive cultural forms. At the same time, feminist theorists of color in the global north and global south challenged universalized views of gender that treated all women as subject to the same gender oppression and that appropriated their cultural practices to support universalist claims. Different theories about connections between anatomical sex, gender, and sexuality shaped dialogues and debates between feminist theories, lesbian feminist and queer theory. They all concur, however, that power relations shape how gender is defined, constituted, sanctioned, identified with, resisted, lived, and reproduced. Together, debates about the importance and composition of differences between women became the generative engine for feminist theory in the 1980s (Sandoval 1991 and McDermott 1994).

DIFFERENCE[12]—As the preceding discussion indicates, "difference" was articulated not only as "gender difference that united women as distinct from men" but also "as an index of incommensurability among women of different races, classes, ethnicities, and sexualities" (Schmitz et al. 1995: 710). As the above quotation from Audre Lorde shows, women of color objected to a gender-only focus in feminist theory. In addition, Frances Beal warned in 1972, that women's liberation would quickly become a white women's movement if it insisted on organizing along the gender lines alone (Sandoval 1991). Such a focus on "women in general" presumed that other dimensions of social life were unimportant in understanding women's experience as women. Moreover, women of color argued, the exclusive focus on gender universalized the particular experience of white, middle-class, heterosexual women residing in the global north as the normal/normative situation of "women in general," and dismissed their experiences and perspectives (Lorde 1981; Spelman 1988; and Thompson Reading 5).

To illustrate how false universals silence difference, recall the earlier example of average height. The contrast of men and women treats each group as homogenous. Differences among women (and among men) vanish, especially differences in privilege and disadvantage within each group. Hierarchies of difference within each group ensure that the general case represents the situation, perspective, interests of the dominant group. bell hooks illuminated the flawed logic of false universals when she famously asked, "Which men do women want to be equal to" (hooks 1984: 18)? Because they are not also subordinated by race, class, (neo)colonialism, or homophobia, white middle-class, heterosexual women of the global north mistook their situation to be a case of pure sexism. As if privileges of race, class, nation, sexuality did not shape their lives (Spelman 1988). This reasoning also overlooks the relational processes by which systems of domination confer privileges on some and deprivations on others. As Barkley Brown reminds us, "We need to recognize" that "middle-class women live the lives they do precisely because working class women lead the lives they do. White women and women of color not only live different lives, but white women live the lives they do in large part because women of color live the ones they do" (Barkley Brown 1992: 298). Intertwining race, class, heterosexual, and imperialist privilege gave (and continue to give) white, middle-class, heterosexual women of the global north greater means for articulating their perspectives. This culturally and economically dominant group's perspectives thus came to define the terms of feminist debate, against which women located otherwise have had to situate themselves.

The effects of hierarchical differences are evident in the essays by Elizabeth Martinez (Reading 12) Combahee River Collective (Reading 13), and Charlotte Bunch (Reading 15) who directed their arguments against the "hegemonic feminist" subject (Thompson Reading 5). Their arguments reflect the terms of inclusion/exclusion that women of color and women of the global south confront in feminist theory and politics narrowly focused on gender. Either they must ignore dimensions of their situations to locate themselves within "women in general" or they must mark themselves by their differences from that group. In contrast, the essays by Carole Pateman (Reading 11) and Shulamith Firestone (Reading 14) speak about "women in general," without specifying which women and where. Nor do they consider how their accounts might change if they did specify which women and which men they meant. Charlotte Bunch must counter the heterosexism by which the specific issues confronting heterosexual women are assumed automatically to be issues for all women, while lesbian issues are not. However, Elizabeth Martinez notes, the "revolutionary Chicana does not identify with the so-called women's liberation movement" (Reading 12). She rejects feminist separatism because it would require her to ignore the grounds of solidarity Chicanas have with Chicanos in fighting racism and imperialism. In their arguments that an adequate feminist theory and practice would need to account for all hierarchies of difference, these readings also clearly convey the anger and disillusionment caused by exclusionary practices. As Barbara Smith, lead author of the Combahee River Collective, argues "Racism is a feminist issue" because "feminism is the political theory and practice that struggles to free *all* women. ... Anything less than this vision of total freedom is not feminism, but merely female self-aggrandizement" (Hull et al. 1982: 49).

Those excluded from dominant feminist theories turned the concept of difference to their own ends, opening intellectual space to theorize the ways that women's lives are shaped by race, nationality, class, and sexuality, as well as by gender. However, specifying differences between women also raised new issues. Initially, questions focused on how to think about connections between systems of differences. Did the combination of race and gender oppression produce a kind of double jeopardy, in which the injuries of sexism and racism added up to a double dose of oppression (Beal 1970)? What would happen if one were also subject to class-based domination, (neo)-colonialism, or heterosexual domination? Did that constitute a situation of multiple jeopardy in which subordinations add up to even greater misery (King 1988)? Did each new element of domination in this additive model produce greater suffering and the possibility of greater insight? Was there a hierarchy of oppressions, in which some forms of domination were more fundamental to social change? Marxist movements traditionally argued that the class system is the basic division of society and that racism, imperialism, and sexism derive from it. Radical feminist theorists sometimes argued that the oppression of women by men was the original oppression, and served as the model for all others (Burris 1973; Rich 1979; Bunch Reading 15). Alternatively, some contended, racism, sexism, and class-domination were produced by separate, interrelated, systems (Combahee Reading 13; Hartmann Reading 19).[13]

In the course of often-contentious discussions, the additive model of oppression gave way to the model of simultaneous oppressions (Lorde 1984; Spelman 1988). In an early example, the women of the Combahee River Collective argue that the conditions of our lives result from the synthesis of simultaneous and "interlocking systems of domination" based on racial, sexual, heterosexual, and class oppression (Reading 13). By the 1990s, multiracial feminist theorists conceptualized interacting oppressions that compose our lives as a matrix of domination (Dill and Zinn 1996; Hill Collins 1990). In this view, specific locations within the matrix consist of specific simultaneous effects of multiple systems of oppression. These complex locations can include combinations of both privileges and oppressions. Yet these insights would come later.

The Combahee River Collective and Martinez readings signal a central feature of feminist politics in the 1980s: fragmentation along lines of identity politics.[14] Identity politics are based on the premise that those who experience specific configurations of oppression are best suited to understand that oppression and develop strategies for change. As Combahee authors observed "the most profound and potentially the most radical politics come directly out of our own identity, as opposed to working to end somebody else's oppression." Black feminism, they note, grew out of involvement in the "Second Wave of the American women's movement" and "the movement for Black liberation," both of which failed to address the unique political struggles of black women adequately (Reading 13). Organizing groups along lines of identity provided intellectual and emotional space in which to grapple with specific situations of multiple oppression.

Elaboration of the operations of multiple oppressions in women's lives produced new questions of identity, connection, and belonging. Who are "we" who are outside the boundaries of the northern white women's movement and feminist theory? How might "we" work, think, and organize together. By what name should "we" be known?

One answer to that question, the term, women of color, emerged at the 1981 National Women's Studies Association Conference in Storrs, Connecticut. The conference became a watershed event in U.S. women's studies. The conference topic was "Women Respond to Racism" and it included breakout sessions structured by identity. The categories available for white women to select from included specificities of class, sexuality, and immigrant status. Women who did not identify as white found their differences collapsed into the single category, "women of color." The women of color involved in organizing the conference offered the category in response to criticism that the discussions of racism among U.S. feminists often dichotomized race as black and white. The Combahee River Collective (Reading 13) provides an example of the erasure of racial differences beneath the hegemony of black/white definitions in the U.S. The authors position themselves as fighting against the oppressions faced by all women of color. Yet, the essay theorizes racism from the specific location as African-American women. At the conference, the term "women of color" was intended to be more inclusive of the variety of women's racial identities and experiences of racism. However, conference participants intensely deliberated whether this was an appropriate concept for thinking through different racisms. They were well aware of what the term "threatened to hide" including, "for example, culture, ethnicity, national associations, religion, skin color, race, language, class, and sexual differences" (cited in King 1994: 64). Despite such trepidations, the term "women of color" was widely used in multi-racial feminist dialogues and alliances.

Other possible terms included "Third World women." The term, the Third World, widely used in the 1970s and 1980s, originated in the context of the Cold War. The First World label designated the industrialized liberal-capitalist nations of Western Europe and the North America. The Second World referred to the communist and socialist nations. The Third World referred to those new nations emerging through anti-colonialist movements and decolonization.[15] The term highlighted relational geopolitical location as a factor in gender identity formation. While the label "women of color" highlights race as the grounds of common oppression and political solidarity, "Third World women" highlights colonialism as the grounds of oppression and solidarity. In the U.S. in the 1980s and 1990s, "women of color" came to designate the multifaceted nexus of race, nation, colonialism, and globalization. On the other hand, "Third World women" continued to denote non-U.S. locations and identities (Mohanty 1991b). Both can imply the notion of a diasporic identity.

More recently, the term transnational has been used to refer to people and ideas that travel between locations in the global south and north. It invokes the complex legal, material, and emotional processes involved in crossing geopolitical borders and identity boundaries. The term multiracial feminism has been used to convey the conjuncture of anti-racist and anti-patriarchal activisms engaged in by women of color and anti-racist white women (Thompson Reading 5; Dill and Zinn 1996). The location of such individuals within the political struggles of their originary cultures can be quite complicated. As Aihwa Ong asks, "do Third World feminists who now write in the Anglophone world enjoy a privileged positionality in representing the 'authentic experiences' of women from our ancestral cultures or not?" As Lydia Liu notes, it is not clear, "exactly how the post-colonial theorist relates to the 'Third world' except that s/he travels in and out of it and points out its difference from that of the 'First world.'" The term transnational tries to capture the notion that such scholars are, as Ong notes, "multiply inscribed subjects," who engage complicated cultural power relations in crossing national boundaries (as quoted in Kim and McCann 1998: 117).

Despite the unstable nature of the terms, "women of color," "Third World women," "transnational feminist," and "multiracial feminist," they can denote a political commitment, strategic unity, a community of belonging, from which oppositional consciousness and significant theoretical insights can emerge (Spivak 1990). However, unity constructed by these terms is necessarily contingent and subject to renegotiation.

The voices of transnational feminists, feminists of color and feminists in the global south have often been relegated to the margins of U.S. feminist theorizing. Nonetheless, dialogues spurred by those counter voices have moved U.S. feminist theory to develop more nuanced understandings of the multiple power relations that shape women's situations. One key insight to emerge from the work of multiracial and transnational feminist theories is that it is always necessary to specify the when, where, and who in feminist theory and politics.

WOMEN'S EXPERIENCES—In displacing the notion that natural sex differences made male domination inevitable, the concept of gender created another problem. Without resorting to the female body/soul/nature as the thing that makes women, *women*, what else can account for women's shared identity? On what grounds would women come together as a group to demand change? What would be the basis of women's political agency? The concept of experience seemed to provide the answer. Many feminist theorists have asserted that women's identity as a distinct and specific social group begins with their "lived experiences" as women—beings whose lives, rights, opportunities, pleasures, and responsibilities are often dictated by the value their cultures give to the perceived sex of their bodies as distinct from that of men. Thus, shared "common experiences" of oppression define women as a social group who can act in concert to resist gender oppression and improve their lives. Moreover, critical examination of these "lived experiences" provides the grounds for building a feminist theory.

That is, feminist theorists have argued, the existing "knowledge" about women justifies male domination and, therefore, it is untrustworthy.[16] Thus, such theorists conclude, the value and meaning of women's lives must be defined from women's point of view, from the inside of their experiences rather than from some outside view.

In 1970s feminist activism, consciousness-raising held a privileged place as a source of critical knowledge that could inform resistance to oppression.[17] As T. V. Reed (Reading 9) notes in his essay on the poetics of mid-twentieth-century feminism, consciousness-raising involved structured conversations in which small groups of women shared experiences on specific topics. By sharing experiences, the common elements would surface, thus clarify the systematic nature of women's subordination. In turn, through these conversations women would come to identify with each other, would build solidarity around the most pressing issues confronting them, and would be able to devise strategies for change. Reed's discussion of poetry as a tool of feminist theorizing illuminates the high regard for the expressive power of language in feminist identity formation. As he notes, new insights demanded new language, and feminist poetics has been a vital creative tool with which to learn how to speak about what had previously been unspeakable. Reed's analysis also illuminates the conditions of emergence for the feminist poetry movement, and traces its connections to feminist politics and movements. Muriel Rukeyser's classic poem (Reading 8) expresses the energy and hopefulness of consciousness-raising, a process that facilitates her decision to renounce masks and mythologies. The poem ends with hope and anticipation as she embarks on a journey of self-discovery emblematic of consciousness-raising and of the feminist poetry movement.

As noted above, claims that women shared a common experience were vigorously debated in feminist circles. Those excluded from hegemonic feminism contended that differences in women's social positions and cultural contexts are so extensive that there is no "common experience of women." Moreover, they argued because consciousness-raising groups often consisted of women with similar backgrounds and situations, hierarchies of power that interacted with gender ensured that the experiences of white, middle-class, heterosexual women in metropolitan centers dominated the feminist agenda. Yet even while women of color and lesbians around the world challenged the notion of a "common women's experience" they have also embraced the concept in theorizing their specific, local situations. Black feminism, the Combahee River Collective argued, emerges from "the political realization that comes from the seemingly personal experiences of individual Black women's lives" (Reading 13). This linkage of experience, identity, and knowledge through consciousness-raising formed the basis for the identity politics articulated by women of color. Claims based in "lived experience" run through the readings in this section.[18]

Questions about which experiences, whose experiences, and how experience can serve to build effective knowledge generated much feminist scholarship. Deniz Kandiyoti (Reading 10) introduces an analytic tool with which to specify the where and when of specific women's experiences. She proposes the term "patriarchal bargain" to describe contextually specific strategies women pursue "within a set of concrete constraints" that shape "women's gendered subjectivity" and life options. Kandiyoti illustrates this concept using two examples: the autonomy and protest form in sub-Saharan Africa and the subservience and manipulation of classic patriarchy found in the Middle East, South Asia, and East Asia. Ultimately, Kandiyoti demonstrates that "patriarchal bargains are not timeless and immutable entities, but are susceptible to historical transformations that open up new areas of struggle and renegotiation …" (Reading 10). This analytic tool applied to lived experience can help us understand strategies of compliance and to identify conditions of emergence of resistance in relationship to specific ideological, material, and political constraints

THE PERSONAL IS POLITICAL—An initial answer to the question of which experiences should inform feminist theory and politics is captured in the phrase, "the personal is political." This phrase started out as a political slogan used by self-named radical feminists in the United States to convey several related notions. It encapsulates the theory underlying the practice of consciousness-raising, that experience is the best grounds for building feminist knowledge and is the best way to define effective feminist politics. At the same time, it expresses the claim that the system of male domination is deeply entrenched in intimate relationships between women and men (Hanisch 1970 and Grant 1993). Many of the top issues for feminists in the north involve women's most personal and intimate experiences—inequality in marriage, male-centered sexuality, reproduction self-determination, and sexual and domestic violence.[19] Examination of those experiences through consciousness-raising, it was argued, would reveal the system of male domination, and would expose the underlying power relations that bound those personal experiences together. The concept also challenges the conventional view of politics as limited to formal processes of government in the public sphere, which tend to treat, sexuality, reproduction, and sexual violence as non-political because they are part of private life. Instead, feminists define politics as relations of power that operate within all human relationships in which "one group rules another" (Millet 1970: 111 as cited in Grant 1993: 34). The exercise of power makes these relationships political. This view of politics was articulated against criticisms from the U.S. left and liberals that the issues that U.S. women sought to address were personal problems, not political issues (Grant 1993).

Shulamith Firestone's 1970 book, the *Dialectic of Sex*, addresses the underlying power relations to such personal issues. Working at the intersection of radical and socialist feminist theorizing, Firestone utilized Marxist analytic categories to explicate the situation of women. The book is best remembered for its call for extra-uterine reproduction. The reading included here (Reading 14) focuses on another central concern in mid-twentieth-century U.S. feminisms, the sexual objectification of women. Picking up on de Beauvoir's theme that women are defined by what men desire, Firestone muses on the process by which women come to embody that desire. She argues that as "the biological bases of sex class crumbles male supremacy must shore itself up with artificial institutions and exaggerations …" Women are called into conformity with the standards of conventional feminine beauty through the discourse of romance, which makes women want to be individually attractive to men. The culture of romance, she concludes, "is a tool of male power to keep women from knowing their conditions." Men's sexuality is also shaped by this culture, but, she argues, the situation is more complicated and exploitative for women who must embody "the Image of Sex Appeal" (Reading 14). She ends by noting that changing this culture will be difficult precisely because romance and eroticism are exciting.

The notion of the personal is political is not limited to changes in private relationships, however. It also recognizes the need for change in the public world. Carole Pateman (Reading 11) offers another angle on feminist genealogies, one that is focused on the dialogues and conflicts between feminist theory and the "Western tradition" of social and political theory, specifically liberalism and socialism. Situating her account with those who have characterized that tradition as "male-stream" thought, Pateman argues that feminist theory challenges traditional philosophical arguments about justice, freedom, and equality. Moreover, she argues, feminism should not be "domesticated" to fit within traditional arguments. Gender inequality is not just one more form of injustice that fine-tuning the system can redress. To the contrary, the system depends on the exclusion of women. Both liberal and socialist theories, she notes, split the world into public and private domains before the question of freedom and justice are raised. Women are written out before the articulation of rights and opportunities. Therefore, the individual subject of freedom and justice is a disembodied individual who is implicitly masculine. Sex difference cannot simply be accommodated, because that "leaves intact the sexually particular characterization of the public world, the individual, and his capacities." By writing out women, the individual of traditional theory lacks capacities "that men don't possess"—bodies that can give birth. Feminist theory that starts from embodied individuals thus challenges "theory that masquerades as universalism" (Reading 11). Instead of gender-neutral equality, which continues to deny the embodiment of individuals, Pateman argues that feminists should be more concerned with autonomy.

The concept of autonomy is central to Sônia Correa and Rosalind Petchesky (Reading 16) who discuss feminist theorizing at this intersection of the personal and political: reproductive health and rights. They show that the feminist claim to reproductive self-determination relies on the liberal right of bodily integrity, the right not to be interfered with by government in matters concerning one's body and its processes. However, this liberal right is only one of four principles that Correa and Petchesky use to articulate a flexible feminist framework for reproductive justice. The others are equality, personhood, and diversity. In describing each of these principles, they incorporate the insights developed by transnational and multiracial feminists. As they make clear, of sexual and reproductive health matters must always be considered within specific social-historical locations, taking full account of women's situation.

The essay gives a glimpse into the north–south collaborations on sexual and reproductive health and safety that Amrita Basu (Reading 6) identified as among the strongest global coalitions.[20] At the same time, women of the south have questioned the extent to which feminist theory in the north privileges personal experiences in private life. For instance, Basu expresses the sentiment that feminists in the north overemphasize individual sexual issues in contrast to questions of poverty and basic needs that are more likely to be raised by feminists of the south. For feminists in the global south, economic justice and sustainable development are often the most pressing issues. In addition, multiracial feminists argued that the concept should be read in reverse as well—the political is personal. That is, they argue, feminists must also commit to work on issues that do not directly affect them. One need not be subject to racism, homophobia, or xenophobia, they argue, to know that it is wrong and to work to end it (Thompson Reading 5). Therefore, as with other core feminist concepts, the meaning and importance of the personal is political concept is an ongoing subject of debate locally and globally.

INTERSECTIONALITY—The various ways of being women, shaped along axes of domination such as race, class, nation, and sexual orientation that intertwine with gender, means that "the paradox at the heart of feminism" is how to weigh the things women have in common with the differences among us (Spelman 1988: 3). As noted earlier, in the 1990s the initial additive model of oppression gave way to a more fluid and flexible understanding of the interactions of systems of domination. The concept of intersectionality was developed by Kimberlé Crenshaw to understand the complex interactions of racism and sexism that erase the specific experiences of routine violence experienced by African-American women. It describes the simultaneous, multiple, overlapping, and contradictory systems of power that shape our lives and political options. She argued that "through an awareness of intersectionality, we can better acknowledge and ground the differences among us and negotiate the means by which these differences will find expression in constructing group politics" (Crenshaw 1993). Intersectional feminist theory "locates its analysis within systems of ideological, political, and economic power as they are shaped by historical patterns of race, class, gender, sexuality, nation, ethnicity, and age." With this concept, scholars have produced a wealth of interdisciplinary scholarship focusing on "how structures of difference combine to create new and distinct social, cultural, and artistic forms" (Dill et al. 2007: 629). In particular, the concept destabilizes existing power relations grounded in the lived experiences of the marginalized, it allows counterhegemonic narratives to come into focus.

As an "analytic strategy," intersectionality also provides guidance on how to move beyond fragmented identity politics (Dill and Zambrana Reading 18). It suggests that by specifying differences and commonalities it becomes possible to find the ground on which to build alliances and principled coalitions (Collins 1990). However, such moments of coalescence are historically contingent. "The meaning of our sisterhood will change. If society's powers are ever mobile and in flux, as they are, then our oppositional moves must not be ideologically limited to one, single, frozen, 'correct' response" (Sandoval 1990: 66). In the readings that follow, students can trace the strands of oppositional thinking by feminists that in tandem and in dialogue as feminist theory moved from initial static concepts to the cusp of more flexible intersectional analyses, which are taken up in Section II.

Notes

1. The first usage of this term was apparently in the preface of Kate Millett's book, *Sexual Politics*, one of the earliest feminist critiques published by a mainstream press. See also Nicholson Reading 4 and Thompson Reading 6.
2. This question reverberates with those asked in earlier centuries by, for instance, by Mary

Wollstonecraft [1792]1975; John Stuart Mill 1883; and Harriet Taylor [1851]1983. In the eighteenth and nineteenth centuries they asked what women's character might be like if curtailed by what pleased men.

3. There has been much debate about the quality of the 1953 translation with some arguing that it essentialized de Beauvoir's argument. A more recent translation by French feminist scholars was published in 2010. We decided to stay with the version read by English speakers at the time. See de Beauvoir 2010.

4. Radical feminists took the name *radical* from the new left politics of the moment that positioned itself as radical in contrast to both liberalism and the old left of the 1950s. See Grant 1993: 18–19.

5. This famous statement is attributed to Sigmund Freud, whose theorized sex differences at the intersections of biological and psychological sciences. Morgan 2006 notes that the concept of gender has not been as earth shattering for speakers of other languages because it does not translate well.

6. Two early collections are Michelle Rosaldo and Louise Lamphere, eds., *Woman, Culture, and Society* (Palo Alto: Stanford University Press, 1974) and Rayna Reiter, ed., *Toward an Anthropology of Women* (New York: Monthly Review Press, 1975).

7. As it was first used in 1599, the term, exotic, simply meant "alien, introduced from abroad, not indigenous." By the end of the nineteenth century, however, the term had come to connote something, exciting, stimulating, and slightly dangerous with which to "spice up" the more mundane domestic world (Ashcroft et al. 1998: 94).

8. See for example Rubin 1975: 166, 168, 172, 174–5, 181. We do not intend to single Rubin and Oakley out for criticism. Rather, we highlighted their work because they exemplify the conversations and debates of their time—in their strengths and their weaknesses.

9. Audre Lorde offers an exemplary critique of this practice in her classic essay, "An Open Letter to Mary Daly," in Moraga and Anzaldúa 1981. See also Mary Daly 1978; Chandra Talpade Mohanty 1991b; and bell hooks 1984. For feminist definitions of patriarchy, see Hartmann Reading 18; Gayle Rubin 1975; Zillah Eisenstein 1978; and Maria Mies 1986.

10. In widely cited published interviews, Feinberg expresses a preference for the gender-neutral pronouns ze and hir, which we follow.

11. For instance, Suzanne Kessler (2000) examines the practice of surgical alteration of the ambiguous genitalia of intersexed persons to fit medical categories of sexually dimorphic bodies. Although feminist theorists, including Kessler, argued for socially constructed genders, they, nonetheless, easily fell into step with the medical logic of two distinct sexes and two distinct genders, both marked by distinct body types. See also Ann Fausto-Sterling (2000), which examines how biological knowledge of sex, gender, and sexuality shapes and is shaped by politics and culture and how both are literally embodied in our physiology.

12. A vast literature on significance of differences between women and men was produced in the 1980s, including debates about gender differences in moral reasoning (Carol Gilligan 1982), in knowledge production (Mary Belenky et al. 1986 and Hester Eisenstein and Alice Jardine 1980), in relationality (Nancy Chodorow 1978 and Sara Ruddick 1989), and in sexuality (Catharine MacKinnon 1987). Because of space limitations, this strand of feminist theory is not well represented in this anthology.

13. See also Omi and Winant (1994) whose concept of racial formation argues that race is independent but connected to capitalism and imperialism. Similarly, post-colonial theorists argue that colonialism has generated relations of power that are related to but independent of capitalism. See Bhabha 1990 and 1998.

14. Section III discusses some of the problematic implications of identity politics for feminist theories of subjectivity and agency.

15. The term, "Third World" is generally attributed to French demographer, Alfred Sauvy. The term rapidly developed pejorative and racialized connotations in Western usage. On use of the term by U.S. feminists of color, see Burris 1971; Anzaldúa Reading 25; and Sandoval 1990.

16. Section III includes readings that question the trustworthiness of experience as a basis for knowledge building.

17. Feminist consciousness-raising owes much to the theories of oppression developed by W. E. B. Du Bois (1969) and Paulo Freire (1970).

18. The continuing importance of experiential narratives for women of the south and women of color can be seen in Shari Stone-Mediatore 2000 and The Latina Feminist Group 2001. See also Grant 1993: 27.

19. Published guidelines for consciousness-raising groups helped set up this process of defining the most pressing issues by providing lists of suggested topics. See "Consciousness Raising" (1970). This piece defines the appropriate composition and process for consciousness-raising groups and lists the topics of family, childhood and adolescence, men, marital status, motherhood, sex, women, behavior, ambitions, and movement activity.

20. This essay is from a collection that sought to extend the influence of feminist reproductive and sexual health networks on the 1994 Cairo conference on Development and Population. Rosalind Petchesky is feminist political scientist and activist based in the U.S., and Sônia Correa, based in Brazil, coordinates research on sexual and reproductive health for Development Alternatives with Women for a New Era (DAWN).

FEMINIST MOVEMENTS

1.
THE DAY THE MOUNTAINS MOVE
Yosano Akiko
(1911)

The day the mountains move has come.
I speak, but no one believes me.
For a time the mountains have been asleep,
But long ago they danced with fire.
It doesn't matter if you believe this,
My friends, as long as you believe:
All the sleeping women
Are now awake and moving.

2.
RE-ROOTING AMERICAN WOMEN'S ACTIVISM: GLOBAL PERSPECTIVES ON 1848

Nancy A. Hewitt

(2001)

For many American women's historians trained in the 1960s and 1970s, interest in the field was inspired by their engagement with women's liberation. They were compelled by their politics to recover the roots of modern feminism. Many radical feminists initially found foremothers in the likes of Louise Michel, Emma Goldman, Crystal Eastman, and other turn-of-the-century socialist and anarchist women. Though women's historians of this generation were driven by competing visions of feminism and thus embraced different foremothers, many sought to understand the present through a genealogical excavation of the past. This was particularly true for those studying women's political activism, who moved from contemporary debates about sex equity back through suffrage (socialism too quickly fell by the wayside in the US) and then Seneca Falls. This chapter explores the implications of reaching Seneca Falls through this reverse chronological trajectory, and then suggests how we might rethink the history of women's activism by re-embedding Seneca Falls in the world of 1848.

What a world it was—revolutions erupted across Europe; Irish peasants and later defeated German revolutionaries migrated to the United States *en masse*; the Treaty of Guadalupe Hidalgo ended the Mexican-American War, adding new territories and peoples to the United States; the *Communist Manifesto* was published; the Seneca Nation embraced a written constitution for the first time; John Humphrey Noyes established a utopian community at Onedia, New York; New York State granted property rights to married women; slavery was abolished in the French West Indies; US slaves fled North to find freedom; the first Chinese immigrants to North America arrived in San Francisco; the Gold Rush began; the Free Soil Party and spiritualism were founded and both attracted thousands of devotees. This remarkable array of events shaped the meaning of Seneca Falls and the trajectories of women's activism in the mid-nineteenth-century US.

Yet rarely is the 1848 women's rights convention conceived as part of these revolutionary developments. Instead, it is most often defined as foremother to the federal suffrage amendment passed in the US in 1920. Disentangling Seneca Falls from suffrage is no easy task. These two events were identified as the touchstones of American women's history long before the field was created. Until quite recently, Betsy Ross stitching the American flag and the Salem Witch Trials were the only other widely-known 'women's' events in American history. In 1959, Eleanor Flexner's *Century of Struggle* reinvigorated the narrative that carried women's activism from Seneca Falls to suffrage, but the original story line was crafted by pioneer feminists themselves. In their six-volume *History of Woman's Suffrage*, published between 1881 and 1922, editors Susan B. Anthony, Elizabeth Cady Stanton and Matilda Joslyn Gage claimed Seneca Falls as the birthplace of the women's movement and the Nineteenth Amendment mandating women's suffrage as that movement's greatest achievement.[1]

In recent years, scholars studying African American, immigrant and working-class women have challenged certain aspects of the story.[2] Focusing on the post-Civil War suffrage campaign rather than its antebellum antecedents, historians have detailed the racist, nativist and elitist tendencies of many white women activists and highlighted the exclusion of poor, black and immigrant women from the political organizations and agendas of more well-to-do white suffragists. These challenges have tarnished the image of several pioneer figures and added a few women of colour and working women to the pantheon of feminist foremothers, but the dominant story of women's political activism as the struggle for enfranchisement has been left largely intact.[3]

By focusing the analysis synchronically—that is, on events occurring concurrently with the emergence of women's rights in 1848—we leave aside the question of how women moved from Seneca Falls to suffrage. We can then ask, instead, how women of various racial, ethnic and economic backgrounds and of diverse religious, regional and ideological perspectives defined women's rights in the 1840s? How were these views shaped by the Mexican-American War, mass immigration, European revolutions, debates over slavery, race and Native American rights? And to what extent did the agenda crafted at Seneca Falls and later women's rights conventions speak to the concerns expressed by female radicals in Europe and by other communities of women in the US? The answers offered here are speculative, the intention being merely to open up the landscape of 1848, to relocate Seneca Falls within a more panoramic frame, and to suggest how this might help us write new histories of American women's activism by reclaiming alternative narratives of women's rights.

First, the legend of the Seneca Falls Woman's Rights Convention—a legend well-entrenched in historical texts and popular memory—must be challenged. The classic version of the story was penned by Elizabeth Cady Stanton in her 1898 autobiography.[4] In 1840, Stanton found herself, 26 years old and newly married, 'seated behind a curtain at the World's Anti-Slavery Convention in London in company with the forty-two year old Lucretia Mott (a well-known Quaker abolitionist). The unwillingness of the convention to seat women delegates led the two to an animated discussion about the discrimination they were experiencing' and to the decision to call a women's rights convention on their return to the States.

'Eight years and several children later, Stanton, restless and yearning for intellectual stimulation in the isolated town of Seneca Falls, New York, met Mott again.' Joined by three friends of Mott, they drew up a Declaration of Sentiments, modelled on the Declaration of Independence, listing women's grievances. They then sent out a call inviting 'interested men and women to discuss the subject of women's rights' at the local Wesleyan Chapel. Much to the organizers' surprise, some three hundred women and men showed up. The result of the Seneca Falls convention 'was a surge of interest in the "woman question" and the launching of a vigorous debate that was destined to increase in scope and volume through the next seventy-two years', culminating in the achievement of women suffrage.

Most current accounts of this event accept Stanton's narrative and focus on her leadership and the demand for political equality. The history is thus written as one woman's struggle to craft a public role for herself and to inspire a political movement in support of suffrage. The main actors are nearly all native-born white women, assisted by a few good men—such as Lucretia Mott's husband James, who chaired the Seneca Falls convention, and abolitionist leader Frederick Douglass, the lone African American participant, who argued vigorously for women's right to vote.

Many other versions of this story could be told, however, highlighting other organizers, other participants and other agendas. Judith Wellman, for instance, has traced three distinct political networks—Free Soilers, legal reformers, and Quaker abolitionists—who converged at the 1848 convention. Nancy Isenberg has just completed a book that places Seneca Falls in the context of contemporary struggles over church politics, property rights, and moral reform. More than a decade ago, I too tried to recast the history of woman's rights, by placing radical Quakers at centre stage.[5] Led by Lucretia Mott, these feminist Friends dominated the Seneca Falls organizing committee (Stanton was the sole non-Quaker) and provided somewhere between a quarter and a third of the 100 individuals who signed the convention's Declaration of Sentiments. A more complete challenge must also examine the links between women activists in the US and their counterparts in Europe as well as between the agendas of Anglo-American women's rights advocates and the concerns of African American, Native American, Mexican American, immigrant and working-class women.

A new history of women's rights might begin by replacing Elizabeth Cady Stanton with Lucretia Mott as the central figure at the Seneca Falls Convention. Mott was, after all, the magnet that attracted such a large Quaker contingent to the meeting. …

The path that Mott … took to Seneca Falls was traversed by many women who shared the faith and politics of these radical Quakers; it is a path that links women's rights to decidedly different historical connections and contexts than those claimed by Stanton. … Like her Quaker co-workers, she was immersed in efforts to end slavery, advance the rights of free blacks and Indians, protest the US war with Mexico, and secure property reform. …

Events in Europe were widely covered that summer in the antislavery as well as the mainstream press.[6] Several American women who later embraced women's rights had forged bonds with their abolitionist sisters in England during the 1830s and 1840s. Now they reached out to like-minded women in France, Germany and other parts of Europe, creating a set of international alliances among pioneer feminists.[7] Evidence of these connections appears in the reports of the early women's rights conventions. In the Syracuse proceedings … a letter appeared from French revolutionaries Pauline Roland and Jeanne Deroin, sent to the 'Convention of American Women' from their Parisian prison cell in June 1851. In it, they applauded the courage of the American women and reminded them that the chains of the throne and the scaffold, the church and the patriarch, the slave, the worker and the woman must all be broken simultaneously if 'the kingdom of Equality and Justice shall be realized on Earth'.[8]

Deroin was a seamstress, a committed Saint Simonian socialist, and a revolutionary. In June 1848, she demanded that her male counterparts recognize women's political and social rights. She claimed the right to vote, ran for the legislative assembly, organized workers, and wrote for *La Voix des Femmes*, an early French feminist newspaper.[9] The events that enveloped Deroin were closely followed by abolitionists and women's rights advocates in the US. The abolition of slavery in the French West Indies, for instance, was applauded by Lucretia Mott, who urged her American compatriots to 'take courage' from such advances abroad. 'We cannot separate our own freedom from that of the slave'; they are 'inseparably connected ... in France', she noted, and are 'beginning to be so in other countries'.[10] In Rochester, emancipation in the French West Indies was marked by a city-wide celebration on 1 August, just one day before women's rights advocates gathered at the city's Unitarian church to complete the deliberations begun at Seneca Falls.[11]

After a July visit to the Seneca (Indian) Nation, Mott claimed that Native Americans, too, were learning 'from the political agitations abroad ... imitating the movements of France and all Europe and seeking a larger liberty ...'.[12] This concept of a 'larger liberty' was central to important segments of revolutionary movements in France and Germany and of radical abolition and women's rights movements in England and the US. These segments comprised largely women and men who emerged from utopian socialist societies and radical separatist congregations—followers of Charles Fourier, French Saint Simonians, German religious dissidents, and Quakers who rejected the Society of Friends' restrictions on worldly activity and complete sexual and racial equality.[13] These were revolutionaries who believed that to truly transform society meant rooting out oppression in all its forms—in the family, the church, the community, the economy, the polity—simultaneously. To them, emancipation of any group—slaves, for instance—was inextricably intertwined with emancipation for all groups—workers, women, prisoners and other subjugated peoples. Ultimately, a cooperative commonwealth based on shared labour and shared resources must replace older forms of rule—monarchies, autocracies, even bourgeois democracies. These radical activists advocated individual rights, but only in so far as they complemented rather than competed with communitarian ideals.

Thus revolutionaries like Deroin and women's rights advocates like Mott ... supported voting rights for those currently excluded from the body politic, viewing suffrage as a necessary but not a sufficient means for achieving change. The question was complicated in the US by Quaker women's and men's refusal to participate in a government that tolerated violence against slaves and employed military might in the conquest of Mexico. Members of the Friends of Human Progress, a radical Quaker association founded in summer 1848, argued that women should have the same right to refuse to vote as men, but suffrage was not high on their political agenda. Instead, for them, the women's rights movement provided one more building block in a multifaceted campaign to achieve racial, economic and gender justice in America.[14]

Radical Quaker analyses of European revolutionaries turned on the inclusiveness of their vision. They applauded Jeanne Deroin and Pauline Roland in this regard, but their enthusiasm for Hungarian freedom fighter Louis Kossuth waned during his visit to the US in the early 1850s, when he failed to speak out against slavery.[15] For Mott … and like-minded co-workers, rights for women remained tied to rights for slaves, free blacks, landless labourers, industrial workers, Native Americans and Mexicans. When radical Quakers organized the second US women's rights convention in Rochester two weeks after the Seneca Falls meeting, a woman presided, two local seamstresses were invited to discuss women's economic oppression, and two black abolitionist leaders fresh from the Emancipation Day celebration—Frederick Douglass and William C. Nell—were listed as featured speakers. The convention participants called for equal property rights, pay, access to education and occupations, authority in the church and home, and voting rights, for all women regardless of 'complexion', that is race. A month later, a gathering of the Friends of Human Progress added to this list land reform, Native American rights, and the abolition of capital punishment.[16]

Two weeks after the Rochester convention, Frederick Douglass carried the women's rights message into a new arena—the National Convention of Colored Freemen, held in Cleveland, Ohio. He introduced a resolution providing for the full and equal participation of women and men.[17] William Nell, who three years earlier had successfully advocated women's rights in the militant New England Freedom Association (a group that aided fugitive slaves), spoke on behalf of the resolution. By the mid-1850s, nearly every major free black organization in the North granted voting rights to women and a few included women among their officers.

Though the record among predominantly white antislavery organizations was more uneven, those societies that counted a large number of Quakers and some number of free blacks in their membership—such as the Philadelphia Female Anti-Slavery Society and the Western New York Anti-Slavery Society—were in the vanguard. They consistently sought and recognized the support of their African American colleagues; and, as a result, a small circle of black women and men regularly joined women's rights conventions as speakers, delegates and officers. …

Free blacks recognized the potential power of these interracial alliances for achieving their primary goals—access to education and jobs, abolition and aid to fugitive slaves. During 1848, free black women in several cities also demonstrated their own brand of women's rights, one inextricably entwined with racial justice. Charlotte Forten, a member of an affluent free black family of Philadelphia, pursued her work for education, fugitive slaves, abolition and women's rights quietly and with the support of Lucretia Mott and the Philadelphia Female Anti-Slavery Society. Her counterparts across the North—many from less wealthy backgrounds—organized fundraising fairs, challenged school segregation, and refused to consume slave-produced goods. Some embraced more dramatic strategies. In Cincinnati, for instance, in the summer of 1848, freedwomen used washboards and shovels to fend off slavecatchers harassing blacks in the city.[18] Other free women armed themselves with even more deadly weapons to protect fugitive slaves.

In the South, more drastic measures were required if black women were going to participate in these larger freedom struggles. One particularly daring escape was planned in fall 1848 by Ellen Craft, a slave woman from Macon, Georgia. Married to William Craft, a free black cabinetmaker, the light-skinned Ellen dressed herself as a young gentleman, swathed her jaw in bandages to make it appear she was ill, and boarded a train and then a steamer to Philadelphia, with William posing as her/his manservant. They arrived safely in port on Christmas morning, and became noted abolitionist speakers in the US and England.[19] Ellen literally embodied the meaning of women's rights for slaves—the right to control over one's person and one's family. These were property rights, but of a different sort than those envisioned by most white women. …

As early as 1848, the rejection of feminine fashion and the embrace of more liberated, and more masculine, dress had become one sign of revolutionary commitment for women radicals in Europe and the US. Believing that clothes made the man while corsets confined the woman, a number of radical women sought to free themselves and their sisters from restrictive clothing. Replacing bone stays, cinch waists, and long skirts with turkish trousers, loose blouses and knee-length jackets, dress reformers assumed that ease of movement would aid in women's public as well as private labours. In her bid for freedom, Ellen Craft readily exchanged women's skirts for men's pants. In the case of slaves, however, and others who regularly performed extensive manual labour—Native American farmers, Mexican artisans, and Irish factory workers—women already wore less restrictive clothing than their white middle-class counterparts. Yet the freer clothing donned by these women was not usually linked to emancipation. Rather, the failure of poor and working women or any woman from another culture to wear middle-class white American fashions was viewed by those with wealth and power as a reflection of loose morals and a cry for patriarchal control.

Between 1846 and 1848, the issues of women's dress and men's control intersected with the path of western conquest as the Mexican-American War brought vast new territories under US authority. …

Under Spanish law and, after 1821, Mexican law, women retained rights to property after marriage; they could inherit, loan, convey or pawn property whether single or married; they shared custody of children; and they could sue in court without a male relative's approval.[20] These rights were almost uniformly denied under Anglo-American law. In the areas that came under US control, women's rights had been expanded further during the 1830s and 1840s by residents' distance from the district courts of Mexico. They may also have been influenced by their proximity to Pueblo villages, in which women had traditionally held rights to property and a public voice though such rights had been severely curtailed after the Spanish conquest. In Mexican communities, extended kin groups, communal farming patterns, and collective decision-making as well as more egalitarian legal codes defined notions of women's rights and responsibilities.

Northern Mexico was no feminist utopia, however, as the number and range of court cases against abusive husbands, adultery, assault, property disputes and debts make clear. Nonetheless, conditions worsened with the signing of the Treaty of Guadalupe Hidalgo. As the region came under US control, government officials, Protestant missionaries, and white settlers used portrayals of local women as sexually promiscuous and culturally inferior to justify the imposition of Anglo-American authority. At the very same time, then, as participants at the Seneca Falls Convention were demanding rights to property, inheritance, and custody, 'New' Mexican women were losing precisely those rights as they came under US jurisdiction. Mexican women were losing not only rights, but also claims to respectability by virtue of their dark skin and now 'foreign' ways. All but the most affluent were compared, as were their Native American counterparts in the Southwest and California, to southern slaves. Indeed, any group of women in the US considered non-white might be defined as morally and socially inferior.

In the northeastern US non-white women had long been affected by the influx of Euro-Americans. Prior to and for more than a century after contact with Europeans, the Seneca—like other Iroquois groups and like the Pueblo—passed names and property through the mother's line, husbands moved into their wives' households upon marriage, and women controlled agricultural production. Seneca women also held positions of religious and political authority, though chiefs and *sachems* were almost always men. Over the course of two centuries of trade, warfare, disease, missionary efforts and governmental pressure, however, the Seneca had lost most of their tribal lands, moved to reservations, and converted to patrilineal descent and men's control of agriculture. In July 1848, they also adopted a new 'republican' form of government and a written constitution. Women, who once held veto power over a range of decisions—from the appointment of chiefs to the signing of treaties—were divested of some of their authority, but retained the right to vote. And though Seneca men and women would now elect judges and legislators by majority vote, 3/4 of all voters and 3/4 of all *mothers* had to ratify legislative decisions.[21]

Several Quaker women's rights advocates were in correspondence with Seneca residents on the Cattaragus reservation, and Quaker missionary women described in detail the specific voting privileges accorded women, and mothers, there.[22] Lucretia Mott visited the reservation just before travelling to Seneca Falls; and just after the Declaration of Sentiments was published, the Seneca women produced a remarkably similar document. For the next 70 years, white suffragists would point, with some ambivalence, to the Iroquois as emblems of politically empowered women, recognizing the ways that communal ownership of property, matrilineal descent, and shared political and religious authority established foundations for female equality.[23] Yet Iroquois women themselves, like their Mexican and Pueblo counterparts, would slowly lose both rights and respectability as they were forced to embrace Anglo-American laws and customs. And in the post-Civil War period, most women's rights advocates, having accepted the individual right of suffrage as their primary goal, no longer embraced the communitarian vision of equality and justice that allowed their antebellum foremothers to see the Seneca as a model rather than a problem.

There are other threads to follow as we contextualize women's rights and women's activism in the 1840s: exiled revolutionaries (whose radical politics led to the support of women's and workers' rights in the German-language press); Irish immigrants (812 of whom arrived in New York harbour while the Seneca Falls convention was in session); the Gold Rush and western migration (which pulled apart but also extended the radical Quaker network with new circles of activity forming in Michigan, Indiana, and California). Yet the examples above are sufficient to suggest the potential richness of a synchronic analysis.

In rethinking Seneca Falls, it is important to remember that the movement Elizabeth Cady Stanton championed—a movement based on liberal conceptions of self-ownership, individual rights and suffrage—was born there. But it was not alone, nor was it yet triumphant. Rather, the vision held by the largest and most active contingent of feminist foremothers was rooted in communitarian values and organic conceptions of both oppression and liberation. Linked to agendas promoted by utopian socialists and religious radicals in Europe's revolutionary circles, the ideas advanced by feminist Friends also echoed—if sometimes unintentionally—the experiences of women in those African American, Mexican and Native American communities founded on extended kinship networks, communal labour and collective rights. Self-consciously engaged in campaigns against slavery, war and western conquest, and for religious freedom, economic justice and political equality, radical Quakers connected the women's rights agenda to a broader programme of social transformation and more diverse networks of activists. Even with all the limitations and shortcomings of such utopian endeavours and knowing that a more liberal, rights-based vision would ultimately dominate, the legacy of women's rights radicals is worth reclaiming. For it provides an alternative foundation for modern feminism, one that incorporates race and class issues, critiques of colonialism, socialist foremothers, and an internationalist perspective.

Notes

1. E. Flexner, Century *of Struggle: The Women's Rights Movement in the United States* (Cambridge, Mass: Belknap Press, 1959); E. C. Stanton, S. B. Anthony, and M. j. Gage (eds), *History of Women Suffrage*, 6 volumes. …

2. Some of those most important works in this area are R. Terborg-Penn, *African American Women in the Struggle for the Vote, 1850–1920* (Bloomington: Indiana University Press, 1998) and R. Terborg-Penn, 'Discrimination Against Afro-American Women in the Woman's Movement, 1830–1920' in R. Terborg-Penn and S. Harley (eds), *The Afro-American Woman: Struggles and Images* (Port Washington, NY: Kennikat Press, 1978) pp. 17–27; P. Giddings, *When and Where I Enter: The Impact of Black Women on Race and Sex in America* (New York: William Morrow, 1984); Y. Azize, 'Puerto Rican Women and the Vote', reprinted in E. DuBois and V. Ruiz (eds), *Unequal Sisters: A Multicultural History of Women in the United States* (New York: Routledge, 1994) pp. 260–7; J. Jensen, '"Disfranchisement is a Disgrace": Women and Politics in New Mexico, 1900–1940' in J. M. Jensen and D. Miller (eds), *New Mexico Women: Intercultural Perspectives* (Albuquerque: University of New Mexico Press, 1990) pp. 301–31; E. C. DuBois, 'Working Women, Class Relations, and Suffrage Militance: Harriet Stanton Blatch and the New York Woman Suffrage Movement, 1894–1909', *Journal of American History*, 74 (June 1987) pp. 34–58.

3. See, for instance, the treatment of woman's rights and suffrage in S. Evans, *Born for Liberty: A History of Women in America* (New York: The Free Press, 1989) …

4. E. C. Stanton, *Eighty Years and More: Reminiscences, 1815–1897* (New York: T. Fisher Unwin, 1898). The version sketched below, based on Stanton's autobiography, comes from A. F. Scott, *Natural Allies: Women's Association in American History* (Urbana: University of Illinois Press, 1992), pp. 54–5. This version parallels that found in most women's history and American history texts. For two articles that suggest a more complex origin for the Seneca Falls Convention, and women's rights more generally, see J. Wellman, 'The Seneca Falls Woman's Rights Convention: A Study of Social Networks', *Journal of Women's History*, 3 (Spring 1991) pp. 9–37; and Nancy A. Hewitt, 'Feminist Friends: Agrarian Quakers and the Emergence of Woman's Rights in America', *Feminist Studies*, 12 (Spring 1986) pp. 27–49.

5. Wellman, 'The Seneca Falls Woman's Rights Convention'; N. Isenberg, *Sex and Citizenship in Antebellum America* (New York: University of North Carolina Press, 1998); and Hewitt, 'Feminist Friends.'

6. See especially Frederick Douglass' *North Star*, which had just begun publication in early 1848 and covered events in Europe extensively during that spring and summer.

7. See B. Anderson, *Joyous Greetings: The First International Women's Movement, 1830–1860* (New York: Oxford University Press, 2000) for a pathbreaking analysis of these early international connections.

8. *Proceedings of the Woman's Rights Convention*, quote p. 35; letter pp. 32–5.

9. On the life of Jeanne Deroin, see C. Goldberg Moses, *French Feminism in the Nineteenth Century* (Albany: State University of New York Press, 1984); and Moses and L. Wahl Rabine (eds), *The Word and the Act: French Feminism in the Age of Romanticism* (Bloomington: Indiana University Press, 1992).

10. Lucretia Mott, 'Law of Progress,' in D. Greene (ed.), *Lucretia Matt: Her Complete Speeches and Sermons* (New York: Edwin Mellen Press, 1980) p. 75. Thanks to Bonnie Anderson for bringing this speech to my attention.

11. The *North Star* provided lengthy coverage of the upcoming Emancipation Day celebration in its July 14, 1848 issue, the same issue in which the announcement of the Seneca Falls Woman's Rights Convention appeared.

12. Mott to Quincy, *The Liberator*, 6 October 1848.

13. See Moses, *French Feminism*; C. M. Prelinger, 'Religious Dissent, Women's Rights, and the Hamburger Hochshule fuer das Weibliche Geschlecht in Mid-Nineteenth-century Germany', Church History, 45 (1976) pp. 42–55; and Hewitt, 'Feminist Friends'.

14. On the political vision of the Friends of Human Progress (also known as the Congregational Friends and the Progressive Friends), see Proceedings of the Yearly Meeting of Congregational Friends, Held at Waterloo, NY, from the Fourth to the Sixth of the Sixth Month, Inclusive, with an Appendix, 1849 (Auburn, NY: Oliphant's Press, 1849); and Yearly Meeting of Congregational Friends, *Proceedings of the Woman's Rights Convention* (Auburn, NY: Henry Oliphant, 1850).

15. See, for instance, Mary Robbins Post to Dear All [Isaac and Amy Post], 5 May, 185[1], Post Family Papers.

16. On Rochester Convention, see Report, 'Rochester Woman's Rights Convention,' 2 August 1848, Phoebe Post Willis Papers, University of Rochester, Rochester, New York; and Hewitt, 'Feminist Friends'.

17. Material in this paragraph is taken from Terborg-Penn, 'Afro-Americans in the Struggle for Woman's Suffrage', Chapter 1; and Benjamin Quarles, 'Frederick Douglass and the Woman's Rights Movement', History 2000 Occasional Papers Series, No. 1–1993 (Baltimore, Md: Morgan State University Foundation, 1993).

18. On black women's antislavery activity, see D. Sterling (ed.), *We Are Your Sisters: Black Women in the Nineteenth Century* (New York: WW Norton, 1984) Part II; and J. Roy Jeffrey, *The Great Silent Army of Abolitionism: Ordinary Women in the Antislavery Movement* (Chapel Hill: UNC Press, 1998) Chapter 4.

19. Described in Sterling, *We Are Your Sisters*, pp. 62–4.

20. Magoffin quoted in J. Lecompte, 'The Independent Women of Hispanic New Mexico', *Western Historical Quarterly*, 22, 1 (1981) pp. 17–35.

21. For an overview of Seneca women's status, see J. M. Jensen, 'Native American Women and Agriculture' in K. K. Sklar and T. Dublin (eds), *Women and Power in American History*, volume 1 (Englewood Cliffs, NJ: Prentice-Hall, 1991) pp. 8–23. See also, S. R. Wagner, *The Untold Story of the Iroquois Influence on Early Feminists* (Aberdeen, South Dakota: Sky Carrier Press, 1996); and H. S. C. Caswell, *Our Life Among the Iroquois Indians* (Boston and Chicago: Congregational Sunday School and Publishing Society, 1892) and Mott to Quincy, *The Liberator*, 6 October 1848.

22. For a detailed account by a Quaker missionary of Seneca Indian life, see Caswell, *Our Life Among the Iroquois Indians* especially pp. 79–80 on the new 1848 constitution.

23. For a discussion of this interest and ambivalence about Indian women in the women's movement, see D. Janiewski, 'Giving Women a Future: Alice Fletcher, the "Woman Question" and "Indian Reform"' in N. A. Hewitt and S. Lebsock (eds), *Visible Women: New Essays on American Activism*, (Urbana: University of Illinois Press, 1993) pp. 325–44.

3.

THE SECOND SEX: INTRODUCTION
Simone de Beauvoir
(1952)

For a long time I have hesitated to write a book on woman. The subject is irritating, especially to women; and it is not new. Enough ink has been spilled in the quarreling over feminism, now practically over, and perhaps we should say no more about it. It is still talked about, however, for the voluminous nonsense uttered during the last century seems to have done little to illuminate the problem. After all, is there a problem? And if so, what is it? Are there women, really? Most assuredly the theory of the eternal feminine still has its adherents who will whisper in your ear: "Even in Russia women still are *women*"; and other erudite persons-sometimes the very same-say with a sigh: "Woman is losing her way, woman is lost." One wonders if women still exist, if they will always exist, whether or not it is desirable that they should, what place they occupy in this world, what their place should be. "What has become of women?" was asked recently in an ephemeral magazine.[1]

But first we must ask: what is a woman? "*Total mulier in utero,*" says one, "woman is a womb." But in speaking of certain women, connoisseurs declare that they are not women, although they are equipped with a uterus like the rest. All agree in recognizing the fact that females exist in the human species; today as always they make up about one half of humanity. And yet we are told that femininity is in danger; we are exhorted to be women, remain women, become women. It would appear, then, that every female human being is not necessarily a woman; to be so consider she must share in that mysterious and threatened realm known as femininity. Is this attribute something secreted by the ovaries? Or is it a Platonic essence, a product of the philosophic imagination? Is a rustling petticoat enough to bring it down to earth? Although some women try zealously to incarnate this essence, it is hardly patentable. It is frequently described in vague and dazzling terms that seem have been borrowed from the vocabulary of the seers, and indeed in the times of St. Thomas it was considered an essence as certainly defined as the somniferous virtue of the poppy. …

If her functioning as a female is not enough to define woman, if we decline also to explain her through "the eternal feminine," and if nevertheless we admit, provisionally, that women do exist, then we must face the question: what is a woman?

To state the question is, to me, to suggest, at once, a preliminary answer. The fact that I ask it is in itself significant. A man would never get the notion of writing a book on the peculiar situation of the human male.[2] But if I wish to define myself, I must first of all say: "I am a woman"; on this truth must be based all further discussion. A man never begins by presenting himself as an individual of a certain sex; it goes without saying that he is a man. The terms *masculine* and *feminine* are used symmetrically only as a matter of form, as on legal papers. In actuality the relation of the two sexes is not quite like that of two electrical poles, for man represents both the positive and the neutral, as is indicated by the common use of *man* to designate human beings in general; whereas woman represents only the negative, defined by limiting criteria, without reciprocity. In the midst of an abstract discussion it is vexing to hear a man say: "You think thus and so because you are a woman"; but I know that my only defense is to reply: "I think thus and so because it is true," thereby removing my subjective self from the argument. It would be out of the question to reply: "And you think the contrary because you are a man," for it is understood that the fact of being a man is no peculiarity. A man is in the right in being a man; it is the woman who is in the wrong. It amounts to this: just as for the ancients there was an absolute vertical with reference to which the oblique was defined, so there is an absolute human type, the masculine. Woman has ovaries, a uterus; these peculiarities imprison her in her subjectivity, circumscribe her within the limits of her own nature. It is often said that she thinks with her glands. Man superbly ignores the fact that his anatomy also includes glands, such as the testicles, and that they secrete hormones. He thinks of his body as a direct and normal connection with the world, which he believes he apprehends objectively, whereas he regards the body of woman as a hindrance, a prison, weighed down by everything peculiar to it. "The female is a female by virtue of a certain *lack* of qualities," said Aristotle; "we should regard the female nature as afflicted with a natural defectiveness." And St. Thomas for his part pronounced woman to be an "imperfect man," an "incidental" being. This is symbolized in Genesis where Eve is depicted as made from what Bossuet called "a supernumerary bone" of Adam.

Thus humanity is male and man defines woman not in herself but as relative to him; she is not regarded as an autonomous being. Michelet writes: "Woman, the relative being …:" And Benda is most positive in his *Rapport d' Uriel*: "The body of man makes sense in itself quite apart from that of woman, whereas the latter seems wanting in significance by itself. … Man can think of himself without woman. She cannot think of herself without man." And she is simply what man decrees; thus she is called "the sex," by which is meant that she appears essentially to the male as a sexual being. For him she is sex—absolute sex, no less. She is defined and differentiated with reference to man and not he with reference to her; she is the incidental, the inessential as opposed to the essential. He is the Subject, he is the Absolute—she is the Other.[3] …

Thus it is that no group ever sets itself up as the One without at once setting up the Other against itself. If three travelers chance to occupy the same compartment, that is enough to make vaguely hostile "others" out of all the rest of the passengers on the train. In small-town eyes all persons not belonging to the village are "strangers" and suspect; to the native of a country all who inhabit other countries are "foreigners"; Jews are "different" for the anti-Semite, Negroes are "inferior" for American Racists, aborigines are "natives" for colonists, proletarians are the "lower class" for the privileged. …

The parallel drawn by Bebel between women and the proletariat is valid in that neither ever formed a minority or a separate collective unit of mankind. And instead of a single historical event it is in both cases a historical development that explains their status as a class and accounts for the membership of *particular individuals* in that class. But proletarians have not always existed, whereas there have always been women. They are women in virtue of their anatomy and physiology. Throughout history they have always been subordinated to men, and hence their dependency is not the result of a historical event or a social change—it was not something that *occurred*. The reason why otherness in this case seems to be an absolute is in part that it lacks the contingent or incidental nature of historical facts. A condition brought about at a certain time can be abolished at some other time, as the Negroes of Haiti and others have proved; but it might seem that a natural condition is beyond the possibility of change. In truth, however, the nature of things is no more immutably given, once for all, than is historical reality. If woman seems to be the inessential which never becomes the essential, it is because she herself fails to bring about this change. Proletarians say "We"; Negroes also. Regarding themselves as subjects, they transform the bourgeois, the whites, into "others." But women do not say "We," except at some congress of feminists or similar formal demonstration; men say "women," and women use the same word in referring to themselves. They do not authentically assume a subjective attitude. The proletarians have accomplished the revolution in Russia, the Negroes in Haiti, the Indo-Chinese are battling for it in Indo-China; but the women's effort has never been anything more than a symbolic agitation. They have gained only what men have been willing to grant; they have taken nothing, they have only received.[4]

The reason for this is that women lack concrete means for organizing themselves into a unit which can stand face to face with the correlative unit. They have no past, no history, no religion of their own; and they have no such solidarity of work and interest as that of the proletariat. They are not even promiscuously herded together in the way that creates community feeling among the American Negroes, the ghetto Jews, the workers of Saint-Denis, or the factory hands of Renault. They live dispersed among the males, attached through residence, housework, economic condition, and social standing to certain men—fathers or husbands—more firmly than they are to other women. If they belong to the bourgeoisie, they feel solidarity with men of that class, not with proletarian women; if they are white, their allegiance is to white men, not to Negro women. The proletariat can propose to massacre the ruling class, and a sufficiently fanatical Jew or Negro might dream of getting sole possession of the atomic bomb and making humanity wholly Jewish or black; but woman cannot even dream of exterminating the males. The bond that unites her to her oppressors is not comparable to any other. The division of the sexes is a biological fact, not an event in human history. Male and female stand opposed within a biological fact, not an event in human history. Male and female stand opposed within a primordial *Mitsein*, and woman has not broken it. The couple is a fundamental unity with its two halves riveted together, and the cleavage of society along the line of sex is impossible. Here is to be found the basic trait of woman: she is the Other in a totality of which the two components are necessary to one another. ...

Master and slave, also, are united by a reciprocal need, in this case economic, which does not liberate the slave. In the relation of master to slave the master does not make a point of the need that he has for the other; he has in his grasp the power of satisfying their need through his own action; whereas the slave, in his dependent condition, his hope and fear, is quite conscious of the need he has for his master. Even if the need is at bottom equally urgent for both, it always works in favor of the oppressor and against the oppressed. That is why the liberation for the working class, for example, has been slow.

Now, woman has always been mans dependent, if not his slave; the two sexes have never shared the world in equality. And even today woman is heavily handicapped, though her situation is beginning to change. Almost nowhere is her legal status the same as man's, and frequently it is much to her disadvantage. Even when her rights are legally recognized in the abstract, long-standing custom prevents their full expression in the mores. In the economic sphere men and women can almost be said to make up two castes; other things being equal, the former hold the better jobs, get higher wages, and have more opportunity for success than their new competitors. In industry and politics men have a great many more positions and they monopolize the most important posts. In addition to all this, they enjoy a traditional prestige that the education of children tends in every way to support, for the present enshrines the past—and in the past all history has been made by men. At the present time, when women are beginning to take part in the affairs of the world, it is still a world that belongs to men—they have no doubt of it at all and women have scarcely any. To decline to be the Other, to refuse to be a party to the deal—this would be for women to renounce all the advantages conferred upon them by their alliance with the superior caste. Man-the-sovereign will provide woman-the-liege with material protection and will undertake the moral justification of her existence; thus she can evade at once both economic risk and the metaphysical risk of a liberty in which ends and aims must be contrived without assistance. Indeed, along with the ethical urge of each individual to affirm his subjective existence, there is also the temptation to forgo liberty and become a thing. This is an inauspicious road, for he who takes it—passive, lost, ruined—becomes henceforth the creature of another's will, frustrated in his transcendence and deprived of every value: But it is an easy road; on it one avoids the strain involved in undertaking an authentic existence. When man makes of woman the *Other*, he may, then, expect her to manifest deep-seated tendencies toward complicity. Thus, woman may fail to lay claim to the status of subject because she lacks definite resources, because she feels the necessary bond that ties her to man regardless of reciprocity, and because she is often very well pleased with her role as the *Other*.

But it will be asked at once: how did all of this begin? It is easy to see that the duality of the sexes, like any duality, gives rise to conflict. And doubtless the winner will assume the status of absolute. But why should man have won from the start? It seems possible that women could have won the victory; or that the outcome of the conflict might never have been decided. How is it that this world has always belonged to the men and that things have begun to change only recently? Is this change a good thing? Will it bring about an equal sharing of the world between men and women? …

It was only later, in the eighteenth century, that genuinely democratic men began to view the matter objectively. Diderot, among others, strove to show that woman is, like man, a human being. Later John Stuart Mill came fervently to her defense. But these philosophers displayed unusual impartiality. In the nineteenth century the feminist quarrel became again a quarrel of partisans. One of the consequences of the industrial revolution was the entrance of women in to productive labor, and it was just here that the claims of the feminist emerged from the realm of theory and acquired an economic basis, while their opponents became the more aggressive. Although landed property lost power to some extent, the bourgeoisie clung to the old morality that found the guarantee of private property in the solidity of the family. Woman was ordered back into the home the more harshly as her emancipation became a real menace. Even within the working class the men endeavored to restrain woman's liberation, because they began to see the women as dangerous competitors—the more so because they were accustomed to work for lower wages.[5]

In proving woman's inferiority, the antifeminists then began to draw not only upon religion, philosophy, and theology, as before, but also upon science—biology, experimental psychology, etc. At most they were willing to grant "equality in difference" to the *other* sex. That profitable formula is most significant; it is precisely like the "equal but separate" formula of the Jim Crow laws aimed at the North American Negroes. As is well known, this so-called equalitarian segregation has resulted only in the most extreme discrimination. The similarity just noted is in no way due to chance, for whether it is a race, a caste, a class, or a sex that is reduced to a position of inferiority, the methods of justification are the same. "The eternal feminine" corresponds to "the black soul" and to "the Jewish character." True, the Jewish problem is on the whole very different from the other two—to the anti-Semite the Jew is not so much an inferior as he is an enemy for whom there is to be granted no place on earth, for whom annihilation is the fate desired. But there are deep similarities between the situation of woman and that of the Negro. Both are being emancipated today from a like paternalism, and the former master class wishes to "keep them in their place"—that is, the place chosen for them. In both cases the former masters lavish more or less sincere eulogies, either on the virtues of "the good Negro" with his dormant, childish, merry soul—the submissive Negro—or on the merits of the woman who is "truly feminine"—that is, frivolous, infantile, irresponsible—the submissive woman. In both cases the dominant class bases its argument on a state of affairs that it has itself created. As George Bernard Shaw puts it, in substance, "the American white relegates the black to the rank of shoeshine boy; and he concludes from this that the black is good for nothing but shining shoes." This vicious circle is met with in all analogous circumstances; when an individual (or a group of individuals) is kept in a situation of inferiority, the fact is that he *is* inferior. But the significance of the verb *to be* must be rightly understood here; it is in bad faith to give it a static value when it really has the dynamic Hegelian sense of "to have become." Yes, women on the whole *are* today inferior to men; that is, their situation affords them fewer possibilities. The question is: should that state of affairs continue?

… But men profit in many more subtle ways from the otherness, the alterity of woman. Here is miraculous balm for those afflicted with an inferiority complex, and indeed no one is more arrogant toward women, more aggressive or scornful, than the man who is anxious about his virility. Those who are not fear-ridden in the presence of their fellow men are much more disposed to recognize a fellow creature in woman; but even to these the myth of woman, the Other, is precious for many reasons.[6] They cannot be blamed for not cheerfully relinquishing all the benefits they derive from the myth, for they realize what they would lose in relinquishing woman as they fancy her to be, while they fail to realize what they have to gain from the woman of tomorrow. Refusal to pose oneself as the Subject, unique and absolute, requires great self-denial. Furthermore, the vast majority of men make no such claim explicitly. They do not *postulate* woman as inferior, for today they are too thoroughly imbued with the ideal of democracy not to recognize all human beings as equals.

In the bosom of the family, woman seems in the eyes of childhood and youth to be clothed in the same social dignity as the adult males. Later on, the young man, desiring and loving, experiences the resistance, the independence of the woman desired and loved; in marriage, he respects woman as wife and mother, and in the concrete events of conjugal life she stands there before him as a free being. He can therefore feel that social subordination as between the sexes no longer exists and that on the whole, in spite of differences, woman is an equal. As, however, he observes some points of inferiority—the most important being unfitness for the professions—he attributes these to natural causes. When he is in a co-operative and benevolent relation with woman, his theme is the principle of abstract equality, and he does not base his attitude upon such inequality as may exist. But when he is in conflict with her, the situation is reversed: his theme will be the existing inequality, and he will even take it as justification for denying abstract equality.[7]

So it is that many men will affirm as if in good faith that women *are* the equals of man and that they have nothing to clamor for, while *at the same time* they will say that women can never be the equals of man and that their demands are in vain. It is, in point of fact, a difficult matter for man to realize the extreme importance of social discriminations which seem outwardly insignificant but which produce in woman moral and intellectual effects so profound that they appear to spring from her original nature.[8] The most sympathetic of men never fully comprehend woman's concrete situation. And there is no reason to put much trust in the men when they rush to the defense of privileges whose full extent they can hardly measure. We shall not, then, permit ourselves to be intimidated by the number and violence of the attacks launched against women, nor to be entrapped by the self-seeking eulogies bestowed on the "true woman," nor to profit by the enthusiasm for woman's destiny manifested by men who would not for the world have any part of it.

We should consider the arguments of the feminists with no less suspicion, however, for very often their controversial aim deprives them of all real value. If the "woman question" seems trivial, it is because masculine arrogance has made of it a "quarrel"; and when quarreling, one no longer reasons well. People have tirelessly sought to prove that woman is superior, inferior, or equal to man. Some say that, having been created after Adam, she is evidently a secondary being; others say on the contrary that Adam was only a rough draft and that God succeeded in producing the human being in perfection when He created Eve. Woman's brain is smaller; yes, but it is relatively larger. Christ was made a man; yes, but perhaps for his greater humility. Each argument at once suggests its opposite, and both are often fallacious. If we are to gain understanding we must get out of these ruts; we must discard the vague notions of superiority, inferiority, equality which have hitherto corrupted every discussion of the subject and start afresh.

Very well, but just how shall we pose the question? And, to begin with, who are we to propound it at all? Man is at once judge and party to the case; but so is woman. What we need is an angel—neither man nor woman—but where shall we find one? Still, the angel would be poorly qualified to speak, for an angel is ignorant of all the basic facts involved in the problem. With a hermaphrodite we should be no better off, for here the situation is most peculiar; the hermaphrodite is not really the combination of a whole man and a whole woman, but consists of parts of each and thus is neither. It looks to me as if there are, after all, certain women who are best qualified to elucidate the situation of woman. Let us not be misled by the sophism that because Epimenides was a Cretan he was necessarily a liar; it is not a mysterious essence that compels men and women to act in good or in bad faith, it is their situation that inclines them more or less toward the search for truth. Many of today's women, fortunate in the restoration of all the privileges pertaining to the estate of the human being, can afford the luxury of impartiality—we even recognize its necessity. We are no longer like our partisan elders; by and large we have won the game. In recent debates on the status of women the United Nations has persistently maintained that the equality of the sexes is now becoming a reality, and already some of us have never had to sense in our femininity an inconvenience or an obstacle. Many problems appear to us to be more pressing than those which concern us in particular, and this detachment even allows us to hope that our attitude will be objective. Still, we know the feminine world more intimately than do the men because we have our roots in it, we grasp more immediately than do men what it means to a human being to be feminine; and we are more concerned with such knowledge. I have said that there are more pressing problems, but this does not prevent us from seeing some importance in asking how the fact of being women will affect our lives. What opportunities precisely have been given us and what withheld? What fate awaits our younger sisters, and what directions should they take? It is significant that books by women on women are in general animated in our day less by a wish to demand our rights than by an effort toward clarity and understanding. As we emerge from an era of excessive controversy, this book is offered as one attempt among others to confirm that statement.

But it is doubtless impossible to approach any human problem with a mind free from bias. The way in which questions are put, the points of view assumed, presuppose a relativity of interest; all characteristics imply values, and every objective description, so called, implies an ethical background. Rather than attempt to conceal principles more or less definitely implied, it is better to state them openly at the beginning. This will make it unnecessary to specify on every page in just what sense one uses such words as *superior, inferior, better, worse, progress, reaction*, and the like. If we survey some of the works on woman, we note that one of the points of view most frequently adopted is that of the public good, the general interest; and one always means by this the benefit of society as one wishes it to be maintained or established. For our part, we hold that the only public good is that which assures the private good of the citizens; we shall pass judgment on institutions according to their effectiveness in giving concrete opportunities to individuals. But we do not confuse the idea of private interest with that of happiness, although that is another common point of view. Are not women of the harem more happy than women voters? Is not the housekeeper happier than the working-woman? It is not too clear just what the word *happy* really means and still less what true values it may mask. There is no possibility of measuring the happiness of others, and it is always easy to describe as happy the situation in which one wishes to place them.

In particular those who are condemned to stagnation are often pronounced happy on the pretext that happiness consists in being at rest. This notion we reject, for our perspective is that of existentialist ethics. Every subject plays his part as such specifically through exploits or projects that serve as a mode of transcendence; he achieves liberty only through a continual reaching out toward other liberties. There is no justification for present existence other than its expansion into an indefinitely open future. Every time transcendence falls back into immanence, stagnation, there is a degradation of existence into the "*en-soi*"—the brutish life of subjection to given conditions—and of liberty into constraint and contingence. This downfall represents a moral fault if the subject consents to it; if it is inflicted upon him, it spells frustration and oppression. In both cases it is an absolute evil. Every individual concerned to justify his existence feels that his existence involves an undefined need to transcend himself, to engage in freely chosen projects.

Now, what peculiarly signalizes the situation of woman is that she—a free and autonomous being like all human creatures—nevertheless finds herself living in a world where men compel her to assume the status of the Other. They propose to stabilize her as object and to doom her to immanence since her transcendence is to be overshadowed and forever transcended by another ego (*conscience*) which is essential and sovereign. The drama of woman lies in this conflict between the fundamental aspirations of every subject (ego)—who always regards the self as the essential—and the compulsions of a situation in which she is the inessential. How can a human being in woman's situation attain fulfillment? What roads are open to her? Which are blocked? How can independence be recovered in a state of dependency? What circumstances limit woman's liberty and how can they be overcome? These are the fundamental questions on which I would fain throw some light. This means that I am interested in the fortunes of the individual as defined not in terms of happiness but in terms of liberty.

Quite evidently this problem would be without significance if we were to believe that woman's destiny is inevitably determined by physiological, psychological, or economic forces. Hence I shall discuss first of all the light in which woman is viewed by biology, psychoanalysis, and historical materialism. Next I shall try to show exactly how the concept of the "truly feminine" has been fashioned—why woman has been defined as the Other—and what have been the consequences from man's point of view. Then from woman's point of view I shall describe the world in which women must live; and thus we shall be able to envisage the difficulties in their way as, endeavoring to make their escape from the sphere hitherto assigned them, they aspire to full membership in the human race.

Notes

1. *Franchise*, dead today.
2. The Kinsey Report [Alfred C. Kinsey and others: *Sexual Behavior in the Human Male* (W. B. Saunders Co., 1948)] is no exception, for it is limited to describing the sexual characteristics of American men, which is quite a different matter.
3. E. Lévinas expresses this idea most explicitly in his essay *Temps et l'Autre*. "Is there not a case in which otherness, alterity [*altérité*], unquestionably marks the nature of a being, as its essence, an instance of otherness not consisting purely and simply in the opposition of two species of the same genus? I think that the feminine represents the contrary in its absolute sense, this contrariness being in no wise affected by any relation between it and its correlative and thus remaining absolutely other. Sex is not a certain specific difference ... no more is the sexual difference a mere contradiction. ... Nor does this difference lie in the duality of two complementary terms, for two complementary terms imply a pre-existing whole. ... Otherness reaches its full flowering in the feminine, a term of the same rank as consciousness but of opposite meaning."

   I suppose that Lévinas does not forget that woman, too, is aware of her own consciousness, or ego. But it is striking that he deliberately takes a man's point of view, disregarding the reciprocity of subject and object. When he writes that woman is mystery, he implies that she is mystery for man. Thus his description, which is intended to be objective, is in fact an assertion of masculine privilege.
4. See Part II, ch. viii.
5. See Part II, pp. 129–31.
6. A significant article on this theme by Michel Carrouges appeared in No. 292 of the *Cahiers du Sud*. He writes indignantly: "Would that there were no woman-myth at all but only a cohort of cooks, matrons, prostitutes, and bluestockings serving functions of pleasure or usefulness!" That is to say, in his view woman has no existence in and for herself; she thinks only of her *function* in the male world. Her reason for existence lies in man. But then, in fact, her poetic "function" as a myth might be more valued than any other. The real problem is precisely to find out why woman should be defined with relation to man.
7. For example, a man will say that he considers his wife in no wise degraded because she has no gainful occupation. The profession of housewife is just as lofty, and so on. But when the first quarrel comes he will exclaim: "Why, you couldn't make your living without me!"
8. The specific purpose of Book II of this study is to describe this process.

4.
FEMINISM IN "WAVES": USEFUL METAPHOR OR NOT?
Linda Nicholson
(2010)

By the early 1990s, it had become clear that the kind of feminist activity that had blossomed from the late 1960s through the late 1980s in the United States was no longer present. Consequently, many began to ask: what was the present state of feminism? One idea put forth in the early 1990s was that feminism had not died but was merely in a "third wave"—a younger form of feminism that looked very different from earlier forms.[1] Here I would like to turn to the question of the current state of feminism, not through asking whether we are in a "third wave," but through reflecting upon the general use of the wave metaphor in feminist self-understanding. In seeing what has been useful, or not, in this metaphor, we can generate some tools in understanding the contemporary state of U.S. feminism.

Let me begin then with some reflections on the wave metaphor. In the late 1960s, it was very useful for feminists to begin to describe their movement as the "second wave" of feminism. It was useful because it reminded people that the then current women's rights and women's liberation movements had a venerable past—that these movements were not historical aberrations but were part of a long tradition of activism. The late 1960s and early 1970s was a time when feminists began to rewrite U.S. history. Involved in that rewriting were new understandings of the suffrage movement, including the recognition that the suffrage movement was part of a larger nineteenth century movement around women's issues. One could expand the meaning of the suffrage movement and tie it to 1960s activism by referring to the former as the first wave of U.S. feminism and to the 1960s movement as the second wave. Thus the wave metaphor both showed the 1960s movement as something other than an historical aberration and also framed the nineteenth century movement as far larger and more historically significant than most of us had been taught.

But the wave metaphor has outlived its usefulness. For one, the places where it mostly gets mentioned, among those who are committed to some version or another of feminism, are those places where people mostly now know this history, i.e. know about the larger significance of the nineteenth century women's movement and know that 1960s activism emerged from a long history of struggle around women's issues. But it is not only that the wave metaphor has outlived its usefulness. It is also that the wave metaphor tends to have built into it an important metaphorical implication that is historically misleading and not helpful politically. That implication is that underlying certain historical differences, there is one phenomenon, feminism, that unites gender activism in the history of the United States, and that like a wave, peaks at certain times and recedes at others. In sum, the wave metaphor suggests the idea that gender activism in the history of the United States has been for the most part unified around one set of ideas, and that set of ideas can be called feminism.[2]

But as the historical record has increasingly illustrated, that is not how best to understand the past in the United States. The different kinds of activism around gender that have taken place since the early nineteenth century in this country cannot be reduced to one term, feminism. That kind of reduction obfuscates the historical specificity of gender activism in the history of the United States. It obscures the differences in the ideas that have motivated different groups of people to pursue different kinds of political goals at different moments in time. For example, to call the nineteenth century movement "the first wave" suggests an underlying similarity between the political goals of this movement with those of the movements that began to emerge in the 1960s. But as Nancy Cott argued in her groundbreaking book, *The Grounding of Modern Feminism*, it is not even appropriate to call much of the activism around gender issues in the nineteenth century, and particularly the nineteenth century suffrage movement, a "feminist" movement. For one, those active in this movement did not use the term. Moreover, many who supported suffrage had more limited political goals than did those who began to use the word feminism in the early twentieth century. Many of those who supported suffrage did so not on the basis of a general idea of women's equality with men, or because they thought of women as individuals similar to men—ideas that would become important for many of those beginning to call themselves feminists in the early twentieth century—but because they believed, for a variety of reasons, that women should have the vote. As Cott quotes an early twentieth century feminist, "All feminists are suffragists, but not all suffragists are feminists."[3]

Not recognizing these distinctions has led some scholars to be puzzled about why feminism "died" after the nineteenth amendment was passed. My own view is that it did not die because at that moment in time it had not yet been born, at least not as the type of large-scale social movement that suffrage had become. In the early twentieth century, while there were a large number of people who supported women's suffrage and who were working to improve women's situation in other ways, such as through supporting protective labor legislation for women, their support did not translate into what was then becoming understood as feminism. An important strand of the feminist vision of the time—that women and men were similar in fundamental ways and on that basis should be treated as equals—was the position of only a small number of women, mostly those in professional or gender neutral jobs. That kind of feminist position, as reflected in the National Women's Party endorsement of an Equal Rights Amendment, was strongly opposed by many who saw such an amendment undermining the protective labor legislation that women had only recently won. The relative isolation of this kind of feminist position remained the case up until the early 1960s.[4]

But even in the period between the passage of the nineteenth amendment and the early 1960s, real changes in gender roles and relationships were taking place. During the

1920s and 1930s, ordinary women were challenging older notions of womanhood in a myriad number of ways, from cutting their hair, to adopting new norms about sexuality, to developing new understandings of their relationship to wage labor. Particularly in the post World War II period, a growing number of women were entering the paid labor force for a larger period of their lives. In the 1940s and 1950s, women in unions were beginning to make many of the same kinds of political demands that had become associated with the label feminism in the early part of the century—such as equal pay for equal work. Connections began to be made among those who occupied leadership positions in such unions with others who were arguing for women's rights in other arenas, laying the groundwork for the kind of political activism that began to surface in a more public way in the early 1960s.[5] This complex history tends to be obscured by the use of the wave metaphor.

Moreover, the use of the wave metaphor becomes particularly unhelpful when we turn our attention back to the present. During the 1960s, 1970s and 1980s, feminism began to expand its meaning, including not only those who supported what many now think of as a liberal understanding of feminism, but also those who took this worldview in new directions. The 1960s through the 1980s was a period of great theoretical and political creativity and activity, making possible a very broad understanding of feminism. But after that kind of creative activity began to die down in the 1990s, people began to wonder whether or not we were in a third wave of feminism. The appeal of this way of thinking was that it kept up the hope that gender activism had not really died down but merely had taken a somewhat different, more youthful and jazzier form. But when I think about what has transpired in the period from the 1990s to today, I don't think that the metaphor of a third wave is the best way to describe what has gone on. Instead, let me offer a different kind of analysis about what has happened.

Since the early 1990s, we have been in a period where the feminism that emerged in the 1960s, 1970s, and 1980s has both flourished in many areas and stalled in others, and this complexity cannot be adequately captured by the metaphor of a wave. Rather, we need to understand the areas in which it has flourished and the areas in which it has stalled to have a realistic assessment both of where we are as well as to better figure out where we need to go.

Let me begin with the more optimistic perspective on how feminism has been flourishing. Following the mass transformation of consciousness that was the great legacy of the mass movements of the 1960s, 1970s, and 1980s, feminism began the quiet, but very important job of institutionalizing itself. The phrase that has sometimes been used to describe this process is "the long walk through the institutions." We all are aware of many of the results of that process: the creation of women's studies programs, the establishment of rape crisis centers and shelters for the victims of domestic abuse, the creation of women's caucuses in many organizations, the formation of women's political organizations, such as Emily's List, etc., etc. What we tend to be less conscious of is how many of these institutionalized manifestations of 1960s, 1970s, and 1980s feminism are not static but have continued to grow and develop, more quietly perhaps than was the case with their inauguration, but still happening. Women's Studies programs are no longer small isolated ghettos in liberal arts schools but have spread into law schools, medical schools, and schools of architecture and journalism. Emily's List has grown into a powerful organization that almost succeeded in helping make a woman president of the United States. The women's ordination movement in many religious denominations has either achieved its goals or, in the case of some churches, such as the Roman Catholic Church, has continued to grow.[6] Women make up an increasing percentage of those receiving doctorates in the United States, indeed surpassing the percentage of men in 2003.[7] While employed women still do a disproportionate share of housework and childrearing, that share has decreased over time.[8] And gender is talked about in more sophisticated and more public ways than would have been heard even in the glory days of the 1970s. Within Women's Studies settings, feminists recognize today in more conceptually developed ways than they did even in the 1980s, how phenomena such as gender, race, and class intersect in constituting an individual's social identity. Among the wider public, in the last presidential campaign, even conservative Republican women used the word sexism to disparage many of the criticisms Democrats were making of Sarah Palin. For all of the hypocrisy that one might see in their responses—when exactly did Phyllis Schlafly change her mind about the appropriateness of a woman with a four-month-old baby entering the work force?—still, that these conservative women and men saw the adjective "sexist" as rhetorically powerful, meant that feminism was not only far from dead but was in a state of growth.

THAT IS THE GOOD NEWS. The bad news, however, is also not hard to find. The wage gap between women and men continues to exist. Rigid and narrow standards of beauty continue to dominate the lives of women, perhaps even more so today than even forty years ago.[9] A sexual double standard among young women and men continues to be in place.[10] And no one could claim that many of the other encompassing goals of the radical and socialist feminist movements of the 1960s, 1970s and 1980s—such as for the elimination of racial and class inequality—have been attained.

The question then is why the feminism of the 1960s, 1970s, and 1980s has advanced so far in some ways and gone nowhere in others. And here again, this is a question for which the wave metaphor supplies little help. Instead, what we need to do is examine the reasons why we are where we are by looking at the very specific contexts of the lives of diverse groups of women. I can't come up with a full answer to this question, but instead let me offer a few reflections.

One of the reasons why 1960s, 1970s and 1980s feminism did generate the kind of mass attention that it did was because a lot of it spoke to the real conflicts many women were experiencing as they were entering the workforce. As I noted earlier, the post World War II period was one of an important change in the gendered nature of the paid labor force. Women had been entering the work force in increasing numbers since the early twentieth century. But prior to World War II, a lot of this labor had been associated with women who were poor, black, single, or childless. After World War II, more married women, more white women, more middle class women, more women with children at home, became part of the paid labor force. Moreover, they were entering jobs that were not as sex stereotyped as those in which most women had been employed before the war. The consequences of these changes were numerous. Among union women, it meant that while older demands such as protective labor legislation were still important, such legislation began to diminish in importance in relation to newer issues such as equal pay for equal work and the elimination of gender segregated seniority lists.[11] Among middle class women, the older ideology that one was either a wife and mother or a career woman began to diminish in favor of the newer ideology that women could be both—a happy wife and mother and a successful contributor to the household economy.[12] The consequence was that in the early 1960s, the ideology of liberal feminism—that women are equal to men, and that women, like men, should be judged as individuals—the very ideology that could NOT generate a mass following in the 1920s, could now begin to generate such a mass following. And because this understanding of feminism continues to speak to the real concerns of many women, this understanding of feminism continues to flourish in contemporary society.

But, as we know, liberal feminism was only one part of the feminist movement of the 1960s, 1970s and 1980s. Also constituting an important part of this movement was radical feminism. In some respects, the radical feminism of the 1960s, 1970s, and 1980s also expressed ideas that responded to the conflicts of many. Radical feminism's slogan that "the personal is political" captured the tensions experienced by many women who found themselves subject to older sex role stereotypes within domestic settings as they were also beginning to negotiate a more equal economic arena. In bringing attention to the politics of housework or the phenomenon of domestic abuse, radical feminists were drawing attention to phenomena with which many could identify. In using such terminology as "sex roles," radical feminists were also employing the kind of psychological/sociological language that was becoming more prevalent in ordinary discourse. In all of these respects, radical feminism also has become a part of mainstream America.

But there were aspects of radical feminism that could have been advanced only by a small group of relatively privileged women at a certain point in their lives and that therefore could not be sustained by many over time. The idea that women should separate from men could not appeal to the very large population of American heterosexual women who saw marriage and motherhood as representing some of the best of what life has to offer. And because so many American women have and still do see romantic relationships as central parts of their lives, other aspects of radical feminism also became impossible to implement in a mass way, for example that women should abandon the task of making themselves more beautiful or sexually desirable. These were ideas that young women in small radical enclaves might have adopted at a certain moment in their lives. But looking back now from the perspective of forty years later, it seems unlikely that these kinds of political ideals could have reached many or made themselves part of the general culture in any kind of sustained way.

And if many aspects of radical feminism could speak only to a small segment of the U.S. population, the same is even more true of an even smaller and less influential segment of the feminism of the 1960s, 1970s, and 1980s, its Marxist and socialist wings. The ideals of this part of women's liberation—eliminating racism, sexism, and class inequality—while theoretically understandable given the heady sense of optimism of the time, did not resonate with a significant segment of the U.S. population. This point responds to one of the criticisms that sometimes has been made against women's liberation as well as against the Black Power movement of the 1960s and 1970s, that both "sold out," were "co-opted," or undermined the left because neither sufficiently advanced an economic agenda that would have pushed this country in a socialist direction. But this kind of criticism blames Black Power and women's liberation for failing to achieve what neither could have achieved given the political climate of the United States in that period. That socialist movements within both movements were always relatively small is only one sign of the fact that America in the 1960s, 1970s and 1980s was not ready to make encompassing social structural changes either in terms of economic, racial, or gender relations.[13]

In short, what I am saying is that the feminism of the 1960s, 1970s, and 1980s achieved and continues to achieve what it has to the extent its message has resonated with the felt needs of many. Certain aspects of those movements that did speak to problems and tensions expressed by many have continued to generate change, often in more extensive and sophisticated ways than was true of the earlier period. Others that were less in tune with the lives and desires of ordinary women and men have fared less well. In short, we are in a period now where the kind of feminism many of us experienced in the 1960s, 1970s, and 1980s is both flourishing and quiescent. Gender is alive and well as a focus of attention in public discourse and public life even as some of the issues associated with the feminism of the earlier period have retreated from sight. That kind of complexity cannot be captured with the metaphor of a wave.

To be sure, there is one use that the wave metaphor is suited for—to identify those moments in history when issues of gender mobilize large numbers of people in very public, noisy, and challenging ways, that is, when such issues are able to generate large scale social or political movements. We are not in that kind of period, which makes the description of feminist activism today as a "third wave" even more questionable. But if we look back at other periods in U.S. history where that kind of activism was also not present, say, for example, in the period between the 1920s and the 1960s, the lack of such very public activity does not necessarily mean the lack of changes in gender norms and gender ideology. Consequently, younger feminists are correct in claiming that there are possibilities for gender activism today that are different from the forms of activism that flourished in the 1960s, 1970s, and 1980s. We can acknowledge those differences and also acknowledge the connections such activism might have to the activism of the 1960s, 1970s, and 1980s without the use of the "wave" metaphor. A more useful way of thinking about these changes as well as other changes in activism over time can be suggested by the metaphor of a kaleidoscope. At any given moment in time, the view in a kaleidoscope is complex, showing distinct colors and patterns. With a turn of the kaleidoscope, some of these colors and patterns become more pronounced, others less so, and new patterns and colors have emerged. This kind of metaphor suggests a better way to think about the changes that have marked the history of gender activism in the United States than does one that likens such changes to an ocean's ebbs and swells.[14]

Notes

1. An essay that was influential in introducing the phrase "third wave" was Rebecca Walker's "Becoming the Third Wave" in Ms. (January/February 1992) pp. 39–41. The term received fur-

ther prominence through the publication of Jennifer Baumgardner and Amy Richard's, *ManifestA: Young Women, Feminism and the Future* (New York: Farrar, Straus and Giroux, 2000). Several books that were published in the 1990s that also focused on the idea of a next generation of feminism include: Barbara Findlen, ed., *Listen Up: Voices from the Next Feminist Generation* (Seattle, Washington: Seal Press, 1995); Rebecca Walker, ed., *To Be Real: Telling the Truth and Changing the Face of Feminism* (N.Y.: Anchor Books, 1995); and Leslie Heywood and Jennifer Drake, eds., *Third Wave Agenda* (Minneapolis: University Of Minnesota Press, 1997).

2. Ednie Kaeh Garrison also argues against the wave metaphor in feminist historiography because of its suggestion that feminism represents a unified phenomenon. She suggests replacing the metaphor of an ocean wave with the metaphor of radio waves in part because of the plurality that the latter metaphor suggests. See Edna Kaeh Garrison, "Are We On a Wavelength Yet? On Feminist Oceanography, Radios and Third Wave Feminism," pp. 237–256 in Jo Reger, ed., *Different Wavelengths: Studies of the Contemporary Women's Movement* (New York and London: Routledge, 2005).

3. Nancy Cott, *The Grounding of Modern Feminism* (New Haven and London: Yale University Press, 1987). For this last quote see p. 15.

4. I elaborate this argument in Linda Nicholson, *Identity Before Identity Politics* (Cambridge, England: Cambridge University Press, 2008), pp. 142–161.

5. Dorothy Sue Cobble, *The Other Women's Movement: Workplace Justice and Social Rights in Modern America* (Princeton and Oxford: Princeton University Press, 2004). See also, Leila J. Rupp and Verta Taylor, *Survival in the Doldrums: The American Women's Rights Movement, 1945 to the 1960s* (New York and Oxford: Oxford University Press, 1987).

6. Catherine Wessinger, ed., *Religious Institutions and Women's Leadership: New Roles Inside the Mainstream* (Columbia, South Carolina: University of South Carolina Press, 1996).

7. Scott Smallwood, "American Women Surpass Men in Earning Doctorates," The Chronicle of Higher Education, December 12, 2003, in "The Faculty" p. 10.

8. By the mid 1990s, men were still doing only about a third of the housework. However, this contribution represented a doubling of their share from the mid 1960s. Suzanne M. Bianci, Melissa A. Milkie, Liana C. Sayer and John P. Robinson, "Is Anyone Doing the Housework—Trends in the Gender Division of Household Labor," pp. 191–228 in *Social Forces*, September 2000, 79 (1): 191.

9. Naomi Wolf, *The Beauty Myth: How Images of Beauty Are Used Against Women* (New York: William Morrow and Company, Inc., 1991). This book, published in the early 1990s, shows the continuance of rigid beauty standards even twenty years following the emergence of radical feminism. Eighteen years later, there is no evidence that the power of beauty standards has diminished.

10. I base this claim upon reports from my undergraduates at Washington University in St. Louis.

11. Dennis A. Deslippe, *"Rights, Not Roses" Unions and the Rise of Working-Class Feminism* (Urbana and Chicago: University of Illinois Press, 2000), p. 32.

12. Joanne Meyerowitz, "Beyond the Feminine Mystique," pp. 229–262 in Joanne Meyerowitz, ed. *Not June Cleaver: Women and Gender in Postwar America, 1945–1960* (Philadelphia, PA: Temple University Press, 1994). See particularly, p. 231.

13. Adolph L. Reed Jr., "Black Particularity Reconsidered," in Eddie S. Glaude Jr., *Is It Nation Time: Contemporary Essays on Black Power and Black Nationalism,"* pp. 39–66 talks about the ways in which Black Power deviated from what was possible in the 1960s and in this sense "sold out" the left. Nancy Fraser talks about the cooptation of feminism within the context of an emerging neoliberalism in Nancy Fraser, "Feminism, Capitalism and the Cunning of History," pp. 97–117 in *New Left Review*, 56, March/April 2009. …

14. It is not clear that all those who have expressed the idea of a "third wave" require the use of this metaphorical phrase. Their point seems to be more importantly that there exists a younger generation of feminists whose politics both are similar and different from those of an earlier generation of activists. The lack of need for this particular metaphor is illustrated by Rebecca Walker in a 2004 introduction to the volume *The Fire This Time: Young Activists and the New Feminism,* eds., Vivien Labaton and Dawn Lundy Martin (N.Y.: Anchor, 2004). …

5.

MULTIRACIAL FEMINISM: RECASTING THE CHRONOLOGY OF SECOND WAVE FEMINISM

Becky Thompson

(2002)

In the last several years, a number of histories have been published that chronicle the emergence and contributions of Second Wave feminism.[1] Although initially eager to read and teach from these histories, I have found myself increasingly concerned about the extent to which they provide a version of Second Wave history that Chela Sandoval refers to as "hegemonic feminism."[2] This feminism is white led, marginalizes the activism and world views of women of color, focuses mainly on the United States, and treats sexism as the ultimate oppression. Hegemonic feminism deemphasizes or ignores a class and race analysis, generally sees equality with men as the goal of feminism, and has an individual rights-based, rather than justice-based vision for social change.

Although rarely named as hegemonic feminism, this history typically resorts to an old litany of the women's movement that includes three or four branches of feminism: liberal, socialist, radical, and sometimes cultural feminism.[3] The most significant problem with this litany is that it does not recognize the centrality of the feminism of women of color in Second Wave history. Missing too, from normative accounts is the story of white antiracist feminism which, from its emergence, has been intertwined with, and fueled by the development of, feminism among women of color.[4]

Telling the history of Second Wave feminism from the point of view of women of color and white antiracist women illuminates the rise of multiracial feminism—the liberation movement spearheaded by women of color in the United States in the 1970s that was characterized by its international perspective, its attention to interlocking oppressions, and its support of coalition politics.[5] Bernice Johnson Reagan's naming of "coalition politics"; Patricia Hill Collins's understanding of women of color as "outsiders within"; Barbara Smith's concept of "the simultaneity of oppressions"; Cherrie Moraga and Gloria Anzaldúa's "theory in the flesh"; Chandra Talpade Mohanty's critique of "imperialist feminism"; Paula Gunn Allen's "red roots of white feminism"; Adrienne Rich's "politics of location"; and Patricia Williams's analysis of "spirit murder" are all theoretical guideposts for multiracial feminism.[6] Tracing the rise of multiracial feminism raises many questions about common assumptions made in normative versions of Second Wave history. Constructing a multiracial feminist movement time line and juxtaposing it with the normative time line reveals competing visions of what constitutes liberation and illuminates schisms in feminist consciousness that are still with us today.

The Rise of Multiracial Feminism

Normative accounts of the Second Wave feminist movement often reach back to the publication of Betty Friedan's *The Feminine Mystique* in 1963, the founding of the National Organization for Women in 1966, and the emergence of women's consciousness-raising (CR) groups in the late 1960s. All signaled a rising number of white, middle-class women unwilling to be treated like second-class citizens in the boardroom, in education, or in bed. Many of the early protests waged by this sector of the feminist movement picked up on the courage and forthrightness of 1960s' struggles—a willingness to stop traffic, break existing laws to provide safe and accessible abortions, and contradict the older generation. For younger women, the leadership women had demonstrated in 1960s' activism belied the sex roles that had traditionally defined domestic, economic, and political relations and opened new possibilities for action.

This version of the origins of Second Wave history is not sufficient in telling the story of multiracial feminism. Although there were Black women involved with NOW from the outset and Black and Latina women who participated in CR groups, the feminist work of women of color also extended beyond women-only spaces. In fact, during the 1970s, women of color were involved on three fronts—working with white-dominated feminist groups; forming women's caucuses in existing mixed-gender organizations; and developing autonomous Black, Latina, Native American, and Asian feminist organizations.[7]

This three-pronged approach contrasts sharply with the common notion that women of color feminists emerged in reaction to (and therefore later than) white feminism. In her critique of "model making" in Second Wave historiography, which has "all but ignored the feminist activism of women of color," Benita Roth "challenges the idea that Black feminist organizing was a later variant of so-called mainstream white feminism."[8] Roth's assertion—that the timing of Black feminist organizing is roughly equivalent to the timing of white feminist activism—is true about feminist activism by Latinas, Native Americans, and Asian Americans as well.

One of the earliest feminist organizations of the Second Wave was a Chicana group —Hijas de Cuauhtemoc (1971)—named after a Mexican women's underground newspaper that was published during the 1910 Mexican Revolution. Chicanas who formed this *femenista* group and published a newspaper named after the early-twentieth-century Mexican women's revolutionary group, were initially involved in the United Mexican American Student Organization which was part of the Chicano/a student movement.[9] Many of the founders of Hijas de Cuauhtemoc were later involved in launching the first national Chicana studies journal, *Encuentro Feminil.*

An early Asian American women's group, Asian Sisters, focused on drug abuse intervention for young women in Los Angeles. It emerged in 1971 out of the Asian American Political Alliance, a broad-based, grassroots organization largely fueled by the consciousness of first-generation Asian American college students. Networking between Asian American and other women during this period also included participation by a contingent of 150 Third World and white women from North America at the historic Vancouver Indochinese Women's Conference (1971) to work with Indochinese women against U.S. imperialism.[10] Asian American women provided services for battered women, worked as advocates for refugees and recent immigrants, produced events spotlighting Asian women's cultural and political diversity, and organized with other women of color.[11]

The best-known Native American women's organization of the 1970s was Women of All Red Nations (WARN). WARN was initiated in 1974 by women, many of whom were also members of the American Indian Movement which was founded in 1968 by Dennis Banks, George Mitchell, and Mary Jane Wilson, an Anishinabe activist.[12] WARN's activism included fighting sterilization in public health service hospitals, suing the U.S. government for attempts to sell Pine Ridge water in South Dakota to corporations, and networking with indigenous people in Guatemala and Nicaragua.[13] WARN reflected a whole generation of Native American women activists who had been leaders in the takeover of Wounded Knee in South Dakota in 1973, on the Pine Ridge reservation (1973–76), and elsewhere. WARN, like Asian Sisters and Hijas de Cuauhtemoc, grew out of—and often worked with—mixed-gender nationalist organizations.

The autonomous feminist organizations that Black, Latina, Asian, and Native American women were forming during the early 1970s drew on nationalist traditions through their recognition of the need for people of color-led, independent organizations.[14] At the same time, unlike earlier nationalist organizations that included women and men, these were organizations specifically for women.

Among Black women, one early Black feminist organization was the Third World Women's Alliance which emerged in 1968 out of the Student Nonviolent Coordinating Committee (SNCC) chapters on the East Coast and focused on racism, sexism, and imperialism.[15] The foremost autonomous feminist organization of the early 1970s was the National Black Feminist Organization (NBFO). Founded in 1973 by Florynce Kennedy, Margaret Sloan, and Doris Wright, it included many other well-known Black women including Faith Ringgold, Michelle Wallace, Alice Walker, and Barbara Smith. According to Deborah Gray White, NBFO, "more than any organization in the century … launched a frontal assault on sexism and racism."[16] Its first conference in New York was attended by 400 women from a range of class backgrounds.

Although the NFBO was a short-lived organization nationally (1973–75), chapters in major cities remained together for years, including one in Chicago that survived until 1981. The contents of the CR sessions were decidedly Black women's issues— stereotypes of Black women in the media, discrimination in the workplace, myths about Black women as matriarchs, Black women's beauty, and self-esteem.[17] The NBFO also helped to inspire the founding of the Combahee River Collective in 1974, a Boston-based organization named after a river in South Carolina where Harriet Tubman led an insurgent action that freed 750 slaves. The Combahee River Collective not only led the way for crucial antiracist activism in Boston through the decade, but it also provided a blueprint for Black feminism that still stands a quarter of a century later. From

Combahee member Barbara Smith came a definition of feminism so expansive that it remains a model today. Smith writes that "feminism is the political theory and practice to free *all* women: women of color, working-class women, poor women, physically challenged women, lesbians, old women, as well as white economically privileged heterosexual women. Anything less than this is not feminism, but merely female self-aggrandizement" (Hull 1982: 49).

These and other groups in the early and mid-1970s provided the foundation for the most far-reaching and expansive organizing by women of color in U.S. history. These organizations also fueled a veritable explosion of writing by women of color, including Toni Cade's pioneering, *The Black Woman: An Anthology* in 1970, Maxine Hong Kingston's *The Woman Warrior* in 1977, and in 1981 and 1983, respectively, the foundational *This Bridge Called My Back: Writings by Radical Women of Color and Home Girls: A Black Feminist Anthology*. While chronicling the dynamism and complexity of a multidimensional vision for women of color, these books also traced for white women what is required to be allies to women of color.

By the late 1970s, the progress made possible by autonomous and independent Asian, Latina, and Black feminist organizations opened a space for women of color to work in coalition across organizations with each other. During this period, two cohorts of white women became involved in multiracial feminism. One group had, in the late 1960s and early 1970s, chosen to work in anti-imperialist, antiracist militant organizations in connection with Black Power groups—the Black Panther Party, the Black Liberation Army—and other solidarity and nationalist organizations associated with the American Indian, Puerto Rican Independence, and Chicano Movements of the late 1960s and early 1970s. These women chose to work with these solidarity organizations rather than work in overwhelmingly white feminist contexts. None of the white antiracist feminists I interviewed (for a social history of antiracism in the United States) who were politically active during the civil rights and Black Power movements had an interest in organizations that had a single focus on gender or that did not have antiracism at the center of their agendas.

Militant women of color and white women took stands against white supremacy and imperialism (both internal and external colonialism); envisioned revolution as a necessary outcome of political struggle; and saw armed propaganda (armed attacks against corporate and military targets along with public education about state crime) as a possible tactic in revolutionary struggle. Although some of these women avoided or rejected the term "feminist" because of its association with hegemonic feminism, these women still confronted sexism both within solidarity and nationalist organizations and within their own communities. In her autobiographical account of her late-1960s' politics, Black liberation movement leader Assata Shakur writes: "To me, the revolutionary struggle of Black people had to be against racism, classism, imperialism and sexism for real freedom under a socialist government."[18] During this period, Angela Davis was also linking anti-capitalist struggle with the fight against race and gender oppression.[19] Similarly, white militant activist Marilyn Buck, who was among the first women to confront Students for a Democratic Society (SDS) around issues of sexism, also spoke up for women's rights as an ally of the Black Liberation Army.

Rarely, however, have their stories—and those of other militant antiracist women—been considered part of Second Wave history. In her critique of this dominant narrative, historian Nancy MacLean writes: "Recent accounts of the rise of modern feminism depart little from the story line first advanced two decades ago and since enshrined as orthodoxy. That story stars white middle-class women triangulated between the pulls of liberal, radical/cultural, and socialist feminism. Working-class women and women of color assume walk-on parts late in the plot, after tendencies and allegiances are already in place. The problem with this script is not simply that it has grown stale from repeated retelling. It is not accurate. ..."[20]

The omission of militant white women and women of color from Second Wave history partly reflects a common notion that the women's movement followed and drew upon the early civil rights movement and the New Left, a trajectory that skips entirely the profound impact that the Black Power movement had on many women's activism. Omitting militant women activists from historical reference also reflects a number of ideological assumptions made during the late 1960s and early 1970s—that "real" feminists were those who worked primarily or exclusively with other women; that "women's ways of knowing" were more collaborative, less hierarchical, and more peace loving than men's; and that women's liberation would come from women's deepening understanding that "sisterhood is powerful."

These politics were upheld both by liberal and radical white feminists. These politics did not, however, sit well with many militant women of color and white women who refused to consider sexism the primary, or most destructive, oppression and recognized the limits of gaining equality in a system that, as Malcolm X had explained, was already on fire. The women of color and white militant women who supported a race, class, and gender analysis in the late 1960s and 1970s often found themselves trying to explain their politics in mixed-gender settings (at home, at work, and in their activism), sometimes alienated from the men (and some women) who did not get it, while simultaneously alienated from white feminists whose politics they considered narrow at best and frivolous at worst.

By the late 1970s, the militant women who wanted little to do with white feminism of the late 1960s and 1970s became deeply involved in multiracial feminism. By that point, the decade of organizing among women of color in autonomous Black, Latina, and Asian feminist organizations led militant antiracist white women to immerse themselves in multiracial feminism. Meanwhile, a younger cohort of white women, who were first politicized in the late 1970s, saw feminism from a whole different vantage point than did the older, white, antiracist women. For the younger group, exposure to multiracial feminism led by women of color meant an early lesson that race, class, and gender were inextricably linked. They also gained vital experience in multiple organizations—battered women's shelters, conferences, and health organizations—where women were, with much struggle, attempting to uphold this politic.[21]

From this organizing came the emergence of a small but important group of white women determined to understand how white privilege had historically blocked cross-race alliances among women, and what they, as white women, needed to do to work closely with women of color. Not surprisingly, Jewish women and lesbians often led the way among white women in articulating a politic that accounted for white women's position as both oppressed and oppressor—as both women and white.[22] Both groups knew what it meant to be marginalized from a women's movement that was, nevertheless, still homophobic and Christian biased. Both groups knew that "there is no place like home"—among other Jews and/or lesbians—and the limits of that home if for Jews it was male dominated or if for lesbians it was exclusively white. The paradoxes of "home" for these groups paralleled many of the situations experienced by women of color who, over and over again, found themselves to be the bridges that everyone assumed would be on their backs.

As the straight Black women interacted with the Black lesbians, the first-generation Chinese women talked with the Native American activists, and the Latina women talked with the Black and white women about the walls that go up when people cannot speak Spanish, white women attempting to understand race knew they had a lot of listening to do. They also had a lot of truth telling to reckon with, and a lot of networking to do, among other white women and with women of color as well.

Radicals, Heydays, and Hot Spots

The story of Second Wave feminism, if told from the vantage point of multiracial feminism, also encourages us to rethink key assumptions about periodization. Among these assumptions is the notion that the 1960s and early 1970s were the height of the radical feminist movement. For example, in her foreword to Alice Echols's *Daring to Be Bad: Radical Feminism in America, 1967–1975*, Ellen Willis asserts that by the mid-1970s, the best of feminism had already occurred.[23] In her history of the women's liberation movement, Barbara Ryan writes that the unity among women evident in the early 1970s declined dramatically by the late 1970s as a consequence of divisions within the movement.[24]

Looking at the history of feminism from the point of view of women of color and antiracist white women suggests quite a different picture. …

… Although the late 1960s and early 1970s might have been the "heyday" for white "radical" feminists in CR groups, from the perspective of white antiracists, the early 1970s were a low point of feminism—a time when many women who were committed to an antiracist analysis had to put their feminism on the back burner in order to work with women and men of color and against racism.

Coinciding with the frequent assumption that 1969 to 1974 was the height of "radical feminism," many feminist historians consider 1972 to 1982 as the period of mass mobilization and 1983 to 1991 as a period of feminist abeyance.[25] Ironically, the years that sociologists Verta Taylor and Nancy Whittier consider the period of mass mobilization for feminists (1972–82) are the years that Chela Sandoval identifies as the period when "ideological differences divided and helped to dissipate the movement from within."[26] For antiracist women (both white and of color), the best days of feminism were yet to come when, as Barbara Smith explains, "Those issues that had divided many of the movement's constituencies—such as racism, anti-Semitism, ableism, ageism, and classism—were put out on the table."[27] …

In fact, periodization of the women's movement from the point of view of multiracial feminism would treat the late 1960s and early 1970s as its origin and the mid-1970s, 1980s, and 1990s as a height. A time line of that period shows a flourishing multiracial feminist movement. In 1977, the Combahee River Collective Statement was first published; in 1979, *Conditions: Five*, the Black women's issue, was published, the First National Third World Lesbian Conference was held, and Assata Shakur escaped from prison in New Jersey with the help of prison activists. In 1981, Byllye Avery founded the National Black Women's Health Project in Atlanta; Bernice Johnson Reagan gave her now-classic speech on coalition politics at the West Coast Women's Music Festival in Yosemite; and the National Women's Studies Association held its first conference to deal with racism as a central theme, in Storrs, Connecticut, where there were multiple animated interventions against racism and anti-Semitism in the women's movement and from which emerged Adrienne Rich's exquisite essay, "Disobedience and Women's Studies."[28] Then, 1984 was the year of the New York Women against Rape Conference, a multiracial, multiethnic conference that confronted multiple challenges facing women organizing against violence against women—by partners, police, social service agencies, and poverty. In 1985, the United Nations Decade for Women conference in Nairobi, Kenya, took place; that same year, Wilma Mankiller was named the first principal chief of the Cherokee Nation. In 1986, the National Women's Studies Association conference was held at Spelman College. The next year, 1987, the Supreme Court ruled that the Immigration and Naturalization Service must interpret the 1980s' Refugee Act more broadly to recognize refugees from Central America, a ruling that reflected the work on the part of thousands of activists, many of whom were feminists, to end U.S. intervention in Central America.

In 1991, Elsa Barkely Brown, Barbara Ransby, and Deborah King launched the campaign called African American Women in Defense of Ourselves, within minutes of Anita Hill's testimony regarding the nomination of Clarence Thomas to the Supreme Court. Their organizing included an advertisement in the *New York Times* and six Black newspapers which included the names of 1,603 Black women. The 1982 defeat of the ERA did not signal a period of abeyance for multiracial feminism. In fact, multiracial feminism flourished in the 1980s, despite the country's turn to the Right.

Understanding Second Wave feminism from the vantage point of the Black Power movement and multiracial feminism also shows the limit of the frequent assignment of the term "radical" only to the white antipatriarchal feminists of late 1960s and early 1970s. Many feminist historians link the development of radical feminism to the creation of several antipatriarchy organizations—the Redstockings, Radicalesbians, WITCH, and other CR groups. How the term "radical" is used by feminist historians does not square, however, with how women of color and white antiracists used that term from the 1960s through the 1980s. What does it mean when feminist historians apply the term "radical" to white, antipatriarchy women but not to antiracist white women and women of color (including Angela Davis, Kathleen Cleaver, Marilyn Buck, Anna Mae Aquash, Susan Saxe, Vicki Gabriner, and Laura Whitehorn) of the same era whose "radicalism" included attention to race, gender, and imperialism and a belief that revolution might require literally laying their lives on the line? These radical women include political prisoners—Black, Puerto Rican, and white—some of whom are still in prison for their antiracist activism in the 1960s and 1970s. Many of these women openly identify as feminists and/or lesbians but are rarely included in histories of Second Wave feminism.

What does it mean when the term "radical" is only assigned to white, antipatriarchy women when the subtitle to Cherríe Moraga and Gloria Anzaldúa's foundational book, *This Bridge Called My Back*, was "*Writings by Radical Women of Color*"?[29] To my mind, a nuanced and accurate telling of Second Wave feminism is one that shows why and how the term "radical" was itself contested. Recognizing that there were different groups who used the term "radical" does not mean that we then need an overarching definition of "radical feminism" that includes all these approaches. It does mean understanding that white feminists … do not have exclusive rights to the term. An expansive history would emphasize that Second Wave feminism drew on the civil rights movement, the New Left, *and* the Black Power movement which, together, helped to produce three groups of "radical" women.

Principles of a Movement

Although analysis of the feminist movement that accounts for competing views of what it means to be "radical" is a step forward in developing a complex understanding of Second Wave history, what most interests me about comparing normative feminist history with multiracial feminism are the contestations in philosophy embedded in these coexisting frameworks. Both popular and scholarly interpretations of Second Wave feminism typically link two well-known principles to the movement—"Sisterhood Is Powerful" and the "Personal Is Political." From the point of view of multiracial feminism, both principles are a good start but, in themselves, are not enough.

… Lorraine Bethel's poem, "What Chou Mean *We* White Girl? or the Cullud Lesbian Feminist Declaration of Independence" ("Dedicated to the proposition that all women are not equal, i.e., identical/ly oppressed"), clarifies that a "we" between white and Black is provisional, at best.[30] …

Cross-racial struggle made clear the work that white women needed to do in order for cross-racial sisterhood to *really* be powerful. Among the directives were the following: Don't expect women of color to be your educators, to do all the bridge work. White women need to be the bridge—a lot of the time. Do not lump African American, Latina, Asian American, and Native American women into one category. History, culture, imperialism, language, class, region, and sexuality make the concept of a monolithic "women of color" indefensible. Listen to women of color's anger. It is informed by centuries of struggle, erasure, and experience. White women, look to your own history for signs of heresy and rebellion. Do not take on the histories of Black, Latina, or American Indian women as your own. They are not and never were yours.

A second principle associated with liberal and radical feminism is captured in the slogan "The Personal Is Political," first used by civil rights and New Left activists and then articulated with more depth and consistency by feminist activists. The idea behind the slogan is that many issues that historically have been deemed "personal"—abortion, battery, unemployment, birth, death, and illness—are actually deeply political issues.

Multiracial feminism requires women to add another level of awareness—to stretch the adage from "The Personal Is Political" to, in the words of antiracist activist Anne Braden, "The Personal Is Political and The Political Is Personal."[31] Many issues that have been relegated to the private sphere are, in fact, deeply political. At the same time, many political issues need to be personally committed to—whether you have been victimized by those issues are not. In other words, you don't have to be part of a subordinated group to know an injustice is wrong and to stand against it. White women need not be victims of racism to recognize it is wrong and stand up against it. Unless that is done, white women will never understand how they support racism. If the only issues that feminists deem political are those they have experienced personally, their frame of reference is destined to be narrowly defined by their own lived experience.

The increasing number of antiracist white women who moved into mixed-gender, multi-issue organizations in the 1980s and 1990s after having helped to build women's cultural institutions in the 1970s and 1980s may be one of the best examples of an attempt to uphold this politic. …

The tremendous strength of autonomous feminist institutions—the festivals, conferences, bookstores, women's studies departments, women's health centers—were the artistic, political, and social contributions activists helped to generate. All of these cultural institutions required women to ask of themselves and others a pivotal question Audre Lorde had posited: Are you doing your work? And yet, by the mid-1980s, the resurgence of the radical Right in the United States that fueled a monumental backlash against gays and lesbians, people of color, and women across the races led multiracial feminists to ask again: Where and with whom are you doing your work? Many antiracist feminists who had helped to build the largely women-led cultural institutions that left a paper trail of multiracial feminism moved on, into mixed-gender, multiracial grassroots organizations, working against the Klan, in support of affirmative action and immigrant rights, and against police brutality and the prison industry. It is in these institutions that much of the hard work continues—in recognizing that "sisterhood is powerful" only when it is worked for and not assumed and that the "personal is political" only to the extent that one's politics go way beyond the confines of one's own individual experience.

Blueprints for Feminist Activism

There are multiple strategies for social justice embedded in multiracial feminism: a belief in building coalitions that are based on a respect for identity-based groups; attention to both process and product but little tolerance for "all-talk" groups; racial parity at every level of an organization (not added on later but initiated from the start); a recognition that race can not be seen in binary terms; a recognition that racism exists in your backyard as well as in the countries the United States is bombing or inhabiting economically; and a recognition of the limits to pacifism when people in struggle are up against the most powerful state in the world. Multiracial feminism is not just another brand of feminism that can be taught alongside liberal, radical, and socialist feminism.

Multiracial feminism is the heart of an inclusive women's liberation struggle. The race-class-gender-sexuality-nationality framework through which multiracial feminism operates encompasses and goes way beyond liberal, radical, and socialist feminist priorities—and it always has. Teaching Second Wave feminist history requires chronicling how hegemonic feminism came to be written about as "the" feminism and the limits of that model. Teaching Second Wave history by chronicling the rise of multiracial feminism challenges limited categories because it puts social justice and antiracism at the center of attention. This does not mean that the work done within hegemonic feminism did not exist or was not useful. It does mean that it was limited in its goals and effectiveness.

Although the strategies for multiracial feminism were firmly established in the 1970s and 1980s, I contend that these principles remain a blueprint for progressive, feminist, antiracist struggle in this millennium. …

Because written histories of social movements are typically one generation behind the movements themselves, it makes sense that histories of the feminist movement are just now emerging. That timing means that now is the time to interrupt normative accounts before they begin to repeat themselves, each time, sounding more like "the truth" simply because of the repetition of the retelling. This interruption is necessary with regard to Second Wave feminism as well as earlier movements. …

… I want young women to know the rich, complicated, contentious, and visionary history of multiracial feminism and to know the nuanced controversies within Second Wave feminism. I want them to know that Shirley Chisholm ran for president in 1972; that Celestine Ware wrote a Black radical feminist text in the 1970s which offered an inspiring conception of revolution with a deep sense of humanity; that before Mab Segrest went to work for an organization against the Klan in North Carolina, she and others published an independent lesbian journal in the 1970s that included some of the most important and compelling race-conscious writing by white women and women of color to date.[32] I want people to know that there are antiracist feminist women currently in prison for their antiracist activism in the 1960s and since.[33] … [T]he work of … multiracial feminist activists help show that the struggle against racism is hardly linear, that the consolidation of white-biased feminism was clearly costly to early Second Wave feminism, and that we must dig deep to represent the feminist movement that does justice to an antiracist vision.

Notes

1. For examples of histories that focus on white feminism, see Sheila Tobias, *Faces of Feminism: An Activist's Reflections on the Women's Movement* (Boulder: Westview Press, 1997); Barbara Ryan, *Feminism and the Women's Movement: Dynamics of Change in Social Movement Ideology and Activism* (New York: Routledge, 1992); Alice Echols, *Daring to Be Bad: Radical Feminism in America, 1967–1975* (Minneapolis: University of Minnesota Press, 1989).
2. Chela Sandoval, *Methodology of the Oppressed* (Minneapolis: University of Minnesota Press, 2000), 41–42.
3. Of these branches of feminism (liberal, socialist, and radical), socialist feminism, which treats sexism and classism as interrelated forms of oppression, may have made the most concerted effort to develop an antiracist agenda in the 1970s. … For early socialist feminist documents, see

Rosalyn Baxandall and Linda Gordon, eds., *Dear Sisters: Dispatches from the Women's Liberation Movement* (New York: Basic Books, 2000).

4. For an expanded discussion of the contributions and limitations of white antiracism from the 1950s to the present, see Becky Thompson, *A Promise and a Way of Life: White Antiracist Activism* (Minneapolis: University of Minnesota Press, 2001).

5. … Maxine Baca Zinn and Bonnie Thornton Dill, "Theorizing Difference from Multiracial Feminism," *Feminist Studies* 22 (summer 1996): 321–31.

6. … Paula Gunn Allen, "Who Is Your Mother? Red Roots of White Feminism," in her *The Sacred Hoop* (Boston: Beacon Press, 1986), 209–21; Adrienne Rich, *Blood, Bread, and Poetry* (New York: Norton, 1986) [ed. for others, see Works Cited herein].

7. Here I am using the term "feminist" to describe collective action designed to confront interlocking race, class, gender, and sexual oppressions (and other systematic discrimination). Although many women in these organizations explicitly referred to themselves as "feminist" from their earliest political work, others have used such terms as "womanist," "radical women of color," "revolutionary," and "social activist." … The tendency not to include gender-conscious activism by women of color in dominant versions of Second Wave history unless the women used the term "feminist" fails to account for the multiple terms women of color have historically used to designate activism that keeps women at the center of analysis and attends to interlocking oppressions. …

8. Benita Roth, "The Making of the Vanguard Center: Black Feminist Emergence in the 1960s and 1970s," in *Still Lifting, Still Climbing: African American Women's Contemporary Activism*, ed. Kimberly Springer (New York: New York University Press, 1999), 71.

9. Sherna Berger Gluck, "Whose Feminism, Whose History? Reflections on Excavating the History of (the) U.S. Women's Movement(s)," in *Community Activism and Feminist Politics: Organizing across Race, Class, and Gender*, ed. Nancy A. Naples (New York: Routledge, 1998), 38–39.

10. Miya Iwataki, "The Asian Women's Movement: A Retrospective," *East Wind* (spring/summer 1983): 35–41; Gluck, 39–41.

11. Sonia Shah, "Presenting the Blue Goddess: Toward a National Pan-Asian Feminist Agenda," in *The State of Asian America: Activism and Resistance in the 1990s*, ed. Karin Aguilar-San Juan (Boston: South End Press, 1994), 147–58.

12. M. Annette Jaimes with Theresa Halsey, "American Indian Women: At the Center of Indigenous Resistance in Contemporary North America," in *The State of Native America: Genocide, Colonization, and Resistance*, ed. M. Annette Jaimes (Boston: South End Press, 1992), 329.

13. Stephanie Autumn, "… This Air, This Land, This Water—If We Don't Start Organizing Now, We'll Lose It," *Big Mama Rag* 11 (April11983): 4, 5.

14. For an insightful analysis of the multidimensionality of Black nationalism of the late 1960s and early 1970s, see Angela Davis, "Black Nationalism: The Sixties and the Nineties," in *The Angela Davis Reader*, ed. Joy James (Malden, Mass.: Blackwell, 1998), 289–96.

15. Ibid., 15, 314.

16. Deborah Gray White, *Too Heavy a Load: Black Women in Defense of Themselves* (New York: Norton, 1999), 242.

17. Ibid., 242–53.

18. Assata Shakur, *Assata: An Autobiography* (Chicago: Lawrence Hill Books, 1987), 197.

19. Angela Davis, *Angela Davis: An Autobiography* (New York: Random House, 1974).

20. Nancy MacLean, "The Hidden History of Affirmative Action: Working Women's Struggles in the 1970s and the Gender of Class," *Feminist Studies* 25 (spring 1999): 47.

21. As a woman who was introduced to antiracist work through the feminist movement of the late 1970s—a movement shaped in large part by women of color who called themselves "womanists," "feminists," and "radical women of color"—I came to my interest in recasting the chronology of Second Wave feminism especially hoping to learn how white antiracist women positioned themselves vis-á-vis Second Wave feminism. I wanted to learn how sexism played itself out in the 1960s and how antiracist white women responded to Second Wave feminism. And I wanted to find out whether the antiracist baton carried in the 1960s was passed on or dropped by feminist activists. …

22. Several key Jewish feminist texts that addressed how to take racism and anti-Semitism seriously in feminist activism were published during this period and included Evelyn Torton Beck, ed., *Nice Jewish Girls: A Lesbian Anthology* (Trumansburg, N.Y.: Crossing Press, 1982); Melanie Kaye/Kantrowitz and Irena Klepfisz, eds., *The Tribe of Dina: A Jewish Women's Anthology* (Boston: Beacon Press, 1989), first published as a special issue of *Sinister Wisdom*, nos. 29/30 (1986); Melanie Kaye/Kantrowitz, *The Issue Is Power: Essays on Women, Jews, Violence, and Resistance* (San Francisco: Aunt Lute, 1992); Irena Klepfisz, Periods of Stress (Brooklyn, N.Y.: Out & Out Books, 1977), and *Keeper of Accounts* (Watertown, Mass.: Persephone Press, 1982).

    For key antiracist lesbian texts, see Adrienne Rich, *On Lies, Secrets, and Silence: Selected Prose, 1966–1978* (New York: Norton, 1979); Joan Gibbs and Sara Bennett, *Top Ranking: A Collection of Articles on Racism and Classism in the Lesbian Community* (New York: Come! Unity Press, 1980); Mab Segrest, *My Mama's Dead Squirrel: Lesbian Essays on Southern Culture* (Ithaca, N.Y.: Firebrand Books, 1985); Elly Bulkin, Minnie Bruce Pratt, and Barbara Smith, *Yours in Struggle: Three Feminist Perspectives on Anti-Semitism and Racism* (Brooklyn, N.Y.: Long Haul Press. 1984).

23. Ellen Willis, foreword to *Daring to Be Bad*, vii.

24. Barbara Ryan.

25. Verta Taylor and Nancy Whittier, "The New Feminist Movement," in *Feminist Frontiers IV*, ed. Laurel Richardson, Verta Taylor, and Nancy Whittier (New York: McGraw-Hill, 1997), 544–45.

26. Chela Sandoval 1990, 55.

27. Barbara Smith, "'Feisty Characters' and 'Other People's Causes'" in *The Feminist Memoir Project*, ed. R. B. DuPlessis and A. Snitow (New York: Three Rivers Press), 479–80.

28. Adrienne Rich, "Disobedience and Women's Studies," *Blood, Bread, and Poetry*, 76–84.

29. Moraga and Anzaldúa.

30. Lorraine Bethel, "What Chou Mean *We*, White Girl," in *Conditions: Five* (1979): 86.

31. Thompson. See also Anne Braden, *The Wall Between* (Knoxville: University of Tennessee Press, 1999); Anne Braden, "A Second Open Letter to Southern White Women," *Southern Exposure* 6 (winter 1977): 50.

32. See *Feminary: A Feminist Journal for the South Emphasizing Lesbian Visions*. Schlesinger Library at the Radcliffe Institute for Advanced Study at Harvard University has scattered issues of *Feminary*. Duke University Rare Book, Manuscript, and Special Collection Library has vols. 5–15 from 1974–1985. …

33. Marilyn Buck, Linda Evans, Laura Whitehorn, and Kathy Boudin are among the white political prisoners who are either currently in prison or, in the case of Laura Whitehorn and Linda Evans, recently released, serving sentences whose length and severity can only be understood as retaliation for their principled, antiracist politics.

6.
GLOBALIZATION OF THE LOCAL/ LOCALIZATION OF THE GLOBAL: MAPPING TRANSNATIONAL WOMEN'S MOVEMENTS
Amrita Basu
(2000)

It may be time to replace the bumper sticker that exhorts, "Think Globally, Act Locally," with one that reads, "Think Locally, Act Globally." Or perhaps it's time simply to retire the bumper sticker, for with the growth of transnational social movements, we need to rethink entirely relations between the local and the global.

I am interested in exploring the implications for women's movements in the South of the growth of the transnational networks, organizations, and ideas. In the essay that follows I want to ask how North–South tensions around the meaning of feminism and the nature of women's movements have changed. What new opportunities have emerged and what new tensions have surfaced? What is the relationship between the transnationalism of the '90s and the feminism of the '60s and '70s, when Robin Morgan aptly and controversially claimed, "Sisterhood Is Global?"

My point of departure is an anthology of writings I edited in preparation for the 1995 Beijing women's conference entitled *The Challenge of Local Feminisms: Women's Movements in Global Perspective.* I found myself attempting to navigate twin dangers: resisting, on the one hand, the tendency narrowly to equate women's movements with autonomous urban, middle-class feminist groups, and, on the other hand, of defining women's movements so broadly that the term includes virtually all forms of women's activism. I highlighted the local origins and character of women's movements crossnationally and argued that women's movements must be situated within the particular political economics, state policies, and cultural politics of the regions in which they are active.

The question I now propose to ask is whether we need to rethink once again the relationship between local and global feminisms. Is it possible that the 1995 Beijing conference, which my book was designed to commemorate, in fact marked the coming of age of transnational feminism and the eclipse of locally based women's movements? This question is prompted by the appearance of more transnational women's movement activity than we ever have seen.

Before proceeding, a word about my terms: I am aware that *local* can connote the supposed particularism, provincialism and primordialism, of the Third World while *global* may connote the breadth and universality that is often associated with Western feminism. By contrast, I use the term *local* to refer to indigenous and regional, and *global* to refer to the transnational. I employ these terms because they correspond to the levels at which a great deal of women's activism is organized, namely at the grass roots and transnational levels. As I will discuss, it is also important to inject into that dynamic attention to the national level.

There is considerable controversy about the significance of transnational movements, NGOs, networks, and advocacy groups. While some scholars speak of the emergence of a global civil society, others are more skeptical.[1] How to evaluate the transnationalization of women's movements is no less complicated. From one perspective it represents a signal achievement—particularly for women in the South. For example, Valentine Moghadam (1996) argues that transnational networks are organizing women around the most pressing questions of the day: reproductive rights, the growth of religious fundamentalism, and the adverse effects of structural adjustment policies. Moghadam also comments favorably in the recent emergence of networks, which she believes have a broader and more far reaching impact than local movements.[2] From another perspective as women's movements have become more transnational, their commitment to grass roots mobilization and cultural change has diminished. Sonia Alvarez (1997, 1998, 2000) argues that women's movements are becoming increasingly bureaucratized as they have come to work more closely with NGOs, political parties, state institutions, and multilateral agencies.[3] What explains the differences in these two perspectives? Which is correct?

I emphasize the indeterminate character of transnational activism in the late 1990s and early 2000s. It is inaccurate to depict local women's movements as simply being subsumed by global ones or as engaging in sustained overt resistance to global influences. Rather what prevails is more complex and varied situation in which local and transnational movements often exist independently of one another and experience similar challenges and dilemmas. Furthermore, while transnational ideas, resources, and organizations have been extremely successful around certain issues in some regions, their success with these issues is more circumscribed elsewhere. ...

Women's Movements in Global Perspective

The international women's conferences that occurred in Mexico City (1975), Copenhagen (1980) Nairobi (1985) and Beijing (1995) provide a fruitful opportunity to explore changing relationships among women's organizations transnationally. The two-tier system of conferences, namely the United Nations-convened official conferences of heads of states, and the non-governmental conferences convened by women's groups and movements, provide insights into the workings of the international state system and of what some describe as a burgeoning global civil society.

International feminism might be periodized as comprising two broad phases. The first phase, between 1975 and 1985, was marked by bitter contestation over the meaning of feminism and over the relationship between the local and the global. The second decade-long phase, which begin with the Nairobi conference in 1985 and culminated in the Beijing conference in 1995, was marked by a growth of networks linking women's activism at the local and global levels.

Fierce struggles over the meaning and significance of feminism took place at international women's conferences of activists and policy makers from 1975 to 1985. Some of these debates identified the South with the local and the North with the global. A typical scenario would be one in which women from the South would argue that women's major priorities were both local and material, for instance, the needs for potable drinking water, firewood for fuel, and more employment opportunities. Meanwhile, women from the North typically would focus on women's broad transnational identities and interests.

It would be inaccurate to imply that tensions along North–South lines had disappeared entirely by the 1995 Beijing women's conference. Even today the organizations that sponsor campaigns to extend women's civil and political rights are Northern-based while Southern-based groups are more apt to address poverty, inequality, and basic needs. Esther Ngan-ling Chow (1996) notes, "Even when they agree on the importance of all issue such as human rights, women from various world regions frame it differently. While Western women traditionally have based their human rights struggles on issues of equality, non-discrimination and civil and political rights, African, Asian and Latin American women have focused their struggles on economic, social and cultural rights."[4]

These differences, however, were less striking at the Beijing conference than significant areas of agreement that were established across North–South lines. Charlotte Bunch and Susan Fried (1996) argue that the entire Platform of Action was an affirmation of the human rights of women: "The incorporation of women's human rights language and concepts by governments and organizations from all parts of the world and in all manner of ways indicates more than a rhetorical gesture. It represents a shift in analysis that moves beyond single-issue politics or identity-based organizing and enhances women's capacity to build global alliances based on collective political goals and a common agenda."[5]

One important explanation for the diminution of tension between women's movements in the North and South is the increasingly important influence of women of color in shaping debates about feminism in the United States. Recall that some of the earliest and most important critiques of feminist universalism came from African American and Latina women in the United States. Years later, in preparation for the 1995 Beijing women's conference, American women of color formed a coalition with women from the South and drafted language for the platform document about women who face multiple forms of discrimination.[6]

At the same time, women from the South increasingly have worked to correct nationalism's exclusions by proposing non-discriminatory policies in newly formed states. Thanks to the influence of its women's movement, Namibia's constitution forbids sex discrimination, authorizes affirmative action for women, and recognizes only those forms of customary law which do not violate the constitution. The South African constitution similarly provides equal rights for women and prohibits discrimination on grounds of sexual orientation. Palestinian women have drafted a bill of rights and sought legislation protecting women from family violence.

Furthermore, with the end of the Cold War, the character of international gatherings changed quite significantly. Early meetings, like the Mexico City conference in 1975, were dominated by national political leaders who sought to use these forums to pursue their own agendas. Whereas many of the delegates attending the 1975 Mexico City conference were the wives, daughters, and widows of male politicians, by the 1985 Nairobi conference, the representatives included many women who were powerful in their own right. Even more important was the growth of women's movements globally and their increasingly important roles relative to those of states.

As nongovernmental organizations and movements have grown, they have become more diverse, and divisions that cross-cut the North–South and East–West divide have become more salient. Both transnational networks of feminists and of conservative activists have grown. For example, a coalition of conservative Islamic groups and Christian anti-abortion activists sought to shape the agenda of the Cairo conference on population and development in 1994 and to influence the World Plan of Action at the Beijing conference in 1995.[7] The coalition included some powerful nongovernmental organizations, such as the International Right to Life Committee and Human Life international; religious bodies, like the Vatican; and some states, preeminently the Islamic Republic of Iran. Like women's organizations, this coalition functions at local, national, and transnational levels.

The growth of transnational networks of the religious Right has reduced North-South polarization. Some of the staunchest opponents of feminism are North American or European, and among its staunchest supporters are Asians, Africans, and Latin Americans. The ability of Muslim, Protestant, and Catholic groups to transcend national differences and arrive at common positions on motherhood, pornography, abortion, homosexuality, and premarital sexuality has encouraged feminist groups similarly to seek out areas of agreement.

Charting the Terrain

It is tempting to treat international conferences as synonymous with transnational women's movements, since they have grown simultaneously. However to conflate the two is to underestimate the extent to which new forms of transnationalism emerge from civil society and include a diverse array of organizations, including NGOs social movements, issue and identity networks, project coalitions, and issue-based campaigns.

The growth of transnational women's movements entails the spread and growing density of groups and linkages among groups within transnational civil society. It also refers to a flow of resources, generally from the North to the South, to support women's organizations. Southern-based NGOs have come to rely heavily on financial support from Northern affiliates, foundations, and academic institutions. But it is not just individuals, groups, and currencies that cross borders with greater ease and frequency than in the past. Certain discourses—and this is a second dimension—have acquired greater importance among women in both the North and the South. One of the most important is that the violation of women's rights is a human rights abuse. Thus women's movements can be said to have become increasingly transnational when they appeal to universal principles of human rights and seek redress in global arenas.

The past few years have witnessed the growth of all these dimensions of transnational activism. There also has been a vast expansion in the number of NGOs which engage in international networking, from the one hundred fourteen that attended the NGO forum in Mexico City in 1975 to the three thousand that participated in the Beijing NGO forum in 1995. Today, tens of thousands of NGOs participate in international conferences and gatherings. Many of these are organized at the regional level by women activists from the South, independent of both the United Nations and national governments.

In keeping with the multifaceted character of globalization, transnational women's movements are themselves extremely diverse. A minority among them seek to challenge the feminization of poverty and class inequality that globalization entails. One important example is Development Alternatives with Women for a New Era (DAWN), which researchers and activists formed in 1984 to promote alternative approaches to state sponsored macroeconomic policies. DAWN includes membership from the Caribbean, Latin America, Africa, South and South-East Asia, and the Middle East. It earlier was based in Bangalore and now is based in Rio.

A much larger group of women's organizations has sought to extend women's civic and political rights, particularly to address violence against women and the denial of women's rights by religious nationalists. An important example is the coalition of one hundred thirty women's and human rights groups— including the National Organization for Women, the Feminist Majority, Human Rights Watch, the National Political Congress of Black Women, and the Women's Alliance for Peace and Human Rights— which organized a campaign protesting the repressive measures that the Taleban has exercised against Afghan women since assuming power in September 1996 and urging the international community to deny investments and recognition to the Taleban. It has organized a website documenting the Taleban's abuses, a petition campaign and demonstrations protesting them, and various fundraising activities. Among its victories has been to dissuade Unocal, an American oil company, from building a pipeline through Afghanistan.

The amount of international funding available for women's organizations, women's studies programs, and women's movements has grown dramatically over the past decade. Grants by major U.S. foundations to groups working on women's rights and violence against women increased from $241,000 in 1988 to $3,247,000 in 1993 (Keck and Sikkink 1998). The Ford Foundation underwrote almost half of this amount. In India alone, for example, the large majority of women's NGOs receive foreign funding.

As far as transnational discourses are concerned, neither conventions on international human rights nor the campaign for women's human rights is new. What is relatively new is the extent to which coalitions of transnational women's organizations have lobbied to demand recognition for women's rights as human rights. The year 1993 marked a turning point for the women's human rights movement, for during that year the Vienna Human Rights Declaration and Program of Action and the UN declaration on the Elimination of Violence Against Women recognized violence against women as a human rights abuse and defined gender violence to include violence against women in the public and the private sphere. Women's human rights activists consolidated their gains at the Beijing conference and since have increasingly employed human rights appeals. With the collapse of communism and the decline of the organized Left, democratic movements have taken the place formerly occupied by socialism, and liberal principles of human rights have become hegemonic.

What are the implications of the transnationalization of women's movements for women in the South? Does the diminution of overt North–South tensions at the Beijing conference and other international forums reflect the increasingly important leadership and agenda-setting roles of women from the South? Or, conversely, are Southern-based organizations less able to oppose Northern domination because of their greater dependence on Northern funding sources? There is no one simple response to this question.

It would be inaccurate to see transnational networks and movements simply as vehicles for Northern domination. Networks like DAWN and WLUML (Women Living under Muslim Law) were organized by and for women from the South. Although these networks accept external funding, they formulate their objectives independently of donor organizations. Furthermore, certain problems may be more effectively addressed at the transnational than at the local level. A good example concerns some of the problems women face as a result of the growth of religious fundamentalism. Afghan women's groups are subject to such extreme repression that they could not organize effectively without outside support. Furthermore transnational networks of women have been a vital counterweight to transnational networks of the religious right.

The campaign against the Taleban also illuminates the possibilities of combining global and local appeals. While the campaign has made extensive use of the website and of e-mail petition campaigns, it also has organized demonstrations locally, including one in Amherst, MA, where women marched through the town commons with banners in their hands and pieces of mesh fabric pinned to their lapels to evoke the *burqua* (veil). Terming the campaign an attempt to stop "gender apartheid" in Afghanistan, the coalition identified the crimes against Afghan women with the evils of apartheid in South Africa. This simple, indeed simplistic characterization, provided an effective means of generating support for the campaign.

Another tool that the campaign against the Taleban and other campaigns against religious fundamentalism have employed is to record the stories of women who are stoned, beaten, or publically humiliated for having worked, married, divorced, or done nothing at all. These individual narratives not only permit a personal identification with the victims but also invite activism against those who perpetrate abuse. The coalition against sexual apartheid in Afghanistan distributes a video entitled "A Shroud of Silence" which recounts these stories in a particularly graphic form.

The very conditions for the success of global campaigns like the one against the Taleban in Afghanistan suggest some of the limitations of the strategy. Global Campaigns are much more likely to succeed when women's civil and political rights rather than their economic rights (food, shelter, housing) have been violated. They are more effective in challenging physical violence than structural violence against women.

Although this organizing problem exists locally, it is much more significant at the transnational level.

Struggles opposing violence against women are nested within the context of women's class and sometimes ethnic struggles more often at the local than at the transnational level. In India struggles against marital abuse often have emerged amidst social movements of the urban and rural poor. Women who protest the complicity of the state with illicit liquor producers in Andhra Pradesh, for example, readily appreciate the connections between violence against women and unemployment, state corruption, and a range of other issues. By contrast, when women come together in global forums as victims of gender violence, their identities as Bosnian, African American, or poor women may be muted.

Women's groups most enthusiastically have supported transnational campaigns against sexual violence in countries where the state is repressive or indifferent and women's movements are weak. Conversely, transnationalism has provoked more distrust in places where women's movements have emerged, grown, and defined themselves independently of Western feminism. Indeed, one explanation for the differences between the positions of Valentine Moghadam (1996) and Sonia Alvarez (1998) is that they examine such different contexts. Moghadam's optimism about the role of transnational networks may be born of the pessimism she feels about the potential for women's movements in face of the growth of Islamic fundamentalism in the Middle East. By contrast, Alvarez expresses concern about cooptation because historically women's movements in Latin America have been strong and closely tied to left-wing parties and human rights movements.

It is precisely in situations where women's movements are grappling with how to organize more inclusively to overcome social hierarchies that transnational linkages may pose the greatest challenge. In such situations, transnationalism may deepen divisions between globalized elites, who belong to transnational networks, and the large majority of women, who do not. The result may be a deradicalization of women's movements. Or there may be growing rifts between those who have access to international funding and those who do not. In this event, some activists become more mobile, while others remain stuck at the local level. The dependence of transnational activists on the internet, which requires specialized skills and technology, further accentuates class divisions among activists. …

How should we evaluate the growing exchanges among women's movements transnationally? To what extent are transnational forms of activism overcoming the tensions that until recently bedeviled women's movements across North–South lines? Are new networks, coalitions, and alliances addressing the key issues that women face transnationally? These questions are of more than academic relevance. The major funding organizations are committed to strengthening civil society both locally and cross-nationally and have identified women's movements as key to this endeavor. For women's movement activists in the South, the question of what kind of transnational alliances to forge and resources to accept is a key concern.

Transnational networks, campaigns, and discourses seem to be most effective where support for a particular demand exists locally, but its expression is constrained where the state is either indifferent or repressive towards women; and where the violation involves physical violence and redress can be found by asserting women's civil and political rights. Examples of such situations include the mass rape of Bosnian women, the Taleban's violence against Afghan women, and the recalled plight of East Asian comfort women during the Second World War. By contrast, transnational networks, campaigns, and discourses have been less effective in strengthening women's movements where strong local movements already exist. Furthermore, activists derive less benefit from transnational connections when the state concedes, however partially, to their demands.

Although transnational women's networks have grown considerably, there is a danger of both crediting and blaming them too much. In India, as in many other places, the principal location of the women's movements is the national rather than the transnational level. Its priority is to influence the state. Women's groups have formed vital roles in nation-building in Namibia, South Africa and Nicaragua; in conflict resolution in war-torn Ireland, Israel, and Bosnia-Herzegovia; and in the democratization of authoritarian states in central Europe and Latin America.[8]

In all contexts, transnational linkages are likely to be most effective when redress can be sought by asserting women's civil and political rights, rather than their economic well-being, and when transnational linkages are not primarily designed to provide resources. The extent to which women's organizations in the South have come to depend on Northern funding has impeded the open-ended, two-way flow of ideas that has been so critical to the development of feminism. Economic reliance on Western foundations fosters the ever-present possibility of dependence and resentment. These problems are quite independent of the intentions of Northern-based funding organizations, many of which have become quite sensitive to the issues.

Meanwhile, women's economic situation remains perilous. Women constitute 70 percent of the 1.3 billion people living in absolute poverty and two-thirds of the world's illiterate population. Accordingly, the Beijing platform for action called on non-governmental women's organizations to strengthen antipoverty programs and improve women's health, education, and social services. It called on NGOs to take responsibility for ensuring women's full and equal access to economic resources, including the right to inheritance, ownership of land, and natural resources. Interestingly, the only recommendation that NGOs have seriously embraced is to provide women with greater access to savings and credit mechanisms and institutions. Important as microcredit schemes are in allowing women a larger share of the pie, they do not contribute to rethinking the implications of macroeconomic policies for women.[9]

Transnational networks and activists seem to be most effective when the basis for mobilization is sexual victimization. Moreover, the victims who generate the most sympathy generally are women from the South who experience genital mutilation, stoning, or public humiliation. Important as campaigns like the coalition against gender apartheid in Afghanistan may be, they draw sympathy partly because of pervasive anti-Arab sentiment in the U.S., which is gendered. Muslim women often are considered victims of the Islamic faith and of the misogyny of men of their community. The dissemination of pieces of mesh fabric to signify the *burqua* by the coalition against the Taleban certainly implies that the *purdah* is inevitably associated with the degradation of women, thereby inadvertently exacerbating anti-Muslim sentiment.

That there is an alternative to the choice between a religious politics which undermines women's rights and universalist, liberal feminism, which undermines women's religious and nationalist loyalties, is illustrated by the network Women Living under Muslim Law (WLUML). Established in 1985, it provides information, solidarity, and support both to women in Muslim countries and to Muslim women living elsewhere. The network was formed in response to the rise of religious "fundamentalist" movements and the attempt by certain states to institute family codes that would deny women full citizenship rights. By making Muslim women both its objects of concern and its leaders, and by showing how Islam provides both sympathetic and adverse characterizations of women's rights, the WLUML avoids disparaging characterizations of Muslim women. What the WLUML Campaign suggests is that global visions need to be further infused with local realities, while appreciating that the local is not merely local, but infused with global influences.

Notes

1. For a sampling of the debates on global civil society, see Lipschutz (1992) Wapner (1995), and Keck and Sikkink (1998).
2. Moghadam (1996a).
3. Alvarez (1998, 1997, and 2000).
4. Chow (1996).
5. Bunch and Fried (1996).
6. Chow (1996), 189.
7. Moghadam (1996b).
8. Cockburn (1998).
9. Cecelia Lynch points to the ineffectiveness of social movements in confronting globalization in (1998).

7.

THE IDEA OF ANCESTRY: OF FEMINIST GENEALOGIES AND MANY OTHER THINGS[1]

Michelle V. Rowley
(2012)

Are waves transatlantic? This is an inevitable question for transnational feminists placed in a North American Women's Studies classroom. The language of first, second, and third waves continues to bring an inordinate measure of comforting order and logic to feminist theorizing. Yet, for a transnational feminist, such a logic can be anything but comforting and we feel compelled to consider how we might undermine the very organizing premises of the field we have asked our students to enter into without undermining their confidence in us as the instructor.

The use of a wave metaphor has been used within U.S. feminist theorizing to mark historical eras (Roth, 2000), to demarcate the emergence of different kinds of lobbies, activisms, and their related organizing frames (Nicholson, 1997), and to signal a different generational ethos (Walker, 1990; Baumgardner and Richards, 2000). Feminist scholars have attached different visual and aural symbols to the metaphor: for some, "waves" represent the sea (Jones, 2010); for others, waves represent radio signals (Garrison, 2010).

The entrenched nature of "waves" as an organizing metaphor within feminist theorizing may very well account for why we continue to narrate feminist history to our students as we do. If we question this metaphor, we immediately open ourselves to many other contentious musings. For example, what is the purpose and value of feminist chronologies? Are these chronologies transferable? Do the advocacy and political categories that help demarcate one era from the other translate when articulated in other cultural contexts? In other words, I ask again, are waves transatlantic?

Of course, the value of theorizing via a wave metaphor does not rest in its ability to travel. That is to say, even if the wave metaphor could travel unimpeded by context and particularity, the inherent problems with linear and originary narratives would still remain. As my colleague Lisa Hogeland has noted:

> Generational thinking is always unspeakably generalizing: one reason we react so vehemently to accounts of "our" generation is that changes in feminist ideas, and the social, political, and institutional impact of feminism itself have been so uneven. No account can be sufficiently inclusive, and to feel ourselves excluded from or marginalized within "our" generation causes pain. (110)

If we are to have any chance at challenging the exclusionary practices that Hogeland suggests attends generational thinking, then my argument here is that we must, at this juncture, expand our feminist literacy. How, then, might we begin to envision an alternative way of feminist remembering that may actually transfer and enable us to talk about feminist histories in different ways without privileging the importance of one site or historical narrative above the other? Would it not be wonderful if we could find theoretical language that explicates feminist histories in ways that actually reflect the violent, volatile, and unpredictable connectivity that characterizes waves, rather than the present contradiction of a wave metaphor that is, in its operation, calmly divisive?

Why Do Genealogies Matter?

Despite my earlier skepticism with regard to generational thinking, genealogical narratives, whether at the individual, societal, or national level, do important work in providing a sense of belonging for those who narrate these narratives. For example, the title for this piece is taken from Etheridge Knight's poem entitled "The Idea of Ancestry"; we may find that there is much to learn by turning toward poetry. In this piece, Knight's individual identity and sense of belonging are intimately bound up with his sense of family and history. While incarcerated, Knight writes:

> Taped to the wall of my cell are 47 pictures: 47 black /faces: my father, mother, grandmothers (1 dead), grand-/ fathers (both dead), brothers, sisters, uncles, aunts,/ cousins (1st and 2nd), nieces, and nephews. They stare/ across the space at me sprawling on my bunk. I know/ their dark eyes, they know mine. (12)

Known for his unconventional punctuation, Knight uses the colon in a way that may help us understand the seductive persistence of generational narratives. Unlike a period which separates, a colon functions like a connector. A colon tells us that what follows explains what has preceded it. The colons that punctuate the first three lines of this poem emphasize the importance of being tangibly surrounded (47 photographs) by a genealogy that is known and recognizable ("I know their dark eyes, they know mine"). Separated by colons, the pictures, black faces, father, mother, grandmothers, grandfathers, brothers, sisters, uncles, aunts, cousins, all explain each other and each intervening colon reminds us that we cannot fully understand one aspect of the sentence without resorting to a prior articulation. Genealogies therefore are deeply enmeshed networks. The first sentences of the poem would also suggest to us that genealogies truncate time and space. Despite the poet's individual incarceration, it is the *idea* of ancestry that triumphs over the separation of time and space to sustain him ("They stare across the space at me sprawling on my bunk").

The first stanza of the poem concludes as follows:

> I have the same name as 1 grandfather, 3 cousins, 3 nephews,/ and 1 uncle. The uncle disappeared when he was 15, just took/ off and caught a freight (they say). He's discussed each year/ when the family has a reunion, he causes uneasiness in/ the clan, he is an empty space. My father's mother, who is 93/ and who keeps the Family Bible with everbody's birth dates/

(and death dates) in it, always mentions him. There is no/ place in her Bible for "whereabouts unknown." (ibid.)

As we learn our respective genealogies, they become readily accessible, always at hand to be invoked, narrated, and re-told. Through sequences of naming, enumeration, calling forth births and deaths and his central positioning of archival practices (the family bible), Knight artfully participates in this task of genealogical narration. One of the reasons that I love this poem is because I remain haunted by the lyrical beauty, emptiness, and desire that sit in the phrase "whereabouts unknown." "Whereabouts unknown" does indeed cause a sense of "uneasiness." It is against the order of things; it defies the ease with which we can tell these readily accessible genealogies. "Whereabouts unknown" should and does give us pause.

If we are instructed by Knight's piece, we will see that genealogies, when invoked positively, are invoked to do very precise work. They offer a sense of belonging and history. They often provide a belief system—a credo or world view—that is in some way reflective of those who tell their narratives. Think of how genealogies are invoked in our own family framework: it is to tell a story.

However, in my quest for an expanded feminist literacy on generational thinking, I am excited by what rests in the interstices of "whereabouts unknown." It is here that I think we should begin to explore the relevance and parameters of feminist genealogies.

Whereabouts Unknown: Expanding Our Feminist Genealogical Narratives

I've deliberately started with Etheridge Knight's work, not to superimpose a feminist consciousness on him, but to alert us to the importance of unexpected, diverse, and surprising beginnings in the expansion of our feminist literacy.

Notwithstanding my own skepticism about how well the metaphor of feminist waves travels, the fact is that as an organizing principle it carries such hegemonic heft that it has indeed traveled, albeit choppily. In such travel we often find that feminist theorists work hard to designate a similar set of historical watershed periods despite the theorists' very disparate political geographies. Alternatively, there is the compulsion to condense and distill a set of activist themes or activist issues that supposedly define their respective wave, hoping all the while that these themes mirror as much as possible the ones that are found within U.S. genealogies. Reproductive rights? Check. Consciousness-raising groups? Check. This is followed by a sigh of belonging. We, too, have a second wave.

For example, drawing on the Anglophone Caribbean for illustrative purposes, the mid to late 1990s signaled an emerging tendency to make sense of Caribbean feminist realities by deploying a wave analytic. As I have argued elsewhere, in this literature there is both an awareness and strident critique of the universalizing aspects of the wave metaphor, but nonetheless, a continued need to draw on the metaphor as a way of making sense of local specificities; such is the hegemonic nature of the analytic.[2] For example, in her piece "Issues of Difference," Caribbean feminist Rawidda Baksh

Soodeen draws on a transnational feminist critique to call out the limitations of deploying a wave analytic outside of a western context. However, while she critiques the presumed universality of women's subordination that attended the feminist second wave, she goes on to argue that the automatic dismissal of feminist theory as ethnocentric marks a failure to "distinguish between the application of feminist theories to the historical, political, and socio-cultural specificities of black/Third World women and the notion of all theory as 'white'" (1998, 76). She then identifies the Caribbean "second wave" as a period beginning in the 1970s and critiques the Afro-centricity of this era. From this overview, we see an example of how a wave analytic can be invoked in a non-U.S. context to address a specific feminist political history. Baksh-Soodeen's deploys the wave analytic in order to first demarcate the consolidation of a specific historical period and to then argue that Caribbean "feminist discourses gave pre-eminence to this historical experiences and present day situation of African-Caribbean people, leading to an Afro-centric rather than a multicultural paradigm."[3] Her efforts to apply the theory "to the historical, political, and socio-cultural specificities of black/Third World women" is laudable. Yet, the seeming inevitability of deploying the idea of a "wave" analytic should give us pause. Ann Braithwaite reminds us that "feminist theory or theorizing … is not a matter (only) of learning and using terms and concepts that have been passed on from elsewhere. It is also … the necessity—to put it in other words—to always 'think about how we think about' whatever term or concept is being used" (2004, 97). That a wave analytic is narrated repeatedly contributes to our sense of its inevitability and, therefore, becomes the way that we think about the field; in other words, the concepts that we use begin to shape the seeming axiomatic parameters of the field and, as such, lock us into a cycle of conceptual usage.

However, on return to the theoretical possibilities of Etheridge Knight's "whereabouts unknown," my concern with Baksh's approach are twofold. First, it continues to name the wave *the* analytic that frames all possibilities; in other words, the whereabouts are "already known." Second, it privileges a watershed period rather than an analytical question of specific area of investigation. With regard to the latter critique, beginning with a designated time period as a wave analytic encourages us to potentially privilege this watershed period, rather than place the watershed in service of the research question, which allows for new rather than descriptive knowledges to emerge[4] (Rowley, 2007, 86). In other words, rather than going in search of a set of themes or watershed periods that have been argued to characterize a particular wave, we may well be better served by exploring why moments emerge as meaningful and by what the initiating and connecting impulses are locally, globally, and regionally.

In an effort to explore such an approach and expand what I have been referring to as a feminist literacy to take us beyond the hegemonic and thereby prescriptive nature of a wave analytic, I have in the past used the term *politics and conditions of emergence*. I've defined this approach as "a praxis that foregrounds differently named theoretical trajectories, attends to the locally specific ways in which feminists have responded and contributed to a wider body of feminist knowledge through the naming of their locally specific realities, and acknowledges the ways in which feminists in the North have structured their own theoretical formulations as a result of these contributions"(2007, 87).

Using the politics and conditions of emergence as a way of narrating feminist histories opens us to the productive value of "whereabouts unknown." As a guiding principle, the politics and conditions of emergence frees us from designated, historical points of departure. In its stead, we place emphasis on the power dynamics and context that lead to specific feminist issues and responses coming to full force. Second, the politics and conditions of emergence in its generic articulation has no country of origin; it has no home and, as such, does not privilege one geopolitical region as the model by which we tell our respective histories. Third, the politics and conditions of emergence, by emphasizing issues of power and context, encourages us to remain open to surprising, unexpected, and constantly shifting points of departure as we tell multiple feminist histories. In other words, driven by a sense of "whereabouts unknown," it frees us to go in search of *all* of the possible actors (male, female, differing abilities, gender identification, nationalities) who may have contributed to the genealogical story that we wish tell about our named feminism. Fourth, referencing Knight's poem once more—"there is no place in her Bible for whereabouts unknown," the politics and conditions of emergence allows us to both use and challenge traditional archival modes of telling feminist stories. The concept, when coupled with my use of Knight's work, reminds us that it is okay that these unexpected and surprising points of departure will indeed cause "uneasiness in the clan."

Finally, the politics and context of emergence by no means dispenses with the importance of history. It simply challenges the idea of one narrative or mode by which we can tell such a history. On the other hand, the politics and conditions of emergence is also painstakingly attentive to time and space as felt within their historical contexts. As contemporary communication technologies speed up the ways in which subsequent generations experience time, the politics and conditions of emergence should also encourage us to use the classroom as a space in which we attend to the temporality of our historical narratives. As time speeds up, we need to remind students that the revolution was truly not televised—and definitely not tweeted. As such, the progression of events, the experience of time, the technologies that communicated and dictated the pace of social change are all integral to my use of the politics and conditions of emergence.

I have been deliberate in my effort to move eclectically between and among scholars based in multiple locations as I have been in my attempt to use different modes of disciplinary analyses, drawing on literary figures who at best stand on the periphery of traditional feminist narratives. I have maneuvered in this way to point toward the choppiness and unpredictability suggested by the parameters of the politics and conditions of emergence versus a neatly packaged wave critique. At the beginning of this piece, I voiced a sense of anxiety at the prospect of encouraging my students to take an oppositional stance to many of the narratives that shape their women's studies education. Encouraging such an oppositional location as instructors is often a taken for granted, in fact, necessary aspect of graduate education. Such an oppositional stance seems more complicated at the undergraduate level where the student's desire for a stable narrative may possibly be stronger. However, as a way of encouraging such intellectual dissent within the field but particularly at the undergraduate level, it be time for us to re-visit what we see to be integral to women's studies education (May, 2002, 137). For many reasons, some institutional, others intellectual, this is no easy task. Robyn Wiegman reminds us that the investment that we have in telling stories about our feminist past is very much implicated in the desire for a feminist future (in Braithwaite, 101). However, if women's studies is to have a future that is diverse, multiple, and shifting in its possibilities, then it needs to envision a past that has similar characteristics attached to it. It is my hope that by being guided by the politics and conditions of emergence we free ourselves to inhabit an adventure that takes us to our disciplinary whereabouts unknown.

Notes

1. This piece expands on ideas first articulated in my piece "Feminist Visions for Women in a New Era: An Interview with Peggy Antrobus," *Feminist Studies* 33, no. 1 (Spring 2007): 64–87.
2. See, for example, Rawwida Baksh-Soodeen's "Issues of Difference in Contemporary Caribbean Feminism," *Feminist Review* 59 (1998): 78. Patricia Mohammed, "Like Sugar in Coffee: Third Wave Feminism and the Caribbean" *Social and Economic Studies* 52, no. 3 (2003): 5–30; and "The Future of Feminism in the Caribbean" in the *Feminist Review*, no. 64 (Spring 2000): 116–19.
3. The Caribbean's ethnic and racial diversity is such that to give pre-eminence to any Afro-based group, which holds regional numerical majority, *may* signal the marginalization of individuals of Indo-, indigenous, Chinese, or Syrian descent.
4. I emphasize "descriptive" knowledge because often when we are led by a watershed period rather than by an investigative question, we tend to describe what has occurred in this period rather than to pursue a critical engagement with the issue or question at hand; these, however, are not mutually exclusive approaches and work best when they inform each other.

LOCAL IDENTITIES AND POLITICS

8.
THE POEM AS MASK
Muriel Rukeyser
(1968)

Orpheus
When I wrote of the women in their dances and wildness,
    it was a mask,
on their mountain, god-hunting, singing, in orgy,
it was a mask; when I wrote of the god,
fragmented, exiled from himself, his life, the love gone
    down with song,
it was myself, split open, unable to speak, in exile from
    myself.

There is no mountain, there is no god, there is memory
of my torn life, myself split open in sleep, the rescued child
beside me among the doctors, and a word
of rescue from the great eyes.

No more masks! No more mythologies!

Now, for the first time, the god lifts his hand,
the fragments join in me with their own music.

9.
THE POETICAL IS THE POLITICAL: FEMINIST POETRY AND THE POETICS OF WOMEN'S RIGHTS
T. V. Reed
(2005)

> For women, poetry is not a luxury. It is a vital necessity of our existence. It forms the quality of the light within which we predicate our hopes and dreams toward survival and change, first made into language then into idea, and then into more tangible action. Poetry is the way we give name to the nameless so it can be thought.
>
> > – Audre Lorde, "Poetry Is Not a Luxury," *Sister Outsider*

No social movement in the past fifty years has had a greater cultural impact than the women's movement, which reemerged in the 1960s and has grown in multifaceted ways into the present. The tremendous impact of feminism in everyday life includes, but extends far beyond, changes in laws legislation, and political institutions. The texture of the life of every single person living in the United States was changed by the new feminism. …

As with most social movements, however, the people who came to support these views often distance themselves from the means by which the ideas came into being—feminist activism—as something too radical to identify with.

In this chapter I will trace the social movement process by which the once radical idea that women were entitled to equality with men moved from the margins to the center, from the unimaginable to common sense. … I'll use feminist poetry as a case study for how feminist ideas were formed in women's movement cultures and subsequently projected out into the wider culture. One key aspect of this process was something called "consciousness-raising." Feminist consciousness-raising in the late 1960s involved women meeting in small discussion/action groups to share their personal experiences in order to turn them into analyses of common political and structural sources of inequality for women. Consciousness-raising, while certainly not the only women's movement method, touched all realms of feminist action.

Compared to the drama of civil disobedience of sit-ins, or the shock of tragic shootouts with the police, the poetic "dramas of consciousness-raising" described in this chapter may at first sound quite tame. But part of my point is to suggest that they are anything but tame in their effects. Feminists did and do engage in many large, dynamic public demonstrations, and "zap actions" (small group acts of civil disobedience) were a key part of the movement, especially in the early years. These included the infamous attack on the Miss America pageant in 1968 that earned feminists the misnomer "bra burners" (no bras were burned, but many were thrown in a freedom trash can to symbolize the throwing off of the constraints of male-dominated notions of femininity and women's body image). But to argue that poems are every bit as dramatic as these demonstrations, or as confrontations with police, is to make a feminist point: what counts as dramatic has often been defined in limiting ways based on male-centered views of heroic performance. If the goal is to change the world, there is reason to believe that publicly performed or privately read poems have been a force as powerful as any other. Before the 1960s poetry was still mainly a genteel, feminized but male-dominated form, and that aura still lingers around it. But there was nothing genteel about the raucous, often sexually frank, and always politically charged poetry that came out of the women's movement. Moving poetry from polite lecture halls and quiet living rooms out into the streets was part of many 1960s movements, but no one did it more intensely or effectively than the poets of the women's movement, and in doing so they reclaimed public space as women's space. …

"Poetry Is Not a Luxury": Poems and/as Consciousness-Raising

Consciousness-raising was crucial in forming feminist thought on a whole range of issues, from economics to government to education, but it was particularly useful in giving a name to the "nameless" forms of oppression felt in realms previously relegated to the nonpolitical arena of "personal" relations. The premise of this chapter comes primarily from an essay by feminist poet/activist/theorist Audre Lorde, quoted in the chapter epigraph. As a child of Jamaican immigrants, a working-class black woman, a mother, a lesbian, and a socialist, Lorde richly embodied the complex multiplicities within and around feminism. In her landmark essay "Poetry Is Not a Luxury," Lorde provides one of the strongest and clearest cases for the value of consciousness-raising without ever using the word. What she describes instead is the process of writing a poem. This is no coincidence, I will argue, but rather a convergence. For both consciousness-raising and poetry writing make the subjective objective, make the inner world of "personal" experience available for public "political" discussion. While poetry is often thought of as pure expression of personal feelings, only very bad poetry does that. Good poetry makes personal experience available to others by giving it an outward form.

As I look at poetry in this chapter as *one* key place where women's movement ideas, attitudes, positions, and actions were formed, expressed, and circulated to wider communities, I will also be using poetry as a metaphor for the larger process of inventing feminist analysis and diffusing feminist ideas and actions throughout the culture. …

… As African American feminist Cellestine Ware characterized it in her brilliant book, *Woman Power* (1970), the role of CR groups was to express, compare, analyze, theorize, and then organize against all the ways in which women were oppressed. This meant thinking about and challenging the specific sexist structures in every "public" and "private" social space: the factory, sweatshop, kitchen, bedroom, classroom, board-room, playing field, courtroom, or the halls of Congress. From the beginning, the new feminists realized that this largely unexplored set of analyses needed to be made from the ground up, through a process of comparing individual women's stories and turning them into a set of structural analyses. The point was to move from collected personal experiences to theorized general conditions, and then to further actions flowing from the analyses.[1]

A new language had to be invented to characterize the experiences of oppression and liberation that had no name. Sometimes this meant literally inventing new words; for instance, the newly minted concept "sexism" was used to examine the ways in which discrimination against women was built into the very structure of the language. Women challenged every generic use of *man* or *he* claiming to speak for all "human-ity," and they invented or adopted words to displace the presumptive "man" at the center of all public activity: *firefighter* for *fireman, worker* for *workman,* business execu-tive for *businessman, chair* for chairman, police officer for *policeman, representative* or *senator* for *congressman,* and so on across all the various social spaces and places where women were absent or underrepresented. This task also moved in the opposite direc-tion, replacing feminized and invariably lesser female versions of terms. Thus, *flight attendant* replaced *stewardess,* or more to the point of this chapter, *poet* came to be used in place of the condescending *poetess.* But beyond neologisms, the deeper task was to find language to express oppressions and liberations that had no name.

Whether from formal CR groups, informal discussions, or shared writings there emerged from consciousness-raising a host of new issues for the agenda of women's liberation. Shared stories moved women from the isolation of battering to a collective analysis of domestic violence, from a personal sense of sexual inadequacy to calls for equal sexual pleasure for women, from a sense of the social "double jeopardy" of being a woman and of color to women-of-color feminisms, from personal fears about preg-nancy or forced sterilization to calls for reproductive rights, from poverty viewed as personal failure to analyses of welfare rights and the feminization of poverty, from per-sonal experiences of intimidation by the boss to the concept of sexual harassment, and so on for dozens of issues that were moved from the personal to the political through collective dialogue, discussion, and debate.

The formal CR group, according to the early women's movement activist Pam Allen, proceeded through four stages: opening up (revealing personal feelings); sharing (through dialogue with other group members); analyzing (seeking general patterns by comparing to other experiences); and abstracting (creating a theory). Sometimes mis-understood as therapy, which it no doubt became on some occasions in some groups, CR was intended to strengthen the theoretical basis for revolutionary action. As femi-nist theorist and women's movement historian Katie King notes, the aim of "CR is not to exchange or relive experience, nor is it cathartic. Rather, its purpose is to teach women to think abstractly, and the purpose of thinking abstractly is to create theory in order to clarify and clear the ground for action."[2] Much important feminist thought and action emerged from this process, and was presented in written form in such early feminist anthologies as *Sisterhood Is Powerful* (1970), *The Black Woman* (1970),

Radical Feminism (1973) (which collects material from three earlier collections, *Notes from the First Year, Second Year* and *Third Year*), and, in poetic form, *No More Masks! An Anthology of Poems by Women* (1973).

As several feminist critics have argued, some kind of positing of group commonality plays a necessary heuristic role in all feminist organizing (or any other movement that includes an element of collective identity).[3] The problem arises with the rush to give that heuristic concept a specific content. Some feminists can be justly accused of this kind of "essentialism," arguments that homogenize all women as essentially alike (in oppression or in resistance).[4] But there has always been a way of drawing on experiences, a way of doing consciousness-raising, that suggests a path through this dilemma. Rather than simply being replaced, consciousness-raising can be and often has been, *re*-placed into a more varied public space where conflicting and complementary "experiences" have provided the bases for painful but productive arguments within feminism that have broadened and deepened the movement(s). This is precisely what happened in many parts of the early feminist movement, and has continued to happen ever since. As I suggested, formal consciousness-raising groups in the women's movement of the late 1960s and early 1970s were just the particular form of a larger, more general process of raising consciousness that goes on in many movements and many forms. In women's movements, one of the key forms, though hardly the only one, has been the writing, reading, and performing of poetry.

Women's Movement Poetry and the Range of Feminist Issues

Poems about women in economic poverty and spiritual poverty; poems about battering and resistance to battering; poems about sisterly solidarity and unsisterly betrayal; poems about factory work and maid work; poems about men as oppressors or men as lovers or men as loving oppressors; poems about women loving women; poems about the power in menstruation and the beauty of vaginas; poems about bad sex and good sex; poems in Spanglish and Niuyorican, black English and white Wellesley diction; poems about the pain of abortion and the pain of childbirth; poems about sterilization of poor women and the sterile lives of upper-class women; poems about women's history and women's future; poems about reform and revolution; poems about women in barrios and Chinatowns, Indian reservations and ghettos; poems revaluing traditional women's work and celebrating women breaking barriers into male-dominated jobs; poems about women lumberjacks and women quilters; poems about witches and bitches, *brujas* and voodoo queens; poems about women athletes and bookish women; poems about breast-feeding and breast cancer; poems about laundry and feminist theology; poems about war and peace; poems about women in Vietnam and Spanish Harlem; poems about Harriet Tubman and Marilyn Monroe; poems about Wall Street and Main Street; poems about changing diapers and changing lives; even poems about writing poems. Poems poured forth by the hundreds from the new wave of feminist activity crystallizing in the late 1960s.

Andrea Chessman and Polly Joan assert in their *Guide to Women's Publishing* that "poetry was the medium of the movement," and that while "every revolutionary movement has had its poets and its poetry, no other movement has been so grounded in poetry as Feminism."[5] I do not think it is necessary to call poetry "the" medium of the movement, but it has certainly played a very important role for many feminists. One reason for this is that no movement has had a more sweeping need for epistemological transformation, for transformation in the nature and scope of knowledge. In effect, the feminist movement claims that half of the world's population has largely been excluded from production of what counts as knowledge about that world. As noted above, the women's movement has transformed every field of human knowledge, from business to science to politics to art and literature to "home economics."

Feminist poetry is certainly not alone in bringing about this profound transformation, but it touches all these social and cultural realms, among others. But feminism also has brought about a more general transformation of consciousness above and beyond these particular realms. To get at these two different dimensions, I will look first at "women's movement poetry" as a general tool of social change, and then at a more narrowly defined "feminist poetry movement" as an example of a formation aimed at one particular cultural sphere, the profession of poem-making.

The movement understood that knowledge was power, and that knowledge/power was vested in language. At the center of this was the notion that dimensions of women's voices had been silenced, distorted, or trivialized for centuries. Thus poetry, as one of the richest tools for exploring the dynamic meaning-making processes of language, was bound to become an important movement resource. Poetry is particularly well equipped to challenge two crucial dichotomies: the separation of private and public spheres, and the split between "emotion" and "intellect." Poems had practical advantages as well. They could be produced in the interstices of the busy multitasking lives most women lead. They took far less time to write than books, and they were far easier to reproduce and circulate. They could be nailed to trees and telephone poles, taped to windows, and slid under doors. They lent themselves to performance in public during a highly dramatic, performative era. They could also be set to music, turned into song.

The whole panoply of feminist issues that emerged from format CR groups and from dozens of other sites of consciousness-raising activity can be found in poetry produced in and around the movement. In addition to anthologies of feminist poetry, most of the general anthologies of feminist thought from the new movement included poetry. The widely circulated collection, *Sisterhood Is Powerful: An Anthology of Writings from the Women's Liberation Movement* (1970), for example, was edited by a poet, Robin Morgan, and included a section entitled "The Hand That Cradles the Rock: Poetry as Protest?' And one of the first major collections of feminist writings to center on women of color, *The Black Woman*, was edited by fiction writer/poet Toni Cade [Bambara], and privileged poems as the first set of readings. This is not because poetry "reflected" feminist issues, but because poetry was one of the main tools used to identify, name, formulate, and disseminate those issues. Poetry was consciousness-raising. Poetry was theory. Poetry was feminist practice.

When the radical women's liberation phase, with its emphasis on interconnections between race, class, and gender, was being displaced in the mid-1970s by a more mainstream brand of feminism, poetry became a key site for the articulation and contestation of feminisms. Poets like Adrienne Rich, Audre Lorde, Janice Mirikitani, Sonia Sanchez, Susan Griffin, Nikki Giovanni, Mice Walker, Wendy Rose, Judy Grahn, Pat Parker, Irena Klepfitz, Robin Morgan, Nellie Wong, Chrystos, June Jordan, Marge Piercy, Lorna Dee Cervantes, Joy Harjo, and Cherrie Moraga used poetry as part of an ongoing dialogue about the nature(s) and purpose(s) of feminism(s). In this context poems become mediators between a collective "woman" and particular communities of "women." Poetry plays an important role in diffusing these subject positions out into the wider culture where their impact is often independent of knowledge of their movement origins.

For some people who might be recruited to a movement and for some people already in it, poems (and other forms of art) are more effective in conveying movement ideology than are manifestos and other directly political forms. Katie King has argued that what she calls "art theoretical" discourses, including poetry, were central to the production of feminist cultures that were in turn "the primary location of feminist identity politics in the 70s and 80s."[6] These "art theoretical" "writing technologies" (King includes "song" and "story" alongside "poetry") were especially important in the struggles of various women-of-color feminists to dislodge white, middle-class women from the center of feminist thought. In this sense, poetry as theory and consciousness-raising did much to challenge the limits of theory emerging from the often fairly segregated movement groups.

Two poets edited one of the most influential books in the history of feminist thought, *This Bridge Called My Back: Radical Writing by Women of Color*, and much of its content takes the form of poetry. *This Bridge* not only featured poetry alongside more conventional forms of analysis, but also insisted that poetry was a form of feminist theory. Poems in that anthology (and others like it) drew upon personal experience mediated through race and ethnicity as well as gender, to show up the limiting "whiteness" of the identity proffered as normative in much women's movement culture. While poetry was by no means the only medium through which this critique was offered, it was a particularly powerful one.

Many other forms and forums of writing—manifestos, academic books and articles, novels and short stories, speeches, debates, and that close cousin to poetry, the song lyric—also contributed greatly to this process. King notes that mixed genres were particularly effective as their challenging of generic boundaries embodied their efforts to challenge the borders of what counted as feminism and feminist theory. This category would include, for example, Audre Lorde's mixing of autobiography, poetry, fiction, legend, and essay in her "biomythography" *Zami* (1982), or the mixing of *poemas*, *cuentos*, and *essais* in Gloria Anzaldúa's *Borderlands/La Frontera* (1987) and Cherrie Moraga's *Loving in the War Years* (1983).[7] The writing of poems, however, preceded even these longer works. Lorde suggests why this might be so: she notes that poetry is economical not only in terms of expression but also in terms of the material support needed to produce it: "poetry can be done between shifts, in the hospital pantry, on the subway, on scraps of surplus paper. Over the last few years writing a novel on tight finances, I came to appreciate the enormous differences in the material demands between poetry and prose. As we reclaim our literature, poetry has been the major voice of poor, working class [women], and [women of color]."[8]

This Bridge uses poetry to articulate both a collective "women-of-color position" and various ethnic-specific positionings. Other collections of writings, again invariably mixing poetry with prose fiction and nonfiction, focused on specific ethno-racialized communities of women. These texts identify points of solidarity and difference within such groups as Chicanas/Latinas (*Making Face, Making Soul: Hacienda Caras*), African American women (*The Black Woman, and Home Girls: A Black Feminist Anthology*), native women (*Reinventing the Enemy's Language: Contemporary Native American Women's Writings of North America*), and Asian/Pacific American women (*Making Waves: An Anthology of Writings by and about Asian American Women*). Lesbians of color played significant roles in all of these volumes, and each deals seriously with issues of sexuality as interwoven with class and other differences within communities of color. Similar volumes like *Nice Jewish Girls: A Lesbian Anthology* did much the same for a variety of self-defined feminist movement subcultures.[9] In these volumes poetry does much of the work of "auto-ethnography," of showing the experience of the self to be part of and in tension with the experience of the collective, the social group. The poems also become what Young calls "auto-theoretical" works in which self-exploration, as in all good consciousness-raising, is the beginning, not the end, of a process leading to theory and action. Again, the point is that poetry does not simply "reflect" ideas already in the air, but rather in giving "form" brings the ideas into public existence, and helps to invent identities, not merely to express them. Movements in general are highly productive places, sites of a great deal of "cultural poetics"—the bringing into visibility and audibility of new thoughts and feelings. In this case, the cultural poetics occurs through actual poetry. But the lines across genres in this respect are constantly transgressed; Rich, Lorde, and Anzaldúa are as well known for their essays as for their poems, and each reinforces and adds nuance to the other.

The process of feminist consciousness-raising continues. As it does so, poetry plays a role in each new site or phase of activity, helping to form new issues and new feminist identities. The rise of antimilitarist, environmentalist feminisms in the 1980s and early 1990s, for example, was inspired in part by poet Susan Griffin's lyrical study *Women and Nature* (1978), and various "ecofeminist" anthologies used poetry to present new ways of thinking about relations between the devaluing of women and the denigration of nature.[10] And the critically important challenges to the ethnocentric dimension of U.S. feminisms, emerging under the impact of feminist movements in the Southern Hemisphere and of postcolonial theory in the universities, have also used poetry as one key mode of contestation. Figures like Chandra Mohanty, Gayatri Spivak, Trinh T. Minh-ha, Lata Mani, Caren Kaplan, Inderpal Grewal, and Rey Chow gained prominence in the early 1990s by analyzing and countering homogenizing, racist conceptions of "women in the Third World" found in much U.S. feminism. This process gained support from poets whose defamiliarizing verses challenged dominant Anglo-American feminist paradigms. Trinh's poetic, auto-ethnographic *Woman/Native/Other* offers one example, while Spivak's literary critical essays on Bengali women poets and storytellers present another.[11] Over time, virtually every constituency or position within the wide terrain of feminisms has been constructed in part through poetry, from the most essentialist statements of universal womanhood to the most deconstructive celebrations of postmodern fragmented subjectivities.

The Feminist Poetry Movement as a Cultural Formation

Let us turn now from "women's movement poetry" to the "feminist poetry movement." The distinction is partly artificial, since the two forms of activity overlap and intertwine, but it is useful to separate them in order to understand the full cultural impact of feminism(s). The distinction can be put this way: in "women's movement poetry" the movement comes first and is the central focus, with poetry as one of many means of serving the movement, while in the "feminist poetry movement" poetry comes first and the central concern is to establish a new kind of poetry.[12] The feminist poetry movement is a cultural formation by and aimed at professional poets and the cultural institutions (publishing houses, literature departments, bookstores) surrounding them. The feminist poetry movement is both inside and beyond the women's movement It is what British cultural theorist Raymond Williams calls a "formation," an intellectual or cultural school of thought, like impressionism in painting or naturalism in fiction waiting, that can have "significant and sometimes decisive influence on the active development of a culture, and which [has] a variable and often oblique relation to formal institutions."[13]

As historian of the feminist poetry movement Kim Whitehead puts it, "feminist poetry began in a hundred places at once, in writing workshops and at open readings, on the kitchen tables of self-publishing poet/activists, and in the work of already established poets who began slowly to transform their ideas about formal strategies and thematic possibilities."[14] The grassroots troops of the new feminist poetry movement grew out of the hundreds of consciousness-raising groups and collectives. As these radical new feminist poets began to emerge, they caught the attention of some powerful, already-established women poets whose own poetry began to change under the influence of the movement. Poets like Adrienne Rich, June Jordan, and Gwendolyn Brooks were in varying degrees part of the poetry establishment when the women's movement emerged. The movement helped them understand ways in which they felt marginalized, stifled, or distorted by the male-dominated institutions and formations of the poetry world. At the same time, some of these poets had anticipated feminist themes in their work and with increasing self-consciousness brought that work to bear in the context of creating the women's movement This led not only to a reworking by these poets of their own work, but also to a rethinking and researching of the role of women in the history of poetry.

Among living links to a longer legacy, no poet was more important to the movement than Muriel Rukeyser. A winner of the prestigious Yale Younger Poets prize in 1935, Rukeyser had given up a career of safe verse-making to immerse herself in the social and political struggles of the Depression years, a commitment she brought with her into the movements she associated with in the 1960s. Rukeyser, along with younger but established poets like Rich (who also had won the Yale prize for her first, premovement volume) became indefatigable teachers of poetry and poetics to the emerging generation of women's movement poets. Over time this process moved the category "woman poet" from a dismissive term to one charged with possibility.

As it emerged, the feminist poetry movement drew upon several other compatible developments in the field of poetry. Three strands from existing schools of poetry were particularly influential as rewritten into the terms of an emerging feminist poetic consciousness. First, the beat poets had begun in the 1950s a return of poetry to public performance. Poetry had become a rather genteel affair, more often read in libraries or living rooms. Beat poets like Allen Ginsburg were infamous for their raucous public poetry rituals. This process was then taken up by many protest poets in the 1960s, particularly antiwar poets (including Ginsburg himself) and poets in the black arts and other cultural nationalist movements. No group developed this return to poetry as performance, rather than silent reading, more powerfully than feminist poets who fostered hundreds of public readings in feminist bookstores, music festivals, and demonstrations. Second, the confessional school of poets, founded by figures like Robert Lowell in the 1950s and including some proto-feminist poets like Sylvia Plath and Anne Sexton, had opened up possibilities for personal psychological exploration that played well into the intimate psychological dynamics of emerging feminist experience. And third, the Black Mountain poets, among others, had begun moving poetry away from rigid formal lines to more open, free-verse forms. These forms were both better suited to the open explorations of self-in-society of feminist poets, and less daunting than rigid metrical poetry for women excluded from formal literary training.

Just as the early feminist movement scoured all history for examples of women struggling to liberate themselves from male-defined institutions and social roles, when the feminist poetry movement emerged, it naturally set out to find its poetic precursors. This task entailed both uncovering women poets buried under male-centered poetic histories, and rereading and reinterpreting female poets who had managed to find some hold in the mostly male-defined pantheon of important poets. In the United States it was nineteenth-century poet Emily Dickinson who served most often as a distant American foremother to the feminist poetry formation. The full range of Dickinson's poetry had only recently become available in the 1950s, and as her reputation grew as one of the two great poets of the latter half of the nineteenth century (alongside Walt Whitman), feminists struggled to rescue her from those who would ignore the powerful things she had to say about the minds and spirits of women.

Several poetry anthologies appearing in the early years of the new women's movement played a key role in solidifying the formation. The most successful of these was *No More Masks! An Anthology of poems by Women* (1973), edited by Florence Howe (co-founder of Feminist Press) and Ellen Bass.[15] The collection starts with poems by Amy Lowell, Gertrude Stein, and other members of the modernist poetry movement of the early twentieth century, then presents an array of contemporary poets shaped in the women's liberation movement." The collection includes 220 pieces from 86 poets, about 20 of them women of color. The title comes, not surprisingly, from a feminist poem by Rukeyser telling women to take off the false faces put upon them by patriarchy, and the subtitle indicates that the search for "poems by women" did not necessarily restrict the collection to a political definition of "feminist poet."

Howe reports in the preface to a later edition of the anthology that the book began as something of a "lark, a game" of collecting women poets that she engaged in with her then student Bass. As she puts it, "in the early seventies it was still possible to use a card catalog under the word 'women' and find 'poets,' though we could not have known then that many poets had slipped away, out of that net into invisibility." This process of scouring library card catalogs netted about fifty established women poets for the collection, and then, Howe notes, the "younger poets found us: Word spread quickly in the early seventies through women's liberation newspapers and newsletters. We received three hundred submissions through the mail?"[16] From this Howe and Bass culled the collection, with only their "inchoate" feminism and an insistence that the "poem please us aesthetically" to guide them. This second criterion, the aesthetic one, is the mark of the formation on their efforts. The larger task, which might define the formation, is expressed by Howe as a set of questions in the preface to the original edition: "A nagging doubt: are women victims of prejudiced editors or are women poets out of the mainstream of modern poetry? What is the mainstream? And what do women write about?"[17]

No More Masks! was one of several anthologies that took on the task of answering these questions by making available for the first time a wide range of historical and contemporary poems by women, Other, similar volumes emerged in this same time period. It was clearly the moment when the formation was strong enough to begin shaping its own tradition. One such work was *Rising Tides: Twentieth-Century American Women Poets* (1973), whose goals were stated baldly in a prefatory paragraph: "Because representation in most poetry anthologies of the past has not gone beyond tokenism, most women writers have remained minor figures in the male-dominated literary world. This book is an attempt to make both men and women aware of the vital force women poets today represent." As the back cover put it, "Rising out of the same growing consciousness that spawned the women's liberation movement, this book is a feminist statement in the largest sense."[18] A year later came *The World Split Open: Four Centuries of Women Poets in England and America, 1552–1950* (1974), a collection whose title, again from a Rukeyser poem (What would happen if one woman told the truth about her life? / The world would split open"), shows its connection to the movement and whose subtitle indicates that it is aimed at helping to establish a still longer tradition.

By the end of the twentieth century, this literary formation had contributed mightily to a rewriting of the entire history of poetry. It is now possible to go to any literary bookstore in America and find dozens of anthologies dedicated to one or another of numerous strands and schools of feminist and/or women's poetry. Under the onslaught of this formation, and interrelated formations in ethnic and gay writing, literary history has been rewritten. It now not only includes but has been radically changed by the presence of a panoply of female (and often feminist) poets. And the future of poetry by women has been forever shaped by this remaking of the universe of poetry into an available *tradition* for women to build upon, just as surely as the wider culture was radically rewritten from top to bottom by feminist challenges to dominant paradigms of thought and action. ...

Building Feminist Cultural Institutions

Both women's movement poetry and the feminist poetry movement depended upon the creation and development of parallel, feminist institutions. I have argued that, given the centrality of experience, emotion, language reformation, and intimate spheres of action to the feminist process of consciousness-raising, poetry with its linguistic and affective precision was well suited to play a major role in diffusing feminist ideas out into the world. But a very concrete process of institution building underwrote this predisposition. Drawing on the tradition found in the civil rights, new left, and ethnic nationalist movements of creating "parallel institutions" to challenge inadequate or corrupt ones in the dominant society, all strands of women's movements built formal alternative cultural structures. Many CR groups, the first level of institutionalization, for example, became writing groups. Feminist CR/writing groups in turn produced at first feminist broadsides, and then underground journals run by feminist publishing collectives. Feminist publishing collectives sponsored poetry readings and poetry festivals that widened the audience, encouraging small feminist presses to move into bigger projects. These processes produced and rediscovered enough writing to justify the creation of small feminist bookstores, and small feminist bookstores encouraged the creation of larger feminist presses. Larger feminist presses proved the existence of a market for women's writing that mainstream publishing houses could not ignore. They began then to broker deals with mainstream publishing houses that guaranteed a wider audience for feminist writers, and netted the feminist presses profits that allowed them to bring more radical writers into print.[19] By 1978 a phenomenal seventy-three feminist periodicals and sixty-six feminist presses had sprung up, along with dozens of women's bookstores.[20]

While institutionalization certainly involved some watering down upon entry into the "mainstream" many feminist writers resisted and continue to resist that process and the individualizing, divide-and-conquer strategy it often entails. When, for example, white feminist poet Adrienne Rich won the National Book Award in 1974, she indicated, as part of a joint statement written with two African American feminist poets, fellow nominees Alice Walker and Audre Lorde, that she accepted the award "not as an individual but in the name of all women whose voices have gone and still go unheard in a patriarchal world." More generally, poets and editors negotiate between movement and nonmovement sites, making individual and collective decisions about when to support feminist presses and when to send their work out as incursions into the wider world.

The process of feminist institution building also includes an academic institution, women's studies departments, with a strong literary component that assisted the feminist poetry movement and used literature as one means of classroom consciousness-raising. This led to efforts to rewrite the canon of literature to include far more women's literature and a significant amount of feminist literature. This process moved from movement anthologies to women's studies textbooks to such major revisionist works as the *Heath Anthology of American Literature*, which in turn forced a reworking of such mainstream collections as the *Norton Anthology of American Literature*. This process has taken several decades, but from these small group beginnings there has emerged a vast body of feminist writing that has touched every level, layer, and corner of American society. There is now a great body of feminist thought enmeshed in virtually every literary anthology available for use in the classroom or by the casual reader.

Ultimately, Toni Morrison's Nobel Prize for literature, and the vast women-of-color literary movement she embodies, grows out of movement contexts through these layers of mediation. As usual, by the time that point is reached, the originating movement contexts have been lost in the mists of time (and hegemony), but their diffusion is nevertheless movement work. One might note by way of materially tracing this process that Morrison edited and wrote introductions for both the first collection of Huey Newton's Black Panther writings, *To Die for the People*, and one of the most important early collections of black feminist thought, *The Black Woman*, compiled by Toni Cade [Bambara]. Again, this can stand as but one example of a massive *diffusing* of feminist and other radical movement ideas into the mainstream. That this process also involves some *defusing*, some lessoning of the explosive impact found when texts are produced and received within a movement culture, is no doubt true. But that just suggests the need for ongoing movement struggle, struggle that should include taking far more credit for the powerful impact already achieved by the incorporation of feminist ideas into common-sense, mainstream thought and action.

Third Wave Poetics?

The debates within feminism in the 1980s and 1990s are interpreted differently. To some liberal white women committed to maintaining a status quo, the debates were seen as divisive, particularly in the context of a "backlash" against feminism in the years of Reaganism and Christian conservatism.[21] To women in the Third World, U.S. women of color, and their white allies who believe feminism should not be dominated by one set of privileged voices, the turmoil, however painful, has been healthy and transformative. Similar ferment surrounds the language and concept of a "third wave" of feminism. Some suggest that the critique of "hegemonic feminism" by lesbians and women of color in the United States and the Third World itself constituted a third-wave movement. Others see this as a process that has cleared the way, making it possible for a younger generation to take the movement in new directions. For others still, the wave metaphor is always falsely homogenizing, untrue to the variety of sites of feminist movement activity. But however one characterizes it, feminist activity is alive and well in the twenty-first century, both in the form of ongoing women's movements and in the impact of feminism within other progressive movements.

It is also clear that as these movements continue, poetry will continue to be a powerful feminist tool. The feminist music movement, which has always been closely linked to feminist poetry, was given renewed energy in the 1990s by new feminist music, most notably the independent folk/rock of Ani DiFranco, the post-punk energy of Riot Grrrls, and feminist rap by performers like Queen Latifah. The feminist poetry movement is also one of the forces behind the renewed energy in performed or "spoken word," poetry. Growing as well out of the powerful hip-hop culture pioneered by black and Latino/a youth (which in turn owes much to black power and Latino/a nationalist poetics), spoken word performance is an important site of feminist consciousness-raising for younger women (and men) and a sign that poetry will continue to be one key site of feminist action for years to come.

Notes

1. Cellestine Ware, *Woman Power* (New York: Tower, 1970). King analyzes this text astutely in *Theory in Its Feminist Travels*, 126–30.

2. King, *Theory in Its Feminist Travels*, 127.

3. As important as these feminist groups were, they were only as strong ultimately as the diversity within them. And many were not very diverse racially. The preference of women of color for struggling within ethnic nationalist movements during the early years left many early feminist groups all white in composition. …

4. … Two books that are particularly useful in examining the question of essentialism in feminism are Diana Fuss, *Essentially Speaking* (New York: Routledge, 1989); and Elizabeth Spelman, *Inessential Woman* (Boston: Beacon Press, 1988). Among other interesting attempts to mediate the essentialist/constructionist debate, see Linda Alcoff, "Cultural Feminism versus Post-structuralism," *Signs* 13 (Spring 1988): 405–36; and several of the articles in the special issue "The Essential Difference," *Differences* 1, no. 2 (Summer 1989). Alice Echols in *Daring to Be Bad* implicates CR groups and "cultural feminism" in the rise of essentialism. For a rethinking of this claim, see King, *Theory in Its Feminist Travels.*

5. I am indebted throughout this section to Kim Whitehead, *The Feminist Poetry Movement* (Jackson: University Press of Mississippi, 1996). See also Jan Montefiore, *Feminism and Poetry* (London: Pandora, 1995).

6. King, *Theory in Its Feminist Travels*, 122.

7. Audre Lorde, *Zami* (Watertown, MA: Persephone, 1982); Gloria Anzaldúa, *Borderlands/La Frontera* (San Francisco: Aunt Lute, 1987); Cherríe Moraga, *Loving in the War Years* (Boston: South End, 1983).

8. Lorde, *Sister Outsider* (Freedom, CA: Crossing Press, 1984), 116.

9. Gloria Anzaldúa, ed., *Making Face, Making Soul* (San Francisco: Aunt Lute, 1990); Cade, ed., *Black Woman*; Smith, ed. Home Girls; Joy Harjo and Gloria Bird, eds., *Reinventing the Enemy's Language* (New York: W. W. Norton, 1998); Diane Yen-Mei Wong and Emilya Cachapero, eds., *Making Waves* (Boston: Beacon Press, 1989); and Evelyn Tortow Beck, ed., *Nice Jewish Girls* (New York: Crossing Press, 1984).

10. See Susan Griffin, *Women and Nature* (San Francisco: Harper and Row, 1978); and Irene Diamond and Gloria Orenstein, eds., *Reweaving the World* (San Francisco: Sierra Club Books, 1990). The best treatment of the strengths and weaknesses of this school of feminism is Noël Sturgeon, *Ecofeminist Natures* (New York: Routledge, 1997).

11. See Trinh T. Minh-ha, *Woman/Native/Other* (Bloomington: Indiana University Press, 1989); and Gayatri Chakravarty Spivak, *In Other Wor(l)ds* (New York: Routledge, 1988). Many of the founding essays in this line of critique are gathered in Chandra Mohanty, Ann Russo, and Lourdes Torres, eds., *Third World Women and the Politics of Feminism* (Bloomington: Indiana University Press, 1991).

12. See Kim Whitehead, *The Feminist Poetry Movement* (Jackson: University Press of Mississippi, 1996).

13. Raymond Williams, *Marxism and Literature* (Oxford: Oxford University Press, 1977), 117.

14. Whitehead, *Feminist Poetry Movement*, 3.

15. Florence Howe and Ellen Bass, eds., *No More Masks!* (New York Anchor/Doubleday, 1973).

16. Howe, in the preface to the revised and expanded edition of *No More Masks!* (New York: Harper Collins, 1993). The subtitle of this revised edition, "An Anthology of *Twentieth Century American* Women Poets," acknowledges the historical and national boundaries of the collection not noted by the earlier subtitle "Poems by Women."

17. Howe and Bass, *No More Masks!* (1973), xxviii.

18. Laura Chester and Sharon Barba, eds., *Rising Tides* (New York: Pocket Books, 1973), i.

19. Stacey Young in *Changing the Wor(l)d* details how feminist editors and publishers, by carefully brokering this process, continue to move work originally associated with movement contexts out into wider public spaces and then into more mainstream locations.

20. Statistics from Chesman and Joan's *Guide to Women's Publishing*, cited in Whitehead, *Feminist Poetry Movement*, 19.

21. The reaction against feminism in the 1980s is accessibly chronicled in journalist Susan Faludi's *Backlash* (New York: Anchor, 1992).

10.
BARGAINING WITH PATRIARCHY
Deniz Kandiyoti
(1988)

Of all the concepts generated by contemporary feminist theory, patriarchy is probably the most overused and, in some respects, the most undertheorized. This state of affairs is not due to neglect, since there is a substantial volume of writing on the question, but rather to the specific conditions of development of contemporary feminist usages of the term. While radical feminists encouraged a very liberal usage, to apply to virtually any form or instance of male domination, socialist feminists have mainly restricted themselves to analyzing the relationships between patriarchy and class under capitalism. As a result, the term *patriarchy* often evokes an overly monolithic conception of male dominance, which is treated at a level of abstraction that obfuscates rather than reveals the intimate inner workings of culturally and historically distinct arrangements between the genders.

It is not my intention to provide a review of the theoretical debates around patriarchy (Barrett 1980; Beechey 1979; Delphy 1977; Eisenstein 1978; Hartmann 1981; McDonough and Harrison 1978; Mies 1986; Mitchell 1973; Young 1981). Instead, I would like to propose an important and relatively neglected point of entry for the identification of different forms of patriarchy through an analysis of women's strategies in dealing with them. I will argue that women strategize within a set of concrete constraints that reveal and define the blueprint of what I will term the *patriarchal bargain*[1] of any given society, which may exhibit variations according to class, caste, and ethnicity. These patriarchal bargains exert a powerful influence on the shaping of women's gendered subjectivity and determine the nature of gender ideology in different contexts. They also influence both the potential for and specific forms of women's active or passive resistance in the face of their oppression. Moreover, patriarchal bargains are not timeless or immutable entities, but are susceptible to historical transformations that open up new areas of struggle and renegotiation of the relations between genders.

By way of illustration, I will contrast two systems of male dominance, rendered ideal-typical for the purposes of discussing their implications for women. I use these ideal types as heuristic devices that have the potential of being expanded and fleshed out with systematic, comparative, empirical content, although this article makes no pretense at providing anything beyond a mere sketch of possible variations. The two types are based on examples from sub-Saharan Africa, on the one hand, and the Middle East, South Asia, and East Asia on the other. My aim is to highlight a continuum ranging from less corporate forms of householding, involving the relative autonomy of mother-child units evidenced in sub-Saharan polygyny, to the more corporate male-headed entities prevalent in the regions identified by Caldwell (1978) as the "patriarchal belt." In the final section, I analyze the breakdown and transformation of patriarchal bargains and their relationship to women's consciousness and struggles.

Autonomy and Protest: Some Examples from Sub-Saharan Africa

I had one of my purest experiences of culture shock in the process of reviewing the literature on women in agricultural development projects in sub-Saharan Africa (Kandiyoti 1985). Accustomed as I was to only one type of patriarchy (which I shall describe in some detail later, under the rubric of classic patriarchy), I was ill prepared for what I found. The literature was rife with instances of women's resistance to attempts to lower the value of their labor and, more important, women's refusal to allow the total appropriation of their production by their husbands. Let me give some examples.

Wherever new agricultural schemes provided men with inputs and credit, and the assumption was made that as heads of household they would have access to their wives' unremunerated labor, problems seemed to develop. In the Mwea irrigated rice settlement in Kenya, where women were deprived of access to their own plots, their lack of alternatives and their total lack of control over men's earnings made life so intolerable to them that wives commonly deserted their husbands (Hanger and Moris 1973). In Gambia, in yet another rice- growing scheme, the irrigated land and credit were made available to men only, even though it was the women who traditionally grew rice in tidal swamps, and there was a long-standing practice of men and women cultivating their own crops and controlling the produce. Women's customary duties with respect to labor allocation to common and individual plots protected them from demands by their husbands that they provide free labor on men's irrigated rice fields. Men had to pay their wives wages or lend them an irrigated plot to have access to their labor. In the rainy season, when women had the alternative of growing their own swamp rice, they created a labor bottleneck for the men, who simply had to wait for the days women did not go to their own fields (Dey 1981).

In Conti's (1979) account of a supervised smallholder settlement project in Upper Volta, again, the men were provided with land and credit, leaving the women no independent resource base and a very inadequate infrastructure to carry out their daily household chores. The result was vocal protest and refusal to cooperate. ...

In short, the insecurities of African polygyny for women are matched by areas of relative autonomy that they clearly strive to maximize. Men's responsibility for their wives' support, while normative in some instances, is in actual fact relatively low. Typically, it is the woman who is primarily responsible for her own and her children's upkeep, including meeting the costs of their education, with variable degrees of assistance from her husband. Women have very little to gain and a lot to lose by becoming totally dependent on husbands, and hence they quite rightly resist projects that tilt the delicate balance they strive to maintain. In their protests, wives are safeguarding already existing spheres of autonomy.

Documentation of a genuine trade-off between women's autonomy and men's responsibility for their wives can be found in some historical examples. Mann (1985) suggests that despite the wifely dependence entailed by Christian marriage, Yoruba women in Lagos accepted it with enthusiasm because of the greater protection they thought they would receive. … Commenting on Ashanti marriage, Abu (1983, p. 156) singles out as its most striking feature "the separateness of spouses' resources and activities and the overtness of the bargaining element in the relationship." Polygyny and, in this case, the continuing obligations of both men and women to their own kin do not foster a notion of The family or household as a corporate entity.

Clearly, there are important variations in African kinship systems with respect to marriage forms, residence, descent, and inheritance rules (Guyer and Peters 1987). These variations are grounded in complete cultural and historical processes, including different modes of incorporation of African societies into the world economy (Mbilinyi 1982; Murray 1987; S. Young 1977). Nonetheless, it is within a broadly defined Afro-Caribbean pattern that we find some of the clearest instances of noncorporateness of the conjugal family both in ideology and practice, a fact that informs marital and marketplace strategies for women. Works on historical transformations (for example, Etienne and Leacock 1980) suggest that colonization eroded the material basis for women's relative autonomy (such as usufructary access to communal land or traditional craft production) without offering attenuating modifications in either marketplace or marital options. The more contemporary development projects discussed above also tend to assume or impose a male-headed corporate family model, which curtails women's options without opening up other avenues to security and well-being. The women perceive these changes, especially if they occur abruptly, as infractions that constitute a breach of their existing accommodations with the male-dominated order. Consequently, they openly resist them.

Subservience and Manipulation: Women Under Classic Patriarchy

These examples of women's open resistance stand in stark contrast to women's accommodations to the system I will call *classic patriarchy*. The clearest instance of classic patriarchy may be found in a geographical area that includes North Africa, the Muslim Middle East (including Turkey, Pakistan. and Iran), and South and East Asia (specifically, India and China).[2]

The key to the reproduction of classic patriarchy lies in the operations of the patrilocally extended household, which is also commonly associated with the reproduction of the peasantry in agrarian societies (E. Wolf 1966). Even though demographic and other constraints may have curtailed the numerical predominance of three-generational patrilocal households, there is little doubt that they represent a powerful cultural ideal. It is plausible that the emergence of the patriarchal extended family, which gives the senior man authority over everyone else, including younger men, is bound up in the incorporation and control of the family by the state (Ortner 1978), and in the transition from kin-based to tributary modes of surplus control (E. Wolf 1982). The implications of the patrilineal-patrilocal complex for women not only are remarkably uniform but also entail forms of control and subordination that cut across cultural and religious boundaries, such as those of Hinduism, Confucianism, and Islam.

Under classic patriarchy, girls are given away in marriage at a very young age into households headed by their husband's father. There, they are subordinate not only to all the men but also to the more senior women, especially their mother-in-law. The extent to which this represents a total break with their own kin group varies in relation to the degree of endogamy in marriage practices and different conceptions of honor. ...

Whether the prevalent marriage payment is dowry or bride-price, in classic patriarchy, women do not normally have any claim on their father's patrimony. Their dowries do not qualify as a form of premortem inheritance since they are transferred directly to the bridegroom's kin and do not take the form of productive property, such as land (Agarwal 1987; Sharma 1980). In Muslim communities, for a woman to press for her inheritance rights would be tantamount to losing her brothers' favor, her only recourse in case of severe ill-treatment by her husband or divorce. The young bride enters her husband's household as an effectively dispossessed individual who can establish her place in the patriliny only by producing male offspring.

The patrilineage totally appropriates both women's labor and progeny and renders their work and contribution to production invisible. Woman's life cycle in the patriarchally extended family is such that the deprivation and hardship she experiences as a young bride is eventually superseded by the control and authority she will have over her own subservient daughters-in-law. The cyclical nature of women's power in the household and their anticipation of inheriting the authority of senior women encourages a thorough internalization of this form of patriarchy by the women themselves. In classic patriarchy, subordination to men is offset by the control older women attain over younger women. However, women have access to the only type of labor power they can control, and to old-age security, through their married sons. Since sons are a woman's most critical resource, ensuring their lifelong loyalty is an enduring preoccupation. Older women have a vested interest in the suppression of romantic love between youngsters to keep the conjugal bond secondary and to claim sons' primary allegiance. Young women have an interest in circumventing and possibly evading their mother-in-law's control. There are culturally specific examples of how this struggle works to the detriment of the heterosexual bond (Boudhiba 1985; Johnson 1983; Mernissi 1975; M. Wolf 1972), but the overall pattern is quite similar.

The class or caste impact on classic patriarchy creates additional complications. Among the wealthier strata, the withdrawal of women from nondomestic work is frequently a mark of status institutionalized in various seclusion and exclusion practices, such as the purdah system and veiling. The institution of purdah, and other similar status markers, further reinforces women's subordination and their economic dependence on men. However, the observance of restrictive practices is such a crucial element in the reproduction of family status that women will resist breaking the rules, even if observing them produces economic hardship. They forego economically advantageous options, such as the trading activities engaged in by women in parts of Africa, for alternatives that are perceived as in keeping with their respectable and protected domestic roles, and so they become more exploitable. ...

Thus, unlike women in sub-Saharan Africa who attempt to resist unfavorable labor relations in the household, women in areas of classic patriarchy often adhere as far and as long as they possibly can to rules that result in the unfailing devaluation of their labor. The cyclical fluctuations of their power position, combined with status considerations, result in their active collusion in the reproduction of their own subordination. They would rather adopt interpersonal strategies that maximize their security through manipulation of the affections of their sons and husband. As M. Wolf's (1972) insightful discussion of the Chinese uterine family suggests, this strategy can even result in the aging male patriarch losing power to his wife. Even though these individual power tactics do little to alter the structurally unfavorable terms of the overall patriarchal script, women become experts in maximizing their own life chances.

Commenting on "female conservatism" in China, Johnson (1983, p. 21) remarks: "Ironically, women through their actions to resist passivity and total male control, became participants with vested interests in the system that oppressed them." …

In other areas of classic patriarchy, changes in material conditions have seriously undermined the normative order. As expressed succinctly by Cain et al. (1979, p. 410), the key to and the irony of this system reside in the fact that "male authority has a material base, while male responsibility is normatively controlled." Their study of a village in Bangladesh often an excellent example of the strains placed by poverty on bonds of obligation between kin and, more specifically, on men's fulfillment of their nonnative obligations toward women. …

… In the next section, I will analyze some of the implications of such processes of transformation.

The Demise of Patriarchal Bargains: Retreat into Conservatism or Radical Protest?

The material bases of classic patriarchy crumble under the impact of new market forces, capital penetration in rural areas (Kandiyoti 1984), or processes of chronic immiseration. While there is no single path leading to the breakdown of this system, its consequences are family uniform. The domination of younger men by older men and the shelter of women in the domestic sphere were the hallmarks of a system in which men controlled some form of viable joint patrimony in land, animals, or commercial capital. Among the propertyless and the dispossessed, the necessity of every household member's contribution to survival turns men's economic protection of women into a myth.

The breakdown of classic patriarchy results in the earlier emancipation of younger men from their fathers and their earlier separation from the paternal household. While this process implies that women escape the control of mothers-in-law and head their own households at a much younger age, it also means that they themselves can no longer look forward to a future surrounded by subservient daughters-in-law. For the generation of women aught in between, this transformation may represent genuine personal tragedy, since they have paid the heavy price of an earlier patriarchal bargain, but are not able to cash in on its promised benefits. M. Wolf's (1975) statistics on suicide among women in China suggest a clear change in the trend since the 1930s, with a sharp increase in the suicide rates of women who are over 45, whereas previously the rates were highest among young women, especially new brides. She relates this change explicitly to the emancipation of sons and their new possibility of escaping familial control in the choice of their spouse, which robs the older woman of her power and respectability as mother-in-law.

Despite the obstacles that classic patriarchy puts in women's way, which may far outweigh any actual economic and emotional security, women often resist the process of transition because they see the old normative order slipping away from them without any empowering alternatives. In a broader discussion of women's interest, Molyneux (1985, p. 234) remarks:

> This is not just because of "false consciousness" as is frequently supposed—although this can be a factor—but because such changes realized in a piecemeal fashion could threaten the short-term practical interests of some women, or entail a cost in the loss of forms of protection that are not then compensated for in some way.

Thus, when classic patriarchy enters a crisis, many women may continue to use all the pressure they can muster to make men live up to their obligations and will not, except under the most extreme pressure, compromise the basis for their claims by stepping out of line and losing their respectability. Their passive resistance takes the form of claiming their half of this particular patriarchal bargain—protection in exchange for submissiveness and propriety.

The response of many women who have to work for wages in this context may be an intensification of traditional modesty markers, such as veiling. Often through no choice of their own, they are working outside their home and are thus "exposed"; they must now use every symbolic means at their disposal to signify that they continue to be worthy of protection. It is significant that Khomeini's exhortations to keep women at home found enthusiastic support among many Iranian women despite the obvious elements of repression. The implicit promise of increased male responsibility restores the integrity of their original patriarchal bargain in an environment where the range of options available to women is extremely restricted. Younger women adopt the veil, Azari (1983, p. 68) suggests, because "the restriction imposed on them by an Islamic order was therefore a small price that had to be paid in exchange far the security, stability and presumed respect this order promised them."

This analysis of female conservatism as a reaction to the breakdown of classic patriarchy does not by any means exhaust the range of possible responses available to women. It is merely intended to demonstrate the place of a particular strategy within the internal logic of a given system, parallels to which may be found in very different contexts, such as the industrialized societies of Western Europe and the United States. Historical and contemporary analyses of the transformation of the facts and ideologies of Western domesticity imply changes in patriarchal bargains. Gordon's (1982) study of changing feminist attitudes to birth control in the nineteenth and twentieth century describes the strategy of voluntary motherhood as part of a broader calculus to improve women's situation. …

For the modern era, Ehrenreich (1983) provides an analysis of the breakdown of the white middle-class patriarchal bargain in the United States. She traces the progressive opting out of men from the breadwinner role starting in the 1950s, and suggests that women's demands for greater autonomy came at a time when men's conjugal responsibility was already much diminished and alternatives for men outside the conjugal union had gained considerable cultural legitimacy. Despite intense ideological mobilization, involving experts such as doctors, counselors, and psychologists who tried to reinforce the idea of the responsible male breadwinner and the domesticated housewife, alternative trends started to emerge and to challenge the dominant normative order. Against this background, Ehrenreich evaluates the feminist and the antifeminist movements and says, "It is as if, facing the age-old insecurity of the family wage system, women chose opposite strategies: either to get out (figuratively speaking) and fight for equality of income and opportunity, or to stay home and attempt to bind men more tightly to them" (1983, p. 151). The familism of the antifeminist movement could therefore be interpreted as an attempt to reinstate an older patriarchal bargain, with feminists providing a convenient scapegoat on whom to blame current disaffection and alienation among men (Chafetz and Dworkin 1987). Indeed, Stacey (1987, p. 11) suggests that "feminism serves as a symbolic lightning rod for the widespread nostalgia and longing for lost intimacy and security that presently pervade social and political culture in the United States."

However, the forms of consciousness and struggle that emerge in times of rapid social change require sympathetic and open-minded examination, rather than hasty categorization. Thus Ginsburg (1984) evaluates antiabortion activism among women in the United States as strategic rather than necessarily reactionary. She points out that disengaging sexuality from reproduction and domesticity is perceived by many women as inimical to their best interests, since, among other things, it weakens the social pressure on men to take responsibility for the reproductive consequences of sexual activity. This concern and the general anxiety it expresses are by no means unfounded (English 1984) and speak to the current lack of viable alternatives for the emotional and material support of women with children. ...

At the ideological level, broken bargains seem to instigate a search for culprits, a hankering for the certainties of a more traditional order, or a more diffuse feeling that change might have gone either too far or badly wrong. ...

Conclusion

Systematic analyses of women's strategies and coping mechanisms can help to capture the nature of patriarchal systems in their cultural, class-specific, and temporal concreteness and reveal how men and women resist, accommodate, adapt, and conflict with each other over resources, rights, and responsibilities. Such analyses dissolve some of the artificial divisions apparent in theoretical discussions of the relationships among class, race, and gender, since participants' strategies are shaped by several levels of constraints. Women's strategies are always played out in the context of identifiable patriarchal bargains that act as implicit scripts that define, limit, and inflect their market and domestic options. The two ideal-typical systems of male dominance discussed in this article provide different baselines from which women negotiate and strategize, and each affects the forms and potentialities of their resistance and struggles. Patriarchal bargains do not merely inform women's rational choices but also shape the more unconscious aspects of their gendered subjectivity, since they permeate the context of their early socialization, as well as their adult cultural milieu (Kandiyoti 1987a, 1987b).

A focus on more narrowly defined patriarchal bargains, rather than on an unqualified notion of patriarchy, offers better prospects for the detailed analysis of processes of transformation. In her analysis of changes in sexual imagery and mores in Western societies, Janeway (1980) borrows Thomas Kuhn's (1970) terminology of scientific paradigms. She suggests, by analogy, that widely shared ideas and practices in the realm of sexuality may act as sexual paradigms, establishing the rules of normalcy at any given time, but also vulnerable to change when "existing rules fail to operate, when anomalies can no longer be evaded, when the real world of everyday experience challenges accepted causality" (1980, p. 582). However, sexual paradigms cannot be fully comprehended unless they are inscribed in the rules of more specifically defined patriarchal bargains, ...

To stretch the Kuhnian analogy even further, patriarchal bargains can be shown to have a normal phase and a crisis phase, a concept that modifies our very interpretation of what is going on in the world. Thus, during the normal phase of classic patriarchy, there were large numbers of women who were in fact exposed to economic hardship and insecurity. They were infertile and had to be divorced, or orphaned and without recourse to their own natal family, or unprotected because they had no surviving sons or—even worse—had "ungrateful" sons. However, they were merely considered "unlucky," anomalies and accidental casualties of a system that made sense otherwise. It is only at the point of breakdown that every order reveals its systemic contradictions. The impact of contemporary socio-economic transformations upon marriage and divorce, on household formation, and on the gendered division of labor inevitably lead to a questioning of the fundamental, implicit assumptions behind arrangements between women and men.

However, new strategies and forms of consciousness do not simply emerge from the ruins of the old and smoothly produce a new consensus, but are created through personal and political struggles, which are often complex and contradictory (see Strathern 1987). The breakdown of a particular patriarchal system may, in the short run, generate instances of passive resistance among women that take the paradoxical form of bids for increased responsibility and control by men. A better understanding of the short-and medium-term strategies of women in different social locations could provide a corrective influence to ethnocentric or class-bound definitions of what constitutes a feminist consciousness.

Notes

1. Like all terms coined to convey a complex concept, the term *patriarchal bargain* represents a difficult compromise. It is intended to indicate the existence of set rules and scripts regulating gender relations, to which both genders accommodate and acquiesce, yet which may nonetheless be contested, redefined, and renegotiated. Some suggested alternatives were the terms *contract*, *deal*, or *scenario*; however, none of these fully captured the fluidity and tension implied by bargain. I am grateful to Cynthia Cockburn and Nels Johnson for pointing out that the term

bargain commonly denotes a deal between more or less equal participant, so it does not accurately apply to my usage, which clearly indicates an asymmetrical exchange. However, women as a rule bargain from a weaker position.

2. I am excluding not only Southeast Asia but also the Northern Mediterranean, despite important similarities in the latter regarding codes of honor and the overall importance attached to the sexual purity of women, because I want to restrict myself to areas where the patrilocal-patrilineal complex is dominant. This, societies with bilateral kinship systems, such as Greece, in which women do inherit and control property and receive dowries that constitute productive property, do not qualify despite important similarities in other ideological respects. This is not, however, to suggest that an unqualified homogeneity of ideology and practice exists within the geographical boundaries indicated. For example, there are critical variations within the Indian subcontinent chat have demonstrably different implications for women (Dyson and Moore 1983). Conversely, even in areas of bilateral kinship, there may be instance, in which all the facets of classic patriarchy, namely, property, residence, and descent through the male line, may coalesce under specified circumstances (Denich 1974). What I am suggesting is that the most clear-cut and easily identifiable examples of classic patriarchy may be found within the boundaries indicated in the text.

11.
INTRODUCTION: THE THEORETICAL SUBVERSIVENESS OF FEMINISM
Carole Pateman
(1986)

Over the past decade an impressive and original body of feminist criticism of social and political theory has been created. ... [It] show[s] very clearly how feminist theorists are now challenging the most fundamental presuppositions and categories of what Mary O'Brien (1981) has aptly called male-stream theory. Virtually all the social and political theory that is enshrined in the classic works and contemporary textbooks, radical as well as conservative, is malestream thought. This means that feminist theorists are in an exposed position. Their arguments are as potentially subversive of conventionally radical theory, including marxism, as of other theories, and those radicals who might be expected to be the allies of feminist scholars are as often as not hostile or, at best, indifferent. To ask embarrassing questions about the relation between women and men, and to argue that sexual domination is central to, though unacknowledged in, modern social and political theory, is to touch on some emotions, interests, and privileges very different from those disturbed by arguments about class.

Feminist theory has taken a variety of forms during its long history, and there are many continuities in the arguments of present-day feminists and their predecessors of the past three centuries. The new development in feminism is that contemporary work is distinguished by a radical challenge to the most fundamental aspects of existing social and political theory. One of the first undertakings of the present generation of feminist theorists was to reread and reinterpret the classic texts (largely political theory texts) to establish what the great writers had said about women, and what place was allotted to them in their theories (see especially Moller-Okin, 1979b; Clark and Lange, 1979; Elshtain, 1981; Pitkin, 1984; Lloyd, 1984). Such work is essential because the standard commentaries and textbooks usually either pass over the (often very lengthy) discussions of women and the relation between the sexes in the classic texts as peripheral to the real concerns of the authors, or offer an exposition of patriarchal arguments that assumes their validity is self-evident. Nor do the standard works show any awareness of the way in which classic theories are bound up with a defence of masculinity against the dangers of femininity (Pitkin, 1984). Feminist scholars have succeeded in throwing a great deal of new light onto the theoretical fathers and the manner in which their theories are constructed, and have thus illuminated the basic presuppositions of the conventional understanding of 'political', 'social' and 'historical' inquiry. For many of us at least, the classics can no longer be read as we were taught to read them.

The manner in which the theorists and the works included in the 'Western Tradition' of social and political thought are chosen has also been questioned: why do standard discussions ignore J.S. Mill's 'The Subjection of Women'? Why is Paine's reply to Burke's polemic against the French revolution studied, but not Mary Wollstonecraft's earlier reply? Why have the early socialists, who were concerned with relations between the sexes and new modes of household organisation, been dismissed as 'utopian'? Why, more generally, are none of the feminist theorists' writing from the seventeenth century onward discussed, when the most minor male figures are given their due? ...

Some of the central concepts of social and political theory have come under feminist scrutiny too, and a wide range of traditional problems have been discussed, such as consent, power, equality of opportunity, and justice. The revival of the organised feminist movement has also led to the appearance of new problems on the theoretical agenda, such as sexuality, abortion, motherhood and housework. Some of these new problems, notably abortion, have been much discussed in conventional theoretical circles, and the way in which certain problems, but not others, have been carried into the male-stream, together with the manner in which they have been defined and discussed, raises a larger and difficult question. The question is also highlighted by recent attempts by some scholars to look at the history of political thought from a specifically feminist perspective (see especially O'Brien, 1981; Hartsock, 1983; Eisenstein, 1981), and is suggested by the phrase 'male-stream' thought. The question is: what is, and should be, the relationship of feminist theorists to the classics and to conventional theoretical methods?

When contemporary feminists first began to discover the full extent and the outspokenness of the misogyny in many of the texts, and began to appreciate fully that the classic theorists were patriarchalists, almost to a man, one immediate response was to declare that the whole tainted heritage must be rejected and that feminist theorists must make a new start. Similarly, when faced with numerous recent philosophical examples of methodologically impeccable discussions of abortion that conspicuously fail to acknowledge that only women can become pregnant, there is a strong temptation to insist that feminism and philosophy should go their separate ways. However, it is impossible completely to turn our backs on the classics or on contemporary methodology, because all modes of discourse reflect and are implicated in the past to a greater or lesser degree. Moreover, there are valuable insights to be gained and lessons to be learned from male-stream theory. This is not to say that the task is to put women on an equal theoretical footing with men in existing theory. Okin's pathbreaking study showed that such a goal was illusory. More recent investigations have been uncovering further how the understanding of 'theory' is dependent on an opposition to women and all that is symbolised by the feminine and women's bodies, and why, traditionally, women's intuition and deficiency in rationality have been presented as the antithesis of the logic, order and reason required of theorists. The question, then, is not how feminists are to create theory *ab initio*, but how we are to develop the most appropriate forms of criticism and our own, distinctive approaches, in order to dismantle and transform social and political theory. ...

More generally, the discussions also show that although feminist scholarship deals with the social position of women, not all theoretical work that discusses women and women's problems is feminist. This is not to say that feminist theorists all argue in the same way or agree with each other; quite the contrary … To appreciate the difference between discussions of 'women's issues' and distinctively feminist argument, it is necessary to distinguish two forms of inquiry. On the one hand, there is work which draws on the rich source of new topics for theoretical discussion provided by the women's movement, but which treats these merely as additional problems to be investigated through existing analytical techniques and theoretical perspectives. On the other hand, there is work which proceeds from a distinctive feminist theoretical standpoint, and so asks specific kinds of questions and uses particular forms of argument.

It is perhaps an indication of the impact that feminism—and work falling into the second category—has already made on social and political theory, that several recent discussions have insisted that feminist theory is nothing more than the inclusion of women and the relation between the sexes into existing theories. Feminist criticism is thus blunted and feminism made safe for academic theory. …

[That] [d]omesticated feminism seems neither to be theoretically innovative nor to be raising questions that have not already been asked, albeit in different contexts, by conventional social and political theorists. This is inevitable, because domesticated feminism denies that sexual domination is at issue, or that feminism raises a problem, the problem of patriarchy, that is repressed in other theories. From ancient times, theorists have struggled over the question of how the rule of some people over others could be justified, but in all the long controversy over rule by slave-masters, by kings, by lords, by elites, by representatives, by the ruling class, by the vanguard party, sexual domination has remained virtually unquestioned. Men's domination of women has formed the taken-for-granted natural basis for social and political life, even in the visions of the most revolutionary theorists. If domesticated versions of feminism recognise sexual power, it is taken to pose no special problems or to have no special status, since it is assumed that relations between men and women can be analysed in the same way, using the same categories, as relations between any other superiors and subordinates.

Feminists reject this assumption, and this not only sets them apart from theorists busily domesticating feminism, but also brings them into direct conflict with liberals and socialists. The conflict with liberalism began as soon as feminist arguments appeared in the seventeenth century, when the fundamental assumptions and categories of modern social and political theory were first developed. Strictly, it is anachronistic to refer to these early writings as feminist; the term 'feminism' (coined in France) did not come into general use until the end of the nineteenth century (Offen, 1985). However, the arguments of seventeenth- and eighteenth-century writers, such as Mary Astell (1668–1731) and the much better known Mary Wollstonecraft, establish a long tradition of argument, still relevant and heard today, that is unequivocally 'feminist' (see Goreau, 1985). Moreover, anachronism notwithstanding, if this tradition is not named, it can all too easily disappear from view once again.

Feminist theory has always led a subterranean existence, never acknowledged by academic theorists (or by most of the theoretical leaders of social and political movements). Nor is the neglect mere oversight. If the full history of 300 years of feminist theory is ever written, it will reveal how feminists have persistently criticised a body of radical thought, liberal and socialist, that has not just happened to exclude women—an omission that could be remedied within the theories as they stand—but which is constructed from within a division between the public (the social, the political, history) and the private (the personal, the domestic, the familial), which is also a division between the sexes. The classic theorists … are explicit enough about women's lack of the capacities required by the free and equal 'individuals' who can take their place in the public realm (see also Brennan and Pateman, 1979; Pateman, 1980b; 1983b). The masculine, public world, the universal world of individualism, rights, contract, reason, freedom, equality, impartial law, and citizenship, is taken to be the proper concern of social and political theory. 'Theory' has been constructed within the sexual division between the private and public spheres, and theorists look to the latter sphere. But they cannot acknowledge that the public sphere gains its meaning and significance only in contrast with, and in opposition to, the private world of particularity, natural subjection, inequality, emotion, love, partiality—and women and femininity; if they did so, they would have to question their conception of theoretical inquiry. The patriarchal separation of the two spheres and the sexes is therefore repressed in contemporary theory, and the private sphere is treated as the natural foundation of civil life that requires no critical theoretical scrutiny. … The ultimate irony is that feminists are now accused of introducing an irrelevant and harmful separation between women and men into theoretical inquiry.

There are few problems about the relationship of feminism and conservatism, which is a theory of inequality and subjection. The difficulties arise with liberalism and socialism. The latter, like feminism, are specifically modern doctrines, sharing common origins in the proclamation of the natural freedom and equality of individuals. Liberalism and socialism are presented as theories of individual freedom and equality—interpreted very differently, of course, by liberals and socialists—that are universal in their scope. It is all too easy to take the claim of universalism at face value, and so suppose that feminism is no more than a generalisation of liberal or socialist assumptions and arguments to women. Appearances are misleading here. Both theories are patriarchal, which means that their apparently universal categories, such as the 'individual', the 'worker', the 'social', or the 'political', are sexually particular, constructed on the basis of male attributes, capacities and modes of activity. Despite the long history of leftist criticism of liberalism, the critics rarely questioned its patriarchalism. It is therefore not surprising that the problem of men's domination of women is absent from modern social and political theory; if it is admitted, fundamental theoretical principles are thrown into question.

One of the most important and complex legacies of the past for feminism is the construction of the ostensibly universal 'individual' within the division between private and public. The sexually particular character of the individual is at the heart of the problem of equality and sexual difference … The 'individual' is masculine, but, because he appears universal and because the categories of liberalism and socialism appear to hold out a universal promise, it seems either (for liberals) that the task of feminism is to make good this promise and incorporate women into existing institutions as equals, or (for socialists) to carry out the class revolution which will bring true universalism into being. The difficulty, in both cases, is that feminism is seen as a matter of fitting women into a unitary, undifferentiated framework that assumes that there is only one—universal—sex. Or, to put this another way, it is easy to suppose, in the face of the long history of assertion that women's capacities necessitate our exclusion from public life, that the only appropriate response is to insist that sexual difference is irrelevant. However, this line of argument leaves intact the sexually particular characterisation of the public world, the individual and his capacities.

Since the seventeenth century, one of the major feminist arguments has been that women possess the same capacities and abilities as men, and, if only educated properly, can do everything that men can do. The argument is admirable, as far as it goes. What it glosses over is that there is a womanly capacity that men do not possess, and thus it implicitly denies that birth, women's bodies and the feminine passions inseparable from their bodies and bodily processes have any political relevance. Mary O'Brien (1981) has explored some of the reasons why our theoretical heritage lacks 'a philosophy of birth', and other feminist scholars have drawn attention to the manner in which the conventional understanding of the 'political' is built upon the rejection of physical birth in favour of the masculine creation of (giving birth to) social and political order (see also Hartsock, 1983; Pitkin, 1984; Pateman, 1984). It is thus hardly surprising that much current feminist theory ... is concerned with women's bodies.

When feminism is taken to be about nothing more than equality in the sense of women attaining the same status as individuals, workers or citizens as men, it is difficult to find a convincing defence against the longstanding anti-feminist charge that feminists want to turn women into men. The 'universal' standing that is to be won is that of a being with masculine characteristics engaging in masculine activities. Existing patriarchal theory has no place for women *as women*; at best, women can be incorporated as pale reflections of men. ... [F]eminists should be more concerned with autonomy than equality. The formal, liberal civil and political equalities are important, of course, and now that women have attained a large measure of formal equality with men, and legal reforms to promote equality of opportunity are being enacted, the contradictions in taking individualism and universalism at face value are being revealed; equality of opportunity and 'gender-neutral' laws, policies and language all too frequently result in absurdities, or work against women. In the USA, where these trends are most developed, maternity benefits, for example, have been defended as 'provided to help the existence of the human race ... If a man could bear children he would be under the same law'. On the other hand, the exclusion of pregnancy from California disability insurance was declared constitutional in 1974 because it was based on a disability, namely pregnancy, not upon sex; the programme, it was said, 'divides potential recipients into two groups—pregnant women and non-pregnant persons ... The fiscal and actuarial benefits thus accrue to members of both sexes' (quotations are from Midgley and Hughes, 1983: 160–61). The very difficult question is where, theoretically, do we go from these kinds of absurdities?

There have been many famous critiques of the abstract character of liberal individualism, but none has ever questioned the most fundamental abstraction of all: the abstraction of the 'individual' from the body. In order for the individual to appear in liberal theory as a universal figure, who represents anyone and everyone, the individual must be disembodied. That is to say, a natural fact of human existence, that humankind has two bodies, female and male, must be disregarded. The theorists who recognised this fact, whether radical like Rousseau or conservative like Hegel, invariably assumed that women's bodies had no place in the public world. The public 'individual' was masculine, yet, at the same time, this figure was presented as universal, which means that, for universalism to be maintained, the attributes of the individual are implicitly abstracted from the body. If they were not so abstracted it would become clear that 'the' individual has the body of one sex. Feminists are thus bringing women's bodies to the centre of theoretical argument, but current discussions are very different from those of the classic writers. Nor should they be confused with the recent revival of patriarchal argument … [that] leads necessarily to a complete identification of women with the private sphere, maternity and childcare, and who rejects 'artificial' birth control, abortion and pain relief in childbirth. …

Feminist theory, for the first time, opens up the possibility of new approaches that reject what, until now, have been seen as the only alternatives; either 'gender-neutral' abstract individualism, or a social individualism that prescribes that women's bodies, bodily processes and passions entail our submission to men's will and judgments. …

It is, however, very apparent that distinctively feminist theory begins from the recognition that individuals are feminine and masculine, that individuality is not a unitary abstraction but an embodied and sexually differentiated expression of the unity of humankind. To develop a theory in which women and femininity have an autonomous place means that the private and the public, the social and the political, also have to be completely reconceptualised; in short, it means an end to the long history of sexually particular theory that masquerades as universalism. Whether or not patriarchal theory is ultimately subverted, … recent feminist theory shows that a very rich and exciting beginning has been made.

12.
LA CHICANA
Elizabeth Martinez
(1972)

The history and problems of La Chicana are similar to those of Latin-American women. Although the native Indian women of the Americas was, before the Spanish conquest, far from being completely free, she often participated more fully in the life of the society than did her sister under Spanish rule. The coming of the European, with his Catholic Church and feudal social system, was a turning point. Our roots lie in the act of rape: the rape of women, the rape of an entire continent and its people.

Inside the borders of the United States, the women of La Raza lived first under Spanish rule, then Mexican rule, and beginning in 1848 under U.S. imperialist rule. That year, the process of rape was resumed. The Chicana was raped by the invading gringo both in the literal, physical sense as well as in the sense of those forms of oppression imposed on all our people, both men and women.

Today we can say that the Chicana suffers from a triple oppression. She is oppressed by the forces of racism, imperialism and sexism. This can be said of all non-white women in the United States. Her oppression by the forces of racism and imperialism is similar to that endured by our men. Oppression by sexism, however, is hers alone. (By sexism, we mean oppression based on sex just as racism is oppression based on race. Sexism includes both social structures and attitudes of male superiority that are rooted in those structures.)

The Chicana of working class origin, like her Third World sisters in the United States, is born into a life pattern that we see again and again. If she finishes her secondary education, she is lucky. The Chicana who does agricultural work is almost never able to accomplish this; she must go to work in the fields at an early age, along with other members of the family, and move with them around the country as they search for work. Eventually, the Chicana will marry and become pregnant—or simply become pregnant. After one, two or three children, it is likely that her husband will leave the home. This will not necessarily happen because he does not love the woman and children but more often because of economic pressures. He simply cannot find work to support the family. Even if he doesn't leave the home, the situation is very hard and psychological tension grows between the couple.

This tension is increased when the woman is able to find work while the man cannot. This often happens because certain kinds of jobs, such as domestic service or working in the garment industry, are available to uneducated women. One of the ugliest forms of these economic pressures arises from the U.S. welfare system. Under that system, a woman with children cannot receive financial aid if there is a man in the house (her husband or any other). But she can receive it if there is no man. Some couples deliberately separate so that the woman and children can qualify for welfare aid. This was the case of Reies López Tijerina, leader of the land struggle in New Mexico, and his first wife Maria Escobar.

Despite the hard life faced by the working class Chicana—and we have barely suggested it here—she is expected to live according to attitudes and prejudices imposed by sexism. These include ideas about virginity, false definitions of femininity and the double standard (one standard of sexual behavior for women, a different standard for men). The Chicana may be working 16 hours a day to support and care for her children, but she will still be viewed as a sexual object rather than as a human being. Unless she is over the age of 35 or 40, she will be seen more as a face and body than as a fellow worker and fellow victim of oppression.

All this holds true not only for the working class Chicana—who forms the great majority of our women—but also for the Chicana of Middle Class origin. Often the spiritual growth of this Chicana is even more stunted. From birth, her life is a predestined pattern based on passing from her parents' control to that of her husband. She goes through high school acquiring a strong sense of competition with other Chicanas for the attention of the boys. This is the dominant feature of her high school years Although she is expected to become a wife and mother, the whole subject of sexual functions and physiology is treated like a dark secret. Femininity is turned into capitalist consumerism. Her womanhood is channeled into buying clothes and makeup and driving her husband to worry about making more money so that he can buy more material possessions that will give the family "status."

In the last 10 or 20 years, there has been a growing number of Chicanas from Middle Class backgrounds who go on from high school to university study and sometimes become professional workers. This group also falls prey to the values of consumerism, but some members do develop a stronger political awareness. This group has added a new element to the picture of the Chicana today.

Today—with literally thousands of Chicano women drawn into activity—there is a wide variety in positions held by Chicanas concerning their role. They might be drawn out as follows:

- The position that women should seek no change in their roles and should never challenge the status quo. This position is found among Chicanas of all classes and ages.
- The position that women are very capable, and can make important contributions as women without raising a fuss about it—in other words, without challenging the present, general situation. This position is generally held by older, working class Chicanas who often have strong individual personalities.
- The position that women must fight sexism constantly, but as an isolated phenomenon. This position is generally held by younger Chicanas, often university students.
- The position that women should and can be revolutionaries at every level of the

struggle. They should struggle against sexism without fear, but within the context of our whole struggle as a people.

We win not win our liberation struggle unless the women move together with the men rather than against them. We must work to convince the men that our struggle will become stronger if women are not limited to a few, special roles. We also have the right to expect that our most enlightened men will join in the fight against sexism; it should not be our battle alone.

We have only begun to grapple with the question of La Chicana and we have much to learn.

What has been the reaction of the men to all this? In some cases, the men have seen how they themselves are oppressed by the sexist attitudes that we call "machismo." They perceive how Chicanos waste time, energy and even their lives in so-called fights over women. They perceive how our oppressor uses "machismo" against us—for example, by appealing to a Chicano's sense of supposed manhood in order to get him to kill Vietnamese. Sexism is a useful tool to the colonizer; the men are oppressed but they can beat and mistreat women, who thus serve as targets for a frustration that might otherwise become revolutionary. Some men understand very well that the full participation of women is needed if our people are to win the liberation struggle.

The truth is that we need to reexamine and redefine our culture. Some of us do not believe that in our culture, femininity has always meant: weak, passive delicate looking … in other words, qualities that inflate the male ego. The woman of La Raza is traditionally a fighter and revolutionary. In the history of Mexico the nation closest to us, we find a long line of heroines-from the war of independence against Spain through the 1910 revolution and including the rebellions of the Yaqui Indians. The same holds true for other nations.

The woman of La Raza is also, by tradition, a worker. These are the traditions, this is the culture, that the revolutionary Chicana wants to revive. These are the traditions that a revolutionary nationalism will revive.

The revolutionary Chicana does not identify with the so-called women's liberation movement in the United States because up to now that movement has been dominated by white women of middle class background. Some of the demands of that movement have real meaning for the Chicana—such as free day-care centers for children and reform of the welfare system. But more often our demands and concerns do not meet with theirs. For example, the women's liberation movement has rejected traditional family. For us, the family has been a source of unity and our major defense against the oppressor.

Up to now, the U.S. women's liberation movement has been mainly concerned with sexism and ignored or denied the importance of racism. For the Chicana, the three types of oppression cannot be separated. They are all a part of the same system, they are three faces of the same enemy. They must all be fought with all our courage and strength. As we said earlier, the rape of our continent, our people, is historically linked. To undo the wrong, we Chicanas must understand that link, and struggle as a united force with our men and our allies.

13.
A BLACK FEMINIST STATEMENT
The Combahee River Collective[1]
(1977)

We are a collective of black feminists who have been meeting together since 1974.[2] During that time we have been involved in the process of defining and clarifying our politics, while at the same time doing political work within our own group and in coalition with other progressive organizations and movements. The most general statement of our politics at the present time would be that we are actively committed to struggling against racial, sexual, heterosexual, and class oppression and see as our particular task the development of integrated analysis and practice based upon the fact that the major systems of oppression are interlocking. The synthesis of these oppressions creates the conditions of our lives. As black women we see black feminism as the logical political movement to combat the manifold and simultaneous oppressions that all women of color face.

We will discuss four major topics in the paper that follows: (1) The genesis of contemporary black feminism; (2) what we believe, i.e., the specific province of our politics; (3) the problems in organizing black feminists, including a brief herstory of our collective; and (4) black feminist issues and practice.

1. The Genesis of Contemporary Black Feminism

Before looking at the recent development of black feminism we would like to affirm that we find our origins in the historical reality of Afro-American women's continuous life-and-death, struggle for survival and liberation. Black women's extremely negative relationship to the American political system (a system of white male rule) has always been determined by our membership in two oppressed racial and sexual castes. As Angela Davis points out in "Reflections on the Black Woman's Role in the Community of Slaves," black women have always embodied, if only in their physical manifestation, an adversary stance to white male rule and have actively resisted its inroads upon them and their communities in both dramatic and subtle ways. There have always been black women activists—some known, like Sojourner Truth, Harriet Tubman, Frances E. W. Harper, Ida B. Wells Barnett, and Mary Church Terrell, and thousands upon thousands unknown—who had a shared awareness of how their sexual identity combined with their racial identity to make their whole life situation and the focus of their political struggles unique. Contemporary black feminism is the outgrowth of countless generations of personal sacrifice, militancy, and work by our mothers and sisters.

A black feminist presence has evolved most obviously in connection with the second wave of the American women's movement beginning in the late 1960s. Black, other Third World, and working women have been involved in the feminist movement from its start, but both outside reactionary forces and racism and elitism within the movement itself have served to obscure our participation. In 1973 black feminists, primarily located in New York, felt the necessity of forming a separate black feminist group. This became the National Black Feminist Organization (NBFO).

Black feminist politics also have an obvious connection to movements for black liberation, particularly those of the 1960s and 1970s. Many of us were active in those movements (civil rights, black nationalism, the Black Panthers), and all of our lives were greatly affected and changed by their ideology, their goals, and the tactics used to achieve their goals. It was our experience and disillusionment within these liberation movements, as well as experience on the periphery of the white male left, that led to the need to develop a politics that was antiracist, unlike those of white women, and antisexist, unlike those of black and white men.

There is also undeniably a personal genesis for black feminism, that is, the political realization that comes from the seemingly personal experiences of individual black women's lives. Black feminists and many more black women who do not define themselves as feminists have all experienced sexual oppression as a constant factor in our day-to-day existence.

Black feminists often talk about their feelings of craziness before becoming conscious of the concepts of sexual politics, patriarchal rule, and, most importantly, feminism, the political analysis and practice that we women use to struggle against our oppression. The fact that racial politics and indeed racism are pervasive factors in our lives did not allow us, and still does not allow most black women, to look more deeply into our own experiences and define those things that make our lives what they are and our oppression specific to us. In the process of consciousness-raising, actually life-sharing, we began to recognize the commonality of our experiences and, from that sharing and growing consciousness, to build a politics that will change our lives and inevitably end our oppression.

Our development also must be tied to the contemporary, economic and political position of black people. The post World War II generation of black youth was the first to be able to minimally partake of certain educational and employment options, previously closed completely to black people. Although our economic position is still at the very bottom of the American capitalist economy, a handful of us have been able to gain certain tools as a result of tokenism in education and employment which potentially enable us to more effectively fight our oppression.

A combined antiracist and antisexist position drew us together initially, and as we developed politically we addresses ourselves to heterosexism and economic oppression capitalism.

2. What We Believe

Above all else, our politics initially sprang from the shared belief that Black women are inherently valuable that our liberation is a necessity not as an adjunct to somebody else's but because of our need as human persons for autonomy. This may seem so obvious as to sound simplistic, but it is apparent that no other ostensibly progressive movement has ever considered our specific oppression a priority or worked seriously for the ending of that oppression. Merely naming the pejorative stereotypes attributed to black women (e.g., mammy, matriarch, Sapphire, whore, bulldagger), let alone cataloguing the cruel, often murderous, treatment we receive, indicates how little value has been placed upon our lives during four centuries of bondage in the Western hemisphere. We realize that the only people who care enough about us to work consistently for our liberation is us. Our politics evolve from a healthy love for ourselves, our sisters, and our community which allows us to continue our struggle and work.

This focusing upon our own oppression is embodied in the concept of identity politics. We believe that the most profound and potentially the most radical politics come directly out of our own identity, as opposed to working to end somebody else's oppression. In the case of Black women this is a particularly repugnant, dangerous, threatening, and therefore revolutionary concept because it is obvious from looking at all the political movements that have preceded us that anyone is more worthy of liberation than ourselves. We reject pedestals, queenhood, and walking ten paces behind. To be recognized as human, levelly human, is enough.

We believe that sexual politics under patriarchy is as pervasive in black women's lives as are the politics of class and race. We also often find it difficult to separate race from class from sex oppression because in our lives they are most often experienced simultaneously. We know that there is such a thing as racial-sexual oppression which is neither solely racial nor solely sexual, e.g., the history of rape of black women by white on as a weapon of political repression.

Although we are feminists and lesbians, we feel solidarity with progressive black men and do not advocate the fractionalization that white women who are separatists demand. Our situation as black people necessitates that we have solidarity around the fact of race, which white women of course do not need to have with white men, unless it is their negative solidarity as racial oppressors. We struggle together with black men against racism, while we also struggle with black men about sexism.

We realize that the liberation of all oppressed peoples necessitates the destruction of the political-economic systems of capitalism and imperialism as well as patriarchy. We are socialists because we believe the work must be organized for the collective benefit of those who do the work and create the products and not for the profit of the bosses. Material resources must be equally distributed among those who create these resources. We are not convinced, however, that a socialist revolution that is not also a feminist and antiracist revolution will guarantee our liberation. We have arrived at the necessity for developing an understanding of class relationships that takes into account the specific class position of black women who are generally marginal in the labor force, while at this particular time some of us are temporarily viewed as doubly desirable tokens at white-collar and professional levels. We need to articulate the real class situation of persons who are not merely raceless, sexless workers, but for whom racial and sexual oppression are significant determinants in their working/economic lives. Although we are in essential agreement with Marx's theory as it applied to the very specific economic relationships he analyzed, we know that this analysis must be extended further in order for us to understand our specific economic situation as black women.

A political contribution which we feel we have already made is the expansion of the feminist principle that the personal is political. In our consciousness-raising sessions, for example, we have in many ways gone beyond white women's revelations because we are dealing with the implications of race and class as well as sex. Even our black women's style of talking/testifying in black language about what we have experienced has a resonance that is both cultural and political. We have spent a great deal of energy delving into the cultural and experiential nature of our oppression out of necessity because none of these matters have ever been looked at before. No one before has ever mentioned the multilayered texture of black women's lives

As we have already stated, we reject the stance of lesbian separatism because it is not a viable political analysis or strategy for us. It leaves out far too much and far too many people, particularly black men, women, and children. We have a great deal of criticism and loathing for what men have been socialized to be in this society: what they support, how they act, and how they oppress. But we do not have the misguided notion that it is their maleness, per se—i.e., their biological maleness—that makes them what they are. As black women we find any type of biological determinism a particularly dangerous and reactionary basis upon which to build a politic. We must also question whether lesbian separatism is an adequate and progressive political analysis and strategy, even for those who practice it, since it so completely denies any but the sexual sources of women's oppression, negating the facts of class and race.

3. Problems in Organizing Black Feminists

During our years together as a black feminist collective we have experienced success and defeat, joy and pain, victory and failure. We have found that it is very difficult to organize around black feminist issues, difficult even to announce in certain contexts that we are black feminists. We have tried to think about the reasons for our difficulties, particularly since the white women's movement continues to be strong and to grow in many directions. In this section we will discuss some of the general reasons for the organizing problems we face and so talk specifically about the stages in organizing our own collective.

The major source of difficulty in our political work is that we are not just trying to fight oppression on one front or even two, but instead to address a whole range of oppressions. We do not have racial, sexual, heterosexual, or class privilege to rely upon nor do we have even the minimal access to resources and power that groups who possess any one of these types of privilege have.

The psychological toll of being a black woman and the difficulties this presents in reaching political consciousness and doing political work can never be underestimated. There is a very low value placed upon black women's psyches in this society, which is both racist and sexist. As an early group member once said, "We are all damaged people merely by virtue of being black women." We are dispossessed psychologically and on every other level, and yet we feel the necessity to struggle to change our condition and the condition of all black women. In "A Black Feminist's Search for Sisterhood," Michele Wallace arrives at this conclusion:

> We exist as women who are black who are feminists, each stranded for the moment, working independently because there is not yet an environment in this society remotely congenial to our struggle—because, being on the bottom, we would have to do what no one else has done: we would have to fight the world.[3]

Wallace is not pessimistic but realistic in her assessment of black feminists' position, particularly in her allusion to the nearly classic isolation most of us face. We might use our position at the bottom, however, to make a clear leap into revolutionary action. If black women were free, it would mean that everyone else would have to be free since our freedom would necessitate the destruction of all the systems of oppression.

Feminism is, nevertheless, very threatening to the majority of black people because it calls into question some of the most basic assumptions about our existence, i.e., that gender should be a determinant of power relationships. Here is the way male and female roles were defined in a black nationalist pamphlet from the early 1970s.

> We understand that it is and has been traditional that the man is the head of the house. He is the leader of the house/nation because his knowledge of the world is broader, his awareness is greater, his understanding is fuller and his application of this information is wiser. … After all, it is only reasonable that the man be the head of the house because he is able to defend and protect the development of his home. … Women cannot do the same things as men—they are made by nature to function differently. Equality of men and women is something that cannot happen even in the abstract world. Men are not equal to other men, i.e., ability, experience, or even understanding. The value of men and women can be seen as in the value of gold and silver—they are not equal but both have great value. We must realize that men and women are a complement to each other because there is no house/family without a man and his wife. Both are essential to the development of any life.[4]

The material conditions of most black women would hardly lead them to upset both the economic and sexual arrangements that seem to represent some stability in their lives. Many black women have a good understanding of both sexism and racism, but because of the everyday constrictions of their lives cannot risk struggling against them both.

The reaction of black men to feminism has been notoriously negative. They are, of course, even more threatened than black women by the possibility that black feminists might organize around our own needs. They realize that they might not only lose valuable and hard-working allies in their struggles but that they might also be forced to change their habitually sexist ways of interacting with and oppressing black women. Accusations that black feminism divides the black struggle are powerful deterrents to the growth of an autonomous black women's movement.

Still hundreds of women have been active at different times during the three-year existence of our group. And every black women who came, came out of a strongly felt need for some level of possibility that did not previously exist in her life.

When we first started meeting early in 1974 after the NBFO first eastern regional conference, we did not have a strategy for organizing, or even a focus. We just wanted to see what we had. After a period of months of not meeting, we began to meet again late in the year and started doing an intense variety of consciousness-raising. The overwhelming feeling that we had is that after years and years we had finally found each other. Although we were not doing political work as a group, individuals continued their involvement in lesbian politics, sterilization abuse and abortion rights work, Third World Women's International Women's Day activities, and support activity for the trials of Dr. Kenneth Edelin, Joan Little, and Inez Garcia. During our first summer, when membership had dropped off considerably, those of us remaining devoted serious discussion to the possibility of opening a refuge for battered women in a black community. (There was no refuge in Boston at that time.) We also decided around that time to become an independent collective since we had serious disagreements with NBFOs bourgeois-feminist stance and their lack of a clear political focus.

We also were contacted at that time by socialist feminists, with whom we had worked on abortion rights activities, who wanted to encourage us to attend the National Socialist Feminist Conference in Yellow Springs. One of our members did attend and despite the narrowness of the ideology that was promoted at that particular conference, we became more aware of the need for us to understand our own economic situation and to make our own economic analysis.

In the fall, when some members returned, we experienced several months of comparative inactivity and internal disagreements which were first conceptualized as a lesbian-straight split but which were also the result of class and political differences. During the summer those of us who were still meeting had determined the need to do political work and to move beyond consciousness-raising and serving exclusively as an emotional support group. At the beginning of 1976, when some of the women who had not wanted to do political work and who also had voiced disagreements stopped attending of their own accord, we again looked for a focus. We decided at that time, with the addition of new members, to become a study group. We had always shared our reading with each other, and some of us had written papers on black feminism for group discussion a few months before this decision was made. We began functioning as a study group and also began discussing the possibility of starting a black feminist publication. We had a retreat in the late spring which provided a time for both political discussion and working out interpersonal issues. Currently we are planning to gather together a collection of black feminist writing. We feel that it is absolutely essential to demonstrate the reality of our politics to other black women and believe that we can do this through writing and distributing our work. The fact that individual black feminists are living in isolation all over the country, that our own numbers are small, and that we have some skills in writing, printing, and publishing makes us want to carry out these kinds of projects as a means of organizing black feminists as we continue to do political work in coalition with other groups.

4. Black Feminist Issues and Practice

During our time together we have identified and worked on many issues of particular relevance to black women. The inclusiveness of our politics makes us concerned with any situation that impinges upon the lives of women, Third World, and working people. We are of course particularly committed to working on those struggles in which race, sex, and class are simultaneous factors in oppression. We might, for example, become involved in workplace organizing at a factory that employs Third World women or picket a hospital that is cutting back on already inadequate health care to a Third World community, or set up a rape crisis center in a black neighborhood. Organizing around welfare or daycare concerns might also be a focus. The work to be done and the countless issues that this work represents merely reflect the pervasiveness of our oppression.

Issues and projects that collective members have actually worked on are sterilization abuse, abortion rights, battered women, rape, and health care. We have also done many workshops and educationals on black feminism on college campuses, at women's conferences, and most recently for high school women.

One issue that is of major concern to us and that we have begun to publicly address is racism in the white women's movement. As black feminists we are made constantly and painfully aware of how little effort white women have made to understand and combat their racism, which requires among other things that they have a more than superficial comprehension of race, color, and black history and culture. Eliminating racism in the white women's movement is by definition work for white women to do, but we will continue to speak to and demand accountability on this issue.

In the practice of our politics we do not believe that the end always justifies the means. Many reactionary and destructive acts have been done in the name of achieving "correct" political goals. As feminists we do not want to mess over people in the name of politics. We believe in collective process and a nonhierarchical distribution of power within our own group and in our vision of a revolutionary society. We are committed to a continual examination of our politics as they develop through criticism and self-criticism as an essential aspect of our practice. As black feminists and lesbians we know that we have a very definite revolutionary task to perform and we are ready for the lifetime of work and struggle before us.

Notes

1. Editor's note: The Combahee River Collective is a Black feminist group in Boston whose name comes from the guerrilla action conceptualized and led by Harriet Tubman on June 2, 1863, in the Port Royal region of South Carolina. This action freed more than 750 slaves and is the only military campaign in American history planned and led by a woman.
2. This statement is dated April 1977.
3. Michele Wallace, "A Black Feminist's Search for Sisterhood," *The Village Voice*, 28 July 1975, pp. 6–7.
4. Mumininas of Committee for Unified Newark, *Mwanamke Mwananchi (The Nationalist Woman)*, Newark, N.J., c. 1971, pp. 4–5.

14.
THE CULTURE OF ROMANCE
Shulamith Firestone
(1970)

So far we have not distinguished 'romance' from love. ... When love takes place in a power context, everyone's 'love life' must be affected. Because power and love don't make it together.

So when we talk about romantic love we mean love corrupted by its power context—the sex class system—into a diseased form of love that then in turn reinforces this sex class system. We have seen that the psychological dependence of women upon men is created by continuing real economic and social oppression. However, in the modern world the economic and social bases of the oppression are no longer *alone* enough to maintain it. So the apparatus of romanticism is hauled in. (Looks like we'll have to help her out. Boys!)

Romanticism develops in proportion to the liberation of women from their biology. As civilization advances and the biological bases of sex class crumble, male supremacy must shore itself up with artificial institutions, or exaggerations of previous institutions, e.g., where previously the family had a loose, permeable form, it now tightens and rigidifies into the patriarchal nuclear family. Or, where formerly women had been held openly in contempt, now they are elevated to states of mock worship.[1] Romanticism is a cultural tool of male power to keep women from knowing their conditions. It is especially needed—and therefore strongest—in Western countries with the highest rate of industrialization. Today, with technology enabling women to break out of their roles for good—it was a near miss in the early twentieth century—romanticism is at an all-time high.

How does romanticism work as a cultural tool to reinforce sex class? Let us examine its components, refined over centuries, and the modern methods of its diffusion—cultural techniques so sophisticated and penetrating that even men are damaged by them.

(1) *Eroticism.* A prime component of romanticism is eroticism. All animal needs (the affection of a kitten that has never seen heat) for love and warmth are channelled into genital sex: people must never touch others of the same sex, and may touch those of the opposite sex only when preparing for a genital sexual encounter ('a pass'). Isolation from others makes people starved for physical affection; and if the only kind they can get is genital sex, that's soon what they crave. In this state of hypersensitivity the least sensual stimulus has an exaggerated effect, enough to inspire everything from schools of master painting to Rock 'n' Roll. Thus *eroticism is the concentration of sexuality—often into highly-charged objects ('Chantilly Lace')—signifying the displacement of other social/affection needs on to genital sex.* To be plain old needy-for-affection makes one a 'drip',

to need a kiss is embarrassing, unless it is an erotic kiss; only 'sex' is OK, in fact it proves one's mettle. Virility and sexual performance become confused with social worth.

Constant erotic stimulation of male sexuality coupled with its forbidden release through most normal channels are designed to encourage men to look at women as only things whose resistance to entrance must be overcome. For notice that this eroticism operates in only one direction. Women are the only 'love' objects in our society, so much so that women regard *themselves* as erotic.[2] This functions to preserve direct sex pleasure for the male, reinforcing female dependence: women can be fulfilled sexually only by vicarious identification with the man who enjoys them. Thus eroticism preserves the sex class system.

The only exception to this concentration of all emotional needs into erotic relationships is the (sometimes) affection within the family. But here, too, unless they are *his* children, a man can no more express affection for children than he can for women. Thus his affection for the young is also a trap to saddle him into the marriage structure, reinforcing the patriarchal system.

(2) *The sex privatization of women.* Eroticism is only the topmost layer of the romanticism that reinforces female inferiority. As with any lower class, group awareness must be deadened to keep them from rebelling. In this case, because the distinguishing characteristic of women's exploitation as a class is sexual, a special means must be found to make them unaware that they are considered all alike sexually ('cunts'). Perhaps when a man marries he chooses from this undistinguishable lot with care, for as we have seen, he holds a special high place in his mental reserve for 'The One', by virtue of her close association with himself; but in general, he can't tell the difference between chicks (blondes, brunettes, redheads). And he likes it that way. ('A wiggle in your walk, a giggle in your talk, THAT'S WHAT I LIKE!') When a man believes all women are alike, but wants to keep women from guessing, what does he do? He keeps his beliefs to himself, and pretends, to allay her suspicions, that what she has in common with other women is precisely what makes her different. Thus her sexuality eventually becomes synonymous with her individuality. *The sex privatization of women is the process whereby women are blinded to their generality as a class which renders them invisible as individuals to the male eye.* Is not that strange Mrs. Lady next to the President in his entourage reminiscent of the discreet black servant at White House functions?

The process is insidious: When a man exclaims, 'I love Blondes!' all the secretaries in the vicinity sit up; they take it personally because they have been sex-privatized. The blonde one feels personally complimented because she has come to measure her worth through the physical attributes that differentiate her from other women. She no longer recalls that any physical attribute you could name is shared by many others, that these are accidental attributes not of her own creation, that her sexuality is shared by half of humanity. But in an authentic recognition of her individuality, her blondeness would be loved, but in a different way: she would be loved first as an irreplaceable totality, and then her blondeness would be loved as one of the characteristics of that totality.

The apparatus of sex privatization is so sophisticated that it may take years to detect—if detectable at all. It explains many puzzling traits of female psychology that take such form as:

Women who are personally complimented by compliments to their sex, i.e., 'Hats off to the Little Woman!'

Women who are not insulted when addressed regularly and impersonally as Dear, Honey, Sweetie, Sugar, Kitten, Darling, Angel, Queen, Princess, Doll, Woman.

Women who are secretly flattered to have their asses pinched in Rome. (Much wiser to count the number of times other girls' asses are pinched!)

The joys of 'prickteasing' (generalized male horniness taken as a sign of personal value and desirability).

The 'clotheshorse' phenomenon. (Women, denied legitimate outlets for expression of their individuality, 'express' themselves physically, as in 'I want to see something "different".')

These are only some of the reactions to the sex privatization process, the confusion of one's sexuality with one's individuality. The process is so effective that most women have come to believe seriously that the world needs their particular sexual contributions to go on. ('She thinks her pussy is made of gold.') But the love songs would still be written without them.

Women may be duped, but men are quite conscious of this as a valuable manipulative technique. That is why they go to great pains to avoid talking about women in front of them ('not in front of a lady')—it would give their game away. To overhear a bull session is traumatic to a woman: so all this time she has been considered only 'ass', 'meat', 'twat', or 'stuff', to be gotten a 'piece of', 'that bitch', or 'this broad' to be tricked out of money or sex or love! To understand finally that she is no better than other women but completely indistinguishable comes not just as a blow but as a total annihilation. But perhaps the time that women more often have to confront their own sex privatization is in a lover's quarrel, when the truth spills out: then a man might get careless and admit that the only thing he ever *really* liked her for was her bust ('Built like a brick shithouse') or legs anyway ('Hey, Legs!'), and he can find that somewhere else if he has to.

Thus sex privatization stereotypes women: it encourages men to see women as 'dolls' differentiated only by superficial attributes—not of the same species as themselves—and it blinds women to their sexploitation as a class, keeping them from uniting against it, thus effectively segregating the two classes. A side-effect is the converse: if women are differentiated only by superficial physical attributes, men appear more individual and irreplaceable than they really are.

Women, because social recognition is granted only for a *false* individuality, are kept from developing the tough individuality that would enable breaking through such a ruse. If one's existence in its generality is the only thing acknowledged, why go to the trouble to develop real character? It is much less hassle to 'light up the room with a smile'—until that day when the 'chick' graduates to 'old bag', to find that her smile is no longer 'inimitable'.

(3) *The beauty ideal.* Every society has promoted a certain ideal of beauty over all others. What that ideal is is unimportant, for any ideal leaves the majority out; ideals, by definition, are modelled on *rare* qualities. For example, in America, the present fashion vogue of French models, or the erotic ideal Voluptuous Blonde are modelled

on qualities rare indeed: few Americans are of French birth, most don't look French and never will (and besides they eat too much); voluptuous brunettes can bleach their hair (as did Marilyn Monroe, the sex queen herself), but blondes can't develop curves at will—and most of them, being Anglo-Saxon, simply aren't built like that. If and when, by artificial methods, the majority can squeeze into the ideal, the ideal changes. If it were attainable, what good would it be?

For the exclusivity of the beauty ideal serves a clear political function. Someone— most women—will be left out. And left scrambling, because as we have seen, women have been allowed to achieve individuality only through their appearance—looks being defined as 'good' not out of love for the bearer, but because of her more or less success- ful approximation to an external standard. This image, defined by men (and currently by homosexual men, often misogynists of the worst order), becomes the ideal. What happens? Women everywhere rush to squeeze into the glass slipper, forcing and muti- lating their bodies with diets and beauty programmes, clothes and makeup, anything to become the punk prince's dream girl. But they have no choice. If they don't the penal- ties are enormous: their social legitimacy is at stake.

Thus women become more and more look-alike. But at the same time they are expected to express their individuality through their physical appearance. Thus they are kept coming and going, at one and the same time trying to express their similarity and their uniqueness. The demands of Sex Privatization contradict the demands of the Beauty Ideal, causing the severe feminine neurosis about personal appearance.

But this conflict itself has an important political function. When women begin to look more and more alike, distinguished only by the degree to which they differ from a paper ideal, they can be more easily stereotyped as a class: they look alike, they think alike, and even worse, they are so stupid they believe they are not alike.

* * *

These are some of the major components of the cultural apparatus, romanticism, which, with the weakening of 'natural' limitations on women, keep sex oppression going strong. The political use of romanticism over the centuries became increasingly complex. Operating subtly or blatantly, on every cultural level, romanticism is now— in this time of greatest threat to the male power role—amplified by new techniques of communication so all-pervasive that men get entangled in their own line. How does this amplification work?

With the cultural portrayal of the smallest details of existence (e.g., deodorizing one's underarms), the distance between one's experience and one's perceptions of it becomes enlarged by a vast interpretive network; if our direct experience contradicts its interpretation by this ubiquitous cultural network, the experience must be denied. This process, of course, does not apply only to women. The pervasion of image has so deeply altered our very relationships to ourselves that even men have become objects— if never *erotic* objects. Images become extensions of oneself; it gets hard to distinguish the real person from his latest image, if indeed the Person Underneath hasn't evapo- rated altogether. Arnie, the kid who sat in back of you in the sixth grade, picking his nose and cracking jokes, the one who had a crook in his left shoulder, is lost under successive layers of adopted images: the High School Comedian, the Campus Rebel, James Bond, the Salem Springtime Lover, and so on, each image hitting new highs of sophistication until the person himself doesn't know who he is. Moreover, he deals with others through this image-extension (Boy-Image meets Girl-Image and consummates Image-Romance). Even if a woman could get beneath this intricate image façade—and it would take months, even years, of a painful, almost therapeutic relationship—she would be met not with gratitude that she had (painfully) loved the man for his real self, but with shocked repulsion and terror that she had found him out. What he wants instead is the Pepsi-Cola Girl, to smile pleasantly to his Johnny Walker Red in front of a ski-lodge fire.

But, while this reification affects both men and women alike, in the case of women it is profoundly complicated by the forms of sexploitation I have described. Woman is not only an Image, she is the Image of Sex Appeal. The stereotyping of women expands: now there is no longer the excuse of ignorance. Every woman is constantly and explicitly informed on how to 'improve' what nature gave her, where to buy the products to do it with, and how to count the calories she should never have eaten—indeed, the 'ugly' woman is now so nearly extinct even she is fast becoming 'exotic'. The competition becomes frantic, because everyone is now plugged into the same circuit. The current beauty ideal becomes all-pervasive ('Blondes have more fun …').

And eroticism becomes erotomania. Stimulated to the limit, it has reached an epidemic level unequalled in history. From every magazine cover, film screen, TV tube, subway sign, jump breasts, legs, shoulders, thighs. Men walk about in a state of constant sexual excitement. Even with the best of intentions, it is difficult to focus on anything else. This bombardment of the senses, in turn, escalates sexual provocation still further: ordinary means of arousal have lost all effect. Clothing becomes more provocative: hemlines climb, bras are shed. See-through materials become ordinary. But in all this barrage of erotic stimuli, men themselves are seldom portrayed as erotic objects. Women's eroticism, as well as men's, becomes increasingly directed towards women.

One of the internal contradictions of this highly effective propaganda system is to expose to men as well as women the stereotyping process women undergo. Though the idea was to better acquaint women with their feminine role, men who turn on the TV are also treated to the latest in tummy-control, false eyelashes, and floor waxes (Does she … or doesn't she?). Such a crosscurrent of sexual tease and exposé would be enough to make any man hate women, if he didn't already.

Thus the extension of romanticism through modern media enormously magnified its effects. If before culture maintained male supremacy through Eroticism, Sex Privatization, and the Beauty Ideal, these cultural processes are now almost too effectively carried out: the media are guilty of 'overkill'. The regeneration of the women's movement at this moment in history may be due to a backfiring, an internal contradiction of our modern cultural indoctrination system. For in its amplification of sex indoctrination, the media have unconsciously exposed the degradation of 'femininity'.

In conclusion, I want to add a note about the special difficulties of attacking the sex class system through its means of cultural indoctrination. Sex objects *are* beautiful. An attack on them can be confused with an attack on beauty itself. Feminists need not get so pious in their efforts that they feel they must flatly deny the beauty of the face on the cover of *Vogue*. For this is not the point. The real question is: is the face beautiful in a *human* way—does it allow for growth and flux and decay, does it express negative as well as positive emotions, does it fall apart without artificial props—or does it falsely imitate the very different beauty of an *inanimate* object, like wood trying to be metal?

To attack eroticism creates similar problems. Eroticism is *exciting*. No one wants to get rid of it. Life would be a drab and routine affair without at least that spark. That's just the point. Why has all joy and excitement been concentrated, driven into one narrow, difficult-to-find alley of human experience, and all the rest laid waste? When we demand the elimination of eroticism, we mean not the elimination of sexual joy and excitement but its rediffusion over—there's plenty to go around, it increases with use—the spectrum of our lives.

Notes

1. Gallantry has been commonly defined as 'excessive attention to women without serious purpose', but the purpose is very serious: through a false flattery, to keep women from awareness of their lower-class condition.
2. Homosexuals are so ridiculed because in viewing the male as sex object they go doubly against the norm: even women don't read Pretty Boy magazines.

15.
LESBIANS IN REVOLT
Charlotte Bunch
(1972)

The development of lesbian-feminist politics as the basis for the liberation of women is our top priority; this article outlines our present ideas. In our society, which defines all people and institutions for the benefit of the rich, white male, the lesbian is in revolt. In revolt because she defines herself in terms of women and rejects the male definitions of how she should feel, act, look, and live. To be a lesbian is to love oneself, woman in a culture that denigrates and despises women. The lesbian rejects male sexual/political domination; she defies his world, his social organization, his ideology, and his definition of her as inferior. Lesbianism puts women first while the society declares the male supreme. Lesbianism threatens male supremacy at its core. When politically conscious and organized, it is central to destroying our sexist, racist, capitalist, imperialist system.

Lesbianism Is a Political Choice

Male society defines lesbianism as a sexual act, which reflects men's limited view of women: they think of us only in terms of sex. They also say lesbians are not real women, so a real woman is one who gets fucked by men. We say that a lesbian is a woman whose sense of self and energies, including sexual energies, center around women—she is woman-identified. The woman-identified-woman commits herself to other women for political, emotional, physical, and economic support. Women are important to her. She is important to herself. Our society demands that commitment from women be reserved for men.

The lesbian, woman-identified-woman, commits herself to women not only as an alternative to oppressive male/female relationships but primarily because she *loves* women. Whether consciously or not, by her actions, the lesbian has recognized that giving support and love to men over women perpetuates the system that oppresses her. If women do not make a commitment to each other, which includes sexual love, we deny ourselves the love and value traditionally given to men. We accept our second-class status. When women do give primary energies to other women, then it is possible to concentrate fully on building a movement for our liberation.

Woman-identified lesbianism is, then, more than a sexual preference; it is a political choice. It is political because relationships between men and women are essentially political: they involved power and dominance. Since the lesbian actively rejects that relationship and chooses women, she defies the established political system.

Lesbianism, by Itself, Is Not Enough

Of course, not all lesbians are consciously woman-identified, nor are all committed to finding common solutions to the oppression they suffer as women and lesbians. Being a lesbian is part of challenging male supremacy, but not the end. For the lesbian or heterosexual woman, there is no individual solution to oppression.

The lesbian may think that she is free since she escapes the personal oppression of the individual male/female relationship. But to the society she is still a woman, or worse, a visible lesbian. On the street, at the job, in the schools, she is treated as an inferior and is at the mercy of men's power and whims. (I've never heard of a rapist who stopped because his victim was a lesbian.) This society hates women who love women, and so, the lesbian, who escapes male dominance in her private home, receives it doubly at the hands of male society; she is harassed, outcast, and shuttled to the bottom. Lesbians must become feminists and fight against woman oppression, just as feminists must become lesbians if they hope to end male supremacy.

U.S. society encourages individual solutions, apolitical attitudes, and reformism to keep us from political revolt and out of power. Men who rule, and male leftists who seek to rule, try to depoliticize sex and the relations between men and women in order to prevent us from acting to end our oppression and challenging their power. As the question of homosexuality has become public, reformists define it as a private question of whom you sleep with in order to sidetrack our understanding of the politics of sex. For the lesbian-feminist, it is not private; it is a political matter of oppression, domination, and power. Reformists offer solutions that make no basic changes in the system that oppresses us, solutions that keep power in the hands of the oppressor. The only way oppressed people end their oppression is by seizing power: people whose rule depends on the subordination of others do not voluntarily stop oppressing others. Our subordination is the basis of male power.

Sexism Is the Root of All Oppression

The first division of labor, in prehistory, was based on sex: men hunted, women built the villages, took care of children, and farmed. Women collectively controlled the land, language, culture, and the communities. Men were able to conquer women with the weapons that they developed for hunting when it became clear that women were leading a more stable, peaceful, and desirable existence. We do not know exactly how this conquest took place, but it is clear that the original imperialism was male over female: the male claiming the female body and her services as his territory (or property).

Having secured the domination of women, men continued this pattern of suppressing people, not on the basis of tribe, race, and class. Although there have been numerous battles over class, race, and nation during the past three thousand years, none has brought the liberation of women. While these other forms of oppression must be ended, there is no reason to believe that our liberation will come with the smashing of capitalism, racism, or imperialism today. Women will be free only when we concentrate on fighting male supremacy.

Our war against male supremacy does, however, involve attacking the latter-day dominations based on class, race and nation. As lesbians who are outcasts from every group, it would be suicidal to perpetuate these man-made divisions among ourselves. We have no heterosexual privileges, and when we publicly assert our Lesbianism, those of us who had them lose many or our class and race privileges. Most of our privileges as women are granted to us by our relationships to men (fathers, husbands, boyfriends) whom we now reject. This does not mean that there is no racism or class chauvinism within us, but we must destroy these divisive remnants of privileged behavior among ourselves as the first step toward their destruction in the society. Race, class, and national oppressions come from men, serve ruling-class white male interests, and have no place in a woman-identified revolution.

Lesbianism Is the Basic Threat to Male Supremacy

Lesbianism is a threat to the ideological, political, personal and economic basis of male supremacy. The lesbian threatens the ideology of male supremacy by destroying the lie about female inferiority, weakness, passivity, and by denying women's "innate" need for men. Lesbians literally do not need men, even for procreation.

The lesbian's independence and refusal to support one man undermines the personal power that men exercise over women. Our rejection of heterosexual sex challenges male domination in its most individual and common form. We offer all women something better than submission to personal oppression. We offer the beginning of the end of collective and individual male supremacy. Since men of all races and classes depend on female support and submission for practical tasks and feeling superior, our refusal to submit will force some to examine their sexist behavior, to break down their own destructive privileges over other humans, and to fight against those privileges in other men. They will have to build new selves that do not depend on oppressing women and learn to live in social structures that do not give them power over anyone.

Heterosexuality separates women from each other; it makes women define themselves through men; it forces women to compete against each other for men and the privilege that comes through men and their social standing. Heterosexual society offers women a few privileges as compensation if they give up their freedom: for example, mothers are "honored," wives or lovers are socially accepted and given some economic and emotional security, a woman gets physical protection on the street when she stays with her man, etc. The privileges give heterosexual women a personal and political stake in maintaining the status quo.

The lesbian receives none of these heterosexual privileges or compensations since she does not accept the male demands on her. She has little vested interest in maintaining the present political system since all of its institutions—church, state, media, health, schools—work to keep her down. If she understands her oppression, she has nothing to gain by supporting white rich male America and much to gain from fighting to change it. She is less prone to accept reformist solutions to women's oppression.

Economics is a crucial part of woman oppression, but our analysis of the relationship between capitalism and sexism is not complete. We know that Marxist economic theory does not sufficiently consider the role of women or lesbians, and we are presently working on this area.

However, as a beginning, some of the ways that lesbians threaten the economic system are clear: in this country, women work for men in order to survive, on the job and in the home. The lesbian rejects this division of labor at its roots; she refuses to be a man's property, to submit to the unpaid labor system of housework and child care. She rejects the nuclear family as the basic unit of production and consumption in capitalist society.

The lesbian is also a threat on the job because she is not the passive/part-time woman worker that capitalism counts on to do boring work and be part of a surplus labor pool. Her identity and economic support do not come through men, so her job is crucial and she cares about job conditions, wages, promotion, and status. Capitalism cannot absorb large numbers of women demanding stable employment, decent salaries, and refusing to accept their traditional job exploitation. We do not understand yet the total effect that this increased job dissatisfaction will have. It is, however, clear that as women become more intent upon taking control of their lives, they will seek more control over their jobs, thus increasing the strains on capitalism and enhancing the power of women to change the economic system.

Lesbians Must Form Our Own Movement to Fight Male Supremacy

Feminist-lesbianism, as the most basic threat to male supremacy, picks up part of the women's liberation analysis of sexism and gives it force and direction. Women's liberation lacks direction now because it has failed to understand the importance of heterosexuality in maintaining male supremacy, and because it has failed to face class and race as real differences in women's behavior and political needs. As long as straight women see lesbianism as a bedroom issue, they hold back the development of politics and strategies that would put an end to male supremacy and they give men an excuse for not dealing with their sexism.

Being a lesbian means ending identification with, allegiance to, dependence on, and support of heterosexuality. It means ending your personal stake in the male world so that you join women individuality and collectively, in the struggle to end your oppression. Lesbianism is the key to liberation and only women who cut their ties to male privilege can be trusted to remain serious in the struggle against male dominance. Those who remain tied to men individually or in political theory, cannot always put women first. It is not that heterosexual women are evil or do not care about women. It is because the very essence, definition, and nature of heterosexuality is men first. Every woman has experienced that desolation when her sister puts her man first in the final crunch heterosexuality demands that she do so. As long as women still benefit from heterosexuality, receive its privileges and security they will at some point have to betray their sisters, especially lesbian sisters who do not receive those benefits.

Women in women's liberation have understood the importance of having meetings and other events for women only. It has been clear that dealing with men divides us and saps our energies, and that it is not the job of the oppressed to explain our oppression to the oppressor. Women also have seen that collectively, men will not deal with their sexism until they are forced to do so. Yet, many of these same women continue to have primary relationships with men individually and do not understand why lesbians find them oppressive. Lesbians cannot grow politically or personally from the situation which denies the basis of our politics: that lesbianism is political, that heterosexuality is crucial to maintaining male supremacy.

Lesbians must form our own political movement in order to grow. Changes that will have more than token effects in our lives will be led by woman-identified lesbians who understand the nature of our oppression and are therefore in a position to end it.

Notes

1. "Lesbians in Revolt," first appeared in *The Furies*, vol. I, no. 1 (January 1972).

16.
REPRODUCTIVE AND SEXUAL RIGHTS: A FEMINIST PERSPECTIVE

Sônia Correa and Rosalind Petchesky
(1994)

In current debates about the impact of population policies on women, the concept of reproductive and sexual rights is both stronger and more contested than ever before. Those who take issue with this concept include religious fundamentalists, as well as opponents of human rights in general, who associate human rights with individualist traditions deriving from Western capitalism. Some feminists, too, are skeptical about the readiness with which advocates of fertility reduction programs, whose primary concern is neither women's health nor their empowerment, have adopted the language of reproductive rights to serve their own agendas.

As a Southern and a Northern feminist who have written about and organized for women's reproductive health for many years, we are conscious of the tensions and multiple perspectives surrounding this conceptual territory. Our purpose in this chapter is not to impose a concept, but to explore a different way of thinking about it in order to advance the debate. We define the terrain of reproductive and sexual rights in terms of power and resources: power to make informed decisions about one's own fertility, childbearing, child rearing, gynecologic health, and sexual activity; and resources to carry out such decisions safely and effectively. This terrain necessarily involves some core notion of "bodily integrity," or "control over one's body." However, it also involves one's relationships to one's children, sexual partners, family members, community, caregivers, and society at large; in other words, the body exists in a socially mediated universe. …

Epistemological and Historical Premises

Contrary to many social critics, we are not convinced that reproductive and sexual rights (or human rights) are simply a "Western" concept. As Kamla Bhasin and Nighat Khan (1986) have argued with regard to feminism in South Asia, "an idea cannot be confined within national or geographic boundaries." Postcolonial writers and Southern governments have readily adopted, and adapted, the theories of Marx, Malthus, or Milton Friedman to suit their own purposes. Democracy movements in postcolonial societies easily invoke rights when it comes to voting, or forming political parties or trade unions. Why should concepts like "reproductive rights," "bodily integrity," and women's rights to sexual selfdetermination be any less adaptable? …

The term "reproductive rights" is of recent—and probably North American[1]—origins, but its roots in ideas of bodily integrity and sexual self determination have a much older and culturally broader genealogy. The idea that a women in particular must be able "to decide whether, when, and how to have children" originated in the feminist birth control movements that developed at least as early as the 1830s among the Owenite socialists in England and spread to many parts of the world over the course of a century (Chesler 1992; Gordon 1976; Huston 1992; Jayawardena 1993; Ramusack 1989; Weeks 1981). Leaders of these movements in Western countries, like Margaret Sanger in North America and Stella Browne in England, linked "the problem of birth control" not only with women's struggle for social and political emancipation, but also with their need to "own and control" their bodies and to obtain sexual knowledge and satisfaction (Sanger 1920). Their counterparts among women's rights advocates in 19th-century Europe and America and among the early birth control pioneers in 20th-century Asia, North Africa, and Latin America were more reticent about women's sexuality, emphasizing instead a negative right: that of women (married or single) to refuse unwanted sex or childbearing.

Underlying both the defensive and the affirmative versions of these early feminist prototypes of reproductive rights language were the same basic principles of *equality*, *personhood*, and *bodily integrity*. They held a common premise: in order for women to achieve equal status with men in society, they must be respected as full moral agents with projects and ends of their own; hence they alone must determine the uses—sexual, reproductive, or other—to which their bodies (and minds) are put.[2]

In the late 1970s and early 1980s, women's health movements emerged throughout Asia, Latin America, Europe and North America (DAWN 1993; Garcia-Moreno and Claro 1994). These movements aimed at achieving the ability of women, *both* as individuals *and* in their collective organizational forms and community identities, to determine their own reproductive and sexual lives in conditions of optimum health and economic and social well-being. They did not imagine women as atoms completely separate from larger social contexts; rather, they consciously linked the principle of "women's right to decide" about fertility and childbearing to "the social, economic and political conditions that make such decisions possible" (Women's Global Network for Reproductive Rights 1991).

Increasingly, as women of color in Northern societies and women from Southern countries have taken leadership in developing the meanings of sexual and reproductive rights for women, these meanings have expanded. They have come to encompass both a broader range of issues than fertility regulation (including, for example, maternal and infant mortality, infertility, unwanted sterilization, malnutrition of girls and women, female genital mutilation, sexual violence, and sexually transmitted diseases); and a better understanding of the structural conditions that constrain reproductive and sexual decisions (such as reductions in social sector expenditures resulting from structural adjustment programs; lack of transportation, water, sanitation, and child care; illiteracy; and poverty). In other words, the concept of sexual and reproductive *rights* is being enlarged to address the *social needs* that erode reproductive and sexual choice for the majority of the world's women, who are poor (Desai 1994; Petchesky and Weiner 1990).

In the past decade, the integral tie between reproductive rights and women's sexual self-determination, including the right to sexual pleasure, has gained recognition not only in the North, but in Latin America, Africa and Asia.[3] As the Women's Resource and Research Center (WRRC) in the Philippines states in its Institutional Framework and Strategies on Reproductive Rights (Fabros 1991), "self-determination and pleasure in sexuality is one of the primary meanings of the idea of 'control over one's body' and a principal reason for access to safe abortion and birth control." Anchoring the possibility of women's *individual* right to health, well-being, and "self-determined sexual lives" to the *social* changes necessary to eliminate poverty and empower women, this framework dissolves the boundary between sexuality, human rights, and development. It thus opens a wider lens not only on reproductive and sexual rights, but on rights in general.

Rights Discourse: Rethinking Rights as Individual and Social

The discourse of (human) rights has come under heavy assault in recent years, from, among others, feminist, Marxist, and postmodernist sources (Olsen 1984; Tushnet 1984; Unger 1983). …

While these criticisms are theoretically compelling, they offer no alternative discourse for social movements to make collective political claims. Whatever its theoretical weaknesses, the polemical power of rights language as an expression of aspirations for justice across widely different cultures and political-economic conditions cannot easily be dismissed (Heller 1992). In practice, then, the language of rights remains indispensable but needs radical redefinition.

Feminist theorists and activists have figured prominently in efforts to shed the abstract universality, formalism, individualism and antagonism encumbering rights language (Bunch 1990; Crenshaw 1991; Friedman 1992; Nedelsky 1989; Petchesky 1994; Schneider 1991; Williams 1991). Allying themselves with worldwide struggles for democratization among indigenous peoples, ethnic minorities, sexual minorities, immigrant groups, and oppressed majorities—all of whom invoke the language of "human rights"—they seek to recast rights discourse in a more inclusive "referential universe" (Williams 1991). The purpose is to transform the classical liberal rights model in order: (1) to emphasize the *social*, not just individual, nature of rights, thus shifting the major burden of correlative duties from individuals to public agencies; (2) to acknowledge the *communal* (relational) *contexts* in which individuals act to exercise or pursue their rights; (3) to foreground the *substantive* basis of rights in human needs and a redistribution of resources; and (4) to recognize the bearers of rights in their self defined, multiple identities, including their gender, class, sexual orientation, race, and ethnicity. …

Feminist writings and actions in defense of women's human rights build on these critiques to challenge the customary reluctance of states and international agencies to intervene in traditionally defined "family matters." Through vigorous international campaigns leading up to and beyond the United Nations Human Rights Conference in Vienna in 1993, they have called for national and international sanctions against gender-based violations of human rights, and they have shown how such violations occur most frequently in the supposedly private realms of family, reproduction, and sexuality (for example, through endemic violence against women). Inaction by public authorities in response to such violations—whether at the hand of state officials, nongovernmental organizations (NGOs), or spouses—constitutes, they argue, a form of acquiescence (Bunch 1990; Cook 1993b; Copelon 1994; Freedman and Isaacs 1993; Heise 1992).

By prying open the "citadel of privacy," feminist legal and political theory offers a wedge with which to challenge the claims of "tradition" and "local culture" used to defeat domestic application of international human rights norms (see Boland, Rao and Zeidenstein, 1994). Feminist deconstructions of the public-private division also point to a model of reproductive and sexual behavior that is socially contextualized. …

A social model of human behavior does not assume that individuals make decisions in a vacuum or that "choices" are equally "free" for everyone. Group identities that are complex and "intersectional" (across gender, class, ethnicity, religion, age, nationality) pull women's decisions in multiple directions. Moreover, because of existing social inequalities, the resources and range of options women have at their disposal differ greatly, affecting their ability to exercise their rights (Crenshaw 1991; Eisenstein 1994; Williams 1991).

How does this interactive, socially embedded model of personal decisionmaking apply to the realm of sexual and reproductive rights? Qualitative data across a variety of cultural and historical settings suggest that the extent to which reproductive and sexual decisions are "freely" made eludes easy classification; but "free" or "voluntary," whatever its meaning, is not the same as isolated or individualistic. In each concrete case we must weigh the multiple social, economic, and cultural factors that come to bear on a woman's decision and constitute its local meaning. Women's decisions about whether or not to bring a pregnancy to term are most frequently made in consultation with, under the constraint of, and sometimes in resistance against networks of significant others—mothers, mothers-in-law, sisters, other kin, neighbors; sometimes husbands or male partners, sometimes not (Adams and Castle 1994; Ezeh 1993; Gilligan 1982; Jeffery, Jeffery and Lyon 1989; Khattab 1992; Petchesky 1990). …

Here we confront the nagging problem, always a dilemma for feminist advocates, of how to critique the kinds and range of choices available to women without denigrating the decisions women do make for themselves, even under severe social and economic constraints.[4] The debate concerning sterilization prevalence rates in Brazil provides a striking illustration. In a context of rapid fertility decline, female sterilization has become a "preferred" method in Brazil, used by 44 percent of current contraceptors. In some regions, the sterilization rate reaches more than 64 percent, as in the case of the Northeast, and the average age of sterilization has rapidly declined since the early 1980s (15 percent of sterilized women in the Northeast are under 25 years of age). A complex mix of factors explains this trend: concerns about the side effects or effectiveness of reversible contraception, failure of the public health system to provide adequate information about and access to other methods, severe economic conditions, women's employment patterns, and cultural and religious norms making sterilization less "sinful" than abortion (Correa 1993; Lopez 1993; Petchesky 1979).

In their analysis of the sterilization trends, Brazilian feminists are caught between the urgent need to denounce the inequities in sterilization rates—particularly among black women—and the evidence of research findings that many women have consciously chosen and paid for the procedure and are satisfied with their decision. On the one hand, this is a clear example of the "constrained choices" that result from circumstances of gender, poverty, and racism; the very notion that women in such conditions are exercising their "reproductive rights" strains the meaning of the term (Lopez 1993). On the other hand, the call for criminal sanctions against sterilization by some groups in Brazil seems a denial of women's moral agency in their search for reproductive self-determination.

We need to develop analytical frameworks that respect the integrity of women's reproductive and sexual decisions, however constrained, while also condemning social, economic, and cultural conditions that may force women to "choose" one course over another. Such conditions prevail in a range of situations, curtailing reproductive choices and creating dilemmas for women's health activists. Women desperate for employment may knowingly expose themselves to reproductively hazardous chemicals or other toxins in the workplace. Women hedged in by economic dependence and the cultural preference for sons may "choose" abortion as a means of sex selection. Where female genital mutilation is a traditional practice, women must "choose" for their young daughters between severe health risk and sexual loss on the one hand, and unmarriageable pariah status on the other.

For reproductive decisions to be in any real sense "free," rather than compelled by circumstance or desperation, requires the presence of certain *enabling conditions*. These conditions constitute the foundation of reproductive and sexual rights and are what feminists mean when they speak of women's "empowerment." They include material and infrastructural factors, such as reliable transportation, child care, financial subsidies, or income supports, as well as comprehensive health services that are accessible, humane, and well staffed. The absence of adequate transportation alone can be a significant contributor to higher maternal mortality and failure to use contraceptives (see Asian and Pacific Women's Resource Collection Network 1990; and McCarthy and Maine 1992). They also include cultural and political factors, such as access to education, earnings, self-esteem, and the channels of decisionmaking. Where women have no education, training, or status outside that which comes from bearing sons, childbearing may remain their best option (Morsy 1994; Pearce 1994; Ravindran 1993).

Such enabling conditions, or social rights, are integral to reproductive and sexual rights and directly entail the responsibility of states and mediating institutions (for example, population and development agencies) for their implementation. Rights involve not only *personal liberties* (domains where governments should leave people alone), but also *social entitlements* (domains where affirmative public action is required to ensure that rights are attainable by everyone). They thus necessarily imply public responsibilities and a renewed emphasis on the linkages between personal well-being and social good, including the good of public support for gender equality in all domains of life.

This is not meant to suggest a mystical "harmony of interests" between individual women and public authorities, nor to deny that conflicts between "private" and "public" interests will continue to exist. ... These realities prompt us to rethink the relationship between the state and civil society, and to map out an ethical framework for reproductive and sexual rights in the space where the social and the individual intersect.

The Ethical Content of Reproductive and Sexual Rights

We propose that the grounds of reproductive and sexual rights for women consist of four ethical principles: *bodily integrity*, *personhood*, *equality*, and *diversity*. Each of these principles can be violated through acts of invasion or abuse—by government officials, clinicians and other providers, male partners, family members, and so on or through acts of omission, neglect, or discrimination by public (national or international) authorities. Each also raises dilemmas and contradictions that can be resolved only under radically different social arrangements from those now prevailing in most of the world.

Bodily Integrity

Perhaps more than the other three principles, the principle of bodily integrity, or the right to security in and control over one's body, lies at the core of reproductive and sexual freedom. As suggested in our introduction, this principle is embedded in the historical development of ideas of the self and citizenship in Western political culture. Yet it also transcends any one culture or region, insofar as some version of it informs all opposition to slavery and other involuntary servitude, torture, rape, and every form of illegitimate assault and violence. As the Declaration of the International Women's Year Conference in Mexico City put it in 1975, "the human body, whether that of women or men, is inviolable and respect for it is a fundamental element of human dignity and freedom" (quoted in Freedman and Isaacs 1993).

To affirm the right of women to "control over" or "ownership of" their bodies does not mean that women's bodies are mere things, separate from themselves or isolated from social networks and communities. Rather, it connotes the body as an integral part of one's self, whose health and wellness (including sexual pleasure) are a necessary basis for active participation in social life. Bodily integrity, then, is not just an individual but a social right, since without it women cannot function as responsible community members (Freedman and Isaacs 1993; Petchesky 1990, 1994). Yet in its specific applications, the bodily integrity principle reminds us that while reproductive and sexual rights are necessarily social, they are also irreducibly *personal*. While they can never be realized without attention to economic development, political empowerment, and cultural diversity, ultimately their site is individual women's bodies (DAWN 1993; Petchesky 1990).

Bodily integrity includes both "a woman's right *not to be alienated from her sexual and reproductive capacity* (e.g., through coerced sex or marriage, ... [genital mutilation], denial of access to birth control, sterilization without informed consent, prohibitions on homosexuality) and ... her right to the *integrity of her physical person* (e.g., freedom from sexual violence, from false imprisonment in the home, from unsafe contraceptive methods, from unwanted pregnancies or coerced childbearing, from unwanted medical interventions)" (Dixon-Mueller 1993). ...

But bodily integrity also implies *affirmative* rights to enjoy the full potential of one's body—for health, procreation, and sexuality. Each of these raises a host of complex questions we can only touch upon here. In regard to health, the very term "integrity" connotes *wholeness*—treating the body and its present needs as a unity, not as piecemeal mechanical functions or fragments. ...

The question of whether there is a "fundamental right to procreate" based in one's biological reproductive capacity is clearly more complicated than whether one has a right, as a matter of bodily integrity, to prevent or terminate a pregnancy. Yet we can recognize that childbearing has consequences for others besides an individual woman, man, or lineage without subscribing to the claim that women have a duty to society (or the planet!) to abstain from reproducing. Such a duty could begin to exist only when all women are provided sufficient resources for their well-being, viable work alternatives, and a cultural climate of affirmation outside of childbearing so that they no longer depend on children for survival and dignity (Berer 1990; Freedman and Isaacs 1993). And even then, antinatalist policies that depend on coercion or discriminate against or target particular groups would be unacceptable.

Our hesitancy about a "right to procreate" is not based on any simple correlation between population growth, environmental degradation, and women's fertility, ... Rather, it comes from apprehensions about how patriarchal kinship systems throughout history have used such claims to confine and subordinate women, who alone have bodies that can be impregnated. Procreative rights are, however, an important part of reproductive and sexual rights. They include the right to participate in the basic human practice of raising and nurturing children; the right to bring wanted pregnancies to term in conditions of safety, decency, and good health, and to raise one's children in such conditions; and the right of gay and lesbian families to bear, foster, or adopt children in the same dignity as other families. They also include a transformation in the prevailing gender division of labor so that men are assigned as much responsibility for children's care as women.

Finally, what shall we say of the body's capacity for sexual pleasure and the right to express it in diverse and nonstigmatized ways? If the bodily integrity principle implies such a right, as we believe, its expression surely becomes more complicated and fraught with dangers for women and men in the context of rising prevalence of HIV and STD infection (Berer 1993a; DAWN 1993). In addition to these immediate dangers—compounded by the now well-documented fact that many STDs increase women's susceptibility to HIV—there is the "vicious cycle" in which "women suffering the consequences of sexually transmitted disease find themselves in a social circumstance that further increases their risk of exposure to sexually transmitted infections and their complications" (Elias 1991). This cycle currently affects sub-Saharan African women most drastically, but is rapidly becoming a worldwide phenomenon. It includes women's lack of sexual self-determination; the high risk they incur of infertility and ectopic pregnancy from STD infection; their dependence on men and in-laws for survival; the threat of ostracism or rejection by the family or male partner following infection or infertility;

then the threat of unemployment, impoverishment, and prostitution, followed by still greater exposure to STD and HIV infection (Elias 1991; Wasserheit 1993).

The global crisis of HIV and AIDS complicates but does not diminish the right of all people to responsible sexual pleasure in a supportive social and cultural environment. For women and men of diverse sexual orientations to be able to express their sexuality without fear or risk of exclusion, illness, or death requires sex education and male and female resocialization on a hitherto unprecedented scale. This is why bodily integrity has a necessary social rights dimension that, now more than ever, is a matter of life and death.

Personhood

Listening to women is the key to honoring their moral and legal personhood—that is, their right to self-determination. This means treating them as principal actors and decision-makers in matters of reproduction and sexuality—as subjects, not merely objects, and as ends, not only means, of population and family planning policies. As should be clear from our earlier discussion emphasizing a relational-interactive model of women's reproductive decisions, our concept of decisionmaking autonomy implies respect for how women make decisions, the values they bring to bear, and the networks of others they choose to consult; it does not imply a notion of solitude or isolation in "individual choices." Nor does it preclude full counseling about risks and options regarding contraception, prenatal care, childbearing, STDs and HIV, and other aspects of gynecologic health.

At the clinical level, for providers to respect women's personhood requires that they trust and take seriously women's desires and experiences, for example, concerning contraceptive side effects. When clinicians trivialize women's complaints about such symptoms as headaches, weight gain, or menstrual irregularity, they violate this principle. Qualitative studies of clinical practices regarding the use of Norplant® in the Dominican Republic, Egypt, Indonesia, and Thailand found that women's concerns about irregular bleeding were often dismissed, and their requests for removal of the implant not honored (Zimmerman et al. 1990).

Respect for personhood also requires that clients be offered a complete range of safe options, fully explained, without major discrepancies in cost or government subsidization. When some contraceptive methods are *de facto* singled out for promotion (for instance, longacting implants or sterilization), or clinical practices manifest strong pronatalist or antinatalist biases (as in programs governed by demographic targets), or safe legal abortion is denied, respect for women's personhood is systematically abused. "Quality of care" guidelines, which originated in women's health activism and were codified by Judith Bruce, reflect not only good medical practice but an ethic of respect for personhood (Bruce 1990; DAWN 1993; Jain, Bruce and Mensch 1992; Mintzes 1992).

At the level of national and international policies and programs, treating women as persons in sexual and reproductive decisionmaking means assuring that women's organizations are represented and heard in the processes where population and health policies are made and that effective mechanisms of public accountability, in which women participate, are established to guard against abuses. It also means abandoning demographic targets in the service of economic growth, cost containment, or ethnic or nationalist rivalries and replacing them with reproductive health and women's empowerment goals (see Jain and Bruce 1994). Demographic targeting policies that encourage the use of material incentives or disincentives often work to manipulate or coerce women, particularly those who are poor, into accepting fertility control methods they might otherwise reject, thus violating their decisionmaking autonomy.

The question of "incentives" is clearly a complicated one, since in some circumstances they may expand women's options and freedom (Dixon-Mueller 1993). Feminists and human rights activists have justly criticized programs that promote particular fertility control methods or antinatalist campaigns through monetary inducements or clothing to "acceptors," fines or denials of child care or health benefits to "offenders," or quotas reinforced with "bonuses" for village officials or clinic personnel (Freedman and Isaacs 1993; Ravindran 1993). What would be our reaction, however, to a system of women-managed comprehensive care clinics that provided child care or free transportation to facilitate clinic visits? A distinct difference exists between these two cases, since the former deploys the targeting and promotional strategies that undermine women's personhood, whereas the latter incorporates the kinds of enabling conditions we earlier found necessary for equalizing women's ability to exercise their reproductive rights. To distinguish *supportive* or *empowering* conditions from *coercive* incentives or disincentives, we need to assure that they respect all four ethical principles of reproductive rights (bodily integrity, personhood, equality, and diversity). When poor or incarcerated women are expected to purchase other rights "for the price of their womb" (for example, a job for sterilization or release from prison for Norplant®), "incentives" become corrupted into bribes (Williams 1991). Women's social location determines whether they are able to make sexual and reproductive decisions with dignity.

Equality

The principle of equality applies to sexual and reproductive rights in two main areas: relations between men and women (gender divisions), and relations among women (conditions such as class, age, nationality, or ethnicity that divide women as a group). With respect to the former, the impetus behind the idea of reproductive rights as it emerged historically was to remedy the social bias against women inherent in their lack of control over their fertility and their assignment to primarily reproductive roles in the gender division of labor. "Reproductive rights" (or "birth control") was one strategy within a much larger agenda for making women's position in society equal to men's. At the same time, this notion contains the seeds of a contradiction, since women alone are the ones who get pregnant, and in that sense, their situation—and degree of risk—can never be reducible to men's.

This tension, which feminists have conceptualized in the debate over equality versus "difference," becomes problematic in the gender neutral language of most United Nations documents pertaining to reproductive rights and health. For example, article

16(e) of the Convention on the Elimination of All Forms of Discrimination against Women (CEDAW) gives men and women "*the same rights* to decide freely and responsibly on the number and spacing of their children and to have access to the information, education and means to enable them to exercise these rights [emphasis added]." Might this article be used to mandate husbands' consent to abortion or contraception? Why should men and women have "the same" rights with regard to reproduction when, as not only childbearers but those who in most societies have responsibility for children's care, women have so much greater stake in the matter—when, indeed, growing numbers of women raise children without benefit of male partners? (The language of "couples" in family planning literature raises the same kinds of questions.)

If we take the issue of contraception as an illustration, the principle of equality would seem to require that, where contraceptive methods carry risks or provide benefits, those risks and benefits must be distributed on a fair basis between women and men, as well as among women. This would suggest a population policy that puts greater emphasis on encouraging male responsibility for fertility control and scientific research into effective "male" contraceptives. In fact, many women express a sense of unfairness that they are expected to bear nearly all the medical risks and social responsibility for avoiding unwanted pregnancies (Pies n.d.). But such a policy might also conflict with the basic right of women to control their own fertility and the need many women feel to preserve that control, sometimes in conditions of secrecy and without "equal sharing" of risks.

On the surface, this dilemma seems to be a contradiction within feminist goals, between the opposing principles of equality and personhood. The feminist agenda that privileges women's control in reproductive rights would seem to reinforce a gender division of labor that confines women to the domain of reproduction. Yet exploring the problem more deeply reveals that women's distrust of men's taking responsibility for fertility control and reluctance to relinquish methods women control are rooted in other kinds of gendered power imbalances that work against a "gender equality" approach to reproductive health policies. These include social systems that provide no educational or economic incentives toward men's involvement in child care and cultural norms that stigmatize women's sexuality outside the bounds of heterosexual monogamy. Thus, while a reproductive health policy that encourages the development and use of "male methods" of contraception may increase the total range of "choices," in the long run it will not help to realize women's social rights nor gender equality until these larger issues are also addressed.

Applying the equality principle in the implementation of sexual and reproductive rights also requires attention to potential inequalities *among* women. This means, at the least, that risks and benefits must be distributed on a fair basis and that providers and policy makers must respect women's decisionmaking authority without regard to differences of class, race, ethnic origin, age, marital status, sexual orientation, nationality, or region (North–South). Returning to our example of contraception, there is certainly ample evidence that access to safe methods of fertility control can play a major role in improving women's health, but some contraceptive methods can have negative consequences for some women's health (National Research Council 1989). Issues of equal treatment may arise when certain methods—particularly those that carry medical risks or whose long-term effects are not well known—are tested, targeted, or promoted primarily among poor women in Southern or Northern countries. Indeed, when clinical trials are conducted among poor urban women, who tend to move frequently or lack transportation, the necessary conditions for adequate medical follow-up may not exist, and thus the trials themselves may be in violation of the equality principle. Meanwhile, issues of discrimination arise when safe, beneficial methods such as condoms or diaphragms, low-dose hormonal pills, or hygienic abortion facilities are available only to women with the financial resources to pay for them.

For governments and international organizations to promote sexual and reproductive rights in ways that respect equality among women requires addressing at least the most blatant differences in power and resources that divide women within countries and internationally. In the case of safe, effective methods of contraception, laws that guarantee the "freedom" of all women to use whatever methods they "choose" are gratuitous without geographic access, high-quality services and supplies, and financing for all women who need them. We are saying that the economic and political changes necessary to create such conditions are a matter not just of development, but of (social) *rights*; indeed, they are a good example of why development *is* a human right and why women's reproductive rights are inseparable from this equation (Sen 1992).

Diversity

While the equality principle requires the mitigation of inequities among women in their access to services or their treatment by health providers and policy makers, the diversity principle requires respect for differences among women—in values, culture, religion, sexual orientation, family or medical condition, and so on. The universalizing language of international human rights instruments, reflecting a Western liberal tradition, needs to be reshaped to encompass such differences (see Freedman and Isaacs 1993; Cook 1993 a, b). While defending the universal applicability of sexual and reproductive rights, we must also acknowledge that such rights often have different meanings, or different points of priority, in different social and cultural contexts.

Differences in cultural or religious values, for example, affect attitudes toward children and childbearing, influencing how diverse groups of women think about their entitlements in reproduction. In her study of market women in Ile-Ife, Nigeria, anthropologist Tola Olu Pearce (1994) found that the high value placed on women's fertility and the subordination of individual desires to group welfare in Yoruba tradition made the notion of a woman's individual right to choose alien. Yet Yoruba women in Ile-Ife have also used methods of fertility control to space their children and "avoid embarrassment" for untold generations and no doubt consider it part of their collective "right" as women to do so. A similar communal ethic governing women's reproductive decisions emerges in a study of Latina single mothers in East Harlem (New York City), who consider their "reproductive rights" to include the right to receive public assistance in order to stay home and care for their children (Benmayor, Torruellas, and Juarbe 1992).

Local religious and cultural values may also shape women's attitudes toward medical technologies or their effects, such as irregular menstrual bleeding. Clinic personnel involved in disseminating Norplant® have not always understood the meanings menstrual blood may have in local cultures and the extent to which frequent bleeding—a common side effect of Norplant®—may result in the exclusion of women from sex, rituals, or community life (Zimmerman et al. 1990). Imposing standards of what is "normal" or "routine" bleeding (for example, to justify refusal to remove the implant upon request) could constitute a violation of the diversity principle, as well as the bodily integrity and personhood principles.[5]

It is important to distinguish between the feminist principle of respect for difference and the tendency of male-dominated governments and fundamentalist religious groups of all kinds to use "diversity" and "autonomy of local cultures" as reasons to deny the universal validity of women's human rights.[6] In all the cases cited above, women's assertion of their particular needs and values, rather than denying the universal application of rights, clarifies what those rights mean in specific settings. Women's multiple identities—whether as members of cultural, ethnic, and kinship groups, or as people with particular religious and sexual orientations, and so forth—challenge human rights discourse to develop a language and methodology that are pluralistic yet faithful to the core principles of equality, personhood, and bodily integrity. This means that the diversity principle is never absolute, but always conditioned upon a conception of human rights that promotes women's development and respects their self-determination. Traditional patriarchal practices that subordinate women—however local or time-worn, or enacted by women themselves (for example, genital mutilation)—can never supersede the social responsibility of governments and intergovernmental organizations to enforce women's equality, personhood, and bodily integrity, through means that respect the needs and desires of the women most directly involved.

Bringing a Feminist Social Rights Approach to Population and Development Policies

The above analysis has attempted to show that the individual (liberty) and the social (justice) dimensions of rights can never be separated, as long as resources and power remain unequally distributed in most societies. Thus the affirmative obligations of states and international organizations become paramount, since the ability of individuals to exercise reproductive and sexual rights depends on a range of conditions not yet available to many people and impossible to access without public support. In this respect, the language of "entitlement" seems to us overly narrow, insofar as it implies claims made by individuals on the state without expressing the idea of a mutual *public* interest in developing empowered, educated, and politically responsible citizens, including all women. Likewise, the language of "choosing freely and responsibly" still contained in most international instruments that address family planning and reproductive rights is at best ambiguous and at worst evasive (see Boland, Rao, and Zeidenstein 1994). What does it mean to choose "responsibly"? Who, in fact, is responsible, and what are the necessary conditions—social, economic, cultural—for individuals to act in socially responsible ways? The correlative duties associated with sexual and reproductive rights belong not only to the bearers of those rights, but to the governmental and intergovernmental agencies charged with their enforcement. …

Documents developed in preparation for the 1994 International Conference on Population and Development (ICPD), in Cairo, have begun to reflect the vision of reproductive and sexual rights as social rights that we have presented here. This is true not only of documents produced by women's NGOs, but also of official conference preparatory meetings and summaries, where for the first time in international population discourse, issues of gender equality and women's empowerment overshadow demographic targets and economic growth and are recognized as part of "sustainable development." …

… Years of organizing and advocacy by women's health groups throughout the world have clearly had an important effect *at the level of official rhetoric* on intergovernmental forums concerned with "population" issues. To what extent are we likely to see governments, UN agencies, and international population organizations move from awareness to action to translate this rhetoric into concrete policies and programs that truly benefit women?

Many women's health groups, in both the South and the North, are concerned that feminist sounding rhetoric is being used by international population agencies to legitimate and gloss over what remain instrumentalist and narrowly quantitative ends. Perceiving the history of population control policies and programs as all too frequently oblivious to women's needs and the ethical principles outlined above, they fear the language of reproductive rights and health may simply be co-opted by the Cairo process to support business as usual.

Our position is slightly note optimistic but nonetheless cautious. Feminists are putting pressure on population and family planning agencies to acknowledge women's self-defined needs and our conceptions of reproductive and sexual rights. This should move us closer to social and policy changes that empower women, but whether it does will depend on even more concerted action by women's NGOs, including alliances with many other groups concerned with health, development, and human rights. One such action should be to insist on full participation by women's rights and health groups in all relevant decisionmaking bodies and accountability mechanisms. In the long run, however, it is not enough that we call population agencies to account. To bridge the gap between rhetoric about reproductive and sexual rights and the harsh realities most women face demands a much larger vision. We must integrate, but not subordinate, those rights with health and development agendas that will radically transform the distribution of resources, power, and wellness within and among all the countries of the world (DAWN 1993; Sen 1992). These are the enabling conditions to transform rights into lived capacities. For women, Cairo is just a stop along the way.

Notes

1. The term seems to have originated with the founding of the Reproductive Rights National Network (R2N2) in the United States in 1979. R2N2 activists brought it to the European-based International Campaign for Abortion Rights in the early 1980s; at the International Women and Health Meeting

in Amsterdam in 1984, the Campaign officially changed its name to the Women's Global Network for Reproductive Rights (Berer 1993b [personal communication]). Thereafter, the concept rapidly spread throughout women's movements in the South (for example, in 1985, under the influence of feminist members who had attended the Amsterdam meeting, the Brazilian Health Ministry established the Commission on the Rights of Human Reproduction). See also Garcia-Moreno and Claro 1994.

2. In fact, the principle of "ownership of one's body and person" has much deeper roots in the history of radical libertarian and democratic thought in Western Europe. Historian Natalie Zemon Davis traced this idea to 16th-century Geneva, when a young Lyonnaise girl, brought before the Protestant elders for sleeping with her fiancé before marriage, invoked what may have been a popular slogan: "*Paris est au roi, et mon corps est à moi*" (Paris is the king's, and my body is mine). The radical Levellers in 17th-century England developed the notion of a "property in one's person," which they used to defend their members against arbitrary arrest and imprisonment (Petchesky 1994). But the principle is not only of European derivation. Gandhi's concept of *Brahmacharya*, or "control over the body," was rooted in Hindu ascetic traditions and the Vedas' admonition to preserve the body's vital fluids. Like that of 19th-century feminists and the Catholic church, Gandhi's concept was theoretically gender-neutral, requiring both men and women to engage in sexual restraint except for purposes of procreation (Fischer 1962; O'Flaherty 1980). Islamic law goes further toward a sexually affirmative concept of self-ownership. Quranic provisions not only entitle women to sexual satisfaction in marriage, as well as condoning abortion and contraception; they also allow that, upon divorce—which wives as well as husbands may initiate—a woman regains her body. (Ahmed 1992; Musallam 1983; Ruthven 1984).

3. In Latin America, a new resolution of the Colombian Ministry of Public Health "orders all health institutions to ensure women the right to decide on all issues that affect their health, their life, and their sexuality, and guarantees rights 'to information and orientation to allow the exercise of free, gratifying, responsible sexuality which cannot be tied to maternity'" (quoted in Cook 1993a). In North Africa, Dr. Hind Khattab's field research among rural Egyptian women has revealed strong sentiments of their sexual entitlement to pleasure and gratification from husbands (Khattb 1993 [personal communication]).

4. Feminist theory and practice have witnessed a long history of division over this question. Whether with regard to protective labor legislation, prostitution, pornography, or providing contraceptive implants to teenagers or poor women, conflicts between "liberals" (advocates of "freedom to choose") and "radicals" (advocates of social protection or legal prohibition) have been bitter and protracted.

5. Not only clinicians but feminist activists maybe guilty of imposing their own values and failing to respect diversity. Feminist groups that condemn all reproductive technologies (for examples, technologies that artificially assist fertility) as instruments of medical control over women against "nature" ignore the ways that such technologies may expand the rights of particular women (for example, lesbians seeking pregnancy through artificial insemination or in vitro fertilization).

6. It seems crucial to us to recognize that religious fundamentalist movements are on the upswing in all the world's regions and major religions—Catholicism, Protestantism, Judaism, and Hinduism as well as Islam. Despite vast cultural and theological differences, these fundamentalisms share a view of women as reproductive vessels that is antipathetic to any notion of women's reproductive rights. In an otherwise excellent discussion of the clash between religious and customary law and human rights, Lynn Freedman and Stephen Isaacs (1993) place undue emphasis on Muslim countries and Islamic law.

17.
TRANSGENDER LIBERATION: A MOVEMENT WHOSE TIME HAS COME
Leslie Feinberg
(1992)

This pamphlet is an attempt to trace the historic rise of an oppression that, as yet, has no commonly agreed-upon name. We are talking here about people who defy the "man"-made boundaries of gender.

Gender: self-expression, not anatomy.

All our lives we've been taught that sex and gender are synonymous—men are "masculine" and women are "feminine." Pink for girls and blue for boys. It's just "natural," we've been told. But at the turn of the century in this country, blue was considered a girl's color and pink was a boy's. Simplistic and rigid gender codes are neither eternal nor natural. They are changing social concepts.

Nevertheless, there's nothing wrong with men who are considered "masculine" and women whose self-expression falls into the range of what is considered "feminine." The problem is that the many people who don't fit these narrow social constraints run a gamut of harassment and violence.

This raises the question: Who decided what the "norm" should be? Why are some people punished for their self-expression?

Many people today would be surprised to learn that ancient communal societies held transgendered people in high esteem. It took a bloody campaign by the emerging ruling classes to declare what had been considered natural to be its opposite. That prejudice, foisted on society by its ruling elite, endures today.

Yet even in a society where there are harsh social penalties for not fitting, a large part of the population can't or won't change their nature. It is apparent that there are many ways for women and men to be; everything in nature is a continuum.

Many of the terms used to describe us are words that cut and sear.

When I first worked in the factories of Buffalo as a teenager, women like me were called "he-shes."

Although "he-shes" in the plants were most frequently lesbians, we were recognized not by our sexual preference but by the way we expressed our gender.

There are other words used to express the wide range of "gender outlaws": transvestites, transsexuals, drag queens and drag kings, cross-dressers, bull-daggers, stone butches, androgynes, diesel dykes or berdache—a European colonialist term.

We didn't choose these words. They don't fit all of us. It's hard to fight an oppression without a name connoting pride, a language that honors us.

In recent years a community has begun to emerge that is sometimes referred to as the gender or transgender community. Within our community is a diverse group of people who define ourselves in many different ways. Transgendered people are demanding the right to choose our own self-definitions. The language used in this pamphlet may quickly become outdated as the gender community coalesces and organizes—a wonderful problem.

We've chosen words in this pamphlet we hope are understandable to the vast majority of working and oppressed people in this country, as a tool to battle bigotry and brutality. We are trying to find words, however inadequate, that can connect us, that can capture what is similar about the oppression we endure. We have also given careful thought to our use of pronouns, striving for both clarity and sensitivity in a language that only allows for two sexes.

Great social movements forge a common language—tools to reach out and win broader understanding. But we've been largely shut out of the progressive movement.

It was gay transvestites who led the 1969 battle at the Stonewall Inn in New York City that gave birth to the modern lesbian and gay movement.

But just as the lesbian and gay movement had to win over the progressive movement to the understanding that struggling shoulder to shoulder together would create a more powerful force for change, the transgendered community is struggling to win the same understanding from the lesbian and gay movement.

Many people think that all "masculine" women are lesbians and all "feminine" men are gay. That is a misunderstanding. Not all lesbians and gay men are "cross"-gendered. Not all transgendered women and men are lesbian or gay. Transgendered people are mistakenly viewed as the cusp of the lesbian and gay community. In reality the two huge communities are like circles that only partially overlap.

While the oppressions within these two powerful communities are not the same, we face a common enemy. Gender-phobia—like racism, sexism and bigotry against lesbians and gay men—is meant to keep us divided. Unity can only increase our strength.

Solidarity is built on understanding how and why oppression exists and who profits from it. It is our view that revolutionary changes in human society can do away with inequality, bigotry and intolerance.

In the spirit of building that fighting movement, we offer this view of the sweeping patterns in history, the commonality of women and men who have walked the path of the berdache, of the transgendered—walked that road whether we were held in high esteem or reviled.

Look at us. We are battling for survival. Listen. We are struggling to be heard.

Transgender Predates Oppression

Jazz musician Billy Tipton died in 1989 at the age of 74. He will be remembered most not for his music, but for the revelation that Tipton was born a woman. Tipton died of an untreated bleeding ulcer rather than visit a doctor and risk exposure.

After his death this debate began: Did Tipton live as a man simply in order to work as a musician in a male-dominated industry or because of lesbian oppression?

It is true that women's oppression, especially under capitalism, has created profound social and economic pressures that force women to pass as men for survival. But this argument leaves out transgendered women—women who are considered so "masculine" in class society that they endure extreme harassment and danger. Many of these women are forced to "pass" in order to live. Of course transgendered women also experience the crushing weight of economic inequity and, in many cases, anti-lesbian oppression. These factors also play a role in forcing "masculine" women as well as non-transgendered women to pass.

If "masculine" women are acknowledged at all, it is implied that they're merely a product of decadent patriarchal capitalism and that when genuine equality is won, they will disappear.

It's "Passing" That's New

Transgendered women and men have always been here. They are oppressed. But they are not merely products of oppression. It is *passing* that's historically new. Passing means hiding. Passing means invisibility. Transgendered people should be able to live and express their gender without criticism or threats of violence. But that is not the case today.

There are legions of women and men whose self-expression, as judged by Hollywood stereotypes, is "at odds" with their sex. Some are forced underground or "pass" because of the repression and ostracism they endure.

Today all gender education teaches that women are "feminine," men are "masculine;" and an unfordable river rages between these banks. The reality is there is a whole range of ways for women and men to express themselves.

Transgender is a very ancient form of human expression that pre-dates oppression. It was once regarded with honor. A glance at human history proves that when societies were not ruled by exploiting classes that rely on divide-and-conquer tactics, "cross-gendered" youths, women and men on all continents were respected members of their communities.

"She Is a Man"

"Strange country, this," a white man wrote of the Crow nation on this continent in 1850, "where males assume the dress and perform the duties of females, while women turn men and mate with their own sex."

Randy Burns, a founder of the modern group Gay American Indians, wrote that GAI's History Project documented these alternative roles for women and men in over 135 North American Native nations.

The high incidence of transgendered men and women in Native societies on this continent was documented by the colonialists who referred to them as *berdache*.

Perhaps the most notable of all berdache Native women was Barcheeampe, the Crow "Woman Chief," the most famous war leader in the history of the upper Missouri nations. She married several wives and her bravery as a hunter and warrior was honored in songs. When the Crow nation council was held, she took her place among the chiefs, ranking third in a band of 160 lodges.

Today transgender is considered "anti-social" behavior. But amongst the Klamath nations transgendered women were given special initiation ceremonies by their societies.

Among the Cocopa, Edward Gifford wrote, "female transvestites were called war hameh, wore their hair and pierced their noses in the male fashion, married women and fought in battle alongside men."

Wewha, a famous Zuni berdache who was born a man, lived from 1849 to 1896. She was among the tallest and strongest of all the Zuni. When asked, her people would explain, "She is a man." Wewha was sent by the Zuni to Washington, D.C., for six months where she met with President Grover Cleveland and other politicians who never realized she was berdache.

Osh-Tische (Finds Them and Kills Them), a Crow berdache or báde who was also born a man, fought in the Battle of the Rosebud. When a colonial agent tried to force Osh-Tisch to wear men's clothing, the other Native people argued with him that it was against her nature and they kicked the agent off their land. They said it was a tragedy, trying to change the nature of the bade.

A Jesuit priest observed in the 1670s of the berdache, "They are summoned to the Councils, and nothing can be decided without their advice."

But the missionaries and colonialist military reacted to the Native berdache in this hemisphere with murderous hostility. Many berdache were tortured and burnt to death by their Christian conquerors. Other colonial armies sicced wild dogs on the berdache.

Why Such Hostility?

Why were the European colonialists so hostile to transgendered women and men? The answer can be found back on the European continent in the struggles that raged between the developing classes of haves and have-nots.

Ancient societies on the European continent were communal. Thousands of artifacts have been unearthed dating back to 25,000 B.C. that prove these societies worshipped goddesses, not gods. Some of the deities were transgendered, as were many of their shamans or religious representatives.

We have been taught that the way things are now is roughly the way they have always been—the "Flintstones" school of anthropology. The strong message is: Don't bother trying to change people. But a glance at history proves that human society has undergone continuous development and change.

A great debate has raged for more than 150 years about the role of women in ancient societies. To hear Jesse Helms and his ilk rant, you'd think that the patriarchal nuclear family has always existed. That's not true.

Twentieth century anthropologists recognize that matrilineal communal societies existed all over the world at an early stage in social development. Women were the heads of *gens* or clans that bore little resemblance to today's "family." ...

When Bigotry Began

In the fertile river valleys of Eurasia and Northeast Africa, during the period of about 4500 BC to 1200 B.C., human labor became more productive and abundance accumulated as wealth. The old communal systems were gradually and unconsciously transformed.

A tremendous societal change took place. The desire to pass on wealth to male heirs demanded wifely monogamy; the patriarchal family became the new economic unit of society.

But the respect the ancient communal societies accorded transgendered men and women, and same-sex love, endured long after these societies underwent dramatic changes.

An Egyptian sculpture of a bearded Queen Hat-shepsut dressed in the garb of a pharaoh (1485 B.C.), for example, shows the persistence of popular folklore about the bearded woman as a sacred symbol of power and wisdom.

A link between transvestism and religious practice is also found in ancient myths associated with Greek gods and heroes. The myth of Achilles notes that he lived and dressed as a woman at the Court of Lycomedes in Scyros before he acquired his martial skills. ...

To "justify" the new economic system and break the spirit of people who had lived and worked communally, a systematic downgrading of the status of women and an assault on the transgendered population began.

An early prohibition against transgender was codified in the Mosaic Law of the Hebrews, one of the earliest patriarchal societies: "The woman shall not wear that which pertaineth unto a man, neither shall a man put on a woman's garment; for all that do so are abomination unto the Lord thy God" (*Deuteronomy*, 22:5).

The rise of the Greek city-states during the 8th to 6th centuries B.C., is another example of the subjugation of women. The new patriarchal economic system couldn't co-exist with matrilineage. But in many areas transgender, same-sex love and many of the old religious practices of transvestism continued to flourish, because they didn't yet threaten the new ruling order.

The slave-owners developed an ideology degrading women in order to justify overturning women's equality in society. Many of the early Greek myths and the numerous depictions in artwork of battles against Amazon warriors symbolized the overthrow of matrilineal communal societies and their replacement with patriarchal slave societies.

Patriarchal gods like the Greek deity Dionysos arose to overpower the pre-class goddesses. Dionysos was one of the Greek gods that replaced goddess worship. But Greek painters and writers portrayed Dionysos as feminine or dressed in women's apparel. Transvestism also persisted in the rituals of Dionysos, which endured even after Christianity became a state religion of the ruling elite.

The attitude toward women partly accounts for the growing hostility of the ruling classes toward transgendered men. But another aspect of the campaign against "effeminate" men, and Dionysos in particular, might have been to create a Rambo mentality, like the extreme appeal to "manhood" of the Nazi war machine or today's Pentagon.

These were "expand or die" militaristic societies. Unlike the war god Ares, Dionysos was a "make love, not war" god who encouraged soldiers to desert their posts in battle. …

The Persistence of Transgender

Although ruling attitudes toward cross-gendered expression were changing and becoming repressive, ancient respect for transgender proved difficult to eradicate and transgendered women and men continued to be present in all classes of society. …

The Natural Becomes "Unnatural"

Ancient religion, before the division of society into classes, combined collectively held beliefs with material observations about nature. Christianity as a mass religion really began in the cities of the Roman empire among the poor, and incorporated elements of collectivism and hatred of the rich ruling class. But over several hundred years, Christianity was transformed from a revolutionary movement of the urban poor into a powerful state religion that served the wealthy elite.

Transgender in all its forms became a target. In reality it was the rise of private property, the male dominated family and class divisions led to narrowing what was considered acceptable self-expression. What had been natural was declared its opposite.

As the Roman slave-based system of production disintegrated it was gradually replaced by feudalism. Laborers who once worked in chains were now chained to the land.

Christianity was an urban religion. But the ruling classes were not yet able to foist their new economic system, or the religion that sought to defend it, on the peasantry. The word pagan derives from the Latin paganus, which meant rural dweller or peasant. It would soon become a codeword in a violent class war.

Even after the rise of feudalism, remnants of the old pagan religion remained. It was joyously prosexual—lesbian, gay, bisexual and straight. Many women were among its practitioners. Many shamans were still transvestites. And transvestism was still a part of virtually all rural festivals and rituals.

In the medieval Feast of Fools, laymen and clergy alike dressed as women. The Faculty of Theology at the University of Paris reported priests "who danced in the choir dressed as women."

But in order for the land-owning Catholic church to rule, it had to stamp out the old beliefs that persisted from pre-class communal societies, because they challenged private ownership of the land.

Ancient respect for transgendered people still had roots in the peasantry. Transvestism played an important role in rural cultural life. Many pagan religious leaders were transgendered. So it was not surprising that the Catholic church hunted down male and female transvestites, labeling them as heretics, and tried to ban and suppress transvestism from all peasant rituals and celebrations.

By the 11th century, the Catholic church—by then the largest landlord in Western Europe—gained the organizational and military strength to wage war against the followers of the old beliefs. The campaign was carried out under a religious banner—but it was a class war against the vestiges of the older communal societies. ...

Transgender Endures

... Throughout the Middle Ages and into early industrial capitalism, transvestism continued to play an important role in many militant struggles as a form of social and political rebellion against class rule. ...

As the old land-based feudal order was replaced by capitalism, the very existence of transvestite and other transgendered women and men had been largely driven underground. Many were forced to pass as the opposite sex in order to survive. Transvestite women passed as men and became soldiers, pirates and highway robbers. Yet transvestism continued to emerge culturally throughout Europe in holiday celebrations, rituals, carnival days, masquerade parties, theater and opera.

These transgender traditions persist today in the Mummer's Festival, Mardi Gras and Halloween. In contemporary imperialist Japan cross-gendered roles are still at the heart of ancient Noh drama and Kabuki theater. But these are not merely vestiges of tradition. Transgendered women and men still exist, no matter how difficult their struggle for survival has become.

Transgender Around the World

Our focus has been on European history, and consciously so. The blame for anti-transgender laws and attitudes rests squarely on the shoulders of the ruling classes on that continent. The seizures of lands and assets of the "accused" during the witch trials and Inquisition helped the ruling classes acquire the capital to expand their domination over Asia, Africa and the Americas. The European elite then tried to force their ideology on the peoples they colonized around the world.

But despite the colonialists' racist attempts at cultural genocide, transvestism and other transgendered expression can still be observed in the rituals and beliefs of oppressed peoples. It is clear that they held respected public roles in vast numbers of diverse societies in cultures continents apart.

Since the 16th century, "transvestite shamans have ... been reported among the Araucanians, a large tribe living in southern Chile and parts of Argentina. ... Male transvestite shamans have also been reported for the Guajira, a cattle-herding people of northwest Venezuela and north Colombia, and the Tebuelche, hunter-gatherers of Argentina" (*Construction*).

"Transvestism also used to be practiced by shamans in the Vietnamese countryside, Burma, in India among the Pardhi, a hunting people, and in the southeast, by the Lhoosais, as well as in Korea" (*Construction*).

Transgender in religious ceremony is still reported in areas of West Africa. "One of the principal deities of the Aborney pantheon is Lisa-Maron, a figure which incorporates both man and woman; the great god Shango can be represented as either male or female; and contemporary shamans in Brazil worship Yansan, who is the 'man-woman'" (*Dressing Up*).

"The mugawe, a powerful religious leader of the Kenyan Meru, is considered a complement to the male political leaders and consequently must exemplify feminine qualities: he wears women's clothing and adopts women's hairstyles; he is often homosexual, and sometimes marries a man. Among the Kwayama, a tribe of Angolan Bantu cultivators and herders, many diviners, augerers, and diagnosers of illness wear women's clothing, do women's work, and become secondary spouses of men whose other wives are female. South African Zulu diviners are usually women, but roughly 10 percent are male transvestites" (*Construction*).

Male-to-female transgender that doesn't appear to have a special religious significance has been reported in the pastoral Nandi of Kenya, the Dinka and Nuer of the Sudan, the agricultural Konso and Amhara of Ethiopia, the Ottoro of Nubia, the Fanti of Ghana, the Ovimbundu of Angola, the Thonga farmers of Zimbabwe, the Tanala and Bara of Madagascar, the Wolof of Senegal, and the Lango, Iteso, Gisu, and Sebei of Uganda (*Construction*).

Cross-dressing is still a feature in Brazilian and Haitian ceremonies derived from West African religions (*Construction*).

The Chukchee, Kamchadal, Koryak, and Inuits—all Native peoples of the Artic Basin—had male shamans who dressed as women.

"In India, the Vallabha sect, devotees of Krishna, dressed as women … Reports, of the 1870s and 1930s, describe the priests (*bissu*) of the Celebes who live and dress as women" (*Dressing Up*). …

Passing for Survival

By the time the Industrial Revolution in Europe had forged plowshares into weapons and machinery, prejudice against transgendered women and men was woven deep into the tapestry of exploitation.

But mercantile trade and early industrial capitalism created opportunities for anonymity that seldom existed under feudalism, where the large serf families and their neighbors lived and worked on the land.

Capitalism unchained the peasants from the land—but chained them to machinery as wage slaves, or sent them off in armies and armadas to conquer new land, labor and resources.

Not only transgendered women but men now had the opportunity to pass. The oppression of women under capitalism forced many thousands of women who weren't transgendered to pass as men in order to escape the economic and social inequities of their oppression.

The consequences for passing were harsh. At the close of the 17th century the penalty in England was to be placed in the stocks and dragged through the streets in an open cart. In France as late as 1760 transvestites were burned to death.

Despite the criminal penalties, women passed as men throughout Europe—most notably in the Netherlands, England and Germany. Passing was so widespread during the 17th and 18th centuries that it was the theme of novels, fictionalized biographies and memoirs, art, plays, operas and popular songs. …

… [D]espite long being termed "illegal" and "unnatural" and still carrying with it an "unofficial" death penalty, transvestism is still a part of human expression.

Transvestites and other transgendered people were leaders of the first wave of gay liberation that began in the 1880s in Germany. That movement enjoyed the support of many in the mass Socialists parties.

Magnus Hirschfeld, a Jewish gay leader of the first wave of gay liberation in Germany in the 1880s, was also reported to be transvestite. He wrote a ground-breaking work on the subject. Most of the valuable documentation this movement uncovered about transgender throughout history, along with research about lesbians and gay men, was burned in a pyre by the Nazis. …

Transgendered roles are still seen—most frequently as "comedy"—on television and in film, theater, literature, dance and music. But the social penalties for transgendered people who try to live and work in dignity and respect are still cruel and frequently violent.

Christine Jorgensen Battled Bigotry

The development of anesthesia and the commercial synthesis of hormones are relatively recent discoveries of this century. These breakthroughs opened the possibility for individuals to change their sex to conform with their gender. Since that time, tens of thousands of transsexuals in this country alone have made the same life decision that Christine Jorgensen made.

While Jorgensen was not the first person to have a sex-change, she was by far the most well-publicized. She died May 3, 1989, at age 62 after a battle with cancer. Jorgensen was remembered in mainstream media obituaries as George Jorgensen, the Bronx-born ex-GI and photographer who traveled to Denmark in the early 1950s to become Christine—the first reported sex-change.

These accounts admit to an "international fuss" over her life decision, but add that she was "transformed into an instant celebrity. She traveled the lecture and nightclub circuit, met royalty and celebrities and ended up rich" (*New York Daily News*, May 4, 1989).

Sounds like a Harlequin novel, doesn't it? This is sheer hypocrisy coming from the media—and the ruling powers guiding their pens—that made Jorgensen the object of universal ridicule. Not once during her lifetime did anyone who controls this society say that Christine Jorgensen was a human being deserving respect.

The news of Jorgensen's sex change was leaked to the press in late 1952—one of the deepest periods of political reaction in the history of the United States. It was the height of the notorious McCarthy witch hunts, when hundreds were dragged into court and put in prison simply for their political views. The Rosenbergs were sitting on death row, awaiting electrocution at Sing-Sing. Pentagon planes bombed Korea and tested the hydrogen bomb in the South Pacific.

Jim Crow laws still ruled the South. Gay men and lesbians were fighting for survival without a movement. Transvestism was only acceptable when it was "Uncle Milty" Berle putting on drag for guffaws.

When the news about Christine Jorgensen hit, all hell broke loose. From appalled news commentators to cruel talk show hosts, she was attacked so viciously it seemed she was exiled from the human race.

What had been an important private decision was seized on by a hostile media and vulgarized. Her personal life was no longer her own. She was relentlessly hounded. Jorgensen told the media a year before her death: "I'm not that recognizable anymore. I can actually go into a supermarket and people don't know who I am, which is just wonderful and suits me just fine.

"Things don't hurt the way they did then," she added.

Somehow she paid this punishing emotional price and survived with grace and dignity. It took great courage.

The attacks on Jorgensen were part of a campaign meant to enforce conformity, but it was too late in history for this to succeed.

Jorgensen told the press in 1986:"I could never understand why I was receiving so much attention. Now, looking back, I realize it was the beginning of the sexual revolution, and I just happened to be one of the trigger mechanisms."

From Joan of Arc to Stonewall

In the last decades, the development of technology rendered many of the occupational divisions between men and women obsolete. Women were joining the work force in larger numbers, becoming a part of the working class in the most active and immediate sense. This shaped a whole new consciousness.

The contraceptive pill, first produced in 1952, virtually revolutionized social relations for many women, and allowed women to participate in all phases of life with the same freedom from unwanted pregnancies as men.

Rigidly enforced gender boundaries should also have been scrapped. But the motor force of capitalism still drives prejudice and inequity as a vehicle for division. It took monumental struggles—and still greater ones remain on the horizon—to right these wrongs.

The civil rights and national liberation movements of the 1950s and 1960s, and the massive resistance to the Vietnam war, rocked the world and helped give rise to the women's liberation struggle as well.

In 1969, militant young gay transvestites in New York City's Greenwich Village led a fight against cops who tried to raid the Stonewall Inn. The battles lasted for four nights running. The Stonewall Rebellion gave birth to a modern lesbian and gay rights movement that will never again be silenced behind closet doors.

From peasant uprisings against feudalism in the Middle Ages to the Stonewall Rebellion in the 20th century, transvestites and other transgendered people have figured in many militant struggles, both in defense of the right of personal expression and as a form of political rebellion.

But from the violence on the streets to the brutality of the police, from job discrimination to denial of health care and housing—survival is still a battle for the transgendered population.

Transgendered people are the brunt of cruel jokes on television and in films. Movies like "*Psycho*," "*Dressed to Kill*" and "*Silence of the Lambs*" create images of transgendered people as dangerous sociopaths.

In "*Silence of the Lambs*," a sort-of-transvestite, wanna-be-transsexual kills women and skins them in order to sew a woman's body for himself. The film turns reality upside down: It is actually transvestites and transsexuals who have been the victims of grisly murders.

This point was driven home by activists who disrupted the National Film Society awards in spring 1992. They passed out fliers highlighting the real-life murder of transsexual Venus Xtravaganza, who appeared in the documentary "*Paris is Burning*." Xtravaganza was murdered before the film on Harlem's drag balls was finished.

"*Silence of the Lambs*" swept the Academy Awards. "*Paris is Burning*" wasn't even nominated.

Fighting for a Better World

The institutionalized bigotry and oppression we face today have not always existed. They arose with the division of society into exploiter and exploited. Divide-and-conquer tactics have allowed the slave-owners, feudal landlords and corporate ruling classes to keep for themselves the lion's share of wealth created by the laboring class.

Like racism and all forms of prejudice, bigotry toward transgendered people is a deadly carcinogen. We are pitted against each other in order to keep us from seeing each other as allies.

Genuine bonds of solidarity can be forged between people who respect each other's differences and are willing to fight their enemy together. We are the class that does the work of the world, and can revolutionize it. We can win true liberation.

The struggle against intolerable conditions is on the rise around the world. And the militant role of transgendered women, men and youths in today's fight-back movement is already helping to shape the future.

SECTION II

THEORIZING INTERSECTING IDENTITIES

INTRODUCTION

The 1980s saw the explosion of writings by women of color and transnational feminist scholars that redirected the focus of feminist theory. These writings embody vibrant debates about the intersections of race, nation, colonialism, sexuality, class, and gender for understanding women's complex situations. In this way, marginalized experiences of women situated otherwise were not simply told or uncovered. They expressed an "oppositional consciousness" that intervened in the flow of "hegemonic feminist theory" (Sandoval 1990). The intellectual efforts to understand intersecting differences, however, have been located in separate, although often overlapping and sometimes fractious, intellectual communities. Scholars in multiple identity-based sites across the world struggled to understand the connections and disconnections between gender and specific intersections of greatest concern to them. The readings in this section were assembled with these tensions in mind. Like a kaleidoscope in which a jumble of objects are refracted through a prism in constantly shifting patterns, the readings offer as a shifting prism of difference through which to examine the mobile and multiple configurations of domination in our lives.

The readings are arranged in two subsections that approach the task of theorizing intersectionality from different angles. The readings in subsection, Social Processes/Configuring Differences, refer to those social spaces and practices in which bodies, institutions, and ideologies meet, interact, and shape each other. The readings offer intersectional analyses of gender relations with different combinations of class, race, ethnicity, nationality, and sexuality. Not all the readings deal with all of these intersections, each brings specific intersections into focus. In so doing, the readings highlight the ways in which feminist theorists conceptualize relational differences of class, race/ethnicity, nation, and sexuality. Recognizing that social processes always involve "the interplay of structures and agency," the second subsection, Boundaries and Belongings, presents experiential perspectives on intersecting identities (Parreñas Reading 20). Written by scholars and theorists, each reading reflects on tensions pervading experiences of intersecting identities in their personal history, intellectual work, and/or their activism. The readings narrate the challenges involved in crossing boundaries and negotiating the terms of belonging in community. Together they demonstrate the value of lived experiences in intersectional analyses and give depth to the meaning of the politics of location.[1]

Social Processes/Configuring Differences

As noted in the Section I Introductory Essay, the conversations about differences between women, which at first relied on an additive model of oppression, led to a more fluid, flexible model for conceptualizing difference—intersectionality. As initially articulated by Kimberle Crenshaw, intersectionality offered a "methodology that ultimately will disrupt the tendencies to see race and gender as exclusive or separable" (Crenshaw 1993: 1244).[2] Recent intersectional analyses builds on her formulation by paying attention to the "relationships and interactions between multiple axes of identity and multiple dimensions of social organization—at the same time" (Dill and Zambrana Reading 18).

Bonnie Thornton Dill and Ruth Enid Zambrana provide a comprehensive review of intersectionality as feminist "analytic strategy" in Reading 18. They trace intersectional thinking back to early women's and ethnic studies, but note that it has roots in social justice movements as well. They note that "inequality and oppression are deeply woven into the tapestry of American life." And yet, because social scientific theories of inequality have ignored the ways "dimension[s] of inequality" are co-constituted, they cannot adequately account for the experiences of women of color. The intersectional approach identifies subjects that "occupy multiple social locations," attends to the complexity of their experiences, and all the while remains committed to social justice. This commitment is articulated through building knowledge that "incorporates the many contradictory and overlapping ways that human life is experienced," while paying attention to how power operates in and through social structures, interpersonal relationships, discourse, and representation (Reading 18). Ultimately, the authors argue that intersectionality offers four interventions: (1) It grounds theory in the lived experiences of the marginalized so as to identify counterhegemonic narratives. This allows theorists to identify not just oppression but also to pay attention to privilege. (2) It pushes theory beyond essentialized identity categories by allowing for nuanced accounts of complexity and variation within and across difference. It forces us to consider the various possible meanings of terms, like Latino/a, African American, Asian American, and white, as well as the heterogeneity held within the category. (3) It attends to the multiple domains of power (structural, disciplinary, hegemonic, and interpersonal) that operate with and through each other in the people's lives. (4) Intersectionality maintains a political commitment to empower its subjects through work that combines "advocacy, analysis, policy development, theorizing, and education." Highlighting examples of intersectionality at work in global and national activism, Dill and Zambrana conclude that "transformative is perhaps one of the best words to characterize this scholarship" because it transforms knowledge and uses that knowledge to transform society" (Reading 18).

Heidi Hartmann presents the socialist-feminist concept of class (Reading 19) thorough her discussion of the 1970s debates about how to understand the relationship of gender and class.[3] Her essay, which circulated in mimeographed form for many years before it was formally published, elaborates on one socialist-feminist solution: dual systems theory, which treated class and patriarchy as separate systems that worked in tandem.[4]

Hartmann begins with Marx's notion of historical materialism. Marx famously said, "As people express their lives, so they are." He meant that the ways people organized the activities of making the things they need to live—food, clothing, shelter, tools—and to make human beings themselves are the key factors that shape history (Marx 1977: 161, 162; see also Engels 1972). Historical materialism, as a method for understanding society and history, focuses on this material reality, the forces and relations of production and reproduction. In this scheme, an individual's class is determined by their location in relationship to the dominant mode of production in a given historical period. For Marx, capitalism involved a two-class system: The working class, or proletariat, who do not own property (capital[5]) and have only their labor power with which to make a living, and the capitalist class, the bourgeoisie, who own capital and therefore have the power to define the conditions of life and work for everyone. This economic inequality is normalized through cultural ideology that valorizes the bourgeoisie and deprecates the working classes.

In practice, as Hartmann notes, Marx and Marxists ignore the relations and forces of reproduction and with it the system of patriarchy that, she argues, subordinates women. She defines patriarchy as the "set of social relations between men … though hierarchical … enables them to dominate women." She argues that, like the class system, patriarchy has a material base: men's control of women's sexuality and their access to resources. Where Marx mistakenly saw the sexual division of labor as natural, Hartmann theorizes it as social. Following Gayle Rubin, Hartmann calls the system that underlies patriarchy the sex/gender system, and details how the system secures male-domination by restricting women's access to resources and by constraining their sexuality. She also examines the uneasy partnership that developed historically between capitalism and patriarchy. She concludes that because the capitalist class system alone does not produce women's subordination, socialism alone will not eliminate it. Feminist theory and activism is needed as well. While Hartman does note that race, like gender, serves as a system of domination, she does not elaborate a theory of the intersections of gender and class with race and nation.

As a system of domination, race is generally recognized as a categorization of humans into groups who possess distinct phenotypic appearances (Omi and Winant 1994). Yet, race has never been just about skin color or character, it is part of the "construction and naturalization of unequal forms of inter-cultural relations" (Ashcroft et al. 1998: 46). Racial classifications developed in the context of European capitalist and colonialist expansion that began four hundred years ago. The fullest articulation of racial categories came in European and American racial sciences of the late nineteenth century. The concept of race has been central to organizing global inequality that accompanied colonial expansion and accomplished European cultural and economic imperialism. Colonialism refers to the processes of empire-building—imperialism—in which regions outside of Europe were claimed by European nations, and organized into economic, bureaucratic, military, and ideological relationships with them. This occupation of territory was justified through a racialized discourse of civilization. Racial classifications lent credibility to the claim of natural superiority by which European nations sought to legitimate their occupation and domination of other cultures (Ashcroft et al. 1998 and Stoler 2000). Likewise, racial classifications provided a natural basis for the rigid hierarchy of difference between the colonizer and the colonized and between slaves and slave owners.

Conventional histories of 'Western Civilization' note that colonialism involved the dispersal of Europeans across the world, a "Europeanization of the globe" (Ashcroft et al. 1998: 123). However, colonialism also involved the movement of many peoples from their homelands to other regions. For instance, the slave trade involved the involuntary movement of millions of Africans to North and South America and the Caribbean. In addition, after slavery was outlawed in Europe in the nineteenth century, systems of indenture "resulted in worldwide colonial diasporas."[6] "[L]arge populations of agricultural laborers from population rich areas, such as India and China, [were transported] to areas where they were needed to service plantations." Descendants of these groups have developed their own cultures, which "preserve and extend" their "originary cultures." Today, the major diasporic movements also involve the movement of "colonized peoples back to the metropolitan centers" (Ashcroft et al. 1998: 69–70). As Rhacel Parreñas notes, historical and contemporary diasporas involve complicated relationships to homelands and "many elsewheres" (Reading 20).

Like the classification of humans by race, the idea of the nation, is a product of European expansion. The nation, a "natural and immutable formation based on shared collective values," is the entity for which the colonies were claimed (Ashcroft et al. 1998: 151). National wellbeing justified the subordination of other people and places. However, the nation, itself, is "an imagined community" (Anderson 1983). Most citizens will never know or even meet most of their compatriots, but national myths, holidays, and patriotic rituals, such as commemorations on Independence Day, bind citizens to one another in their imaginations. These beliefs and rituals hold the nation together and tie it to territory. Its position relative to other nations is central to the imaginary community of a nation. As Edward Said has demonstrated the imagined community of European and European American nations was built on an "imaginary geography" of Orientalism that mirrored "the West's" self-proclaimed superiority to the rest of the world, but particularly 'the East' (Said 1978). At the same time, the boundaries between the nation (us) and the colonized (them), erased internal differences homogenizing myths and rituals of national tradition (Ashcroft et al. 1998).[7] The nation has not been limited to "the West." It extended into the colonized world as liberation movements directed at ending colonialism established new nations. These new nations likewise depend on imagined common identity and the erasure of internal difference. Mrinalini Sinha (Reading 22) notes that the nation is thus always unstable, because such erasures are never complete, and re-emerging differences disrupt hegemonic national myths.[8]

Intensified globalization in the last decades of the twentieth century has also undermined the sovereignty of nations. Global networks of cultures and markets have existed for centuries, certainly. Recent processes, however, differ from earlier periods in the greater speed and farther reach of communications and financial technologies. Financial markets are so closely integrated across time and space that national economies are no longer autonomous. With the increasing movement of capital, commodities, and people across their borders, the boundaries of nations are blurred and nations have struggled to build a stable basis for sovereignty (Parreñas Reading 20).

Chandra Talpade Mohanty enormously influential article, "Under Western Eyes: Feminist Scholarship and Colonial Discourses," published in 1986 challenged hegemonic feminism from a transnational feminist perspective (see Mohanty Reading 48). In a meticulous analysis of the conventional representations of "Third World Women" in

First World feminist texts, Mohanty illuminates how those texts reproduce elements of colonial discourse. As Mohanty says, "the point" of feminist texts "is not just 'to record' one's history of struggle or consciousness, but how they are recorded; the way we read, receive and disseminate such imaginative records is immensely significant" (Mohanty 1991a: 34). With this analysis, intellectual space opened to prioritize the politics of geopolitical location. The essays by Rhacel Parreñas (Reading 20), Lila Abu-Lughod (Reading 21), and Mrinalini Sinha (Reading 22) make clear that gender is central to historical racial and colonial discourses as well as to contemporary globalization processes. Transnational feminist scholars, they attend to the contradictions of globalization and how asymmetrical power relations structure feminist texts, coalitions, and solidarities.

Rhacel Parreñas (Reading 20) provides an overview of recent globalization processes. Drawing on the work of feminist economist Saskia Sassen, she elaborates the characteristic features of current global capitalism. In particular, she notes that the last two decades have seen the formation of global cities characterized by high-end financial profits centers and low wage jobs, massive movements of people to fill those low wage jobs, and the feminization of the international division of labor. In response, nations have tightened the restrictions on citizenship. Thus, people may gain entrance into the nation, but not necessarily membership in it. With this background, Parreñas investigates how the social processes of state regulation, familial separations, and exploitative working conditions shape the situation of Filipina migrant domestic workers. These social processes, she argues, configure the women as "dislocated" subjects. Observing that individual agency is configured in and through the "situations and statuses conferred" on persons, she argues that "subjects cannot be removed from external forces that constitute the meanings of their existence." In the case of Filipina migrant workers, "non-belonging" defines the "boundaries of existence and exercise of agency" in their lives (Reading 20). Agency, she notes, is both enabled and limited by institutional processes, and she details how the women negotiate these processes as they build their lives.

Lila Abu-Lughod (Reading 21) introduces the concepts of colonial discourse and especially Orientalism. Although Edward Said did not initially account for gender, she notes that feminists in the global south have used this analytic tool extensively. Abu-Lughod begins with the observations that "the power of Orientalism comes from its power to construct the very object it speaks about" (Reading 21). That is, Orientalism is not just a system of representations. Orientalist discourses are part of the wider "Western style of dominating, restructuring, and having authority over the Orient" (Said 1978: 3). These power relations pose specific dilemmas for Middle East feminist scholars, because their work is "implicated in projects that establish Western authority and cultural difference." Abu-Lughod notes four strands of feminist research that engage Orientalism. The first is the extensive work done to "explore gender and sexuality in Orientalist discourses." The second uses history and anthropology to counter stereotypes of Muslim and Middle East gender relations. The third investigates the history of Middle East feminism. Finally, "politically engaged scholarship" engages the "peculiar way that feminist critique" circulates in an asymmetrical global context. She reminds readers that the flow is not simply in one direction. A conceptual framework that relies on monolithic binaries between West/non-West, ignores the "worldliness of all cultural production" and the multidirectional flows connecting them (Reading 21).

Mrinalini Sinha (Reading 22) summarizes feminist scholarship on the place and meaning of gender in the social processes of nation and nationalism. She notes that national myths often rely on kinship imagery to ground the "blood" and "bond" of national belonging. Moreover, national identities are gendered through normative formulations of masculinity and femininity in figures of good men and women—the heroic and the honorable—on which the nation's wellbeing depends. Such norms are configured in bodies, dress codes, and sexual behavior. Sinha details the gendering of citizenship. That is, in many nations the right to vote, to serve in public office or the military, as well as the right to marry, divorce, have children, and travel are also differentiated by gender. Such differentiation often institutionalizes gender subordination and discounts women's contributions to struggles to establish nationhood.

Sinha focuses in particular on the complex intertwining of gender and nation in colonialism. Colonial rulers often justified their cultural intervention in the name of improving the status of women. Such practices make women's situation a political token within the hierarchical relationships of patriarchal colonialism. She notes, "Womanhood has been used to embody both the promise and the threat of modernity" Women and their status can signal the move towards modernity as well as the limits that must be placed on it. When the status of women is used in this way, it becomes very challenging for feminists in/from post-colonial cultures to criticize the gender politics of our culture. To do so could result in our complaints being taken as evidence that the men of our culture are not as civilized as Western men are, and thus, our complaints may be seen as traitorous to our cultures.[9] The accusation of betrayal can be a powerful force to silence gender contestation. Yet, at the same time, the deprecating representations of colonial discourse can foster greater embrace of national gender norms. These themes are taken up by several readings in the Boundaries and Belongings subsection.

A distinct but overlapping strand of conversation and debate in the 1980s and 1990s dealt with the complex relationships of sex, gender, and sexuality. Feminist discussions of sexuality shifted in the mid-1980s and 1990s as a multi-gendered LGBT community coalesced in response to the homophobic politics surrounding the AIDS epidemic. In that moment, lesbian feminists moved beyond earlier separatist perspectives and began a new dialogue about the queer commonalities across gender differences. At the same time, lesbian feminists began to raise new questions about the relationship of gender, sex, and sexuality in feminist theory (see Calhoun Reading 38 and Walters Reading 49). An early perspective on the politics of lesbian feminism is represented by Monique Wittig's essay (Reading 23). She frames lesbian politics, around her analysis of the relation between women and the myth of woman—the dominant cultural representation that "marks" actual women as different from but "belong[ing] to men." The myth of woman is that representation of the "natural" woman to which actual women must conform in "servitude" to men. Thus, as does de Beauvoir, Wittig argues that women are made by culture and not born in nature. However, she extends this claim, observing that heterosexuality is the means by which women are bound to men. Given the ties that bind women to the myth of woman, Wittig poses a political question: How can we distinguish strategies for the liberation of women from strategies for securing the dominion of the myth of woman? How can we distinguish when women are speaking for the myth of woman and when they are resisting it? The answers to these questions hinge on developing the insights of the lesbian feminist. Concurring with Charlotte Bunch (Reading 15), Wittig's lesbian feminist "refusal to become (or to remain) heterosexual" amounts to "the refusal of the economic, ideological, and political power of a man." Outside of the category of woman, the lesbian has a unique vantage point from which to begin to define "a new personal and subjective definition for all humankind." In her view, movement beyond the categories of sex "can be accomplished only by the destruction of heterosexuality as a social system," the system that produces the doctrine of sex differences to justify the oppression of women (Reading 23)

The field of masculinity studies also emerged in the 1990s to investigate social processes that configure experiences of masculinity. In her essay, Raewyn Connell, a leading theorist in masculinity studies, defines gender as the "social processes of configuring practices" involving bodies and the "everyday conduct of life" in relation to the "reproductive arena" (Reading 24). That is, the practices that enact, for instance, family life, birthing, parenting, marriage and love, are shaped by social processes that constrain which individuals can participate in which of these practices and when. As an example, consider the current debates about the right to marry. For Connell, hegemonic forms of femininity and masculinity configure (and are configured through) these gender practices. Using the concept of hegemonic masculinity, Connell investigates how patriarchal power relations, gendered market relations, and heteronormative structures of desire subordinate women and valorize men. Hegemonic masculinity, Connell argues, depends upon the complicity of men, the subordination of some masculinities, and marginalization of non-normative patterns of gender relations. The subordination of gay men is, in her estimation, a central feature of contemporary hegemonic masculinity. At the same time, she argues, the global gender regime hinges on the racialized discourses by which men of color and of the global south are likewise marginalized. In both cases, unfavorable contrasts to femininity feature prominently.

Boundaries and Belongings

One of the most important writings during this period was *This Bridge Called My Back*, published in 1981. It was one of the first anthologies by U.S. self-defined women of color and it constructed women of color as an identity of positive acclamation, not the negation of whiteness. In a variety of genres, the contributors use their marginalized experience "to remember and to renarrate everyday experiences of domination and resistance, and to situate these experiences in relation to broader historical phenomena" (Stone-Mediatore 2000: 117). Donna Kate Rushin's "The Bridge Poem" (Reading 25), first appeared in *This Bridge*, and it represents the tone of the anthology—"pain and anger, faith, and fervor" (Foster 1983: 133). Rushin's words, express the frustration of a woman of color who has continually been used as a bridge to connect people in different locations. She has had enough of doing work for others so that they can realize the limits and potentials of their positions. The bridge in the poem, and in the anthology title, thus signifies how women of color have been walked over, literally and figuratively, as others find themselves and their freedom. She tells the reader to either "stretch or drown," because she is no longer going to be there to fill the gap. Instead, she is going to focus her energies on building a bridge "to her own power" to her "true self." In the Forward to the second edition, the anthology editor, Gloria Anzaldúa, declares, "There are no more bridges, one builds them as one walks" (1981: n.p.). The poem captures the emotions that informed investment in identity politics and disengagement from difficult dialogues across asymmetrical differences. It also exemplifies the call to accountability women of color issued to those women represented by hegemonic feminism to investigate the mechanism of privilege that they enjoy.

June Jordan's (Readings 26) thoughtful meditation of the shifting processes of race, class, gender, and sexuality in her professional and personal life leads her to reconsider the processes identification and connection. The essay highlights the knowledge that can come through reflexive analysis of experience as Jordan reflects on the complex interplay of bodies, institutions, and ideologies as she travels from Boston to the Bahamas. The essay considers the shifting historical nexus of race, nation, colonialism, and global capitalism that comes into focus and conflict at different moments in her trip. She finds that the experiential basis for collective action is not always as obvious as categories of race, class, and sexuality might lead us to believe. Instead, the potential for making common cause is fluid. Shifting experiences of power can facilitate or hinder identification with others. Connection can come in unexpected ways.

An exemplar of the generative insights of reconfiguring experience can be seen in Gloria Anzaldúa's work. In her now classic volume, *Borderlands/La Frontera: The New Mestiza,*she traces her shifting identity as a Mexican American lesbian as she crosses boundaries of community. These experiences of shifting identity, she argues, are the grounds for a "new higher consciousness" of the multiple logics of power, which she calls "mestiza consciousness" (Anzaldúa 1987).[10] Residing in the borderlands, the new mestiza learns to shift identities between contexts, to bridge cultures, and thus, to come up with new strategies (Mohanty 1991a). While the experiences of multiple shifting identities is painful, the mestiza not only "sustains contradictions, she turns the ambivalence into something else," a perspective that "includes rather than excludes" (Anzaldúa 1987).

Written some years later, the essay included here (Reading 27) "claims multicultural education as a centerpiece of the mestiza nation." Reflecting on her location as a "Chicana Tejana dyke from a working-class background" and college professor, she argues for a pedagogy that represents the marginalized, an approach that does not silence "alter-narratives," but includes them. Such pedagogy would highlight the links between "lived experience … political struggles, and art-making." Speaking to the challenges of building this new curriculum, she argues that the new mestiza risks being "worn down by the costs of an exclusionary education." Working in the "oppressor's terrain makes for a complex identity." She risks being co-opted or "assimilated." Yet, as a "luminal subject," she is someone who "lives in borderlands" and bridges communities. A new and effective "methodology of resistance," she concludes "asks how people negotiate multiple worlds every day" (Reading 27). She recommends a process of conscious positioning, of always asking how one can engage accountably from one's own specific location within the intersecting categories of difference—gender, race, ethnicity, class, sexuality, and nation.

In her essay, Minnie Bruce Pratt (Reading 28) discusses her complicated relationship with notions of "home," and how her identity and embodied experiences shape her relations with others as she moves through the landscape of her neighborhood and her personal history. Reflecting on her position as a white woman from the U.S. south, she considers what pull myths of home can have for white women. She ponders the dimensions of race, class, and First World privilege and asks how we can be accountable to them. How can we reposition ourselves in interactions across differences? Arguing that we must "walk into change," she reviews what she learned in the landscape of her privileged and constrained youth, and asks what she was taught not to see. In this way, she illustrates how white women might learn to draw from the strengths of their heritage and culture and yet reject racist and Orientalist appeals to national belonging. She concludes that we must "expand [our] constricted eye" if we are to make effective coalitions with women of color in the U.S and the global south (Reading 28).

Throughout her writings, Audre Lorde, continuously draws attention to the interconnectedness of gender, race, and sexual identity As a lesbian of color, she criticized the strategy of lesbian separatism advocated by Charlotte Bunch (Reading 15) and Monique Wittig (Reading 23) as an unworkable strategy for lesbians of color (Lorde 1984). As Barbara Smith has noted, lesbians of color have good reasons for solidarity with men of color (Smith and Smith 1981; Smith 1983). Yet while separatism is unworkable, Lorde sees that organizing across differences is very challenging for black women as well. In the piece included here (Reading 29), Lorde addresses the exclusions lesbians of color have had to confront within their racial/ethnic/cultural communities. She illuminates the complexity of heterosexism and homophobia by which her identity as a lesbian is subsumed under her identity as a black woman in race-based identity politics, forcing her to hide to gain inclusion. She notes, "Heterosexism and homophobia are two grave barriers to organizing among Black women," and she challenges African-American women to see how they have clung to heterosexual privilege as one of the few privileges afforded them. Laying claim to kinship, Lorde recounts her antiracist activism as a lesbian and asserts, "I want to be recognized. I am a Black lesbian, and I am your sister." Black women, she concludes, must find ways to organize across "genuine" differences without either "denying them" or "blowing them out of proportion" (Reading 29). Lorde delineates the challenges of organizing around differences, with specific reference to homophobia within the U.S. black community. However, the observations can be extended to a variety of contexts within the intersections of oppressions.

In Reading 30, Lionel Cantu et al. raise issues of sexuality for transnational communities of color and weigh the challenges of organizing around issues of sexual identity in diaspora. Reacting to the pejorative cultural representations required of political asylum seekers, the authors argue that social processes enacted in controlling national boundary crossings replicate conventional ideologies of gender and sexuality. In reaffirming gender and sexual conventions, this boundary work helps the nation reaffirm its identity in the face of transnational movements of people, cultures, and commodities. In particular, the essay discusses the complex performance of race, gender, and sexuality required of gay asylum seekers. The logic of the U.S. asylum hearing requires a demonstration of an "immutably gay identity" by petitioners and positions the United States as saving the petitioners from "the tyranny of their timeless cultures and communities ..." Thus these processes affirm an "essentialized construction of sexuality that functioned within strictly nationalist logic" of U.S. progressiveness and Third World backwardness (Reading 30). Cantu's analysis, drawn from his experiences as an expert witness at such hearings, illuminates how shifting contexts of queer identity can replicate colonial dominations in the pursuit of sexual freedom.

Leila Ahmed (Reading 31) also engages the complex politics of location in the contemporary world. A feminist scholar, she has made an extensive study of "the first debate on the veil in the Muslim world." In the essay here, she examines the politics and meanings of veiling in American Muslim communities in the post-9/11 world. Attuned to the complex history of veiling, she traces the grounds for three "master narratives of the veil." The first master narrative emerged British colonial discourse, which disparaged Egyptian society and culture. This discourse identified the veil as a marker of the backwardness that justified British rule. The British colonial regime advocated unveiling to free women from uncivilized male domination, thus participating in the discourse of "white men saving brown women from brown men." The second master narrative emerged from Westernizing Egyptian elites for whom unveiling served as a marker of their embrace of the project of modernizing Egypt. Advocacy of women's rights was part of this discourse, and Egyptian feminists contributed to it. The third master narrative, the Islamist discourse, emerged in resistance to the pejorative image of Muslims in colonial discourse. It embraced veiling, not as a marker of the primitive, but as a specifically Muslim modernity. While this discourse embraced elements of women's rights, such as to education, those rights were limited by "divinely ordained" male dominance.

With this historical background, Ahmed considers the current politics of veiling. She notes that young women in the U.S. narrate their decision to veil in terms of choice rather than obligation, endeavoring to "empty it [the veil] of its patriarchal meaning." Moreover, she notes that indeed it serves very different purposes, including identification with and commitment to a minority community subjected to prejudice and repression. Yet, she argues, these new meanings are very local. The veil "could not have the same meaning in Saudi Arabia or Iran or any other place where there is no commitment to ideals of justice and equality for all." In such locations, "women ultimately are not free to make their own decisions." She concludes that globally the three master narratives are so intertwined that all are called forth in our perceptions and responses to the veil. Because "we are all mired in the meanings and histories of our times," what the veil will mean, how new local and existing global discourse will matter in the future, will depend on our commitment to social justice for all (Reading 31).

Obioma Nnaemeka (Reading 32) is a Nigerian scholar of women and development studies who resides and works in the United States. In the essay included here, she draws on the Igbo metaphor of masquerade to characterize the "history of feminist engagement (as theory and practice) nationally and globally." Following the lessons of the Igbo masquerade, feminist engagement, she argues, involves "shifting patterns, territorial claims, locations, movement, aesthetics, paradox, and perspectives." She notes that throughout its history feminism has faced the challenge of "articulating simultaneously commonality and difference." So far, it has not done so satisfactorily. First World "feminist arrogance" has marginalized African women and feminists through a "mindset" of "the West and the Rest of Us," that tends to lump together all women situated otherwise. From her perspective, race alone is not the issue. The complex politics of location that she describes involves both geography and status. Thus, she eschews the label, woman of color. She notes "naming and location converge" in the shifting acceptance and rejection of the label feminist by African women's advocates. African feminists prioritize their geo-political location within imperialism and its consequences in calling themselves African feminists. She concludes, that "naming feminism is an act of (agency) resistance that sustains its dynamism and expands its horizon." To name "one's location and struggle" sets an agenda and claims power. Self-named, we must then follow the example of the chameleon in "this journey that is feminist engagement." We must be "adaptable, tolerant, and accommodating" (Reading 32).

Native American feminist activist scholar Andrea Smith (Reading 33) discusses native women's engagement with feminism in the United States. She argues that gender and sexual violence in native communities are inextricably linked through processes of colonization and genocide. It was through sexual violence and imposition of their European gender norms and relations on native communities that Europeans were able to colonize native peoples in the first place. Rejecting a rigid binary of feminist/not feminist, Smith examines the complex and heterogeneous political stances, identities, and practices within Native American women's movements, which exist at the intersection of sovereignty and sexism. She draws on her activist experiences with issues of domestic violence and sexual violence against women and children in native communities to show that "issues of survival," often conceived exclusively in terms of sovereignty, are also issues of sexism. Women, therefore, she concludes, are in the center of movements for sovereignty and national survival. Moreover, as long as patriarchal gender systems are in place, a true decolonization and sovereignty will never be fully achieved. She argues that developing a native feminist politic around sovereignty requires a more critical and complex analysis of sexism and of feminism in native communities.

In the final section of the article, Smith questions the legitimacy of the United States and questions the western notion of nation-state as a form of domination and power over others. She argues that the nation-building project in native communities is a project of imagination, one that emphasizes interconnectedness, interdependency, and inclusiveness. In doing so, she sets apart the project of sovereignty from nationalist models (and from separatist models as well) by highlighting the importance of taking power from the status quo but using that power to build an alternative form of governance that is not based on domination, coercion, and control. This "utopian" society cannot be "fully imagined" in advance, but is a "collective, creative process" that is made "as we walk" (Reading 33).

Section II ends with an essay by Mari Matsuda (Reading 34), which examines the challenges of building coalitions across communities of difference. The occasion of her reflection is the 1990 Conference on Women of Color and the Law. Matsuda returns to a theme that has resonated across contemporary feminist movements.[11] She warns against the false comfort of avoiding "hard conversations" because it "seduces us into ignorance about the experiences of others and about the full meaning of our own lives." The essay incorporates accounts of three women's approaches to coalitions. For Matsuda, the value of these examples is that they provide a basis for building "theory out of coalition." The hard work of building coalitions has revealed that "all forms of subordination are interlocking and mutually reinforcing." She offers readers a method of intersectional analysis that she calls "ask the other question." In the face of one form of subordination, she suggests that we ask, what else is going on here? What are the "non-obvious relationships of domination in this situation?" That is, for example, when you "see something that looks racist ... ask where is the patriarchy in this?" When "something looks homophobic ... ask what are the class interests here?" (Reading 34). By asking the other questions, we may be better able to build our understanding of complex intersecting dominations and to negotiate more effective coalitional agendas for change.

As a whole, the readings in Section II illuminate the complex and recurrent dilemma of feminist theory: how to weigh differences both in terms of individual identities and in terms of political configurations of feminist activism. The readings demonstrate that the boundaries of difference within the social group, women, are ever in flux and must continually be defined, redefined, and always negotiated in specific times and places. As Patricia Williams has explained,

> while being black has been the most powerful social attribution in my life, it is only one of a number of governing narratives or presiding fictions by which I am constantly reconfiguring myself in the world. Gender is another, along with ecology, pacifism, my peculiar brand of colloquial English, and Roxbury, Massachusetts. The complexity of role identification, the politics of sexuality, the inflections of professionalized discourse—all describe and impose boundary in my life, even as they confound one another in unfolding spirals of confrontation, deflection, and dream. (Patricia Williams 1991: 256)

As Williams eloquently describes, gender is one axis of the matrix of domination that, along with others, imposes boundaries on any woman. Furthermore, a woman's identity can never be collapsed to a single dimension because identity is not only always relational, ever changing and fluid, but also inherently contradictory, layered, and conflicting. Because of these multi-layered differences, including the inherent differences "within" us, feminist scholars have argued that it is difficult to render identity as a secure anchor for politics (e.g. Minh-Ha 1989; Butler 1990; Scott 1992; and Brown 1995). They argue that "appeals to experience risk naturalizing ideologically conditioned categories that structure our experiences of self and world" (Stone-Mediatore 2000: 110). Likewise, they note, that "the evidence of experience ... becomes evidence for the fact of difference, rather than a way of exploring how difference is established, how it operates, how and in what ways it constitutes subjects who see and act in the world" (Scott 1992: 25). Even with these limitations, as Mohanty argues, "Stories of experiences have been vital to Third World feminist praxis" (Stone-Mediatore 2000: 116). So how do feminist theorists proceed? How can we weigh differences effectively? How can we assess the shifting identities and alliances produced by the intersecting boundaries within the matrix of domination? How can we ground feminist political practices? Finally, can our experiences usefully inform our knowledge? Section III delineates two important currents of feminist theorizing in a transnational world that offer thoughtful responses to these questions.

Notes

1. On the politics of location, see Kaplan and Grewal 1994; Rich 2001; and Mani Reading 41.
2. Crenshaw envisions intersectionality as "a provision concept linking contemporary politics with postmodern theory" (1244).
3. See, for example, Combahee River Collective Reading 13, Humphries 1977, Eisenstein 1978, and Sen 1980.
4. Iris Young coined the label dual systems theory. See Young 1980 and 1981.
5. Capital is a unique kind of property that has the ability to create more value. It includes things such as stocks bonds, and real estate.
6. Diaspora, first used to describe the situation of Jews in the Middle Ages, has come to refer to "the voluntary and involuntary movement of peoples from their homelands to other regions" (Ashcroft et al. 1998: 68).
7. The idea of the nation also conceals the power and practices of the nation-state. Thus, the nation is a "contentious site, on which ideas of self-determination and freedom, of identity, and unity collide with suppression and force, of domination and exclusion" (Ashcroft et al. 1998: 151).
8. Erasures and reemergence of difference are not enacted only in national myths, but as the twentieth century histories of genocide demonstrate, they are often violently enacted on national landscapes. See Powers 2002 for the history of twentieth-century genocides and U.S. knowledge and complicity.
9. This judgment also rebounds to European and First World women whose complaints of mistreatment are often dismissed with the response that they are well treated in comparison with women of other nations and, therefore, should be grateful.
10. Although past editions of this reader included an excerpt from *Borderlands/La Frontera*, we were unable to secure permission for this edition.
11. For an early vision of twenty-first-century feminist politics based on coalitions, see Bernice Johnson-Reagon 1983.

SOCIAL PROCESSES/
CONFIGURING DIFFERENCES

18.
CRITICAL THINKING ABOUT INEQUALITY: AN EMERGING LENS
Bonnie Thornton Dill and Ruth Enid Zambrana
(2009)

Inequality and oppression are deeply woven into the tapestry of American life. As a result large disparities exist on measures of income, wealth, education, housing, occupation, and social benefits. These disparities are neither new nor randomly distributed throughout the population, but occur in patterns along such major social divisions as race, gender, class, sexuality, nationality, and physical ability. Social scientists have traditionally analyzed inequalities by isolating these factors and treating them as if they are independent of one another. Even when their interactions are discussed they are still conceptualized as if they are largely independent forces that happen to overlap under specific conditions. For example, studies of race often focus upon contrasting Whites with Blacks and other racially identifiable groups without taking into account historical modes of incorporation of each group. Historical linkages and systemic interrelationships that reveal the underlying ways any one dimension of inequality is shaped by another are rarely fully examined. A problematic result is that the experiences of whole groups are ignored, misunderstood, or erased, particularly those of women of color.

This chapter discusses intersectionality as an innovative and emerging field of study that provides a critical analytic lens to interrogate racial, ethnic, class, physical ability, age, sexuality, and gender disparities and to contest existing ways of looking at these structures of inequality. It identifies and discusses four theoretical interventions that we consider foundational to this interdisciplinary intellectual enterprise. We argue that intersectionality challenges traditional modes of knowledge production in the United States and illustrate how this theory provides an alternative model that combines advocacy, analysis, theorizing, and pedagogy—basic components essential to the production of knowledge as well as the pursuit of social justice and equality.

Research and teaching that focuses on the intersections of race, ethnicity, gender, and other dimensions of identity is a relatively new approach to studying inequality. (Inequality for these purposes is defined as institutionalized patterns of unequal control over and distribution of a society's valued goods and resources such as land, property, money, employment, education, healthcare, and housing.) Intersectionality has gained its greatest influence in the post-civil rights era and has been developed and utilized most prominently in the new scholarship created in the interdisciplinary fields of ethnic studies,[1] women's studies, area studies, and, more recently, lesbian, gay, bisexual, and transgender studies, cultural studies, critical legal studies, labor studies, multicultural studies, American studies, and social justice education. Intersectional analysis begins with the experiences of groups that occupy multiple social locations and finds approaches and ideas that focus on the complexity rather than the singularity of human experience.

Traditional disciplinary boundaries and the compartmentalization and fixity of ideas are challenged by these emerging interdisciplinary fields. These fields seek not only to reexamine old issues in new ways, but also to shift the lens through which humanity and social life are viewed—identifying new issues, new forms, and new ways of viewing them. Thus intersectional scholarship reflects an ongoing intellectual and social justice mission that seeks to: (1) reformulate the world of ideas so that it incorporates the many contradictory and overlapping ways that human life is experienced; (2) convey this knowledge by rethinking curricula and promoting institutional change in higher education institutions; (3) apply the knowledge in an effort to create a society in which all voices are heard; and (4) advocate for public policies that are responsive to multiple voices. …

The Intersectional Lens: An Emerging Perspective

Discussion of the origins of intersectionality most often begins with the research, writings, and teaching by and about women of color in the United States (both native and migrant). Women of color scholars have used the idea of intersections to explain our own lives and to critique the exclusion of our experiences, needs, and perspectives from both White, Eurocentric, middle-class conceptualizations of feminism and male dominated models of ethnic studies. We have laid claim to a U.S. scholarly tradition that began in the nineteenth century with women like Maria Stewart and men like W.E.B. DuBois, whose work of "cultural social analysis," according to ethnic studies scholar Johnella Butler, claimed the right to articulate a sense of self and act on it.[2] Contemporary women of color have continued this legacy by locating ideas that explore the intersections of race, gender, ethnicity, and sexuality at the center of their thinking about their own lives and those of women, men and families of color (Baca Zinn & Dill, 1994; Collins, 1998, 2000; Crenshaw, 1993a and b; Davis, 1983; Anzaldúa, 1999; Dill, 1983; hooks, 1992; Moraga & Anzaldúa, 2002; Hull, Bell Scott, & Smith, 2003). Intersectionality is a product of seeking to have our voices heard and lives acknowledged.

Although considerable ground work for this kind of scholarship was laid first in the fields of ethnic and women's studies—areas that perhaps have the longest published record of grappling with these issues—as this body of ideas and knowledge grew and developed, new ways of thinking, which were emerging in other fields, began to influence one another, broadening the intellectual appeal and practical applicability of intersectional approaches to questions of identity and social life.

In addition to its academic and intellectual concerns, intersectional scholarship matters outside the academy because day-to-day life and lived experience is the primary domain in which the conceptualization and under-standing of these constructs is and has been grounded. Scholars emphasize that the work itself grew out of movements with a social justice agenda such as those focused on civil rights, women's rights, and the struggles to include ethnic studies within university curricula. Thus this work is not seen as emanating solely from a series of linked theoretical propositions but from an effort to improve society, in part, by understanding and explaining the lives and experiences of marginalized people and by examining the constraints and demands of the many social structures that influence their options and opportunities. For example, rather than think that one could understand the responses of young Black women to hip-hop music merely through an analysis that focuses on race, an intersectional framework would analyze the relationships among sexuality, gender, class, and popular culture, within an historical as well as a contemporary framework, in order to shed light on this phenomenon (Crenshaw, 1993a; Rose, 1994; Morgan, 1999; Pough, 2004).

One point of general agreement among intersectional scholars is that the experiences and texts of traditionally marginalized groups were not considered knowledge thirty years ago. Yet the writings, ideas, experiences, and perspectives of people whose lives were once considered unimportant are increasingly influencing traditional disciplines. In the field of sociology, for example, inter-sectional analysis has extended and combined traditional subareas of stratification, race and ethnicity, and family by drawing on conflict theory, theories of racialization (Omi & Winant, 1994; Oliver & Shapiro, 1995; Massey & Denton, 1993) and gender stratification (Lorber, 1994, 1998; Gardiner, 2002; Kimmel, 2000; Myers, Anderson, & Risman, 1998). These subareas, combined with ideas drawn from ethnic studies, critical legal theory, and postmodernism, explore the ways identity flows from and is entangled in those relationships and how systems of inequality (race, ethnicity, class, gender, physical ability, and sexuality) are embedded in and shape one another. Intersectionality is both a reflection of and influence upon some of the newer directions in fields such as history, sociology, legal studies, and anthropology to name a few. It does this by examining relationships and interactions between multiple axes of identity and multiple dimensions of social organization—at the same time.

… [W]e treat intersectionality as an analytical strategy—a systematic approach to understanding human life and behavior that is rooted in the experiences and struggles of marginalized people. The premises and assumptions that underlie this approach are: inequalities derived from race, ethnicity, class, gender, and their intersections place specific groups of the population in a privileged position with respect to other groups and offer individuals unearned benefits based solely on group membership; historical and systemic patterns of disinvestment in nonprivileged groups are major contributors to the low social and economic position of those groups; representations of groups and individuals in media, art, music, and other cultural forms create and sustain ideologies of group and individual inferiority/superiority and support the use of these factors to explain both individual and group behavior; and individual identity exists within and draws from a web of socially defined statuses some of which may be more salient than others in specific situations or at specific historical moments.

As Weber (2001) points out, intersectional analysis operates on two levels: at the individual level, it reveals the way the intermeshing of these systems creates a broad range of opportunities for the expression and performance of individual identities. At the societal/structural level, it reveals the ways systems of power are implicated in the development, organization, and maintenance of inequalities and social injustice. In both writing and teaching, scholars engaged in this work are challenged to think in complex and nuanced ways about identity and to look at both the points of cohesion and fracture within groups (Dill & Johnson, 2002; Weber, 2001) as they seek to capture and convey dynamic social processes in which individual identities and group formations grow and shift in continuous interaction with one another, within specific historical periods and geographic locations.

Additionally intersectional analysis provides an important lens for reframing and creating new knowledge because it asserts new ways of studying power and inequality and challenges conventional understandings of oppressed and excluded groups and individuals. Collins (2000) in her discussion of Black feminist thought as critical social theory states:

> For African American women, the knowledge gained at intersecting oppressions of race, class and gender, provides the stimulus for crafting and passing on the subjugated knowledge of Black women's critical social theory. As a historically oppressed group, U.S. Black women have produced social thought designed to oppose oppression.

Thus, to use Collins's language, intersectional analysis is a tool that reveals the subjugated knowledges of people of color and produces social thought that can be considered critical social theory. One of the key ways this is accomplished is through the unveiling of power in interconnected structures of inequality. Intersectional analysis explores and unpacks relations of domination and subordination, privilege and agency, in the structural arrangements through which various services, resources, and other social rewards are delivered; in the interpersonal experiences of individuals and groups; in the practices that characterize and sustain bureaucratic hierarchies; and in the ideas, images, symbols and ideologies that shape social consciousness (Collins, 2000). It is characterized by the following four theoretical interventions: (1) Placing the lived experiences and struggles of people of color and other marginalized groups as a starting point for the development of theory; (2) Exploring the complexities not only of individual identities but also group identity, recognizing that variations within groups are often ignored and essentialized; (3) Unveiling the ways interconnected domains of power organize and structure inequality and oppression; and (4) Promoting social justice and social change by linking research and practice to create a holistic approach to the eradication of disparities and to changing social and higher education institutions.

Intersectionality's Theoretical Interventions

Centering the Experiences of People of Color

The intersectional approach to the study of inequality, as it has developed in U.S. social thought, is rooted in illuminating the complexities of race and ethnicity as it intersects with other dimensions of difference. In doing this, the multiple and intersectional influences of these characteristics become clear. For example, for African American men and women, if we begin with their own understandings of the ways race is used to limit their life choices and chances, we see that opportunity is not just structured by race, but by the confluence of race, class, gender, and other dimensions of difference. Similarly the opportunity for a college preparatory K-12 education is influenced by one's race but also by class position in the society and within that racial group, as well as by gender and the perceptions and expectations of one's gender based on class, race, region, ability, and so on. (A low-income woman from Appalachia, who is White, faces a different set of opportunities and constraints on the path to a college degree than a middle-income woman who is White and living in New York City.)

As discussed earlier, intersectional knowledge is distinctive knowledge generated by the experiences of previously excluded communities and multiply oppressed groups. It tells, interprets, and analyzes the stories of Black, Latino/a,[3] Asian American, and Native American Indian women and/or of gay men, lesbians, and transgender people of all racial and ethnic groups in the United States.[4] It is knowledge based upon and derived from what intersectional scholars have called the "outsider-within," "subaltern," and "border-land"[5] voices of society, creating counterhistories and counternarratives to those based primarily on the experiences of social elites. Importantly this approach focuses on the relationships of opportunity and constraint created by the dimensions of inequality so that racism, for example, is analyzed not only in terms of the constraints it produces in the lives of people of color but also in terms of the privileges it creates for Whites.

An example can be found in some of the earliest work in what has come to be termed "Whiteness studies." Other scholars (Frankenberg, 1993; Waters, 1990; Brodkin, 1998; Lipsitz, 1998; Roediger, 1991) have extended the concept of race to Whites and revealed the unacknowledged privilege that is derived from White skin, a privilege that is taken for granted and remains invisible.

Complicating Identity

Both individual and group identity are complex—influenced and shaped not simply by a person's race, class, ethnicity, gender, physical ability, sexuality, religion, or nationality—but by a combination of all of those characteristics. Nevertheless, in a hierarchically organized society, some statuses are more valued than others. Within groups, there is far greater diversity than appears when, for analytical purposes people are classified with a single term.

For example, the term Latino/a—as a gendered, ethnic, and racial construct—is interconnected with multiple discourses on social stratification and political/national identity. Its meaning varies depending on the social context in which it is employed and the political meanings associated with its usage.

The term Latino/ a challenges the privileging of Spanish or Hispanic lineage over the other indigenous and African lineages of Spanish-speaking individuals in the United States. Nevertheless Latino/a as a social construct needs to be problematized because its underlying political discourse seeks to disrupt "neat" categories of what is now perceived as the Latino or brown race. Thus, by homogenizing all Latino/as into one category, the discourse on national identity is dismissed and the effects of the intersection of race, ethnic subgroup, and socioeconomic status on Latinas are overlooked.[6]

Identity for Latinos, African Americans, Asian, and Native Americans, is complicated by differences in national origin or tribal group, citizenship, class (both within the sending and host countries—for recent migrants), gender as well as race and ethnicity. A contemporary example is found in the controversy surrounding whether or not Black students who migrated from Africa or the West Indies to the United States should be permitted to take advantage of scholarships designed for historically underrepresented African Americans. In several articles it has been argued that in their pursuit of diversity, universities have redefined the original remedies of civil rights law to include immigrant Africans and Afro-Caribbean's as substitutes for native born African American Blacks (Guinier, 2004; Bell, 2004). An intersectional approach necessitates acknowledging such intragroup differences in order to address them.

Unveiling Power in Interconnected Structures of Inequality

Collins, in *Black Feminist Thought* (2000, 275) conveys a complex understanding of power by describing it as *both* a force that some groups use to oppress others *and* "an intangible entity that operates throughout a society and is organized in particular domains." This complex notion of power provides tools for examining the ways that people experience inequalities are organized and maintained through four interrelated domains:

1. the structural domain, which consists of the institutional structures of the society including government, the legal system, housing patterns, economic traditions, and educational structure;
2. the disciplinary domain, which consists of the ideas and practices that characterize and sustain bureaucratic hierarchies;
3. the hegemonic domain, which consists of the images, symbols, ideas, and ideologies that shape social consciousness (Collins, 2000).
4. the interpersonal domain, which consists of patterns of interaction between individuals and groups.

Intersectional analyses, as knowledge generated from and about oppressed groups, unveil these domains of power and reveal how oppression is constructed and maintained through multiple aspects of identity simultaneously. Understanding these aspects of power draws on knowledge of the historical legacies of people who have experienced inequality due to discriminatory practices and policies based on combinations of race, class, gender, ethnicity, and other dimensions of difference. Because arrangements of power shift and change over time and in different cultural contexts, individuals and groups experience oppression and inequalities differently according to their social, geographic, historical, and cultural location (Weber, 2001).

Structural Power

Within the structural domain, we are particularly interested in the ways "institutions are organized to reproduce subordination over time" (Collins, 2000, 277). In U.S. history, people of color have been controlled by policies in every institution of the society. These included, but are not limited to, racial segregation, exclusion acts, internment, forced relocation, denial of the right to own property, and denial of the right to marry and form stable families. Within each of these forms of institutional subordination, the various categories intersect to provide distinctive experiences for groups of individuals.

For example, in a recent essay using an intersectional approach to Latina health, we argue that the location of health services in relationship to low-income Latino communities structures access to healthcare and is a major factor affecting the health of Latino women, children, and families. The distribution of governmental resources, ranging from funding for research to the provision of public health services, is examined in terms of historical patterns and political considerations, which have led to a concentration of health resources in middle- and upper-income communities and the prioritization of research on diseases and illnesses, which are more prevalent in those populations (Zambrana & Dill, 2006).

Intersectional analysis also directs us to look at structural inequities by examining questions of social and economic justice, both to reveal the sources of these inequities and to begin to redress them. Poverty is primarily the result of the unequal distribution of society's goods and resources and the concentration of wealth in the hands of a few. When one examines the interaction of poverty with race/ethnicity and gender, it is apparent that these factors, taken together, have a disproportionately negative effect on people of color, especially women (Higginbotham & Romero, 1997; Williams & Collins, 1995), and result in an over concentration of detrimental social, economic, and political outcomes for them and their families.

Race, ethnicity, and geography matter, as they are all determinants of access to social capital or social resources (Massey & Denton, 1993).[7] Intersectional analysis draws attention to the policies, practices, and outcomes of institutional racism and discrimination, one result of which is the concentration of low-income people of color in resource poor neighborhoods with poorly financed and underdeveloped public systems such as schools and public health services.

Disciplinary Power

In addition to formal policies or the location of resources away from some communities, intersectional analyses draw attention to the bureaucratic practices that perpetuate and maintain inequality. Linda Gordon, in her book: *Pitied but Not Entitled: Single Mothers and the History of Welfare, 1890–1935* (1994) provides an analysis that illustrates the intertwining of structural and disciplinary power. The book focuses upon the ways in which U.S. social welfare policies and their implementation have resulted in the impoverishment of single mothers. Gordon's history outlines the development during the New Deal of a two-tier welfare system; a nationally supported social insurance system of generous benefits for workers who were disproportionately White and male, and a poorly funded, state supported system of "means-tested" morally evaluated benefits for those who were irregularly employed, a disproportionate number of whom were women and minorities. In her telling of this story, Gordon reveals the behind the scenes politics, rivalries, and values within the Children's Bureau in which "feminist" social workers of the progressive era became the advocates of a system of maternal and child health that gave primacy to women's role as mother and advocated for states to implement these policies. An unintended consequence was that the primary program for single mothers, Aid to Families with Dependent Children (AFDC), became subject to state politics and local bureaucratic practices. It was, therefore, more likely to be governed by state legislation that openly discriminated on the basis of race or immigrant status and to bureaucratic practices that gave or denied benefits on the basis of morality, political loyalty, and the value judgments of individual caseworkers.

In sum, Gordon's work shows how disciplinary power administered through case workers at the national and state levels combined with structural power organized in state and federal legislation shaped historical patterns of racial and gender relations within the U.S. system of social welfare. This example is repeated throughout the society not only in public welfare systems but across all public systems including education, housing, and employment.

Hegemonic Power

Hegemonic power refers to the cultural ideologies, images, and representations that shape group and individual consciousness and support or justify policies and practices in the structural and disciplinary domains. Through the manipulation of ideology it links social institutions—structural power, organizational practices—disciplinary power, and everyday experiences—interpersonal power (Collins, 2000, 284). These ideas influence the ways members of various social groups are viewed and depicted in the society at large and the expectations associated with these depictions (hooks, 1992; Chin & Humikowski, 2002; Zambrana, Mogel, & Scrimshaw, 1987). Intersectional analyses challenge us to interrogate those ideologies and representations, to locate and uncover their origins and multiple meanings, and to examine the reasons for their existence and persistence.

For example, dominant representations of people of color build upon and elaborate ideas, images, and stereotypes that are deeply rooted in American history and become the rationale for the differential treatment of groups and individuals (Portes, 2000). In the case of Latinas, scholars have argued that stereotypes of Latinas as aliens, hypersexual, exotic, and passive promote the myth that they need to be controlled by state institutions through such policies as those that deny prenatal care or force sterilization. These false representations affect not only the ways dominant culture healthcare providers treat their Latina patients but the kinds of public policies that are designed to determine access to healthcare. (Silliman, et al., 2004, 216).

Welfare reform provides another example of the ways stereotypes and representations affect social policies, access to services, and the location of groups within the social structure. An essay written by Dill, Baca Zinn, and Patton examines this issue in depth. This essay demonstrates that representations of single motherhood as the cause of delinquency, crime, violence, abandonment, abuse, and gangs and depictions of single mothers as self-centered, free-loading, idle, and sexually promiscuous, have been nationally linked to Black women, Latinas—especially on the West Coast and in the Mexican border states—and Native American women in the West. These representations have been used to justify welfare reform strategies specifically designed to promote work and decrease childbirth among low-income women. In the essay we argue that a major source of the power and appeal of welfare reform was its effort to discipline and control the behavior of Black women, other women of color, and by example, White women (1999).

These stereotypes exist, are interpreted, understood, and reinscribed within larger social and historical narratives that have a long history in U.S. society. Another example discussed at length in the Dill, Baca Zinn, and Patton essay cited above, relies heavily on scholar Rickie Solinger's book, *Wake up Little Susie: Single Pregnancy and Race before* Roe v. Wade (1992).

According to Solinger, social services available to pregnant single women in the post-World War II era were strikingly dissimilar based on race. Young, White, middle-class women who got pregnant during this era were typically sent to homes for unwed mothers far away from their communities where they were heavily counseled that giving up their children for adoption and "forgetting" the experience was the only psychologically acceptable thing to do (Cole & Donley, 1990; Solinger, 1992). During this same time period, however, she shows that African American women were excluded from most homes for unwed mothers on the basis of race, and there were very few all-Black homes. In contrast to White women, African American women went virtually unserved in the child welfare system. Black women were frequently turned away from adoption agencies (Day, 1979) and directed to public welfare departments. Thus the stereotype of the Black welfare mother was both drawn on and enforced by policies that limited African American women's access to social resources while maintaining the myth of White moral superiority (Dill, Baca Zinn, & Patton, 1999).

Interpersonal Power

Interpersonal power refers to "routinized, day-to-day practices of how people treat one another. Such practices are systematic, recurrent and so familiar that they often go unnoticed." They have been referred to as everyday racism or everyday sexism, etc. and are powerful "in the production and reinforcement of the status quo" (Collins, 2000, 287; Bonilla Silva, 2006, 26; Essed, 1991). Everyday racism is entwined with the implementation of disciplinary and hegemonic power. It is exemplified in the simple acts of referring to White men as "men" and men of color with a racial modifier in news reports; or reports by White women of experiencing feelings of threat or fear when encountering a Black man on the street in the evening.

In her book, *Understanding Everyday Racism*, Essed analyzes interviews with fifty-five women of African descent in the Netherlands and the United States who recount experiences of everyday racism. She argues that these accounts are not ad hoc stories but have a specific structure with several recurring elements and reflect the fact that Whites in the Netherlands and the United States have very different and narrower definitions of racism than Blacks. For Whites, racism is seen as extreme beliefs or actions that endorse White supremacy. For Blacks, the emphasis is on a wide variety of actions including White supremacy as well as Eurocentrism, avoidance of contact with other ethnic groups, underestimating the abilities of minorities, and passive tolerance of racist behavior by others.

Within intersectional analyses, unveiling the workings of power, which is understood as both pervasive and oppressive, is vitally important. It reveals both the sources of inequality and its multiple and often conflicting manifestations. It provides a way to examine how different identity markers overlay or intersect with one another at all levels of social relations (structural/institutional/ideological/macro and interpersonal/everyday/micro) in different historical and geographical, contexts (Collins, 1998; Crenshaw, 1993b; Weber, 2001).

Promoting Social Justice and Social Change

Grounded in the everyday lives of people of diverse backgrounds, intersectional knowledge reveals the various impacts of the presence of racial and gender disparities, and is a critical first step toward eliminating inequality. The social justice agenda of the intersectional approach is inextricably linked to its utility in unveiling power. It also provides an analytical framework for combining the different kinds of work that need to be included in the pursuit of social justice: advocacy, analysis, policy development, theorizing, and education. Because intersectional work validates the lives and stories of previously ignored groups of people, it is seen as a tool that can be used to help empower communities and the people in them. Implicitly the production of this knowledge offers the potential for creating greater understanding among groups of people.

The Declaration of the NGO (nongovernmental) Forum of the UN Conference on Racism in 2001 included in its opening statement the following under the topic gender:

> 119. An intersectional approach to discrimination acknowledges that every person be it man or woman exists in a framework of multiple identities, with factors such as race, class, ethnicity, religion, sexual orientation, gender identity, age, disability, citizenship, national identity, geopolitical context, health, including HIV/AIDS status and any other status are all determinants in one's experiences of racism, racial discrimination, xenophobia and related intolerances. An intersectional approach highlights the way in which there is a simultaneous interaction of discrimination as a result of multiple identities. (Declaration & Programme of Action, 2001)

This statement, in an international document that begins with an assessment of the contemporary circumstances of discrimination in a global context and continues by laying out a program of action that individual nation-states are encouraged to follow is an excellent example of the ways the ideas of intersectionality are linked to social action. In this case, the statement about gender immediately links gender issues to a variety of other issues for which specific action steps are delineated. In effect, it is argued that gender, as part of a complex set of relationships, must be also considered within each of the concerns delineated in the plan of action.

A second example of the link between intersectional thinking, social justice, and social change is the work of LatCrit. LatCrit, Latina and Latino Critical Legal Theory,

Inc., describes itself as "an intellectual and social community of people engaged in critical 'outsider jurisprudence' that centers Latino/as in all of their diversity." One of its goals is "to develop a critical, activist, and interdisciplinary discourse on law and policy toward Latinas/os and to foster both the development of coalitional theory and practice as well as the accessibility of this knowledge to agents of social and legal transformation" (www.LatCrit.org). To accomplish these goals, LatCrit supports projects at a number of law schools around the country. One project that exemplifies the link between theory and activism is the Community Development Externship Network, "an experiential learning project designed to provide legal assistance to local communities or activists working on social justice efforts in rural and urban sites in the U.S. and the Americas. Central to this project is that students are engaged in the work of securing material remedies to social injustices suffered both by groups and individuals, including land reclamation projects and other kinds of reparations-oriented efforts."

In conclusion, transformation of knowledge and of individual lives is a fundamental aspect of intersectional work. Strong commitments and desires to create more equitable societies that recognize and validate differences drive the research of scholars and the practice of activists. Among these scholars, discussions of social change focus not just on changing the society at large but also on changing structures of knowledge within institutions of higher learning and the relationship of colleges and universities to the society. *Transformative* is perhaps one of the best words to characterize this scholarship because it is seen not only as transforming knowledge but using knowledge to transform society.

Notes

1. Throughout this book we often use the term "ethnic studies" to refer to the group of departments and programs that include African American (Black) studies, Chicano (Mexican American) studies, Puerto Rican studies, American Indian studies, and Asian American studies. In some institutions all of these programs are combined into a department called American Ethnic Studies. In other universities some exist as separate departments.
2. Johnella Butler, Spelman College, personal communication.
3. The term Latina/o is used interchangeably with Hispanics, consistent with federal standards. Under the category of Hispanic/Latino are included persons of Spanish-speaking origin from the Spanish-speaking Caribbean, Central America, Mexico, and Latin America. Hispanics/Latinos may be of any race and/or mixed race but have a preference for identifying with their national origin.
4. Examples include: E. N. Glenn, *Unequal Citizens*; R. Ferguson, *Aberrations in Black*, P. Hondagneau-Sotelo, *Domestica*, Audre Lorde, *Sister Outsider*, P. H. Collins, *Black Feminist Thought*, A. Hurtado, *The Color of Privilege*, among many others.
5. These terms are drawn from the work of Patricia Hill Collins, Gayatri Spivak, and Gloria Anzaldúa, respectively.
6. For an excellent historical account of the role of race and class and exclusionary racial practices in the United States and Latin American countries, see C. E. Rodriguez, 2000.
7. Social capital broadly refers to access to resources that improve educational, economic, and social position in society (Bourdieu, 1985; Ellen & Turner, 1997).

19.

THE UNHAPPY MARRIAGE OF MARXISM AND FEMINISM: TOWARDS A MORE PROGRESSIVE UNION

Heidi Hartmann

(1981)

The "marriage" of marxism and feminism has been like the marriage of husband and wife depicted in English common law: marxism and feminism are one, and that one is marxism.[1] Recent attempts to integrate marxism and feminism are unsatisfactory to us as feminists because they subsume the feminist struggle into the "larger" struggle against capital. To continue our simile further, either we need a healthier marriage or we need a divorce.

The inequalities in this marriage, like most social phenomena, are no accident. Many marxists typically argue that feminism is at best less important than class conflict and at worst divisive of the working class. This political stance produces an analysis that absorbs feminism into the class struggle. Moreover, the analytic power of marxism with respect to capital has obscured its limitations with respect to sexism. We will argue here that while marxist analysis provides essential insight into the laws of historical development, and those of capital in particular, the categories of marxism are sex-blind. Only a specifically feminist analysis reveals the systemic character of relations between men and women. Yet feminist analysis by itself is inadequate because it has been blind to history and insufficiently materialist. Both marxist analysis, particularly its historical and materialist method, and feminist analysis, especially the identification of patriarchy as a social and historical structure, must be drawn upon if we are to understand the development of western capitalist societies and the predicament of women within them. In this essay we suggest a new direction for marxist feminist analysis. … [W]e try to use the strengths of both marxism and feminism to make suggestion both about the development of capitalist societies and about the present situation of women. We attempt to use marxist methodology to analyze feminist objectives, correcting the imbalance in recent socialist feminist work, and suggesting a more complete analysis of our present socioeconomic formation. We argue that a materialist analysis demonstrates that patriarchy is not simply a psychic, but also a social and economic structure. We suggest that our society can best be understood once it is recognized that it is organized both in capitalistic and in patriarchal ways. While pointing out tensions between patriarchal and capitalist interests, we argue that the accumulation of capital both accommodates itself to patriarchal social structure and helps to perpetuate it. We suggest in this context that sexist ideology has assumed a peculiarly capitalist form in the present, illustrating one way that patriarchal relations tend to bolster capitalism. We argue, in short, that a partnership of patriarchy and capitalism has evolved. ...

I. Marxism and the Woman Question

The woman question has never been the "feminist question." The feminist question is directed at the causes of sexual inequality between women and men, of male dominance over women. Most marxist analyses of women's position take as their question the relationship of women to the economic system, rather than that of women to men, apparently assuming the latter will be explained in their discussion of the former. Marxist analysis of the woman question has taken three main forms. All see women's oppression in our connection (or lack of it) to production. Defining women as part of the working class, these analyses consistently subsume women's relation to men under workers' relation to capital. First, early marxists, including Marx, Engels, Kautsky, and Lenin, saw capitalism drawing all women into the wage labor force, and saw this process destroying the sexual division of labor. Second, contemporary marxists have incorporated women into an analysis of everyday life in capitalism. In this view, all aspects of our lives are seen to reproduce the capitalist system and we are all workers in the system. And third, marxist feminists have focused on housework and its relation to capital, some arguing that housework produces surplus value and that houseworkers work directly for capitalists. ...

Engels, in *Origins of the Family, Private Property and the State*, recognized the inferior position of women and attributed it to the institution of private property.[2] In bourgeois families, Engels argued, women had to serve their masters, be monogamous, and produce heirs who would inherit the family's property and continue to increase it. Among proletarians, Engels argued, women were not oppressed, because there was no private property to be passed on. Engels argued further that as the extension of wage labor destroyed the small-holding peasantry, and women and children were incorporated into the wage labor force along with men, the authority of the male head of household was undermined, and patriarchal relations were destroyed.[3]

For Engels, then, women's participation in the labor force was the key to their emancipation. Capitalism would abolish sex differences and treat all workers equally. Women would become economically independent of men and would participate on an equal footing with men in bringing about the proletarian revolution. After the revolution, when all people would be workers and private property abolished, women would be emancipated from capital as well as from men. Marxists were aware of the hardships women's labor force participation meant for women and families, which resulted in women having two jobs, housework and wage work. Nevertheless, their emphasis was less on the continued subordination of women in the home than on the progressive character of capitalism's "erosion" of patriarchal relations. Under socialism housework too would be collectivized and women relieved of their double burden.

The political implications of this first marxist approach are clear. Women's liberation requires first, that women become wage workers like men, and second, that they join with men in the revolutionary struggle against capitalism. Capital and private property, the early marxists argued, are the cause of women's particular oppression just as capital is the cause of the exploitation of workers in general.

Though aware of the deplorable situation of women in their time the early marxists failed to focus on the *differences* between men's and women's experiences under capitalism. They did not focus on the feminist questions—how and why women are oppressed as women. They did not, therefore, recognize the vested interest men had in women's continued subordination. As we argue in Part III below, men benefited from not having to do housework, from having their wives and daughters serve them, and from having the better places in the labor market. Patriarchal relations far from being an atavistic leftovers, being rapidly outmoded by capitalism, as the early marxists suggested, have survived and thrived alongside it. And since capital and private property do not cause the oppression or women as *women* their end alone will not result in the end of women's oppression. …

Marxist feminist who have looked at housework have also subsumed the feminist struggle into the struggle against capital. Mariarosa Dalla Costa's theoretical analysis of housework is essentially an argument about the relation of housework to capital and the place of housework in capitalist society and not about the relations of men and women as exemplified in housework.[4] Nevertheless, Dalla Costa's political position, that women should demand wages for housework, has vastly increased consciousness of the importance of housework among women in the women's movement. The demand was and still is debated in women's groups all over the United States.[5] By making the claim that women at home not only provide essential services for capital by reproducing the labor force, but also create surplus value through that work,[6] Dalla Costa also vastly increased the left's consciousness of the importance of housework, and provoked a long debate on the relation of housework to capital.[7]

Dalla Costa uses the feminist understanding of housework as real work to claim legitimacy for it under capitalism by arguing that it should be waged work. Women should demand wages for housework rather than allow themselves to be forced into the traditional labor force, where, doing a "double day," women would still provide housework services to capital for free as well as wage labor. Dalla Costa suggests that women who receive wages for housework would be able to organize their housework collectively, providing community child care, meal preparation, and the like. Demanding wages and having wages would raise their consciousness of the importance of their work; they would see its *social* significance, as well as its private necessity, a necessary first step toward more comprehensive social change.

Dalla Costa argues that what is socially important about housework is its necessity to capital. In this lies the strategic importance of women. By demanding wages for housework and by refusing to participate in the labor market women can lead the struggle against capital. Women's community organizations can be subversive to capital and lay the basis not only for resistance to the encroachment of capital but also for the formation of a new society.

Dalla Costa recognizes that men will resist the liberation of women (that will occur as women organize in their communities) and that women will have to struggle against them, but this struggle is an auxiliary one that must be waged to bring about the ultimate goal of socialism. For Dalla Costa, women's struggle are revolutionary not because they are feminist, but because they are anti-capitalist. Dalla Costa finds a place in the revolution for women's struggle by making women producers of surplus value, and as a consequence part of the working class. This legitimates women's political activity.[8]

The women's movement has never doubted the importance of women's struggle because for feminists the *object* is the liberation of women, which can only be brought about by women's struggles. Dalla Costa's contribution to increasing our understanding of the social nature of housework has been an incalculable advance. But like the other marxist approaches reviewed here her approach focuses on capital—not on relations between men and women. The fact that men and women have differences of interest, goals, and strategies is obscured by her analysis of how the capitalist system keeps us all down, and the important and perhaps strategic role of women's work in this system. The rhetoric of feminism is present in Dalla Costa's writing (the oppression of women, struggle with men) but the focus of feminism is not. If it were, Dalla Costa might argue for example, that the importance of housework as a social relation lies in its crucial role in perpetuating male supremacy. That women do housework, performing labor for men, is crucial to the maintenance of patriarchy.

Engels ... and Dalla Costa ... fail to analyze the labor process within the family sufficiently. Who benefit from women's labor? Surely capitalists, but also surely men, who as husbands and fathers receive personalized services at home. The content and extent of the services may vary by class or ethnic or racial group, but the fact of their receipt does not. Men have a higher standard of living than women in terms of luxury consumption, leisure time, and personalized service.[9] A materialist approach ought not ignore this crucial point.[10] It follows that men have a material interest in women's continued oppression. ...

... The focus of marxist analysis has been class relations; the object of marxist analysis has been understanding the laws of motion of capitalist society. While we believe marxist methodology can be used to formulate feminist strategy, these marxist feminist approaches discussed above clearly do not do so; their marxism clearly dominates their feminism.

As we have already suggested, this is due in part to the analytical power of marxism itself. Marxism is a theory of the development of class society, of the accumulation process in capitalist societies, of the reproduction of class dominance, and of the development of contradictions and class struggle. Capitalist societies are driven by the demands of the accumulation process, most succinctly summarized by the fact that production is oriented to exchange, not use. In a capitalist system production is important only insofar as it contributes to the making of profits, and the use value of products is only an incidental consideration. Profits derive from the capitalists' ability to exploit labor power, to pay laborers less than the value of what they produce. The accumulation of profits systematically transforms social structure as it transforms the relations of production. The reserve army of labor, the poverty of great numbers of people and the near-poverty of still more, these human reproaches to capital are by-products of the accumulation process itself. From the capitalist's point of view, the reproduction of the working class may "safely be left to itself."[11] At the same time, capital creates an ideology, which grows up along side it, of individualism, competitiveness, domination, and in our time, consumption of a particular kind. Whatever one's theory of the genesis of ideology one must recognize these as the dominant values of capitalist societies.

Marxism enables us to understand many aspects of capitalist societies: the structure of production, the generation of a particular occupational structure, and the nature of the dominant ideology. Marx's theory of the development of capitalism is a theory of the development of "empty places." Marx predicted, for example, the growth of the proletariat and the demise of the petit bourgeoisie. More precisely and in more detail, Braverman among others has explained the creation of the "places" clerical worker and service worker in advanced capitalist societies.[12] Just as capital creates these places indifferent to the individuals who fill them, the categories of marxist analysis, class, reserve army of labor, wage-laborer, do not explain why particular people fill particular places. They give no clues about why *women* are subordinate to *men* inside and outside the family and why it is not the other way around. *Marxist categories, like capital itself, are sex-blind.* The categories of marxism cannot tell us who will fill the empty places. Marxist analysis of the woman question has suffered from this basic problem. ...

II. Radical Feminism and Patriarchy

The great trust of radical feminist writing has been directed to the documentation of the slogan "the personal is political." Women's discontent, radical feminists argued, is not the neurotic lament of the maladjusted, but a response to a social structure in which women are systematically dominated, exploited, and oppressed. Women's inferior position in the labor market, the male-centered emotional structure of middle class marriage, the use of women in advertising, the so-called understanding of women's psyche as neurotic—popularized by academic and clinical psychology—aspect after aspect of women's lives in advanced capitalist society was researched and analyzed. The radical feminist literature is enormous and defies easy summary. At the same time, its focus on psychology is consistent. The New York Radical Feminists' organizing document was "The Politics of the Ego." "The personal is political" means for radical feminists, that the original and basic class division is between the sexes, and that the motive force of history is the striving of men for power and domination over women, the dialectic of sex.[13]

Accordingly, Firestone rewrote Freud to understand the development of boys and girls into men and women in terms of power.[14] Her characterizations of what are "male" and "female" character traits are typical of radical feminist writing. The male seeks power and domination; he is egocentric and individualistic, competitive and pragmatic; the "technological mode," according to Firestone, is male. The female is nurturant, artistic, and philosophical; the "aesthetic mode" is female.

No doubt, the idea that the aesthetic mode is female would have come as quite a shock to the ancient Greeks. Here lies the error of radical feminist analysis: the dialectic of sex as radical feminists present it projects male and female characteristics as they appear in the present back into all of history. The radical feminist analysis has greatest strength in its insights into the present. Its greatest weakness is a focus on the psychological which blinds it to history.

The reason for this lies not only in radical feminist method, but also in the nature of patriarchy itself, for patriarchy is a strikingly resilient form of social organization. Radical feminists use patriarchy to refer to a social system characterized by male domination over women. Kate Millett's definition is classic:

> Our society … is a patriarchy. The fact is evident at once if one recalls that the military, industry, technology, universities, science, political offices, finances—in short, every avenue of power within the society, including the coercive force of the police, is entirely in male hands.[15]

This radical feminist definition of patriarchy applies to most societies we know of and cannot distinguish among them. The use of history by radical feminists is typically limited to providing examples of the existence of patriarchy in all times and places.[16] For both marxist and mainstream social scientists before the women's movement, patriarchy referred to a system of relations between men, which form the political and economic outlines of feudal and some pre-feudal societies, in which hierarchy followed ascribed characteristics. Capitalist societies are understood as meritocratic, bureaucratic, and impersonal by bourgeois social scientists; marxists see capitalist societies as systems of class domination.[17] For both kinds of social scientists neither the historical patriarchal societies nor today's western capitalist societies are understood as systems of relations between men that enable them to dominate women.

Towards a Definition of Patriarchy

We can usefully define patriarchy as a set of social relations between men, which have a material base, and which, though hierarchical, establish or create interdependence and solidarity among men that enable them to dominate women. Though patriarchy is hierarchical and men of different classes, races, or ethnic groups have different places in the patriarchy, they also are united in their shared relationship of dominance over their women; they are dependent on each other to maintain that domination. Hierarchies "work" at least in part because they create vested interests in the status quo. Those at the higher levels can "buy off" those at the lower levels by offering them power over those still lower. In the hierarchy of patriarchy, all men, whatever their rank in the patriarchy, are bought off by being able to control at least some women. There is some evidence to suggest that when patriarchy was first institutionalized in state societies, the ascending rulers literally made men the heads of their families (enforcing their control over their wives and children) in exchange for the men's ceding some of their tribal resources to the new rulers.[18] Men are dependent on one another (despite their hierarchical ordering) to maintain their control over women.

The material base upon which patriarchy rests lies most fundamentally in men's control over women's labor power. Men maintain this control by excluding women from access to some essential productive resources (in capitalist societies, for example, jobs that pay living wages) and by restricting women's sexuality.[19] Monogamous heterosexual marriage is one relatively recent and efficient form that seems to allow men to control both these areas. Controlling women's access to resources and their sexuality, in turn, allows men to control women's labor power, both for the purpose of serving men in many personal and sexual ways and for the purpose of rearing children. The services women render men, and which exonerate men from having to perform many unpleasant tasks (like cleaning toilets) occur outside as well as inside the family setting. Examples outside the family include the harassment of women workers and students by male bosses and professors as well as the common use of secretaries to run personal errands, make coffee, and provide "sexy" surroundings. Rearing children, whether or not the children's labor power is of immediate benefit to their fathers, is nevertheless a crucial task in perpetuating patriarchy as a system. Just as class society must be reproduced by schools, work places, consumption norms, etc., so must patriarchal social relations. In our society children are generally reared by women at home, women socially defined and recognized as inferior to men, while men appear in the domestic picture only rarely. Children raised in this way generally learn their places in the gender hierarchy well. Central to this process, however are the areas outside the home where patriarchal behaviors are taught and the inferior position of women enforced and reinforced: churches, schools, sports, clubs, unions, armies, factories, offices, health centers, the media, etc.

The material base of patriarchy, then, does not rest solely on childrearing in the family, but on all the social structures that enable men to control women's labor. The aspects of social structures that perpetuate patriarchy are theoretically identifiable, hence separable from their other aspects. Gayle Rubin has increased our ability to identify the patriarchal element of these social structures enormously by identifying "sex/gender systems":

> a "sex/gender system" is the set of arrangements by which a society transform, biological sexuality into product, of human activity, and in which these transformed sexual needs are satisfied.[20]

We are born female and male, biological sexes but we ate created woman and man, socially recognized gender. *How* we are so created is that second aspect of the *mode* of production of which Engels spoke, "the production of human beings themselves, the propagation of the species."

How people propagate the species is socially determined. If, biologically, people are sexually polymorphous, and society were organized in such a way that all forms of sexual expression were equally permissible, reproduction would result only from some sexual encounters, the heterosexual ones. The strict division of labor by sex, social invention common to all known societies, creates two very separate genders and a need for men and women to get together for economic reasons. It thus helps to direct their sexual needs toward heterosexual fulfillment, and helps to ensure biological reproduction. In more imaginative societies, biological reproduction might be ensured by other techniques, but the division of labor by sex appears to be the universal solution to date. Although it is theoretically possible that a sexual division of labor not imply inequality between the sexes, in most known societies, the socially acceptable division of labor by sex is one which accords lower status to women's work. The sexual division of labor is also the underpinning of sexual subcultures in which men and women experience life differently; it is the material base male power which is exercised (in our society) not just in not doing housework and securing superior employment, but psychologically as well.

How people meet their sexual needs, how they reproduce, how they inculcate social norms in new generation, how they learn gender, how it feels to be a man or woman— all occur in the realm Rubin labels the sex/gender system. Rubin emphasizes the influence of kinship (which tells you with whom you can satisfy sexual needs) and the development of gender specific personalities via childrearing and "oedipal machine." In addition, however, we can use the concept of the sex/gender system to examine all other social institutions for the roles they play in defining and reinforcing gender hierarchies. Rubin notes that theoretically a sex/gender system could be female dominant, male dominant, or egalitarian, but declines to label various known sex/gender systems or to periodize history accordingly. We choose to label our present sex/gender system patriarchy, because it appropriately captures the notion of hierarchy and male dominance which we see as central to the present system.

Economic production (what marxists are used to referring to as *the* mode of production) and the production of people in the sex/gender sphere both determine "social organization under which the people of a particular historical epoch and particular country live," according to Engels. The whole of society, then, can be understood by looking at both these types of production and reproduction, people and things.[21] There is no such thing as "pure capitalism," nor does "pure patriarchy" exist, for they must of necessity coexist. What exists is patriarchal capitalism, or patriarchal feudalism, or egalitarian hunting/gathering societies, or matriarchal horticultural societies, or patriarchal horticultural societies, and so on. There appears to be no necessary connection between *changes* in the one aspect of production and changes in the other. A society could undergo transition from capitalism to socialism, for example, and remain patriarchal.[22] Common sense, history, and our experience tell us, however, that these two aspects of production are so closely intertwined, that change in one ordinarily creates movement, tension, or contradiction in the other.

Racial hierarchies can also be understood in this context. Further elaboration may be possible along the lines of defining color/race systems, arenas of social life that take biological color and turn it into a social category, race. Racial hierarchies, like gender hierarchies, are aspects of our social organization, of how people are produced and reproduced. They are not fundamentally ideological; they constitute that second aspect of our mode of production, the production and reproduction of people. It might be most accurate then to refer to our societies not as, for example, simply capitalist, but as patriarchal capitalist white supremacist. In Part III below, we illustrate one case of capitalism adapting to and making use of racial orders and several examples of the interrelations between capitalism and patriarchy.

Capitalist development creates the places for a hierarchy of workers, but traditional marxist categories cannot tell us who will fill which places. Gender and racial hierarchies determine who fills the empty places. *Patriarchy is not simply hierarchical organization,* but hierarchy in which *particular* people fill *particular* places. It is in studying patriarchy that we learn why it is women who are dominated and how. While we believe that most known societies have been patriarchal, we do not view patriarchy as a universal, unchanging phenomenon. Rather patriarchy, the set of interrelations among men that allow men to dominate women, has changed in form and intensity over time. It is crucial that the hierarchy among men, and their differential access to patriarchal benefits, be examined. Surely, class, race, nationality, and even marital status and sexual orientation, as well as the obvious age, come into play here. And women of different class, race, national, marital status, or sexual orientation groups are subjected to different degrees of patriarchal power. Women may themselves exercise class, race, or national power, or even patriarchal power {through their family connections) over men lower in the patriarchal hierarchy than their own male kin.

To recapitulate, we define patriarchy as a set of social relations which has a material base and in which there are hierarchical relations between men and solidarity among them which enable them in turn to dominate women. The material base of patriarchy is men's control over women's labor power. That control is maintained by excluding women from access to necessary economically productive resources and by restricting women's sexuality. Men exercise their control in receiving personal service work from women, in not having to do housework or rear children, in having access to women's bodies for sex, and in feeling powerful and being powerful. The crucial elements of patriarchy as we *currently* experience them are: heterosexual marriage (and consequent homophobia), female childrearing and housework, women's economic dependence on men (enforced by arrangements in the labor market), the state, and numerous institutions based on social relations among men—clubs, sports, unions, professions, universities, churches, corporations, and armies. All of these elements need to be examined if we are to understand patriarchal capitalism.

Both hierarchy and interdependence among men and the subordination of women are *integral* to the functioning of our society; that is, these relationships are *systemic.* We leave aside the question of the creation of these relations and ask, can we recognize patriarchal relations in capitalist societies? Within capitalist societies we must discover those same bonds between men which both bourgeois and marxist social scientists claim no longer exist or are, at the most, unimportant leftovers. Can we understand how these relations among men are perpetuated in capitalist societies? Can we identify ways in which patriarchy has shaped the course of capitalist development?

III. The Partnership of Patriarchy and Capital

How are we to recognize patriarchal social relations in capitalist societies? It appears as if each woman is oppressed by her own man alone; her oppression seems a private affair. Relationships among men and among families seem equally fragmented. It is hard to recognize relationships among men, and between men and women, as *systematically* patriarchal. We argue, however, that patriarchy as a system of relations between men and women exists in capitalism, and that in capitalist societies a healthy and strong partnership exists between patriarchy and capital. Yet if one begins with the concept of patriarchy and an understanding of the capitalist mode of production, one recognizes immediately that the partnership of patriarchy and capital was not inevitable; men and capitalists often have conflicting interests, particularly over the use of women's labor power. Here is one way in which this conflict might manifest itself: the vast majority of men might want their women at home to personally service them. A smaller number of men, who are capitalists, might want most women (not their own) to work in the wage labor market. In examining the tensions of this conflict over women's labor power historically, we will be able to identify the material base of patriarchal relations in capitalist societies, as well as the basis for the partnership between capital and patriarchy. ...

The argument that capital destroys the family also overlooks the social forces which make family life appealing. Despite critiques of nuclear families as psychologically destructive, in a competitive society the family still meets real needs for many people. This is true not only of long-term monogamy, but even more so for raising children. Single parents bear both financial and psychic burdens. For working class women, in particular, these burdens make the "independence" of labor force participation illusory. Single parent families have recently been seen by policy analysts as transitional family formations which become two-parent families upon remarriage.[23]

It could be that the effects of women's increasing labor force participation are found in a declining sexual division of labor within the family, rather than in more frequent divorce, but evidence for this is also lacking. Statistics on who does housework, even in families with wage-earning wives, show little change in recent years; women still do most of it.[24] The double day is a reality for wage-working women. This is hardly surprising since the sexual division of labor outside the family, in the labor market, keeps women financially dependent on men—even when they earn wage themselves. The future of patriarchy does not, however, rest solely on the future of familial relations. For patriarchy, like capital, can be surprisingly flexible and adaptable.

Whether or not the patriarchal division of labor, inside the family and elsewhere, is "ultimately" intolerable to capital, it is shaping capitalism now. As we illustrate below, patriarchy both legitimates capitalist control and delegitimates certain forms of struggle against capital.

Ideology in the Twentieth Century

Patriarchy, by establishing and legitimating hierarchy among men (by allowing men of all groups to control at least some women), reinforces capitalist control, and capitalist values shape the definition of patriarchal good.

The psychological phenomena Shulamith Firestone identifies are particular examples of what happens in relationships of dependence and domination. They follow from the realities of men's social power—which women are denied—but they are shaped by the fact that they happen in the context of a capitalist society.[25] If we examine the characteristics of men as radical feminists describe them—competitive, rationalistic, dominating—they are much like our description of the dominant values of capitalist society.

This "coincidence" may be explained in two ways. In the first instance, men, as wage laborers, are absorbed in capitalist social relations at work, driven into the competition these relations prescribe, and absorb the corresponding values.[26] The radical feminist description of men was not altogether out of line for capitalist societies. Secondly, even when men and women do not actually behave in the way sexual norms prescribe, men *claim for themselves* those characteristics which are valued in the dominant ideology. So, for example, the authors of *Crestwood Heights* found that while the men, who were professionals, spent their days manipulating subordinates (often using techniques that appeal to fundamentally irrational motives to elicit the preferred behavior), men and women characterized men as "rational and pragmatic." And while the women devoted great energies to studying scientific methods of child-rearing and child development, men and women in Crestwood Heights characterized women as "irrational and emotional."[27]

This helps to account not only for "male" and "female" characteristics in capitalist societies, but for the particular form sexist ideology takes in capitalist societies. Just as women's work serves the dual purpose of perpetuating male domination and capitalist production, so sexist ideology serves the dual purpose of glorifying male characteristics/capitalist values, and denigrating female characteristics/social need. If women were degraded or powerless in other societies, the reasons (rationalizations) men had for this were different. Only in a capitalist society does it make sense to look down on women as emotional or irrational. As epithets, they would not have made sense in the renaissance. Only in a capitalist society does it make sense to look down on women as "dependent." "Dependent" as an epithet would not make sense in feudal societies. Since the division of labor ensures that women as wives and mothers in the family are largely concerned with the production of use values, the denigration of these activities obscures capital's inability to meet socially determined need at the same time that it degrades women in the eyes of men, providing a rationale for male dominance. An example of this may be seen in the peculiar ambivalence of television commercials. On one hand, they address themselves to the real obstacles to providing for socially determined needs: detergents that destroy clothes and irritate skin, shoddily made goods of all sorts. On the other hand, concern with these problems must be denigrated; this is accomplished by mocking women, the workers who must deal with these problems.

A parallel argument demonstrating the partnership of patriarchy and capitalism may be made about the sexual division of labor in the work force. The sexual division of labor places women in low-paying jobs, and in tasks thought to be appropriate to women's role. Women are teachers, welfare workers, and the great majority of workers in the health fields. The nurturant roles that women play in these jobs are of low status because capitalism emphasizes personal independence and the ability of private enterprise to meet social needs, emphases contradicted by the need for collectively provided social services. As long as the social importance of nurturant tasks can be denigrated because women perform them, the confrontation of capital's priority on exchange value by a demand for use values can be avoided. In this way, it is not feminism, but sexism that divides and debilitates the working class.

IV. Towards a More Progressive Union

Many problems remain for us to explore. Patriarchy as we have used it here remains more a descriptive term than an analytic one. If we think marxism alone inadequate, and radical feminism itself insufficient, then we need to develop new categories. What makes our task a difficult one is that the same features, such as the division of labor, often reinforce both patriarchy and capitalism, and in a thoroughly patriarchal capitalist society, it is hard to isolate the mechanisms of patriarchy. Nevertheless, this is what we must do. We have pointed to some starting places: looking at who benefits from women's labor power, uncovering the material base of patriarchy, investigating the mechanisms of hierarchy and solidarity among men. The questions we must ask are endless. ...

The struggle against capital and patriarchy cannot be successful if the study and practice of the issues of feminism is abandoned. A struggle aimed only at capitalist relations of oppression will fail, since their underlying supports in patriarchal relations of oppression will be overlooked. And the analysis of patriarchy is essential to a definition of the kind of socialism useful to women. While men and women share a need to overthrow capitalism they retain interests particular to their gender group. It is not clear—from our sketch, from history, or from male socialists—that the socialism being struggled for is the same for both men and women. For a humane socialism would require not only consensus on what the new society should look like and what a healthy person should look like, but more concretely, it would require that men relinquish their privilege.

As women we must not allow ourselves to be talked out of the urgency and importance of our tasks, as we have so many times in the past. We must fight the attempted coercion, both subtle and not so subtle, to abandon feminist objectives.

This suggests two strategic considerations. First, a struggle to establish socialism must be a struggle in which groups with different interests form an alliance. Women should not trust men to liberate them after the revolution, in part, because there is no reason to think they would know how; in part, because there is no necessity for them to do so. In fact their immediate self-interest lies in our continued oppression. Instead we must have our own organizations and our own power base. Second, we think the sexual division of labor within capitalism has given women a practice in which we have learned to understand what human interdependence and needs are. While men have long struggled *against* capital, women know what to struggle *for*.[28] As a general rule, men's position in patriarchy and capitalism prevents them from recognizing both human needs for nurturance, sharing, and growth, and the potential for meeting those needs in a nonhierarchical, nonpatriarchal raise their consciousness, men might assess the potential gains against the potential losses and choose the status quo. Men have more to lose than their chains.

As feminist socialists, we must organize a practice which addresses both the struggle against patriarchy and the struggle against capitalism. We must insist that the society we want to create is a society in which recognition of interdependence is liberation rather than shame, nurturance is a universal, not an oppressive practice, and in which women do not continue to support the false as well as the concrete freedoms of men.

Notes

Earlier drafts of this essay appeared in 1975 and 1977 coauthored with Amy B. Bridges. Unfortunately, because of the press of current commitments, Amy was unable to continue with this project, joint from its inception and throughout most of its long and controversial history.

1. Often paraphrased as "the husband and wife are one and that one is the husband," English law held the "by marriage, the husband and wife are one person in law: that is, the very being or legal existence of the women is suspended during the marriage, or at least is incorporated and consolidated into that of the Husband, " I. Blackstone, *Commentaries*, 1965, pp. 442–445, cited in Kenneth M. Davidson, Ruth B. Ginsburg, and Herma H. Kay, *Sex Based Discrimination* (St. Paul, Minn.: West Publishing Co., 1974), p. 117.

2. Frederick Engels, *The Origin of the Family, Private Property and the State*, edited, with an introduction by Eleanor Burke Leacock (New York: International Publishers, 1972).

3. Frederick Engels, *The Condition of the Working Class in England* (Stanford, Calif.: Stanford University Press, 1958). See esp. pp. 162–66 and p. 296.

4. Mariarosa Dalla Costa, "Women and the Subversion of the Community," in *The Power of Women and the Subversion of the Community* by Mariarosa Dalla Costa and Selma James (Bristol, England: Falling Wall Press, 1973; second edition) pamphlet, 78 pps.

5. It is interesting to note that in the original article (cited in n. 7 above) Dalla Costa suggests that wages for housework would only further institutionalize woman's housewife role (pp. 32,34) but in a note (n. 16, pp. 52–52) she explains the demand's popularity and its use as a consciousness raising tool. Since then she has actively supported the demand. See Dalla Costa, " A General Strike," in *All Work and No Pay*, ed. Wendy Edmond and Suzie Fleming (Bristol, England: Falling Wall Press, 1975).

6. The text of the article reads: "We have to make clear that, within the wage, domestic work produces not merely use values, but is essential to the production of surplus value" (p. 31). Note 12 reads: "What we mean precisely is that housework as work is *productive* in the Marxian sense, that is, producing surplus value" (p. 52, original emphasis). To our knowledge this claim has never been made more rigorously by the wages for housework group. Nevertheless marxists have responded to the claim copiously.

7. The literature of the debate includes Lise Vogel, "The Earthly Family," *Radical America*, Vol. 7, nos. 4–5 July-October 1973), pp. 9–50; Ira Gerstein, "Domestic Work and Capitalism," *Radical America*, Vol. 7, nos. 4–5 July-October 1973, pp. 101–128; John Harrison, "Political Economy of Housework," *Bulletin of the Conference of Socialist Economists*, Vol. 3, no. 1 (1973); Wally Seccombe, "The Housewife and her Labour under Capitalism," *New Left Review*, no. 83 January-February 1974), pp. 3–24; Margaret Coulson, Branka Magas, and Hilary Wainwright, "The Housewife and her Labour under Capitalism,' A Critique," *New Left Review*, no. 89 (January-February 1975), pp. 59–71; Jean Gardiner, "Women's Domestic Labour," *New Left Review*, no. 89 (January-February 1975), pp. 47–58; Ian Cough and John Harrison, "Unproductive Labour and Housework Again," *Bulletin of the Conference of Socialist Economists*, Vol. 4, no. 1 (1975); Jean Gardiner, Susan Himmelweit and Maureen Mackintosh, "Women's Domestic Labour," *Bulletin of the Conference of Socialist Economists*, Vol. 4, no. 2 (1975); Wally Seccombe, "Domestic Labour: Reply to Critics," *New Left Review*, no. 94 (November-December 1975), pp. 85–96; Terry Fee, "Domestic Labor," *Review of Radical Political Economics*, Vol. 8, no. 1 (Spring 1976), pp. 1–8; Susan Himmelweit and Simon Mohun, "Domestic Labour and Capital," *Cambridge Journal of Economics*, Vol. 1, no. 1 (March 1977), pp. 15–31.

8. In the U.S., the most often heard political criticism of the wages for housework group has been its opportunism.

9. Laura Oren documents this for the working class in "Welfare of Women in Laboring Families: England, 1860–1950," *Feminist Studies*, Vol. 1, nos. 3–4 (Winter-Spring 1973), pp. 107–25.

10. The late Stephen Hymer pointed out to us a basic weakness in Engels' analysis in *Origins*, a weakness that occurs because Engels fails to analyze the labor process within the family. Engels argues that men enforced monogamy because they wanted to leave their property to their own children.

> Hymer argued that far from being a 'gift,' among the petit bourgeoisie, possible inheritance is used as a club to get children to work for their fathers. One must look at the labor process and who benefits from the labor of which others [sic].

11. This is a paraphrase. Karl Marx wrote: "The maintenance and reproduction of the working class is, and must ever be, a necessary condition to the reproduction of capital. But the capitalist may safely leave its fulfillment to the labourer's instincts of self-preservation and propagation." [*Capital* (New York: International Publishers, 1967), Vol. 1, p. 572.]

12. Harry Braverman, *Labor and Monopoly Capital* (New York: Monthly Review Press, 1975).

13. "Politics of Ego: A Manifesto for New York Radical Feminists," can be found in *Rebirth of Feminism*, ed. Judith Hole and Ellen Levine (New York: Quadrangle Books, 1971), pp. 440–443. "Radical feminists" are those feminists who argue that the lost fundamental dynamic of history is men's striving to dominate women. 'Radical' in this context does *not* mean anti-capitalist, socialist, counter-cultural, etc., but has the specific meaning of this particular set of feminist beliefs or group of feminists. Additional writings of radical feminists, of whom the New York Radical Feminists are probably the most influential, can be found in *Radical Feminism*, ed. Ann Koedt (New York: Quadrangle Press, 1972).

14. Focusing on power was an important step forward in the feminist critique of Freud. Firestone argues, for example, that if little girls "envied" penises it was because they recognized that little boys grew up to be members of a powerful class and little girls grew up to be dominated by them. Powerlessness, not neurosis, was the heart of women's situation. More recently, feminists have criticized Firestone for rejecting the usefulness of the concept of the unconscious. In seeking to explain the strength and continuation of male dominance, recent feminist writing has emphasized the fundamental nature of gender-based personality differences, their origins in the unconscious, and the consequent difficulty of their eradication. See Dorothy Dinnerstein, The *Mermaid and the Minotaur* (New York: Harper Colophon Books, 1977), Nancy Chodorow, *The Reproduction of Mothering* (Berkeley: University of California Press, 1978), and Jane Flax, "The Conflict Between Nurturance and Autonomy in Mother-Daughter Relationships and Within Feminism," *Feminist Studies*, Vol. 4, no. 2 June 1978), pp. 141–189.

15. Kate Millett, *Sexual Politics* (New York: Avon Books, 1971), p. 25.

16. One example of this type of radical feminist history is Susan Brownmiller's *Against Our Will, Men, Women, and Rape* (New York: Simon & Shuster, 1975).

17. For the bourgeois social science view of patriarchy, see, for example, Weber's distinction between traditional and legal authority, *Max Weber: The Theories of Social and Economic Organization*, ed. Talcott Parson (New York: The Free Press, 1964), pp. 328–357. These views are also discussed in Elizabeth Fee, "The Sexual Politics of Victorian Social Anthropology," *Feminist Studies*, Vol. 1, nos. 3–4 (Winter-Spring 1973), pp. 23–29, and in Robert A. Nisbet, *The Sociological Tradition* (New York: Basic Books, 1966), especially Chapter 3, "Community."

18. See Viana Muller, "The Formation of the State and the Oppression of Women," *Review of Radical Political Economics*, Vol. 9, no. 3 (Fall 1977), pp. 7–21.

19. The particular ways in which men control women's access to important economic resources and restrict their sexuality vary enormously, both from society to society, from subgroup to subgroup, and across time. The examples we use to illustrate patriarchy in this section, however, are drawn primarily from the experience of whites in western capitalist countries. The diversity is shown in *Toward on Anthropology of Women*, ed. Rayna Rapp Reiter (New York: Monthly Review Press, 1975), *Woman, Culture and Society*, ed. Michelle Rosaldo and Louise Lamphere (Stanford, California: Stanford University Press, 1974), and *Females, Males, Families: A Biosocial Approach*, by Liba Leibowitz (North Scituate, Massachusetts: Duxbury Press, 1978). The control of women's sexuality is tightly linked to the place of children. An understanding of the demand (by men and capitalists) for children is crucial to understanding changes in women's subordination.

 Where children are needed for their present or future labor power, women's sexuality will tend to be directed toward reproduction and childrearing. When children are seen as superfluous, women's sexuality for other than reproductive purposes is encouraged, but men will attempt to direct it towards satisfying male needs. The Cosmo girl is a good example of a woman "liberated" from childrearing only to find herself turning all her energies toward attracting and satisfying men. Capitalists can also use female sexuality to their own ends, as the success of Cosmo in advertising consumer products shows.

20. Gayle Rubin, "The Traffic in Women," in *Anthropology of Women*, ed. Reiter, p. 159.

21. Himmelweit and Mohun point out that both aspects of production (people and things) are logically necessary to describe a mode of production because by definition a mode of production must be capable of reproducing itself. Either aspect alone is not self-sufficient. To put it simply the production of things requires people, and the production of people requires things. Marx, though recognizing capitalism's need for people did not concern himself with how they were produced or what the connections between the two aspects of production were. See Himmelweit and Mohun, "Domestic Labour and Capital" (note 7 above).

22. For an excellent discussion of one such transition to socialism, see Batya Weinbaum, "Women in Transition to Socialism: Perspectives on the Chinese Case," *Review of Radical Political Economics*, Vol. 8, no. 1 (Spring 1976), pp. 34–58.

23. Heather L. Ross and Isabel B Sawhill, *Time of Transition The Growth of Families Headed by Women* (Washington, D.C.: The Urban Institute, 1975).

24. See Kathryn E Walker and Margaret E. Woods *Time Use A Measure of Household Production of Family Goods and Services* (Washington D.C.: American Home Economics Association, 1976; and Heidi I. Hartmann, "The Family as the Locus of Gender, Class, and Political Struggle: The Example of Housework," *Signs*, Vol. 6, no. 3 (Spring 1981).

25. Richard Sennett's and Jonathan Cobb's *The Hidden Injuries of Class* (New York: Random House, 1973) examines similar kinds of psychological phenomena within hierarchical relationships between men at work.

26. This should provide some clues to class differences in sexism, which we cannot explore here.

27. See John R. Seeley, et al., *Crestwood Heights* (Toronto: University of Toronto Press, 1956), pp. 382–394. While men's place may be characterized as "in production" this does not mean that women's place is simply "not in production"—her tasks, too, are shaped by capital. Her non-wage work is the resolution, on a day-to-day basis, of production for exchange with socially determined need, the provision of use values in a capitalist society (this is the context of consumption). See Weinbaum and Bridges, "The Other Side of the Paycheck," for a more complete discussion of this argument. The fact that women provide "merely" use values in a society dominated by exchange values can be used to denigrate women.

28. Lise Vogel, "The Earthly Family" (see n. 7).

20.
SERVANTS OF GLOBALIZATION: WOMEN, MIGRATION, AND DOMESTIC WORK
Rhacel Salazar-Parreñas
(2001)

Migrant Filipina Domestic Workers in Rome and Los Angeles

Diwaliwan, a glossy monthly magazine published in Hong Kong, caters to Filipino/a migrant workers around the globe. While pictures of Philippine movie stars and "Ms. Diwaliwan" monthly beauty contest winners usually grace the front page of the magazine, the most striking image on the cover is the notation of the price in the Hong Kong dollar, Australian dollar, Canadian dollar, Japanese yen, Italian lire, Spanish peseta, and at least a dozen other currencies. While the widespread circulation of *Diwaliwan* points to the existence of the Filipino/a diaspora, the magazine's contents reveal some aspects of its readership.[1] This magazine periodically covers issues concerning overseas domestic work. This is because the majority of Filipina migrants scattered all over the globe are domestic workers.

The outflow of women from the Philippines and their entrance into domestic service in morn than 130 countries represent one of the largest and widest flows of contemporary female migration (Tyner, 1999). Filipino women are the quintessential service workers of globalization. … According to nongovernmental organizations in the Philippines, there are approximately 6.5 million Filipino migrants. Since the early 1990s, women have composed more than half of deployed Filipino migrant workers (Asis, 1992). Of these women, two-thirds are employed in domestic service (Tolentino, 1996). By definition, domestic workers are employees paid by individuals or families to provide elderly care, childcare, and/or housecleaning in private homes.

This study enters the world of migrant Filipina domestic workers by comparing their experiences of migration and settlement in the two cities with the largest populations of Filipino migrants in Italy and the United States: Rome and Los Angeles (King and Rybaczuk, 1993; U.S. Census, 1993). I focus my study on Italy and the United States first because they are the two most popular destinations of Filipino migrants in Western countries. Second, the Philippines has particular colonial tie to both countries As suggested by migration systems theory, migration streams are not randomly selected but instead emerge from prior links established through colonialism or preexisting cultural and economic ties (Castles and Miller 1998) While the United States maintains enormous economic dominance in relation to the Philippines, Italy indirectly enjoys cultural dominance through the institution of the Roman Catholic Church. Third, contemporary Filipino migration flows to these two countries did nor originate in a formal recruitment policy as they did for most other destinations of Filipino overseas laborers (for example, Hong Kong and Saudi Arabia). The movements of domestic workers into these two countries are for the most part informal streams that are not monitored by the state. In Italy, migrant women from the Philippines, Cape Verde, and Peru are concentrated in domestic service (Andall, 1992). In the United States, domestic work has been an occupation historically relegated to women of color and immigrant women (Dill, 1994 Glenn, 1986; Rollins, 1985; Romero, 1992). Notably, however, Filipina migrants are not concentrated in domestic service in the United States labor market.

My study looks at the politics of incorporation of migrant Filipina domestic workers. It does not concentrate solely on domestic work as an occupational issue. Instead, I view the experiences of migrant Filipina domestic workers through the lens of four key institutions of migration—the nation-state, family labor market, and the migrant community. Within each institution, I examine a particular process of migration. Accordingly, they are (1) the outflow of migration, (2) the formation of the migrant household, (3) the entrance into the labor market, and (4) the formation of the migrant community.

In conducting a cross-national study, I found that migrant Filipina domestic workers in Rome and Los Angeles encounter similar issues of migration with each of the institutional processes that I set out to analyze. They experience partial citizenship vis-à-vis the nation-state. In terms of the family, the majority of women in both cities maintain transnational households. As such, they share the pain of family separation. In both cities, many of them perform domestic work with a college education in hand. From this they share the experience of contradictory class mobility or an inconsistent social status in the labor market. Finally, they encounter both social exclusion and feelings of nonbelonging in the formation of the migrant community, albeit from different sources—in Rome from the dominant society and in Los Angeles from middle-class members of the Filipino migrant community. Still, in both cities they face alienation from other migrants. My examination of institutional processes focuses on these four issues, which I refer to as *dislocations*, meaning the positions into which external forces in society constitute the subject of migrant Filipina domestic workers. My analysis of dislocations illustrates their process of constitution and the means by which migrant Filipina domestic workers resist (attempt to eliminate) or negotiate (attempt to mitigate) the effects of these dislocations in their everyday lives. From this perspective, the experience of migration is embodied in dislocations. ...

This study's underlying question asks, why do migrant Filipina domestic workers in cities with different "contexts of reception" encounter similar dislocations?[2] The answer lies mostly in their shared role as low-wage laborers in global capitalism. As such, this study provides a "cross-national comparison" to emphasize the similarities engendered by globalization among the low-wage migrant workers demanded in the economic centers of global capitalism (Portes, 1997). My discussion foregrounds the position and shared experiences of migrant Filipina domestic workers as the global servants of global capitalism. These shared experiences of dislocations are the tropes of alliance among them. That is, they may draw cross-national alliances on the basis of these dislocations and consequently perceive themselves as part of a global community of workers dislocated into low-wage labor by the economic turmoil caused by global restructuring in the Philippines. ...

Why a Cross-National Perspective on Migrant Filipina Domestic Workers?

... In contrast to other studies, I present a comparative study of migrant Filipina domestic workers. ...

Calling forth a comparative study of migration globalization requires a shift from a unilocal to multilocal perspective in the analysis of economic activities. A comparative study ensures that a focus on the local does not overlook the global (Mufti and Shohat, 1997). With the relocation of production in globalization, the decline in manufacturing activities in Pittsburgh, for example, can no longer be understood without the simultaneous consideration of manufacturing activities in other localities, such as export processing in Mexico and informal manufacturing in New York. Though not constituting a traceable relocation such as production activities, low-wage service labor—such as domestic work—should also be understood in a multilocal perspective to emphasize the expansion of reserve armies of cheap labor with the formation of a (low-wage) labor diaspora and the demands for low-wage service workers by the economic bloc of postindustrial nations.

Hence, by showing the emergence of similarities among migrant Filipina domestic workers in different contexts, this study brings to the forefront the significance of their shared position in the global economy. Despite the differences in the particularities of their destinations, migrant Filipina domestic workers do fulfill a similar economic role in globalization. In both Rome and Los Angeles, they are part of the low-wage service workforce of the economic bloc of postindustrial nations. With this in mind, we can see more clearly that a cross-national perspective allows us to truly situate migration flows in globalization and its corresponding macrostructural trends.

Finally, I conduct a comparative study so as to situate the lives of Filipino Americans in a diasporic instead of a domestic perspective (Wong, 1995).[3] A turn toward a diasporic perspective follows the trajectory established by Lisa Lowe (1996) in *Immigrant Acts* of placing the analysis of Asian American experiences in an "international context," one that is mindful of the construction of Asian American subjects in the globalization of the economy, the foreign policies of the United States, and the resulting migration of Koreans, Southeast Asians, and Filipinos from the wars and foreign presence of the United States in Asia. ...

The large contingent of Filipino labor migrants to the United States is conceivably part of a larger outflow of a hierarchical labor diaspora from the Philippines. Professionals, semiprofessionals, and low-wage workers make up this diaspora. Moreover, the presence of Filipina domestic workers in the midst of the more visible professional migrants in the United States points to this country's inclusion in the Filipina domestic worker diaspora. Indeed, a large number of undocumented Filipina women in the

United States end up in domestic work (Hogeland and Rosen, 1990). The case of the United States invites an assessment of the larger structural forces and migrant institutions that propel a distinct subgroup of Filipinas into domestic work. Thus, I situate the experiences of Filipina domestic workers in a diasporic terrain, one that cannot be understood without the simultaneous consideration of the experiences of their counterparts in other countries. The Filipino labor diaspora is conceivably composed of one labor force in the global economy. By making this point, I do not mean to imply that migrant Filipina domestic workers or Filipino labor migrants have the same experiences the world over. ... [T]he Filipino labor diaspora is segmented by gender and class. Despite my seemingly contradictory findings, I do maintain that experiences in this diaspora are differentiated by social, political, legal, historical, and economic contexts of incorporation. Yet by drawing out existing similarities in their experiences, I wish to move toward finding a cross-national coalitional ground for the Filipino diasporic subject.

Filipinos in Globalization: An Imagined Global Community of Filipina Domestic Workers

As political economist Saskia Sassen states, "International migrations are produced, they are patterned, and they are embedded in specific historical phases" (1993: 97). The contemporary outmigration of Filipinas and their entrance into domestic work is a product of globalization; it is patterned under the role of the Philippines as an export-based economy in globalization; and it is embedded in the specific historical phase of global restructuring. The global economy is the stage that migrant Filipina domestic workers in Rome and Los Angeles have entered in their pursuit of the accumulation of capital. Considering that they perform the same role on the same stage (but in different places) for the same purpose, the emergence of similarities between them becomes less surprising despite the different contexts of their destinations.

The existence of an "imagined (global) community," using Benedict Anderson's conceptualization of the nation, reinforces the presence of similarities in their lives.[4] The imagined global community of Filipina migrants emerges, in part, from the simultaneity of their similar experiences as domestic workers across geographic territories. A Filipina domestic worker in Rome may "imagine" the similar conditions faced by domestic workers in Singapore, London, and Kuwait. Notably, they are only able to conceive of a global community because of the existence of shared interests and practices among them.[5]

The dislocations that are constituted in their labor migration are these shared experiences. As such, they are the premise of their community and from which they carve a symbolic transnational ethnic identity as Filipino diasporic subjects. Dislocations, or "narratives of displacement," as Stuart Hall refers to them, are the conjunctures or specific positionings of subjects in social processes (Hall, 1998, 1991a, 1991b). As mentioned, the dislocations of migrant Filipina domestic workers include partial citizenship, the pain of family separation, the experience of contradictory class mobility, and the feeling of social exclusion or nonbelonging in the migrant community.

... Dislocations represent conjunctures from which migrant Filipina domestic workers develop a cross-national allegiance. ... based on the effects of systems of inequality. ... Hence, dislocations are neither essential nor exclusive to migrant Filipina domestic workers but instead emerge from the specificities and conjunctures in their location in the political economy of globalization and its corresponding institutional processes The sharing of these dislocations enables the formation of an imagined global community.

Yet this imagined global community does not emerge solely from the sharing of experiences but comes from, borrowing the words of social theorist Michel de Certeau, the creation of continuously traveled "bridges" across geographic territories ("frontiers") in migration. As Arjun Appadarai (1996) notes, imagination is not a fantasy that can be divorced from actions. This imagined global community is constituted by circuits like those identified by anthropologist Roger Rouse as tying together sending and receiving communities of migration into a singular community through the "continuous circulation of people, money, goods, and information" (1991: 14) or what anthropologists Linda Basch, Nina Glick-Schiller, and Christina Szanton Blanc (1994) refer to as "transnational social fields" in their seminal study on tansnationalism, *Nations Unbound.*[6]

Migrant Filipina domestic workers maintain transnational projects that connect the Philippines to various geographical locations. For example ethnic goods circulate from the Philippines to the United States, other countries of Asia, the Middle East, and Europe. However, these webs are not restricted to a binary flow that is directed solely to and from the Philippines. Tangible and imagined links also weave the multiple migrant communities that make up the Filipino labor diaspora more closely together. Instead of just a transnational community, these links forge the creation of a global community.

In the case of the Filipino diaspora, circuits function multinationally. First, the circulation of goods occurs in a multinational terrain. In Europe, for instance, ethnic goods circulate to connect multiple Filipino migrant communities with their shipment from the Philippines to the United Kingdom and only then to other European nation-states. Moreover, multinational ethnic enclave businesses have sprouted with franchises of remittance agencies in Europe, Asia, the Middle East, and North America. Philippine bank-sponsored remittance centers such as Far East Bank-SPEED and PCI Bank compete with carriers such as LBC across continents. Although money does not usually circulate between migrant communities, remittance agencies represent collective locations among geographically distanced migrant workers.

In addition, transnational family ties of migrants are not limited to the Philippines. Intimate decisions involved in family maintenance transcend multiple borders. The families of the following handful of women vividly show that migration creates multinational households in various forms, an observation previously made by Khandelwal (1996) regarding contemporary Indian migrant families. Vanessa Dulang, a single woman who followed two of her sisters to Rome in 1990, is the seventh of eleven siblings who decided to work abroad, as two of her sisters and brother live in Kentucky while an older brother navigates to different countries as a seaman. The youngest among her siblings, Ruth Mercado works in Rome while her oldest sister is a barmaid in Switzerland, her brother a tricycle driver in Manila, and her other sister cares for the elderly in Saudi Arabia. Her retired parents stay in the Philippines, where they depend on the remittances sent by their daughters from three different nations. A trained nurse, Gloria Diaz works as a domestic worker in Rome while her oldest sister works as a nurse in the United States and another sister as a nurse in Manila. A domestic worker in Los Angeles, Dorothy Espiritu had previously worked in Saudi Arabia, during which time her oldest daughter began working in Japan and another daughter in Saudi Arabia, Finally, there is the family of Libertad Sobredo, a domestic worker in Los Angeles. Her nine children are either working outside of the Philippines, in Saudi Arabia and Greece, or pursuing their college degrees in Manila. These families exemplify the formation of a multinational, and not just binational household structure among Filipino labor migrants. The interdependency among members of multinational families results in the circulation of money from multiple counties to the Philippines, where economically dependent family members usually reside. Accentuating the experience of a multinational family, Libertad Sobredo, for example, usually deals with family crises occurring across the Pacific in the Philippines by making transatlantic phone calls to her eldest son in Greece.

Finally, magazines that cater to Filipino labor migrants provide additional solid evidence of a circuit that links the multiple migrant communities of Filipinos across the globe. The distribution of the monthly publication *Tinig Filipino* and the aforementioned *Diwaliwan* in more than a dozen countries signifies the presence of a diasporic community from which these magazines profit and which in turn is perpetuated by their circulation of information (to say the least) across geographic borders. As print language created the "imagined community" of the nation in the 1800s, it now provides a tangible link connecting geographically dispersed migrant Filipina domestic workers. A vehicle for creating the notion of a global community and instilling "in the minds of each … the image of their communion" (Anderson, 1983: 6) *Tinig Filipino* aptly describes itself as the "Linking Force Around the World." …

This study centers on the narratives of displacement, or dislocations, of migrant Filipina domestic workers. I explain their experience of migration by mapping out the dislocations that they encounter in migration and that serve as the basis of their identity as Filipino diasporic subjects in this age of late capitalism and globalization. In the process, I also explain how these dislocations form and are contested. In doing so, I address the question of why migrant Filipina domestic workers in host societies with different "contexts of reception" have similar experiences. As I will show, the answer rests largely on their positioning in globalization as part of the secondary tier labor force of the economic bloc of postindustrial nations. …

The Dislocation of Migrant Filipina Domestic Workers

Filipina domestic workers face four key dislocations in migration: partial citizenship, the pain of family separation, contradictory class mobility, and nonbelonging. In this [section], I explain how I identify these dislocations by using three levels of analysis— macrostructural, intermediate, and subject level—to lay out the theoretical foundation of my study.

Two dominant approaches are used to explain the processes of migration. The macroapproach documents macroprocesses that control the flows of migration and the labor market incorporation of migrants (Sassen, 1988). One of the best-known macrostructural approach is the world-system model. The second method, an intermediate level, centers its analysis on institutions (for example, households and social networks) to document social processes of migration and settlement (Massey et al., 1987). Social processes by definition are processes shaped by the interplay of structures and agency. Offering equally valid but different perspectives on the processes of migration, these two approaches neither contradict nor oppose one another. For example, both criticize the traditional microlevel approach to the study of migration from the level of the individual for disregarding structural determinants of migration and settlement (Pedraza-Bailey, 1990).

Another way of examining migratory processes is from the level of the subject. This perspective examines how migrants are situated in social processes of migration and how migrants in turn navigate through these constitutive processes. Analyzing migration from the level of the subject does not retreat to the widely critiqued analysis of migration from the level of the individual because the theoretical conception of a subject differs from that of an individual. In contrast to the "free will" ascribed to an individual, a subject is not free reigning but instead is "something at the behest of forces greater than it" (Smith, 1988: xxxiii). Joan Scott writes: "They are not unified, autonomous individuals exercising free will, but rather subjects whose agency is created through situations and statuses conferred on them. Being a subject means being 'subject to definite conditions of existence, conditions of endowment of agents, and conditions of exercise'" (1992: 34). In other words, subjects cannot be removed from the external forces that constitute the meanings of their existence. At the same time, agency is not denied in this conception. Instead, in this view agency is enabled and limited by the structures that constitute subjects.

The three levels of analysis that I utilize in this study reveal different aspects of migratory processes. The macrolevel approach clarifies our understanding of the structural processes that determine patterns of migration and settlement. The intermediate level of analysis documents the institutional transformations and shifts in social relations that are engendered in migration. Finally, the subject level approach broadens our understanding of migratory experiences by examining the positionings of migrants within institutional processes.

Globalization and the Macrolevel of Analysis

As I noted, globalization is a framework that needs to be considered in order to achieve a complete understanding of the local (Dirlik, 1996; Grewal and Kaplan, 1994; Kearney, 1995). Anthropologist Michael Kearney defines globalization as "social, economic, cultural and demographic processes that take place within nations but also transcend them, such that attention limited to local processes, identities, and units of analysis yields incomplete understanding of the local" (1995: 548). Sassen further qualifies that globalization "is not an encompassing umbrella" (1998: 3). Instead, it operates in specific institutional and geographical contexts and thereby reaches the "most molecular elements in society" (Foucault, 1980: 99). Globalization, through its corresponding macroprocesses, shapes the subject formation of migrant Filipina domestic workers and the position of these subjects in institutions (Dirlik 1996; Grewal and Kaplan, 1994 Ong, 1999; Sassen, 1998). We need to thus consider macroprocesses to understand the dislocations of migration. These macroprocesses include the formation of the "global city" (Cohen, 1992; Sassen, 1988, 1994, 1996c, 1996d), the feminization of the international labor force (Sassen, 1988, 1996a), the "opposite turns of nationalism" (Sassen, 1996b), and the formation of an economic bloc of postindustrial nations (Reich, 1991; Sassen, 1993).

As firmly established in the literature on migration, global capitalism functions through and maintains an overarching world-system that organizes nations into unequal relations and creates a larger structural linkage between sending and receiving countries in migration (Portes and Walton, 1981; Sassen, 1984; Zolberg, 1983). Migrants are "part of the ongoing circulation of resources, both capital and labor, within the boundaries of a single global division of labor, that is between a dominant core and a dependent periphery" (Friedman-Kasaba, 1996: 24). In the case of the Philippines, this division of labor emerges in the direct recruitment of its citizens to provide labor to more advanced capitalist nations in Europe, the Americas, Asia, and the Middle East (Battistella and Paganoni, 1992), One can arguably look at the destinations of migrant Filipina domestic workers as an economic bloc that solicits lower-wage labor from less advanced nations in the global economy.

Contributing an insightful theoretical framework on the position of women in the global economy, Sassen (1984, 1988) establishes a structural link between the feminization of wage labor and globalization. According to Sassen, globalization simultaneously demands the low-wage labor of women from traditionally Third World countries in export-processing zones of developing countries and in secondary tiers of manufacturing and service sectors in advanced capitalist countries (Sassen, 1984).[7] The case of women in the Philippines provides an exemplary illustration. While Filipino women comprised 74 percent of the labor force in export-processing zones by the early 1980s (Rosca 1995), they constituted 55 percent of the migrants by the early 1990s (Asis, 1992).

Under the global capitalist system, the penetration of manufacturing production in developing countries directly leads to socioeconomic restructuring in advanced capitalist countries such as Italy and the United States. First, the manufacturing production that remains in these latter countries (such as garment, electronics, and furniture) must compete with low production costs in developing countries. This results in the decentralization and deregulation of the few remaining manufacturing jobs in these nations (Sassen, 1996c).

Second, multinational corporations with production facilities across the globe, by and large, maintain central operations in new economic centers, or "global cities" (Sassen 1994), where specialized professional services (for example, legal, financial, accounting, and consulting tasks) are concentrated. Examples of such cities in the United States and Italy are New York, Los Angeles, Miami, and Milan. The rise of these geographic centers in which decision making in the operation of overseas production takes place demands low-wage service labor to maintain the lifestyles of their professional inhabitants. For the most part, immigrants, many of whom are female, respond to these demands (Sassen, 1984). …

Another macroprocess that corresponds with global restructuring is the "opposite turns of nationalism" (Sassen, 1996b). One turn has already been described, that is, the "denationalization of economies." The other turn is the "renationalization of politics," which refers to increasing sentiments of nationalism. In postindustrial nations, renationalization partially results from the use of immigrants as scapegoats against the economic displacement faced by middle-income workers in the deindustrialization of the economy (Sassen, 1996b; Ong, 1999). An apt example of renationalization at work is the "orientalization" of Asians in the United States as shown by the campaign contribution crises that recently plagued the Democratic Party (Ong, 1999). While the denationalization of economies causes the renationalization of politics, the former also overturns or at the very least eases the impacts of the latter. An example is the selective incorporation of foreign-born skilled workers, an adjustment allowed by state regimes to maximize the benefits of global capitalism (Ong, 1999).

Macroprocesses in globalization provide the condition for the subjection of migrant Filipina domestic workers. As such the questions directing this study can be reformulated around these macroprocesses to emphasize their centrality in the formation of dislocations. How does the opposite turn of nationalism situate migrant Filipina domestic workers in various institutional settings? How do the feminization of the labor force and the relegation of these women to low-wage service work in postindustrial nations situate them in the global labor market? Finally, how does the rise of the "global city" place them in a contradictory position in the family and community?

As this study intends to show, these macroprocesses impose dislocations on migrant Filipina domestic workers. To provide an introductory synopsis, the opposite turns of nationalism, for instance, consigns them to the position of partial citizenship in host societies with their rejection as citizens by the renationalization of politics and acceptance as low-wage workers by the denationalization of economies. Another example is the demand for their labor in globalization and its corresponding macroprocess of the feminization of the labor force; this predicament relegates them to low-wage service work regardless of their level of educational attainment and thereby leads to their contradictory class mobility. Finally, their concentration in "global cities" promotes the formation of transnational households and consequently results in the dislocation of the pain of family separation as the low wages of domestic work cannot cover the high costs of raising a family in the geographic centers of global capitalism.

Intermediate Level of Analysis

Studies that apply an intermediate level of analysis to the examination of migration diverge from those using a macrostructural level of analysis by recognizing agency in their systematic view of migratory processes. At the same time they build from and depend on these latter studies for the structural context of their discussions about institutional and social processes. By amending the conspicuous absence of agency in the macrolevel approach, various intermediate level studies have been able to expand the scope of our understanding of migratory processes (Pedraza, 1994). They address questions that macrolevel discussions cannot answer, for example, those concerning the constitution of migration flows, such as why migration flows are concentrated in specific communities, why they persist after the initial causal factors of migration have eroded, and why there is a specific gender and class constitution to migration (Grasmuck and Pessar, 1991; Hondagneu-Sotelo, 1994).

In this approach, migrants are shown to respond to larger structural forces through the manipulation of institutions (for instance, social networks) in the creation of migrant communities, in the maintenance of migration flows, or in easing and securing one's social and labor market incorporation upon settlement. These are a few examples of the social processes captured in the intermediate level of analysis. Notably, the development of the intermediate level of analysis by Douglas Massey and his colleagues (1987) has led to the further expansion of migration studies in the areas of transnationalism and gender studies. Studies in these areas have returned the favor by theoretically advancing the intermediate level of analysis in their consideration of social relations in institutional and social processes of migration (Hondagneu-Sotelo, 1994; Kibria, 1993). As they have significantly advanced the field of migration studies, I turn to the two burgeoning areas of transnationalism and gender studies to look at how this approach directs us to the identification of dislocations.

Transnationalism

In this age of globalization, migrants no longer inhabit an enclosed space, as their daily practices are situated simultaneously in both sending and receiving communities of migration (Rouse, 1991). As such, they can now be conceived of as "transmigrants," meaning "immigrants whose daily lives depend on multiple and constant interconnections across international borders and whose public identities are configured in relationships to more than one nation-state" (Glick-Schiller et al., 1995: 48). This category moves us beyond the long-standing binary construction of settlement in migration studies that is split between migrants (temporary settlers) and immigrants (permanent settlers).

Just as globalization "installs itself in very specific structures," transnational processes do not supersede but instead are embedded in the institution of the nation-state (Sassen, 1998: 3; Guarnizo and Smith, 1998; Ong, 1999). Numerous studies have shown a variety of ways that "transnational processes are anchored in" nation-states (Kearney, 1995: 548). For instance, transnationalism functions along juridical territories (Ong, 1999). Moreover, nation-states institutionalize transnational processes with programs that advocate concrete financial and political ties between sending and receiving communities of migration (Glick-Schiller and Fouron, 1998; Mahler, 1998; Smith, 1998).

Transmigration is fostered by the compression of space and time in globalization (Harvey, 1989). In other words, the option of transmigration is promoted by the greater access of migrants to advanced forms of communication. Yet why do migrants turn to transnational institutions? Migrants usually do so to negotiate their stunted integration in settlement. They create transnational institutions (such as transnational families and hometown associations) because they have not been fully incorporated into the host society (Glick-Schiller et al., 1995; Ong, 1999). By situating themselves in "transnational social fields," migrants counteract their marginal status in the host society (Appadarai, 1996; Basch et al., 1994; Goldring, 1998). For example, they benefit from their higher social status in the sending community as well as from the higher purchasing power of their wages (Basch et al., 1994; Goldring, 1998).

In the introduction to their collection of essays *Transnationalism from Below*, Guarnizo and Smith (1998) propose the use of a "mesostructural" or intermediate, level of analysis to the study of transnational processes. ... From research on transnationalism, we have learned about the formation of transnational institutions in which migrants function, whether they are families (Laguerre, 1994; Basch et al., 1994), networks (Rouse, 1991, 1992), community organizations such as hometown associations (Smith, 1998), political groups (Glick-Schiller and Fouron, 1998), or business enterprises (Ong, 1999). At the same time we have learned that it is important to look within these institutional formations of migration and account for the "everyday practices of ordinary people" that take place in transnational institutions (Guarnizo and smith, 1998). Indeed, transnational institutions, while determined by structural constraints, are created by the everyday practices of migrants. This indicates that the intermediate and subject levels of analyses are intimately related analytic approaches that are differentiated mostly by a question of emphasis between social process and subjection.

Gender

By considering the constitution of social relations in institutions, feminist scholars of migration have significantly advanced the intermediate level of analysis. For one, they have rightly shown that institutions are sites of patriarchal ideologies (Pessar, 1999).

An analysis of social relations illuminates social patterns in institutional processes. Feminist scholars of migration have shown, for example, that the social relation of gender organizes, shapes, and distinguishes the immigration patterns and experiences of men and women (Hondagneu-Sotelo, 1994; Pedraza, 1991). They have brought to the foreground the different labor market concentration and incorporation of male and female migrants (Hondagneu-Sotelo, 1994; Mahler, 1995); the different social spaces and networks men and women create and inhabit in the migrant community (Hagan, 1994; Hondagneu-Sotelo, 1994); and the different experiences of men and women in the migrant family (Friedman-Kasaba, 1996; Grasmuck and Pessar, 1991; Hondagneu-Sotelo, 1994; Kibria, 1993). Accounting for social relations in institutions underscores the divergences caused by gender, class, and/or generation in migration and shows that these divergences come not without social conflicts (Hondagneu-Sotelo, 1994, 1999; Kibria, 1993).

Literature on female migration has also illustrated the reconstitution of gender within migratory processes. In particular, studies have concluded that migration, which involves the movement "from one system of gender stratification to another" (Zlotnick, 1990), reconstitutes the position of women in the labor market and household (Glenn, 1986; Grasmuck and Pessar 1991; Hondagneu-Sotelo, 1994). In the receiving country, migrant women experience a certain degree of gender liberation because of their greater contribution to household income and participation in public life (Hondagneu-Sotelo, 1994; Kibria, 1993). However, studies are careful to point out that even with these advances, patriarchy is not eliminated but is somehow retained in migration (Pessar, 1999).

Researchers have also included gender in discussions of the causes of migration. In a study of Central American refugees in Washington, D.C., Repak (1995) establishes that gender is a determinant of migration by showing that the greater demand for low-wage female workers in this particular receiving community initiated the primary migration of women. Yet for the most part, women remain secondary migrants (Donato, 1992). That is, they migrate to create or reunify a family. Even so, this does not necessarily mean that women play a secondary role in migration (Hondagneu-Sotelo, 1994). As Toro-Morn (1995) argues using the case of Puerto Rican migrants, the secondary migration of women is part of a family strategy for survival.

Scholars of gendered migration generally warn against ghettoizing gender as applicable only to women (Pessar, 1999; Tyner, 1999). As a solution, they recommend comparative studies of male and female gendered experiences. Though I recognize this need in migration research, I nonetheless opted to focus solely on migrant women. The absence of men in my study does not represent a digression from viewing gender as a central analytical principle in the study of migration. A sole focus on the experiences of women in various institutional settings can still advance gendered migration research. Such studies can continue the new direction in migration research that accounts for the intersections of race, class, gender, and foreign status in the lives of male and female migrants (Pessar, 1999; Espiritu, 1997). One way of doing so is through the lens of migration as a process of subject formation. Thus, the next section focuses on the constitution of the subject and their dislocations which are shaped by multiple forms of oppression. This accounts for the intersections of race, class, gender and citizenship in the lives of migrant Filipina domestic workers.

Subject Level of Analysis

The subject level of analysis diverges from the intermediate level by not centering its analysis on social processes and the social relations constituted within these processes This approach does not seek to document the formation of social processes. Instead, social processes are considered settings for the process of subjection. This mode of analysis moves beneath the structural and institutional bases of social processes to deconstruct their minute effects on the subject. It does so to identify the subject-positions constituted within social processes.

In this view, social processes generate boundaries of "existence" and "exercise." Taking place in institutional agencies—which, according to Foucault, maintain "regimes of truth and power" (Ong, 1999)—social processes produce discourses. In its broadest sense, discourse refers to a particular system of meanings communicated by language and practices (Weedon, 1997). ... Discourses are emitted through institutional agencies, which in turn are given meaning by these "regimes of truth and power." From the discourse produced in institutional regimes arise subject-positions, which are "a contradictory mix of confirming and contending 'identities'" (O'Sullivan et al. 1994: 310). ...

As subject-positions are generated by discourses that maintain institutional agencies, I examine social processes not only to document the institutional transformations engendered in migration (for example, community formation constitution of migration flow, labor market incorporation, and transformation of household) but also to establish social processes and their corresponding institutions as the contexts in which a migrant subject exists and acts, the contexts from which emerge particular subject-positions. By defining the subjectivity of migrant Filipina domestic workers, I seek to identify their multiple subject-positions, or what I prefer to call "dislocations" or "narratives of displacement" to emphasize the subordinate conditions of their migration.

Dislocations are the challenges that Filipina domestic workers encounter as they navigate through social processes of migration. They are the segmentations embodying their daily practices in migration and settlement. As such, they are the stumbling blocks and sources of pain engendered within social processes of migration. Dislocations define the experience of migration from the perspective of the migrant subject. They are "the conscious and unconscious thoughts and emotions of the individual, her sense of self, and her ways of understanding her relations to the world" (Weedon, 1997: 32).

Dislocations stem specifically from the structural location inhabited by the migrant. In the case of migrant Filipina domestic workers, they emerge from their structural location as racialized women, low-wage workers, highly educated women from the Philippines, and members of the secondary tier of the transnational workforce in global restructuring.

By examining the subject-positions of migrant Filipina domestic workers I follow the trajectory established by women of color feminist theorists on ways to account for the multiple intersections of race, class, gender, sexuality, and nation (Alarcón, 1990; Grewal and Kaplan, 1994; Lorde, 1984; Mohanty, 1991; Trinh, 1989). First, this approach avoids universalisms and instead follows the analytic trajectory established in women of color feminism to emphasize specificities in location (Lorde, 1984; Mohanty, 1991). At the same time it stresses the specific position of subjects in sets of relationships. Women of color feminist theorists tend to account for the specific contexts of experiences in order to avoid the exclusivity unavoidably rendered by universal notions of race, class, and/or gender (Grewal, 1994). Thus, they insist that subjects are constituted only in their situatedness in multiple and intersecting axes of domination (Alarcón, 1990; Sandoval, 1991).

Second, ... [b]y placing in the foreground the dislocations that constitute the conjuncture-based identity of migrant Filipina domestic workers, I underscore their marginal location in multiple discursive spaces of race, gender, nation, and class. I highlight how these intersecting axes of domination leave them "decentered" and "fragmented" subjects (Grewal and Kaplan, 1994; Grewal 1994). By focusing my analysis on dislocations, I ... promote the feminist project advocated by theorists such as Norma Alarcon,

Stuart Hall, and Gayatri Spivak to view identity as an incomplete and ongoing process. With this in mind, my study provides only a partial picture of the complicated positioning of migrant Filipina domestic workers in "webs of power relations" (Foucault, 1983).

Why do I insist on viewing migration as a process of subjectivization? Only by documenting the subjectivity of migrant Filipina domestic workers can I account for their experience of migration. Dislocations are the defining characteristics of experience. As such, my study interrogates the meanings of these dislocations to explain the experience of migration. As Joan Scott says, "Experience is, in this approach, not the origin of our explanation, but that which we want to explain" (1992: 38). In this case, the experience that I want to explain is the constitution of parallel lives among migrant Filipina domestic workers in different locations.

A subject level approach is not at all foreign in the social sciences. In her groundbreaking study of transnational practices in the Chinese diaspora, *Flexible Citizenship* (1999), Aihwa Ong is one of the first scholars to apply a subject level of analysis to the study of migration and transnationalism. ... In the process she shows that analyzing everyday practices is a viable approach to understanding global and institutional processes of migration. In other studies of migration, the subject level of analysis comes closest in the consideration of the "politics of location," which recognizes that relationships and experiences are determined by one's structural location in multiple axes of domination (Mohanty, 1991). ...

My analysis of migration as a process of subject formation does not end with a documentation of dislocations. It includes an equal consideration of the actions undertaken by migrant Filipina domestic workers to ease and resist their dislocations. Judith Butler contends, "The analysis of subjection is always double, tracing the conditions of subject formation and tracing the turn against these conditions for the subject—and its perspective—to emerge" (1997: 29). In the formulation of migration as a process of subject formation, migrants resist larger structural forces by responding to the dislocations that these forces have generated in their lives. In making this point I want to emphasize that the average migrant Filipina domestic worker does not come to realize her world through the understanding of larger systems such as patriarchy and global capitalism. She instead does so through the particular dislocations that these systems have generated in her everyday experience of migration (see Foucault, 1983: 212).

Foucault refers to such resistances to power as "immediate struggles" (Foucault, 1978, 1983). The notion of immediate struggle is precisely what Butler describes as the "turn" taken by subjects against the conditions of their formation. Because immediate struggles are always present in relations of power, functioning within their circuits, they do not necessarily have to directly confront larger structures in society to be effective tools for change.[8] For their strength, immediate struggles rely on their multiplicity, irregular forms, and constant presence `within the operation of power.

Even though the forms of resistance that migrant Filipina domestic workers deploy against dislocations do not involve the direct diminishment of structural or institutional power, their acts of resistance must be credited with possible interventions against the ways that structural inequalities operate in shaping their everyday lives. ... In other words, dislocations emerge from exercises of power imposed on migrant

Filipina domestic workers by agents—a category that includes these women—of the state, labor market, family, and community. The macro-processes that dislocate migrant Filipina domestic workers are deployed only in action. As such, dislocations are not ontologically rooted in institutions. Instead, they are constituted by the practices that create and maintain institutions. Consequently, they can be negotiated through the realignment of these constitutive practices.

Yet negotiation does not necessarily signify elimination. The means by which migrant Filipina domestic workers choose to ameliorate the dislocations they encounter in migration ironically involve conforming to these dislocations. In fact, the means by which migrant Filipina domestic workers resist their dislocations actually re-create structural inequalities. This is the "bind of agency" that Butler (1997) speaks of, the subject's simultaneous "recuperation" and "resistance" of power. Agency is at the same time "a resistance that is *really* a recuperation of power" and "a recuperation that is *really* a resistance" (Butler, 1997: 13). This occurs because a subject can never be completely removed from the process of its constitution. As I stated, agency is conditioned and therefore limited by the social processes from which it emerges and takes place. This means that resistance, as it recuperates power, does not necessarily bring positive change.

This contention actually raises a larger theoretical question regarding agency. If agency emerges within and not outside the process of subjection, how is agency possible? ...

For the subject, the "conditions of its own subordination" is disabling and enabling, because the enactment of power involves a shift from power as externally "acting on" to constitutively "acted by" subjects (Butler, 1997: 12, 15). ... In the process, the subject does not escape the external forces "to which it is bound," but instead its actions exceed the forces of its constitution (Butler, 1997: 17). It is precisely through this conditioned agency that subjects intervene to shape the process and condition of their constitution.

Consequently, when acting against dislocations, migrants do not necessarily impose interventions against structural processes but may also intensify and re-create hierarchies among migrants and their families, migrants and their employers, and migrants and other migrants. As mothers, for example migrant Filipina domestic workers cope with the pain of family separation by intensifying filial authority through the suppression of their own and their children's emotional needs. As domestic workers, they resist the downward mobility of migration by emphasizing and taking advantage of their higher social status compared to that of poorer women in the Philippines. For instance, they hire their own domestic workers. As a final example, domestics in Rome heighten the alienation that they experience in the migrant community by expediting the accumulation of savings through the commercialization of friendships in the community (for example, charging a fee for personal favors) when resisting the dislocation of nonbelonging.

In summary, my study maps the subject formation of migrant Filipina domestic workers through the illustration of how particular subject-positions or dislocations are constituted in migration. Following Butler, I frame my analysis of subjection around two questions: What are the particular dislocations that define the experience of migration for Filipina domestic workers in Rome and Los Angeles? How do they then turn against these dislocations?

Conclusion

… I approach the study of migration from three levels of analysis. These approaches neither contradict nor override one another. Moreover, the subject level approach builds from the two other approaches so as to interrogate the constitution of the migrant as a subject regulated by various axes of domination. Following the process of this constitution requires an understanding of the contexts in which it takes place. Thus, it requires an understanding of globalization and its corresponding macrostructural trends as well as the institutional processes that function as the regimes in which the subject is regulated by structural forces in society.

Notes

1. I use the term *diaspora* to refer to the forced dispersal of a particular group of people from their homeland to a multitude of countries. I recognize that the term has come to mean more in recent years. In cultural studies, "'diaspora' refers to the doubled relationship or dual loyalty that migrants, exiles, and refugees have to places—their connections to the space they currently occupy and their continuing involvement with 'back home'" (Lavie and Swedenburg, 1996: 14). There is a lively debate between these two views. See Clifford (1997) for a thorough overview of various theoretical conceptions of diaspora. Though the experiences of contemporary Filipino migrants fit the two meanings of diaspora, I advocate for a return to its classic definition so as to underscore the dispersal of Filipino labor migrants into more than 130 countries as a unique and particular result of globalization. The fact is the transnational ties of migrant Filipinos, are not restricted to the homeland. Ties exist between various Filipino communities. This particular "diasporic" reality is discounted by the view of diaspora as "dual loyalty."
2. Though I use Portes and Rumbaut's (1996) formulation of immigrant incorporation as the foundational backbone of my study, I recognize the limits in their conception. …
3. According to Wong, "*a diasporic perspective* emphasizes Asian Americans as one element in the global scattering of peoples of Asian origin," while a domestic perspective "stresses the status of Asian Americans as an ethnic/ racial minority within the national boundaries of the U.S." (1995: 2).
4. Jonathan Okamura (1998) also applies the concept of "imagined community" to the Filipino diaspora.
5. As migration scholar Luin Goldring notes, "*Community* involves a sense of shared history and identity, mutually intelligible meanings" (1998: 173).
6. According to Basch et al. (1994), transnational social fields form from family connections, business enterprises that market and sell ethnic commodities, and organizations that promote ties to the homeland.
7. There are many studies that document the increasing labor market participation of women in developing countries due to global restructuring. See Nash and Fernandez Kelly (1983) and Ward (1990).
8. At the same time, one cannot assume that subjects passively accept and conform to their dislocations. As Foucault reminds us, "'the other' (the one over whom power is exercised) [must] be thoroughly recognized and maintained to the very end as a person who acts; and that faced with a relationship of power, a whole field of responses, reactions, and results, and possible interventions may open up" (1983: 220).

21.
ORIENTALISM AND MIDDLE EAST FEMINIST STUDIES
Lila Abu-Lughod
(2001)

The events marking the twentieth anniversary of the publication of Edward Said's 1978 *Orientalism* provide an excellent occasion to reflect on the book's impact on Middle East gender and women's studies. In some ways *Orientalism* and feminist studies have, in Marilyn Strathern's memorable phrase, an awkward relationship.[1] Despite the fact that the book is attuned, perhaps surprising for its time, to issues of gender and sexuality, its main focus lies elsewhere: the way in which the Orient has been represented in Europe through an imaginative geography that divides East and West, confirming Western superiority and enabling, if not actually constituting, European domination of those negatively portrayed regions known as "East."[2] *Orientalism* was not meant to be a work of feminist scholarship or theory. Yet it has engendered feminist scholarship and debate in Middle East studies as well as far beyond the field.

In this essay I consider four ways in which Said's work has had an impact. First, *Orientalism* opened up the possibility for others to go further than Said had in exploring the gender and sexuality of Orientalist discourse itself. Second, the book provided a strong rationale for the burgeoning historical and anthropological research that claimed to be going beyond stereotypes of the Muslim or Middle Eastern woman and gender relations in general. Third, the historical recovery of feminism in the Middle East, emerging from this new abundance of research has, in turn, stimulated a reexamination of that central issue in *Orientalism*: East/West politics. Finally, Said's stance, that one cannot divorce political engagement from scholarship, has presented Middle East gender studies and debates about feminism with some especially knotty problems, highlighting the peculiar ways that feminist critique is situated in a global context.

Correctives

The first studies inspired by *Orientalism* augmented Said's work with a closer focus on gender. One might point to works of the mid-1980s like Rana Kabbani's *Europe's Myths of Orient* that examined literature and Malek Alloula's *The Colonial Harem* that turned back the gaze of French photographic postcards of Algerian women. After the initial wave of corrective projects, with books like Billie Melman's 1992 historical study, *Women's Orients: English Women and the Middle East, 1718–1918: Sexuality, Religion, and Work;* Judith Mabro's 1991 edited collection, *Veiled Half-Truths;* and a theoretically sophisticated analysis by a scholar not working specifically within Middle East studies, Lisa Lowe's 1991 *Critical Terrains: French and British Orientalisms,* scholars examined the way that gender inflected Western discourses on the Orient. These books asked specifically how European colonial women, mostly travelers, writers, and missionaries, represented "the Orient" A few essays in Zehra Arat's 1998 published collection, *Deconstructing Images of "The Turkish Woman,"* also take up this intriguing theme.

However, a 1998 book by Meyda Yegenoglu, a Turkish scholar trained in the United States, entitled *Colonial Fantasies: Toward a Feminist Reading of Orientalism,* takes to a new level the underexamined question of the gender and sexuality of Orientalism. Written with sometimes numbing sophistication, the book explores the neglected term in Said's important distinction between latent" and "manifest" Orientalism. Yegenoglu suggests that "latent" Orientalism, which it to "the nature and extent of the sexual implications of the unconscious site of Orientalism," should be at the core of our analysis. Drawing on psychoanalysis, especially in its Lacanian and feminist versions, as well as a range of poststructuralist theories on the constitution of the subject, she faults Said for treating "images of woman and images of sexuality in Orientalist discourse" simply as "a trope limited to the representation of Oriental woman and of sexuality" (p. 25). In other words, she challenges the way Said and others relegate gender and sexuality to a subfield in their analysis of colonial discourse. Taking a more radical position, she sets out to analyze instead "how representations of cultural and sexual difference are constitutive of each other" (p. 1). ...

The "Real" Orient

If works such as these are meant as correctives to Said's relative "neglect" of gender and sexuality the bulk of work within Middle East gender studies has seen *Orientalism* instead as providing a strong rationale for careful and sympathetic research. Recognizing that stereotypes of the Middle Eastern woman have been crucial to negative depictions of the region and its culture(s), many scholars have sought through ethnographic or social historical research to reveal the complex "realities" of gender and women in the Middle East or, through literary study, to explore how Middle Eastern women represent themselves. In books like the 1965 *Guests of the Sheik,* Elizabeth Warnock Fernea pioneered the sympathetic portrayal of women behind the veil. Further Fernea's work to translate and publish Middle Eastern women's writings, in books beginning with *Middle Eastern Muslim Women Speak* (with Basima Berzigan), published around the same lime as *Orientalism,* has made available to new audiences the many voices of Middle Eastern women.

Whereas in the 1960s and early 1970s, research and scholarly writing on Middle Eastern women focused on questions of role and status, the late 1970s marked an important shift as Cynthia Nelson pointed out in a review of the field. In recent decades, an enormous body of scholarship (mostly in anthropology, sociology and history) has enhanced our knowledge of women and gender relations in various parts of the Middle East.[3] Two exemplary new books allow us to reflect both on the achievements and limitations of this sensitive, theoretically informed, post-Orientalist empirical work.

As we have come to expect, the promotional copy justifying the importance of Homa Hoodfar's 1997 *Between Marriage and the Market: Politics and Survival in Cairo* claims that "Hoodfar overturns stereotypes about women. Islam, and the Middle East and North Africa in general." And indeed, this extraordinarily rich book shows the resourcefulness of lower-class women in Cairo. Documenting with insight the strategies people use, whether in work or marriage, to cope with the economic shifts entailed by the structural adjustment policies the government has adopted. The author offers perceptive analyses of the manipulations of gender ideologies and religious beliefs. The anthropologist, of Iranian origin, writes with wonderful honesty, clarity, and generosity about the subjects she clearly came to like and respect.

Judith Tucker's 1998 *In the House of the Law: Gender and Islamic Law in Syria and Palestine* is a detailed and lively study based on jurists' legal opinions and the Islamic court records of Damascus, Nablus, and Jerusalem. Written by one of the pioneers of Middle East women's social history, the book subtly argues that although Islamic legal doctrines were based on female/male differences, judges opted in practice for broader and more flexible interpretations based on a desire for justice and for the stability of the community. Arguing against an essential and rigid association of Islamic law with patriarchy. Tucker concludes that it is only in recent times, when law became codified and linked to the state, that there developed "the enshrinement of gendered right and privilege without the accompanying flexibility and judicial activism that had been the hallmark of Islamic justice" (p. 186).

It must be recalled, however, that *Orientalism* was not just about representations or stereotypes of the Orient but about how these were linked and integral to projects of domination that were ongoing. This raises an uncomfortable question about all our work of the combating-stereotype-sort—and I would include here not just these books but many others that show how active, practical, powerful, and resourceful (as opposed to passive, silent, and oppressed) Middle Eastern women are or how complex gender relations are, including my own ethnography of the Awlad 'Ali, *Writing Women's Worlds: Bedouin Stories.* First, we have to ask what Western liberal values we may be unreflectively validating in proving that "Eastern" women have agency too. Second, and more importantly, we have to remind ourselves that although negative images of women or gender relations in the region are certainly to be deplored, offering positive images or "nondistorted" images will not solve the basic problem posed by Said's analysis of Orientalism. The problem is about the production of knowledge in and for the West. As Yegenoglu puts it, following Said's more Foucauldian point, the power of Orientalism comes from its power to construct the very object it speaks about and from its power to produce a regime of truth about the other and thereby establish the identity and the power of the subject that speaks about it" (pp. 90–91). As long as we are writing for the West about "the other," we are implicated in projects that establish Western authority and cultural difference.

Middle Eastern Feminisms

This particular dilemma has underscored the often quite polarized debates in the last decade among scholars who have turned to the study of feminist organizations, jour-

nals, and more generally, the modernizing projects of remaking women and gender relations. The richest historical work has been on Egypt, with such studies as Leila Ahmed's
1992 *Women and Gender in Islam*; Margot Badran's 1995 *Feminists, Islam, and Nation:
Gender and the Making of Modern Egypt*; Beth Baron's 1994 *The Women's Awaken-
ing in Egypt*; Marilyn Booth's forthcoming *May Her Likes Be Multiplied*; and Cynthia
Nelson's 1996 *Doria Shafik, Egyptian Feminist*. The parallels for Turkey are described
by contributors to Zehra Arat's *Deconstructing Images of "The Turkish Woman"* and
by scholars writing mostly in Turkish. For Iran, Parvin Paidar's 1995 *Women and the
Political Process in Twentieth-Century Iran* and Afsaneh Najmabadi's series of articles,
soon to be part of a book, stand out. One central question is whether local feminisms,
especially those of the early decades of this century, should be considered "indigenous"
or imported, liberating or disciplinary. This debate has consequences for current discussions about what kind of feminism is appropriate for the Middle East.

In a collection of essays I recently brought together under the title *Remaking Women:
Feminism and Modernity in the Middle East* (1998), some scholars took up these questions, showing indeed that colonial constructions of women as the locus of Eastern backwardness shaped anticolonial nationalisms and that feminist projects relied on Western
discourses on women's public roles, marriage, domesticity, and scientific childrearing.
But these essays also explored the selectiveness with which Western ideas and models
were appropriated; the significant changes that were introduced when European ideas
were translated into local contexts; and the very ways that middle-class women themselves were able to make positive use of what seemed like new systems of discipline and
regulation. Following one of the most productive lines of thought made possible by *Orientalism*, with the division between East and West (and representation of each) to be
understood *not* as a natural geographic or cultural fact but as a product of the political
and historical encounter of imperialism. We argued that condemning "feminism" as an
inauthentic Western import is just as inaccurate as celebrating it as a local or indigenous
project. The first position assumes such a thing as cultural purity; the second underestimates the formative power of colonialism in the development of the region.

This takes me to the fourth way in which Said's work has been—or perhaps could
be—crucial to Middle East gender studies: sorting out the politics of contemporary
Middle East feminisms. The issues raised here are relevant for many other Third World
feminisms. Said's greatest intellectual contribution has been to reveal the "worldliness" of all cultural production, even academic. I have always understood the tensions
in *Orientalism* between a humanism that looks beyond cultural difference and the
Foucauldian project of tracking the relationship between power and knowledge as arising from Said's need to grasp and expose what many of us have experienced: the pain
of identifying with a community (the Palestinians) regarded with antipathy in the West
and heated brutally on the ground.

Feminist scholarship too is, by definition, an engaged scholarship because it is
premised on a concern about the condition of women and usually involves a critique
of the structures that oppress them. It too is linked to personal experience. A good deal
of the most interesting feminist theorizing inside and outside of Middle East studies
has been about the importance of positionality (the social location from which one

analyzes the world), related to the insights of *Orientalism*. However, as the work of a number of outspoken feminists from the Middle East reveals, and I will just take some examples from the Arab world here, to launch feminist critiques in a context of continuing Western hegemony is to risk playing into the hands of Orientalist discourse. There are analogies to be made with what happens what Edward Said goes beyond criticizing Israel or the United States and instead denounces authoritarian Arab regimes or deplores the lack of democracy in Arafat's Palestine National Authority.

Feminists from the Middle East, especially those who write in English or French, are inevitably caught between the sometimes incompatible projects of representing Middle East women as complex agents (that is, not as passive victims of Islamic or "traditional" culture), mostly to the West and advocating their rights at home, which usually involves a critique of local patriarchal structures. The problem with the latter is that it can easily be appropriated as native confirmation of already negative and simplistic images, as when American missionary women at the turn of the century cited Qasim Amin for evidence of the lovelessness, and therefore inferiority, of marriage under Islam.[4] Qasim Amin, author of the controversial *The Liberation of Women* in 1899, is often credited in the Middle East with being a champion of women's emancipation.

Let me try to give some examples of the tricky situations in which Arab feminists find themselves. Moroccan sociologist Fatima Mernissi is a good example because her sophistication, creativity and political courage are stunning; and yet her work, when it moves between her home in the Arab world and the Western context in which it is so well received, can be troubling. Her 1994 memoir of coming of age is called *Dreams of Trespass: Tales of a Harem Girlhood*. Instead of refusing to reproduce the old Orientalist stereotype of women in harems, she brings to life the world of women and patriarchal authority in the enclosed household of her wealthy Fez family. Conjuring up a rich emotional world and capturing exquisitely family dynamics and women's experiences, she nevertheless anchors the memoir in her "innocent" interrogation of the meaning of boundaries, the invisible rules of space, and sexual difference. In the end, despite her celebration of women's traditional powers of beauty, she unambivalently pits her mother's strong wish for modernity—for a little girl dressed in Western clothes who will attend school learn French, and become liberated—against all the restricting forces of tradition and the harem. Tradition and Modernity. Harems and Freedom. Veiling and Unveiling. These are the familiar terms by which the East has long been apprehended (and devalued) and the West has constructed itself as superior. These are some of what Said calls the dogmas of Orientalism, and they are the very terms that feminist scholars like Lata Mani, in her belatedly published book on colonial India, *Contentious Traditions*, have brilliantly called into question.

For many feminists from the region, not just "tradition" but Islamism is also seen as a threat to women. Again, one has to ask what the class politics and ideological assumptions of a local opposition to this might be and what views of the incompatibility of Islam with women's rights such opposition unwittingly affirms. Can one both recognize that organizations such as Women against Fundamentalism and Women Living under Islamic Laws are working against some serious abuses of women and yet be open to the many women activists working from within the Islamic tradition to bring out new interpretations of religious texts or the many nonelite women searching for an alternative modernity that is not secular? Feminists In the context of the Islamic Republic of Iran, in many ways like Islamic modernists earlier in the century and feminist lslamist contemporaries in Egypt, Jordan, and Turkey are themselves arguing for a more dynamic and historically sensitive vision of what Islam is or could be for women. They are publishing journals and magazines in Persian, Arabic, and Turkish—work that is not directed to the West and is largely unknown here except through scattered studies published in English, including the work of Afsaneh Najmabadi ("Feminisms in an Islamic Republic," in Yvonne Haddad and John Esposito's 1998 *Islam, Gender, and Social Change*). Nilufer Cole (*The Forbidden Modern: Civilization and Veiling*, 1996), and Aynur Ilyasoglu ("Islamist Women in Turkey: Their Identity and Self-Image," In Arat's *Deconstructing Images of "The Turkish Woman"*). Some of their voices are recorded by Elizabeth Fernea in her wide-ranging exploration, In *Search of Islamic Feminism: One Woman's Global Journey*, a 1998 book that never quite clarifies what "Islamic feminism" might mean.

In her 1997 address to the Middle East Women's Studies Association at the Middle East Studies Association annual meetings, the Cairo-based anthropologist Soraya Altorki spoke with great eloquence about the problems confronted by women who work in three Arab women's groups in Egypt—the Women and Memory Forum, the New Woman, and Nour—devoted to "feminist" research and advocacy.[5] Her remarks on these groups could be paralleled by discussion of other groups, such as the Women's Studies Program at Birzeit University in Palestine, where feminists are working within national contexts for the study and advocacy of women, not only teaching, running for office, and organizing women's centers but also publishing studies that might shape policymaking by the national governing authorities.[6] They are all put on the defensive by some activities of feminists abroad and by the Western media's sensationalism when presenting Islam and women. They must also reckon with international funding agencies with their own priorities regarding women's issues, priorities that often differ from those working in what Altorki calls a "nationalist context." As a number of the participants in the first Arab regional women's/gender studies workshop noted (proceedings of which were published in a volume edited by Cynthia Nelson and Soraya Altorki for *Cairo Papers in Social Science*), their projects and stances are inevitably read, and undertaken, in relation to these outside constructions and interventions that they admit are linked, in Altorki's words, to "the legacy of colonial rule and present hegemony."[7]

The dilemmas are sharp because of this global context. As the Women and Memory Forum, a group in Egypt, puts it, "identifying exclusively with the west means rejecting the Arab heritage, while rejecting the west and cleaving to 'tradition' means accepting patriarchal structures of subordination and inferiorization."[8] The solution is to refuse the tradition/Western modernity divide, but how sophisticated do you have to be to manage this?

One strategy seems to be to publish in regional languages as well as English or French, and to initiate local projects, both academic and activist. The recently established Women and Memory Forum in Egypt holds conferences, publishes a newsletter called *Letters from Memory* (as of the January 1999 issue, in both English and Arabic), and has published a few books in Arabic. The editors creatively rewrite Arab folktales from "a gender-sensitive perspective," recover the writings and activities of forgotten women from the past (whether feminists like Malak Hifni Nassef or an eighteenth-century aristocrat who forced the invading French to respect her while standing up for the rights of others), and rewrite Arab history from a gendered perspective.[9]

Nour, a research and publishing house for work on and by Arab women, has commissioned and published books, including some translations; organized the first Arab women's book fair; and regularly publishes a book review journal by the name *Nour*. The journal, now in its fourteenth issue (with recent special issues devoted to Palestinian and Lebanese women), cover a wide range of books, some in English but most in Arabic, in the social sciences and literature. These organizations are run by academic or professional women and, like the Women's Studies Programs at universities in Palestine and Yemen, have been partially supported by European (especially Dutch) funds, opening them up to occasional suspicion.

The work of the New Woman Research Center in Egypt is perhaps more controversial, however, because it concentrates on the problem of violence against women.[10] The center's field research has shown how widespread the problems are; but one can also imagine what uses publicity about this issue might be put to in the wider world, a world already primed to think of the Middle East as a place of violence against women, especially because of the highly publicized issue of female circumcision. And what accusations will be leveled against these feminists by government authorities and other defenders of Egypt's image?

The problems faced by feminists in various countries of the Middle East vary because such groups work in such different political contexts, both internally and vis-à-vis the West. For example, feminists in Turkey have similarly taken up the question of violence against women, opening the Purple Roof Women's Shelter in Istanbul, and a similar one in Ankara, along with taking on less controversial projects such as founding the Women's Library and Information Center. Each national context is configured differently. Turkish feminists are subject to less criticism in the name of Turkey's image abroad. Instead they must confront not just the growing presence of Islamists (whom they, as secularists, find threatening) but also the challenge they represent to the state which, based on Kemalist ideology and reforms, sees itself as having solved "the woman question" long ago. In Iran under the Islamic Republic, feminism in its various guises and expressed through various media, including a number of women's journals, faces yet other alignments and minefields.

Some feminist scholars in the field have worried that the influence of Said's *Orientalism*, and the broader approaches known variously as postcolonial and postmodern, have led us away from criticism of local institutions and political forces. Haideh Moghissi, a Canadian-based Iranian feminist scholar, goes so far as to accuse Middle East intellectuals of undertaking "a costly intellectual experiment" when they are so anxious to be anti-Orientalist that they develop an "uncritical fascination with Western postmodernism" In her 1999 *Feminism and Islamic Fundamentalism: The Limits of Postmodern Analysis*, she asserts that this inclines them to celebrate difference and local voices. She fears that in recognizing and respecting what they call Islamic feminisms in Iran, they "inadvertently lend support to the most effectively cloaked repressive movement in the region: Islamic fundamentalism" (p. 63). Her targets are other European-based Iranian feminist scholars such as Haleh Afshar (*Islam and Feminisms: An Iranian Case Study*, 1998) and Afsaneh Najmabadi, who no longer see Islamic feminism as an oxymoron, and even Ziba Mir-Hosseini, whose detailed 1999 study of the internal religio-legal debates about gender and women in the Islamic Republic in the 1990s (*Islam and Gender: The Religious Debate in Contemporary Iran*) makes a case for a lively range of opinion among clerics and laypeople and whose argument is that the processes of social change set in motion by the Islamic Revolution in 1979 have "nurtured not only a new school of jurisprudence, which is slowly trying to respond to social realities, but also a new gender consciousness" (p. 179).

Deniz Kandiyoti, whose earlier groundbreaking *Women, Islam, and the State* had brought to the fore issues of nationalism and state policy, moving discussion away from essentialist cultural arguments about "women and Islam," also worries about the impact of Said's *Orientalism*. In a sweeping review in the introduction to her recent edited volume, *Engendering Middle East Studies*, she argues that the field of Middle East gender studies has been negatively affected by the arguments of *Orientalism* in three ways: social analysis has been devalued in favor of analysis of representations; binary thinking about East and West has trained us to focus too much on the West and not enough on the internal heterogeneity of Middle Eastern societies; and, finally, it has also deflected attention away from "local institutions and cultural processes that are implicated in the production of gender hierarchies and in forms of subordination based on gender" (p. 18). Kandiyoti argues for the necessity of internal critique of gendered power in Middle Eastern societies.

Said, I believe, would not disagree. I even think he offers Middle East feminists and feminist scholars a model for the kinds of entangled political engagements they inevitably face. He has braved accusations and condemnations coming from many sides as he both criticizes the various forms and instruments of Western domination *and* the failures of Middle Eastern societies and political systems. What enables him to steer a clear course is the integrity of his position. He is a critic who is consistent in his advocacy of justice on a global scale, and of democratic principles, wherever. As feminists we would do well to be similarly consistent, aware of the complex ground we tread and criticizing the multiple forms of injustice we find.

Notes

1. Marilyn Strathern. "An Awkward Relationship," *Signs* 12 (winter 1987): 276–93.
2. Some have charged that Said had relatively little to say about women and gender in his book, although he was to correct for this slightly in his 1985 article, "Orientalism Reconsidered," *Race and Class* 27, no. 2 (1965): 1–15, and in his *Culture and Imperialism* (New York Knopf, 1993). It must be recalled that *Orientalism* was published as feminist scholarship was beginning to take off in the United States and at just the same moment that the first major readers on women in the Middle East came out: Lois Beck and Nikki Keddie, eds. *Women in the Muslim World* (Cambridge Harvard University Press, 1978), and Elizabeth Fernea and Basima Bezirgan's *Middle Eastern Muslim Women Speak* (Austin: University of Texas Press, 1977).
3. Cynthia Nelson. "Old Wine in New Bottles," in *The Contemporary Study of the Arab World*, ed. Earl Sullivan and Jacqueline Ismael (Edmonton, Alberta: Alberta University Press, 1991), 127–52.

4. I discuss this in "The Marriage of Islamism and Feminism in Egypt Selective Repudiation as a Dynamic of Postcolonial Cultural Politics," in my *Remaking Women* (Princeton: Princeton University Press, 1998).

5. Soraya Altorki, "Feminist Groups in Contemporary Egypt," *The Review of the Association for Middle East Women's Studies* 7, no. 4 (1996): 16.

6. Lisa Taraki, Rita Giacaman Penny Johnson and Rema Hammami, *Palestinian Women: A Status Report* (Birzeit, Palestine: Women's Studies Program, Birzeit University 1997).

7. Altorki, 16.

8. Quoted in Altorki, 16.

9. See Hoda Elsadda, Somaya Ramadan, and Anita Abu-Bakr, eds., *Women's Time and Alternative Memory* (Zaman al-nisa' w al-dhakira al-badila) (Cairo: Women and Memory Forum, 1998).

10. The New Woman Research and Study Center has many projects besides this one on violence against women. For example, they commissioned and published, in Arabic and English, a comparative study, *The Feminist Movement in the Arab World* (Cairo: Dar El-Mostaqbal Al Arabi, 1996).

22.
GENDER AND NATION
Mrinalini Sinha
(2004)

What does gender have to do with the study of the nation or nation with the study of gender? …

If the scholarship on nationalism had demonstrated a certain indifference to gender as a category of analysis, feminist scholarship was equally guilty of neglecting the study of the nation and of nationalism. That was especially true of certain strands within feminist scholarship shaped by an assumption of the apparent naturalness of the nation for women in North America and Northwestern Europe. This scholarship tended to assume that women's relation to the nation was best summed up in that famous quotation from a character in Virginia Woolf's novel *Three Guineas*: "[A]s a woman I have no country. As a woman I want no country. As a woman my country is the whole world."[1]

The quotation invokes, of course, the history of Europe and North America, where women had to wage a separate struggle for the right to vote and to be included as citizens of the nation. On the basis of this particular history, moreover, the quotation also assumes that feminism has an apparently natural antipathy for, and an ability to transcend, the nation. A feminist scholarship that took this history as axiomatic tended to dismiss the salience of the nation and of nationalism for women and for feminism.

Here again, it was feminist scholarship of the "third world" (the colonized and semiperipheral areas of the world) that took the lead in engaging the study of nationalism as a feminist concern. Women's engagement in nationalist struggles against imperialism often led to a very different trajectory for feminism in the third world. At roughly the same time as the publication of Woolf's *Three Guineas,* for example, the anticolonial nationalist struggle in India produced a different dynamics for bourgeois women's investment in the nation. The dynamics of this relation were nicely captured in a popular nationalist slogan: "India cannot be free until its women are free and women cannot be free until India is free." In many colonized and semiperipheral areas of the world, the struggle for women's emancipation occurred in tandem with anticolonial nationalist struggles. It should come as no surprise, therefore, that third-world feminist scholarship once again was at the forefront in engaging with the phenomenon of nationalism.[2] More recently, feminist scholarship more generally has recognized the equally important ways in which the nation has also shaped, and been shaped by, gender relations and gender identities in the older, more established nation-states of the world. Indeed, the history of anticolonial nationalisms has played a formative role in shaping the scholarly agenda on gender and nation more generally.

What follows is a review of more than a decade of scholarship that has brought the study of gender and of the nation together and demonstrated the critical interdependence of the two. …

Definitional Clarifications

Contemporary scholarship proceeds from an underlying assumption that both genders and nations are socially constructed around ideological systems of "difference" that implicate them in relations of social power. There are certain key terms in this scholarship, however, that may still need some broad clarifications. The *nation* may be defined as a group whose members, on the basis of some combination of beliefs in a common origin, a common history, and a common destiny, constitute themselves as a community and lay claim to a specified territory and political representation, ranging from cultural autonomy to political statehood. There is, however, no one universal and inevitable form of the nation. Nations are necessarily constructed around a myth of their own uniqueness. The closest thing to a broad understanding of the nation, perhaps, is Benedict Anderson's characterization of nations as *limited imagined communities*. Nations are always limited because even the largest of nations has "finite, if elastic boundaries, beyond which lie other nations." They are necessarily imagined because the "members of even the smallest nation will never know most of their fellow-members, meet them, or even hear of them, yet in the minds of each lives the image of their communion." Nations also function as communities "because, regardless of the actual inequality and exploitation that may prevail in each, the nation is always conceived as a deep, horizontal comradeship."[3] This broad understanding of the nation provides a helpful framework for identifying the specificity of the nation as a community and its investment in gender difference.

That understanding of the nation also provides the basis for some broad definitions of such related terms as *nationalism, national identity, citizenship,* and the *nation-state.* … In its most general sense, … scholars have defined nationalism to include both the belief in nationhood and the goal to establish statehood for the nation. The definitions of "national identity" emphasize that it is "constructed" and subject to a continuous process of articulations and rearticulations. Because the construction of national identity does not "depend on the existence of any objective linguistic or cultural differentiation but on the subjective experience of difference," it necessarily entails a continuous process of defining itself against a host of "others."[4] "Citizenship," likewise, is a "slippery concept"; it works through implicit and explicit mechanisms to exclude various groups from full citizenship, both within and from without the nation-state. The term may be broadly defined to refer to the status bestowed on those who are "full members of a community," which includes political, social, and economic rights and duties. …

The relation between the terms *nation* and *state* requires a little more clarification. Most scholars are at pains to point out that the two terms are in no way synonymous and should be kept analytically distinct.[5] The frequent conflation of the two terms— through an obliteration of the hyphen from the term *nation-state*—leads to considerable confusion. The state is never an automatic political extension of the nation; the fit between nation and state, in fact, is never perfect. Even the most seemingly homogenous nation-states contain within their borders people who are only partially, if at all, integrated into the hegemonic construction of the nation. Furthermore, the boundaries of a national community—as in the contemporary example of the Kurds or of nationals who live outside their specified countries—may cut across the political boundaries of a state. Finally, there are stateless nations and multinational states. …

… Far from resting on a secure natural foundation, therefore, nations arise out of creative acts of human labor or imagination, including the emergence of national bureaucracies and communication systems; the creation of national histories and nationwide educational systems; and the spread of national myths, rituals, and "invented traditions" that masquerade as timeless.[6]

This view, of course, does not deny that nations are "real" in that they become instituted and renewed through countless ordinary, and extraordinary, practices that insinuate a nation into the very structure of society and the collective consciousness of people. Instead, it emphasizes the role of invention—both in the sense of fabrication and in the sense of the novel recombination of existing elements—that is necessary for the formation of national communities. Feminist scholarship has usefully pushed the analysis of the "invented" character of the nation to demonstrate its reliance on the discourse of gender. If nations are not natural, then their self-representation through gendered language and imagery acquires new significance. So, for example, the preponderance of female personifications in the representations of the nation—as in Germania (Germany), Marianne (France), or Mother India—require explanation. …

… Because women are often constructed as the symbolic "bodyguards" of a culture, those who carry the group's "honor" and are responsible for the intergenerational reproduction of its culture, they cannot be marginalized easily from cultural analyses of the nation.[7]

… Scholars have also emphasized the legacy of imperialism and colonialism to reframe the study of the nation in both the metropole and the colony. They argue that the history of nationalism has been directly implicated in the project of European domination of the world. As such, therefore, the "rule of colonial difference" (the maintenance of a supposedly essential difference of the rulers from the ruled) has shaped the history of the nation in the metropole as much as in the colony.[8] The direction of imperial influence flowed not just from the metropole to the colony but also in the reverse. …

The further point, however, is that nationalisms in the colonial world did not simply replicate the "modular" form of the nation as it had been previously imagined elsewhere in Europe and the New World. …

The real imaginative labor of anticolonial nationalism, therefore, lay in constructing its project as "different but modem" in relation to the modem West. In so doing, the project of anticolonial nationalism was often mediated through a logic of gender difference. The discourse of Indian nationalism, for example, produced the figure of the "modern Indian woman" as the unique signifier of Indianness and of the national culture's absolute difference from the West. This scholarship has thus contributed in making gender central to the analysis of the nation. …

Contributions of Feminist Scholarship

...

Much of the scholarship on nationalism—despite the contributions of feminist scholarship—associated nationalism typically with the domain of the "public," from which women have been excluded, and women with the domain of the "private." The contribution of women to the construction and maintenance of national communities and national identities was thus minimized in this allegedly gender-neutral scholarship on nationalism. Yet as feminist scholarship has long demonstrated, the origins and separation of the modern domains of the public and private were not "natural." The thrust of both feminist theoretical and historical scholarship has been to demonstrate a much more contingent, and interconnected, history of the gendered divisions of the modern public and private.

The constitution of the modern domains of the public and the private took place on the basis of a prior "sexual contract," which gendered these domains masculine and feminine, respectively.[9] ...

The ideological construction of gender difference, therefore, has historically shaped the modern "public" world of politics as much as it has the "private" world of familial relations in large parts of the world that came to be constituted as the "West." ...

... Although women may have been marginalized from the domain of the public, they have clearly played a significant role in the production and maintenance of national communities and national identities all over the world. Women, for example, are conspicuous in nationalist discourses as symbols of national culture and, through the control of women's sexuality, as the markers of community boundaries. Hence concerns about interracial and intercommunal sexual relations have typically centered on the access to, and availability of, women.

The most visible contribution of women to nationalist projects, of course, has been the mobilization of women, along with men, as active participants in various nationalist projects. From the peasant women whose bread riots ignited the French Revolution (1789) and the Russian Revolution (1917) to the contribution of elite and bourgeois women in various nationalist movements, the range of women's activities has been varied. Women have contributed to social reform and public education movements, they have participated in various public rituals and protests that constitute the "national public," and they have mobilized on behalf of national liberation and revolutionary struggles. ... [W]omen fought alongside men as guerillas in the Land and Freedom Army during the Mau Man uprising in Kenya (1952–59). ...[10] Equally significant, however, is the invocation of the supposedly "traditional" roles of women—as mothers, as objects of reverence and of protection, and as signifiers or markers of a group's innermost identity—in projects of nationalism.

Feminist scholarship, indeed, has demonstrated a variety of ways in which women contribute to the project of the nation:

• as biological reproducers of the members of ethnic collectivities;
• as reproducers of the boundaries of ethnic/national groups;

- as participants in the ideological reproduction of the collectivity and as transmitters of its culture;
- as signifiers of ethnic/national difference—as a focus and symbol in ideological discourses used in the construction, reproduction, and transformation of ethnic/national categories; and
- as participants in national, economic, political, and military struggles.[11]

Yet women are themselves always differentiated by race, class, age, education, religion, ethnicity, and urban/rural residence, all of which affect the nature and extent to which they are included in the national embrace. Their contributions and commitments to the nation have been shaped not just by their difference from men but by differences among women themselves. … What this scholarship, despite its difference in emphasis, seems to suggest is that women's experience of the project of modern nationhood has been distinct from that of men's.

Because gender is not a synonym for women, however, a gendered analysis of the nation does not rest simply on making women visible in the project of nationalism. The challenge posed by feminist scholarship has to do not just with the visibility of "women" but, more important, with the constitution of the nation itself in the "sanctioned institutionalization of gender *difference*."[12] The discourse of the nation is implicated in particular elaborations of masculinity as much as of femininity. As such, it contributes to their normative constructions. It becomes a privileged vehicle in the consolidation of dichotomized notions of "men" and "women" and of "masculinity" and "femininity." We thus have "fathers" and "mothers," and "sons" and "daughters," of the nation, each with their own gendered rights and obligations. This is the sense in which the discourses of gender and the nation can be seen as symbiotic. On the one hand, national narratives rely heavily on the supposedly natural logic of gender differences to consolidate new political identities around the nation. On the other hand, the discourse of nationalism provides legitimacy to normative gendered constructions of masculinity and femininity.[13]

The concern of many a feminist scholar, therefore, has been as much with men and masculinity as with women and femininity.[14] … So, for example, nationalist movements often involve reasserting masculinity and reclaiming male honor, and moments of nationalist fervor frequently center around a remasculinization of national culture.[15] At the same time, as many studies have shown, women have enthusiastically supported the nation and nationalism. Although we may thus debate the extent to which nations are best understood as inherently masculinist constructs, nations in one form or another have relied on a discourse of gender difference. One of the "gender ironies" of nationalism, in fact, is that the nation, for all its emphasis on a "deep horizontal comradeship," constitutes its members differentially in distinctly gendered ways.[16]

The discourse of the nation is thus inevitably implicated in gender power. The hierarchical construction and institutionalization of gender difference in nationalist discourse has typically meant that the costs and benefits of nationhood and of national belonging fall unevenly on men and women. Even when nationalist projects have invited women to stand alongside men in sacrificing for the nation, they often reassert the "traditional" roles of women once the moment of national crisis is over. …

Gender itself is never constituted only through the ideological construction of sexual difference. One "becomes a woman," or for that matter a man, not just in opposition to members of the other sex but also in opposition to other women and to other men.[17] "When President Theodore Roosevelt famously compared the "cowardly" and "selfish" woman who neglected her duty to be a mother with the man who "fears to do his duty in battle when the country calls him," his vision of the gendered national duties of Americans was based not just on a notion of sexual difference. His admonition, in fact, was directed very specifically to the "well-born white woman" who through "willful sterility" was guilty of "race suicide."[18] "Womanhood" in Roosevelt's rhetoric of the nation, then, was already also a class-bound and racialized construct. Nations, indeed, are not only gendered but also simultaneously "raced" and constituted by other axes of difference. The discourse of race—the fiction of a "racial identity"—is no less constitutive than the discourse of gender in the construction of nations.[19]

The further point, however, is that the various axes of difference—of gender, race, ethnicity, class, sexuality, and of colonizer and colonized—are not only mutually constitutive but also differently constituted. Hence they often intersect in the articulation of nations in uneven and unpredictable ways. ...

To ignore the various modes of organizing "difference" in the articulation of the nation, therefore, would reproduce the "gender blindness of previous historians of nations and nationalism in another key."[20] One of the most challenging and rewarding agendas for feminist scholarship, indeed, has been to account for the mutual constitution, and the often contradictory and uneven mediation, of multiple axes of difference in the articulation of both genders and nations.

Major Themes

The gendered articulation of the nation—no less than its articulation in other forms of organizing difference—can be examined only in concrete historical situations. Nations and national identities are continuously being formed and reformed in relation to various categories of difference. All nations are gendered, but there is no one privileged narrative of the gendering of nations. ...

Nevertheless, a decade or so of scholarship on the subject has offered some broad themes for analyzing the intersection between the discourses of gender and of the nation. These, for the sake of convenience, may be divided as the constitution of the nation in gender difference, the gendered modes of national belonging, and the relation between feminisms and nationalisms.

The Constitution of the Nation in Gender Difference

One of the most striking features of nationalist discourses, as numerous scholars have observed, is the pervasiveness of familial and gendered imagery. All nations are imagined as "domestic genealogies."[21] The very term *nation* comes from the Latin *natio* (to be born). People are "born" into a nation, and foreigners "adopt" a nation or are "naturalized" into national citizenship.[22] Individuals are assigned their place within the national family, and nations themselves belong within the global family of nations. The nation is often constituted as *Heimat* (homeland). The relations of people to specific lands, languages, cultures, or shared histories are expressed as motherlands or fatherlands, mother tongues, mother cultures, and "founding fathers" or "mothers of the nation." Feminist scholars, therefore, justifiably raise questions about the reasons for, and implications of, the ubiquitousness of gendered and familial imagery in nationalist discourses.

The family—constructed as a "natural" heterosexual and patriarchal unit—performs a variety of critical ideological services in the constitution of the nation. The first, perhaps most obvious, function is in representing the nation as an innate or organic community whose members, like those of the family, are constituted by "natural" ties rather than by mere accident or choice. The familial imagery thus offers the "invented" nation a powerful legitimizing language of naturalization. In order to do so, however, the institution of the family itself is first removed from history and made into a timeless and natural unit of social organization. The family is thus depoliticized in the discourse of the nation; it is constructed as prior to history and thus immune to political challenge or to change.[23]

The history of the nation, however, has been closely associated with a particular historical form of the family—the heterosexual bourgeois nuclear family—and the resulting normative constructions of sexuality and gender identities that sustain this family form. The history of their mutual reinforcement can be seen in their development in Europe. There, the rise of the middle class from the eighteenth century onward produced a unique differentiation of gender roles and a distinctive code of bourgeois "respectability" that emphasized the control of sexual passions by both men and women and presented marriage as the only acceptable sexual relationship.[24] Nineteenth-century European nationalisms entered into a convenient marriage with bourgeois "respectability" and contributed to spreading its norms across classes. The norms of bourgeois sexual respectability, in turn, helped in the construction of the national community as a virile homosocial community whose "proper" male homosocial relations were secured through the identification and exclusion of homosexuality often figured as "effeminacy" or deviant.

The norms of sexual respectability also helped differentiate "pure" from "fallen" women. The former were constructed as the symbolic signifiers of the nation and deployed for the service of the nation in their "naturally" subordinate roles as dutiful mothers, wives, and daughters. In contrast to the "normal" sexuality of respectable men and women of the nation, European nationalisms associated "abnormal" sexuality with a variety of others—such as Jews, Africans, homosexuals, and so on—in their midst. Hence at the same time that white English womanhood was being desexualized, Sara Bartman, a Khoisan woman from the Cape of South Africa, could be brought to England and exhibited in public as an exotic specimen of exaggerated female sexuality.[25] The development of gendered European nationalisms sustained—and were themselves sustained by—the naturalization of a racialized bourgeois heterosexual and patriarchal family form.

The bourgeois ideology of gender, family, and sexuality was further sustained in the imperialist-nationalist projects of the nineteenth century. The norms of bourgeois domesticity and the resulting construction of gender difference in the colonies helped construct and maintain the ideological, economic, and political power of colonizing elites. The Western bourgeois ideal of gender difference was used as the yardstick of "civilization," and any deviation from it became further proof of the "backwardness" of indigenous people. ...

... The ideology of gender, family, and sexuality similarly framed the colonial policies and practices of the other European nations, such as the French, the Dutch, and the Germans in their respective empires.[26] The marriage between European nationalisms and bourgeois respectability, therefore, was cemented not just in Europe but also in the imperial-nationalist process of "domesticating the empire."

... When scholars ignore the significance of the trope of the family for nationalist discourse, therefore, they not only foreclose an examination of the mutually reinforcing logic of nation, gender, and heterosexual identities but also underestimate the force of the representational labor in constructing the nation—like the family—as timeless, natural, and organic.

The second, and related, function of the representation of nations as domestic genealogies—replete with a cast of fathers, mothers, sons, and daughters of the nation—is to provide the nation with its "instrumental passions."[27] The nation, for all its foundational ambivalence, has the capacity to inspire enormous passion and devotion from its members. ...

The language of kinship plays a very important role in allowing the nation to appropriate for itself the kind of elemental passions hitherto associated with the ties of blood. Thus the nation in the form of an abused or humiliated mother appeals to her sons and daughters, albeit often in differently gendered ways, to come to her protection and restore her honor. Similarly, the nation as fatherland calls upon its sons and daughters to obey the father and fulfill their respective gendered duties to the nation. The representation of the nation through a language of love—an "eroticized nationalism"—helps account for the distinctiveness of nationalism as a discourse capable of arousing enormous passions from the members of nations.[28]

In this context, therefore, heterosexual desire is often mapped onto political desire as *amor patrie* (love of country). In Latin America during the nineteenth century, for example, romance novels inspired "passionate patriotism" toward the new nations.[29] The new national ideals in Latin America were reflected in tales of heterosexual desire and marriage. These "foundational fictions," through stories of love that conquers all, offered a figurative conciliation for the many political and social tensions that beset the new nation-states. ... The nation's hold on the emotions of people, indeed, would be hard to understand outside of its investment in gendered kinship relations and in the poetics of heterosexual love.

The further ideological work of the family is to make the various forms of hierarchies both within the nation and between nations seem "natural." Because the family is idealized as a domain in which individual members willingly subsume their interests within the supposedly unified interests of the family (as represented by the male head of household), it becomes a signifier of "hierarchy within unity" for the nation.[30] The myth of the family as a fundamental "unity," of course, is sustained in part through a belief in the allegedly natural subordination of women and children to adult men within the family. The nation's identification with the family to signify the fundamental "unity" of its own members similarly constructs the hierarchies of gender, class, race, and ethnicity within the national community as natural and thus without a history. The familial discourse serves precisely to leave the fundamental "unity" of the nation unchallenged even as actual social relations of power and exploitation divide the members of the nation.

This "family romance" glosses over relations of domination within the family as much as within the nation.[31] The use of the family ideal in the nationalist rhetoric of the United States—as in the rhetoric of "family values" and in the conceptualization of the U.S. nation-state as a national family—renders racial, class, gender, and heterosexual power within the nation as "natural" through invoking the gender and age hierarchies of the family. So, for example, the violence against certain groups, such as Native Americans, Mexican Americans, and African Americans, whose history in the United States was shaped by conquest and slavery rather than voluntary migration, becomes (like "domestic violence") invisible in the narrative of the national family. Similarly, the differential entitlements of citizenship—like birth order in a family—"naturally" privileges groups on the basis of their time of arrival in the United States.[32]

Age and gender hierarchies within a family were also frequently deployed in the context of a developmental narrative of colonial superiority to legitimate European domination abroad. The people of the colonized world were often represented as "children," or "childlike," who needed the benevolent and natural protection of European fathers—and occasionally of European mothers as well. The project of European imperialism and colonialism was thus incorporated within a familial discourse in which the self-representation of imperial nations was that of stem but kindly guardians over people as yet lacking requisite political maturity.

The lack of political maturity was sometimes also explained in explicitly gendered terms, as in the opposition of Sir Lepel Griffin, a diehard nineteenth-century British imperialist in India, to demands for political representation by either Englishwomen or Bengali men. Although he considered the possession of "feminine qualities" by both as grounds for their disqualification from political representation, he also noted an important difference between Englishwomen and Bengali men: "The characteristics of women which disqualify them for public life and its responsibilities are inherent in their sex and are worthy of honour, for to be womanly is the highest praise for women, as to be masculine is her worst reproach, but when men, [such] as the Bengalis are disqualified for political enfranchisement by the possession of essentially feminine characteristics, they must expect to be held in such contempt by stronger and braver races, who have fought for such liberties as they have won or retained."[33] The ideology of gender legitimated the exclusion of certain men as much as women, albeit differently, from political representation. The image of the family performs an important ideological service for the nation in representing a whole range of social inequalities-inside and outside the nation-as "natural" hierarchies. The nation, then, despite its social inequalities, can be represented as a community or a "deep horizontal comradeship." ...

In still other national projects womanhood has been used to embody both the promise and the threat of modernity. This flexibility in the metaphorical role of women for the gendering of tradition and modernity is especially noted in various anticolonial nationalisms. This is, perhaps, itself a testimony of the complex ways in which the problem of tradition and modernity is recast in the context of colonialism and anticolonial nationalism. …

The role of women in various other third-world nationalisms demonstrates a … complexity that goes beyond the mere alignment of women with static and unreformed tradition. Women—more often than not—have had to carry the more complex burden of representing the colonized nation's "betweenness" with respect to precolonial traditions and "Western" modernity.[34] The nationalist project both initiated women's access to modernity and set the limits of the desirable modernity for women. In this context, several early-twentieth-century feminists, such as Halide Edibe in Turkey or Hudá Sha'rawi in Egypt, constructed their dynamic public roles as a duty to the nation rather than as a right.[35] As signifiers of the nation, women needed to be modern, but they could not mark a complete break from tradition. The woman of the anticolonial nationalist imagination, then, was not necessarily a "traditional" woman. She was more likely the "modem-yet-modest" woman who both symbolized the nation and negotiated its tension between tradition and modernity.[36]

Even cultural-revivalist and fundamentalist movements in the third world are seldom traditionalist in any simple way. The call to tradition in these movements is more precisely a response to the modernization of gender relations and to the transformation of gender roles that have already been underway. As one scholar so aptly puts it, "if fundamentalists are calling for the return to the veil, it must be because women have been taking off the veil."[37] The fundamentalist attack against the modernization of gender roles, moreover, is often fueled by class tensions produced by the failure of socioeconomic development and the effects of neocolonialism. The critique of *gharbzahdegi* ("Westoxification") under Ayatollah Khomeini in the Islamic Republic of Iran, for example, reflected both gender and class conflict. The objects of that critique were mainly upper-middle-class and educated women, who, compared with poor and peasant women, had benefited under the previous Pahlavi regime.[38] The important point is that as the "true essence" of national and cultural identity—whether as signifiers of tradition or of modernity—women become vulnerable to different political agendas of the nation.

Gendered Modes of National Belonging

If the ideology of gender difference has been important in the constitution of the nation, then the nation has been equally important for the construction of gender and the performance of masculinity and femininity. Hence, as various scholars have demonstrated, the nation always relates to its members differently as "men" and "women." The project of modern nationhood has largely cast men as "metonymic" (as causes of national history) and women as "metaphorical" or symbolic (analogues of the national soul).[39] In other words, men are defined as consequential to the nation and as its agents, but women are defined as its iconic embodiments. The differential gendered construction of nationalist agency is illustrated in the mottoes of the Hitler youth movement. While boys were asked to "live faithfully; fight bravely; die laughing," girls were expected to "be faithful; be pure; be German."[40]

The trope of sacrifice—one of the most powerful in the narrative of the nation—is similarly gendered. Men are usually called to give their life or die for the nation, and women willingly to surrender their sons and husbands to die for the nation. To be sure, women have historically been agents in the project of the nation and, in some cases, have also died along with men on the battlefields for the sake of the nation. Vietnam, with a tradition of women leading armed resistance against foreign oppression going back to the famous Trung sisters (Trung Trac and Trung Nhi) in 39 C.E., produced a long list of women martyrs during all stages of its nationalist struggles against the Japanese, the French, and the United States.[41] Furthermore, not all men (and not all women) are constructed in similar ways in the project of the nation. Yet the belief in the "natural" difference between men and women has been fairly constant in the constitution of nations, and the nation itself has helped construct the normative constructions of "men" and "women" and of "masculinity" and "femininity."

The focus on the nation as a site for the construction of gender difference has, first, called attention to the hitherto neglected question of the construction of "men" and "masculinity" in nationalist discourse. The nation is implicated in the construction of "men" in various ways. The nation itself is largely modeled as a brotherhood or a fraternity. This, of course, has never included all men. The homosociality of the national brotherhood has depended in large part on the exclusion of homosexuals and men otherwise constructed as deviants. … The nation is not only imagined typically as a fraternity but is also defended and administered through predominantly homosocial institutions. In numerous ways, then, the project of nationhood constructs men as contiguous with each other in the making of the nation.

The discourse of nationalism, moreover, is an important site for the enactment of masculinity. The military—increasingly constructed since at least the second half of the seventeenth century in Europe as an exclusive masculine arena, from which women who traditionally accompanied soldiers to provision, cook, clean, and tend to the wounded were gradually excluded—has constituted a privileged arena in the construction of both modern masculinity and the modern nation.[42] In many cases, indeed, political rights for men have flowed directly from their eligibility to shed blood for the nation. The nationalist project, therefore, is often associated with the production of a militarized masculinity. …

The contours of patriotic masculinity, however, are also produced against, or through the self-conscious rejection of, the feminine or the feminized. That is reflected, for example, in the metamorphosis of Theodore Roosevelt from an "effete" and "weakling" New York state assemblyman to a powerful symbol of turn-of-the-nineteenth-century imperial U.S. masculinity.[43] Roosevelt's self-transformation—which began with his association with the Badlands of South Dakota and a new image as a "muscular cowboy"—was accomplished by bringing together the two dominant themes of turn-of-the-century U.S. nationalism: westward expansion and U.S. imperialism.

Roosevelt's enthusiastic support of the so-called Spanish American War and the role of his "Rough Riders" captured both these themes of patriotic masculinity. The opponents of imperial U.S. intervention in the debate over the "Philippines question" were dismissed as "fossils" and "old women." The project of a patriotic imperial nationalism entailed production of a youthful virile manliness whose opponents were the effete, the feminized, and the old.

The production of nationalist masculinity in national discourse is also enacted via the control/protection of women. The politics of "colonial masculinity" (which informed both colonizers and colonized) in the British Empire illustrates the multiple dimensions in the performance of masculinity.[44] On the one hand, elite "white" British masculinity was constructed both through its difference from feminized or effeminate native men and through its role as the benevolent protector of women. The protection of "Oriental" women—the idea of "white men saving brown women from brown men"—was an important component in the self-definition of white British masculinity in the colonial context.[45] The real or imagined threat to white women from the alleged assaults of native men provided, perhaps, the most dramatic demonstrations of white imperial masculinity in the colonial domain. ... On the other hand, however, "native" men also sought to reclaim their honor and masculinity—from negative representations in colonial discourse—by claiming the right to control/protect "our" women from foreigners and foreign influence. The rhetoric of the protection of women as well as the protection of the nation—itself often represented as a woman—was thus an important component in the production of masculinity.

The nationalist constructions of "women" and "femininity," and women's complicity in those constructions, have also been the subject of much scholarly attention. Despite the historical marginalization of women from the sphere of formal national politics, women are not absent from the domain of the national public. Women, as members of the national family, enter the domain of the national public in numerous ways. The nationalist project assigns them roles not just in biological reproduction but in the larger social and cultural reproduction of the national collectivity. As such, women are called to perform certain important nationalist tasks, such as the preservation and transmission of the national language (the "mother tongue," as it were) and the national culture. Women have emerged as national actors—as mothers, educators, workers, and fighters—in various nationalist projects. ... A further point, however, is that the construction of femininity within nationalist discourse has had important implications for women.

The pervasiveness of powerful female figures—especially the figure of the mother—in the discourse of nationalism provides an important context for understanding the cooperation and complicity of women with such constructions. The image of "motherhood," both in the cultural representation of the nation as "mother" and in women's roles as "mothers of the nation," has been among the most powerful and exalted images of the feminine. The dominant construction of women as mothers—as objects of both national reverence and protection—has been the most important way in which women have been integrated into various nationalist projects. In the United States, white women otherwise excluded from the construction of civic virtues in the young republic enjoyed a status as "republican mothers" who nurtured the heroic sons of the new nation.[46] ...

The relationship between the exaltation of feminine images and the marginalization of women in nationalist projects, however, is not always so straightforward. Women have also successfully mobilized the construction of "motherhood" to stake their claims in national politics. Indeed, women are constructed by (and themselves construct the meaning of) motherhood in nationalist discourse. ... The Argentine Madres de la Plaza de Mayo is, perhaps, the most famous example of women's mobilization of motherhood. ...[47] Women powerfully invoked the image of "motherhood" to denounce political torture and the "disappearance" of political activists. In this sense, then, the construction of powerful female figures in nationalist projects may also empower the mobilization of women.

Yet—to the extent that constructions of "women" and "femininity" are closely bound with considerations of national/cultural identity—these constructions have important implications for women's experience of nationhood. For the sake of the nation, for example, women are often at the receiving end of a wide range of nationalist policies and practices, especially at moments of perceived national crises. The image of a vulnerable "white womanhood" as the embodiment of the honor and prestige of the white race was frequently invoked in colonial contexts to secure colonial power. It sanctioned a variety of colonial policies that entailed control of white women's sexuality in demarcating and policing racialized boundaries for the exercise of colonial power over native populations.[48] Similarly, the critique of modernization and westernization in fundamentalist and cultural revivalist movements is frequently articulated as a call for the "retraditionalization" of women. The systematic use of rape of "enemy" women as a nationalist strategy during times of war, as in the conflicts in Bangladesh in 1971 and in Bosnia-Herzegovinia in the 1990s, is the most dramatic illustration of the consequences for women of being symbols of national culture and vulnerable to violation by national enemies.

There are numerous other ways, however, in which national concerns about the health, demographic future, racial composition, or cultural identity of a nation have entailed the adoption of policies that target women. The Zionist-nationalist discourse and its project of settlement in Palestine, for example, enlists Jewish women in the state of Israel in a "demographic race" against Palestinian Arabs to bear more children. ...[49] The aggressive pro-natalist policies directed at Jewish women under the Israeli state were legitimated as a nationalist priority.

It is, indeed, "women" who become subject in nationalist projects to shifting definitions and redefinitions of national priorities and interests. For women, nationalist projects have often entailed a transition from a "private patriarchy," where women are under the patriarchal control of individual heads of families, to a "public patriarchy," where they experience the patriarchal control of an ethnic collectivity or a larger community of men.[50] The nationalist construct of "women," therefore, produces an anomalous experience of nationhood for women.

Finally, nationalist projects construct "women" primarily through a heterosexual relationship to men that emphasizes a supposedly "natural" hierarchy between men and women. The identification of women mainly with the private and familial sphere has been the basis for the exclusion of women as citizens or from full membership of the community. The most obvious, of course, is the denial of political rights to women as citizens. In most states in Europe and the Americas, women's suffrage followed well after most men's. It was not until the twentieth century that most of these states granted national female suffrage. Many Asian and African states, however, extended universal suffrage to men and women at the same time during the period of national independence in the twentieth century.

Yet the political disabilities in women's status as citizens go beyond the denial of the right to vote. The history of discrimination against women in relation to education, professional employment, economic independence, and rights within marriage, divorce, inheritance, and the custody of children—all the things that have qualified men for public roles—have constructed women's disqualification from a variety of public roles and made them dependent on fathers and husbands. The legacy continues to haunt women's relations to the nation and the state, well after the granting of formal legal equality.

The anomalous status of women as citizens is reflected in the dual construction of women both as individuals in their own right, subject to the general laws of the state, and as men's legal appendages, subject to the provision of special laws. The nationality and immigration laws in many countries in Europe and North America, for example, have a long legacy of being based on the model of the heterosexual nuclear family, with a male head of household and females subsumed as dependents of men. Until World War II, most countries in Europe, with the exception of the Soviet Union, did not give married women equal access to nationality and citizenship. … A married woman's citizenship derived not from her father or from the country of her birth, but from her husband's citizenship. When women married foreign men, therefore, they lost their nationality and had to take up the nationality of their husband. In the event of a divorce, these women often found themselves "stateless." …

… The nationality and immigration legislations have been an important means through which nation-states maintain and preserve a gender-based as well as racialized community of citizens.

In many third-world countries, the duality in the construction of women as citizens is reflected in the tension between secular law and personal law.[51] In many cases, for example, the domain of family legislation and personal law that affects marriage, divorce, child custody, and maintenance and inheritance law, is based on religious law, even when other legal codes are fully secular. The domain of personal law usually privileges the heterosexual patriarchal family and the rights of men over that of women. The nation-state, therefore, ends up colluding with the patriarchal family in circumscribing women's legal equality as citizens of the state. … Recognition by various nationalist projects of women as citizens in their own rights, therefore, is often compromised by the construction of women primarily through a heterosexual relationship to men.

The Relation Between Feminisms and Nationalisms

… [T]he relationship between feminisms and nationalisms is not given but rather shaped in specific historical conjunctures.

In Europe, feminist movements for suffrage and other rights for women generally emerged after, and in response to, the projects of modern nationhood. As such, therefore, they called attention to the inequality of women in the constitution of the nation as a community. ...

Although the self-representation of European feminism may be aligned with radical ideologies that were often explicitly international—and even antinational—in orientation, that does not mean that early European feminists were not staunchly nationalist or that their feminist project was not invested in the racial and imperial politics of their nations. European feminists, as much as their counterparts in the United States and elsewhere, articulated their feminisms as explicitly racialized and imperialist projects precisely for the sake of acceptance and inclusion in the imperial nation. Victorian and Edwardian middle-class British feminists, for example, framed their demand for female suffrage in terms of their imperial-nationalist responsibility. When British feminists elaborated on the image of the supposedly helpless and degraded Indian woman, this was not merely incidental to their feminist project. Rather, they deployed the plight of Indian woman precisely to justify their own claims—as of the "white woman's burden"—for political inclusion in the imperial nation.[52]

... [T]he internationalism of European and U.S. feminists did not necessarily entail the transcendence of nationalist politics. In the United States, where an organized anti-black women suffrage strategy had already emerged by the 1890s, white suffragists readily identified with the racial and imperial priorities of the nation. At the Inter-American Women's Congress in Panama in 1926, for example, feminists representing the United States abstained from voting on a resolution for woman suffrage in all American nations on the grounds that Latin American women were not ready to exercise political rights.[53]

The point is, notwithstanding the inhospitable climate for feminism within many nationalist projects in Europe, that the feminism of middle-class white European feminists, like that of their counterparts in the United States, was informed by the racial and imperial politics of their respective projects of nationhood.

In many colonized and semiperipheral regions, as also in some Eastern European countries, the development of feminism and nationalism was often self-consciously connected.[54] That was partly because here the nationalist projects stimulated the transformation of women's position through a broader concern with national rejuvenation and social reforms. These projects often sought to counter colonial portrayals of the plight of women by turning to a golden age in the ancient past where women supposedly enjoyed equality with men. ...

The development of feminism alongside nationalism, however, does not necessarily provide safeguards. In many third-world nationalist projects the articulation of women's interests has often been subordinated to the interests of the nation. Feminist demands, for example, are expected to be framed only within the parameters of anticolonial nationalism. In some nationalist movements, moreover, feminists are advised to shelve demands until the nationalist emergency is over; they are told "not now, later."[55] In other cases, feminists have been portrayed as "traitors to the nation" and feminism identified as a bourgeois and Westernized project that is irrelevant to the more urgent concerns of the nation. Ironically, the nationalist project in post-Soviet

Russia has similarly delegitimized feminism for its association with the "old order" and with state emancipation. The end of women's emancipation is thus hailed as a positive result of the collapse of the USSR.[56] In still others, the hospitable climate for feminism created during nationalist liberation struggles has been overturned with the attainment of independence. The most famous example is of the Algerian war of liberation against the French, in which approximately eleven thousand Algerian women participated as *moudjahidates* (freedom fighters), with some two thousand involved in the armed wing of the struggle. Whatever openings emerged for a new gender politics in the course of the struggle were quickly foreclosed in its aftermath. Women were pushed back from the political sphere and officially subordinated to men with the adoption of the Family Code based on the *Shariah* (Islamic canonical law).[57] … To conclude, however, that third-world nationalist projects manipulated women cynically to garner support for nationalism would be to underestimate the importance of the "woman question" in the ideological self-representation of anticolonial nationalisms.

Although the relation between feminism and nationalism has almost always been complex, there is no necessary outcome of this relationship. The more important point is that nowhere has feminism ever been autonomous of the national context from which it has emerged. This has been clearly evident in the history of the international feminist movement. The major liberal-feminist international organizations of the first half of the twentieth century were dominated by women from the United States and Northwestern Europe, many of whom not only assumed feminism's ostensible transcendence of national politics but were also invested in an ideology that insisted on the apparent separation of feminist from nationalist concerns.[58] Feminists from other parts of the world contested and exposed that view. Indian feminists such as Kamaladevi Chattopadhyay, Shareefah Hamid Ali, Dhanvanthi Rama Rau, and others, for example, never missed an opportunity to raise the question of the struggle against imperialism at international feminist conferences like the International Alliance of Women and the Women's International League for Peace and Freedom conferences, throughout the interwar period.[59]

Feminists from different parts of the world not only challenged the "maternalism" that often underwrote the ideology of the international feminist movement but also insisted on making national self-determination into a feminist issue. The real possibility of transnational feminist alliances lies in recognition, rather than transcendence, of the unequal power relations and disparate histories that divide women. That is the kind of hard political work that some women's projects are undertaking in order to build alliances between women of polarized ethnonational groups by challenging the mobilization of their ethnonational identities for war: the Women's Support Network in Belfast in Northern Ireland of Protestant and Catholic women; the Medica Women's Therapy Centre in Zenica in central Bosnia of Bosnian Serb, Croatian, and Muslim women, and Bat Shalom in Israel of Jewish and Palestinian women.[60]

Conclusion

It should be clear by now that the gendered articulation of the nation can be examined only in specific historical contexts and always in relation to a variety of forms of organizing difference. … The future of the scholarship on gender and the nation, indeed, may lie precisely in such densely historicized analysis of the articulation of the nation in specific historical moments. Only then will we begin to make visible the multiple, and often uneven, ways in which particular forms of difference inform, and are produced by, the nation in any given historical moment.

Notes

1. Virginia Woolf, *Three Guineas* (1938, repro London: Hogarth Press, 1947), 197.
2. Kumari Jayawardena, *Feminism and Nationalism in the Third World* (London: Zed Books, 1986).
3. Benedict Anderson, *Imagined Communities* (1983, rev. ed. London: New Left Books, 1991), 15–16.
4. Peter Sahlins quoted in Lloyd Kramer, "Historical Narratives and the Meaning of Nationalism," *Journal of the History of Ideas* 58, no. 3 (1997): 526.
5. See especially Yuval-Davis, *Gender and Nation,* (Thousand Oaks: Sage, 1997): 12–15.
6. For Hobsbawm, the nation is an important example of an "invented tradition." Eric Hobsbawm, "Introduction: Inventing Traditions," in *The Invention of Tradition,* ed. Eric Hobsbawm and Terence Ranger (New York: Cambridge University Press, 1983), 1–14.
7. Yuval-Davis, *Gender and Nation.*
8. Partha Chatterjee, *Nationalist Thought and the Colonial World* (1983, repro Minneapolis: University of Minnesota Press, 1998).
9. Carol Pateman, *The Sexual Contract* (Stanford: Stanford University Press, 1988).
10. Cora Ann Presley, *Kikuyu Women, the Mau Mau Rebellion and Social Change in Kenya* (Boulder: Westview Press, 1992), 136.
11. The list is from the Introduction in *Woman-Nation-State,* ed. Nira Yuval Davis and Floya Anthias (New York: St. Martin's Press, 1989), 7.
12. Anne McClintock, "'No Longer in a Future Heaven': Gender, Race, and Nationalism," in *Dangerous Liaisons,* ed. Anne McClintock, Aaamir Mufti, and Ella Shohat (Minneapolis: University of Minnesota Press, 1997), 89.
13. Tamar Mayer, "Gender Ironies of Nationalism," in *Gender Ironies of Nationalism,* ed. Mayer (New York: Routledge, 2000), 1–24.
14. Joanne Nagel, "Masculinity and Nationalism," *Ethnic and Racial Studies* 21 (March 1998): 242–69.
15. For some examples, see Joseph Massad, "Conceiving the Masculine," *Middle East Journal* 49 (Summer 1995): 467–83; Frances Gouda, "Gender and Hyper-Masculinity as Postcolonial Modernity during Indonesia's Struggle for Independence, 1945–1949," in *Gender, Sexuality and Colonial Modernities,* ed. Antoinette Burton (New York: Routledge, 1999), 161–74; and Susan Jeffords, *The Remasculinization of America* (Bloomington: Indiana University Press, 1989).
16. Mayer, ed., *Gender Ironies of Nationalism.*
17. Norma Alarcon, "The Theoretical Subject(s) of *This Bridge Called My Back* and Anglo-American Feminism," in *Making Face, Making Soul,* ed. Gloria Anzaldúa (San Francisco: Aunt Lute Foundation, 1990), 356–69; Evelyn Brooks Higgenbotham, "African American Women's History and the Metalanguage of Race," *Signs* 17 (Winter 1992): 251–74.
18. Quoted in Ida Blom, "Gender and Nation in International Comparison," in *Gendered Nations,* ed. Ida Blom, Karen Hagemann, and Catherine Hall (New York: Berg, 2000), 17; Yuval-Davis, *Gender and Nation,* 30.
19. Etienne Balibar, "The Nation-Form," in Etienne Balibar and Immanuel Wallerstein, *Race, Nation, Class,* trans. Chris Turner (London: Verso Press, 1991), 86–106. …
20. Quoted in Ruth Roach Pierson, "Nations: Gendered, Racialized, Crossed with Empire," in *Gendered Nations,* ed. Ida Blom, Karen Hagemann, and Catherine Hall (New York: Berg, 2000), 42.
21. Anne McClintock, *Imperial Leather* (New York: Routledge, 1995), 357.

22. McClintock, "'No Longer in a Future Heaven,'" 90–91.

23. Ibid., 91.

24. George L. Mosse, *Nationalism and Sexuality* (Madison: University of Wisconsin Press, 1985).

25. Yvette Abrahams, "Images of Sara Bartman," in *Nation, Empire, Colony,* ed. Ruth Roach Pierson and Nupur Chaudhury (Bloomington: Indiana University Press, 1998), 220–36.

26. Julia Clancy-Smith and Frances Gouda, eds., *Domesticating the Empire* (Charlottesville: University of Virginia Press, 1998); Lora Wildenthal, "Race, Gender, and Citizenship in the German Colonial Empire," in *Tensions of Empire,* ed. Frederick Cooper and Ann Laura Stoler (Berkeley: University of California Press, 1997), 263–86.

27. G. Kitching, "Nationalism," *Capital and Class* 25 (1985): 98–116.

28. Andrew Parker et al., "Introduction," in *Nationalisms and Sexualities,* ed. Andrew Parker et al. (New York: Routledge, 1992), 1.

29. Doris Sommer, *Foundational Fictions* (Berkeley: University of California Press, 1991).

30. McClintock, *Imperial Leather,* 45.

31. Lynn Hunt, *The Family Romance of the French Revolution* (New York: Routledge, 1992).

32. This is from Patricia Hill Collins, "It's All In the Family," *Hypatia* 13 (Summer 1998): 62–82.

33. Quoted in Mrinalini Sinha, *Colonial Masculinity* (New York: St Martin's Press, 1995), 35.

34. Winifred Woodhull cited in Madhu Dubey, "The 'True Lie' of the Nation: Fanon and Feminism," *Differences* 10 (Summer 1998): 1–29.

35. This point is made in Kandiyoti, "Identity and its Discontents," … ; see also Hudá Sha'rawi, *Harem Years,* ed. And trans. By Margot Badran (1986, repr. New York: Feminist Press, 1987); and Margot Badran, *Feminist, Islam and Nation* (Princeton: Princeton University Press, 1995). Afshaneh Najmabadi cited in Kandiyoti, "Identity and Its Discontents," 432.

36. Afshaneh Najmabadi cited in Kandiyoti, "Identity and Its Discontents," 432.

37. Fatima Mernissi, *Beyond the Veil,* quoted in Valentine E. Moghadam, "Introduction: Women and Identity Politics in Theoretical and Comparative Perspective," in *Identity Politics and Women,* ed. Valentine E. Moghadam (Boulder: Westview Press, 1994), 15.

38. Nayareh Tohidi, "Modernity, Islamization and Women in Iran," in *Gender and National Identity,* ed. Valentine M. Moghadam (London: Zed Books, 1994), 110–47; see also Valentine E. Moghadam, "Introduction and Overview," in *Identity Politics and Women,* ed. Valentine E. Moghadam (Boulder: Westview Press, 1994), 1–17.

39. Elleke Boehmer, cited in McClintock, "'No Longer in a Future Heaven,'" 91.

40. Claudia Koontz, *Mothers of the Fatherland* (London: Joanthan Cape, 1986), 196, cited in Yuval-Davis, "Gender and Nation," 29.

41. For examples, see Karen Gottshchang Turner with Phan Thank Hao, *Even the Women Must Fight* (New York: John Wiley, 1998); Thi Tuyet Mai Nguyen, *The Rubber Tree,* ed. Monique Senderowicz (Jefferson: McFarland, 1994).

42. Blom, "Gender and Nation in International Comparison," 15.

43. The discussion is from Nagel, "Masculinity and Nationalism," 249–51; see also Gail Bederman, *Manliness and Civilization* (Chicago: University of Chicago Press, 1995); and Kristin Hoganson, *Fighting for American Manhood* (New Haven: Yale University Press, 1998).

44. Sinha, *Colonial Masculinity.*

45. The phrase is from Gayatri Chakravorty Spivak, "Can the Subaltern Speak? Speculations on Widow Sacrifice," *Wedge* 7–8 (Winter-Spring 1985): 121.

46. Linda Kerber, *The Revolutionary Generation* (Washington: American Historical Association, 1990).

47. Asuncion Lavrin, "International Feminisms: Latin American Alternatives," … in *Feminisms and Internationalism,* ed. Mrinalini Sinha, Donna Guy, and Angela Wollacott (Oxford: Blackwell, 1999), 175–91, 195–204. …

48. Amirah Inglis, *The White Woman's Protection Ordinance* (London: Sussex University, 1975); Ann Laura Stoler, "Making Empire Respectable," in *Dangerous Liaisons,* ed. Anne McClintock, Aaamir Mufti, and Ella Shohat (Minneapolis: University of Minnesota Press, 1997), 344–74; Ann Laura Stoler, "Sexual Affronts and Racial Frontiers," in *Becoming National,* ed. Geoff Ely and Ronald Suny (New York: Oxford University Press, 1996), 286–324.

49. ... Nira Yuval-Davis, "National Reproduction and 'the Demographic Race' in Israel," in *Woman-Nation-State,* ed. Nira Yuval Davis and Floya Anthias (New York: St. Martin's Press, 1989), 92–109.

50. Sylvia Walby, "Women and Nation," in *Mapping the Nation,* ed. Gopal Balakrishnan (London: Verso Press, 1996), 235–54.

51. Kandiyoti, "Identity and Its Discontents," 436–40.

52. Antoinette Burton, *Burdens of History* (Chapel Hill: University of North Carolina Press, 1994).

53. Rosalyn Terborg-Penn, "Enfranchising Women of Color," in *Nation, Empire, Colony,* ed. Ruth Roach Pierson and Nupur Chaudhury (Bloomington: Indiana University Press, 1998), 41–56.

54. Jayawardena, *Feminism and Nationalism in the Third World.*

55. Enloe, *Bananas, Beaches and Bases,* 62.

56. Rosalind March, "Women in Contemporary Russia," in *Women, Ethnicity and Nationalism,* ed. Rick Wilford and Robert C. Miller (New York: Routledge, 1998), 87–119.

57. Cherifa Boutta, "Feminine Militancy," in *Gender and National Identity,* ed. Valentine M. Moghadam (London: Zed Books, 1994), 18–39.

58. Leila J. Rupp, *Worlds of Women* (Princeton: Princeton University Press, 1997); see also *Feminisms and Internationalism,* ed. Sinha et al.

59. Mrinalini Sinha, "Suffragism and Internationalism," *Indian Economic and Social History Review* 36 (Dec. 1999): 461–84, reprinted in *Women's Suffrage in the British Empire,* ed. Ian Fletcher, Laura E. Nym Mayhall, and Philippa Levine (New York: Routledge, 2000), 224–40.

60. Cynthia Cockburn, *The Space Between Us* (London: Zed Books, 1998).

23.
ONE IS NOT BORN A WOMAN
Monique Wittig
(1981)

A materialist feminist[1] approach to women's oppression destroys the idea that women are a "natural group": "a racial group of a special kind, a group perceived *as natural*, a group of men considered as materially specific in their bodies."[2] What the analysis accomplishes on the level of ideas, practice makes actual at the level of facts: by its very existence, lesbian society destroys the artificial (social) fact constituting women as a "natural group." A lesbian society[3] pragmatically reveals that the division from men of which women have been the object is a political one and shows that we have been ideologically rebuilt into a "natural group." In the case of women, ideology goes far since our bodies as well as our minds are the product of this manipulation. We have been compelled in our bodies and in our minds to correspond, feature by feature, with the *idea* of nature that has been established for us. Distorted to such an extent that our deformed body is what they call "natural," what is supposed to exist as such before oppression. Distorted to such an extent that in the end oppression seems to be a consequence of this "nature" within ourselves (a nature which is only an *idea*). What a materialist analysis does by reasoning, a lesbian society accomplishes practically: not only is there no natural group "women" (we lesbians are living proof of it), but as individuals as well we question "woman," which for us, as for Simone de Beauvoir, is only a myth. She said: "One is not born, but becomes a woman. No biological, psychological, or economic fate determines the figure that the human female presents in society: it is civilization as a whole that produces this creature, intermediate between male and eunuch, which is described as feminine."[4]

However, most of the feminists and lesbian-feminists in America and elsewhere still believe that the basis of women's oppression is *biological as well as* historical. Some of them even claim to find their sources in Simone de Beauvoir.[5] The belief in mother right and in a "prehistory" when women created civilization (because of a biological predisposition) while the coarse and brutal men hunted (because of a biological predisposition) is symmetrical with the biologizing interpretation of history produced up to now by the class of men. It is still the same method of finding in women and men a biological explanation of their division, outside of social facts. For me this could never constitute a lesbian approach to women's oppression, since it assumes that the basis of society or the beginning of society lies in heterosexuality. Matriarchy is no less heterosexual than patriarchy: it is only the sex of the oppressor that changes. Furthermore, not only is this conception still imprisoned in the categories of sex (woman and man), but it holds onto the idea that the capacity to give birth (biology) is what defines a woman. Although practical facts and ways of living contradict this theory in lesbian society, there are lesbians who affirm that "women and men are different species or races (the words are used interchangeably): men are biologically inferior to women; male violence is a biological inevitability …"[6] By doing this, by admitting that there is a "natural" division between women and men, we naturalize history, we assume that "men" and "women" have always existed and will always exist. No only do we naturalize the social phenomena which express our oppression, making change impossible. …

A materialist feminist approach shows that what we take for the cause or origin of oppression is in fact only the *mark*[7] imposed by the oppressor: the "myth of woman,"[8] plus its material effects and manifestations in the appropriated consciousness and bodies of women. Thus, this mark does not predate oppression: Colette Guillaumin has shown that before the socioeconomic reality of black slavery, the concept of race did not exist, at least not in its modern meaning, since it was applied to the lineage of families. However, now, race, exactly like sex, is taken as an "immediate given," a "sensible given," "physical features," belonging to a natural order. But what we believe to be a physical and direct perception is only a sophisticated and mythic construction, an "*imaginary formation*,"[9] which reinterprets physical features (in themselves as neutral as any others but marked by the social system) through the network of relationships in which they are perceived. (They are seen as *black*, therefore they *are* black; they are seen as *women*, therefore, they *are* women. But before being *seen* that way, they first had to be *made* that way.) Lesbians should always remember and acknowledge how "unnatural," compelling, totally oppressive, and destructive being "woman" was for us in the old days before the women's liberation movement. It was a political constraint, and those who resisted it were accused of not being "real" women. But then we were proud of it, since in the accusation there was already something like a shadow of victory: the avowal by the oppressor that "woman" is not something that goes without saying, since to be one, one has to be a "real" one. We were at the same time accused of wanting to be men. Today this double accusation has been taken up again with enthusiasm in the context of the women's liberation movement by some feminists and also, alas, by some lesbians whose political goal seems somehow to be becoming more and more "feminine." To refuse to be a woman, however, does not mean that one has to become a man. Besides, if we take as an example the perfect "butch," the classic example which provokes the most horror, whom Proust would have called a woman/man, how is her alienation different from that of someone who wants to become a woman? Tweedledum and Tweedledee. At least for a woman, wanting to become a man proves that she has escaped her initial programming. But even if she would like to, with all her strength, she cannot become a man. For becoming a man would demand from a woman not only a man's external appearance but his consciousness as well, that is, the consciousness of one who disposes by right of at least two "natural" slaves during his life span. This is impossible, and one feature of lesbian oppression consists precisely of making women out of reach for us, since women belong to men. Thus a lesbian *has* to be something else, a not-woman, a not-man, a product of society, not a product of nature, for there is no nature in society.

The refusal to become (or to remain) heterosexual always meant to refuse to become a man or a woman, consciously or not. For a lesbian this goes further than the refusal of the *role* "woman." It is the refusal of the economic, ideological, and political power of a man. This, we lesbians, and nonlesbians as well, knew before the beginning of the lesbian and feminist movement. However, as Andrea Dworkin emphasizes, many lesbians recently "have increasingly tried to transform the very ideology that has enslaved us into a dynamic, religious, psychologically compelling celebration of female biological potential."[10] Thus, some avenues of the feminist and lesbian movement lead us back to the myth of woman which was created by men especially for us, and with it we sink back into a natural group. Having stood up to fight for a sexless society,[11] we now find ourselves entrapped in the familiar deadlock of "woman is wonderful." Simone de Beauvoir underlined particularly the false consciousness which consists of selecting among the features of the myth (that women are different from men) those which look good and using them as a definition for women. What the concept "woman is wonderful" accomplishes is that it retains for defining women the best features (best according to whom?) which oppression has granted us, and it does not radically question the categories "man" and "woman," which are political categories and not natural givens. It puts us in a position of fighting within the class "women" not as the other classes do, for the disappearance of our class, but for the defense of "woman" and its reenforcement. It leads us to develop with complacency "new" theories about our specificity: thus, we call our passivity "nonviolence," when the main and emergent point for us is to fight our passivity (our fear, rather, a justified one). The ambiguity of the term "feminist" sums up the whole situation. What does "feminist" mean? Feminist is formed with the word "femme," "woman," and means: someone who fights for women. For many of us it means someone who fights for women as a class and for the disappearance of this class. For many others it means someone who fights for woman and her defense—for the myth, then, and its reenforcement. But why was the word "feminist" chosen if it retains the least ambiguity? We chose to call ourselves "feminists" ten years ago, not in order to support or reenforce the myth of woman, nor to identify ourselves with the oppressor's definition of us, but rather to affirm that our movement had a history and to emphasize the political link with the old feminist movement.

It is, then, this movement that we can put in question for the meaning that it gave to feminism. It so happens that feminism in the last century could never resolve its contradictions on the subject of nature/culture, woman/society. Women started to fight for themselves as a group and rightly considered that they shared common features as a result of oppression. But for them these features were natural and biological rather than social. They went so far as to adopt the Darwinist theory of evolution. They did not believe like Darwin, however, "that women were less evolved than men, but they did believe that male and female natures had diverged in the course of evolutionary development and that society at large reflected this polarization."[12] "The failure of early feminism was that it only attacked the Darwinist charge of female inferiority, while accepting the foundations of this charge—namely, the view of woman as 'unique.'"[13] And finally it was women scholars—and not feminists—who scientifically destroyed this theory. But the early feminists had failed to regard history as a dynamic process which develops from conflicts of interests. Furthermore, they still believed as men do that the cause (origin) of their oppression lay within themselves. And therefore after some astonishing victories the feminists of this first front found themselves at an impasse out of a lack of reasons to fight. They upheld the illogical principle of "equality in difference," an idea now being born again. They fell back into the trap which threatens us once again: the myth of woman.

Thus it is our historical task, and only ours, to define what we call oppression in materialist terms, to make it evident that women are a class, which is to say that the category "woman" as well as the category "man" are political and economic categories not eternal ones. Our fight aims to suppress men as a class, not through a genocidal, but a political struggle. Once the class "men" disappears, "women" as a class will disappear as well, for there are no slaves without masters. Our first task, it seems, is to always thoroughly dissociate "women" (the class within which we fight) and "woman," the myth. For "woman" does not exist for us: it is only an imaginary formation while "women" is the product of a social relationship. We felt this strongly when everywhere we refused to be called a "*woman's* liberation movement." Furthermore, we have to destroy the myth inside and outside ourselves. "Woman" is not each one of us, but the political and ideological formation which negates "women" (the product of a relation of exploitation). "Woman" is there to confuse us, to hide the reality "women." In order to be aware of being a class and to become a class we first have to kill the myth of "woman" including its most seductive aspects (I think about Virginia Woolf when she said the first task of a woman writer is to kill "the angel in the house"). But to become a class we do not have to suppress our individual selves, and since no individual can be reduced to her/his oppression we are also confronted with the historical necessity of constituting ourselves as the individual subjects of our history as well. I believe this is the reason why all these attempts at new definitions of woman are blossoming now. What is at stake (and of course not only for women) is an individual definition as well as a class definition. For once one has acknowledged oppression, one needs to know and experience the fact that one can constitute oneself as a subject (as opposed to an object of oppression), that one can become *someone* in spite of oppression, that one has one's own identity. There is no possible fight for someone deprived of an identity, no internal motivation for fighting, since, although I can fight only with others, first I fight for myself.

The question of the individual subject is historically a difficult one for everybody. Marxism, the last avatar of materialism, the science which has politically formed us, does not want to hear anything about a "subject." ...

... Marxist theory does not allow women any more than other classes of oppressed people to constitute themselves as historical subjects, because Marxism does not take into account the fact that a class also consists of individuals one by one. Class consciousness is not enough. We must try to understand philosophically (politically) these concepts of "subject" and "class consciousness" and how they work in relation to our history. When we discover that women are the objects of oppression and appropriation, at the very moment that we become able to perceive this, we become subjects in the sense of cognitive subjects, through an operation of abstraction. Consciousness of oppression is not only a reaction to (fight against) oppression. It is also the whole conceptual reevaluation of the social world, its whole reorganization with new concepts, from the point of view of oppression. It is what I would call the science of oppression created by the oppressed. This operation of understanding reality has to be undertaken by every one of us: call it a subjective, cognitive practice. The movement back and forth between the levels of reality (the conceptual reality and the material reality of oppression, which are both social realities) is accomplished through language.

It is we who historically must undertake the task of defining the individual subject in materialist terms. This certainly seems to be an impossibility since materialism and subjectivity have always been mutually exclusive. Nevertheless, and rather than despairing of ever understanding, we must recognize the *need* to reach subjectivity in the abandonment by many of us to the myth "woman" (the myth of woman being only a snare that holds us up). This real necessity for everyone to exist as an individual, as well as a member of a class, is perhaps the first condition for the accomplishment of a revolution, without which there can be no real fight or transformation. But the opposite is also true; without class and class consciousness there are no real subjects, only alienated individuals. For women to answer the question of the individual subject in materialist terms is first to show, as the lesbians and feminists did, that supposedly "subjective," "individual," "private" problems are in fact social problems, class problems; that sexuality is not for women an individual and subjective expression, but a social institution of violence. But once we have shown that all so-called personal problems are in fact class problems, we will still be left with the question of the subject of each singular woman—not the myth, but each one of us. At this point, let us say that a new personal and subjective definition for all humankind can only be found beyond the categories of sex (woman and man) and that the advent of individual subjects demands first destroying the categories of sex, ending the use of them, and rejecting all sciences which still use these categories as their fundamentals (practically all social sciences).

To destroy "woman" does not mean that we aim, short of physical destruction, to destroy lesbianism simultaneously with the categories of sex, because lesbianism provides for the moment the only social form in which we can live freely. Lesbian is the only concept I know of which is beyond the categories of sex (woman and man), because the designated subject (lesbian) is *not* a woman, either economically, or politically, or ideologically. For what makes a woman is a specific social relation to a man, a relation that we have previously called servitude,[14] a relation which implies personal and physical obligation as well as economic obligation ("forced residence,"[15] domestic corvée conjugal duties, unlimited production of children, etc.), a relation which lesbians escape by refusing to become or to stay heterosexual. We are escapees from our class in the same way as the American runaway slaves were when escaping slavery and becoming free. For us this is an absolute necessity; our survival demands that we contribute all our strength to the destruction of the class of women within which men appropriate women. This can be accomplished only by the destruction of heterosexuality as a social system which is based on the oppression of women by men and which produces the doctrine of the difference between the sexes to justify this oppression.

Notes

1. Christine Delphy, "Pour un féminisme matérialiste," *L'Arc* 61 (1975). Translated as "For a Materialist Feminism," *Feminist Issues* 1, no. 2 (Winter 1981).
2. Colette Guillaumin, "Race et Nature: Système des marques, idée de groupe naturel et rapports sociaux," *Pluriel*, no. 11 (1977). Translated as "Race and Nature," *Feminist Issues* 8, no. 2 (Fall 1988).
3. I use the word society with an extended anthropological meaning; strictly speaking, it does not refer to societies, in that lesbian societies do not exist completely autonomously from heterosexual social systems.
4. Simone de Beauvoir, *The Second Sex* (New York: Bantam, 1952), p. 249.
5. Redstockings, *Feminist Revolution* (New York: Random House, 1978), p. 18.
6. Andrea Dworkin, "Biological Superiority: The World's Most Dangerous and Deadly Idea," *Heresies* 6:46.
7. Guillaumin, op. cit.
8. de Beauvoir, op. cit.
9. Guillaumin, op. cit.
10. Dworkin, op. cit.
11. Atkinson, p. 6: "If feminism has any logic at all, it must be working for a sexless society."
12. Rosalind Rosenberg, "In Search of Woman's Nature," *Feminist Studies* 3, no. 1/2 (1975): 144.
13. Ibid., p. 146.
14. In an article published in *L'Idiot International* (mai 1970), whose original title was "Pour un movement de libération des femmes" ("For a Women's Liberation Movement").
15. Christiane Rochefort, *Les stances à Sophie* (Paris: Grasset, 1963).

24.
THE SOCIAL ORGANIZATION OF MASCULINITY
Raewyn Connell
(2005)

… 'Masculinity' is not a coherent object about which a generalizing science can be produced. Yet we can have coherent knowledge about the issues raised in these attempts. If we broaden the angle of vision, we can see masculinity, not as an isolated object, but as an aspect of a larger structure.

This demands an account of the larger structure and how masculinities are located in it. The task of this chapter is to set out a framework based on contemporary analyses of gender relations. This framework will provide a way of distinguishing types of masculinity, and of understanding the dynamics of change.

First, however, there is some ground to clear. The definition of the basic term in the discussion has never been wonderfully clear.

Defining Masculinity

All societies have cultural accounts of gender, but not all have the concept 'masculinity'. In its modern usage the term assumes that one's behaviour results from the type of person one is. That is to say, an unmasculine person would behave differently: being peaceable rather than violent, conciliatory rather than dominating, hardly able to kick a football, uninterested in sexual conquest, and so forth.

This conception presupposes a belief in individual difference and personal agency. In that sense it is built on the conception of individuality that developed in early-modern Europe with the growth of colonial empires and capitalist economic relations …

But the concept is also inherently relational. 'Masculinity' does not exist except in contrast with 'femininity'. A culture which does not treat women and men as bearers of polarized character types, at least in principle, does not have a concept of masculinity in the sense of modern European/American culture.

Historical research suggests that this was true of European culture itself before the eighteenth century. Women were certainly regarded as different from men, but different in the sense of being incomplete or inferior examples of the same character (for instance, having less of the faculty of reason). Women and men were not seen as bearers of qualitatively different characters; this conception accompanied the bourgeois ideology of 'separate spheres' in the nineteenth century.[1]

In both respects our concept of masculinity seems to be a fairly recent historical product, a few hundred years old at most. In speaking of masculinity at all, then, we are 'doing gender' in a culturally specific way. This should be borne in mind with any claim to have discovered transhistorical truths about manhood and the masculine. ...

Rather than attempting to define masculinity as an object (a natural character type, a behavioural average, a norm), we need to focus on the processes and relationships through which men and women conduct gendered lives. 'Masculinity', to the extent the term can be briefly defined at all, is simultaneously a place in gender relations, the practices through which men and women engage that place in gender, and the effects of these practices in bodily experience, personality and culture.

Gender as a Structure of Social Practice

... Gender is a way in which social practice is ordered. In gender processes, the everyday conduct of life is organized in relation to a reproductive arena, defined by the bodily structures and processes of human reproduction. This arena includes sexual arousal and intercourse, childbirth and infant care, bodily sex difference and similarity.

I call this a 'reproductive arena' not a 'biological base' to emphasize the point ... that we are talking about a historical process involving the body, not a fixed set of biological determinants. Gender is social practice that constantly refers to bodies and what bodies do, it is not social practice reduced to the body. Indeed reductionism presents the exact reverse of the real situation. Gender exists precisely to the extent that biology does *not* determine the social. It marks one of those points of transition where historical process supersedes biological evolution as the form of change. Gender is a scandal, an outrage, from the point of view of essentialism. Sociobiologists are constantly trying to abolish it, by proving that human social arrangements are a reflex of evolutionary imperatives.

Social practice is creative and inventive, but not inchoate. It responds to particular situations and is generated within definite structures of social relations. Gender relations, the relations among people and groups organized through the reproductive arena, form one of the major structures of all documented societies.

Practice that relates to this structure, generated as people and groups grapple with their historical situations, does not consist of isolated acts. Actions are configured in larger units, and when we speak of masculinity and femininity we are naming configurations of gender practice.

'Configuration' is perhaps too static a term. The important thing is the *process* of configuring practice. (Jean-Paul Sartre speaks in *Search for a Method* of the 'unification of the means in action'.) Taking a dynamic view of the organization of practice, we arrive at an understanding of masculinity and femininity as *gender projects*. These are processes of configuring practice through time, which transform their starting-points in gender structures. ...[2]

We find the gender configuring of practice however we slice the social world, whatever unit of analysis we choose. The most familiar is the individual life course, the basis of the commonsense notions of masculinity and femininity. The configuration of practice here is what psychologists have traditionally called 'personality' or 'character'. ...

Such a focus is liable to exaggerate the coherence of practice that can be achieved at any one site. It is thus not surprising that psychoanalysis, originally stressing contradiction, drifted towards the concept of 'identity'. Post-structuralist critics of psychology such as Wendy Hollway have emphasized that gender identities are fractured and shifting, because multiple discourses intersect in any individual life.[3] This argument highlights another site, that of discourse, ideology, or culture. Here gender is organized in symbolic practices that may continue much longer than the individual life (for instance: the construction of heroic masculinities in epics; the construction of 'gender dysphorias' or 'perversions' in medical theory).

... [A] third site of gender configuration [are] institutions such as the state, the workplace and the school. Many find it difficult to accept that institutions are substantively, not just metaphorically, gendered. This is, nevertheless, a key point.

The state, for instance, is a masculine institution. To say this is not to imply that the personalities of top male office-holders somehow seep through and stain the institution, It is to say something much stronger: that state organizational practices are structured in relation to the reproductive arena. The overwhelming majority of top office holders are men because there is a gender configuring of recruitment and promotion, a gender configuring of the internal division of labour and systems of control, a gender configuring of policymaking, practical routines, and ways of mobilizing pleasure and consent.[4]

The gender structuring of practice need have nothing biologically to do with reproduction. The link with the reproductive arena is social. This becomes clear when it is challenged. An example is the recent struggle within the state over 'gays in the military', i.e. the rules excluding soldiers and sailors because of the gender of their sexual object-choice. In the United States, where this struggle was most severe, critics made the case for change in terms of civil liberties and military efficiency, arguing in effect that object-choice has little to do with the capacity to kill. The admirals and generals defended the status quo on a variety of spurious grounds. The unadmitted reason was the cultural importance of a particular definition of masculinity in maintaining the fragile cohesion of modern armed forces.

It has been clear since the work of Juliet Mitchell and Gayle Rubin in the 1970s that gender is an internally complex structure, where a number of different logics are superimposed. This is a fact of great importance for the analysis of masculinities. Any one masculinity, as a configuration of practice, is simultaneously positioned in a number of structures of relationship, which may be following different historical trajectories. Accordingly masculinity, like femininity, is always liable to internal contradiction and historical disruption.

We need at least a three-fold model of the structure of gender, distinguishing relations of (a) power, (b) production and (c) cathexis (emotional attachment). This is a provisional model, but it gives some purchase on issues about masculinity.[5]

(a) *Power relations* The main axis of power in the contemporary European/ American gender order is the overall subordination of women and dominance of men—the structure Women's Liberation named 'patriarchy'. This general structure exists despite many local reversals (e.g., woman-headed households, female teachers with male students). It persists despite resistance of many kinds, now articulated in feminism. These reversals and resistances mean continuing difficulties for patriarchal power. They define a problem of legitimacy which has great importance for the politics of masculinity.

(b) *Production relations* Gender divisions of labour are familiar in the form of the allocation of tasks, sometimes reaching extraordinarily fine detail. ... Equal attention should be paid to the economic consequences of gender divisions of labour, the dividend accruing to men from unequal shares of the products of social labour. This is most often discussed in terms of unequal wage rates, but the gendered character of capital should also be noted. A capitalist economy working through a gender division of labour is, necessarily, a gendered accumulation process. So it is not a statistical accident, but a part of the social construction of masculinity, that men and not women control the major corporations and the great private fortunes. Implausible as it sounds, the accumulation of wealth has become firmly linked to the reproductive arena, through the social relations of gender.[6]

(c) *Cathexis* ... [S]exual desire is so often seen as natural that it is commonly excluded from social theory. Yet when we consider desire in Freudian terms, as emotional energy being attached to an object, its gendered character is clear. This is true both for heterosexual and homosexual desire. (It is striking that in our culture the non-gendered object choice, 'bisexual' desire, is ill-defined and unstable.) The practices that shape and realize desire are thus an aspect of the gender order. Accordingly we can ask political questions about the relationships involved: whether they are consensual or coercive, whether pleasure is equally given and received. In feminist analyses of sexuality these have become sharp questions about the connection of heterosexuality with men's position of social dominance.[7]

Because gender is a way of structuring social practice in general, not a special type of practice, it is unavoidably involved with other social structures. It is now common to say that gender 'intersects'—better, interacts—with race and class. We might add that it constantly interacts with nationality or position in the world order.

This fact also has strong implications for the analysis of masculinity. White men's masculinities, for instance, are constructed not only in relation to white women but also in relation to black men, Paul Hoch in *White Hero, Black Beast* more than a decade ago pointed to the pervasiveness of racial imagery in Western discourses of masculinity, White fears of black men's violence have a long history in colonial and post-colonial situations. Black fears of white men's terrorism, founded in the history of colonialism, have a continuing basis in white men's control of police, courts and prisons in metropolitan countries. African-American men are massively over-represented in American prisons, as Aboriginal men are in Australian prisons. This situation is strikingly condensed in the American black expression 'The Man', fusing white masculinity and institutional power. ...

Similarly, it is impossible to understand the shaping of working class masculinities without giving full weight to their class as well as their gender politics. This is vividly shown in historical work such as Sonya Rose's *Limited Livelihoods*, on industrial England in the nineteenth century. An ideal of working-class manliness and self-respect was constructed in response to class deprivation and paternalistic strategies of management, at the same time and through the same gestures as it was defined against working-class women. The strategy of the 'family wage', which long depressed women's wages in twentieth-century economies, grew out of this interplay.[8]

To understand gender, then, we must constantly go beyond gender. The same applies in reverse. We cannot understand class, race or global inequality without constantly moving towards gender. Gender relations are a major component of social structure as a whole, and gender politics are among the main determinants of our collective fate.

Relations Among Masculinities: Hegemony, Subordination, Complicity, Marginalization

With growing recognition of the interplay between gender, race and class it has become common to recognize multiple masculinities: black as well as white, working-class as well as middle-class. This is welcome, but it risks another kind of oversimplification. It is easy in this framework to think that there is *a* black masculinity or *a* working-class masculinity.

To recognize more than one kind of masculinity is only a first step. We have to examine the relations between them. Further, we have to unpack the milieux of class and race and scrutinize the gender relations operating within them. There are, after all, gay black men and effeminate factory hands, not to mention middle-class rapists and cross-dressing bourgeois.

A focus on the gender relations among men is necessary to keep the analysis dynamic, to prevent the acknowledgement of multiple masculinities collapsing into a character typology, as happened with Fromm and the *Authoritarian Personality* research. 'Hegemonic masculinity' is not a fixed character type, always and everywhere the same. It is, rather, the masculinity that occupies the hegemonic position in a given pattern of gender relations, a position always contestable.

A focus on relations also offers a gain in realism. Recognizing multiple masculinities, especially in an individualist culture such as the United States, risks taking them for alternative lifestyles, a matter of consumer choice. A relational approach makes it easier to recognize the hard compulsions under which gender configurations are formed, the bitterness as well as the pleasure in gendered experience.

With these guidelines, let us consider the practices and relations that construct the main patterns of masculinity in the current Western gender order.

Hegemony

The concept of 'hegemony', deriving from Antonio Gramsci's analysis of class relations, refers to the cultural dynamic by which a group claims and sustains a leading position in social life. At any given time, one form of masculinity rather than others is culturally exalted. Hegemonic masculinity can be defined as the configuration of gender practice which embodies the currently accepted answer to the problem of the legitimacy of patriarchy, which guarantees (or is taken to guarantee) the dominant position of men and the subordination of women.[9]

This is not to say that the most visible bearers of hegemonic masculinity are always the most powerful people. They may be exemplars, such as film actors, or even fantasy figures, such as film characters. Individual holders of institutional power or great wealth may be far from the hegemonic pattern in their personal lives. (Thus a male member of a prominent business dynasty was a key figure in the gay/transvestite social scene in Sydney in the 1950s, because of his wealth and the protection this gave in the cold-war climate of political and police harassment.)[10]

Nevertheless, hegemony is likely to be established only if there is some correspondence between cultural ideal and institutional power, collective if not individual. So the top levels of business, the military and government provide a fairly convincing *corporate* display of masculinity, still very little shaken by feminist women or dissenting men. It is the successful claim to authority, more than direct violence, that is the mark of hegemony (though violence often underpins or supports authority).

I stress that hegemonic masculinity embodies a 'currently accepted' strategy. When conditions for the defence of patriarchy change, the bases for the dominance of a particular masculinity are eroded. New groups may challenge old solutions and construct a new hegemony. The dominance of *any* group of men may be challenged by women. Hegemony, then, is a historically mobile relation. Its ebb and flow is a key element of the picture of masculinity …

Subordination

Hegemony relates to cultural dominance in the society as a whole. Within that overall framework there are specific gender relations of dominance and subordination between groups of men.

The most important case in contemporary European/American society is the dominance of heterosexual men and the subordination of homosexual men. This is much more than a cultural stigmatization of homosexuality or gay identity. Gay men are subordinated to straight men by an array of quite material practices.

These practices were listed in early Gay Liberation texts such as Dennis Altman's *Homosexual: Oppression and Liberation.* They have been documented at length in studies such as the NSW Anti-Discrimination Board's 1982 report *Discrimination and Homosexuality.* They are still a matter of everyday experience for homosexual men. They include political and cultural exclusion, cultural abuse (in the United States gay men have now become the main symbolic target of the religious right), legal violence (such as imprisonment under sodomy statutes), street violence (ranging from intimidation to murder), economic discrimination and personal boycotts. It is not surprising that an Australian working-class man, reflecting all his experience of coming out in a homophobic culture, would remark:

You know, I didn't really realize what it was to be gay. I mean it's a bastard of a life.[11]

Oppression positions homosexual masculinities at the bottom of a gender hierarchy among men. Gayness, in patriarchal ideology, is the repository of whatever is symbolically expelled from hegemonic masculinity, the items ranging from fastidious taste in home decoration to receptive anal pleasure. Hence, from the point of view of hegemonic masculinity, gayness is easily assimilated to femininity. And hence—in the view of some gay theorists—the ferocity of homophobic attacks.

Gay masculinity is the most conspicuous, but it is not the only subordinated masculinity. Some heterosexual men and boys too are expelled from the circle of legitimacy. The process is marked by a rich vocabulary of abuse: wimp, milksop, nerd, turkey, sissy, lily liver, jellyfish, yellowbelly, candy ass, ladyfinger, pushover, cookie pusher, cream puff, motherfucker, pantywaist, mother's boy, four-eyes, ear-'ole, dweeb, geek, Milquetoast, Cedric, and so on. Here too the symbolic blurring with femininity is obvious.

Complicity

Normative definitions of masculinity, as I have noted, face the problem that not many men actually meet the normative standards. This point applies to hegemonic masculinity. The number of men rigorously practising the hegemonic pattern in its entirety may be quite small. Yet the majority of men gain from its hegemony, since they benefit from the patriarchal dividend, the advantage men in general gain from the overall subordination of women.

… [A]ccounts of masculinity have generally concerned themselves with syndromes and types, not with numbers. Yet in thinking about the dynamics of society as a whole, numbers matter. Sexual politics is mass politics, and strategic thinking needs to be concerned with where the masses of people are. If a large number of men have some connection with the hegemonic project but do not embody hegemonic masculinity, we need a way of theorizing their specific situation.

This can be done by recognizing another relationship among groups of men, the relationship of complicity with the hegemonic project. Masculinities constructed in ways that realize the patriarchal dividend, without the tensions or risks of being the frontline troops of patriarchy, are complicit in this sense.

It is tempting to treat them simply as slacker versions of hegemonic masculinity—the difference between the men who cheer football matches on TV and those who run out into the mud and the tackles themselves. But there is often something more definite and carefully crafted than that. Marriage, fatherhood and community life often involve extensive compromises with women rather than naked domination or an uncontested display of authority.[12] A great many men who draw the patriarchal dividend also respect their wives and mothers, are never violent towards women, do their accustomed share of the housework, bring home the family wage, and can easily convince themselves that feminists must be bra-burning extremists.

Marginalization

Hegemony, subordination and complicity, as just defined, are relations internal to the gender order. The interplay of gender with other structures such as class and race creates further relationships between masculinities.

... [Elsewhere] I noted how new information technology became a vehicle for redefining middle-class masculinities at a time when the meaning of labour for working-class men was in contention. This is not a question of a fixed middle-class masculinity confronting a fixed working-class masculinity. Both are being reshaped, by a social dynamic in which class and gender relations are simultaneously in play.

Race relations may also become an integral part of the dynamic between masculinities. In a white-supremacist context, black masculinities play symbolic roles for white gender construction. For instance, black sporting stars become exemplars of masculine toughness, while the fantasy figure of the black rapist plays an important role in sexual politics among whites, a role much exploited by right-wing politics in the United States. Conversely, hegemonic masculinity among whites sustains the institutional oppression and physical terror that have framed the making of masculinities in black communities.

Robert Staples's discussion of internal colonialism in *Black Masculinity* shows the effect of class and race relations at the same time. As he argues, the level of violence among black men in the United States can only be understood through the changing place of the black labour force in American capitalism and the violent means used to control it. Massive unemployment and urban poverty now powerfully interact with institutional racism in the shaping of black masculinity.[13]

Though the term is not ideal, I cannot improve on 'marginalization' to refer to the relations between the masculinities in dominant and subordinated classes or ethnic groups. Marginalization is always relative to the *authorization* of the hegemonic masculinity of the dominant group. Thus, in the United States, particular black athletes may be exemplars for hegemonic masculinity. But the fame and wealth of individual stars has no trickledown effect; it does not yield social authority to black men generally.

The relation of marginalization and authorization may also exist between subordinated masculinities. A striking example is the arrest and conviction of Oscar Wilde, one of the first men caught in the net of modern anti-homosexual legislation. Wilde was trapped because of his connections with homosexual working-class youths, a practice unchallenged until his legal battle with a wealthy aristocrat, the Marquess of Queensberry, made him vulnerable.[14]

These two types of relationship—hegemony, domination/subordination and complicity on the one hand, marginalization/authorization on the other—provide a framework in which we can analyse specific masculinities. (This is a sparse framework, but social theory should be hardworking.) I emphasize that terms such as 'hegemonic masculinity' and 'marginalized masculinities' name not fixed character types but configurations of practice generated in particular situations in a changing structure of relationships. Any theory of masculinity worth having must give an account of this process of change.

Historical Dynamics, Violence and Crisis Tendencies

To recognize gender as a social pattern requires us to see it as a product of history, and also as a *producer* of history. ... I define gender practice as onto-formative, as constituting reality, and it is a crucial part of this idea that social reality is dynamic in time. We habitually think of the social as less real than the biological, what changes as less real than what stays the same. But there is a colossal reality to history. It is the modality of human life, precisely what defines us as human. No other species produces and lives in history, replacing organic evolution with radically new determinants of change.

To recognize masculinity and femininity as historical, then, is not to suggest they are flimsy or trivial. It is to locate them firmly in the world of social agency. And it raises a string of questions about their historicity.

The structures of gender relations are formed and transformed over time. It has been common in historical writing to see this change as coming from outside gender—from technology or class dynamics, most often. But change is also generated from within gender relations. The dynamic is as old as gender relations. It has, however, become more clearly defined in the last two centuries with the emergence of a public politics of gender and sexuality.

With the women's suffrage movement and the early homophile movement, the conflict of interests embedded in gender relations became visible. Interests are formed in any structure of inequality, which necessarily defines groups that will gain and lose differently by sustaining or by changing the structure. A gender order where men dominate women cannot avoid constituting men as an interest group concerned with defence, and women as an interest group concerned with change. This is a structural fact, independent of whether men as individuals love or hate women, or believe in equality or abjection, and independent of whether women are currently pursuing change.

To speak of a patriarchal dividend is to raise exactly this question of interest. Men gain a dividend from patriarchy in terms of honour, prestige, and the right to command. They also gain a material dividend. In the rich capitalist countries, men's average incomes are approximately *double* women's average incomes. (The more familiar comparisons, of wage rates for full-time employment, greatly understate gender differences in actual incomes.) Men are vastly more likely to control a major block of capital as chief executive of a major corporation, or as direct owner. For instance, of 55 US fortunes above $1 billion in 1992, only five were mainly in the hands of women—and all but one of those as a result of inheritance from men.

Men are much more likely to hold state power: for instance, men are ten times more likely than women to hold office as a member of parliament (an average across all countries of the world). Perhaps men do most of the work? No: in the rich countries, time-budget studies show women and men work on average about the same number of hours in the year. (The major difference is in how much of this work gets paid.)[15]

Given these facts, the 'battle of the sexes' is no joke. Social struggle must result from inequalities on such a scale. It follows that the politics of masculinity cannot concern only questions of personal life and identity. It must also concern questions of social justice.

A structure of inequality on this scale, involving a massive dispossession of social resources, is hard to imagine without violence. It is, overwhelmingly, the dominant gender who hold and use the means of violence. Men are armed far more often than women. Indeed under many gender regimes women have been forbidden to bear or use arms (a rule applied, astonishingly, even within armies). Patriarchal definition of femininity (dependence fearfulness) amount to a cultural disarmament that may be quite as effective as the physical kind. Domestic violence cases often find abused women, physically able to look after themselves, who have accepted the abusers' definitions of themselves as incompetent and helpless.[16]

Two patterns of violence follow from this situation. First, many members of the privileged group use violence to sustain their dominance. Intimidation of women ranges across the spectrum from wolf-whistling in the street, to office harassment, to rape and domestic assault, to murder by a woman's patriarchal 'owner', such as a separated husband. Physical attacks are commonly accompanied by verbal abuse of women (whores and bitches, in recent popular music that recommends beating women). Most men do not attack or harass women; but those who do are unlikely to think themselves deviant. On the contrary they usually feel they are entirely justified, that they are exercising a right. They are authorized by an ideology of supremacy.

Second, violence becomes important in gender politics among men. Most episodes of major violence (counting military combat, homicide and armed assault) are transactions among men. Terror is used as a means of drawing boundaries and making exclusions, for example, in heterosexual violence against gay men. Violence can become a way of claiming or asserting masculinity in group struggles. This is an explosive process when an oppressed group gains the means of violence—as witness the levels of violence among black men in contemporary South Africa and the United States. The youth gang violence of inner-city streets is a striking example of the assertion of marginalized masculinities against other men, continuous with the assertion of masculinity in sexual violence against women.[17]

Violence can be used to enforce a reactionary gender politics, as in the recent fire bombings and murders of abortion service providers in the United States. It must also be said that collective violence among men can open possibilities for progress in gender relations. The two global wars this century produced important transitions in women's employment, shook up gender ideology, and accelerated the making of homosexual communities.

Violence is part of a system of domination, but is at the same time a measure of its imperfection. A thoroughly legitimate hierarchy would have less need to intimidate. The scale of contemporary violence points to crisis tendencies (to borrow a term from Jürgen Habermas) in the modern gender order.

The concept of crisis tendencies needs to be distinguished from the colloquial sense in which people speak of a 'crisis of masculinity'. As a theoretical term 'crisis' presupposes a coherent system of some kind, which is destroyed or restored by the outcome of the crisis. Masculinity, as the argument so far has shown, is not a system in that sense. It is, rather, a configuration of practice *within* a system of gender relations. We cannot logically speak of the crisis of a configuration; rather we might speak of its disruption or its transformation. We can, however, logically speak of the crisis of a gender order as a whole, and of its tendencies towards crisis.[18]

Such crisis tendencies will always implicate masculinities, though not necessarily by disrupting them. Crisis tendencies may, for instance, provoke attempts to restore a dominant masculinity. "Michael Kimmel has pointed to this dynamic in turn-of-the-century United States society, where fear of the women's suffrage movement played into the cult of the outdoorsman. Klaus Theweleit in *Male Fantasies* traced the more savage process that produced the sexual politics of fascism in the aftermath of the suffrage movement and German defeat in the Great War. More recently Women's Liberation and defeat in Vietnam have stirred new cults of true masculinity in the United States, from violent 'adventure' movies such as the *Rambo* series, to the expansion of the gun cult and what William Gibson in a frightening recent study has called 'paramilitary culture'.[19]

To understand the making of contemporary masculinities, then, we need to map the crisis tendencies of the gender order. This is no light task! …

The vast changes in gender relations around the globe produce ferociously complex changes in the conditions of practice with which men as well as women have to grapple. No one is an innocent bystander in this arena of change. We are all engaged in constructing a world of gender relations. How it is made, what strategies different groups pursue, and with what effects, are political questions. Men no more than women are chained to the gender patterns they have inherited. Men too can make political choices for a new world of gender relations. Yet those choices are always made in concrete social circumstances, which limit what can be attempted; and the outcomes are not easily controlled.

To understand a historical process of this depth and complexity is not a task for *a priori* theorizing. It requires concrete study; more exactly, a range of studies that can illuminate the larger dynamic. …

Notes

1. Bloch 1978 outlines the argument for the Protestant middle classes of England and North America. Laqueur 1999 offers a more sweeping argument on similar lines about views of the body.
2. Sartre 1968: 159–60.
3. Hollway 1984.
4. Franzway et al. 1989, Grant and Tancred 1992.
5. Mitchell 1971, Rubin 1975. The three-fold model is spelt out in Connell 1987.
6. Hunt 1980. Feminist political economy is, however, under way, and these notes draw on Mies 1986, Waring 1988, Armstrong and Armstrong 1990.
7. Some of the best writing on the politics of heterosexuality comes from Canada: Valverde 1985, Buchbinder et al. 1987. The conceptual approach here is developed in Connell and Dowsett 1992.
8. Rose 1992, ch. 6 especially.
9. I would emphasize the dynamic character of Gramsci's concept of hegemony, which is not the functionalist theory of cultural reproduction often portrayed. Gramsci always had in mind a social struggle for leadership in historical change.
10. Wotherspoon 1991 (chapter 3) describes this climate, and discreetly does not mention individuals.

11. Altman 1972; Anti-Discrimination Board 1982. Quotation from Connell, Davis and Dowsett 1993: 122.
12. See, for instance, the white US families described by Rubin 1976.
13. Staples 1982. The more recent United States literature on black masculinity, e.g., Majors and Gordon 1994, has made a worrying retreat from Staples's structural analysis towards sex role theory; its favoured political strategy, not surprisingly, is counselling programs to resocialize black youth.
14. Ellmann 1987.
15. For patterns of wealth, see the survey of US millionaires by Forbes magazine. 19 October 1992. On parliaments, see 1993 survey by Inter-Parliamentary Union reported in San Francisco Chronicle 12 September 1993, and United Nations Development Programme 1992: 145. The results of time-budget studies may surprise some readers; see Bittman 1991.
16. The argument here draws on Russell 1982, Connell 1985, Ptacek 1988, Smith 1989.
17. Messerschmidt 1993: 105–17.
18. For the general concept of crisis tendencies, see Habermas 1976, O'Connor 1987; for its relevance to gender. Connell 1987: 158–63.
19. Kimmel 1987, Theweleit 1987, Gibson 1994.

BOUNDARIES AND BELONGINGS

25.
THE BRIDGE POEM
Donna Kate Rushin
(1981)

I've had enough
I'm sick of seeing and touching
Both sides of things
Sick of being the damn bridge for everybody

Nobody
Can talk to anybody
Without me
Right?

I explain my mother to my father my father to my little sister
My little sister to my brother my brother to the white feminists
The white feminists to the Black church folks the Black church folks
To the ex-hippies the ex-hippies to the Black separatists the
Black separatists to the artists the artists to my friends' parents …

Then
I've got to explain myself
To everybody
I do more translating
Than the Gawdamn U.N.

Forget it
I'm sick of it

I'm sick of filling in your gaps

Sick of being your insurance against
The isolation of your self-imposed limitations
Sick of being the crazy at your holiday dinners
Sick of being the odd one at your Sunday Brunches
Sick of being the sole Black friend to 34 individual white people

Find another connection to the rest of the world
Find someone else to make you legitimate
Find some other way to be political and hip

I will not be the bridge to your womanhood
Your manhood
Your human-ness
I'm sick of reminding you not to
Close off too tight for too long

I'm sick of mediating with your worst self
On behalf of your better selves

I am sick
Of having to remind you
To breathe
Before you suffocate
Your own fool self

Forget it
Stretch of drown
Evolve or die

The bridge I must be
Is the bridge to my own power
I must translate
My own fears
Mediate
My own weaknesses

I must be the bridge to nowhere
But my true self
And then
I will be useful

26.
REPORT FROM THE BAHAMAS
June Jordan
(1985)

I am staying in a hotel that calls itself the Sheraton British Colonial. One of the photographs advertising the place displays a middle-aged Black man in a waiter's tuxedo, smiling. What intrigues me most about the picture is just this: while the Black man bears a tray full of "colorful" drinks above his left shoulder, both of his feet, shoes and trouserlegs, up to ten inches above his ankles, stand in the also "colorful" Caribbean salt water. He is so delighted to serve you he will wade into the water to bring you Banana Daquiris while you float! More precisely, he will wade into the water, fully clothed, oblivious to the ruin of his shoes, his trousers, his health, and he will do it with a smile.

I am in the Bahamas. On the phone in my room, a spinning complement of plastic pages offers handy index clues such as CAR RENTAL and CASINOS. A message from the Ministry of Tourism appears among these travelers tips. Opening with a paragraph of "WELCOME," the message then proceeds to "A PAGE OF HISTORY," which reads as follows:

> New World History begins on the same day that modern Bahamian history begins—October 12, 1492. That's when Columbus stepped ashore—British influence came first with the Eleutherian Adventurers of 1647—After the Revolutions. American Loyalists fled from the newly independent states and settled in the Bahamas. Confederate blockade-runners used the island as a haven during the War between the States, and after the War, a number of Southerners moved to the Bahamas.

There it is again. Something proclaims itself a legitimate history and all it does is track white Mr. Columbus to the British Eleutherians through the Confederate Southerners as they barge into New World surf, land on New World turf, and nobody saving one word about the Bahamian people, the Black peoples, to whom the only thing new in their island world was this weird succession of crude intruders and its colonial consequences.

This is my consciousness of race as I unpack my bathing suit in the Sheraton British Colonial. Neither this hotel nor the British nor the long ago Italians nor the white Delta airline pilots belong here, of course. And every time I look at the photograph of that fool standing in the water with his shoes on I'm about to have a West Indian fit, even though I know he's no fool; he's a middle-aged Black man who needs a job and this is his job—pretending himself a servile ancillary to the pleasures of the rich. (Compared to his options in life, I am a rich woman. Compared to most of the Black Americans arriving for this Easter weekend on a three nights four days' deal of bargain rates, the middle-aged waiter is a poor Black man.)

We will jostle along with the other (white) visitors and join them in the tee shirt shops or, laughing together, learn ruthless rules of negotiation as we, Black Americans as well as white, argue down the price of handwoven goods at the nearby straw market while the merchants, frequently toothless Black women seated on the concrete in their only presentable dress, humble themselves to our careless games:

"Yes? You like it? Eight dollar."

"Five."

"I give it to you. Seven."

And so it continues, this weird succession of crude intruders that, now, includes me and my brothers and my sisters from the North.

This is my consciousness of class as I try to decide how much money I can spend on Bahamian gifts for my family back in Brooklyn. No matter that these other Black women incessantly weave words and flowers into the straw hats and bags piled beside them on the burning dusty street. No matter that these other Black women must work their sense of beauty into these things that we will take away as cheaply as we dare, or they will do without food.

We are not white, after all. The budget is limited. And we are harmlessly killing time between the poolside rum punch and "The Native Show on the Patio" that will play tonight outside the hotel restaurant.

This is my consciousness of race and class and gender identity as I notice the fixed relations between these other Black women and myself. They sell and I buy or I don't. They risk not eating. I risk going broke on my first vacation afternoon.

We are not particularly women anymore; we are parties to a transaction designed to set us against each other.

"Olive" is the name of the Black woman who cleans my hotel room. On my way to the beach I am wondering what "Olive" would say if I told her why I chose the Sheraton British Colonial; if I told her I wanted to swim. I wanted to sleep. I did not want to be harassed by the middle-aged waiter, or his nephew. I did not want to be raped by anybody (white or Black) at all and I calculated that my safety as a Black woman alone would best be assured by a multinational hotel corporation. In my experience, the big guys take customer complaints more seriously than the little ones. I would suppose that's one reason why they're big; they don't like to lose money anymore than I like to be bothered when I'm trying to read a goddamned book underneath a palm tree I paid $264 to get next to. A Black woman seeking refuge in a multinational corporation may seem like a contradiction to some, but there you are. In this case it's a coincidence of entirely different self-interests: Sheraton/cash = June Jordan's short run safety.

Anyway, I'm pretty sure "Olive" would look at me as though I came from someplace as far away as Brooklyn. Then she'd probably allow herself one indignant query before righteously removing her vacuum cleaner from my room; "and why in the first place you come down you without your husband?"

I cannot imagine how I would begin to answer her.

My "rights" and my "freedom" and my "desire" and a slew of other New World values; what would they sound like to this Black woman described on the card atop my hotel bureau as "Olive the Maid"? "Olive" is older than I am and I may smoke a cigarette while she changes the sheets on my bed. Whose rights? Whose freedom? Whose desire?

And why should she give a shit about mine unless I do something, for real, about hers?

It happens that the book that I finished reading under a palm tree earlier today was the novel, *The Bread Givers*, by Anzia Yezierska. Definitely autobiographical. Yezierska lays out the difficulties of being both female and "a person" inside a traditional Jewish family at the start of the 20th century. That any Jewish woman became anything more than the abused servant of her father or her husband is really an improbable piece of news. Yet Yezierska managed such an unlikely outcome for her own life. In *The Bread Givers*, the heroine also manages an important, although partial, escape from traditional Jewish female destiny. And in the unpardonable, despotic father, the Talmudic scholar of that Jewish family, did I not see my own and hate him twice, again? When the heroine, the young Jewish child, wanders the streets with a filthy pail she borrows to sell herring in order to raise the ghetto rent and when she cries, "Nothing was before me but the hunger in our house, and no bread for the next meal if I didn't sell the herring. No longer like a fire engine, but like a houseful of hungry mouths my heart cried, 'herring—herring! Two cents apiece!' who would doubt the ease, the sisterhood of conversation possible between that white girl and the Black women selling straw bags on the streets of paradise because they do not want to die? And is it not obvious that the wife of that Talmudic scholar and "Olive," who cleans my room here at the hotel, have more in common than I can claim with either one of them?

This is my consciousness of race and class and gender identity as I collect wet towels, sunglasses, wristwatch, and head towards a shower.

I am thinking about the boy who loaned this novel to me. He's white and he's Jewish and he's pursuing an independent study project with me, at the State University where I teach whether or not I feel like it, where I teach without stint because, like the waiter, I am no fool. It's my job and either I work or I do without everything you need money to buy. The boy loaned me the novel because he thought I'd be interested to know how a Jewish-American writer used English so that the syntax, and therefore the cultural habits of mind expressed by the Yiddish language, could survive translation. He did this because he wanted to create another connection between us on the basis of language, between his knowledge/his love of Yiddish and my knowledge/my love of Black English.

He has been right about the forceful survival of the Yiddish. And I had become excited by this further evidence of the written voice of spoken language protected from the monodrone of "standard" English, and so we had grown closer on this account. But then our talk shifted to student affairs more generally, and I had learned that this student does not care one way or the other about currently jeopardized Federal Student Loan Programs because, as he explained it to me, they do not affect him. He does not need financial help outside his family. My own son, however, is Black. And I am the only family help available to him and that means, if Reagan succeeds in eliminating Federal programs to aid minority students, he will have to forget about furthering his studies, or he or I or both of us will have to hit the numbers pretty big. For these reasons of difference, the student and I had moved away from each other, even while we continued to talk.

My consciousness turned to race, again, and class.

Sitting in the same chair as the boy, several weeks ago, a graduate student came to discuss her grade. I praised the excellence of her final paper; indeed it had seemed to me an extraordinary pulling together of recent left brain/right brain research with the themes of transcendental poetry.

She told me that, for her part, she'd completed her reading of my political essays. "You are so lucky!" she exclaimed.

"What do you mean by that?"

"You have a cause. You have a purpose to your life."

I looked carefully at this white woman; what was she really saying to me? "What do you mean?" I repeated.

"Poverty. Police violence. Discrimination in general."

(Jesus Christ, I thought: Is that her idea of lucky?)

"And how about you?" I asked.

"Me?"

"Yeah, you. Don't you have a cause?"

"Me? I'm just a middle-aged woman: a housewife and a mother. I'm a nobody."

For a while, I made no response.

First of all, speaking of race and class and gender in one breath, what she said meant that those lucky preoccupations of mine, from police violence to nuclear wipe-out, were not shared. They were mine and not hers. But here she sat, friendly as an old stuffed animal, beaming good will or more "luck" in my direction.

In the second place, what this white woman said to me meant that she did not believe she was "a person" precisely because she had fulfilled the traditional female functions revered by the father of that Jewish immigrant, Anzia Yezierska. And the woman in front of me was not a Jew. That was not the connection. The link was strictly female. Nevertheless, how should that woman and I, another female connect, beyond this bizarre exchange?

If she believed me lucky to have regular hurdles of discrimination then why shouldn't I insist that she's lucky to be a middle class white Wasp female who lives in such well-sanctioned and normative comfort that she even has the luxury to deny the power of the privileges that paralyze her life?

If she deserts me and "my cause" where we differ, if, for example, she abandons me to "my" problems of race, then why should I support her in "her" problems of housewifely oblivion?

Recollection of this peculiar moment brings me to the shower in the bathroom cleaned by "Olive." She reminds me of the usual Women's Studies curriculum because it has nothing to do with her or her job: you won't find "Olive" listed anywhere on the reading list. You will likewise seldom hear of Anzia Yezierska. But yes, you will find, from Florence Nightingale to Adrienne Rich, a white procession of independently well-to-do women writers. (Gertrude Stein/Virginia Woolf/Hilda Doolittle are standard names among the "essential" women writers.)

In other words, most of the women of the world—Black and First World and white who work because we must—most of the women of the world persist far from the heart of the usual Women's Studies syllabus.

Similarly, the typical Black History course will slide by the majority experience it pretends to represent. For example, Mary McLeod Bethune will scarcely receive as much attention as Nat Turner, even though Black women who bravely and efficiently provided for the education of Black people hugely outnumber those few Black men who led successful or doomed rebellions against slavery. In fact, Mary McLeod Bethune may not receive even honorable mention because Black History too often apes those ridiculous white history courses which produce such dangerous gibberish as The Sheraton British Colonial "history" of the Bahamas. Both Black and white history courses exclude from their central consideration those people who neither killed nor conquered anyone as the means to new identity, those people who took care of every one of the people who wanted to become "a person," those people who still take care of the life at issue: the ones who wash and who feed and who teach and who diligently decorate straw hats and bags with all of their historically unrequired gentle love: the women.

> *Oh the old rugged cross*
> *on a hill far away*
> *Well I cherish the old rugged cross*

It's Good Friday in the Bahamas. Seventy-eight degrees in the shade. Except for Sheraton territory, everything's closed.

It so happens that for truly secular reasons I've been fasting for three days. My hunger has now reached nearly violent proportions. In the hotel sandwich shop, the Black woman handling the counter complains about the tourists; why isn't the shop closed and why don't the tourists stop eating for once in their lives. I'm famished and I order chicken salad and cottage cheese and lettuce and tomato and a hard boiled egg and a hot cross bun and apple juice.

She eyes me with disgust.

To be sure, the timing of my stomach offends her serious religious practices. Neither one of us apologizes to the other. She seasons the chicken salad to the peppery max while I listen to the loud radio gospel she plays to console herself. It's a country Black version of "The Old Rugged Cross."

As I heave much chicken into my mouth tears start. It's not the pepper. I am, after all, a West Indian daughter. It's the Good Friday music that dominates the humid atmosphere.

> *Well I cherish the old rugged cross*

And I am back, faster than a 747, in Brooklyn, in the home of my parents where we are wondering, as we do every year, if the sky will darken until Christ has been buried in the tomb. The sky should darken if God is in His heavens. And then, around 3 p.m., at the conclusion of our mournful church service at the neighborhood St. Phillips, and even while we dumbly stare at the black cloth covering the gold altar and the slender unlit candles, the sun should return through the high gothic windows and vindicate our waiting faith that the Lord will rise again, on Easter.

How I used to bow my head at the very name of Jesus: ecstatic to abase myself in deference to His majesty.

My mouth is full of salad. I can't seem to eat quickly enough. I can't think how I should lessen the offence of my appetite. The other Black woman on the premises, the one who disapprovingly prepared this very tasty break from my fast, makes no remark. She is no fool. This is a job that she needs. I suppose she notices that at least I included a hot cross bun among my edibles. That's something in my favor. I decide that's enough.

I am suddenly eager to walk off the food. Up a fairly steep hill I walk without hurrying. Through the pastel desolation of the little town, the road brings me to a confectionary pink and white plantation house. At the gates, an unnecessarily large statue of Christopher Columbus faces me down, or tries to. His hand is fisted to one hip. I look back at him, laugh without deference, and turn left.

It's time to pack it up. Catch my plane. I scan the hotel room for things not to forget. There's that white report card on the bureau.

"Dear Guests:" it says, under the name "Olive." "I am your maid for the day. Please rate me: Excellent. Good. Average. Poor. Thank you."

I tuck this momento from the Sheraton British Colonial into my notebook. How would "Olive" rate *me*? What would it mean for us to seem "good" to each other? What would that rating require?

But I am hastening to leave. Neither turtle soup nor kidney pie nor any conch shell delight shall delay my departure. I have rested, here, in the Bahamas, and I'm ready to return to my usual job, my usual work. But the skin on my body has changed and so has my mind. On the Delta flight home I realize I am burning up, indeed.

So far as I can see, the usual race and class concepts of connection, or gender assumptions of unity, do not apply very well. I doubt that they ever did. Otherwise why would Black folks forever bemoan our lack of solidarity when the deal turns real. And if unity on the basis of sexual oppression is something natural, then why do we women, the majority people on the planet, still have a problem?

The plane's ready for takeoff. I fasten my seatbelt and let the tumult inside my head run free. Yes: race and class and gender remain as real as the weather. But what they must mean about the contact between two individuals is less obvious and, like the weather, not predictable.

And when these factors of race and class and gender absolutely collapse is whenever you try to use them as automatic concepts of connection. They may serve well as indicators of commonly felt conflict, but as elements of connection they seem about as reliable as precipitation probability for the day after the night before the day.

It occurs to me that much organizational grief could be avoided if people understood that partnership in misery does not necessarily provide for partnership for change: *When we get the monsters off our backs all of us may want to run in very different directions.*

And not only that: even though both "Olive" and "I" live inside a conflict neither one of us created, and even though both of us therefore hurt inside that conflict, I may be one of the monsters she needs to eliminate from her universe and, in a sense, she may be one of the monsters in mine.

I am reaching for the words to describe the difference between a common identity that has been imposed and the individual identity any one of us will choose, once she gains that chance.

That difference is the one that keeps us stupid in the face of new, specific information about somebody else with whom we are supposed to have a connection because a third party, hostile to both of us, has worked it so that the two of us, like it or not, share a common enemy. *What happens beyond the idea of that enemy and beyond the consequences of that enemy?*

I am saying that the ultimate connection cannot be the enemy. The ultimate connection must be the need that we find between us. It is not only who you are, in other words, but what we can do for each other that will determine the connection.

I am flying back to my job. I have been teaching contemporary women's poetry this semester. One quandary I have set myself to explore with my students is the one of taking responsibility without power. We had been wrestling ideas to the floor for several sessions when a young Black woman, a South African, asked me for help, after class.

Sokutu told me she was "in a trance" and that she'd been unable to eat for two weeks.

"What's going on?" I asked her, even as my eyes startled at her trembling and emaciated appearance.

"My husband. He drinks all the time. He beats me up. I go to the hospital. I can't eat. I don't know what/anything."

In my office, she described her situation. I did not dare to let her sense my fear and horror. She was dragging about, hour by hour, in dread. Her husband, a young Black South African, was drinking himself into more and more deadly violence against her.

Sokutu told me how she could keep nothing down. She weighed 90 lbs. at the outside, as she spoke to me. She'd already been hospitalized as a result of her husband's battering rage.

I knew both of them because I had organized a campus group to aid the liberation struggles of Southern Africa.

Nausea rose in my throat. What about this presumable connection: this husband and this wife fled from that homeland of hatred against them, and now what? He was destroying himself. If not stopped, he would certainly murder his wife.

She needed a doctor, right away. It was a medical emergency. She needed protection. It was a security crisis. She needed refuge for battered wives and personal therapy and legal counsel. She needed a friend.

I got on the phone and called every number in the campus directory that I could imagine might prove helpful. Nothing worked. There were no institutional resources designed to meet her enormous, multifaceted, and ordinary woman's need.

I called various students. I asked the Chairperson of the English Department for advice. I asked everyone for help.

Finally, another one of my students, Cathy, a young Irish woman active in campus IRA activities, responded. She asked for further details. I gave them to her.

"Her husband," Cathy told me, "is an alcoholic. You have to understand about alcoholics. It's not the same as anything else. And it's a disease you can't treat any old way."

I listened, fearfully. Did this mean there was nothing we could do?

"That's not what I'm saying," she said. "But you have to keep the alcoholic part of the thing central in everybody's mind, otherwise her husband will kill her. Or he'll kill himself."

She spoke calmly. I felt there was nothing to do but to assume she knew what she was talking about.

"Will you come with me?" I asked her, after a silence. "Will you come with me and help us figure out what to do next?"

Cathy said she would but that she felt shy: Sokutu comes from South Africa. What would she think about Cathy?

"I don't know," I said. "But let's go."

We left to find a dormitory room for the young battered wife.

It was late, now, and dark outside.

On Cathy's VW that I followed behind with my own car, was the sticker that reads BOBBY SANDS FREE AT LAST. My eyes blurred as I read and reread the words. This was another connection: Bobby Sands and Martin Luther King Jr. and who would believe it? I would not have believed it; I grew up terrorized by Irish kids who introduced me to the word "nigga."

And here I was following an Irish woman to the room of a Black South African. We were going to that room to try to save a life together.

When we reached the little room, we found ourselves awkward and large. Sokutu attempted to treat us with utmost courtesy, as though we were honored guests. She seemed surprised by Cathy, but mostly Sokutu was flushed with relief and joy because we were there, with her.

I did not know how we should ever terminate her heartfelt courtesies and address, directly, the reason for our visit: her starvation and her extreme physical danger.

Finally, Cathy sat on the floor and reached out her hands to Sokutu.

"I'm here," she said quietly, "Because June has told me what has happened to you. And I know what it is. Your husband is an alcoholic. He has a disease. I know what it is. My father was an alcoholic. He killed himself. He almost killed my mother. I want to be your friend."

"Oh," was the only small sound that escaped from Sokutu's mouth. And then she embraced the other student. And then everything changed and I watched all of this happen so I know that this happened: this connection.

And after we called the police and exchanged phone numbers and plans were made for the night and for the next morning, the young South African woman walked down the dormitory hallway, saying goodbye and saying thank you to us.

I walked behind them, the young Irish woman and the young South African, and I saw them walking as sisters walk, hugging each other, and whispering and sure of each other and I felt how it was not who they were but what they both know and what they were both preparing to do about what they know that was going to make them both free at last.

And I look out the windows of the plane and I see clouds that will not kill me and I know that someday soon other clouds may erupt to kill us all.

And I tell the stewardess No thanks to the cocktails she offers me. But I look about the cabin at the hundred strangers drinking as they fly and I think even here and even now I must make the connection real between me and these strangers everywhere before those other clouds unify this ragged bunch of us, too late.

27.
THE NEW MESTIZA NATION: A MULTICULTURAL MOVEMENT
Gloria Anzaldúa
(c. 1992)

As we near the turn into the twenty-first century, we face a backlash and a dangerous regressive state inside and outside of education. …

Amidst this attack by conservatives, people of color, working-class people, and progressive whites in the academy continue to struggle fiercely to define multiculturalism as a movement that reflects and represents the real United States—the mixed, hybrid, mestiza, character of this country.

I consider myself a mestiza multiculturalist teacher and writer[1] informed by my identity as a ChicanaTejana dyke from a working-class background. I am involved in the anti-colonial struggle against literary assimilation, claiming linguistic space to validate my personal language and history. Mestiza feminists such as myself seek the means to transform pedagogical and institutional practices so that they will represent ethnic people and protect students of color, gay men, and lesbians against racist and heterosexist violence. Women of color and working-class people have been at the forefront of this multicultural movement, before multicultural was even a term widely used. We have been articulating the need for curriculums that represent us, pedagogical approaches that do not silence us, and scholarship that challenges existing power hierarchies. We want our histories, our knowledge, our perspectives to be accepted and validated not only in the universities but also in elementary, junior high, and high schools. The roots of multicultural education lie in the lived experiences and struggles of women of color and working-class people. Nor that others have not also worked for this, but we have been there all along, knowing that education depends upon incorporating all different points of view, white, colored, and mestiza, drawing on and from las lenguas of our peoples.

Through our multi-layered experiences as mestizas, women of color, working-class, and gay people we claim multicultural education as a centerpiece of the mestiza nation. In 1920 José Vasconcelos, a Mexican philosopher, envisioned a mestizo nation, a cosmic race, a fifth race embracing the four major races of the world.[2] We are creating ways of educating ourselves and younger generations in this mestiza nation to change how students and teachers think and read by de-constructing Euro-Anglo ways of knowing; to create texts that reflect the needs of the world community of women and people of color; and to show how lived experience is connected to political struggles and art making.

We bring to the present our political experience which is why we are wary of the ways concepts like multiculturalism, difference, and diversity can get co-opted. These terms can, and have, been used against us, making it seem as though difference and diversity are power neutral, thus diluting or stripping these terms of their emancipatory potential. A radical political agenda is often reduced to superficial efforts to serve international foods, wear ethnic clothes, and decorate corporate complexes and airports with native colors and art. This multicultural appropriation/misappropriation is an attempt to control difference by allocating it to bordered-off sections in the curriculum. Diversity is then treated as a superficial overlay that does not disrupt any comfort zones. It is reduced to a footnote or an appendix in people's psyches. Our cultures, languages, thinking, and art are color-coded, made into commercial products, and reified as exotic cultural tales devoid of human agency. The racial/ethnic other or "nos/otras"—a word I split to show that we and they are both us and other—seeks terms that identify our heritages. Mestiza, which is actually an old term, speaks to our common identity as mixed bloods. I have been exploring this as a new category which is more inclusive than a racial mestizaje. Most Chicanos, Latinos, Asians, and Native Americans are mixed bloods. Many are half and half: half Chicano/half white, half Japanese/half white, and so on. The new mestiza is a category that threatens the hegemony of the neo-conservatives because it breaks down the labels and theories used to manipulate and control us. Punching holes in their categories, labels, and theories means punching holes in their walls.

The Trojan mulas in the academy, those who have been educated and assimilated in universities, run the risk of being white-washed in the academy's acid. …

Identity Crisis

As leaders of this movement, the new mestizas are among those who often feel worn down by the costs of exclusionary education. These costs have been high for feminists of color, queer scholars, activists, and artists who are producing new scholarship and who see the possibility of self-representation in higher education. We, the mestiza multiculturalists, know well the dangers of this border crossing, dangers to be reckoned with as we continue to walk across the firing lines. As a Chicana tejana patlache mujer del nuevo mundo, I am tired of being the counter-emancipatory voice, tired of being the return of the repressed, the token woman with the prominent Indian features.

The United States is struggling with a crisis of identity. The new conservatives want to keep higher education a Euro-Anglo institution. They want to keep a Euro-Anglo country, expanding a Euro-Anglo world, imperializing into the Third World. But we problematize their hegemony. We say, "Yo también soy América." For me, *America* does not stop at the Mexican and Canadian borders. It encompasses North America, Central America, South America, and Canada. We have to stop appropriating the word America to only fit the United States. It is all of this, el Nuevo Mundo.

This crisis of identity is not restricted to the monocultural white heterosexuals denouncing the wave of multiculturalism on campuses. The crisis is also felt by mestizas, people of color, mujeres, and lesbians of color who inhabit so many different worlds. This new racism has pounded hegemonic theories into us, making us feel like we don't fit. We are alienated. We are exiled. Not only are they undermining us by assimilating us, but in turn, *we* are using these very same theories, concepts, and assumptions that we have bought into against ourselves. Mestizas internalize those theories, concepts, and labels that manipulate and control us. We buy into these distortions and then we use them on ourselves. Many of us have become split from our ethnic, racial, and class communities. We are trying to figure out terms and ways of being in the world so that we will not be destroyed, so that we will not be co-opted or assimilated, so that we can make sense out of and teach our histories to ourselves and those who come after us. As we create a more diverse curricula we learn ways of teaching and knowing that are more representative of a mestiza nation.

The new mestiza finds herself inside the ivory tower, inside white-colored walls. It is hard to get through that gate and many do not make it. But once she passes through that gate, she becomes a sort of Trojan horse, a Trojan mula who has infiltrated in order to subvert the system, bringing new ideas with her. This work becomes such a weighty job because she docs triple duty. She studies the dominant culture through the scholarship her professors require her to read. She tries to learn about her own culture, seeks permission to explore topics, write papers, aud design a thesis that interests her. But her interests may extend beyond English or white American scholarship. Overwhelmed by her multiple tasks, she often ends up seduced and subverted by the system instead of subverting it.

If she is a progressive white teacher, she has to fight not only her own white sisters, but also those people of color who think, "What is that gringa doing with our stuff?" As a faculty member of color she does double, triple, quadruple work. She becomes a Trojan mula, stumbling with all this baggage. And sometimes the academy starts chipping away at her walls as she rams the academy's walls with her head to make room for others like herself; she ends upon the floor with a bloodied head as she comes up against classrooms where she and her communities are completely invisible. The mestiza must constantly find the energy to develop strategies, meet with people, form organizations, and build coalitions. And all of this depends upon funding so that she can do the Spanish festival, have lesbian, gay, and bisexual awareness week, invite a woman of color scholar or artist to the speaker series, build alliances among her own people and with other groups.

After the first, second, or third year in college, or by the time the mestiza is in graduate school, chances are she has been stepped on a lot—she has boot tracks on her face. Her head is already bloodied from going up against the walls. I call this *Písando su sombra*, and it takes its toll. She may get subverted instead of doing the subverting. ...

... Without acknowledging the difficulties involved in bridging more than one reality, she is left on her own to do the best she can. Being true to and maintaining ties with her ethnic communities is sometimes at odds with developing her intellectual identities, especially if this intellectualism denies any notion of difference.

My experience is a case in point. When I first entered graduate school. I was one of only two Chicanas in the entire graduate program. ... I felt very isolated and marginalized. I left after completing all of my course work when a couple of advisors told me that we were living in "America" and there was no such thing as Chicano literature. ...

For mestizas such as myself, the areas of study that professors want us to concentrate on do not appeal. We want new books, new areas of inquiry, and new methodologies. We want to study non-English and non-Euro-American literatures. We want more work by women of color on the reading lists. We are bookworms gnawing holes in the canon; we ore termites undermining the canonical curriculum's foundations.

We struggle to make room for ourselves, to change the academy so that it does not invalidate, stamp out, or crush our connections to the communities we come from. For working-class and colored people this means breaking down the barred windows that have kept us out of the universities.

I come from working-class roots, and it has been quite a struggle to negotiate the privilege I have received as a writer. Before gaining privilege, I was shut up, made invisible. As I move from the underclass to working class to middle class, I travel from being on the side of the "have-nots" to finding myself somewhat crossing over into the territory of the "haves," whom I've always viewed as oppressors. I am doing a lot of border crossing. Crossing over into the oppressors' terrain makes for a complex identity (and an identity complex). It problematizes who and what I am. Our attitudes toward money are programmed by our own class of origin. The indoctrination we receive is imprinted so deeply within us that it is hard to break through it. People from working-class origins find it difficult to get through the class barriers that exist in institutions of learning, writing, and art—barriers to being in school, to speaking out, to making our voices heard.

The new mestizas have a connection with particular places, a connection to particular races, a connection to new notions of ethnicity, to a new tribalism that is devoid of any kind of romantic illusions. The new mestiza is a liminal subject who lives in borderlands between cultures, races, languages, and genders. In this state of in-betweenness the mestiza can mediate, translate, negotiate, and navigate these different locations. As mestizas, we are negotiating these worlds every day, understanding that multiculturalism is a way of seeing and interpreting the world, a methodology of resistance.

Theories of Mestizaje: Border Inscriptions

People who are initiating a new politics of difference and who are the carriers of difference must have boundary-crossing visions. As multiculturalists they are developing theories of mestizaje—border inscriptions which draw on a combination of cultural values and traditions that show how certain kinds of knowledge have been conquered and colonized. Notions of mestizaje offer another "reading" of culture, history, and art—that of the dispossessed and marginal. Multicultural texts show the writer's or artist's struggle to decolonize subjectivity. For mestizas it is not sufficient simply to reinscribe the traditional culture they emerged from and set up a we-are-right/they-are-wrong binary opposition. Perspectives based on representation problematize these binaries, asking how people negotiate multiple worlds every day. My identity is always in flux; it changes as I step into and cross over many worlds each day—university, home community, job, lesbian, activist, and academic communities. It is not enough for me to say I am a Chicana. It is not enough for me to say I am an intellectual. It is not enough for me to say I am a writer. It is not enough for me to say I am from working-class origins. All of these and none of these are my primary identity. I can't say, this is the true me, or that is the true me. They are all the true me's.

Progressive whites who have friends from different worlds and who study different cultures become intellectual mestizas. They may not be emotional mestizas and certainly are not biological mestizas. But there can be empathy between people of color and progressive, sensitive, politically aware whites. ...

Creating Work That Cannot Be Assimilated

We need to create poetry, art, research, and books that cannot be assimilated, but is accessible. For example, take *Borderlands/La Frontera*: you can access that book, but hopefully it won't get consumed out of existence or tokenized or assimilated to death. I know that as you read the ideas you will reinterpret them, but the ideas can't be melted down. The components are distinct; they're there to dialogue with one another. The different races and communities that make up the Chicana do not disappear, they are not repressed. In reading *Borderlands*, the intellectual Gloria, the published writer and the person with an academic identity, are present. Behind these Glorias are others: Gloria the campesina, Gloria the clerk worker in temp jobs, the unemployed Gloria who subsisted on potatoes, the coming-into-middle-class Gloria, Gloria the lesbian, Gloria the ex-campesina are all present. When I speak at an academic conference, Gloria the intellectual might take center stage. If I am with a group of Chicanas, the ethnic me comes forward and the other Glorias withdraw backstage. In a room full of socializing and partying dyke friends, a different me comes out. But it doesn't mean that in the different communities some parts of me are repressed; all of me is there. Nor does this mean that I am a fake when I present different faces.

As a mestiza, I have many true faces, depending upon the kind of audience or the area I find myself in. Using *mestiza* an umbrella term means acknowledging that certain aspects of identity don't disappear, aren't assimilated or repressed when they are not in the foreground. Identity is a changing cluster of components and a shape-shifting activity. To refer to a person who is changing identity I use the Náhuatl term *nagual*. The nagual is a shapeshifter, a person who changes from human form to animal form. We shift around to do the work we have to do, to create the identities we need to live up to our potential.

Con los Ojos y la Lengua Como Pluma en la Mano Izquierda

...

To activate the conocimiento and communication we need the hand. The hand is an agent of action. It is not enough to speak and write and talk and communicate. It is not enough to see and recognize and know. We need to act upon what we know, to do something about it. The left hand has always been seen as sinister and strange, associated with the female gender and creativity. But in unison with the right, the left hand can perform great things. It is not enough to theorize and intellectualize—theory needs to connect with action, with activism. When theorizing, we need to ask of ourselves and others: *What does this theory have to do with working-class people, women of color, single women with children? What is the ideological and political function of this particular theory? How is this theory being used as an ideological weapon?*

Multiculturalist mestizas want to connect to all our different communities: the job, straight, and activist communities. The mestiza is in a position to make links. First of all, she is a borderland person, a bridge person. She connects from her ethnic community to the academic community, from the feminist group to non-political groups, from the Spanish language to the English language. She has the choice to be a bridge, a drawbridge, a sandbar, or an island in terms of how she relates to and defines herself in the world. She chooses when to do coalition and alliance work.[3] If she is colored, being a bridge means that she is always out there with white people, translating and mediating. As a drawbridge, she withdraws part of the time and says, "I don't want to have anything to do with straights, whites, males, etc. I need time to be with myself, my people. I need time to recharge, regenerate my batteries." The person who opts to be an island says, "I don't want to have anything to do ever with the straight or white folks." Being an island is basically impossible because we all depend on each other for necessities such as shelter and food. A symbol for another kind of bridge is a sandbar. One type of sandbar goes from island to mainland. That is my choice of a bridge because it's natural and it's underwater, which means I can be alone when I desperately need to, or I can connect to people. My creativity starts with solitude … but it also needs close contact with others in my different communities where we discuss mutual cultural and literary issues and support each other with our theories, experiences, and writing.

Doing bridge work brings up many questions, such as: *Where do I come from? What's my culture like? How do I position myself?* For whites this question means being clear about who you are and what privileges you bring into the group's dynamics. It means asking: *What can I do with my privileges? How can I use them for nos/otras? Instead of women of color being a resource for me, how can I be a resource for them? What kinds of knowledge can I offer nos/otras?* This means using your connections, your networks. It may mean making a way for nos/otras to get recognition, funds, or a grant. Or it could mean just being an empathetic ear.

I've seen that when white people align themselves with the struggles of women of color, their understanding of the struggles changes. When a white woman offers to work with nos/otras, we ask her the same thing we ask ourselves: What's in it for you? What is the motivation behind your crossing? More often than not she'll ask herself: *Am I one more white woman ripping off yet another culture? Am I one more white woman bringing her guilt and wanting to be exonerated? Am I one more white woman coming over and saying,"Look at me, I am not racist; otherwise I would not be working with you."*

All of us carry multiple unconscious motivations—both positive and negative. Half the time we don't know why we do things. Ten years down the road a woman of color may deduce, "Oh! I did that because I wanted white people to like me." Because people of color have been oppressed by white people so much we often seek their validation, love, and acceptance. Because we have been violated, we demand so much, we hunger for that acceptance and love. Muchas veces when we don't get it some of us become hostile or rebellious, some of us knuckle under and assimilate, and still others become bridges. Most of the time we don't know exactly why we respond in certain ways. Ten years down the road when we identify as feminists or lesbians or post-feminists, we might look back and say, "Oh yeah. Back then my thinking was screwed up. What I wanted from these white folk, ethnic community, dykes, etc., was for them to tell me I was okay." This desire is dangerous for both women of color and white women because we get into this dialectic of the la patrona, the great white mother, and the needy colored kid. …

When whites tell nos/otras that white people have no culture, they are oblivious to the fact that this whole country and the dominant culture is their culture. What white people watch on television is their culture. The films that they see on the VCR, the foods they eat and the clothes they buy, the vacations they take—it is from their culture, yet they keep saying, "I have no culture." This statement means that the majority of whites don't have a sense of their historical roots, … That's why they want to appreciate or appropriate black, Latino, Native, or Asian cultures. Appropriation is a dangerous act, es muy peligroso, if they are serious about doing coalition work.

Origins

In the last few years, "origins" has become a bad word because the deconstructionists see everything as socially constructed. According to them there is no such thing as "origins." Deconstructionists and some feminist theorists assert that origins are falsely romanticized and idealized. In some ways this assertion is true. We do tend to romanticize origins and culture, but the new mestiza is aware of the tendency to romanticize. She tries to look at the past and examine the aspects of culture that have oppressed women. The past is constantly being constructed in a number of ways. First, the perspective of the viewer of that history changes from one epoch to another; the perspective of a person changes from year to year. Second, the past has not been represented "truthfully" in history books. Written by the conquerors, history books distort and repress the histories of women and people of color.

Perhaps white theorists say that origins are passé or unattractive because they don't want to delve into their past. …

Crossing cultural and class borders requires that one look at the blood in one's veins, examining the history of one's people, including its religious and spiritual practices. Taken back far enough, one discovers some kind of shamanism in their cultural pasts. Look for and build on the positive.

There is such a thing as collective guilt, just as there is individual guilt. I don't mean that the father's guilt automatically, genetically, is handed down to his children. If today a white person is operating under the same white supremacist ideology as his great great grandfather—the notion that white people are better than people of color—then that person is as guilty as his ancestors. If that white person is not living that ideology, has said, "No, this is not my ideology," then he is not accountable or responsible for the sins of his ancestors. However, the ideology that operated during the slave and early colonial times is still operating today. When Bush opens his mouth, you can still hear that old ideology.

As we continue the snuggle with the new conservatism's onslaught, we find ourselves at an impasse—but we can't go back. We need a reminder of what this struggle is all about. At this time when the term *multiculturalism* is being completely subverted, it is important that this concept be sharply defined. Forcing down foreign concepts into our minds is analogous to the insistence on maintaining "family values"—a sign of how desperate they are to keep things the way they once were, because things have changed. But it's too late, the walls have chinks in them, and we refuse to give up our positions no matter how insistent their backlash. To allow depression or disillusionment to stop our Struggle would lose the ground we've gained. Multiculturalism is about including stories of difference. Se trata de otras narrativas. It is about alter-narratives. The stories of multiculturalism are stories of identity, and narratives of identity are stories of location. A story is always a retelling of an older story. This is my retelling.

Notes

1. I am a seventh generation American whose ancestors lived in a part of Texas that used to be Mexico: before, it was Indian territory. My ancestors were Tejanos from Mexico. Long ago a boundary got drawn up and the Anzaldúas found themselves on this side of the border while the other Anzaldúas (who call themselves Anzaldua without the accent) found themselves split on the other side, and we lost touch with each other. This is what has happened to the Chicano/Mexicano race in this country. We are an in-between race. We are still Mexican in terms of racial ancestry but are Norteamericanos who have been educated in U.S. schools and raised imbibing and consuming the dominant values and customs. I am also a dyke Chicana. I call myself *paltache* which is the Aztec Náhuatl word for dyke. The word lesbian does not fit my background, my experience. The term comes from Lesbos, the Greek Island, and is a term of identity for white middle-class lesbians.
2. See José Vasconcelos, *La Raza Cósmica: Mission de la Raza Ibero-Americana* (México: Aguilar S.A. de Ediciones, 1961). For more discussion of this work and concept, see my "La Consciencia de la Mestiza: Toward a New Consciousness,'" in *Making Face, Making Soul / Haciendo Caras*, ed. Gloria Anzaldúa (San Francisco Aunt Lute, 1990).
3. See my "Bridge, Drawbridge, Sand bar or Island." in *Bridges of Power: Women's Multicultural Alliances*, ed. by Lisa Albrecht [(Philadelphia: New Society Publishers, 1990)].

28.

IDENTITY: SKIN, BLOOD, HEART
Minnie Bruce Pratt
(1983)

I live in a part of Washington, D.C., that white suburbanites called "the jungle" during the uprising of the sixties—perhaps still do, for all I know. When I walk the two-and-a-half blocks to H Street, N.E., to stop in at the bank, to leave my boots off at the shoe-repair-and-lock shop, I am most usually the only white person in sight. I've seen two other whites, women, in the year I've lived here. (This does not count white folks in cars, passing through. In official language, H Street, N.E. is known as the "H Street Corridor"; as in something to be passed through quickly, going from your place on the way to elsewhere.)

When I walk three blocks in a slightly different direction, down Maryland Avenue, to go to my lover's house, I pass yards of Black folks: the yard of the lady who keeps children, with its blue-and-red windmill, its roses of Sharon; the yard of the man who delivers vegetables, with its stacked slatted crates; the yard of, the people next to the Righteous Branch Commandment Church of God (Seventh Day), with its tomatoes in the summer, its collards in the fall. In the summer, folks sit out on their porches or steps or sidewalks. When I walk by, if I lift my head and look toward them and speak, "Hey," they may speak, say, "Hey" or "How you doin'?" or perhaps just nod. In the spring I was afraid to smile when I spoke, because that might be too familiar, but by the end of summer I had walked back and forth so often, I was familiar, so sometimes we shared comments about the mean weather.

I am comforted by any of these speakings for, to tell you the truth, they make me feel at home. I am living far from where I was born; it has been twenty years since I have lived in that place where folks, Black and white, spoke to each other when they met on the street or in the road. So when two Black men dispute country matters, calling across the corners of 8th Street—"Hey, Roland, did you ever see a hog catch a rat?"—"I seen a hog catch a *snake*!"—"How about a rat? Ever see one catch a *rat*?"—I am grateful to be living within sound of their voices, to hear a joking that reminds me, with a startled pain, of my father, putting on his tales for his friends, the white men gathered at the drugstore in the mornings.

The pain, of course, is the other side of this speaking, and the sorrow, when I have only to turn two corners to go back in the basement door of my building, to meet Mr. Boone, the janitor, who doesn't raise his eyes to mine, or his head, when we speak. He is a dark red-brown man from the Yemassee in South Carolina—that swampy land of Indian resistance and armed communities of fugitive slaves, that marshy land at the headwaters of the Combahee, once site of enormous rice plantations and location of Harriet Tubman's successful military action that freed many slaves. When we meet in the hall or on the elevator, even though I may have just heard him speaking in his own voice to another man, he "yes-ma'ams" me in a sing-song; I hear my voice replying in the horrid cheerful accents of a white lady. And I hate my white womanhood that drags between us the long bitter history of our region.

I think how I just want to feel at home, where people know me. Instead I remember, when I meet Mr. Boone, that home was a place of forced subservience, and I know that my wish is that of an adult wanting to stay a child: to be known by others, but to know nothing, to feel no responsibility. Instead I recognize, when I walk out in my neighborhood, that each speaking-to another person has become fraught, for me; with the history of race and sex and class. As I walk I have a constant interior discussion with myself, questioning how I acknowledge the presence of another, what I know or don't know about them, and what how they acknowledge me means. It is an exhausting process, this moving from the experience of the "unknowing majority" (as Maya Angelou has called it) into consciousness. It would be a lie to say this process is comforting.

I meet a white man on Maryland Avenue at ten at night, for instance. He doesn't *look* gay; and he's younger and bigger than me. Just because he's wearing a three-piece suit doesn't mean he won't try something. What's he doing walking here, anyway? One of the new gentry taking over? Maybe that's what the Black neighbors think about me. If I speak, he'll probably assume it's about sex, not about being neighborly. I don't feel neighborly toward him, anyway. If he speaks to me, is that about sex? Or does he still think skin means kin? Or maybe he was raised someplace where someone could say, "I know your mama" if he didn't behave. But he's probably not going to think about her when he does whatever he does *here:* better be careful.

In the space of three blocks, on one evening, I can debate whether the young Black woman didn't speak because she was tired, urban-raised, or hates white women; and ask myself why I wouldn't speak to the young professional white woman on her way to work in the morning, but I do at night (and she doesn't speak at all). Is this about who I think I may need for physical safety?

And I make myself speak to a young Black man; if I don't, it will be the old racial-sexual fear. Damn the past. When I speak directly I usually get a respectful answer. Is that the response violently extorted by history, the taboo on white women? Last week the group of Black men on 10th Street started in on "Can I have some?" when Joan and I walked by. Was that because they were three? We were white? We were lesbian? Or because we didn't speak? What about this man? He is a man. And I would speak to him in the *day*time.

After I speak and he speaks, I think of how my small store of manners, the way I was taught to be "respectful" of others, my middle-class, white-woman, rural Southern Christian manners, gave me no ideas on a past Sunday afternoon, in the northwest part of the city, on how to speak to the Latinos and Latinas socializing on the sidewalks there.

And I think of how I'm walking to visit my Jewish lover. When we walk around the neighborhood together, we look like two white women, except the ladies in my building say we look like sisters, because we're close and they can see we love each other. But I'm blonde and blue-eyed, she dark-haired and brown-eyed; we don't look a bit like sisters. If the white people and the Black people we meet knew she was Jewish as well as white, how would their speaking alter?

I reckon the rigid boundaries set around my experience, how I have been "protected" by the amount of effort it takes me to walk these few blocks being as conscious as I can of myself in relation to history, to race, to culture, to gender. In this city where I am no longer of the majority by color or culture, I tell myself every day: In this *world* you aren't the majority race or culture, and never were, whatever you were raised to think; and are you getting ready to be *in* this world?

And I answer myself back: I'm trying to learn how to live, to have the speaking-to extend beyond the moment's word, to act so as to change the unjust circumstances that keep us from being able to speak to each other; I'm trying to get a little closer to the longed-for but unrealized world, where we each are able to live, but not by trying to make someone less than us, not by someone else's blood or pain. Yes, that's what I'm trying to do with my living now. …

Where does the need come from, the inner push to walk into change, if we are women who, by skin color, ethnicity, birth culture, are in a position of material advantage where we gain at the expense of others, of other women? A place where *we* can have a degree of safety, comfort, familiarity, just by staying put. Where is our *need* to change what we were born into? What do we have to gain?

When I try to think of this, I think of my father. When I was about eight years old, he took me up the front marble steps of the courthouse in my town. He took me inside, up the worn wooden steps, stooped under the feet of folks who had gone up and down to be judged, or to gawk at others being judged, up past the courtroom where my grandfather had leaned back in his chair and judged for over forty years, up to the attic, to some narrow steps that went to the roof, to the clock tower with a walled ledge.

What I would have seen from the top, on the streets down below around the courthouse square: the Methodist church, the grey limestone building with the county Health Department, Board of Education, Welfare Department (my mother worked there), the yellow brick Baptist church, the Gulf station, the pool hall (no women allowed), Cleveland's grocery, Ward's shoestore. Then all in a line, connected: the bank, the post office, Dr. Nicholson's office (one door for whites, one for Blacks). Then separate: the Presbyterian church, the newspaper office, the yellow brick jail, same brick as the Baptist church and as the courthouse.

What I could not have seen from the top: the sawmill, or Four Points where the white mill folks lived, or the houses of Blacks in Veneer Mill Quarters.

This is what I would and would not have seen, or so I think: for I never got to the top. When he told me to go up the steps in front of him, I tried to, crawling on hands and knees, but I was terribly afraid. I couldn't, or wouldn't, do it. He let me crawl down; he was disgusted with me, I thought. I think now that he wanted to show me a place he had climbed to as a boy, a view that had been his father's and his, and would be mine. But I was not him: I had not learned to take that height, that being set apart as my own, a white girl, not a boy.

Yet I was shaped by my relation to those buildings and to the people in the buildings, by ideas of who should be working in the Board of Education, of who should be in the bank handling money, of who should have the guns and the keys to the jail, of who should be *in* the jail; and I was shaped by what I didn't see, or didn't notice, on those streets.

Not the way your town was laid out, you say? True, perhaps, but each of us carries around those growing-up places, the institutions, a sort of backdrop, a stage set. So often we act out the present against a backdrop of the past, within a frame of perception that is so familiar, so safe, that it is terrifying to risk changing it even when we know our perceptions are distorted, limited, constricted by that old view.

So this is one gain for me as I change: I learn a way of looking at the world that is more accurate, complex, multilayered, multidimensioned, more truthful. To see the world of overlapping circles, like movement on the mill pond after a fish has jumped, instead of the courthouse square with me at the middle, even if I am on the ground. I feel the *need* to look differently because I've learned that what is presented to me as an accurate view of the world is frequently a lie: so that to look through an anthology of women's studies that has little or no work by women of color is to be up on that ledge above the town and be thinking that I see the town, without realizing how many lives have been pushed out of sight, beside unpaved roads.

I'm learning that what I think that I *know* is an accurate view of the world is frequently a lie: as when I was in a discussion about the Women's Pentagon Action with several women, four of us Christian-raised, one Jewish, my lover Joan, a photographer. Describing the march through Arlington Cemetery, one of the four mentioned the rows of crosses. I had marched for a long time through that cemetery; I nodded to myself, visualized rows of crosses. No, said Joan, they were *headstones*, with crosses or Stars of David engraved above the names. We four Christians objected; we all had seen crosses. But Joan had photographs she had taken of the march through the cemetery, laid them on the table. We saw rows and rows and rows of rectangular gravestones, and in the foreground, clearly visible, one inscribed with a name and a Star of David.

So I gain truth when I expand my constricted eye, an eye that has only let in what I have been taught to see. But there have been other constrictions: the clutch of fear around my heart when I must deal with the *fact* of folks who exist, with their own lives, in other places besides the narrow circle I was raised in. I have learned that my fear is kin to a terror that has been in my birth culture for years, for centuries—the terror of a people who have set themselves apart and *above*, who have wronged others and feel they are about to be found out and punished. …

The place I wanted to reach was not a childish place, but my understanding of it was childish. I had not admitted that the safety of much of my childhood was because Laura Cates, Black and a servant, was responsible for me; that I had the walks with my father in woods that were "ours" because my people, only three generations back, had driven out the Creeks who had lived there; that I was allowed to have my children and one evening a month with women friends because I was a wife who always came home at night to her husband. Raised to believe that I could be where I wanted and have what I wanted and be who I wanted, as a grown woman I thought I could simply claim my desire, even if this was the making of a new place to live with other women. I had no understanding of the limits that I lived within; nor of how much my memory and my experience of a safe space was based on places that had been secured for me by omission, exclusion, or violence; nor that my continued safety meant submitting to those very limits.

I should have remembered, from my childhood, Viola Liuzzo, who was trying to reach the place by another way, shot down in Lowndes County, Alabama, while driving demonstrators back to their homes during the Selma-to-Montgomery march. Her death was justified by Klan leader Robert Shelton on the grounds that "She had five children by four different husbands … her husband hadn't seen her in two, three months … she was living with two nigger men in Selma … she was a *fat* slob with crud … all over her body … she was bra-less."[1] Liuzzo—Italian, white-but-not-white, gone over to the other side—damned, dead. …

I didn't understand what a limited, narrow space, and how short-lasting, it would be, if only *my* imagination and knowledge and abilities were to go into the making and extending of it. I didn't understand how much I was still inside the restrictions of my culture in my vision of how the world could be. …

… Yet, if we are women who have gained privilege by our white skin or our Christian culture, but who are trying to free ourselves *as* women in a more complex way, we can experience this change as loss. Because it is: the old lies and ways of living—habitual, familiar, comfortable, fitting us like our skin—*were* ours.

Our fear of the losses can keep us from changing. What is it, exactly, that we are afraid to lose? …

When we begin to understand that we have benefitted, in our privilege, from the lives and work of others, when we begin to understand how false much of our sense of self-importance has been, we do experience a loss: our self-respect. To regain it, we need to find new ways to be in the world, those very actions a way of creating a positive self.

Part of this process, for me, has been to acknowledge to myself that there are things that I *do not know*—an admission hard on my pride, and harder to do than it sounds …

Partly I have regained myself-respect by rejecting false self-importance and by acknowledging the foundation of liberation effort in this country in the work of women, and men, who my folks have tried to hold down. For me this has meant not just reading their poetry, fiction, essays, but learning about the long history of political organizing in the U.S. by men and women trying to break the economic and cultural grip a Euro-American system has on their lives. But my hardest struggle has been to admit and honor their daily, constant work when this means their correction of *my* ignorance, resistance to *my* prejudice. Then I have to struggle to remember that I don't rule the world with my thoughts and actions like some judge in a tilt-back chair; and that by *listening* to criticisms, not talking back but listening. I may learn how I might have been acting or thinking like one of the old powers-that-be. …

As I've worked at stripping away layer after layer of my false identity, notions of skin, blood, heart based in racism and anti-Semitism, another way I've tried to regain my self-respect, to keep from feeling completely naked and ashamed of who I am, is to look at what I have carried with me from my culture that could help me in the process. As I have learned about the actual history, and present, of my culture, I didn't stop loving my family or my home, but it was hard to figure out what from there I could be proud and grateful to have, since much of what I *had* learned had been based on false pride. Yet buried under the layers, I discovered some strengths:

I found a sense of connection to history; people, and place, through my family's rootedness in the South; and a comparative and skeptical way of thinking, from my Presbyterian variety of Protestantism, which emphasized doubt and analysis. I saw that I had been using these skills all along as I tried to figure out my personal responsibility in a racist and anti-Semitic culture.

I found that my mother had given me hope, through the constancy of her regard for her mother and sisters and women friends, and through her stubbornness in the undertaking and completing of work. I found that my father had given me his manners, the "Pratts' beautiful manners," which amid demonstrate respectfulness to others, if I paid attention; and he had given me the memory, of his sorrow and pain, disclosing to me his heart that still felt wrongs. Somehow, my heart had learned that from his.

In my looking I also discovered a tradition of white Christian-raised women in the South, who had worked actively for social justice since at least 1849, the year a white woman in Bucktown, Maryland, hid Harriet Tubman during her escape from slavery; in her house on the Underground Railroad.[2] From the 1840s to the 1860s, Sarah and Angelina Grimke of South Carolina, living in the North, had organized both for the abolition of slavery, and for women's rights, linking the two struggles. ...

From the 1920s to the 1940s, Jessie Daniel Ames of Texas led an antilynching campaign, gathering women like herself into the Association of Southern Women for the Prevention of Lynching. Begun several decades after Ida B. Wells first organized, as a Black woman, against lynching, the ASWPL included, by the early 1940s, over 109 women's organizations, auxiliaries of major Protestant denominations, and national and regional federations of Jewish women, with a total membership of over four million. The women used a variety of methods to stop the violence done by the white men who were of their kin or their social group, including: investigative reporting for the collection and publication of facts about lynching locally; attempts to change white-run newspaper reporting of lynchings toward a less sensational and inflammatory treatment; signature campaigns to get written pledges from white sheriffs and other law enforcement officers to prevent lynchings; publication in their communities of the names of white "peace officers" who gave up prisoners to lynch mobs; mobilization of local peer pressure in the white community and face-to-face or over-the-phone confrontations with white men by the women; and direct intervention by the women to persuade a mob to stop its violence, including one ASWPL woman in Alabama who stopped the lynching of a Black man accused of raping her seven-year-old daughter.[3] The Association repudiated the "myth of mob chivalry"; its statement of purpose said that "... the claim of the lynchers [is] that they were acting solely in the defense of womanhood ... we dare not longer permit this claim to pass unchallenged nor allow those bent upon personal revenge and savagery to commit acts of violence and lawlessness in the name of women."[4] ...

... Again, it seems that if we are women who want a place for ourselves and for other women, and our children, in a just, peaceful, free world, we need to be saying: *Not in my name*. ...

And I get hopeful when I think that with this kind of work there is the possibility of friendship, and love, between me and the many other women from whom I have been separated by my culture, and by my own beliefs and actions, for so long. For years, I have had a recurring dream: Sleeping, I dream I am reconciled to a woman from whom I have been parted—my mother, the Black woman who raised me, my first woman lover, a Jewish woman friend. In the dream we embrace, with the sweetness that can come when all is made right. I catch a glimpse of this possibility in my dream. It appears in waking life with my friends sometimes, with my lover: Not an easy reconciliation, but one that may come when I continue the struggle with myself and the world I was born into.

Notes

1. Patsy Sims, *The Klan* (New York: Stein and Day, 1978), pp. 108–109.
2. Bettina Aptheker, "Abolitionism, Woman's Rights, and the Battle Over the Fifteenth Amendment," in *Woman's Legacy* (Amherst: University of Massachusetts Press, 1982), p. 35.
3. Jacquelyn Dowd Hall, *Revolt Against Chivalry* (New York: Columbia University Press, 1979), pp. 175, 223–253.
4. Jessie Daniel Ames, *The Changing Character of Lynching*, 1931–1941 (Atlanta, Georgia: Commission on Interracial Cooperation, 1941), p. 64.

29.

I AM YOUR SISTER: BLACK WOMEN ORGANIZING ACROSS SEXUALITIES
Audre Lorde
(1988)

Whenever I come to Medgar Evers College I always feel a thrill of anticipation and delight because it feels like coming home, like talking to family, having a chance to speak about things that are very important to me with people who matter the most. And this is particularly true whenever I talk at the Women's Center. But, as with all families, we sometimes find it difficult to deal constructively with the genuine differences between us and to recognize that unity does not require that we be identical to each other. Black women are not one great vat of homogenized chocolate milk. We have many different faces, and we do not have to become each other in order to work together.

It is not easy for me to speak here with you as a Black Lesbian feminist, recognizing that some of the ways in which I identify myself make it difficult for you to hear me. But meeting across difference always requires mutual stretching, and until you *can* hear me as a Black Lesbian feminist, our strengths will not be truly available to each other as Black women.

Because I feel it is urgent that we not waste each other's resources, that we recognize each sister on her own terms so that we may better work together toward our mutual survival, I speak here about heterosexism and homophobia, two grave barriers to organizing among Black women. And so that we have a common language between us, I would like to define some of the terms I use: *Heterosexism*—a belief in the inherent superiority of one form of loving over all others and thereby the right to dominance; *Homophobia*—a terror surrounding feelings of love for members of the same sex and thereby a hatred of those feelings in others.

In the 1960s, when liberal white people decided that they didn't want to appear racist, they wore dashikis, and danced Black, and ate Black and even married Black, but they did not want to feel Black or think Black, so they never even questioned the textures of their daily living (why should flesh-colored bandaids always be pink?) and then they wondered, "Why are those Black folks always taking offense so easily at the least little thing? Some of our best friends are Black …."

Well, it is not necessary for some of your best friends to be Lesbian, although some of them probably are, no doubt. But it is necessary for you to stop oppressing me through false judgement. I do not want you to ignore my identity, nor do I want you to make it an insurmountable barrier between our sharing of strengths.

When I say I am a Black feminist, I mean I recognize that my power as well as my primary oppressions come as a result of my Blackness as well as my womanness, and therefore my struggles on both these fronts are inseparable.

When I say I am a Black Lesbian, I mean I am a woman whose primary focus of loving, physical as well as emotional, is directed to women. It does not mean I hate men. Far from it. The harshest attacks I have ever heard against Black men come from those women who are intimately bound to them and cannot free themselves from a subservient and silent position. I would never presume to speak about Black men the way I have heard some of my straight sisters talk about the men they are attached to. And of course that concerns me, because it reflects a situation of noncommunication in the heterosexual Black community that is far more truly threatening than the existence of Black Lesbians.

What does this have to do with Black women organizing?

I have heard it said—usually behind my back—that Black Lesbians are not normal. But what is normal in this deranged society by which we are all trapped? I remember, and so do many of you, when being Black was considered *not normal* when they talked about us in whispers, tried to paint us, lynch us, bleach us, ignore us, pretend we did not exist. We called that racism.

I have heard it said that Black Lesbians are a threat to the Black family. But when 50 percent of children born to Black women are born out of wedlock, and 30 percent of all Black families are headed by women without husbands, we need to broaden and redefine what we mean by *family*.

I have heard it said that Black Lesbians will mean the death of the race. Yet Black Lesbians bear children in exactly the same way other women bear children, and a Lesbian household is simply another kind of family. Ask my son and daughter.

The terror of Black Lesbians is buried in that deep inner place where we have been taught to fear all difference—to kill it or ignore it. Be assured: loving women is not a communicable disease. You don't catch it like the common cold. Yet the one accusation that seems to render even the most vocal straight Black woman totally silent and ineffective is the suggestion that she might be a Black Lesbian.

If someone says you're Russian and you know you're not, you don't collapse into stunned silence. Even if someone calls you a bigamist, or a childbeater, and you know you're not, you don't crumple into bits. You say it's not true and keep on printing the posters. But let anyone, particularly a Black man, accuse a straight Black woman of being a Black *Lesbian*, and right away that sister becomes immobilized, as if that is the most horrible thing she could be, and must at all costs be proven false. That is homophobia. It is a waste of woman energy, and it puts a terrible weapon into the hands of your enemies to be used against you to silence you, to keep you docile and in line. It also serves to keep us isolated and apart.

I have heard it said that Black Lesbians are not political, that we have not been and are not involved in the struggles of Black people. But when I taught Black and Puerto Rican students writing at City College in the SEEK program in the sixties I was a Black Lesbian. I was a Black Lesbian when I helped organize and fight for the Black Studies Department of John Jay College. And because I was fifteen years younger then and less sure of myself, at one crucial moment I yielded to pressures that said I should step back for a Black man even though I knew him to be a serious error of choice, and I did, and he was. But I was a Black Lesbian then.

When my girlfriends and I went out in the car one July 4th night after fireworks with cans of white spray paint and our kids asleep in the back seat, one of us staying behind to keep the motor running and watch the kids while the other two worked our way down the suburban New Jersey street, spraying white paint over the black jockey statues, and their little red jackets, too, we were Black Lesbians.

When I drove through the Mississippi Delta to Jackson in 1968 with a group of Black students from Tougaloo, another car full of redneck kids trying to bump us off the road all the way back into town, I was a Black Lesbian.

When I weaned my daughter in 1963 to go to Washington in August to work in the coffee tents along with Lena Horne, making coffee for the marshals because that was what most Black women did in the 1963 March on Washington, I was a Black Lesbian.

When I taught a poetry workshop at Tougaloo, a small Black college in Mississippi, where white rowdies shot up the edge of the campus every night, and I felt the joy of seeing young Black poets find their voices and power through words in our mutual growth, I was a Black Lesbian. And there are strong Black poets today who date their growth and awareness from those workshops.

When Yoli and I cooked curried chicken and beans and rice and took our extra blankets and pillows up the hill to the striking students occupying buildings at City College in 1969, demanding open admissions and the right to an education, I was a Black Lesbian. When I walked through the midnight hallways of Lehman College that same year, carrying Midol and Kotex pads for the young Black radical women taking part in the action, and we tried to persuade them that their place in the revolution was not ten paces behind Black men, that spreading their legs to the guys on the tables in the cafeteria was not a revolutionary act no matter what the brothers said, I was a Black Lesbian. When I picketed for Welfare Mothers' Rights, and against the enforced sterilization of young Black girls, when I fought institutionalized racism in the New York City schools, I was a Black Lesbian.

But you did not know it because we did not identify ourselves, so now you can say that Black Lesbians and Gay men have nothing to do with the struggles of the Black Nation.

And I am not alone.

When you read the words of Langston Hughes you are reading the words of a Black Gay man. When you read the words of Alice Dunbar-Nelson and Angelina Weld Grimké, poets of the Harlem Renaissance, you are reading the words of Black Lesbians. When you listen to the life-affirming voices of Bessie Smith and Ma Rainey, you are hearing Black Lesbian women. When you see the plays and read the words of Lorraine Hansberry, you are reading the words of a woman who loved women deeply.

Today, Lesbians and Gay men are some of the most active and engaged members of Art Against Apartheid, a group which is making visible and immediate our cultural responsibilities against the tragedy of South Africa. We have organizations such as the National Coalition of Black Lesbians and Gays, Dykes Against Racism Everywhere, and Men of All Colors together, all of which are committed to and engaged in antiracist activity.

Homophobia and heterosexism mean you allow yourselves to be robbed of the sisterhood and strength of Black Lesbian women because you are afraid of being called a Lesbian yourself. Yet we share so many concerns as Black women, so much work to be done. The urgency of the destruction of our Black children and the theft of young Black minds are joint urgencies. Black children shot down or doped up on the streets of our cities are priorities for all of us. The fact of Black women's blood flowing with grim regularity in the streets and living rooms of Black communities is not a Black Lesbian rumor. It is a sad statistical truth. The fact that there is widening and dangerous lack of communication around our differences between Black women and men is not a Black Lesbian plot. It is a reality that is starkly clarified as we see our young people becoming more and more uncaring of each other. Young Black boys believing that they can define their manhood between a sixth-grade girl's legs, growing up believing that Black women and girls are the fitting target for their justifiable furies rather than the racist structures grinding us all into dust, these are not Black Lesbian myths. These are sad realities of Black communities today and of immediate concern to us all. We cannot afford to waste each other's energies in our common battles.

What does homophobia mean? It means that high-powered Black women are told it is not safe to attend a Conference on the Status of Women in Nairobi simply because we are Lesbians. It means that in a political action, you rob yourselves of the vital insight and energies of political women such as Betty Powell and Barbara Smith and Gwendolyn Rogers and Raymina Mays and Robin Christian and Yvonne Flowers. It means another instance of the divide-and-conquer routine.

How do we organize around our differences, neither denying them nor blowing them up out of proportion?

The first step is an effort of will on your part. Try to remember to keep certain facts in mind. Black Lesbians are not apolitical. We have been a part of every freedom struggle within this country. Black Lesbians are not a threat to the Black family. Many of us have families of our own. We are not white, and we are not a disease. We are women who love women. This does not mean we are going to assault your daughters in an alley on Nostrand Avenue. It does not mean we are about to attack you if we pay you a compliment on your dress. It does not mean we only think about sex, any more than you only think about sex.

Even if you *do* believe any of these stereotypes about Black Lesbians, begin to practice acting like you don't believe them. Just as racist stereotypes are the problem of the white people who believe them, so also are homophobic stereotypes the problem of the heterosexuals who believe them. In other words, those stereotypes are yours to solve, not mine, and they are a terrible and wasteful barrier to our working together. I am not your enemy. We do not have to become each other's unique experiences and insights in order to share what we have learned through our particular battles for survival as Black women.

There was a poster in the 1960s that was very popular: HE'S NOT BLACK, HE'S MY BROTHER! It used to infuriate me because it implied that the two were mutually exclusive—*he* couldn't be both brother and Black. Well, I do not want to be tolerated, nor misnamed. I want to be recognized.

I am a Black Lesbian, and I *am* your sister.

30.
WELL-FOUNDED FEAR: POLITICAL ASYLUM AND THE BOUNDARIES OF SEXUAL IDENTITY IN THE U.S.–MEXICO BORDERLANDS

Lionel Cantú Jr. with Eithne Luibhéid and Alexandra Minna Stern

(2005)

Between 1999 and 2002, Cantú served as an expert witness in five cases involving Mexican men who petitioned for asylum in the United States on the basis of persecution for sexual orientation. The cases were processed in California, and all five men were eventually granted asylum. Cantú's participation as an expert witness reflected his commitment to using his sociological training and university faculty status to challenge inequalities and to assist those with less privilege. Having researched the lives of men who have sex with men in Mexico, and in migrant Mexican communities in the United States, Cantú appreciated the struggles and courage that underlay each application for asylum based on sexual orientation. Yet, he also began to observe a similarity to the process through which these asylum claims were adjudicated. While standardization remains the cornerstone to ensuring equal application of the law, it also meant that individual asylum applicants' experiences were elicited and given meaning within larger institutional structures that Cantú began to question.

Two issues particularly drew Cantú's attention. One issue was that to gain asylum on the basis of being persecuted for one's sexual orientation, the applicant has to prove that being gay is an "immutable" aspect of his selfhood. This tricky undertaking runs the risk of reinscribing essentialist notions of gay identity that scholars have spent decades painstakingly challenging. The second issue was that, as Saeed Rahman has described, receiving asylum requires painting one's country in racialist, colonialist terms, while at the same time disavowing the United States' role in contributing to the oppressive conditions that one fled.[1] These two issues converged because narratives about immutable homosexual or gay identities in Third World countries often provide the means to reinforce and remake racialist and colonialist scripts of U.S. "progressiveness"/Third World "backwardness."

Immutably Gay

Legally and historically in the United States, asylum for gay petitioners is complexly positioned between on the one hand, a long-held pattern of pathologizing and othering gays and lesbians, and on the other, discourses of providing a safe haven for persecuted people. … [L]esbian and gay immigrants historically were excluded from entry into the United States based on multiple concerns including morality, public health, and political affiliation, and even though exclusion was stricken from immigration law in 1990, lesbian and gay immigrants still face structural discrimination. Throughout the period of explicit exclusion, the Immigration and Naturalization Service (INS) and the courts relied on constructions of gay identity as immutable, inherent, and undesirable when policing the national boundaries. For instance, in *Boutillier v. INS*, the Supreme Court argued, "the petitioner is not being deported for conduct engaged in after his entry into the United States, but rather, for characteristics he possessed at the time of his entry."[2]

Ironically, while these formal and informal terms for excluding gay immigrants were being articulated, a counterdiscourse of asylum rights was emerging and, by 1994, applied to lesbians and gay men. Since 1980, asylum has technically been available in the United States to those fleeing persecution on account of one of five criteria; race, religion, nationality, political opinion, or membership in a particular social group. The question was, where did gays fit in? While many could credibly demonstrate persecution, this was not enough; to gain asylum, persecution had to have occurred on account of one of the five criteria. Yet the INS and courts remained reluctant to consider gays and lesbians as "a particular social group."

… [T]he move toward recognizing gays and lesbians as a particular social group began in 1986, when a Houston immigration judge barred the INS from deporting a Cuban gay man, Fidel Armando Toboso-Alfonso, based on concerns that he might face persecution for his sexual orientation. When the INS appealed the case in 1990, the Board of Immigration Appeals (BIA) affirmed the prior decision that had argued that gays were a particular social group.[3] In 1993, another immigration judge in San Francisco granted asylum to a Brazilian man, Marcelo Tenorio, based on the same assumption.[4] In 1994, for the first time, the INS granted asylum directly to a gay Mexican man, "Jose Garcia" (pseudonym). Two months later, Attorney General Janet Reno elevated the Toboso-Alfonso case as precedent and affirmed that lesbians and gay men constituted a particular social group for purposes of asylum.

Particularly noteworthy is the fact that these precedent-setting gay asylum cases involved migrants from Latin America. Not only are numbers of Latin American migrants proportionately large when compared to other national origin groups, but also, during the late 1980s and the 1990s, Latin Americans filed the majority of asylum petitions.[5] However, like all political stories, the issue is more complex than sheer numbers. The Toboso-Alfonso case, for instance, was clearly complicated by U.S.–Cuban politics—from a U.S. policy perspective, deporting a Cuban refugee, whatever his sexual orientation, was not expedient during the Cold War. Moreover, elevating the Toboso-Alfonso decision to precedent in 1994 provided President Clinton with an opportunity not only to show support for gay rights,[6] but also to champion human rights in Latin American countries that had been supported by previous U.S. Republican administrations. The exigencies of U.S. relations with Latin America dearly shaped the politics of gay asylum—in ways that demand further research.

While the INS has officially recognized sexual orientation as evidence of membership in a particular social group for purposes of granting asylum, asylum remains difficult to attain. Illustrating these difficulties are statistics estimating that between 1994 and 1997, approximately sixty petitioners were granted asylum on these grounds, but reportedly over one thousand such petitions were filed in the same time frame.[7]

To gain asylum, gays and lesbians must convincingly establish both that they are members of a particular social group and that they experienced or may experience persecution as a result. The legal standards for defining a particular social group are somewhat inconsistent, but *Matter of Acosta* (1985) established a basic framework that guides the courts. *Acosta* defined a particular social group as being comprised by those who share a "common, immutable characteristic" that is either "innate" or arises from "shared past experience." In addition, this characteristic "must be one members of the group can not change or is so fundamental to their individual identities or consciences that they should not be required to change it."[8] Paradoxically, then, the same logic of inherent, immutable identity that used to be deployed to exclude gay immigrants is now required to establish that one is eligible for asylum.[9] Officials require such evidence in part because of exaggerated fears that migrants may falsely claim gay identity in order to become eligible for asylum.[10] While this may happen on rare occasions, the converse—where asylum applicants remain afraid to detail persecution based on sexual orientation—is much more likely.

Racialist and Colonialist Scripts

For an asylum petitioner from Mexico to prove that he is immutably gay, and has been persecuted as a result, is an undertaking fraught with contradictions. Much anthropological and sociological research, especially from the 1970s and 1980s, argued that gay identity as understood in the mainstream U.S. sense did not exist in Mexico. This literature, which continues to be referred to in asylum hearings today, certainly creates difficulties for petitioners who must establish that they are essentially gay. According to scholars, the Mexican sex/gender system is such that only men who assume the "feminized" position during sex with other men are stigmatized as homosexual. Men who assume the "active" position can retain their masculinity and heterosexual status. According to this schema, the quintessential Mexican gay asylum applicant is therefore an effeminate man.

There can be no doubt that effeminate men face discrimination and persecution that may reach life-threatening levels, and their asylum applications should receive the most serious consideration.[11] But the difficulties with the use of these accounts of the Mexican sex/gender system in asylum hearings are that they often reinforce racist and colonialist imagery and relations. Moreover, they may restrict asylum possibilities for those who do not conform to the image of the effeminate gay man.

To understand how the reinscription of racism and colonialism occurs, one must realize that asylum hearings are, as Sherene Razack says "encounter[s] between the powerful and the powerless, and the powerful are always from the First World and mostly white, while the powerless are from the Third World and nearly always racialized or ethnicized? The asylum process constructs Third World asylum seekers as either unworthy claimants or as supplicants begging to be saved from the tyranny of their own cultures, communities, and men."[12] To gain asylum, Third World supplicants must paint their countries in racialist, colonialist terms, while disavowing the United States' role in contributing to the conditions that they fled. If the U.S. government decides to "save" the supplicant by granting asylum, this easily reaffirms the notion of the United States as a land of liberty and a bastion of progress.

Cantú particularly noted that when persecution suffered by applicants is attributed to "culture," understood in a reified manner that divorces it from other variables such as race, gender, class, globalization, neocolonial relationships, and unequal U.S.–Mexico ties, these colonialist effects become realized. "Mexican culture" becomes the prism through which the individual is understood and the sole source of problems and repression in Mexico. Neocolonialism, economic exploitation, and other issues become irrelevant.

In the cases for which Cantú served as an expert witness, narratives of the Mexican sex/gender system, reduced to a manifestation of culture conceived in ahistorical terms, were consistently produced. In those cases, the courts heavily relied on reports written by Andrew Reding, director of the Americas Project of the World Policy Institute and associate editor of Pacific News Service. Reding has published a series of reports about gays in Mexico: *Democracy and Human Rights in Mexico* (1995); *Mexico: Treatment of Homosexuals* (1997); and *Mexico: Update on the Treatment of Homosexuals* (1999). Significantly, this last report is part of a Question and Answer Series distributed to asylum officials to assist them in adjudicating asylum claims. The report offers an analysis of the legal, political, cultural, and historical factors shaping the lives of gays in Mexico. Reding's reports maybe strategic, in the sense of providing clear-cut explanations of cultural difference and oppression that resonate effectively within the logic of the legal system, but some of their implications are troubling.

Relying on prior scholarship, Reding restates the argument that it is not all men who have sex with men, but instead men who assume the feminized role who are stigmatized and persecuted for being gay. He attributes their persecution to a "dominant cultural ideal of hypermasculinity" which he does not situate in material context, but rather treats as a timeless and hermetically sealed mainstream Mexican cultural characteristic.[13] According to Reding, "the potential for violence against homosexuals, especially effeminate men and transvestites, is *inherent* in the culture of machismo" (emphasis added).[14] In the report, culture is explicitly separated from the political and legal realms, areas where significant gains have been made for gays, Reding claims.[15] This eviscerated model of Mexican culture is depicted as existing in a temporal sequence that is anterior to mainstream U.S. culture. For instance, he describes "the strong attachments most Mexicans feel to their families" as "comparable to those that prevailed in the United States a century ago."[16] Reding also suggests that "exposure" to U.S. culture can help to ameliorate "negative" tendencies in Mexican culture. For example, "with Mexican culture highly resistant to change from within, the primary force for change is coming from international contact—primarily the influence of U.S. culture."[17]

In these ways, the United States is discursively constructed as enlightened, progressive, separate from Mexico, and positioned to save Mexican gay men from "the tyranny of their [timeless] cultures, communities, and men."[18] Mexico, by contrast, emerges as backward and oppressive, as evinced by its sex/gender system and treatment of effeminate men, In fairness, Reding does acknowledge that in terms of certain political and legal issues, Mexico is in advance of the United States in providing for gays and lesbians.[19] But since "culture" remains cordoned off from law and politics, these facts do not alter his fundamental narrative of the united States as the savior of feminized brown men who are persecuted by macho men, specifically, and Mexican sex/gender systems, generally, all of which are conceived as manifestations of some sort of essentialized Mexican culture. The role of the United States in materially contributing to conditions in Mexico—including sex/gender conditions as these interact with class and race—is not discussed. Neither is the fact that lesbians and gays in the United States face significant discrimination and repression—and that Mexican gay immigrants in the United States must deal with homophobia, racism, and often severe economic exploitation and language barriers. As Cantú's research showed, in their attempts to escape from one form of bigotry [homophobia], most of the [immigrant] Mexican men I interviewed discovered that not only had they not entirely escaped it but they now faced another [racism]."[20]

Thus, narratives about Mexican culture generally, and about the treatment of gay men specifically, which are produced in the course of asylum hearings, variously draw on and reiterate racialist, colonialist imagery, particularly through the role that is attributed to culture. This approach stands in marked contrast to the ways hat white middle-class gay sexuality tends to be understood. As Cantú writes,

> Among U.S. gay and lesbian scholars in the late twentieth century, "gay" identities were understood as the socially constructed results of modernization. … This view of homosexuality stood in stark contrast to that of less developed countries. Traditional anthropological explanations of homosexuality point [] to "culture" to explain differences in how homosexuality was defined in "other," that is, non-Western, societies. Culture becomes the mechanism that reified difference and reproduced the imagined distance of "the others" in academic discourse itself … Why should our understanding of sexual identities in the developing world give primacy to culture and divorce it from political economy?[21]

The grounding of Mexican homosexuality in a model of "culture" that is divorced from social, economic, and political variables has multiple material consequences, including ignoring or naturalizing inequality in relations with Latin America and discrimination toward Latinos in the United States.[22] Moreover, this exclusive focus on "culture" vis-à-vis sexuality both exoticizes and eroticizes Mexicans, an aspect of U.S.–Mexican relations that Cantú had explored in his research on queer tourism in Mexico and its representation in the United States.[23]

The narratives of the Mexican sex/gender system deployed in the Reding report also materially contribute to difficulties for some asylum petitioners because they conflate gender and sexuality in problematic ways and leave little room for the specificity of lesbian experience or the diversities of gay identity that exist in Mexico. The conflation of sexuality with gender (which is conceived in binary terms) is evident throughout the report. For example, "Effeminate behavior elicits far greater levels of social disapproval than does homosexuality [i.e., homosexual acts] per se ... Effeminacy and cross-dressing are serious violations of the masculine ideal. But the greatest transgression is for a man to assume the sexual role of a woman in intercourse."[24] What is problematic in this passage and elsewhere is that the report does not differentiate between being an effeminate man and being a biological female. Yet Cantú's research makes clear that Mexican men themselves recognize and act on such a distinction:

> Being a joto is not to be a man. Neither a man nor a woman, it is an abomination, a curse. ... Thus, the relationship of homosexuality to femininity is more complex than a synonymous equation implies. Homosexuality is not only the opposite of masculinity, it is a corruption of it, an unnatural form that by virtue of its transgression of the binary male/female order poses a threat that must be contained or controlled.[25]

These important distinctions, between men who are feminized and biological females, are not made in Reding's report. Thus, the report frequently compares the treatment of effeminate men to the treatment of biological women. This strategy means that his report gives short shrift to lesbians and the specificity of their persecution. It also contributes to the courts' difficulties in understanding how gender and sexuality variously intersect to produce specific kinds of persecution that single-axis analyses cannot capture ...[26] Finally, this conflation of gender with sexuality, which results in the production of the feminized gay man as the quintessential asylum applicant, does not allow for the variety of Mexican gay identities that exist today. Scholars including Cantú have described the emergence in the 1980s of identity categories such as "internacional" and the growing popularity of the term "gay" in parts of Mexico.[27] These new identities connect to political and economic changes that Mexico is undergoing, including urbanization, economic restructuring, and new transnational links. Their emergence again underscores that sexuality cannot be analyzed simply by reference to a colonialist notion of "culture"; there must be reference to material, political relations. Reding's report erases the range and complexity of these identities. Options for asylum may be reduced accordingly.

Fear, Loathing, and Other Border Tensions

Based on his experiences as an expert witness, and on his sociological research including in-depth interviews with gay Mexican immigrants in California, Cantú posited that even while globalizing forces had multiplied the range of available sexual identities and political projects, the asylum system was generating new, essentializing constructions of sexuality that functioned within strictly nationalist logics, thereby reinscribing borders that globalization had blurred. These contradictions have been paralleled by the United States' management of the U.S.–Mexico border, historically and at present.

Since the 1990s, the contradictory management of the U.S.–Mexico border has been exemplified by policies such as the North American Free Trade Agreement (NAFTA), which further integrated the economies of Mexico and the United States, even while immigration policies attempted to clearly separate the two countries. As Peter Andreas demonstrates, migrants have continued to cross the increasingly militarized U.S.–Mexico border because the logic of economic integration inevitably increased (rather than reduced) such movement and because U.S. employers continued to demand Mexican labor.[28] While militarization of the U.S.–Mexico border cannot, in Andreas's view, stem the migration of Mexicans, it nonetheless fulfills crucial symbolic functions by providing a means to visibly stage displays of state power, sovereign national boundaries, and distinctive national identity—despite, and indeed because of, globalization. Moreover, these displays have legitimated the further extension of violent and dehumanizing practices, which are directed not only at border crossers but also at those within the United States whose belonging remains in question on racial, sexual, and other grounds. Cantú believed that the INS's construction of the effeminate gay Mexican asylum seeker, whose sexuality and persecution were ascribed to essentialized Mexican cultural characteristics, filled an important role in the symbolic production of images of national difference, which mapped onto distinct sovereign territories— that were then defended through violent means. Cantú was particularly concerned to explore how these discursive constructions translated into material practices that affect border crossers.

Future Research Directions

In this essay, Cantú intended to challenge mainstream accounts of asylum as simply the provision of a haven for the oppressed. To him, the asylum system was more complexly double-edged. On the one hand, it offers hope and security to a small number of individuals. On the other hand, through its processes for eliciting, evaluating, and recirculating individuals' testimonies about persecution and suffering, the asylum system remains part of a governance apparatus that generates racist, colonialist images and relations that greatly affect Latin Americans, U.S. Latinos—and Latin Americans who have been granted asylum in the United States. Moreover, these processes shape the general production of knowledge about immigration and globalization.

Inspired by scholars who suggest that efforts to exclude the Chinese laid the foundation for the entire U.S. immigration apparatus Cantú speculated that shifting U.S. strategies for managing relations with Latin America in the 1980s and 1990s materially shaped U.S. asylum law, policies, and procedures, and he sought to demonstrate that.[29] In terms of chronology, his argument has strong merit because it was only in 1980 that the United States established a standard system for processing and admitting refugees and asylum seekers, through the 1980 Refugee Act.

Using the figure of the Mexican gay asylum seeker to generate a Latin American-focused genealogy of the U.S. asylum system further demonstrates the originality of Cantú's scholarship. Cantú was among a handful of scholars who contributed to the development of tools and theories for studying gay migrants, who remain invisible, insignificant, or even despicable in most scholarship. Relentlessly situating gay migrants' lives in the context of material relations of race, gender, class, sexuality, and geopolitics, Cantú's essay here illuminates with clarity and sympathy the lives, struggles, dignity, and agency of Mexican gay migrants who seek asylum.

Yet, Cantú was no sentimentalist. He had an unerring eye for irony—for example, the irony confronting a Mexican asylum seeker whose testimony garners him legal residence, but also fuels racist and colonialist relations that negatively affect his life (and the lives of his family, friends, and lovers). Cantú also drew attention to the irony of how the U.S. immigration apparatus historically used essentialist constructions to exclude gays and lesbians, but now requires essentializing narratives from gays and lesbians if they are to receive asylum. Cantú also highlighted the incongruity of the U.S. asylum systems production of fixed models of hermetically sealed cultures, even while globalization in general, and U.S.–Mexican relations in particular, have significantly reconfigured cultural and national boundaries.

This essay's provisional and suggestive character invites other scholars to take up the politically and theoretically significant work that Cantú began, but was unable to finish.

Notes

This essay, which Cantú planned to include in the *Queer Moves* collection, interrogates what he called "the birth of the Mexican gay asylee" as a juridical and social category in the United States. Drawing on a draft of this unfinished essay, Eithne Luibhéid and Alexandra Minna Stern describe the main ideas that Cantú was exploring, how they connect to his earlier work, and the research questions they open up.

1. Saeed Rahman, "Shifting Grounds for Asylum," *Columbia Human Rights Law Review* 29 (Spring 1998): 516–17.
2. *Boutillier v. INS* 387 US 118 (1967) at 123.
3. Cited in *Hernandez-Montiel v. INS*, 98070582 (U.S. Court of Appeals, 9th Cir., August 24, 2000), at 10481. The Toboso-Alfonso decision can be found at 20 I&N Dec. 819 (BIA, 1990).
4. *Matter of Tenorio*, A72-093-558 (IJ, July 1993): *Matter of Tenorio*, A72-093-558 (BIA, 1999).
5. For example, according to the INS Statistical Yearbook for 2000, "For over a decade, nationals from Central America dominated the annual number of asylum applications filed in the United States. From 1986 to 1992, about half of all asylum applications were filed by Central Americans. … "The largest number of asylum seekers in 2001 came from Mexico, with 9,178 applying during the year, up dramatically from 3,936 in 2000" (U.S. Committee for Refugees, *World Refugee Survey 2000* [Washington, DC, 2000], 275). See also *Refugee Reports* 22, no. 12 (December 2001): 7, for cumulative U.S. asylum statistics from FY 1989 through 2001.
6. According to Cantú, Clinton needed to show support for gay and lesbian issues after failing to deliver on his promise to end anti-gay discrimination in the military.
7. Personal interview conducted by Cantú with Julie Dorf, executive director of the International Gay and Lesbian Human Rights Commission, 1998.
8. Cited in Jin S. Park, "Pink Asylum," *UCLA Law Review* 42 (April 1995): 1115, 1124–25. The Acosta decision can be found at *In Re Acosta* 19 I&N Dec. 211 (BIA 1985). The *Hernandez-Montiel* decision notes that the First, Third, and Seventh Circuits have adopted Acosta's analysis,' but the Ninth Circuit "suggests a `voluntary associational relationship' requirement" that may conflict with Acosta. See *Hernandez-Montiel* at 10477, 10478.
9. It should be noted that the claim that sexual orientation and sexual identity are immutable, and therefore a basis for membership in a particular social group, is not necessarily intended

to reiterate the same old essentialist thinking. Rather, as the *Hernandez-Montiel* ruling relates, that claim has been used by many gay rights advocates to critique attempts to forcibly "convert" lesbians and gays to heterosexuality, and to challenge the general denigration and ill-treatment of queers (*Hernandez-Montiel* at 10479). Thus, essentialism in the asylum system needs to be carefully situated in terms of who is using it and for what purpose. This is another aspect of the paper that Cantú did not have time to fully work through.

10. For example see Arthur Leonard, "Gay Chinese Men Seek U.S. Asylum," *Gay City News* 2, no, 47 (November 27–December 3, 2003), http://www.gaycitynews.com/gcn_248/ gaychinese.html; and Marina Jiminez, "Refuge from the Stones." *Globe and Mail*, December 6, 2003, http://www. theglobeandmail.com/servlct/ArticleNews/TPPrint/LAC/20031206/FCCENT66/Focus/. …

11. Andrew Reding's *Mexico: Update on the Treatment of Homosexuals*, which we will discuss in more detail, importantly notes the significance of class in ensuring that poor effeminate men have particularly limited possibilities for avoiding persecution: "the poor are most vulnerable" (2), and in all cases the extent to which an individual can lead a fulfilling life as a homosexual depends heavily on that individual's socio-economic status" (16) (Question and Answer Series [Resource Information Center, Immigration and Naturalization Service, U.S. Department of Justice, 1999], http://www.worldpolicy.org/globalrights/sexorient/1999-Mexico-gayrights.htrnl).

12. Sherene Razack, *Looking White People in the Eye: Gender, Race, and Culture in Courtrooms and Classrooms* (Toronto: University of Toronto Press, 1998), 88.

13. Reding, *Mexico*, 1. The report carefully details the existence, and cultural difference from the mainstream, of indigenous groups in Mexico.

14. Ibid., 2. Scholarship that interrogates the ways that Mexican culture gets characterized as macho includes Matthew C. Gutmann, *The Meanings of Being Macho* (Berkeley: University of California Press. 1996); and Pierette Hondagneu-Sotelo and Michael Messner, "Gender Displays and Men's Power," in *Theorizing Masculinities*, ed. Harry Brod and Michael Kaufman (Thousand Oaks, CA: Sage, 1994), 200–18. Readers will note how, in this quote from the Reding report, a series of potentially non-commensurate figures—homosexuals, transvestites, and effeminate men—become collapsed into one.

15. Reding writes that despite an "unfavorable cultural environment," significant legal and political gains are being made for gays in Mexico—in some instances, in ways that are more progressive thin in the United States (*Mexico: Update on the Treatment of Homosexuals*, 14). See the section of the report titled "Political and Legal Gains," 14–16.

16. Ibid., 4. Reding also writes, "Mexican society remains highly prejudiced against homosexuals who are HIV positive. As was the case in the United States several years ago, AIDS continues to be identified as a gay disease" (18).

17. Ibid., 9. He also writes, "As the influence of foreign cultures—especially the United States –grows in Mexico, attitudes [toward sexuality and gender] are beginning to change" (2).

18. Razack, *Looking White People in the Eye*, 58.

19. See note 15.

20. Lionel Cantú, "A Place Called Home," in *Queer Politics, Queer Families*, ed. Mary Bernstein and Renate Reimann (New York: Columbia University Press, 2001). See also Lionel Cantú, "*De Ambiente*: Queer Tourism and the Shifting Boundaries of Mexican Male Sexualities," in "Queer Tourism," special issue, *GLQ* 8, no. 1–2 (2002): 139–66, especially 155–56.

21. Cantú, "*De Ambiente*," 141–42; see also Cantú, "Entre Hombres/Between Men," in *Gay Masculinities*, ed. Peter Nardi (Thousand Oaks, CA: Sage, 2000).

22. This is another way in which colonialism manifests in the construction and deployment of narratives of sexuality, including in the asylum hearings for which Cantú served as an expert witness.

23. Cantú, "*De Ambiente*."

24. Reding, *Mexico*, 5.

25. Cantú, "A Place Called Home," 120. See also Annick Prieur, *Mema's House, Mexico City* (Chicago: University of Chicago Press, 1998); and Ian Lumsden, *Homosexualidad: Sociedad y Estado en Mexico* (Toronto: Solediciones/Canadian Gay Archives, 1991).

26. The intersection of gender and sexuality in lesbian persecution, (or example, had made lesbian asylum claims more difficult for courts to understand and adequately address. See Shannon

Minter, `Lesbians and Asylum," in *Asylum Based on Sexual Orientation,* ed. Sydney Levy (San Francisco: IGLHRC and Lambda Legal Defense and Education Fund, 1996), sec. 1B, 3–16. …

27. Cantú, "*De Ambiente,*" 145–46. See also Hector Carillo, "Cultural Change, Hybridity, and Male Homosexuality in Mexico," *Culture, Health, and Sexuality* 1, no. 3 (1999): 223–38.

28. Peter Andreas, "Borderless Economy, Barricaded Border," *NACLA Report on the Americas* 33, no. 3 (November-December 1999): 14–21, 46. See also Saskia Sassen, "Why Migration?" *NACLA Report on the Americas* 26, no. 1 (July 1992): 14–19, 46–47.

29. On Chinese exclusion as the basis for the U.S. immigration apparatus, see Charles McClain, *In Search of Equality* (Berkeley: University of California Press, 1994).

31.
THE VEIL DEBATE—AGAIN
Leila Ahmed
(2005)

I want to begin this exploration with a quotation, or rather a collage of quotations made up of statements by three American Muslim college women in response to my inquiry about what wearing the hijab means to them: "I don't believe the Qur'an requires hijab," said one, "I believe it's a choice not an obligation. I wear it for the same reason that one of my Jewish friends wears a yarmulke: as a way of openly identifying with a group that people have prejudices about and as a way of saying yes we're here and we have the right to be here and to be treated equally." Another, also stating that she didn't believe the Qur'an required it, said she wore it just because she liked to and then added, "When people stare at me when I am on the T, I find myself thinking that, if there's just one woman out there who begins to wonder when she looks at me why she dresses the way she does and begins to notice the sexism of our society—if I've raised just one person's consciousness, that's good enough for me." A third said: "I started wearing it after I returned from a visit to my relatives in Palestine. I don't believe the Qur'an requires it—for me, wearing it is a way of affirming my community and identity, a way of saying that even as I enjoy the comforts we take for granted here and that people in Palestine totally lack, I will not forget the struggle for justice."

I come to this subject as someone who once studied in great detail the first major debate about the veil ever to occur in the Muslim world. It was triggered by a book which advocated unveiling, published in Cairo in 1899. Called *The Liberation of Woman* (*Tahrir al-Mara'a*), it was written by Qasim Amin, a French-educated, upper-middle-class Egyptian lawyer who was not so much a feminist as a modernizer, someone who was arguing that Muslims needed to follow in the paths of progress and civilization forged by Europe. There was nothing controversial about the practical measures he advocated for women—education, for example, to primary level, which was in fact already taking place. … Only his call for abandoning the "backward" and "uncivilized" practice of veiling and the arguments in which he framed this were controversial. "Do you imagine," he wrote, for instance, to give some sense of what his framing arguments were, "that the men of Europe who have attained such completeness of intellect that they were able to discover the force of steam and electricity … those intellects we so much admire, could possibly fail to know the means of safeguarding woman and preserving her purity? Do you think that such a people would have abandoned veiling if they had seen any good in it?"[1]

Clearly then this call for unveiling made at the end of the nineteenth century, came already marked with notions of who was civilized and who was not, and already replete with the markings of colonizer/colonized, European/non-European. And it came already marked, too, with class divisions, as the Western-educated and Westernizing upper classes, people such as Amin, now advocated unveiling: these were classes which were already, and in distinction to other classes, beginning to adopt the customs and dress-styles of Europe, and European ways of furnishing the home.

The moment at which this debate occurred, the end of the nineteenth century, was two decades into the British occupation of Egypt. And it was the era also when the British empire was at its height and the era of the common circulation of imperial discourses as to the proper hierarchies of peoples, races, customs, civilizations.

Amin's book in fact essentially reproduced the colonial narrative of the day as to the inferior Muslim Other, an inferiority and otherness symbolically connoted in European discourse by the veil. This narrative itself was a variant of the colonial trope designating other cultures and in particular the practices of other cultures in relation to women, as inferior—for Hindus for instance it was *suttee* that was the emblem of this, for Muslims—veiling. All of these were versions of the colonial trope that Gayatri Spivak famously called the trope of "white men saving brown women from brown men."

Besides reproducing the colonial narrative, Amin's book also reproduced the specific views on the veil of Lord Cromer, then the British representative in Egypt—the Paul Bremer as it were of his day. ... The veil, as he put it, was "the fatal obstacle" standing in the way of Egyptian men's "attainment of that elevation of thought and character which should accompany the introduction of Western civilization."[2]

For Cromer, then, the veil clearly did not signify merely male dominance or "patriarchy": Patriarchy and male dominance in their British, Victorian forms at least were, indeed, clearly values that Cromer himself was deeply committed to upholding—as president, for instance, of the Society Opposed to Women's Suffrage. Rather, the veil, this visible emblem of Islam, in Cromer's rhetoric and in colonial rhetoric more generally, was essentially a sign of the backwardness of Islamic moral development and civilization altogether—a shorthand signal for everything that was inferior about Islam as moral order and civilization.

While some Egyptians, like Amin, admired Cromer, others hated him. The topic of the veil and Amin's call for unveiling, echoing that of the colonizer, was clearly already, by this moment in history, fraught with other and volatile issues—issues of class, of "superior" and "inferior" religions and civilizations, etc.—and all of these now were in evidence in the intense controversy around the veil that Amin's book ignited in Cairo and other Muslim capitals. This first debate on the veil, then, was not merely the first but also, as it were, the ur-debate on the subject, bringing together all the elements that, henceforth, to some degree or other, would be at play whenever the veil emerged as major issue: notions of civilized versus uncivilized, patriarchal versus liberated, colonizer or former colonizer versus Other; and then also, as the Islamic counter-narrative began now to be articulated, as affirmation of Islamic purity and its God-ordained values versus the corruption of the West—and all intertwined with class issues.

These elements are still often discernibly at play when the veil emerges as focus of attention. The French ban, for instance, is clearly in some sense a reiteration of elements of the colonial narrative, elements that France had already acted on earlier in its history as it pursued the project of unveiling women in Algeria through the early twentieth century, to the Algerian war of independence in the 1960s. And we saw elements of that narrative at play here, too, in our U.S. media, as we went to war in Afghanistan. As one journalist astutely observed, the burkah became "at once battleflag and moral justification for our going to war."[3] Its fleeting appearance on television could function as explanation enough of what we were doing and why we were at war—packaged into that one image were all those old notions of superior/inferior, saving the women, and moral rightness.

I wrote my analysis of that first debate in my book on women in Islam—a book I finished about fourteen years ago and in which I was, implicitly at least, distinctly not a supporter of veiling.[4]

Now we are in a different place, in the midst of events that compel rethinking. Most importantly we are living through the emergence of Muslims as minorities in Europe and the United States, among whom are women who wear hijab. New happenings are affecting their lives—bans on hijab, harassments or firings at work, and, since 9/11 in the United States, occasionally outright attack. Of course then I find myself first of all wanting to support unequivocally their right to wear whatever they wish. Moreover, since this is a country where Muslims are a minority, one anxiety about the veil is automatically removed—the idea, certainly present in Muslim majority countries, that if Islamists come to power, the veil (and with it, more importantly, a host of laws severely curtailing women's rights) might be imposed on all of us by law.

In the midst of this, though, I have found myself wondering as to how it came about that Muslim women, or some Muslim women anyway, growing up in the United States, came to assume and apparently to accept relatively easily the notion that hijab is somehow an important part of being Muslim. For, here, it is among the younger generation of Muslims most particularly that the practice seems to be prevalent and growing. In contrast to the reports from France of young girls being forced to wear it (and indeed in regard to France too such reports are being contested by other reports), here the more common stories one hears and reads of are of young women who choose to wear it, sometimes against parental wishes.

We are living now through this tumultuous, unfolding present, and the emerging and ever shifting realities and helter-skelter developments we are in the thick of are scarcely yet studied or documented. Some research on Muslim women in the United States. has been done and much more is currently in progress.[5] Inevitably though it will be years before we have documentation and studies available from which we can begin to glean and piece together some fairly rich and comprehensive notions of the nuanced complexity of the history we are living through and of what happened in our times—even with regard to this one matter of the veil, and why young women, members of a religious minority in the United States, are taking it up in this country. …

My readings of such studies as there are and my conversations with Muslim women in hijab and my general observations regarding veiling today in the United States confirm my sense that a vast variety of reasons, explanations, and motivations today shape the decision to veil. Besides my readings of such scholarship as is available on the subject, my preliminary conclusions on the matter are based on interviews I conducted over the years 2002 to 2003 with some sixteen college women in the Cambridge, Massachusetts, area who wear hijab; and also on innumerable informal conversations with students and colleagues who wear hijab, and with personal friends and acquaintances—daughters and parents; and on conversations I have had and observations I have made over the last six years during which I have been regularly attending the conventions of some of the major American Muslim associations and in particular that of the Islamic Society of North America (ISNA).[6] In addition too, of course, I have been an avid reader of the wealth of material, interviews, reports, and stories that our media, particularly since 9/11 has been fairly copiously generating on Muslim women in the United States and on the hijab.

As I looked into why the hijab seemed to have been accepted, by some Muslim women anyway, as a norm here in the United States, I found that there was, as it turned out, a direct connection (to my surprise initially) between that first debate in Egypt with which I began this essay, and how that debate had played out in that country in terms of political and class struggles, and the emergence in the United States in the late twentieth, early-twenty-first century of the notion of hijab as foundational to Islam. ...

To sketch out this connection, I will take as my starting point the Egyptian elite's appropriation in the early twentieth century of the colonial narrative of unveiling as essential to the society's moving forward on the path of progress forged by Europe. The call for unveiling became, among this class, at once emblem both of the project of modernization and of the notion that the advancement of women was key to that project. ... And the government pursued those commitments by opening schools for girls at almost the same rate as those for boys, and opening the national university to women in 1928.

By mid-century the veil had all but disappeared from the country's major cities. After the 1952 revolution, which gave women the vote and equal access to schools and universities, Egypt embarked on the path of secular socialism. Through the 1950s and into the 1960s the veil steadily declined, declining seemingly beyond the possibility of return. In Egypt as in several other Muslim countries, unveiling had seemingly won out.

This of course was not the end of the story. ... In 1928 Hasan al-Banna founded the Islamist organization the Ikhwan Muslimeen, the Muslim Brotherhood. Opposed in every way to the government, which it saw as corrupt and subservient to the British, the Ikhwan took a stand against it with regard to the hijab as well as on other matters—affirming the hijab now as an essential part of Islamic dress.

Although it affirmed the hijab as essential, the Ikhwan did not oppose either women's education or their employment: On the contrary the importance of educating women and of enabling and even encouraging women to work was emphasized by several of the Ikhwan's ideologues. There was, however, a proviso: that women's work had to be understood within the framework of the primacy of women's duties as wives and mothers and within the framework of the notion, divinely ordained as they saw it, of men as the ultimate, deciding authorities in the family in all matters including, of course, whether women worked.

This stance on the part of the Ikhwan of both affirming the essentialness of the hijab and encouraging women's work within the framework of the divinely ordained patriarchal family, is important for us to note. The stance signaled that the Ikhwan stood not for old-style unreconstructed Islam but for something new: a restored, revived Islam that fully embraced modernity and the ideas brought in by the West of the importance of women's education and their active participation in society. …

Fully and even eagerly embracing modernity then, the Ikhwan also embraced some basic elements of feminism—but of a feminism reconceived and redefined within strict, clear limits: a feminism rearticulated now within the framework of the divinely ordained patriarchal family. Even the style of veil they adopted was distinctly not that of any of the traditional veils of Egypt (all of which, in their variety, had distinct class connotations) nor indeed was it the traditional style of hijab of any other country. Rather it was distinctly a new and modern hijab divested of particular class or geographic associations: a style of hijab that signaled the movement's commitment both to modernity and in a way to feminism, but a feminism reconceived within the framework of a divinely revealed order of male dominance. It signaled more broadly the Brotherhood's affirmation of a revived Islam, an Islam reconceived in response to the encounter with modernity. That, though, was not how this reconceived Islam represented itself—as a form of the religion that had been profoundly shaped and informed by the encounter with modernity. Rather, the shaping influence of modernity on this reconceived version of Islam was denied and erased: Those advocating and embracing this new Islam represented themselves rather as returning to a "pure" and "authentic" past Islam. …

We have already emerging here, then, … three distinct meanings of the veil beginning with and following from the first attack on the veil conceived from within the bosom of colonialism and manifested in the debate of 1899. First, there was the meaning developed from within the imperial narratives of superior races, religions, civilizations, and of the white man's moral obligation to dominate, change and civilize: Within this narrative …, the veil was symbol of the inferiority, comprehensively, of the Islamic Other.

Second, there was the somewhat different and indeed still always shifting and developing meaning of the veil that emerged when this thesis was adopted and rearticulated from the perspective and in the voice of the native Westernizing elites. … Within this discourse, abandoning the veil signaled a commitment to the project of modernity and a commitment, with it, to a radical recasting and eventually of wholly reconceiving the position and rights of women. Over the twentieth century the commitment to unveiling and to women's rights has moved from Amin's (and Cromer's) Victorian patriarchal notion of reconceiving the position of women, through Shaarawi's more liberative notion of reforms to expand women's rights to, arguably, Nawal El Saadawi's notion of a continued staunch stand against the veil as signal of a commitment to women's full and equal participation without limit or qualification.

Third, there was the meaning that emerged in the Islamist response to the previous discourse, in which, countering the notion of unveiling as essential for progress and modernity, the veil was affirmed as a way of embracing modernity and feminism—but within the framework and limits set by what was understood to be a divinely ordained order of male dominance. This narrative too, like the narrative of unveiling as a necessary feminist goal, has continued and continues to shift its specific meanings and connotations into our own day. For instance, it is not uncommon now to hear young American Muslim women declare (as I will discuss further below) that they intend their habit of veiling to be understood as, among other things, a deeply feminist gesture.

These seem to be the three key master-narratives of the veil, the narratives that provide the foundational frameworks or scaffolding of the veil's meaning in our times. All of us today, those of us who attack it as irretrievably patriarchal, and those of us who attack it (and sometimes attack also the women who wear it) because it powerfully carries meanings of the inferior Muslim Other, and finally, too, those of us who wear it—all, to some degree, deriving our meanings and our responses to the veil from within the frameworks of these three master-narratives. Even when our intention and objective is to counter or reject those meanings—one or another of them—we are still grounded in and allowing ourselves and our perceptions and responses to this garment to be framed by this tangled history and these clashing, shifting, and intertwining narratives.

To return now to what happened in Egypt following the founding of the Ikhwan Muslimeen and to the connections between that history and the developments under way in the United States today. The Ikhwan grew rapidly through the 1930s and thereafter, drawing its membership primarily from educated men of the lower middle classes. The organization's goal was to bring down the government, through violence if necessary, and to institute a government that would bring about the Islamization of Egypt.

From early on, violence was perpetrated by both the Ikhwan and the government. In the 1940s, the elected prime minister of what was then a democratic Egypt, was gunned down by the Ikhwan, and the government, for its part, killed al-Banna, the Ikhwan's founder—and these were but two of many killings committed by both sides. The confrontation between the Ikhwan and the governments of Egypt would continue into the Nasser era and beyond. Since its founding this organization has been important to Egypt's history and indeed to world history. ...

In cities like Cairo and Alexandria, from which the veil had essentially disappeared by the late 1950s, one might occasionally see back then—I speak now from memory—women wearing the hijab of the Ikhwan. The Ikhwan style of the hijab is now the commonplace style of hijab that one might see anywhere—whether in the United States, Egypt, or elsewhere: But, back then, it was new and distinctive. ... To the ordinary Muslim, that style of hijab denoted not greater piety but, quite simply and directly, membership in a politicoreligious organization. ... (That style of hijab brought into currency by the Ikhwan no longer now implies membership in that organization.) ...

In 1965 the United States changed its immigration laws, opening the way to Muslim immigration. ... Of the many Muslims who immigrated in that era, it was essentially men with connections to the Muslim Brotherhood who would become organizationally and religiously active in the United States. ... In the United States, as throughout the world over the last three decades, funds from oil-rich countries helped support the growth and rapid expansion of such organizations and their mosques, centers, and schools.

These associations and the mosques and schools affiliated with them have been in charge of teaching Islam to the younger generation, and their teachings have reflected, naturally enough, the outlook and the religious and ideological commitments of those original organizations—including obviously their position on the veil.

Of course, organizations merely provide a framework for continuity within which change occurs as generation succeeds generation. Whatever beliefs informed the founding of ISNA and MSA, such beliefs are inevitably changing as the old guard is replaced by the new and as more and more of the latter are American-born.

I have been attending the conventions of different Muslim organizations over the last few years—from ISNA to al-Fatiha, which is a gay, lesbian, bisexual, transgender Muslim organization. At ISNA, despite the organization's conservatism, I listened to talks given by women committed to what I would certainly define as feminist goals. And at al-Fatiha I met young gay and lesbian Muslim activists who had grown up attending ISNA and had got their Islam from American mosque-schools.

With this for background let me now draw together a few final thoughts.

… [T]aking 1899 as starting point, [t]hat date marks the beginnings of the era in which colonizers and local elites began to make concerted efforts, through laws as well as in a variety of other ways, to stamp out the practice of veiling in Cairo, Istanbul, Tehran, and elsewhere.

A hundred years on now and more, the veil has returned in all those cities. …

The cities of the United States and Europe are now fast becoming the centers of the production of meanings of the hijab. On the basis of the formal interviews I have conducted and the numerous informal exchanges. and conversations that I have had on this subject with American Muslims, one fact above all is abundantly dear to me: that women's reasons for wearing it are as varied, multiple, complex, and shifting (and multiple, complex, and shifting for each wearer too) as are the women themselves, and the reasons that women—any women—choose to wear what they choose to wear. Human dress is all about symbolism and about signaling different and sometimes contradictory (whether deliberately or otherwise) meanings. The veil is only different—and also therefore infinitely more charged than most clothing—in its potential meanings, meanings which of course may be quite different for wearer and observer. Because of the historical meanings with which it has been imbued since the rise of European imperialism, it has the power, perhaps uniquely as a garment, to provoke, disturb, unsettle. For over a hundred years now it has served as perhaps the quintessential symbol and flag of civilizational dash, of clashing values, and of struggles between the powers of empire and those resisting imperial powers, and an emblem too of clashing classes and of the struggle between the haves and have-nots within a society. These at any rate are among its meanings in societies in which women are free to choose whether to wear it: In societies such as Saudi Arabia and Iran where it is by law compulsory dress for women, it has, of course, a whole other set of meanings.

But these are its grand, overarching meanings, meanings that we can observe as we analyze national and international political discourses on the veil, whether in France or the United States or Egypt or among the jihadis. …

Meanings such as these, however, were not at all in evidence among the young women in hijab that I spoke with and listened to. The reasons they gave as to why they wore the veil and as to its meanings for themselves were typically individualistic and post-modern in their multiplicity and in their inventive combining and recombining of old meanings in new ways. Strikingly too, those new meanings were critically inflected by the fact that this was the dress now, here, of people who belonged to a minority.

Wearing the veil or headscarf can be, for instance, at this moment in the United States, a statement of religious commitment, a statement of identity, of communal affiliation, national or international, a political statement, and an aesthetic and/or erotic statement. It can also be, to be sure, a statement of a commitment to a belief in men as the natural and God-ordained authorities in our societies, and it can be a silent but forceful rejection and even reversal of the veil as emblem of the inferior Muslim Other (much as the Afro was of African racial inferiority), and a stubborn affirmation, of, on the contrary, full moral equality. And of course too it can evoke and play on any combination of these—and many more—possible meanings.

Let me return now to the three interviewees I quoted at the beginning of this essay. All three began by saying that they did not believe that the Qur'an required the hijab: They wore it by choice, they said, not obligation. This response was striking to me in that it constituted a distinct and important departure from the position on the veil espoused by fundamentalist or Islamist, Ikhwan-type Islam. I heard these statements as indicating that the speakers were tacitly distancing themselves from, and even that they were tacitly rejecting, the idea of the hijab as sign of a God-ordained patriarchy. Thus emptying the sign, first of all, of its patriarchal meanings, these three young women (whose responses were typical of responses I received from the majority of those I interviewed) then went on to imbue it with meanings of their own. And those meanings included, most saliently, meanings which in the first place gave visibility to Muslimness in societies where Muslimness is denigrated and where, therefore, Muslims might be expected, wherever possible, to choose invisibility. The women's intent in wearing it, moreover, was to give visibility to Muslimness in ways which foregrounded issues of ethnic, religious, and gender justice. For example, one woman compares her hijab to a yarmulke; another declares she wears it to signal her solidarity with the Palestinians and thus to signal her commitment to global justice; and a third declares that she hopes her hijab might raise the consciousness of observers as to the sexism of our society— the hijab here, far from being emblem of patriarchy, was evidently conceived of by its wearer as raising issues of gender justice.

It is clear from these meanings and the central importance of justice to all of them, that the fact that the hijab is now the dress of a minority has opened up distinctly new possibilities of meaning. In the first place, simply taking on a negatively charged garment in our society is an act of courageous defiance in the face of prejudice. Certainly in the wake of 9/11 simply putting on and venturing out in a hijab must have entailed daily acts of courage. It was ordinary to read in the news then of women attacked and spat on in the streets of the United States, of women who had beer bottles thrown at them from speeding cars, even of women (as I read in one report in any case) being dangerously forced off a motorway by another car. Evidently some of the

American men in these times deemed it honorable and patriotic to attack women dressed in hijab—women marked by their dress as representatives of the Enemy and inferior Muslim Other. To dress in this way at such a moment in this society is to silently and yet insistently refuse the imputed meanings of the inferior Muslim Other—meanings first forged in the colonial era but still vitally alive in our times. Taking on that symbol rejects and inverts its meaning—in much the same way as the slogan "Black is beautiful" inverted and rejected racial stereotypes of the 1960s. Moreover the Afro, the visual sign and embodiment of that slogan, opened up whole other questions—about aesthetic preconceptions, for example. Thus the Afro simultaneously exposed the limits of conventional aesthetics and opened up new ways of seeing. Similarly, some women today quite self-consciously and deliberately intend the veil to open up aesthetic questions.[7] In taking on the hijab, then, some women—particularly the more intellectually engaged and more feminist among them—are also in effect performatively enacting their rejection of both the patriarchal and the colonial narrative of the veil—rejecting the totalizing narratives of both sides. Quoting, borrowing from, reiterating the symbols and narratives or fragments of the narratives of the past, they are also reinventing them. And so as we live through what looks like the return of the veil, we are living, too, through something quite new. Homi Bhaba's reflections on hybridity are pertinent here—"hybrid agencies," he writes, "deploy the partial culture from which they emerge to construct visions of community and versions of historic memory that give narrative form to the minority positions they occupy."[8]

Doubtless too, though, for many Muslims in the United States wearing the hijab is a sign of conformity and obedience to a belief in the God-given nature of male dominance and authority. There is, of course, some latitude in interpretations of these matters—there are important differences between the interpretations of the government of Saudi Arabia, for example, and that of Iran, and also in the Ikhwan's position on these matters. But in the end all agree that authority resides in men and that women ultimately are not free to make their own decisions as fully the equals of men. Such, however, were not the views I encountered among my interviewees.

In short, all of this indicates that while old meanings of the veil continue to be unquestionably present and alive in our society—its meaning as emblem of patriarchy, and as emblem of the inferior Muslim Other—new meanings, too, are emerging, meanings arising out of Muslim people's location as a minority in this society, meanings that are in conversation at once with old meanings and with daily events of our times as well as with our society's history and its underlying ideals and commitments.

Nor is it only among Muslims that the hijab or headscarf is taking on in our day new and sometimes unexpected meanings. For instance, as reports of attacks on women in hijab began to multiply in the wake of 9/11, groups of non-Muslim women in various towns across the United States declared "headscarf days" and took to wearing headscarves in solidarity with women in hijab who were now at risk because of their dress. In the words of Katrina, one of the organizers of a headscarf day, "We're standing up for Muslim women's right to wear hijabs when they want to." In this context the veil or headscarf clearly stands for—of all things—feminist sisterhood. As one woman put it as she tied a headscarf over dreadlocks: "I am wearing it because I understand how it marks you as an object of someone else's hatred. It's still the same fight, but the symbol means something different."[9]

These are clearly distinctly local and momentary U.S. meanings that arise and take their significance from specific events in this country—a country with very specific and particular commitments and history with regard to women and feminism. This is the case also with regard to the hijab being used to signal a call for and a commitment to justice—as in the responses of the interviewees I quoted. The hijab can emerge as emblem of a call for religious and ethnic justice, for justice for women and for global justice, only because these ideals and the struggle for them form part of the commitments and the history of *this* society.

The veil could not have these meanings in Saudi Arabia or Iran or any other place where there is no commitment to ideals of justice and equality for all. On the contrary, in many such countries the unequal treatment of women and minorities is seen by the ruling powers as the proper national, religious, and God-ordained order.

Meanings of the hijab, then, are intensely local. What it means in the United States, where Muslims are a minority about whom many in the majority have fierce prejudices, will inevitably be different from its meanings in countries where Muslims are the majority. But meanings of the hijab are also global and can follow dominant master-narratives, that are both forceful and international in their reach—compared to the local, specific meanings arising out of particular events and histories. And certainly the rightness of patriarchy and of male authority over women is one of these globally powerful meanings.

We are all mired in the meanings and histories of our times.

During the ISNA conventions members of the Young Muslim Women's Association (an affiliate of ISNA) put on evening performances of poetry, skits, plays, fashion-shows, for women-only audiences. The theme of the veil figured quite prominently on the evenings that I was able to attend. One evening the young women presented a series of short skits that made fun of the assumptions about the veil and its supposed constrictions. I recall one skit in particular: It showed two girls preparing for school in the early morning. Agonizing about what to wear, one girl changes from one outfit to the next, and having finally settled on something, she then puts on makeup and then redoes her hair endless times, despairing about how she looks—and finally she rushes out and is late for school. The other, after performing her prayers, eats breakfast and dresses smartly in Islamic gown and headscarf, unworried about her hair or whether her clothes make her look fat, and leaves for school in good time. Which of these young women, after all—the skit asked—was more controlled and more driven by sexist assumptions and dress-requirements of our society: the one anxious to conform to society's requirements of young women that they be attractive and sexy, or the one who could dress without having to endeavor to be attractive to men or to please and appeal to them?

I not only enjoyed these skits but also found their critique of the sexism of American dress for women entirely persuasive. It was a critique that harkened back, of course, to the critiques of women's dress of the U.S. feminists in the 1960s and 1970s—although I did not get the impression that the young Muslim women knew this and that they had any idea therefore of their debt to U.S. feminism. That, after all, had been what the 1968 protest at the Miss America contest had been all about (which included the tossing of bras, girdles, and other constrictive clothing into the trash can, a protest that gave rise to the "bra-burning" myth) as well as other gestures by some feminists of that era to wear corsets or shave their legs and other such things. Moreover, as I pointed out in my discussion of the debate over the veil in 1899, Western dress in that era, the dress that imperialists considered the only "civilized" dress which people of other cultures should adopt as they became civilized, was hardly unpatriarchal or non-sexist, consisting, as it did, of, among other things, corsets that literally cracked women's ribs (hence the frequent fainting) and high heels that damaged women's bodies. At least the veil, which imperialists denounced so fiercely, caused no physical damage.

And yet, though I found the young women's critiques of the American dress quite convincing, I found myself wishing too that they could make these critiques without, on the other hand, championing the veil. Given that it is emblem, in one of the globally powerful master-narratives of our day, of a reaffirmation of God-ordained patriarchy and the reaffirmation of God-ordained constraints as marking necessary limits to women's aspirations.

But we live in a world crisscrossed by master-narratives. Those of us who go bareheaded might as easily be accused of lending support, inadvertently if not deliberately, to the narrative which defines the Other, who is paramountly today the Muslim and whose symbol is the veil, as innately and irretrievably inferior. But arguably there is, in the end, a difference. The history and even the ongoing and contemporary record of this society in matters of freedom of thought and of justice and equality for all is, to be sure, far from exemplary and, indeed, it has at times been utterly, utterly bleak. But it is still a society that conceives of itself as a social experiment evolving into the future and radically open and committed to forthright criticism, struggle, dissent, and transformation—toward that project of justice for all.

Notes

1. Qasim Amin, *Tahrir al-mar'a, in Al-a'mal al-kamila li Qasim Amin,* 2 vols., Muhammad 'Amara (ed.) (Beirut: Al-mu'assasa al-arabiyya lil-dirasat wa'l nashr, 1976) Vol. 2, p. 67.
2. Earl of Evelyn Baring Cromer, *Modern Egypt,* 2 vols (New York: Macmillan Co., 1908), 2: 538.
3. Polly Toynbee, "Was It Worth It?" *The Guardian,* November 13, 2002.
4. Leila Ahmed, *Women and Gender in Islam: Historical Roots of a Modern Debate* (New Haven: Yale University Press, 1992).
5. Among recent useful works of interest are: *The Muslim Veil in North America: Issues and Debates,* Sajida Sultana Avi and Homa Hoodfar (eds.) (Toronto: Women's Press, 2003), and Carolyn Moxley Rouse, *Engaged Surrender: African American Women and Islam* (Berkley: University of California Press, 2004).
6. I want to take this opportunity to thank the Ford Foundation and most particularly Dr. Constance Buchanan for the generous support which has enabled me to pursue this research.
7. See for instance the numerous articles and visuals on this subject in Azizah magazine.
8. Homi Bhabha, "Culture's In-Between," in Stuart Hall and Paul du Gay (eds.), *Questions of Cultural Identity* (London: Sage, 1996), p. 58.
9. "Women Don Scarves in Solidarity with Female Muslims; Event at Wayne State Is like Ones Elsewhere," *Detroit Free Press,* October 18, 2001.

32.
FOREWORD: LOCATING FEMINISMS/FEMINISTS
Obioma Nnaemeka
(2001)

Adiro akwu ofuebe enene nmanwu / One does not stand in one place to watch a masquerade

—Igbo proverb

In Igboland, to watch a masquerade dance is to watch complexity—elegance, agility, masculinity, beauty (sometimes ugliness), shifting patterns, entertainment, ritual, and art (art that is simultaneously classical and baroque in its complexity and paradox). The constant in all this is movement (paradox!). The masquerade is territorial (literally) in *its* (the masquerade is a spirit, remember!) claims, enforcing shifting distances between performer (masquerade) and audience. An element that is crucial in this interaction takes us back to art—perspective. The Igbo used lessons learned from their encounter with the masquerade to articulate the way they see and relate to/with the world—from different perspectives. The crucial elements in the encounter between the Igbo and the masquerade—shifting patterns, territorial claims, location, movement, aesthetics, paradox, and perspectives—punctuate the history of feminist engagement (as theory and practice) nationally and globally.

Indeed, feminist practice is a pioneer of sorts in the diversity business. Before diversity and multiculturalism became *á la mode* in the academe and popular culture (in the United States, at the least), feminist practice had envisaged diversity and multiculturalism but failed to articulate them satisfactorily. In its enthusiasm/eagerness to establish itself as a true *engagement* (in the Sartrean sense of the word), feminist practice evoked a diversity that is couched in biology—sisterhood; thinking that the evocation of bloodline and lineage would insulate it from the dissonance and possible turmoil that difference can engender. The globality of sisterhood planted assumptions on shaky grounds, specifically by promoting a potent commonality that could contain diverse histories and desires. The strategy backfired. In the 1980s, pressurized diversity blew the lid off the container of sisterhood. Two decades earlier, the feminist will (like a rock) was thrown to disrupt the comfort of the stagnant pool of patriarchy sending off ripples and expanding circles of new perspectives and ways of being and knowing. A decade later, the feminist will (like a rock) was thrown into a different pool—the stagnant pool of feminism—sending off ripples and asserting circles of difference. Feminism faced and still faces the difficulty of articulating simultaneously commonality and difference. ...

This book is about African women's attempts to redefine feminisms for their own purposes. By throwing their rock of feminist will into the feminist pool, African women sent off ripples that expose the politics of location at the heart of feminist theory and practice. While claiming the feminist spirit and ideal—equity based on fairness and justice—in their respective traditional milieu and elsewhere, African women expand the horizon of feminist engagement by posing new questions and imposing new demands. In theory and practice, African women engage feminism's politics of location—location as space/geography (physical, intellectual, and cultural) and location as status (hierarchy). On the one hand, they insist on breathing into feminist theory and practice the specificity of their cultures and locations in the global economy; on the other hand they resist the arrogance, imperialism, and unequal power relations that define location as status (hierarchy).

Indeed, African women argue forcefully for a re-examination of the "race" factor in feminist discourse, particularly as it is adumbrated in the "women of color" discourse on the intersection of race, gender, class, etc. The marginalization of African women (as knowing subjects/the namers) and their inscription (as known objects/the named) in both mainstream White feminist discourse and the "women of color" feminist discourse engenders … resistance … For African women, feminist arrogance and imperialism is not just about race; it is about a mindset that emanates from a specific location and to which different races (black, white, brown, etc) lay claim. Feminist arrogance is about the "First World"/"Third World" ("Second World" where are you?) dichotomy; it is about the "West and the Rest of Us."

Equally of concern to African women is the "coloring" of feminist discourse/ engagement—black women, women of color. African women call themselves *African women*. I am an African woman. I call myself an African woman. In Africa I am called an African woman but in North America I am called a black woman (Europeans will pull out from their dictionaries words ranging from *noire, negra* and *schwarze* to *nera, preta,* and *zwarte* in an effort to name me). While African women speak geography (Africa) feminist discourse speaks color (black; white, women of color). It is astonishing to watch an environment that is steeped in color-consciousness select one segment of its population to bestow upon it the "privilege" of color—women of color, people of color, etc. May the "people of no color" stand!

Naming and location converge in the so-called contradiction in the pronouncements of notable African women (Flora Nwapa, Ama Ata Aidoo, and Buchi Emecheta) regarding their acceptance or denial of the feminist label. One should ask why Flora Nwapa rejects the feminist label in London and New York but accepts and affirms it in Nsukka (Nigeria). What does feminism mean in the three different locations? Under what circumstances and by whom was the question posed? Naming feminism is as intractable as the dynamism of difference that propels it. Naming feminism is an act (agency) of resistance that sustains its dynamism and expands its horizon. "When black feminism emerged as a response to (white) feminism, *womanism* (Walker) and *Africana womanism* (Hudson-Weems) soon followed. Those were the first stones thrown into the feminist pool. Before the ripples could subside, African women threw their own rocks of feminist will, setting off ripples of *stiwanism* (Ogundipe-Leslie), *motherism* (Acholonu), *negofeminism* (Nnaemeka, 1995), and different configurations of *womanism* (Kolawale, Ogunyemi). Each of these African ways of naming feminism has a fundamental concern—the use of different aspects of African cultures, historical moments, and current global imperatives to make sense of feminist engagement.

Many years ago when I coined the word *negofeminism* as a name for "African feminism," I was inspired by the philosophy of give-and-take and negotiation that is at the heart of Igbo culture (as is the case in many African cultures). E. N. Njaka affirms that "the Igbo believes he can negotiate anything ... how to negotiate with Chukwu puzzled him and he created intermediaries ... go-betweens" (14). For me, *negofeminism* stands for the "feminism of negotiation" as well as "no *ego* feminism." The former is embedded in Igbo culture, the latter critiques and cautions against the *ego* trip that engenders feminist arrogance, imperialism, and power struggles. However, the cultural dimension remains the dominant force (Nnaemeka, 1995: 106–109). Indeed, inscribed in *negofeminism* are concerns for multi-perspectives, multidisciplinarity, and intersections of difference. The Yoruba looked up at the sky and saw great lessons in the patterns of flight of birds, looked down and allowed their collective wisdom to shine through a proverb: "The sky is so vast that all birds can fly without colliding." Humans called feminists can learn from the birds.

Some scholars have dismissed as distracting the attempts by different categories of women to name their feminist struggle *their own way*:

> I am more concerned with the participation of Third World women in defining feminism and setting its agenda than changing the terminology ... Since 'modern day' feminism is still in process of incarnation, especially at the international level, I question whether the coining of a new term simply retreats from the debate, running the risk of losing sight of the fair amount of universality in women's oppression. (Johnson-Odim, [1991: 316])

I am not equally dismissive of "coining a new term." To assert the power and right to name one's location and struggle is part of "setting [the] agenda"; it is part of "defining feminism." The definition ("coining of a new term") is a tool and a part of the debate. But where is the debate in this instance? I do not see any debate in the true sense of the word. Unless one would pass as debate the monologue of the knowers/namers that is rife in feminist discourses. African women do not have to fold their arms and wait for the "process of incarnation" to incarnate and for someone to emerge from the other side to name the "incarnation" for all women. The dismissal of voices of dissent or alternatives remains the Achilles heel of feminism. What is at issue here is not the rhetoric of naming but the politics of naming, as Patricia Hill Collins elucidates ([Hill Collins, 2000] 236).

What is at issue here is not terminology. What is at stake is the issue of agency, subjectivity, and power—the power to name oneself, one's location and one's struggle. The renaming of female circumcision (what the practitioners call it) as "female genital mutilation" is not an issue of terminology but an assertion of the power to (re)name. The last time I checked, Geoffrey Dahmer (the Milwaukee man who cut up and stored in his refrigerator human beings he didn't like) was called a murderer not a *mutilator*.

Would mutilator gain acceptance and currency in America if it had been proposed by an African or an African nation? I agree with Gita Sen that "[t]here is and must be a diversity of feminisms, responsive to the different needs and concerns of different women, and defined by them for themselves" [Sen, 1987: 13].

On the eve of my departure for graduate studies in *obodo oyibo* (the land of the white people), my great uncle called me into his *obi* and sounded this note of caution. "My daughter," he said, "when you go to *obodo oyibo*, walk like the chameleon." According to my great uncle, the chameleon is an interesting animal to watch. As it walks, it keeps its head straight but looks in different directions. It does not deviate from its goal and grows wiser through the knowledge gleaned from the different perspectives it absorbs along the way. If it sees a prey, it does not jump on it immediately. First, it throws out its tongue. If nothing happens to its tongue, it moves ahead and grabs the prey. The chameleon is cautious (Western feminists are not when it comes to "Third World" women's matters). When the chameleon comes into a new environment, it takes the color of the environment without taking over (unlike Western feminists who *take over* without *taking on* the color of the environment). The chameleon is adaptable, tolerant and accommodating. Whatever we choose to call our feminism is our prerogative. However, in this journey that is feminist engagement, we need to walk like the chameleon—goal-oriented, cautious, adaptable, open to diverse views, tolerant and accommodating. I hear these concerns in the voices of African women in this book. I add my voice to theirs.

33.
NATIVE AMERICAN FEMINISM, SOVEREIGNTY, AND SOCIAL CHANGE
Andrea Smith
(2005)

When I worked as a rape crisis counselor, every Native client I saw said to me at one point, "I wish I wasn't Indian." My training in the mainstream antiviolence movement did not prepare me to address what I was seeing—that sexual violence in Native communities was inextricably linked to processes of genocide and colonization. Through my involvement in organizations such as Women of All Red Nations (WARN, Chicago), Incite! Women of Color against Violence (www.incite-national.org), and various other projects, I have come to see the importance of developing organizing theories and practices that focus on the intersections of state and colonial violence and gender violence. In my ongoing research projects on Native American critical race feminisms, I focus on documenting and analyzing the theories produced by Native women activists that intervene both in sovereignty and feminist struggles.[1] These analyses serve to complicate the generally simplistic manner in which Native women's activism is often articulated within scholarly and activist circles.

Native Women and Feminism

One of the most prominent writings on Native American women and feminism is Annett Jaimes's (Guerrero) early 1990s article, "American Indian Women: At the Center of Indigenous Resistance in North America." Here, she argues that Native women activists, except those who are "assimilated," do not consider themselves feminists. Feminism, according to Jaimes, is an imperial project that assumes the givenness of U.S. colonial stranglehold on indigenous nations. Thus, to support sovereignty Native women activists reject feminist politics. …[2] According to Jaimes, the message from Native women is the same, as typified by these quotes from one of the founders of WARN, Lorelei DeCora Means:

> We are *American Indian* women, in that order. We are oppressed, first and foremost, as American Indians, as peoples colonized by the United States of America, not as women. As Indians, we can never forget that. Our survival, the survival of every one of us—man, woman and child—*as Indians* depends on it. Decolonization is the agenda, the whole agenda, and until it is accomplished, it is the *only* agenda that counts for American Indians.

> You start to get the idea maybe all this feminism business is just another extension of the same old racist, colonialist mentality.[3]

The critique and rejection of the label of feminism made by Jaimes is important and shared by many Native women activists. However, it fails to tell the whole story. Consider, for instance, this quote from Madonna Thunder Hawk, who cofounded WARN with Means:

> Feminism means to me, putting a word on the women's world. It has to be done because of the modern day. Looking at it again, and I can only talk about the reservation society, because that's where I live and that's the only thing I know. I can't talk about the outside. How I relate to that term feminist, I like the word.
>
> When I first heard, I liked it. I related to it right away. But I'm not the average Indian woman; I'm not the average Indian activist woman, because I refuse to limit my world. I don't like that. … How could we limit ourselves? "I don't like that term; it's a white term." Pssshhh. Why limit yourself? But that's me.

My point is not to set Thunder Hawk in opposition to Means: both talk of the centrality of land and decolonization in Native women's struggle. Although Thunder Hawk supports many of the positions typically regarded as "feminist," such as abortion rights, she contends that Native struggles for land and survival continue to take precedence over these other issues. Rather, my argument is that Native women activists' theories about feminism, about the struggle against sexism both within Native communities and the society at large, and about the importance of working in coalition with non-Native women are complex and varied. These theories are not monolithic and cannot simply be reduced to the dichotomy of feminist versus nonfeminist. Furthermore, there is not necessarily a relationship between the extent to which Native women call themselves feminists, the extent to which they work in coalition with non-Native feminists or value those coalitions, whether they are urban or reservation-based, and the extent to which they are "genuinely sovereigntist." In addition, the very simplified manner in which Native women's activism is theorized straightjackets Native women from articulating political projects that both address sexism and promote indigenous sovereignty simultaneously.

Central to developing a Native feminist politic around sovereignty is a more critical analysis of Native activist responses to feminism and sexism in Native communities. Many narratives of Native women's organizing mirror Jaimes's analysis—that sexism is not a primary factor in Native women's organizing. However, Janet McCloud recounts how the sexism in the Native rights movement contributed to the founding of the Indigenous Women's Network in 1985:

> I was down in Boulder, Colorado and Winona LaDuke and Nilak Butler were there and some others. They were telling me about the different kinds of sexism they were meeting up with in the movement with the men, who were really bad, and a lot of these women were really the backbone of everything, doing a lot of the kind of work that the movement needed. I thought they were getting discouraged and getting ready to pull out and I thought, "wow, we can't lose these women because they have a lot to offer." So, we talked about

organizing a women's conference to discuss all the different problems. … Marsha Gomez and others decided to formally organize. I agreed to stay with them as a kind of a buffer because the men were saying the "Indignant Women's Organization" and blah, blah, blah. They felt kind of threatened by the women organizing.[4]

My interviews with Native women activists also indicate that sexism in Native communities is a central concern. …

And although many Native women do not call themselves feminists for many well thought-out reasons, including but not limited to the reasons Jaimes outlines, it is important to note that many not only call themselves feminist but also argue that it is important for Native women to call themselves feminists. And many activists argue that feminist, far from being a "white" concept, is actually an indigenous concept white women borrowed from Native women.

(Interviewee 1)

I think one of the reasons why women don't call themselves feminists is because they don't want to make enemies of men, and I just say, go forth and offend without inhibition. That's generally why I see women hold back, who don't want to be seen as strident. I don't want to be seen as a man-hater, but I think if we have enough man-haters, we might actually have the men change for once. … I think men, in this particular case, I think men are very, very good at avoiding responsibility and avoiding accountability and avoiding justice. And not calling yourself a feminist, that's one way they do that. Well, feminism, that's for white women. Oh feminists, they're not Indian. They're counterrevolutionary. They're all man-haters. They're all ball-busters. They've gotten out of order. No, first of all that presumes that Native women weren't active in shaping our identity before white women came along. And that abusive male behavior is somehow traditional, and it's absolutely not. So I reject that. That's a claim against sovereignty. I think that's a claim against Native peoples. I think it's an utter act of racism and white supremacy. And I do think it's important that we say we're feminists without apology.

(Interviewee 2)

[On Native women rejecting the term "feminist"] I think that's giving that concept to someone else, which I think is ridiculous. It's something that there has to be more discussion about what that means. I always considered, they took that from us, in a way. That's the way I've seen it. So I can't see it as a bad thing, because I think the origins are from people who had empowered women a long time ago.

This reversal of the typical claim that "feminism" is white then suggests that Native feminist politics is not necessarily similar to the feminist politics of other communities or that Native feminists necessarily see themselves in alliance with white feminists. In addition, the binary between feminist versus nonfeminist politics is false because Native activists have multiple and varied perspectives on this concept. For instance, consider one woman's use of "strategic" feminism with another women's affirmation of feminist politics coupled with her rejection of the term "feminist." These women are not neatly categorized as feminists versus nonfeminists.

(Interviewee 1)

Well, you know I vary that from situation to situation. Because when I'm back home, I'll say I'm a feminist just to rile the guys so they know where I still stand. So there's nothing tricky about who I am and what I'm doing. And when I'm out here in a white women's studies department, I won't call myself, because I don't want to align myself with their politics.

(Interviewee 2)

It's not the term that fits within my culture. I'm an Indian woman, first and foremost. I'm a strong Indian woman, very directed, and I believe in feminism as I understand society, and that I would be a part of that. … The word doesn't equate with any Indian word that I would know. That's what I mean, there isn't a word.

Thus, these analyses suggest that sexism is not necessarily a secondary concern to Native women, and Native women's engagement with feminist politics to address sexism is much more complex that generally depicted.

Native Feminism and Sovereignty

If we successfully decolonize, the argument goes, then we will necessarily eliminate problems of sexism as well. This sentiment can be found in the words of Ward Churchill. He contends that all struggles against sexism are of secondary importance because, traditionally, sexism did not exist in Indian nations. Churchill asks whether sexism exists in Indian country after Native peoples have attained sovereignty? His reply, "Ask Wilma Mankiller," former principal chief of the Cherokee Nation.[5] Well, let's ask Mankiller. She says of her election campaign for deputy chief that she thought people might be bothered by her progressive politics and her activist background. "But I was wrong," she says:

> No one challenged me on the issues, not once. Instead, I was challenged mostly because of one fact—I am female. The election became an issue of gender. It was one of the first times I had ever really encountered overt sexism … (people) said having a female run our tribe would make the Cherokees the laughing stock of the tribal world.[6]

Regardless of its origins in Native communities, then, sexism operates with full force today and requires strategies that directly address it. Before Native peoples fight for the future of their nations, they must ask themselves, who is included in the nation? It is often the case that gender justice is … articulated as being a separate issue from issues of survival for indigenous peoples. Such an understanding presupposes that we could actually decolonize without addressing sexism, which ignores the fact that it has been precisely through gender violence that we have lost our lands in the first place.[7] In my activist work, I have often heard the sentiment expressed in Indian country: we do not have time to address sexual/domestic violence in our communities because we have to work on "survival" issues first. However, Indian women suffer death rates because of domestic violence twice as high as any other group of women in this country.[8] They are clearly not surviving as long as issues of gender violence go unaddressed.

Scholarly analyses of the impact of colonization on Native communities often mini-mize the histories of oppression of Native women. In fact, many scholars argue that men were disproportionately affected by colonization because the economic systems imposed on Native nations deprived men of their economic roles in the communities more so than women.[9] By narrowing our analyses solely to the explicitly economic realm of society, we fail to account for the multiple ways women have disproportion-ately suffered under colonization—from sexual violence to forced sterilization. As Paula Gunn Allen argues:

> Many people believe that Indian men have suffered more damage to their traditional status than have Indian women, but I think that belief is more a reflection of colonial attitudes toward the primacy of male experience than of historical fact. While women still play the traditional role of housekeeper, childbearer, and nurturer, they no longer enjoy the unques-tioned positions of power, respect, and decision making on local and international levels that were not so long ago their accustomed functions.[10]

This tendency to separate the health and well-being of women from the health and well-being of our nations is critiqued in Winona LaDuke's 1994 call to not "cheapen sovereignty." She discusses attempts by men in her community to use the rhetoric of "sovereignty" to avoid paying child support payments.

> What is the point of an Indian Child Welfare Act when there is so much disregard for the rights and well being of the children? Some of these guys from White Earth are saying the state has no jurisdiction to exact child support payments from them. Traditionally, Native men took care of their own. Do they pay their own to these women? I don't think so. I know better. How does that equation better the lives of our children? How is that (real) sovereignty?
>
>   The U.S. government is so hypocritical about recognizing sovereignty. And we, the Native community, fall into the same hypocrisy. I would argue the Feds only recognize Indian sov-ereignty when a first Nation has a casino or a waste dump, not when a tribal government seeks to preserve ground water from pesticide contamination, exercise jurisdiction over air quality, or stop clear-cutting or say no to a nuclear dump. "Sovereignty" has become a politicized term used for some of the most demeaning purposes.[11]

Beatrice Medicine similarly critiques the manner in which women's status is often pit-ted against sovereignty, as exemplified in the 1978 *Santa Clara Pueblo v. Martinez* case. Julia Martinez sued her tribe for sex discrimination under the Indian Civil Rights Act because the tribe had dictated that children born from female tribal members who mar-ried outside the tribe lost tribal status whereas children born from male tribal members who married outside the tribe did not. The Supreme Court ruled that the federal gov-ernment could not intervene in this situation because the determination of tribal mem-bership was the sovereign right of the tribe. On the one hand, many white feminists criticized the Supreme Court decision without considering how the Court's affirma-tion of the right of the federal government to determine tribal membership would con-stitute a significant attack against tribal sovereignty.[12] On the other hand, as Medicine notes, many tribes take this decision as a signal to institute gender-discriminatory practices under the name of sovereignty.[13] For these difficult issues, it is perhaps helpful to consider how they could be addressed if we put American Indian women at the center of analysis. Is it possible to simultaneously affirm tribal sovereignty and challenge tribes to consider how … colonization and Europeanization may impact the decisions they make and programs they pursue in a manner which may ultimately undermine their sovereignty in the long term? Rather than adopt the strategy of fighting for sovereignty first and then improving Native women's status second, as Jaimes suggests, we must understand that attacks on Native women's status are themselves attacks on Native sovereignty. Lee Maracle illustrates the relationship between colonization and gender violence in Native communities in her groundbreaking work, *I Am Woman* (1988):

> If the State won't kill us
> we will have to kill ourselves.
> It is no longer good etiquette to head hunt savages.
> We'll just have to do it ourselves.
> It's not polite to violate "squaws"
> We'll have to find an Indian to oblige us.
> It's poor form to starve an Indian
> We'll have to deprive our young ourselves
> Blinded by niceties and polite liberality
> We can't see our enemy,
> so, we'll just have to kill each other.[14]

It has been through sexual violence and through the imposition of European gender relationships on Native communities that Europeans were able to colonize Native peoples in the first place. If we maintain these patriarchal gender systems in place, we are then unable to decolonize and fully assert our sovereignty.

Native Feminist Sovereignty Projects

Despite the political and theoretical straightjacket in which Native women often find themselves, there are several groundbreaking projects today that address both colonialism and sexism through an intersectional framework. One such … project is the Boarding School Healing Project, which seeks to build a movement to demand reparations for U.S. boarding school abuses. This project, founded in 2002, is a coalition of indigenous groups across the United States, such as the American Indian Law Alliance, Incite! Women of Color against Violence, Indigenous Women's Network, and Native Women of Sovereign Nations of the South Dakota Coalition against Domestic Violence and Sexual Assault. In Canada, Native peoples have been able to document the abuses of the residential school system and demand accountability from the Canadian government and churches. The same level of documentation has not taken place in the United States. The Boarding School Healing Project is documenting these abuses to build a movement for reparations and accountability. However, the strategy of this project is not to seek remedies on the individual level, but to demand collective remedy by developing links with other reparations struggles that fundamentally challenge the colonial and capitalist status quo. In addition, the strategy of this project is to organize around boarding schools as a way to address gender violence in Native communities.

That is, one of the harms suffered by Native peoples through state policy was sexual violence perpetrated by boarding school officials. The continuing effect of this human rights violation has been the internalization of sexual and other forms of gender violence *within* Native American communities. Thus, the question is, how can we form a demand around reparations for these types of continuing effects of human rights violations that are evidenced by violence *within* communities, but are nonetheless colonial legacies. In addition, this project attempts to organize against interpersonal gender violence *and* state violence simultaneously by framing gender violence as a continuing effect of human rights violations perpetrated by state policy. Consequently, this project challenges the mainstream anti-domestic/sexual violence movement to conceptualize state-sponsored sexual violence as central to its work. As I have argued elsewhere, the mainstream antiviolence movement has relied on the apparatus of state violence (in the form of the criminal justice system) to address domestic and sexual violence without considering how the state itself is a primary perpetrator of violence.[15] The issue of boarding schools forces us to see the connections between state violence and interpersonal violence. It is through boarding schools that gender violence in our communities was largely introduced. Before colonization, Native societies were, for the most part, not male dominated. Women served as spiritual, political, and military leaders. Many societies were matrilineal and matrilocal. Violence against women and children was infrequent or unheard of in many tribes.[16] Native peoples did not use corporal punishment against their children. Although there existed a division of labor between women and men, women's and men's labor was accorded similar status.[17] In boarding schools, by contrast, sexual/physical/emotional violence proliferated. Particularly brutalizing to Native children was the manner in which school officials involved children in punishing other children. For instance, in some schools, children were forced to hit other children with the threat that if they did not hit hard enough, they themselves would be severely beaten. Sometimes perpetrators of the violence were held accountable, but generally speaking, even when teachers were charged with abuse, boarding schools refused to investigate. In the case of just one teacher, John Boone at the Hopi school, FBI investigations in 1987 found that he had sexually abused more than 142 boys, but that the principal of that school had not investigated any allegations of abuse.[18] Despite the epidemic of sexual abuse in boarding schools, the Bureau of Indian Affairs did not issue a policy on reporting sexual abuse until 1987 and did not issue a policy to strengthen the background checks of potential teachers until 1989. Although not all Native peoples see their boarding school experiences as negative, it is generally the case that much if not most of the current dysfunctionality in Native communities can be traced to the boarding school era.

The effects of boarding school abuses linger today because these abuses have not been acknowledged by the larger society. As a result, silence continues within Native communities, preventing Native peoples from seeking support and healing as a result of the intergenerational trauma. Because boarding school policies are not acknowledged as human rights violations, Native peoples individualize the trauma they have suffered, thus contributing to increased shame and self-blame. If both boarding school policies and the continuing effects from these policies were recognized as human rights violations, then it might take away the shame from talking about these issues and thus provide an opportunity for communities to begin healing.

Unfortunately, we continue to perpetuate this colonial violence through domestic/sexual violence, child abuse, and homophobia. No amount of reparations will be successful if we do not address the oppressive behaviors we have internalized. Women of color have for too long been presented with the choices of either prioritizing racial justice or gender justice. This dualistic analysis fails to recognize that it is precisely through sexism and gender violence that colonialism and white supremacy have been successful. A question to ask ourselves then is, what would true reparations really look like for women of color who suffer state violence and interpersonal gender violence simultaneously? The Boarding School Healing Project provides an opportunity to organize around the connections between interpersonal gender violence and state violence that could serve as a model for the broader antiviolence movement.

In addition, this project makes important contributions to the struggle for reparations as a whole. That is, a reparations struggle is not necessarily radical if its demands do not call into question the capitalist and colonial status quo. What is at the heart of the issue is that no matter how much financial compensation the United States may give, such compensation does not ultimately end the colonial relationship between the United States and indigenous nations. What is at the heart of the struggle for native sovereignty is control over land and resources rather than financial compensation for past and continuing wrongs. If we think about reparations less in terms of financial compensation for social oppression and more about a movement to transform the neocolonial economic relationships between the United States and people of color, indigenous peoples, and Third World countries, we see how critical this movement could be to all of us. The articulation of reparations as a movement to cancel the Third World debt, for instance, is instructive in thinking of strategies that could fundamentally alter these relations.

Feminism and the Nation State

Native feminist theory and activism make a critical contribution to feminist politics as a whole by questioning the legitimacy of the United States specifically and the nation-state as the appropriate form of governance generally. Progressive activists and scholars, although prepared to make critiques of the U.S. government, are often not prepared to question its legitimacy. A case in point is the strategy of many racial justice organizations in the United States to rally against hate crimes resulting from the attacks of 9/11 under the banner, "We're American too." However, what the analysis of Native women activists suggests is that this implicit allegiance to "America" legitimizes the genocide and colonization of Native peoples, as there could be no "America" without this genocide. Thus by making anticolonial struggle central to feminist politics, Native women make central to their organizing the question of what is the appropriate form of governance for the world in general. Does self-determination for indigenous peoples equal aspirations for a nation-state, or are there other forms of governance we can create that are not based on domination and control?

Questioning the United States, in particular, and questioning the nation state as the appropriate form of governance for the world, in general, allow us to free our political imagination to begin thinking of how we can begin to build a world we would actually want to live in. Such a political project is particularly important for colonized peoples seeking national liberation because it allows us to differentiate "nation" from "nation state." Helpful in this project of imagination is the work of Native women activists who have begun articulating notions of nation and sovereignty that are separate from nation-states. Whereas nation-states are governed through domination and coercion, indigenous sovereignty and nationhood is predicated on interrelatedness and responsibility. As Crystal Ecohawk states:

> Sovereignty is an active, living process within this knot of human, material and spiritual relationships bound together by mutual responsibilities and obligations. From that knot of relationships is born our histories, our identity, the traditional ways in which we govern ourselves, our beliefs, our relationship to the land, and how we feed, clothe, house and take care of our families, communities and Nations.[19]

This interconnectedness exists not only among the nation's members but among all creation—human and nonhuman. ...

The idea of a nation did not simply apply to human beings. We call the buffalo or the wolves, the fish, the trees, and all are nations. Each is sovereign, an equal part of the creation, interdependent, interwoven, and all related.[20] These models of sovereignty are not based on a narrow definition of nation that would entail a closely bounded community and ethnic cleansing. For example, one activist distinguishes between a chauvinistic notion of "nationalism" versus a flexible notion of "sovereignty":

> Nationalism is saying, our way is the only right way. ... I think a real true sovereignty is a real, true acceptance of who and what's around you. And the nationalist doesn't accept all that. ... Sovereignty is what you do and what you are to your own people within your own confines, but there is a realization and acceptance that there are others who are around you. And that happened even before the Europeans came, we knew about the Indians. We had alliances with some, and fights with some. Part of that sovereignty was that acceptance that they were there.

It is interesting to me, for instance, how often non-Indians presume that if Native people regained their landbases, that they would necessarily call for the expulsion of non-Indians from those landbases. Yet, it is striking that a much more inclusive vision of sovereignty is articulated by Native women activists. For instance, this activist describes how indigenous sovereignty is based on freedom for all peoples:

> If it doesn't work for one of us, it doesn't work for any of us. The definition of sovereignty [means that] ... none of us are free unless all of our free. We can't, we won't turn anyone

away. We've been there. I would hear stories about the Japanese internment camps … and I could relate to it because it happened to us. Or with Africans with the violence and rape, we've been there too. So how could we ever leave anyone behind.

This analysis mirrors much of the work currently going on in women of color organizing in the United States and in other countries. Such models rely on this dual strategy of what Sista II Sista (Brooklyn) describes as "taking power" and "making power."[21] That is, it is necessary to engage in oppositional politics to corporate and state power ("taking power"). However, if we only engage in the politics of taking power, we will have a tendency to replicate the hierarchical structures in our movements. Consequently, it is also important to "make power" by creating those structures within our organizations, movements, and communities that model the world we are trying to create. Many groups in the United States often try to create separatist communities based on egalitarian ideals. However, if we "make power" without also trying to "take power" then we ultimately support the political status quo by failing to dismantle those structures of oppression that will undermine all our attempts to make power. The project of creating a new world governed by an alternative system not based on domination, coercion, and control does not depend on an unrealistic goal of being able to fully describe a utopian society for all at this point in time. From our position of growing up in a patriarchal, colonial, and white supremacist world, we cannot even fully imagine how a world not based on structures of oppression could operate. Nevertheless, we can be part of a collective, creative process that can bring us closer to a society not based on domination. To quote Jean Ziegler from the 2003 World Social Forum held in Porto Alegre, Brazil: "We know what we don't want, but the new world belongs to the liberated freedom of human beings. 'There is no way; you make the way as you walk.' History doesn't fall from heaven; we make history."

Notes

1. Quotes that are not cited come from interviews conducted in Rapid City, New York City, Santa Cruz, Minneapolis, and Bemidji in 2001. These interviews are derived primarily from women involved in Women of All Red Nations (WARN) and the American Indian Movement (AIM). All are activists today.
2. M. Annette Jaimes and Theresa Halsey, "American Indian Women: At the Center of Indigenous Resistance in North America," in *State of Native America*, ed. M. Annette Jaimes (Boston: South End Press, 1992), 330–31.
3. Ibid., 314, 332. WARN was established as a sister organization to AIM in 1974.
4. Janet McCloud, "The Backbone of Everything," *Indigenous Woman* 1, no. 3 (n.d.): 50.
5. Ward Churchill, *Struggle for the Land* (Monroe, Maine: Common Courage Press, 1993), 419.
6. Wilma Mankiller, *Mankiller* (New York: St. Martin's Press, 1993), 241.
7. Andrea Smith, "Sexual Violence and American Indian Genocide," in *Remembering Conquest: Feminist/Womanist Perspectives on Religion, Colonization, and Sexual Violence*, ed. Nantawan Lewis and Marie Fortune (Binghamton, N.Y.: Haworth Press, 1999), 31–52.
8. Callie Rennison, "Violent Victimization and Race, 1993–1998" (Washington, D.C: Bureau of Justice Statistics, 2001).
9. Lucy Eldersveld Murphy, "Autonomy and the Economic Roles of Indian Women of the Fox-Wisconsin Riverway Region, 1763–1832," in *Negotiators of Change: Historical Perspectives on*

Native American Women, ed. Nancy Shoemaker (New York: Routledge Press, 1995), 72–89; Theda Purdue, "Women, Men, and American Indian Policy: The Cherokee Response to "Civilization," in *Negotiators of Change*, 90–114.

10. Paula Gunn Allen, *The Sacred Hoop* (Boston: Beacon Press, 1986), 202.

11. Winona LaDuke, "Don't Cheapen Sovereignty," *American Eagle* 4 (May 1996): n.d. www.alphacdc.com/eagle/op0596.html.

12. Catherine MacKinnon, *Feminism Unmodified* (Cambridge: Harvard University Press, 1987), 63–69.

13. Beatrice Medicine, "North American Indigenous Women and Cultural Domination," *American Indian Culture and Research Journal* 17, no. 3 (1993): 121–30.

14. Lee Maracle, *I Am Woman* (North Vancouver: Write-On Press Publishers, 1988).

15. Smith, "Sexual Violence and American Indian Genocide," 31–52.

16. Paula Gunn Allen, "Violence and the American Indian Woman," *The Speaking Profits Us* (Seattle: Center for the Prevention of Sexual and Domestic Violence, n.d.), 5–7. See also *A Sharing: Traditional Lakota Thought and Philosophy Regarding Domestic Violence* (South Dakota: Sacred Shawl Women's Society, n.d.); and *Sexual Assault Is Not an Indian Tradition* (Minneapolis: Division of Indian Work Sexual Assault Project, n.d.).

17. See Jaimes and Halsey, "American Indian Women," 311–44; and Allen, *The Sacred Hoop*.

18. "Hello New Federalism, Goodbye BIA," *American Eagle* 4, no. 6 (1994): 19.

19. Crystal Echohawk, "Reflections on Sovereignty," *Indigenous Woman* 3, no. 1 (1999): 21–22.

20. Sharon Venne, "Mining and Indigenous Peoples," *Indigenous Woman* 2, no. 5 (1998): 23–25.

21. Personal conversations with Sista II Sista members, ongoing from 2001–2005.

34.
BESIDE MY SISTER, FACING THE ENEMY: LEGAL THEORY OUT OF COALITION*
Mari J. Matsuda
(1993)

Introduction

The Third Annual Conference on Women of Color and the Law, held in October 1990 at Stanford Law School, *was* coalition: individuals from divergent social backgrounds and positions coming together to work toward a common goal. From all corners of the country hundreds of women and dozens of men came. For the most part, they were law students, but their differences in size, shape, color, hair, speech and attire were so wondrously dramatic that no one wandering into the large auditorium where they gathered would have thought, "Ah, a meeting of law students." No, it looked more like a convocation of proud tribes. Sitting in the sun on perfect Stanford lawns, conference participants laughed and talked politics as though they did this every weekend. White with Black, native with immigrant, lesbian with straight, teacher with student, women with men—as though the joy of communing across differences was their birthright.

Conference organizers and volunteers—themselves as diverse as their guests—buzzed about busily in their official T-shirts, arranging rides, watching the clock, shepherding speakers, smoothing over misunderstandings. Watching these students work so easily with each other almost made me forget that a year of struggle, anger, tears, fears, and consciousness-raising had brought them to their day in the sun. Each one had asked at some point during that long year preceding the conference, "Is it worth it?"

"Is it worth it?" is the question every person who works in coalition confronts.[1] This essay introduces the work of three writers who themselves have asked and answered that question many times over. By their example, they show that the gains from coalition outweigh the pains. Implicit in their work is a knowledge of self that allows them to act in coalition, all the while knowing that the time may come when they must break coalition in order to preserve their own integrity and purpose.

This essay introduces the works of three writers: Haunani-Kay Trask, June Inuzuka, and Sharon Parker. It then considers the relationship between the process and the substance of coalition, suggesting that the instrumental use of coalition-building to achieve certain political goals is merely the beginning of the worth of this method. The deeper worth of coalition is the way in which it constructs us as ethical beings and knowers of our world. This essay concludes with tentative suggestions of the type of substantive theory that may emerge from work in coalition.[2]

I. Three Women Working

A. Daughter of Pi'ilani[3]

Haunani-Kay Trask is a paradox to those unfamiliar with the world from which she comes. She writes of working in coalition with environmentalists who, in her community of Hawai'i, are often white in-migrants.[4] Expressing bitterness and frustration, Trask recounts the dispossession of Native Hawaiian people—their landlessness, poverty, unemployment, imprisonment, rates of disease, and illiteracy. Trask speaks of the *haole* (Caucasian) colonizers who removed the Hawaiian government by force, leaving wounds in the native population that have never healed.[5] Expressing outrage at the haole-backed takeover of Hawai'i has earned Trask the reputation of "haole-hater." She speaks out in the press.[6] She writes. She debates. Trask is constantly engaged in dialogue with the haole. She works with whites in coalition on a variety of issues, from nuclear testing in the Pacific, to South African divestment, to degradation of the environment through geothermal development.

I have heard people say of Professor Trask, "She would be much more effective if she weren't so angry," as though they expect a Native Hawaiian feminist to work in coalition without anger. There is a politics of anger: who is allowed to get angry, whose anger goes unseen, and who seems angry when they are not.[7]

Once, when I intended to compliment an African-American woman on a powerful speech she had made, I said: "I admire your ability to express anger." She looked at me coolly and replied, "I was not angry. If I were angry I would not be speaking here." Another African-American friend of mine jumped into the conversation. "I'm disappointed in you," she said. "This is what always happens to us when a Black woman speaks her mind. Someone calls us angry."

I remember this exchange because it was an uncomfortable one for me, and because it was a moment of learning. Talking across differences, my colleague told me that if she were hatefully angry, beyond hope of coalition, she would not talk. In this light, Professor Trask's strong words are acts of engagement, not estrangement.

Would Professor Trask be more effective if she were less angry? There is a cost to speaking without anger of the deaths and dislocation that native Hawaiians suffered in post-contact Hawai'i.[8] On the simple, communicative level, failure to express the pain created by this legacy obscures the depth of one's feeling and discounts the subordination experienced by one's community. More significantly, the use of polite, rational tones when one is feeling violation is a betrayal of the self.

Professor Trask's many white and Asian colleagues who choose to remain in the room when she speaks in tones of outrage about the destruction of Hawaiian lives, land, and culture inevitably find their understanding greatly enriched. The discomfort brings with it an opportunity for learning. As a third-generation Japanese-American, I have felt the discomfort and benefitted from the learning when Professor Trask criticizes the role of immigrants in displacing Native Hawaiians. The choice is mine to remain in the conversation, discussing (sometimes with acrimony) the role of colonialism in bringing my peasant ancestors eastward from Asia to work on land that once belonged to indigenous peoples of Hawai'i and North America.

I could shelter myself from conflict by leaving the conversation, but I have come to believe that the comfort we feel when we avoid hard conversations is a dangerous comfort, one that seduces us into ignorance about the experiences of others and about the full meaning of our own lives.[9]

B. *Women of Color and Public Policy*

In her article for this symposium, June Inuzuka writes of coalition as strategy.[10] Her concept of coalition is grounded in the world of practical politics and in the recognition that women of color are a numerical minority in the arena of policy formation. In order to meet the immediate and material need for access to government largess, Inuzuka and others like her have worked within organizations dominated by white, middle-class women. Inuzuka's case study of the Women's Business Ownership Act[11] provides a useful descriptive vehicle for exploring the costs and benefits of coalition. Women of color[12] who worked for the Act's passage chose to integrate with largely white[13] feminist organizations. This choice, as Inuzuka's essay reveals, allowed these women of color to influence public policy.

There is a realpolitik awareness in the way Inuzuka approaches her work. She has chosen to de-emphasize the separate and sometimes conflicting categorizations of "white feminist" and "women of color" in coalition-building. Given her mission—to stop legislative developments that could disadvantage women of color as a group—this choice makes sense. Demanding meaningful representation for women of color in the political process requires the dual coalitions that Inuzuka writes about: the coalition of women of color, and the coalition of women of color united with white feminists.

Inuzuka chooses not to problematize the categories "white feminist" and "women of color." This non-deconstructionist approach contrasts with the work of theorists who challenge our thinking about the make-up of the feminist coalition.[14] Inuzuka is an example of an activist who recognizes differences and who chooses, nonetheless, to work with groups formed around the category of "women."

C. *The Multi-Cultural Feminist*

Sharon Parker begins her essay by telling of her genealogy, and in doing so echoes a practice familiar in native cultures.[15] Like legal theorist Patricia Williams, who lets her readers know that she writes as an African-American woman whose genealogy includes slavery and rape,[16] Parker introduces her work and herself through the prism of her lineal past. Bringing one's genealogy to one's work is more than a demonstration of respect for one's ancestors. It is a claim that theory reflects social position and experience, and it is a critique of theory that fails to disclose the particularities of its origin.

Unlike June Inuzuka, who operates in the world of practical politics, Sharon Parker chooses to complexify the notion of "women of color." She identifies herself as a "multi-ethnic" woman and includes "white" as one of the racial identities she claims. For Parker and the growing number of multi-ethnic feminists like her, the question of separate versus collective identity is both personal and political, implicating culture as much as coalition.

What does it mean to claim white, African, and Native ancestry? Physiognomy is not enough to lay claim to an ethnicity. Without the knowledge that comes from the living of Native American culture, a drop of Native American blood is meaningless.[17] Implicit in Parker's statement of her ancestry is her commitment to the cultures represented by that ancestry, as well as her refusal to fit neatly into a single racial category.

Parker focuses explicitly on "herstory" and spirituality in her essay. More than Trask or Inuzuka, Parker speaks in the broad and visionary terms of cultural feminism and eco-feminism, branches of the feminist tradition that seek a women-centered spirit. Feminist spirituality is not often found in the pages of a law review, and Parker's writing will seem unfamiliar to some readers. We might ask why certain strands of feminism are more palatable to legal audiences. Are they better, more progressive, more theoretically sophisticated, or is it simply that they more closely resemble the discourses of power in the legal academy?

These three writers—Parker, Inuzuka, and Trask—have found work in coalition painful. Each describes the racism and condescension they have experienced. Each recounts the frustration that comes from trying to explain the most important aspects of one's life and creed to listeners who are ill-prepared to understand. Each suggests that coalition has limits of both tolerance and utility.

Why, then, given the frustration of coalition, do these women not retreat into racial separatism? In the quest for a theoretical underpinning for social change movements, women of color have the choice of remaining in coalition or dispersing to do separate work. The emergence of feminist jurisprudence, critical race theory, critical legal studies, and the women of color and the law movement has raised fears of division and parochial separatism in the legal community. If it is so hard to work together, if the gulfs in experience are so wide, if the false universals of the modem age are truly bankrupt, what need binds us? What justifies unity in our quest for self-knowledge?

My answer is that we cannot, at this point in history, engage fruitfully in jurisprudence without engaging in coalition, without coming out of separate places to meet one another across all the positions of privilege and subordination that we hold in relation to one another.

II. Theory out of Coalition

Through our sometimes painful work in coalition we are beginning to form a theory of subordination; a theory that describes it, explains it, and gives us the tools to end it. As lawyers working in coalition, we are developing a theory of law taking sides, rather than law as value-neutral. We imagine law to uplift and protect the sixteen-year-old single mother on crack rather than law to criminalize her.[18] We imagine law to celebrate and protect women's bodies; law to sanctify love between human beings—whether women to women, men to men, or women to men, as lovers may choose to love; law to respect the bones of our ancestors; law to feed the children; law to shut down the sweatshops; law to save the planet.

This is the revolutionary theory of law that we are developing in coalition, and I submit that it is both a theory of law we can *only* develop in coalition, and that it is the *only* theory of law we *can* develop in coalition.

A. Looking at Subordination from Inside Coalition

When we work in coalition, as the writers in this symposium demonstrate, we compare our struggles and challenge one another's assumptions. We learn of the gaps and absences in our knowledge. We learn a few tentative, starting truths, the building blocks of a theory of subordination.

We learn that while all forms of oppression are not the same,[19] certain predictable patterns emerge:

- All forms of oppression involve taking a trait, X, which often carries with it a cultural meaning,[20] and using X to make some group the "other" and to reduce their entitlements and power.
- All forms of oppression benefit someone, and sometimes both sides of a relationship of domination will have some stake in its maintenance.[21]
- All forms of oppression have both material and ideological dimensions. The articles on health, socioeconomics, and violence in this symposium show how subordination leaves scars on the body.[22] The damage is real. It is material. These articles also speak of ideology. Language, including the language of science, law, rights, necessity, free markets, neutrality, and objectivity can make subordination seem natural and inevitable, justifying material deprivation.
- All forms of oppression implicate a psychology of subordination that involves elements of sexual fear, need to control, hatred of self and hatred of others.

As we look at these patterns of oppression, we may come to learn, finally and most importantly, that all forms of subordination are interlocking and mutually reinforcing.

B. Ask the Other Question: The Interconnection of All Forms of Subordination

The way I try to understand the interconnection of all forms of subordination is through a method I call "ask the other question." When I see something that looks racist, I ask, "Where is the patriarchy in this?" When I see something that looks sexist, I ask, "Where is the heterosexism in this?" When I see something that looks homophobic, I ask, "Where are the class interests in this?" Working in coalition forces us to look for both the obvious and non-obvious relationships of domination, helping us to realize that no form of subordination ever stands alone.[23]

If this is true, we've asked each other, then isn't it also true that dismantling anyone form of subordination is impossible without dismantling every other? And more and more, particularly in the women of color movement, the answer is that "no person is free until the last and the least of us is free."

In trying to explain this to my own community, I sometimes try to shake people up by suggesting that patriarchy killed Vincent Chin.[24] Most people think racism killed

Vincent Chin. When white men with baseball bats, hurling racist hate speech, beat a man to death, it is obvious that racism is a cause. It is only slightly less obvious, however, when you walk down the aisles of Toys R Us, that little boys grow up in this culture with toys that teach dominance and aggression, while little girls grow up with toys that teach about being pretty, baking, and changing a diaper. And the little boy who is interested in learning how to nurture and play house is called a "sissy." When he is a little older he is called a "f–g." He learns that acceptance for men in this society is premised on rejecting the girl culture and taking on the boy culture, and I believe that this, as much as racism, killed Vincent Chin. I have come to see that homophobia is the disciplinary system that teaches men that they had better talk like 2 Live Crew or someone will think they "aren't real men," and I believe that this homophobia is a cause of rape and violence against women. I have come to see how that same homophobia makes women afraid to choose women, sending them instead into the arms of men who beat them. I have come to see how class oppression creates the same effect, cutting off the chance of economic independence that could free women from dependency upon abusive men.

I have come to see all of this from working in coalition: from my lesbian colleagues who have pointed out homophobia in places where I failed to see it; from my Native American colleagues who have said, "But remember that we were here first," when I have worked for the rights of immigrant women; from men of color who have risked my wrath to say, "But racism *is* what is killing us. Why can't I put that first on my agenda?"

The women of color movement has, of necessity, been a movement about intersecting structures of subordination. This movement suggests that anti-patriarchal struggle is linked to struggle against all forms of subordination. It has challenged communities of color to move beyond race alone in the quest for social justice.

C. Beyond Race Alone

In coalition, we are able to develop an understanding of that which Professor Kimberlé Crenshaw has called "inter-sectionality."[25] The women of color movement has demanded that the civil rights struggle encompass more than anti-racism. There are several reasons for this demand. First, and most obviously, in unity there is strength. No subordinated group is strong enough to fight the power alone, thus coalitions are formed out of necessity.[26]

Second, some of us have overlapping identities. Separating out and ranking oppression denies and excludes these identities and ignores the valid concerns of many in our constituency. To say that the anti-racist struggle precedes all other struggles denigrates the existence of the multiply oppressed: women of color, gays and lesbians of color, poor people of color, *most* people of color experience subordination on more than one dimension.

Finally, perhaps the most progressive reason for moving beyond race alone is that racism is best understood and fought with knowledge gained from the broader anti-subordination struggle. Even if one wanted to live as the old prototype "race man," it is simply not possible to struggle against racism alone and ever hope to end racism.

These are threatening suggestions for many of us who have worked primarily in organizations forged in the struggle for racial justice. Our political strength and our cultural self-worth is often grounded in racial pride. Our multi-racial coalitions have, in the past, succeeded because of a unifying commitment to end racist attacks on people of color. Moving beyond race to include discussion of other forms of subordination risks breaking coalition. Because I believe that the most progressive elements of any liberation movement are those who see the intersections (and the most regressive are those who insist on only one axis), I am willing to risk breaking coalition by pushing intersectional analysis.

An additional and more serious risk is that intersectional analysis done from on high, that is, from outside rather than inside a structure of subordination, risks misunderstanding the particularity of that structure. Feminists have spent years talking about, experiencing, and building theory around gender. Native Americans have spent years developing an understanding of colonialism and its effect on culture. That kind of situated, ground-up knowledge is irreplaceable. A casual effort to say, "Okay, I'll add gender to my analysis," without immersion in feminist practice, is likely to miss something. Adding on gender must involve active feminists, just as adding on considerations of indigenous peoples must include activists from native communities. Coalition is the way to achieve this inclusion.

It is no accident that women of color, grounded as they are in both feminist and anti-racist struggle, are doing the most exciting theoretical work on race–gender intersections. It is no accident that gay and lesbian scholars are advancing social construction theory and the analysis of sexuality in subordination. In raising this I do not mean that we cannot speak of subordination second-hand. Rather, I wish to encourage us to do this, and to suggest that we can do this most intelligently in coalition, listening with special care to those who are actively involved in knowing and ending the systems of domination that touch their lives.

Conclusion

This essay has suggested a theory of subordination that comes out of work in coalition. The Third National Conference on Women of Color and the Law was a place for this work. The women and men of many races who worked on the conference can tell us that making this place is not easy. The false efficiencies of law schools, where we edit facts out of cases and cabin concepts such as "crime" and "property" into semester-sized courses, ill-prepare us for the long, slow, open-ended efficiencies of coalition. Planning the conference involved more than inviting speakers and sending out registration forms. It took a literal thousand human hours spent talking long into the night, telling stories of self and culture and history, before the Stanford Women of Color and the Law Conference could happen. To lay the foundation of trust upon which people could teach, challenge, listen, learn, and form theory out of coalition took time and patience. As often happens in the slow-cooking school of theory-building, the organizers wondered whether all that talk was getting anywhere. Cutting off discussion and avoiding conflict would have saved hours early on, but coalition at its best never works that way. The slow and difficult early work gives us efficiencies when we need them: when the real challenges come, when justice requires action, when there is no time to argue over how to proceed. The organizers of the conference, like the women writing on coalition for this volume, have forged bonds and created theory that will sustain them in the contentious closing days of this century. When called upon they will answer with a courage and wisdom born in their place of coalition.

Notes

*   This title was inspired by a line from *Pablo Neruda, Los Versos del Capitan* (The Captain's Verses) (New Directions ed. 1972): y en medio de la vida estare' siempre, junto al amigo, frente al enemigo (and in the midst of life I shall be always beside the friend, facing the enemy)

1.   Bernice Johnson Reagon, in her well-known essay on coalition, said, "You don't go into coalition because you just *like* it." Bernice Johnson Reagon, "Coalition Politics," in *Home Girls* 354 (Barbara Smith ed. 1983). She goes on to state: "And you shouldn't look for comfort. Some people will come to a coalition and they rate the success of the coalition on whether or not they feel good when they get there. They're not looking for a coalition: they're looking for a home!" (Ibid. 359). As Professor Kimberlé Crenshaw pointed out to me upon reading this essay: "Comfort means perfect peace or perfect oppression."

2.   For general discussions of anti-subordination principles, see Charles Lawrence, Mari J. Matsuda, Richard Delgado & Kimberle Crenshaw, *Words That Wound* (forthcoming); Mari J. Matsuda, Voices of America, 100 *YALE L. J.* 1329 (1991); Ruth Colker, *Anti-Subordination Above All,* 61 *N.Y.V. L. REV.* 1003 (1986); Lucie E. White, Subordination, Rhetorical Survival Skills, and Sunday Shoes. 38 *BUFF. L. REV.* I (1990).

3.   Professor Haunani-Kay Trask was introduced at the Conference as the genealogical descendant of the Pi'ilani line of Maui, the non-self-governing Native Hawaiians. She is the author of *Eros and Power.*

4.   See Haunani Trask, Coalition-Building Between Natives and Non-Natives, 43 *STAN. L. REV.* 1197 (1993).

5.   See Haunani-Kay Trask, Politics in the Pacific Islands, 16 *AMERASIA* I (1990). The article discusses the effects of imperialism on Hawaiian culture. Trask suggests that the power of Native Hawaiian self-definition was impeded by repression of the Hawaiian language. The ability to conceptualize in Native terms was hampered when all cultural referents became those of non-natives (Ibid. 3). In addition to the psychological and political colonization of Native Hawaiians, Trask notes the physical appropriation of Native lands resulting in the denial of control over the land and its peoples (Ibid. 9).

6.   See Racial Dispute Erupts at UH-Manoa, *Honolulu Advertiser*, Oct. 26, 1980, at A-3.

7.   See Trina Grillo, The Mediation Alternative: Process Dangers for Women, 100 *YALE L.J.* 1545, 1576–81 (1991).

8.   For a historical assessment of the mass deaths and social dislocation in the Native Hawaiian population as a result of western contact, see David E. Stannard, *Before The Horror* (1989).

9.   For a discussion of the costs of silence, see King-Kok Cheung, Don't Tell, 103 *Publications Mod. Language* A. 162 (1988).

10. June K. Inuzuka, Women of Color and Public Policy, 43 *STAN. L. REV.* 1215 (1993).

11. Pub. L. No. 100–533, 102 Stat. 2689 (1988).

12. The group "women of color" itself represents a coalition across lines of ethnicity, class, and sexual orientation. This grouping is neither necessary nor inevitable as a matter of formal logic. It is, however, a powerful grouping politically, and one with a historical basis in the conditions of race and gender oppression in this society.

13. Similarly, "white" is a category derived from both the ideology of white supremacy and from opposition to it. The concept of whiteness, of course, is itself subject to deconstruction. See Neil Gotanda, A Critique of Our Constitution is Color-Blind, 44 *STAN. L. REV.* 1 (1991).

Bernice Johnson Reagon describes the expanding identities of whites who participated in the Civil Rights Movement:

> They were people who came South to work in the movement who were not Black. Most of them were white when they came. Before it was over, that category broke up—you know, some of them were Jewish, not simply white, and some others even changed their names. Say if it was Mary when they came South, by the time they were finished it was Maria, right? At some point, you cannot be fighting oppression and be oppressed yourself and not feel it. (Reagon, *supra* note 1, at 363).

14. See, e.g., Elizabeth Spellman, *Inessential Woman* (1988).
15. Sharon Parker, Understanding Coalition, 43 *STAN. L. REV.* 1193 (1993).
16. See generally Patricia L. Williams, *The Alchemy of Race and Rights* (1991).
17. Unless, of course, there is a degraded meaning attached to that drop of blood by the dominant culture. See Gotanda, *supra* note 13.
18. See Dorothy Roberts, Punishing Drug Addicts Who Have Babies, 104 *HARV. L. REV.* 1419 (1991).
19. Trina Grillo & Stephanie Wildman, Obscuring the Importance of Race, 1991 *DUKE L.J.* 397.
20. See Charles R. Lawrence III, The Id, the Ego, and Equal Protection, 39 *STAN. L. REV.* 317 (1987).
21. For an analysis of Hegel's discussion of the Master and Slave relationship, see Kendall Thomas, A House Divided Against Itself, 10 *CARDOZO L. REV.* 1481 (1989); for consideration of the false consciousness that may keep people in situations that harm them, see Mari J. Matsuda, Pragmatism Modified and the False Consciousness Problem, 63 S. *CAL. L. REV.* 1763 (1990).
22. See G. Chezia Carraway, Violence Against Women of Color. 43 *STAN. L. REV.* 130 I (1993); Kimberlé Crenshaw, Mapping the Margins. 43 *STAN. L. REV.* 1241 (1993); Nilda Rimonte, A Question of Culture. 43 *STAN. L. REV.* 1311 (1993).
23. For an analysis of the relationship between sexism and heterosexism, see Suzanne Pharr, *Homophobia: A Weapon of Sexism* (1988).
24. Vincent Chin, a Chinese American, was murdered in Detroit by assailants who shouted racial slurs while attacking Chin with a baseball bat. See Detroit's Asian Americans Outraged by Lenient Sentencing of Chinese American Man's Killer. Rafu Shimpo, May 5, 1983 (on file with the *Stanford Law Review*). For other accounts of anti-Asian violence, see, for example, William Wong, Anti-Asian Violence. *Forum*, June 1989 (reflections on the Stockton, California massacre of Asian-American school children and the Vincent Chin case); L.A. Group Says Skinheads Tied to Anti-Asian Violence, *Asian Week*, Feb. 23, 1990, at 3; Arnold T. Hiura, The Unfortunate Case of Jim Loo, *The Hawaii Herald*, July 6, 1990, at A-13, col. I (racially motivated murder of Chinese-American man in Raleigh, North Carolina); Asian Pacific American Coalition USA, Report: Stockton Killings Racially Motivated, *APAC Alert*, Oct. 1989, at I.
25. See Kimberlé Crenshaw, Demarginalizing the Intersection of Race and Sex, 1989 *U. CHI. LEGAL F.* 139, 140.
26. In addition to the political power that comes from unity, there is also a joy and empowerment that comes from finding connections to others. As a student participant in the Women of Color Conference said: "The energy that comes from comparing experiences; the nods of 'uh-huh' when one person's story of oppression at one axis triggers another person to remember subordination at a different axis; the making of new friends; the renewal of old friendships; the knowledge that we are not alone in our struggles—all are benefits of coalition work."

SECTION III

THEORIZING FEMINIST KNOWLEDGE AND AGENCY

INTRODUCTION

The variety of experiences and the complexity of intersecting and overlapping forms of oppression make it difficult to see how feminist theories can honor the diversity of women's experiences and yet inform an effective gender politics. Moreover, the strands of conversation in Section II insist that feminist theories must come to grips with the ways in which gender identity/oppression intersects, overlaps, imbricates, or conflicts with other social processes of identity/oppression, especially those of race, class, nation, and sexuality. In theorizing these interconnections, several questions emerge. What are the appropriate boundaries of feminist theorizing and feminist politics? Can we turn the insights from the complex and diverse experiences of women into effective knowledge? Can feminists construct a reliable basis for analyzing social systems and for articulating strategies for change that will improve women's lives?

The readings in the Section III are drawn from two major currents within feminist theory—feminist standpoint theories and poststructural feminist theories—each of which offers answers to the preceding questions. Standpoint theory was developed primarily by social scientists, especially sociologists and political theorists. It extends some of the early insights about consciousness that emerged from Marxist/socialist feminist theories and wider conversations about identity politics. It endeavors to develop a feminist epistemology, or theory of knowledge, that delineates a method for constructing effective knowledge from the insights of women's experiences. Poststructural feminist theory was developed primarily among literary critics and philosophers, as well as by film and cultural studies scholars. It builds on insights about sexual difference and language from psychoanalysis and literary theory, and is concerned with understanding how discursive processes construct knowledge and identity. It focuses on the ways in which power relations shape the social category of women, and the subjectivity of women (Hesford and Kozol 2001). The two currents of theory have had much to say to each other. To understand fully the conversations between these two schools of thought, it is necessary to take a few steps back and investigate the key principles of each theory. The readings illustrate those key principles, provide examples of how the theories have been applied, and illuminate the debates about the multiplicity of women's perspectives in local U.S. and in global contexts.

Standpoint Epistemologies/Situated Knowledges

In Reading 35, Nancy Hartsock defines the elements of a standpoint and delineates the grounds for her claim that a feminist standpoint can be constructed from careful analysis of women's experiences. In many ways, Hartsock's essay is a response to Heidi

Hartmann's earlier call to apply Marxist methods to feminist ends. The notion of a standpoint derives from Marx's view that human consciousness emerges in our interactions with nature and other humans as we work to make our lives. These interactions, especially the work we do, shape our knowledge of our companions, our world, and ourselves. They also set limits on what we can know. Following the insights of Hartmann, among others, Hartsock argues that the sexual division of labor, whereby women are responsible for the activities involved in reproducing children and daily life, provides the grounds for a feminist standpoint: A critical perspective on society from which competent knowledge of women's lives can be developed to inform effective strategies for change. A standpoint is political because, Hartsock argues, power relations shape the different perspectives of different social groups. Thus, the sexual division of labor not only sets up differences between men and women, but also domination of women by men.

Following Marx's theory, Hartsock argues that knowledge produced from the dominant group's perspective distorts reality. As she points out, we can see this in contemporary society. The accumulation of wealth through the production and exchange of goods and services is *the* most important activity, if measured by the economic rewards given to those who engage in that activity, if measured by the attention given to the activity within the society, or if measured by the social resources dedicated to the activity by the government. However, the real point of production and exchange is not profit; it is meeting human needs by using those goods. The point of making and exchanging things should be to allow us to survive. But in capitalism, the real relationships between people are inverted so that the exchange of commodities becomes more important than meeting human needs. Human needs are met accidentally, if at all, as a by-product of business activity. Part of the power of dominance is the ability to make your perspective true, to set the rules of the game to your advantage. Thus, even if capitalism distorts human relationships, we all must engage in (or resist) economic activities set up by the rules of capitalist exchange. For instance, our society devalues the work that caregivers, primarily women, do while engaged in raising children, easing the burdens of sickness and old age, and ensuring that employees are fed, clothed, and rested so they can return to the business of business each morning. This devaluation is clear in the exclusion of these activities from measures of economic productivity in the United States. It does not count as work if you perform it for family members and do not receive a wage. When we do hire people to complete this work, we pay them very low wages in comparison to jobs that manage capital accumulation and exchange.

Given this distorted view of social relationships, subordinated social groups must struggle to see their situation clearly. On the surface, the dominant group's description of the way the world works appears to be sensible and true. It takes concerted effort to get below the surface reality because it requires one to think "against the grain" of dominant culture. Subordinated group members caught in the contradictions between the rules of the dominant culture and the realities of human need are in a unique position to develop knowledge from the perspective of underlying domination. This insight can become the grounds for a critique of dominant culture that points to effective strategies for change. For instance, by living the contradictions between doing the crucial work of caregiving in a society that does not value caregiving, Hartsock asserts, women are in a position to see that dominant culture distorts human relationships. The clearest example of this distortion, for Hartsock, is the fact that Western culture valorizes risking death in battle and disparages giving life through birth and care-taking activities. While Hartsock notes that differences among women shape their experiences, she nonetheless argues that the sexual division of labor constructs a singular unique perspective on society, from which feminists can effectively challenge male domination.

Patricia Hill Collins (Reading 37) also articulates the grounds for a feminist standpoint, in this case a black feminist standpoint, based on the insights of feminist and African-American intellectual traditions. As with all standpoint theories, Hill Collins posits that subordinated social groups can have a unique insight into the power relations that subordinate them. For Hill Collins, this position is that of the outsider-within. Black women are positioned both within and yet remain invisible and outside of white society. There is, however, an important difference between Hill Collins and Hartsock. A central claim made by standpoint theorists, including Hill Collins, is that there are certain positions in society from which it is possible, with effort, to see clearly, and others from which clear vision is not possible (see also Harding 1986; Smith 1987). This claim to superior vision rests on the fact that subordinated groups not only sees the world from their location, which the dominant culture ignores, but they also have to know the dominant culture in order to survive in it. In rejecting all either/or thinking on principle, Hill Collins also rejects the claim that any one social group has *the* best vantage point from which to see the truth.

She sees oppression as a "matrix of domination," an interlocking web of oppressions that work simultaneously in the same social structures. Sometimes they intersect. Sometimes they do not. Sometimes they operate in concert and sometimes in conflict. Moreover, these interconnections grow, shift, and attenuate over time. Through this concept, she posits a very dynamic system of oppressions and with it a vigorous heterogeneity of perspectives. Individual experiences of oppression vary depending on where one falls within the historical web of dominations. These dimensions of a person's life intertwine in ways that affect her life opportunities, her chances, her options for resistance, and so on. They are twisted together in ways that are difficult, or impossible, to untangle and can be constituted by moments of privilege and moments of oppression simultaneously (Reading 37).

Given this complexity, she concludes that everybody has a partial view; nobody has the place to stand and see everything clearly. Nevertheless, a partial view can still produce valuable, if not complete or perfect, knowledge. Some locations make it easier to produce accurate knowledge within these interlocking systems, and from some locations, understanding is more difficult (see also Smith 1987). That is, men have to struggle harder than women do to see and understand sexism. White people have to struggle harder than people of color do to see and understand racism. Residents of the global north have to struggle harder than residents of the global south do to see and understand the impact of (post)colonialism. Heterosexuals must struggle harder to see and understand the operations of heteronormativity. Each group needs its own self-defined standpoint, but change and "new versions of truth" can come only through "dialogue and principled coalitions" (Reading 37). However, she also recognizes that expressing a collective body of knowledge in a subordinated group's own interests is extremely difficult, precisely because the dominant groups have vested interests in subjugating that knowledge. Thus, for Hill Collins, a black feminist standpoint is constituted in and through the politics and continuous interplay between subjugation and agency, thought and activism.

Uma Narayan's essay (Reading 36) challenges key components of Western feminist standpoints, arguing that they have built a feminist epistemology that is "noncontextual and nonpragmatic." In so doing, Western feminist epistemologies can "convert important feminist insights ... into feminist epistemological dogmas." Using her perspective as a South Asian feminist, she cites several limitations of existing standpoint theories. Her first criticism is that Western feminist standpoints run the risk of romanticizing women's experiences. Western women, living in cultures that devalue qualities associated with women, often suggest that one way to change the status of women is to re-value their contributions to society. This is not necessarily a useful strategy in cultures dominated by a strong "traditional discourse," in which women's contributions are valued, as long as women "stay in their place." She notes in such cases, feminist efforts to revalue women's contributions may be "drowned out by the louder and more powerful voices of traditional discourse" which will reaffirm women's prescribed place (Reading 36). In addition, there is a tension for feminists in the South between wanting to affirm the value of their culture in the face of Western colonial prejudices and wanting to critique traditions that oppress women. As she notes, liberalism is the politics of colonialism. So from a non-Western perspective, liberalism is not a politics of freedom, it is the politics of oppression. Yet, at the same time, the liberal concept of individual rights is vital for women's resistance to systems of domination. Without a notion of individual rights, it is difficult to argue effectively for women's rights to autonomy or bodily integrity. It is difficult for non-Western feminists to extract that notion of rights from this history of liberal colonial oppression. For Narayan, the problem is that Western feminist standpoints, because they are noncontextual, gloss over these points of tension. In so doing, Western feminist standpoints assume a solid basis for coalition among women's groups, where Narayan sees a more fluid and highly charged terrain for global feminist politics (see also Spivak 1988).

Finally, Narayan challenges the tendency of Western-feminist standpoint theorists to valorize the situation of contradiction. Hartsock identifies the contradictory demands in women's lives between the public and the private sphere as providing the possibility of liberatory thought. Likewise, Hill Collins values the position of the outsider-within as empowering resistance. To the contrary, Narayan points out, for individuals who must "straddl[e] a multiplicity of contexts," one can cope with contradiction in many ways (Reading 36). One can dichotomize one's life and live by the different rules in different contexts. One can alienate oneself from the knowledge of one of the contexts. Alternatively, sometimes, one can simply be overwhelmed by contradictions. In such cases, contradiction does not provide a place for generating liberatory philosophy but instead it can be very disempowering.

Cheshire Calhoun (Reading 38) examines the points of conflict and coincidence within lesbian theory and feminist theory, providing a thoughtful genealogy of U.S. lesbian-feminist theory building. As Heidi Hartmann did with Marxism and feminism, Calhoun suggests that the coupling of feminist and lesbian theory "risks falling into a similar unhappy marriage." She argues that feminist theory, which treats lesbianism as a special case of gender oppression, has not produced an effective basis for lesbian politics. She argues that so far, lesbian theory has been subsumed by feminist theory. This happens because feminist theories of gender do not have a theory of "hetero(sexuality) as a political structure separable from patriarchy." Thus, feminism cannot account for lesbian oppression as sexual oppression. At the same time, in reaction to "patriarchal biases" in the early gay rights movement, lesbian feminist theory conceptualized heterosexuality as "both a product and essential support of patriarchy," and thus lesbians have "no specifically lesbian relationship to heterosexuality." An adequate lesbian theory requires separating sexual politics and gender politics. In pulling apart the sex/gender system into its gender and sexual currents, Calhoun notes that the agendas of feminist movements and lesbian and gay movements are not the same. "Heterosexuality as a political system" functions to ensure reproduction by making masculinity and femininity fundamental to social structure. It is the private sphere. Intimate relationships outside of that sphere do not enjoy the freedom of privacy. "Just as the heart of male privilege lies in the 'right' of access to women, so the heart of heterosexual privilege lies in the 'right' of access to sexual-romantic-marital-familial relationships" (Reading 38). Moreover, it is possible that the end of patriarchy could be accomplished without compulsory heterosexuality. Likewise, it would be possible to end as a political structure without eliminating patriarchal gender relations. Thus, she concludes lesbian theory must develop an understanding of the specifically lesbian relationship to the heterosexual political structure in order to ground an effective lesbian politics.

Donna Haraway (Reading 39) connects the strengths of standpoint theory with the insights of poststructural feminisms in her discussion of situated knowledge. She argues against the extremes of some social constructionists for whom "facts are part of the powerful art of rhetoric." She rejects the claim of superior vantage point made by standpoint theorists, arguing that there is no singular place from which to see everything clearly. Instead, reminding readers that vision is an embodied sense, she argues for an embodied, situated, and partial feminist knowledge. She posits "the joining of partial views and halting voices into a collective subject position that promises a vision … of living within limits and contradictions—views from somewhere" (Reading 39). These views from somewhere would trust the vantage points of the subjugated, but these vantage points must also be re-examined, decoded, and deconstructed. Haraway also suggests that adequate feminist theory would also account for the world itself as an active agent that shapes our lives in ways we cannot command or control. In an example of the analysis she theorizes, she calls into question the distinction between biological sex and social gender that has prevailed in feminist theory until recently. Haraway's argument reiterates a theme that reverberates across many of the readings in this section: any adequate feminist theory must locate the specific social-historical context of its underlying assumptions.

Poststructuralist Epistemologies

Poststructural feminisms approach the dilemma raised by the challenges of feminist theorizing from another perspective. Poststructuralist feminisms first emerged within intellectual circles in France. Reworking semiotic theories of language and psychoanalytic theories of subjectivity, they have been most concerned with theorizing the ways in which cultural discourses and social practices normalize forms of social organization, knowledge, meaning, subjectivity, and identity. Luce Irigaray provides an example of one such theory. The essay uses semiotics to examine how female sexuality has been "theorized within masculine parameters" (Irigaray Reading 40).[1] While the details of poststructural theories are beyond the scope of this book, some discussion of key elements is crucial for understanding feminist uses of these theories.

In poststructural theory, social reality and human subjectivity are constituted in and through language. What we know about the world and ourselves is defined and contested in the language of historically specific discourses. "Discourses are ways of constituting knowledge, together with the social practices, forms of subjectivity, and power relations which inhere in such knowledge" (Weedon 1997: 105). We can never make sense of the "real" world outside of these discursive fields. However, we can analyze the processes by which order and coherence are imposed on the world through the discourses and practices that make up knowledge of "the real." Poststructuralism provides powerful tools for those analyses.

Poststructural theories of subjectivity are distinctive in viewing subjectivity as an ongoing process. In much of Western thought, humans are represented as possessing some unique essence (human nature, reason, race, sex) that is inherent in the individual and exists prior to and outside of the individuals' interaction with society. In contrast, poststructural theories assert that one's subjectivity, one's sense of self, is constituted in the same process through which one learns language, and it is reconstituted each time one thinks, speaks, or acts. For many poststructural feminist theories, the workings of the language and the structure of one's subjectivity are constructed through psychoanalytic processes in which the structure of sexual difference is a binary opposition between masculinity and femininity. Thus, gender differences are intricately intertwined with the construction of subjectivity, which is one key reason poststructural theories have been of continuing interest to feminist theorists.

The way in which language works to construct identity, however, involves a fundamental misrecognition of oneself as the author of meaning. This misrecognition derives from the belief that language reflects and expresses the meaning inherent in the world. We think of ourselves as generating meaning through our language use, rather than language generating us. Instead, poststructuralists argue, we are using a symbol system, the rules of which we have been learning since we were young, and the meaning of words and gestures are already defined in discourses before we give them voice. When we are speaking, we are speaking the lines from scripts written for subjects of the discourse we enunciate. Discourses are continually competing for individuals to take up their "I" positions, to become the subject of those discourses. When we say, for instance, "I'm a feminist," there are certain topics, issues, postures that we have to situate ourselves in relation to such as feminism/femininity, feelings about men, and sexual orientation. When we say, "I am a feminist of color," there are certain topics, issues, postures that we have to situate ourselves in relationship to including feminism/ femininity, race/racism, feelings about men of our culture and feelings about sexism in our culture. When we say, "I am a Third World feminist" or "I am a transnational feminist," we must situate ourselves in relationship to Western feminism/femininity, colonialism, and feelings about sexism in our culture. Such are the issues invoked by discursive struggles in different locations to set "the rules" about what it means to be a feminist.

Yet there is not a singular discourse of gender or sexuality. There are multiple and competing discourses. Thus, identity becomes a site of continual contest among discourses for allegiance of its subjects. What it means to be a woman or a man is the site of continual struggle over the meanings of femininity and masculinity. The construction of the meanings of femininity, of subject positions, of womanhood, is not just a language game. "Everything we do signifies compliance or resistance to dominant norms of what it is to be a woman" (Weedon 1997: 83). It involves a whole array of speaking parts, a whole range of obligatory gestures, a whole set of appropriate practices. Riot grrl, soccer mom, teenage mother, feminist, girl geek, professional woman, all of these have outfits and activities that go with them. That is what Barbie dolls are all about in dominant culture discourses of femininity: get the female body (white, thin, rich, and blonde) in the right outfits for the right identities. Power operates within these discourses to set the limits of what women can be; and the playing field is not level. As Inderpal Grewal and Caren Kaplan have noted, in India Barbie is marketed in a sari, although Ken remains dressed in "American" clothes. This "universalizes and nationalizes a regional style of dress," and erases "other South Asian women's styles of dress" (1994: 11).

Poststructuralists explode the certainty that the meaning of what we say is transparent, and that we guarantee it. For poststructuralists, one never controls those meanings, at least not for very long. Any temporarily fixed meaning involves "both interests and questions of power." The subject positions created in discourses then are always "implicated in power relations" (Weedon 1997: 171, 174). Power relations are not simple binary oppositions between those who have it and those who do not, but are complex relational fields that are "exercised within discourses in the ways [that] constitute and govern individual subjects" (Weedon 1997: 110).[2]

Because they insist that no category—"women," "experience," "the personal"—can be taken for granted, poststructural theories have been particularly useful for feminist theorists of color worldwide. In particular, the tools of these theories have helped to crack open the normative Western feminist subject on one hand and Orientalist view of women in the global south on the other. Lata Mani's analysis (Reading 41) of the different ways that her study of *sati* (ritual widow death) has been received in Britain, the United States, and in India demonstrates the complexity of gender politics in the context of contemporary global culture. Her analysis examines one specific historical case of a colonial discourse where the status of women became a marker of the level of civilization. This discourse constructed multiple knowledges about women and gender that have persisted though time in different locations. Mani takes up the topic of *sati* in part because of the ethnocentric gestures by which the topic has been addressed in the global north. Colonial discourses constructed the practice of *sati* for Westerners. In other words, Western feminists know about *sati*, and other cultural practices that they have called gender atrocities, from historical sources that helped to legitimate colonial rule. At the same time, in India, Mani confronts arguments about the practice of *sati* that raise complex gender politics as well. Such arguments seem to hinge on problematic assumptions about women's agency, as if the matter can be settled by knowing the widow's intention. Mani argues that the challenge for transnational feminist scholars is to "straddle different temporalities of struggle." Narayan (Reading 36) speaks to this tension when she talks about the desire both to delineate the suffering of women and yet to shield Indian culture from the nearly automatic (post)colonial criticisms.

Sandra Bartky's essay (Reading 42) takes up the normative configuration of bodies, drawing on Michel Foucault's 1979 book, *Discipline and Punish*. In this "striking critique," Foucault argues that modern society instituted an "unprecedented discipline" that "invades the body and seeks to regulate its very forces and operations, the economy and efficiencies of its movements." For feminist scholars who have long argued that femininity imposes a confining regime on women, Foucauldian analysis of the body provides a rich field of investigation. Bartky applies Foucault's concepts to her investigation of the modern "disciplinary practices that produce a body which in gesture and appearance is recognizably feminine." The key to Foucault's analysis of modern disciplinary power is that it depends on discourses of self-mastery and techniques of self-policing. Thus, Bartky notes the "dual character" of "feminine bodily discipline," it both imposes and involves the "initiative and ingenuity displayed by countless women in an attempt to master the rituals of beauty." Nonetheless, femininity is an "inegalitarian sort" of discipline. The "system aims at turning women into the docile and compliant companions of men just as surely as the army aims to turn its raw recruits into soldiers" (Bartky Reading 42). That is, women's subjectivities are structured, in part, through the mastery of technique and specialized knowledge required to move, adorn, and otherwise manage a feminine body.

Returning to de Beauvoir's observation that "one is not born, but becomes a woman," Judith Butler's piece (Reading 43) offers a theory of gender construction through performative acts. That is, she argues, we are the gender we enact: We become the gender whose normative qualities we perform in and through our actions in daily life. "Social agents *constitute* social reality through language, gesture, and all manner of symbolic social sign[s]" (emphasis in original). Nevertheless, Butler says, gender is not a performance that an individual chooses to engage in. One's subjectivity, indeed one's body, is gendered through these performances, which are "compelled by social sanction and taboo." It is a fiction of liberal humanism that an agent freely chooses to act in certain ways. "[G]ender is in no way a stable identity or locus of agency from which various acts proceed; rather, it is an identity tenuously constituted in time—an identity instituted through a *stylized repetition of acts*" (emphasis in original). But gender also constitutes "an illusion" that we—audience and actor—believe to be real (Reading 43). Gender's construction is concealed by the fiction of its naturalness. Moreover, Butler asserts that gender is a function of the heterosexual social contract. Thus, gender is performed in the service of "the cultivation of bodies into discrete sexes with 'natural' appearances and 'natural' heterosexual dispositions" (Reading 43). Gender performances produce and reproduce the fiction of two distinct and opposite sexes that "naturally" fit together to form the basic unit of society.

Butler wants to understand how this gendering process works at the level of the body in order to change gender performances and thus genders, sexes, and sexualities. "If the ground of gender identity is the stylized repetition of acts through time, … then the possibilities of gender transformation are to be found in the … possibility of a different sort of repeating, in the breaking or subversive repetition of that style" (Reading 43). Drawing on the rich gay cultural tradition of camp, she particularly privileges those subversive performances that parody heterosexual normativity. Drag exposes the underlying contingency of the conventional gender norms enacted in the performance. Rather than expressing a natural essence, drag demonstrates that gender is constituted through those normative acts themselves.

* * *

The contentions between standpoint feminisms and poststructural feminisms revolve around the questions of power and agency. Poststructural feminisms critique the standpoint epistemologies, in particular questioning the transparency of women's experiences upon which standpoint theories seem to rely. From the point of view of poststructural theories, standpoint theories rest on the same reflective/expressive model of language underlying the liberal humanism. Standpoint theories, like liberal humanism, attempt to fix the truth of their insights with the guarantee that experience is a reliable source of knowledge about reality. They seem to assume that an individual, with an already formed sense of identity, has the experience of oppression and, in reflecting on experience through talking with others, sees it clearly. However, as poststructural theory suggests, historically specific discourses within the cultural context in which individuals narrate their experience constitute what can be said. Thus, women's articulations of their experience are already implicated in conventional power relations embedded in the rules of narration. Poststructural feminist theorists argue that standpoint theorists have thus only revalued the discursive content of the category women, but they have not altered the power relations that continue to confine women to that category. Effective oppositional strategies must destabilize the operations of power, not just construct a new subject position from which those power relations can be exercised. Given the power relations that inhere in those narratives of experience, poststructural feminists wonder how those narratives can point to liberation (Stone-Mediatore 2000).

On the other hand, standpoint theorists, notably Nancy Hartsock, respond with their own critique of poststructural feminist theories, suggesting that they provide a poor basis for political resistance. They criticize poststructural theorists for proposing so contingent and contradictory a sense of subjectivity that they remove the ground for feminist agency. If individuals are merely the sites of power struggles among competing discourses, what agency is left to them to think of or engage in resistance? Thus, they suggest that a poststructural theory that defines one's identity primarily as an artifact of dominant power relations exercised in discursive fields disempowers effective political struggle against dominant culture. In addition, without some way to guarantee the accuracy of knowledge, standpoint theorists wonder how feminists can distinguish between the merits of competing discourses about women. If subjects are the effects of discourse, is feminism just as good a discourse about women as any other discourse about women? Experience may well be contradictory and changing, however, standpoint theorists argue that it may be the best strategic basis upon which feminists can ground demands for improving the opportunities for autonomy and freedom for women. In addition, they note, it is at exactly the moment in history when those silenced in much of Western thought give voice to their experiences that Western thought declares that experience is an unreliable source of knowledge. It is at the moment when subordinated social groups are demanding recognition of our self-articulated perspectives that doubt is cast on the status of the subject. Perhaps, then poststructuralist feminism also reproduces dominant operations of power (Hartsock 1990: 163–164; see also Moya Reading 50).

Despite their respective shortcomings and omission, both strands of theory have been enormously generative for feminists. A wealth of scholarship has been produced in the last two decades that draws on one or both of these theoretical traditions.

Notes

1. One important introduction of poststructuralist theory was "Special Section on French Feminism," *Signs* 7 (Autumn 1981): 5–86, which included essays by/about Julia Kristeva, Luce Irigaray, and Helene Cixous. See also Moses 1998b.
2. Individuals, however, experience subjectivity as their own, not as an effect of discourse. Teresa de Lauretis argues that "what one 'perceives and comprehends as subjective' is constructed through a continuous process, an ongoing constant renewal based on an interaction with the world, which she defines as experience." quoted in Alcoff 1988: 423, who summarizes Lauretis' argument nicely in contrast to the humanist subject underlying cultural feminism.

STANDPOINT EPISTEMOLOGIES/ SITUATED KNOWLEDGES

35.
THE FEMINIST STANDPOINT: TOWARD A SPECIFICALLY FEMINIST HISTORICAL MATERIALISM

Nancy C. M. Hartsock

(1983)

The different understandings of power put forward by women who have theorized about power implicitly pose the question of the extent to which gender is a world-view-structuring experience. In this chapter I explore some of the epistemological consequences of claiming that women's lives differ systematically and structurally from those of men. In particular, I suggest that, like the lives of proletarians according to Marxian theory, women's lives make available a particular and privileged vantage point on male supremacy, a vantage point that can ground a powerful critique of the phallocratic institutions and ideology that constitute the capitalist form of patriarchy. I argue that on the basis of the structures that define women's activity as contributors to subsistence and as mothers, the sexual division of labor, one could begin, though not complete, the construction of a feminist standpoint on which to ground a specifically feminist historical materialism. I hope to show how just as Marx's understanding of the world from the standpoint of the proletariat enabled him to go beneath bourgeois ideology, so a feminist standpoint can allow us to descend further into materiality to an epistemological level at which we can better understand both why patriarchal institutions and ideologies take such perverse and deadly forms and how both theory and practice can be redirected in more liberatory directions.

The reader will remember that the concept of a standpoint carries several specific contentions. Most important, it posits a series of levels of reality in which the deeper level both includes and explains the surface or appearance. Related to the positing of levels are several claims:

1. Material life (class position in Marxist theory) not only structures but sets limits on the understanding of social relations.
2. If material life is structured in fundamentally opposing ways for two different groups, one can expect that the vision of each will represent an inversion of the other, and in systems of domination the vision available to the rulers will be both partial and perverse.
3. The vision of the ruling class (or gender) structures the material relations in which all parties are forced to participate and therefore cannot be dismissed as simply false.

4. In consequence, the vision available to the oppressed group must be struggled for and represents an achievement that requires both science to see beneath the surface of the social relations in which all are forced to participate and the education that can only grow from struggle to change those relations.

5. As an engaged vision, the understanding of the oppressed, the adoption of a standpoint exposes the real relations among human beings as inhuman, points beyond the present, and carries a historically liberatory role.

Because of its achieved character and its liberatory potential, I use the term "feminist" rather than "women's standpoint." Like the experience of the proletariat, women's experience and activity as a dominated group contains both negative and positive aspects. A feminist standpoint picks out and amplifies the liberatory possibilities contained in that experience.

Women's work in every society differs systematically from men's. I intend to pursue the suggestion that this division of labor is the first, and in some societies the only, division of labor; moreover, it is central to the organization of social labor more generally.[1] On the basis of an account of the sexual division of labor, one should be able to begin to explore the oppositions and differences between women's and men's activity and their consequences for epistemology. While I cannot attempt a complete account, I put forward a schematic and simplified account of the sexual division of labor and its consequences for epistemology. I sketch out a kind of ideal type of the social relations and world view characteristic of men's and women's activity in order to explore the epistemology contained in the institutionalized sexual division of labor. In so doing, I do not mean to attribute this vision to individual women or men (any more than Marx or Lukács meant their theory of class consciousness to apply to any particular worker or group of workers). My focus is instead on institutionalized social practices and on the specific epistemology and ontology manifested by the institutionalized sexual division of labor. Individuals, as individuals, may change their activity in ways that move them outside the outlook embodied in these institutions, but such a move can be significant only when it occurs at the level of society as a whole.

I discuss the "sexual division of labor" rather than "gender division of labor" to stress, first, my desire not to separate the effects of "nature and nurture," or biology and culture, and my belief that the division of labor between women and men cannot be reduced to simply social dimensions. One must distinguish between what Sara Ruddick has termed "invariant and *nearly* unchangeable" features of human life, and those that, despite being "*nearly* universal," are "certainly changeable."[2] Thus the fact that women and not men *bear* children is not (yet) a social choice, but that women and not men rear children in a society structured by compulsory heterosexuality and male dominance is clearly a societal choice. A second reason to use the term "sexual division of labor" is to keep hold of the bodily aspect of existence, perhaps to grasp it overfirmly in an effort to keep it from evaporating altogether. There is some biological, bodily component to human existence. But its size and substantive content will remain unknown until at least the certainly changeable aspects of the sexual division of labor are altered.

On the basis of a schematic account of the sexual division of labor, I begin to fill in the specific content of the feminist standpoint and begin to specify how women's lives structure an understanding of social relations, that is, begin to follow out the epistemological consequences of the sexual division of labor. In addressing the institutionalized sexual division of labor, I propose to lay aside the important differences among women and instead to search for central commonalities across race and class boundaries. I take some justification from the fruitfulness of Marx's similar strategy in constructing a simplified, two-class, two-man model in which everything was exchanged at its value. Marx's schematic account in volume I of *Capital* left out of account such factors as imperialism; the differential wages, work, and working conditions of the Irish; the differences between women, men, and children; and so on. While all these factors are important to the analysis of contemporary capitalism, none changes either Marx's theories of surplus value or alienation, the two most fundamental features of the Marxian analysis of capitalism. My effort here takes a similar form, in an attempt to move toward a theory of the extraction and appropriation of women's activity and women themselves. Still, I adopt this strategy with some reluctance, since it contains the danger of making invisible the experience of lesbians or women of color.[3] At the same time, I recognize that the effort to uncover a feminist standpoint assumes that there are some things common to all women's lives in Western class societies.

The feminist standpoint that emerges through an examination of women's activities is related to the proletarian standpoint, but deepergoing. Women and workers inhabit a world in which the emphasis is on change rather than stasis, a world characterized by interaction with natural substances rather than separation from nature, a world in which quality is more important than quantity, a world in which the unification of mind and body is inherent in the activities performed. Yet there are some important differences, differences marked by the fact that the proletarian (if male) is immersed in this world only during the time his labor power is being used by the capitalist. If, to paraphrase Marx, we follow the worker home from the factory, we can once again perceive a change in the *dramatis personae*. He who before followed behind as the worker, timid and holding back, with nothing to expect but a hiding, now strides in front, while a third person, not specifically present in Marx's account of the transactions between capitalist and worker (both of whom are male) follows timidly behind, carrying groceries, baby, and diapers.

Given what has been said about the life activity of the proletarian, one can see that, because the sexual division of labor means that much of the work involved in reproducing labor power is done by women, and because much of the male worker's contact with nature outside the factory is mediated by a women, the vision of reality which grows from the female experience is deeper and more thoroughgoing than that available to the worker.

The Sexual Division of Labor

Women's activity as institutionalized has a double aspect: their contribution to subsistence and their contribution to childrearing. Whether or not all women do both, women as a sex are institutionally responsible for producing both goods and human beings, and all women are forced to become the kinds of persons who can do both. Although the nature of women's contribution to subsistence varies immensely over time and space, my primary focus here is on capitalism, with a secondary focus on the class societies that preceded it.[4] In capitalism, women contribute both production for wages and production of goods in the home, that is, they, like men, sell their labor power and produce both commodities and surplus value, and produce use values in the home. Unlike men, however, women's lives are institutionally defined by their production of use values in the home.[5] Here we begin to encounter the narrowness of Marx's concept of production. Women's production of use values in the home has not been well understood by socialists. It is no surprise to feminists that Engels, for example, simply asks how women can continue to do the work in the home and also work in production outside the home. Marx, too, takes for granted women's responsibility for household labor. He repeats, as if it were his own, the question of a Belgian factory inspector: If a mother works for wages, "how will [the household's] internal economy be cared for; who will look after the young children; who will get ready the meals, do the washing and mending?"[6]

Let us trace both the outlines and the consequences of women's dual contribution to subsistence in capitalism. Women's labor, like that of the male worker, is contact with material necessity. Their contribution to subsistence, like that of the male worker, involves them in a world in which the relation to nature and to concrete human requirement is central, both in the form of interaction with natural substances whose quality, rather than quantity, is important to the production of meals, clothing, and so forth and in the form of close attention in a different way from men's. While repetition for both the wages and even more in household production involves a unification of mind and body for the purpose of transforming natural substances into socially defined goods. This, too, is true of the labor of the male worker.

There are, however, important differences. First, women as a group work more than men. We are all familiar with the phenomenon of the "double day," and with indications that women work many more hours per week than men.[7] Second, a larger proportion of women's labor time is devoted to the production of use values than men's. Only some of the goods women produce are commodities (however much they live in a society structured by commodity production and exchange). Third, women's production is structured by repetition in a different way from men's. While repetition for both the woman and the male worker may take the form of production of the same object, over and over—whether apple pies or brake linings—women's work in housekeeping involves a repetitious cleaning.[8]

Thus the man, in the process of production, is involved in contact with necessity and interchange with nature as well as with other human beings, but the process of production or work does not consume his whole life. The activity of a woman in the home as well as the work she does for wages keeps her continually in contact with a world of qualities and change. *Her* immersion in the world of use—in concrete, many-qualitied, changing material processes—is more complete than his. And if life itself consists of sensuous activity, the vantage point available to women on the basis of their contribution to subsistence represents an intensification and deepening of the materialist world view available to the producers of commodities in capitalism, an intensification of class consciousness. The availability of this outlook to even nonworking-class women has been strikingly formulated by a novelist: "Washing the toilet used by three males, and the floor and walls around it, is, Mira thought, coming face to face with necessity. And that is why women were saner than men, did not come up with the mad, absurd schemes men developed: they were in touch with necessity, they had to wash the toilet bowl and floor."[9]

The focus on women's subsistence activity rather than men's leads to a model in which the capitalist (male) lives a life structured completely by commodity exchange and not at all by production, and at the farthest distance from contact with concrete material life. The male worker marks a way station on the path to the other extreme— the constant contact with material necessity present in women's contribution to subsistence. There are of course important differences along the lines of race and class. For example, working-class men seem to do more domestic labor than men higher up in the class structure—car repairs, carpentry, and the like. And until very recently, the wage work done by most women of color replicated the housework required by their own households. Still, there are commonalities present in the institutionalized sexual division of labor that makes women responsible for both housework and wage work.

Women's contribution to subsistence, however, represents only a part of women's labor. Women also produce/reproduce men (and other women) on both a daily and a long-term basis. This aspect of women's "production" exposes the deep inadequacies of the concept of production as a description of women's activity. One does not (cannot) produce another human being in anything like the way one produces an object such as a chair. Much more is involved, activity that cannot easily be dichotomized into play or work. Helping another to develop, the gradual relinquishing of control, the experiencing of the human limits of one's actions—all these are important features of women's activity as mothers. Women, as mothers, even more than as workers, are institutionally involved in processes of change and growth, and more than workers, must understand the importance of avoiding excessive control in order to help others grow.[10] The activity involved is far more complex than instrumentally working with others to transform objects. (Interestingly, much of women's wage work—nursing, social work, and some secretarial jobs in particular—requires and depends on the relational and interpersonal skills women learned by being mothered by someone of the same sex.)

This aspect of women's activity, too, is not without consequences. Indeed, it is in the production of men by women and the appropriation of this labor, and women themselves, by men, that the opposition between feminist and masculinist experience and outlook is rooted, and it is here that features of the proletarian vision are enhanced and modified for the woman and diluted for the man. Women's experience in reproduction represents a unity with nature that goes beyond the proletarian experience of interchange with nature. As another theorist has put it, "reproductive labor might be said to combine the functions of the architect and the bee: Like the architect, parturitive woman knows what she is doing; like the bee, she cannot help what she is doing." And just as the worker's acting on the external work changes both the world and the worker's nature, so too "a new life changes the world and the consciousness of the woman."[11] In addition, in the process of producing human beings, relations with others may take a variety of forms with deeper significance than simple cooperation with others for common goals—forms that range from a deep unity with another through the many-leveled and changing connections mothers experience with growing children. Finally, women's experience in bearing and rearing children involves a unity of mind and body more profound than is possible in the worker's instrumental activity.

Motherhood in the large sense, that is, motherhood as an institution rather than an experience, including pregnancy and the preparation for motherhood almost all female children receive in being raised by a woman, results in the construction of female existence as centered within a complex relational nexus.[12] One aspect of this relational existence is centered on the experience of living in a woman's rather than a man's body. There are a series of what our culture treats as boundary challenges inherent in female physiology, challenges that make it difficult to maintain rigid separation from the object world. Menstruation, coitus, pregnancy, childbirth, lactation—all represent challenges to bodily boundaries.[13] Adrienne Rich has described the experience of pregnancy as one in which the embryo was both inside and yet "daily more separate, on its way to becoming separate from me and of-itself. In early pregnancy the stirring of the fetus felt like ghostly tremors of my own body, later like the movements of a being imprisoned in me; but both sensations were *my* sensations, contributing to my own sense of physical and psychic space."[14]

In turn, the fact that women but not men are primarily responsible for young children means that the infant first experiences itself as not fully differentiated from the mother and then as an *I* in relation to an *It* that it later comes to know as female.[15] Nancy Chodorow and Jane Flax have argued that the object-relations school of psychoanalytic theory puts forward a materialist psychology, one that I propose to treat as a kind of empirical hypothesis. If the account of human development provided by object relations is correct, one ought to expect to find consequences—both psychic and social.[16] According to object-relations theory, the process of differentiation from a woman, by both boys and girls, reinforces boundary confusion in women's egos and boundary strengthening in men's. Individuation is far more conflictual for male than for female children, in part because both mother and son experience the other as a definite "other." The experience of oneness on the part of both mother and infant seems to last longer with girls.[17]

The complex relational world inhabited by women has its start in the experience and resolution of the oedipal crisis, cleanly resolved for the boy, whereas the girl is much more likely to retain both parents as love objects. The nature of the crisis itself differs by sex: The boy's love for the mother is an extension of mother–infant unity and thus essentially threatening to his ego and independence. Masculine ego formation necessarily requires repressing this first relation and negating the mother.[18] In contrast, the girl's love for the father is less threatening both because it occurs outside this unity and because it occurs at a later stage of development. For boys, the central issue to be resolved concerns gender identification; for girls, the issue is psychosexual development.[19] Chodorow concludes that girls' gradual emergence from the oedipal period takes place in such a way that empathy is built into their primary definition of self, and they have a variety of capacities for experiencing another's needs or feelings as their own. Put another way, girls, because of female parenting, are less differentiated from others than boys, more continuous with and related to the external object world. They are differently oriented to their inner object world as well.[20]

The more complex female relational world is reinforced by the process of socialization. Girls learn roles from watching their mothers; boys must learn roles from rules that structure the life of an absent male figure. Girls can identify with a concrete example present in daily life; boys must identify with an abstract set of maxims only occasionally concretely present in the form of the father. Thus, not only do girls learn roles with more interpersonal and relational skills, but the process of role learning itself is embodied in the concrete relation with the mother. The male, in contrast, must identify with an abstract, cultural stereotype and learn abstract behaviors not attached to a well-known person. Masculinity is idealized for boys, whereas femininity is concrete for girls.[21]

Women and men, then, grow up with personalities affected by different boundary experiences, differently constructed and experienced inner and outer worlds, and pre-occupations with different relational issues. This early experience forms an important ground for the feminine sense of self as connected to the world and the masculine sense of self as separate, distinct, and even disconnected. By retaining the preoedipal attachment to the mother, girls come to define and experience themselves as continuous with others. In sum, girls enter adulthood with a more complex layering of affective ties and a rich, ongoing inner set of object relations. Boys, with a simpler oedipal situation and a clear and early resolution, have repressed ties to another. As a result, women define and experience themselves relationally, and men do not.[22]

Chodorow's argument receives support from Robert Stroller's work on sexual excitement and his search for the roots of adult sexual behavior in infant experience. Attempting to understand why men are more perverse than women (i.e., why men's sexual excitement seems to require more gross hostility than women's) led him to suggest that boys may face more difficulties in individuating than girls.[23] He puts forward a theory of what he terms "primary femininity." Because the male infant is merged with the mother, who is a woman, the boy may experience himself as female. Stoller suggests that it may be that the boy does not start out as heterosexual, as Freud thought, but must separate himself to achieve heterosexuality. The oneness with the mother must be counteracted.[24] Thus, "masculinity in males starts as a movement away from the blissful and dangerous, forever remembered and forever yearned for, mother–infant symbiosis.[25] To become masculine, the boy must separate himself both externally from his mother's body, and within himself, from his own already formed primary identification with femininity.[26] This requires the construction of barriers to femininity directed both inward and outward. The mother may be represented as an evil creature, a witch, to counteract the wish to merge with her. Or the barrier may be constructed and sustained by fantasies of harming the mother.[27] Inwardly, the boy must develop a character structure that forces the feminine part of himself down and out of awareness.[28] …

Abstract Masculinity and the Feminist Standpoint

This excursion into psychoanalytic theory has served to point to the differences in men's and women's experience of self resulting from the sexual division of labor in childrearing. These different psychic experiences both structure and are reinforced by the differing patterns of men's and women's activity required by the sexual division of labor, and are thereby replicated as epistemology and ontology. This differential life activity in class society leads on the one hand toward a feminist standpoint and on the other toward an abstract masculinity.

Because the problem for the boy is to distinguish himself from the mother and protect himself against the real threat she poses for his identity, his conflictual and oppositional efforts lead to the formation of rigid ego boundaries. The way Freud takes for granted the rigid distinction between the "me and not-me" makes the point well: "Normally, there is nothing of which we are more certain than the feeling of ourself, of our own ego. This ego appears to us as something autonomous and unitary, marked off distinctly from everything else." At least toward the outside, "the ego seems to maintain clear and sharp lines of demarcation."[29] Thus, the boy's construction of self in opposition to unity with the mother, his construction of identity as differentiation from the mother, sets a hostile and combative dualism at the heart of both the community men construct and the masculinity world view by means of which they understand their lives. ...

The construction of the self in opposition to another who threatens one's very being reverberates throughout the construction of both class society and the masculinist world view and results in a deep-going and hierarchical dualism. First, the man's experience is characterized by the duality of concrete versus abstract.[30] Material reality as experienced by the boy in the family provides no model, and is unimportant in the attainment of masculinity. Nothing of value to the boy occurs within the family, and masculinity becomes an abstract ideal to be achieved over the opposition of daily life.[31] Masculinity must be attained by means of opposition to the concrete world of daily life, by escaping from contact with the female world of the household into the masculine world of politics or public life. This experience of two worlds, one valuable, if abstract and deeply unattainable, the other useless and demeaning, if concrete and necessary, lies at the heart of a series of dualisms—abstract/concrete, mind/body, culture/nature, ideal/real, stasis/change. And these dualisms are overlaid by gender; only the first of each pair is associated with the male.

Dualism, along with the dominance of one side of the dichotomy over the other, marks phallocentric society and social theory. These dualisms appear in a variety of forms—in philosophy, sexuality, technology, political theory, and the organization of class society itself. ...

The oedipal roots of these hierarchical dualisms are memorialized in the overlay of masculine and feminine connotations. It is not accidental that women are associated with quasi-human and nonhuman nature, that the woman is associated with the body and material life, that the lives of women are systematically used as examples to characterize the lives of those ruled by their bodies rather than their minds.[32]

Both the fragility and fundamental falseness of the masculinist ideology and the deeply problematic nature of the social relations from which it grows are apparent in its reliance on a series of counterfactual assumptions and contentions. Consider how the following contentions run counter to lived experience: The body is both irrelevant and in opposition to the (real) self, an impediment to be overcome by the mind; the female mind either does not exist (Do women have souls?) or works in such incomprehensible ways as to be unintelligible (the "enigma of woman"); what is real and primary is imperceptible to the senses and impervious to nature and natural change. What is remarkable is not only that these contentions have absorbed a great deal of philosophical energy but, along with a series of other counterfactuals, have structured social relations for centuries.

Interestingly enough, the epistemology and society constructed by men, suffering from the effects of abstract masculinity, have a great deal in common with the society and ideology imposed by commodity exchange. The separation and opposition of social and natural worlds, of abstract and concrete, of permanence and change, the effort to define only the former of each pair as important, the reliance on a series of counterfactual assumptions—all this is shared with the exchange abstraction. Abstract masculinity shares still another of its aspects with the exchange abstraction: It forms the basis for an even more problematic social synthesis. Hegel's analysis makes clear the problematic social relations available to the self that maintains itself by opposition: Each of the two subjects struggling for recognition tries to kill the other. But if the other is killed, the subject is once again alone. In sum, then, masculine experience when replicated as epistemology leads to a world conceived as (and in fact) inhabited by a number of fundamentally hostile others whom one comes to know by means of opposition (even death struggle) and yet with whom one must construct a social relation in order to survive.

Women's construction of self in relation to others leads in an opposite direction— toward opposition to dualisms of any sort; valuation of concrete, everyday life; a sense of a variety of connectednesses and continuities both with other persons and with the natural world. If material life structures consciousness, women's relationally defined existence, bodily experience of boundary challenges, and activity of transforming both physical objects and human beings must be expected to result in a world view to which dichotomies are foreign. Women experience others and themselves along a continuum whose dimensions are evidenced in Adrienne Rich's argument that the child carried for nine months can be defined "*neither* as me or as not-me," and she argues that inner and outer are not polar opposites but a continuum.[33] What the sexual division of labor defines as women's work turns on issues of change rather than stasis—the changes involved in producing both use values and commodities, but more profoundly in the activity of rearing human beings who change in both more subtle and more autonomous ways than any inanimate object. Not only the qualities of things but also the qualities of people are important in women's work; quantity becomes peripheral. In addition, far more than the instrumental cooperation of the workplace is required; the mother-child relation and the maintenance of the family, while it has instrumental aspects, is not defined by them. Finally, the unity of mental and manual labor and the directly sensuous nature of much of women's work leads to a more profound unity of mental and manual labor, social and natural worlds, than is experienced by the male worker in capitalism. The unity grows from the fact that women's bodies, unlike men's, can be themselves instruments of production: In pregnancy, giving birth, or lactation, arguments about a division of mental from manual labor are fundamentally foreign.

That this is indeed women's experience is documented in both the theory and practice of the contemporary women's movement and needs no further development here.[34] The more important question here is whether women's experience and the world view constructed by women's activity can meet the criteria for a standpoint. If we return to the five claims carried by the concept of a standpoint it seems clear that women's material life activity has important epistemological and ontological consequences for both the understanding and construction of social relations. Women's activity, then, does satisfy the first requirement for a standpoint.

I can now take up the second claim made by a standpoint: that women's experience not only inverts that of men but forms a basis on which to expose abstract masculinity as both partial and fundamentally perverse, as not only occupying only one side of the dualities it has constructed but reversing the proper valuation of human activity. The partiality of the masculinist vision and of the societies that support this understanding is evidenced by its confinement of activity proper to the man to only one side of the dualisms. Its perverseness, however, lies elsewhere. Perhaps the most dramatic (though not the only) reversal of the proper order of things characteristic of masculine experience is the substitution of death for life.

The substitution of death for life results at least in part from the sexual division of labor in childrearing. The self surrounded by rigid ego boundaries, certain of what is inner and what is outer, the self experienced as walled city, is discontinuous with others. Georges Bataille has made brilliantly clear the ways in which death emerges as the only possible solution to this discontinuity and has followed the logic through to argue that reproduction itself must be understood, not as the creation of life, but as death. The core experience to be understood is that of discontinuity and its consequences. As a consequence of this experience of discontinuity and aloneness, penetration of ego boundaries, or fusion with another, is experienced as violent. The pair "lover-assailant" is not accidental. Nor is the connection of reproduction and death.

"Reproduction," Bataille argues, "implies the existence of *discontinuous* beings." This is so because "beings which reproduce themselves are distinct from one another, and those reproduced are likewise distinct from each other, just as they are distinct from their parents. Each being is distinct from all others. His birth, his death, the events of his life may have an interest for others, but he alone is directly concerned in them. He is born alone. He dies alone. Between one being and another, there is a *gulf*, a discontinuity."[35] (Clearly the gulf of which he speaks is better characterized as a chasm.) In reproduction, sperm and ovum unite to form a new entity, but they do so from the death and disappearance of two separate beings. Thus, the new entity bears death with itself.

Although death and reproduction are intimately linked, Bataille stresses that "it is only death which is to be identified with [the transition to] continuity," he holds to this position despite his recognition that reproduction is a form of growth. The growth, however, he dismisses as not "ours," as being only "impersonal."[36] This is not the female experience, in which reproduction is hardly impersonal, nor experienced as death. It is, of course, in a literal sense, the sperm that is cut off from its source and lost. Perhaps we should not wonder, then, at the masculinist preoccupation with death, and the feeling that growth is "impersonal," not of fundamental concern to oneself. Beneath Bataille's theorization of continuity as death lies the conflictual individuation of the boy: Continuity with another, continuity with the mother, carries not just danger but inevitable death as a separate being. But this complete dismissal of the experience of another bespeaks a profound lack of empathy and refusal to recognize the very being of another. It manifests the chasm that separates each man from every other being and from the natural world, the chasm that marks and defines the problem of community.

The preoccupation with death instead of life appears as well in the argument that is the ability to kill (and for centuries, the practice) that sets humans above animals. Even Simone de Beauvoir has accepted that "it is not in giving life but in risking life that man is raised above the animal: that is why superiority has been accorded in humanity not to the sex that brings forth but to that which kills."[37] That superiority has been accorded to the sex which kills is beyond doubt. But what kind of vision can take reproduction, the creation of new life, and the force of life in sexuality, and turn it into death, not just in theory but in the practice of rape and sexual murder? Any why give pride of place to killing? That is not only an inversion of the proper order of things but also a refusal to recognize the real activities in which men as well as women are engaged. The producing of goods and the reproducing of human beings are certainly life-sustaining activities. And even the deaths of the ancient heroes in search of undying fame were pursuits of life and represented the attempt to avoid death by attaining immortality. The search for life, then, represents the deeper reality that lies beneath the glorification of death and destruction.

Yet one cannot dismiss the substitution of death for life as simply false. Men's power to structure social relations in their own image means that women too must participate in social relations that manifest and express abstract masculinity. The most important life activities have consistently been held by the powers that be to be unworthy of those who are fully human, most centrally because of their close connections with necessity and life: motherwork (the rearing of children), housework, and until the rise of capitalism in the West any work necessary to subsistence. In addition, these activities in contemporary capitalism are all constructed in ways that systematically degrade and destroy the minds and bodies of those who perform them.[38] The organization of motherhood as an institution in which a woman is alone with her children, the isolation of women from each other in domestic labor, the female pathology of loss of self in service to others—all mark the transformation of life into death, the distortion of what could have been creative and communal activity into oppressive toil, and the destruction of the possibility of community present in women's relational self-definition. The ruling gender's and class's interest in maintaining social relations such as these is evidenced by the fact that when women set up other structures in which the mother is not alone with her children, isolated from others, as is frequently the case in working-class communities or the communities of people of color, these arrangements are described as pathological deviations.

The real destructiveness of the social relations characteristic of abstract masculinity, however, is now concealed beneath layers of ideology. Marxian theory needed to go beneath the surface to discover the different levels of determination that defined the relation of capitalist and (male) worker. These levels of determination and laws of motion or tendency of phallocratic society must be worked out on the basis of female experience. This brings me to the fourth claim for a standpoint: its character as an achievement of both analysis and political struggle occurring in a particular historical space. The fact that class divisions should have proved so resistant to analysis and required such a prolonged political struggle before Marx was able to formulate the theory of surplus value indicates the difficulty of this accomplishment. And despite the time that has passed since the theory was worked out, rational control of production has yet to be achieved.

Feminists have only begun the process of revaluing the female experience, searching for the common threads that connect the diverse experiences of women, and searching for the structural determinants of these experiences. The difficulty of the problem faced by feminist theory can be illustrated by the fact that it required a struggle even to define household labor, if not done for wages, as work, to argue that what are held to be acts of love instead must be recognized as work.[39] Both the revaluation of women's experience and the use of this experience as a ground for critique are required. That is, the liberatory possibilities present in women's experience must be, in a sense, read out and developed. Thus, a feminist standpoint may be present on the basis of the commonalities within women's experience, but it is neither self-evident nor obvious.

Finally, because it provides a way to reveal the perverseness and inhumanity of human relations, a standpoint forms the basis for moving beyond these relations. Just as the proletarian standpoint emerges out of the contradiction between appearance and essence in capitalism, understood as essentially historical and constituted by the relation of capitalist and worker, the feminist standpoint emerges both out of the contradiction between the systematically differing structures of men's and women's life activity in Western cultures. It expresses women's experience at a particular time and place, located within a particular set of social relations. Capitalism, Marx noted, could not develop fully until the notion of human equality achieved the status of universal truth.[40] Despite women's exploitation, both as unpaid reproducers of the labor force and as a sex-segregated labor force available for low wages, then, capitalism poses problems for the continued oppression of women. Just as capitalism enables the proletariat to raise the possibility of a society free from class domination, so too it provides space to raise the possibility of a society free from all forms of domination. The articulation of a feminist standpoint based on women's relational self-definition and activity exposes the world men have constructed and the self-understanding that manifests these social relations as both partial and perverse. More important, by drawing out the potentiality available in the actuality and thereby exposing the inhumanity of human relations, it embodies a distress that requires a solution. The experience of continuity and relation—with others, with the natural world, of mind with body—provide an ontological base for developing a nonproblematic social synthesis, a social synthesis that need not operate through the denial of the body, the attack on nature, or the death struggle between the self and other, a social synthesis that does not depend on any of the forms taken by abstract masculinity.

What is necessary is the generalization of the potentiality made available by the activity of women—the defining of society as a whole as propertyless producer both of use values and of human beings. To understand what such a transformation would require, we should consider what is involved in the partial transformation represented by making the whole of society into propertyless producers of use values: socialist revolution. The abolition of the division between mental and manual labor cannot take place simply by means of adopting worker self-management techniques, but instead requires the abolition of private property, the seizure of state power, and lengthy post-revolutionary class struggle. Thus I am not suggesting that shared parenting arrangements can abolish the sexual division of labor. Doing away with this division of labor would of course require institutionalizing the participation of both women and men in childrearing. But just as the rational and conscious control of the production of goods and services requires a vast and far-reaching social transformation, so too the rational and conscious organization of reproduction would entail the transformation both of *every* human relation and of human relations to the natural world. The magnitude of the task is apparent if one asks what a society without institutionalized gender differences might look like.

Generalizing the human possibilities present in the life activity of women to the social system as a whole would raise, for the first time in human history, the possibility of a fully human community, a community structured by a variety of connections rather than separation and opposition. One can conclude then that women's life activity does form the basis of a specifically feminist materialism, a materialism that can provide a point from which to both critique and work against phallocratic ideology and institutions.

Notes

1. This is Iris Young's point I am indebted to her persuasive arguments for taking what she terms the "gender differentiation of labor" as a central category of analysis. See Young, "Dual Systems Theory," *Socialist Review* 50, 51 (March–June 1980): 185. My use of this category, however, differs to some extent from hers. Young focuses on the societal aspects of the division of labor and chooses to use the term "gender division" to indicate that focus. I want to include the relation to the natural world as well. In addition, Young's analysis of women in capitalism does not seem to include marriage as a part of the division of labor. She is more concerned with the division of labor in capitalism in the productive sector.
2. See Sara Ruddick, "Maternal Thinking," *Feminist Studies* 6, no. 2 (Summer 1980): 364.
3. See, for a discussion of this danger, Adrienne Rich, "Disloyal of Civilization," in *On Lies, Secrets, and Silence* (New York: Norton, 1979), pp. 275–310; Elly Bulkin, "Racism and Writing," *Sinister Wisdom*, no. 6 (Spring 1980); bell hooks, *Ain't I a Woman* (Boston: South End Press, 1981), p. 138.
4. Some cross-cultural evidence indicates that the status of women varies with the work they do. To the extent that women and men contribute equally to subsistence, women's status is higher than it would be if their subsistence work differed profoundly from that of men; that is, if they do none or almost all of the work of subsistence, their status remains low. See Peggy Sanday, "Female Status in the Public Domain," in *Woman, Culture and Society*, ed. Michelle Rosaldo

and Louise Lamphere (Stanford: Stanford University Press, 1974), p. 199. See also Iris Young's account of the sexual division of labor in capitalism, mentioned in note 1.

5. It is irrelevant to my argument here that women's wage labor takes place under different circumstances than men's—that is, their lower wages, their confinement to only a few occupational categories, etc. I am concentrating instead on the formal, structural features of women's work. There has been much effort to argue that women's domestic labor is a source of surplus value, that is, to include it within the scope of Marx's value theory as productive labor, or to argue that since it does not produce surplus value it belongs to an entirely different mode of production, variously characterized as domestic or patriarchal. My strategy here is quite different from this. See, for the British debate, Mariarosa Dalla Costa and Selma James, *The Power of Women and the Subversion of the Community* (Bristol: Falling Wall Press, 1975); Wally Secombe, "The Housewife and Her Labor Under Capitalism," *New Left Review* 83 (January–February 1974); Jean Gardiner, "Women's Domestic Labour," *New Left Review* 89 (March 1975); and Paul Smith, "Domestic Labour and Marx's Theory of Value," in *Feminism and Materialism*, eds Annette Kuhn and Ann Marie Wolpe (Boston: Routledge and Kegan Paul, 1978). A portion of the American debate can be found in Ira Gerstein, "Domestic Work and Capitalism," and Lisa Vogel, "The Earthly Family," *Radical America* 7, nos. 4/5 (July-October 1973); Ann Ferguson, "Women as a New Revolutionary Class," in *Between Labor and Capital*, ed. Pat Walker (Boston: South End Press, 1979).

6. Frederick Engels, *Origins of the Family, Private Property and the State* (New York: International Publishers 1942); Karl Marx, *Capital* (New York: International Publishers, 1967) 1: 671. Marx and Engels have also described the sexual division of labor as natural or spontaneous. See Mary O'Brien, "Reproducing Marxist Man," in *The Sexism of Social and Political Thought*, ed. Lorenne Clark and Lynda Lange (Toronto: University of Toronto Press, 1979).

7. For a discussion of women's work, see Elise Boulding, "Familial Constraints of Women's Work Roles," in *Women and the Workplace*, ed. Martha Blaxall and B. Reagan (Chicago: University of Chicago Press, 1976), esp. pp. 111, 113. An interesting historical note is provided by the fact that Nausicaa, the daughter of a Homeric king, did the household laundry. See M. I. Finley, *The World of Odysseus* (Middlesex, England: Penguin, 1979), p. 73. While aristocratic women were less involved in actual labor, the difference was one of degree. And as Aristotle remarked in the *Politics*, supervising slaves is not a particularly uplifting activity. The life of leisure and philosophy, so much the goal for aristocratic Athenian men, then, was almost unthinkable for any woman.

8. Simone de Beauvoir holds that repetition has a deeper significance and that women's biological destiny itself is repetition. See *The Second Sex*, trans. H. M. Parshley (New York: Knopf, 1953), p. 59. But see also her discussion of housework in ibid., pp. 423 ff. There, her treatment of housework is strikingly negative. For her the transcendence of humanity is provided in the historical struggle of self with other and with the natural world. The oppositions she sees are not really stasis vs. change, but rather transcendence, escape from the muddy concreteness of daily life.

9. Marilyn French, *The Women's Room* (New York: Jove, 1978), p. 214.

10. Sara Ruddick, "Maternal Thinking," presents an interesting discussion of these and other aspects of the thought which emerges from the activity of mothering. Although I find it difficult to speak the language of interests and demands she uses, she brings out several valuable points. Her distinction between maternal and scientific thought is very intriguing and potentially useful (see esp. pp. 350–53).

11. Mary O'Brien, "Reproducing Marxist Man," p. 115, n. 11.

12. It should be understood that I am concentrating here on the experience of women in Western culture. There are a number of cross-cultural differences that can be expected to have some effect. See, for example, the differences that emerge from a comparison of childrearing in ancient Greek society with that of the contemporary Mbuti in central Africa. See Philip Slater, *The Glory of Hera* (Boston: Beacon, 1968); and Colin Turnbull, "The Politics of Non-Aggression," in *Learning Non-Aggression*, ed. Ashley Montagu (New York: Oxford University Press, 1978). See also Isaac Balbus, *Marxism and Domination* (Princeton: Princeton University Press, 1982).

13. See Nancy Chodorow, "Family Structure and Female Personality," in Rosaldo and Lamphere, *Women, Culture, and Society*, p. 59.

14. Adrienne Rich, *Of Woman Born* (New York: Norton, 1976), p. 63.

15. I rely on the analyses of Dinnerstein and Chodorow but there are difficulties in that they are attempting to explain why humans, both male and female, fear and hate the female. My purpose here is to invert their arguments and to attempt to put forward a positive account of the epistemological consequences of this situation. What follows is a summary of Nancy Chodorow, *The Reproduction of Mothering* (Berkeley: University of California Press, 1978).

16. See Chodorow, *Reproduction*; and Jane Flax, "The Conflict Between Nurturance and Autonomy in Mother-Daughter Relations and in Feminism," *Feminist Studies* 6, no. 2 (June 1978).

17. Chodorow, *Reproduction*, pp. 105–9.

18. This is Jane Flax's point.

19. Chodorow, *Reproduction*, pp. 127–31, 163.

20. Ibid., p. 166.

21. Ibid., pp. 174–78. Chodorow suggests a correlation between father absence and fear of women (p. 213), and one should, treating this as an empirical hypothesis, expect a series of cultural differences based on the degree of father absence. Here the ancient Greeks and the Mbuti provide a fascinating contrast. (See above, note 12.)

22. Ibid., p. 198. The flexible and diffuse female ego boundaries can of course result in the pathology of loss of self in responsibility for and dependence on others (the obverse of the male pathology of experiencing the self as walled city).

23. He never considers that single-sex childrearing may be the problem and also ascribes total responsibility to the mother for especially the male's successful individuation. See Robert Stoller, *Perversion* (New York: Pantheon, 1975), p. 154 and p. 161, for an awesome list of tasks to be accomplished by the mother.

24. Ibid., pp. 137–38.

25. Ibid., p. 154 See also his discussion of these dynamics in Chapter 2 of Robert Stoller, *Sexual Excitement* (New York: Pantheon, 1979).

26. Stoller, *Perversion*, p. 99.

27. Ibid., pp. 150, 121 respectively.

28. Ibid., p. 150.

29. Sigmund Freud, *Civilization and Its Discontents* (New York: Norton, 1961), pp. 12–13.

30. I use the terms abstract and concrete in a sense much influenced by Marx "Abstraction" refers not only to the practice of searching for universal generalities but also carries derogatory connotations of idealism and partiality. By "concrete," I refer to respect for complexity and multidimensional causality, and mean to suggest as well as a materialism and completeness.

31. Alvin Gouldner has made a similar argument in his contention that the Platonic stress on hierarchy and order resulted from a similarly learned opposition to daily life rooted in the young aristocrat's experience of being taught proper behavior by slaves who could not themselves engage in this behavior. See Gouldner, *Enter Plato* (New York: Basic Books, 1965), pp. 351–55.

32. See Elizabeth Spelman, "Metaphysics and Misogyny" (mimeo). One analyst has argued that its basis lies in the fact that "the early mother, monolithic representative of nature, is a source, like nature, of ultimate distress as well as ultimate joy. Like nature, she is both nourishing and disappointing, both alluring and threatening ... The infant loves her ... and it hates her because, like nature, she does not perfectly protect and provide for it. ... The mother, then—like nature, which sends blizzards and locusts as well as sunshine and strawberries—is perceived as capricious, sometimes actively malevolent." Dorothy Dinnerstein, *The Mermaid and the Minotaur* (New York: Harper & Row, 1976), p. 95.

33. Rich, *Of Woman Born*, pp. 64, 167. For a similar descriptive account, but a dissimilar analysis, see David Bakan, *The Duality of Human Existence* (Boston: Beacon Press, 1966).

34. My arguments are supported with remarkable force by both the theory and practice of the contemporary women's movement. In theory, this appears in different forms in the work of Dorothy Riddle, "New Visions of Spiritual Power," *Quest: a feminist quarterly* 1, no. 3 (Spring 1975); Griffin, *Woman and Nature*, esp. Book IV, "The Separate Rejoined"; Rich, *Of Woman Born*, esp. pp. 62–68; Linda Thurston, "On Male and Female Principle," *The Second Wave* 1, no 2 (Summer 1971). In feminist political organizing, this vision has been expressed as an opposition of

leadership and hierarchy, as an effort to prevent the development of organizations divided into leaders and followers. It has also taken the forms of an insistence on the unity of the personal and the political, a stress on the concrete rather than on abstract principles (an opposition to theory), and a stress on the politics of everyday life. For a fascinating and early example, see Pat Mainardi, "The Politics of Housework," in *Voices of Women's Liberation*, ed. Leslie Tanner (New York: New American Library, 1970).

35. Georges Bataille, *Death and Sensuality* (New York: Arno Press, 1977), p. 12; italics mine.

36. Ibid., pp. 95–96.

37. de Beauvoir, *The Second Sex*, p. 58.

38. Consider, for example, Rich's discussion of pregnancy and childbirth, chaps. 6, 7, and *Of Woman Born*. And see also Charlotte Perkins Gilman's discussion of domestic labor in *The Home* (Urbana, Ill.: University of Illinois Press, 1972).

39. The Marxist-feminist efforts to determine whether housework produces surplus value and the feminist political strategy of demanding wages for housework represent two (mistaken) efforts to recognize women's activity as work.

40. Marx, *Capital*, 1: 60.

36.
THE PROJECT OF FEMINIST EPISTEMOLOGY: PERSPECTIVES FROM A NONWESTERN FEMINIST

Uma Narayan

(1989)

A fundamental thesis of feminist epistemology is that our location in the world as women makes it possible for us to perceive and understand different aspects of both the world and human activities in ways that challenge the male bias of existing perspectives. Feminist epistemology is a particular manifestation of the general insight that the nature of women's experiences as individuals and as social beings, our contributions to work, culture, knowledge, and our history and political interests have been systematically ignored or misrepresented by mainstream discourses in different areas.

Women have been often excluded from prestigious areas of human activity (for example, politics or science) and this has often made these activities seem clearly "male." In areas where women were not excluded (for example, subsistence work), their contribution has been misrepresented as secondary and inferior to that of men. Feminist epistemology sees mainstream theories about various human enterprises, including mainstream theories about human knowledge, as one-dimensional and deeply flawed because of the exclusion and misrepresentation of women's contributions.

Feminist epistemology suggests that integrating women's contribution into the domain of science and knowledge will not constitute a mere adding of details; it will not merely widen the canvas but result in a shift of perspective enabling us to see a very different picture. The inclusion of women's perspective will not merely amount to women participating in greater numbers in the existing practice of science and knowledge, but it will change the very nature of these activities and their self-understanding.

It would be misleading to suggest that feminist epistemology is a homogenous and cohesive enterprise. Its practitioners differ both philosophically and politically in a number of significant ways (Harding 1986). But an important theme on its agenda has been to undermine the abstract, rationalistic, and universal image of the scientific enterprise by using several different strategies. It has studied, for instance, how contingent historical factors have colored both scientific theories and practices and provided the (often sexist) metaphors in which scientists have conceptualized their activity (Bordo 1986; Keller 1985; Harding and O'Barr 1987). It has tried to reintegrate values and emotions into our account of our cognitive activities, arguing for both the inevitability of their presence and the importance of the contributions they are capable of making to our knowledge (Gilligan 1982; Jaggar [1989] and Tronto [1989]). It has also attacked various sets of dualisms characteristic of western philosophical thinking—reason versus emotion, culture versus nature, universal versus particular—in which the first of each set is identified with science, rationality, and the masculine and the second is relegated to the nonscientific, the nonrational, and the feminine (Harding and Hintikka 1983; Lloyd 1984; Wilshire [1989]).

At the most general level, feminist epistemology resembles the efforts of many oppressed groups to reclaim for themselves the value of their own experience. The writing of novels that focused on working-class life in England or the lives of black people in the United States shares a motivation similar to that of feminist epistemology—to depict an experience different from the norm and to assert the value of this difference.

In a similar manner, feminist epistemology also resembles attempts by third-world writers and historians to document the wealth and complexity of local economic and social structures that existed prior to colonialism. These attempts are useful for their ability to restore to colonized peoples a sense of the richness of their own history and culture. These projects also mitigate the tendency of intellectuals in former colonies who are westernized through their education to think that anything western is necessarily better and more "progressive." In some cases, such studies help to preserve the knowledge of many local arts, crafts, lore, and techniques that were part of the former way of life before they are lost not only to practice but even to memory.

These enterprises are analogous to feminist epistemology's project of restoring to women a sense of the richness of their history, to mitigate our tendency to see the stereotypically "masculine" as better or more progressive, and to preserve for posterity the contents of "feminine" areas of knowledge and expertise—medical lore, knowledge associated with the practices of childbirth and child rearing, traditionally feminine crafts, and so on. Feminist epistemology, like these other enterprises, must attempt to balance the assertion of the value of a different culture or experience against the dangers of romanticizing it to the extent that the limitations and oppressions it confers on its subjects are ignored.

My essay will attempt to examine some dangers of approaching feminist theorizing and epistemological values in a noncontextual and nonpragmatic way, which could convert important feminist insights and theses into feminist epistemological dogmas. I will use my perspective as a nonwestern, Indian feminist to examine critically the predominantly Anglo-American project of feminist epistemology and to reflect on what such a project might signify for women in nonwestern cultures in general and for nonwestern feminists in particular. I will suggest that different cultural contexts and political agendas may cast a very different light on both the "idols" and the "enemies" of knowledge as they have characteristically been typed in western feminist epistemology.

In keeping with my respect for contexts, I would like to stress that I do not see nonwestern feminists as a homogenous group and that none of the concerns I express as a nonwestern feminist may be pertinent to or shared by all nonwestern feminists, although I do think they will make sense to many. ...

Nonwestern Feminist Politics and Feminist Epistemology

Some themes of feminist epistemology may be problematic for nonwestern feminists in ways that they are not problematic for western feminists. Feminism has a much narrower base in most nonwestern countries. It is primarily of significance to some urban, educated, middle-class, and hence relatively westernized women, like myself. Although feminist groups in these countries do try to extend the scope of feminist concerns to other groups (for example, by fighting for childcare, women's health issues, and equal wages issues through trade union structures), some major preoccupations of western feminism—its critique of marriage, the family, compulsory heterosexuality—presently engage the attention of mainly small groups of middle-class feminists.

These feminists must think and function within the context of a powerful tradition that, although it systematically oppresses women, also contains within itself a discourse that confers a high value on women's place in the general scheme of things. Not only are the roles of wife and mother highly praised, but women also are seen as the cornerstones of the spiritual well-being of their husbands and children, admired for their supposedly higher moral, religious, and spiritual qualities, and so on. In cultures that have a pervasive religious component, like the Hindu culture with which I am familiar, everything seems assigned a place and value as long as it keeps to its place. Confronted with a powerful traditional discourse that values woman's place as long as she keeps to the place prescribed, it may be politically counterproductive for nonwestern feminists to echo uncritically the themes of western feminist epistemology that seek to restore the value, cognitive and otherwise, of "women's experience."

The danger is that, even if the nonwestern feminist talks about the value of women's experience in terms totally different from those of the traditional discourse, the difference is likely to be drowned out by the louder and more powerful voice of the traditional discourse, which will then claim that "what those feminists say" vindicates its view that the roles and experiences it assigns to women have value and that women should stick to those roles.

I do not intend to suggest that this is not a danger for western feminism or to imply that there is no tension for western feminists between being critical of the experiences that their societies have provided for women and finding things to value in them nevertheless. But I am suggesting that perhaps there is less at risk for western feminists in trying to strike this balance. I am inclined to think that in nonwestern countries feminists must still stress the negative sides of the female experience within that culture and that the time for a more sympathetic evaluation is not quite ripe.

But the issue is not simple and seems even less so when another point is considered. The imperative we experience as feminists to be critical of how our culture and traditions oppress women conflicts with our desire as members of once colonized cultures to affirm the value of the same culture and traditions.

There are seldom any easy resolutions to these sorts of tensions. As an Indian feminist currently living in the United States, I often find myself torn between the desire to communicate with honesty the miseries and oppressions that I think my own culture confers on its women and the fear that this communication is going to reinforce, however unconsciously, western prejudices about the "superiority" of western culture. I have often felt compelled to interrupt my communication, say on the problems of the Indian system of arranged marriages, to remind my western friends that the experiences of women under their system of "romantic love" seem no more enviable. Perhaps we should all attempt to cultivate the methodological habit of trying to understand the complexities of the oppression involved in different historical and cultural settings while eschewing, at least for now, the temptation to make comparisons across such settings, given the dangers of attempting to compare what may well be incommensurable in any neat terms.

The Nonprimacy of Positivism as a Problematic Perspective

As a nonwestern feminist, I also have some reservations about the way in which feminist epistemology seems to have picked positivism as its main target of attack. The choice of positivism as the main target is reasonable because it has been a dominant and influential western position and it most clearly embodies some flaws that feminist epistemology seeks to remedy.

But this focus on positivism should not blind us to the facts that it is not our only enemy and that nonpositivist frameworks are not, by virtue of that bare qualification, any more worthy of our tolerance. Most traditional frameworks that nonwestern feminists regard as oppressive to women are not positivist, and it would be wrong to see feminist epistemology's critique of positivism given the same political importance for nonwestern feminists that it has for western feminists. Traditions like my own, where the influence of religion is pervasive, are suffused through and through with values. We must fight not frameworks that assert the separation of fact and value but frameworks that are pervaded by values to which we, as feminists, find ourselves opposed. Positivism in epistemology flourished at the same time as liberalism in western political theory. Positivism's view of values as individual and subjective related to liberalism's political emphasis on individual rights that were supposed to protect an individual's freedom to live according to the values she espoused.

Nonwestern feminists may find themselves in a curious bind when confronting the interrelations between positivism and political liberalism. As colonized people, we are well aware of the facts that may political concepts of liberalism are both suspicious and confused and that the practice of liberalism in the colonies was marked by brutalities unaccounted for by its theory. However, as feminists, we often find some of its concepts, such as individual rights, very useful in our attempts to fight problems rooted in our traditional cultures.

Nonwestern feminists will no doubt be sensitive to the fact that positivism is not our only enemy. Western feminists too must learn not to uncritically claim any nonpositivist framework as an ally; despite commonalities, there are apt to be many differences. A temperate look at positions we espouse as allies is necessary since "the enemy of my enemy is my friend" is a principle likely to be as misleading in epistemology as it is in the domain of Realpolitik. ....

... [F]eminists should be cautious about assuming that they necessarily have much in common with a framework simply because it is nonpositivist. Nonwestern feminists may be more alert to this error because many problems they confront arise in nonpositivist contexts.

The Political Uses of "Epistemic Privilege"

Important strands in feminist epistemology hold the view that our concrete embodiments as members of a specific class, race, and gender as well as our concrete historical situations necessarily play significant roles in our perspective on the world; moreover, no point of view is "neutral" because no one exists unembedded in the world. Knowledge is seen as gained not by solitary individuals but by socially constituted members of groups that emerge and change through history.

Feminists have also argued that groups living under various forms of oppression are more likely to have a critical perspective on their situation and that this critical view is both generated and partly constituted by critical emotional responses that subjects experience vis-à-vis their life situations. This perspective in feminist epistemology rejects the "Dumb View" of emotions and favors an intentional conception that emphasizes the cognitive aspect of emotions. It is critical of the traditional view of the emotions as wholly and always impediments to knowledge and argues that many emotions often help rather than hinder our understanding of a person or situation (see Jaggar [1989] Reading 44).

Bringing together these views on the role of the emotions in knowledge, the possibility of critical insights being generated by oppression, and the contextual nature of knowledge may suggest some answers to serious and interesting political questions. I will consider what these epistemic positions entail regarding the possibility of understanding and political cooperation between oppressed groups and sympathetic members of a dominant group—say, between white people and people of color over issues of race or between men and women over issues of gender.

These considerations are also relevant to questions of understanding and cooperation between western and nonwestern feminists. Western feminists, despite their critical understanding of their own culture, often tend to be more a part of it than they realize. If they fail to see the contexts of their theories and assume that their perspective has universal validity for all feminists, they tend to participate in the dominance that western culture has exercised over nonwestern cultures.

Our position must explain and justify our dual need to criticize members of a dominant group (say men or white people or western feminists) for their lack of attention to or concern with problems that affect an oppressed group (say, women or people of color or nonwestern feminists, respectively), as well as for our frequent hostility toward those who express interest, even sympathetic interest, in issues that concern groups of which they are not a part.

Both attitudes are often warranted. On the one hand, one cannot but be angry at those who minimize, ignore, or dismiss the pain and conflict that racism and sexism inflict on their victims. On the other hand, living in a state of siege also necessarily makes us suspicious of expressions of concern and support from those who do not live these oppressions. We are suspicious of the motives of our sympathizers or the extent of their sincerity, and we worry, often with good reason, that they may claim that their interest provides a warrant for them to speak for us, as dominant groups throughout history have spoken for the dominated.

This is all the more threatening to groups aware of how recently they have acquired the power to articulate their own points of view. Nonwestern feminists are especially aware of this because they have a double struggle in trying to find their own voice: they have to learn to articulate their differences, not only from their own traditional contexts but also from western feminism.

Politically, we face interesting questions whose answers hinge on the nature and extent of the communication that we think possible between different groups. Should we try to share our perspectives and insights with those who have not lived our oppressions and accept that they may fully come to share them? Or should we seek only the affirmation of those like ourselves, who share common features of oppression, and rule out the possibility of those who have not lived these oppressions ever acquiring a genuine understanding of them?

I argue that it would be a mistake to move from the thesis that knowledge is constructed by human subjects who are socially constituted to the conclusion that those who are differently located socially can never attain *some* understanding of our experience or *some* sympathy with our cause. In that case, we would be committed to not just a perspectival view of knowledge but a relativistic one. Relativism, as I am using it, implies that a person could have knowledge of only the sorts of things she had experienced personally and that she would be totally unable to communicate any of the contents of her knowledge to someone who did not have the same sorts of experiences. Not only does this seem clearly false and perhaps even absurd, but it is probably a good idea not to have any a priori views that would imply either that all our knowledge is always capable of being communicated to every other person or that would imply that some of our knowledge is necessarily incapable of being communicated to some class of persons.

"Nonanalytic" and "nonrational" forms of discourse, like fiction or poetry, may be better able than other forms to convey the complex life experiences of one group to members of another. One can also hope that being part of one oppressed group may enable an individual to have a more sympathetic understanding of issues relating to another kind of oppression—that, for instance, being a woman may sensitize one to issues of race and class even if one is a woman privileged in those respects.

Again, this should not be reduced to some kind of metaphysical presumption. Historical circumstances have sometimes conspired, say, to making working-class men more chauvinistic in some of their attitudes than other men. Sometimes one sort of suffering may simply harden individuals to other sorts or leave them without energy to take any interest in the problems of other groups. But we can at least try to foster such sensitivity by focusing on parallels, not identities, between different sorts of oppressions.

Our commitment to the contextual nature of knowledge does not require us to claim that those who do not inhabit these contexts can never have any knowledge of them. But this commitment does permit us to argue that it is *easier* and *more likely* for the oppressed to have critical insights into the conditions of their own oppression than it is for those who live outside these structures. Those who actually *live* the oppressions of class, race, or gender have faced the issues that such oppressions generate in a variety of different situations. The insights and emotional responses engendered by these situations are a legacy with which they confront any new issue or situation.

Those who display sympathy as outsiders often fail both to understand fully the emotional complexities of living as a member of an oppressed group and to carry what they have learned and understood about one situation to the way they perceive another. It is a commonplace that even sympathetic men will often fail to perceive subtle instances of sexist behavior or discourse.

Sympathetic individuals who are not members of an oppressed group should keep in mind the possibility of this sort of failure regarding their understanding of issues relating to an oppression they do not share. They should realize that nothing they may do, from participating in demonstrations to changing their lifestyles, can make them one of the oppressed. For instance, men who share household and child-rearing responsibilities with women are mistaken if they think that this act of choice, often buttressed by the gratitude and admiration of others, is anything like the woman's experience of being forcibly socialized into these tasks and of having others perceive this as her natural function in the scheme of things.

The view that we can understand much about the perspectives of those whose oppression we do not share allows us the space to criticize dominant groups for their blindness to the facts of oppression. The view that such an understanding, despite great effort and interest, is likely to be incomplete or limited, provides us with the ground for denying total parity to members of a dominant group in their ability to understand our situation.

Sympathetic members of a dominant group need not necessarily defer to our views on any particular issue because that may reduce itself to another subtle form of condescension, but at least they must keep in mind the very real difficulties and possibility of failure to fully understand our concerns. This and the very important need for dominated groups to control the means of discourse about their own situations are important reasons for taking seriously the claim that oppressed groups have an "epistemic advantage."

The Dark Side of "Double Vision"

I think that one of the most interesting insights of feminist epistemology is the view that oppressed groups, whether women, the poor, or racial minorities, may derive an "epistemic advantage" from having knowledge of the practices of both their own contexts and those of their oppressors. The practices of the dominant groups (for instance, men) govern a society; the dominated group (for instance, women) must acquire some fluency with these practices in order to survive in that society.

There is no similar pressure on members of the dominant group to acquire knowledge of the practices of the dominated groups. For instance, colonized people had to learn the language and culture of their colonizers. The colonizers seldom found it necessary to have more than a sketchy acquaintance with the language and culture of the "natives." Thus, the oppressed are seen as having an "epistemic advantage" because they can operate with two sets of practices and in two different contexts. This advantage is thought to lead to critical insights because each framework provides a critical perspective on the other.

I would like to balance this account with a few comments about the "dark side," the disadvantages, of being able to or of having to inhabit two mutually incompatible frameworks that provide differing perspectives on social reality. I suspect that nonwestern feminists, given the often complex and troublesome interrelationships between the contexts they must inhabit, are less likely to express unqualified enthusiasm about the benefits of straddling a multiplicity of contexts. Mere access to two different and incompatible contexts is not a guarantee that a critical stance on the part of an individual will result. There are many ways in which she may deal with the situation.

First, the person may be tempted to dichotomize her life and reserve the framework of a different context for each part. The middle class of nonwestern countries supplies numerous examples of people who are very westernized in public life but who return to a very traditional lifestyle in the realm of the family. Women may choose to live their public lives in a "male" mode, displaying characteristics of aggressiveness, competition, and so on, while continuing to play dependent and compliant roles in their private lives. The pressures of jumping between two different lifestyles may be mitigated by justifications of how each pattern of behavior is appropriate to its particular context and of how it enables them to "get the best of both worlds."

Second, the individual may try to reject the practices of her own context and try to be as much as possible like members of the dominant group. Westernized intellectuals in the nonwestern world often may almost lose knowledge of their own cultures and practices and be ashamed of the little that they do still know. Women may try both to acquire stereotypically male characteristics, like aggressiveness, and to expunge stereotypically female characteristics, like emotionality. Or the individual could try to reject entirely the framework of the dominant group and assert the virtues of her own despite the risks of being marginalized from the power structures of the society; consider, for example, women who seek a certain sort of security in traditionally defined roles.

The choice to inhabit two contexts critically is an alternative to these choices and, I would argue, a more useful one. But the presence of alternative contexts does not by itself guarantee that one of the other choices will not be made. Moreover, the decision to inhabit two contexts critically, although it may lead to an "epistemic advantage," is likely to exact a certain price. It may lead to a sense of totally lacking roots or any space where one is at home in a relaxed manner.

This sense of alienation may be minimized if the critical straddling of two contexts is part of an ongoing critical politics, due to the support of others and a deeper understanding of what is going on. When it is not so rooted, it may generate ambivalence, uncertainty, despair, and even madness, rather than more positive critical emotions and attitudes. However such a person determines her locus, there may be a sense of being an outsider in both contexts and a sense of clumsiness or lack of fluency in both sets of practices. Consider this simple linguistic example: most people who learn two different languages that are associated with two very different cultures seldom acquire both with equal fluency; they may find themselves devoid of vocabulary in one language for certain contexts of life or be unable to match real objects with terms they have acquired in their vocabulary. For instance, people from my sort of background would know words in Indian languages for some spices, fruits, and vegetables that they do not know in English. Similarly, they might be unable to discuss "technical" subjects like economics or biology in their own languages because they learned about these subjects and acquired their technical vocabularies only in English.

The relation between the two contexts the individual inhabits may not be simple or straightforward. The individual subject is seldom in a position to carry out a perfect "dialectical synthesis" that preserves all the advantages of both contexts and transcends all their problems. There may be a number of different "syntheses," each of which avoids a different subset of the problems and preserves a different subset of the benefits.

No solution may be perfect or even palatable to the agent confronted with a choice. For example, some Indian feminists may find some western modes of dress (say trousers) either more comfortable or more their "style" than some local modes of dress. However, they may find that wearing the local mode of dress is less socially troublesome, alienates them less from more traditional people they want to work with, and so on. Either choice is bound to leave them partly frustrated in their desires.

Feminist theory must be temperate in the use it makes of this doctrine of "double vision"—the claim that oppressed groups have an epistemic advantage and access to greater critical conceptual space. Certain types and contexts of oppression certainly may bear out the truth of this claim. Others certainly do not seem to do so; and even if they do provide space for critical insights, they may also rule out the possibility of actions subversive of the oppressive state of affairs.

Certain kinds of oppressive contexts, such as the contexts in which women of my grandmother's background lived, rendered their subjects entirely devoid of skills required to function as independent entities in the culture. Girls were married off barely past puberty, trained for nothing beyond household tasks and the rearing of children, and passed from economic dependency on their fathers to economic dependency on their husbands to economic dependency on their sons in old age. Their criticisms of their lot were articulated, if at all, in terms that precluded a desire for any radical change. They saw themselves sometimes as personally unfortunate, but they did not locate the causes of their misery in larger social arrangements.

I conclude by stressing that the important insight incorporated in the doctrine of "double vision" should not be reified into a metaphysics that serves as a substitute for concrete social analysis. Furthermore, the alternative to "buying" into an oppressive social system need not be a celebration of exclusion and the mechanisms of marginalization. The thesis that oppression may bestow an epistemic advantage should not tempt us in the direction of idealizing or romanticizing oppression and blind us to its real material and psychic deprivations. ...

37.
DEFINING BLACK FEMINIST THOUGHT
Patricia Hill Collins
(1990)

Widely used yet rarely defined, Black feminist thought encompasses diverse and contradictory meanings. Two interrelated tensions highlight issues in defining Black feminist thought. The first concerns the thorny question of who can be a Black feminist. One current response ... classifies all African-American women, regardless of the content of our ideas, as Black feminists. From this perspective, living as Black women provides experiences to stimulate a Black feminist consciousness. Yet indiscriminately labeling all Black women in this way simultaneously conflates the terms *woman* and *feminist* and identifies being of African descent—a questionable biological category—as being the sole determinant of a Black feminist consciousness. ...

The term *Black feminist* has also been used to apply to selected African-Americans—primarily women—who possess some version of a feminist consciousness. Beverly Guy-Sheftall (1986) contends that both men and women can be "Black feminists" and names Frederick Douglass and William E. B. DuBois as prominent examples of Black male feminists. Guy-Sheftall also identifies some distinguishing features of Black feminist ideas: namely, that Black women's experiences with both racial and gender oppression that result in needs and problems distinct from white women and Black men, and that Black women must struggle for equality both as women and as African-Americans. Guy-Sheftall's definition is helpful in that its use of ideological criteria fosters a definition of Black feminist thought that ecompasses both experiences and ideas. In other words, she suggests that experiences gained from living as African-American women stimulate a Black feminist sensibility. But her definition is simultaneously troublesome because it makes the biological category of Blackness the prerequisite for possessing such thought. Furthermore, it does not explain why these particular ideological criteria and not others are the distinguishing ones.

The term Black feminist has also been used to describe selected African American women who possess some version of a feminist consciousness (Beale 1970; Hooks 1981; Barbara Smith 1983; White 1984). This usage of the term yields the most restrictive notion of who can be a Black feminist. The ground-breaking Combahee River Collective (1982) document "A Black Feminist Statement," implicity relies on this definition. The Collective claims that "as Black women we find any type of biological determinism a particularly dangerous and reactionary basis upon which to build a politic" (p. 17). But in spite of this statement, by implying that only African-American women can be Black feminists, they require a biological prerequisite for race and gender consciousness.

The Collective also offers its own ideological criteria for identifying Black feminist ideas. In contrast to Beverly Guy-Sheftall, the Collective places a stronger emphasis on capitalism as a source of Black women's oppression and on political activism as a distinguishing feature of Black feminism.

Biologically deterministic criteria for the term *black* and the accompanying assumption that being of African descent somehow produces a certain consciousness or perspective are inherent in these definitions. By presenting race as being fixed and immutable—something rooted in nature—these approaches mask the historical construction of racial categories, the shifting meaning of race, and the crucial role of politics and ideology in shaping conceptions of race (Gould 1981; Omi and Winant 1986). In contrast, much greater variation is afforded the term feminist. Feminists are seen as ranging from biologically determined—as is the case in radical feminist thought, which argues that only women can be feminists—to notions of feminists as individuals who have undergone some type of political transformation theoretically achievable by anyone. ...

The ambiguity surrounding current perspectives on who can be a Black feminist is directly tied to a second definitional tension in Black feminist thought: the question of what constitutes Black feminism. The range of assumptions concerning the relationship between ideas and their advocates as illustrated in the works of ... Beverly Guy-Sheftall, [and] the Combahee River Collective ... leads to problems in defining Black feminist theory itself. Once a person is labeled a "Black feminist," then ideas forwarded by that individual often become defined as Black feminist thought. This practice accounts for neither changes in the thinking of an individual nor differences among Black feminist theorists.

A definition of Black feminist thought is needed that avoids the materialist position that being Black and/or female generates certain experiences that automatically determine variants of a Black and/or feminist consciousness. Claims that Black feminist thought is the exclusive province of African-American women, regardless of the experiences and worldview of such women, typify this position. But a definition of Black feminist thought must also avoid the idealist position that ideas can be evaluated in isolation from the groups that create them. Definitions claiming that anyone can produce and develop Black feminist thought risk obscuring the special angle of vision that Black women bring to the knowledge production process.

The Dimensions of a Black Women's Standpoint

Developing adequate definitions of Black feminist thought involves facing this complex nexus of relationships among biological classification, the social construction of race and gender as categories of analysis, the material conditions accompanying these changing social constructions, and Black women's consciousness about these themes. One way of addressing the definitional tensions in Black feminist thought is to specify the relationship between a Black women's standpoint—those experiences and ideas shared by African-American women that provide a unique angle of vision on self, community, and society—and theories that interpret these experiences.[1] I suggest that

Black feminist thought consists of specialized knowledge created by African-American women which clarifies a standpoint of and for Black women. In other words, Black feminist thought encompasses theoretical interpretations of Black women's reality by those who live it.

This definition does not mean that all African-American women generate such thought or that other groups do not play a critical role in its production. Before exploring the contours and implications of this working definition, understanding five key dimension of a Black women's standpoint is essential.

The Core Themes of a Black Women's Standpoint

All African-American women share the common experience of being Black women in a society that denigrates women of African descent. This commonality of experience suggests that certain characteristic themes will be prominent in a Black women's standpoint. For example, one core theme is a legacy of struggle. Katie Cannon observes, "throughout the history of the United States, the interrelationship of white supremacy and male superiority has characterized the Black woman's reality as a situation of struggle—a struggle to survive in two contradictory worlds simultaneously, one white, privileged, and oppressive, the other black, exploited, and oppressed" (1985, 30). Black women's vulnerability to assaults in the workplace, on the street, and at home has stimulated Black women's independence and self-reliance.

In spite of differences created by historical era, age, social class, sexual orientation, or ethnicity, the legacy of struggle against racism and sexism is a common thread binding African-American women. Anna Julia Cooper, a nineteenth-century Black woman intellectual, describes Black women's vulnerability to sexual violence:

> I would beg ... to add my plea for the *Colored Girls* of the South:—that large, bright, promising fatally beautiful class ... so full of promise and possibilities, yet so sure of destruction; often without a father to whom they dare apply the loving term, often without a stronger brother to espouse their cause and defend their honor with his life's blood; in the midst of pitfalls and snares, waylaid by the lower classes of white men, with no shelter, no protection. (Cooper 1892, 140)

Yet during this period Black women struggled and built a powerful club movement and numerous community organizations (Giddings 1984, 1988; Gilkes 1985).

Age offers little protection from this legacy of struggle. Far too many young Black girls inhabit hazardous and hostile environments. In 1975 I received an essay entitled "My World" from Sandra, a sixth-grade student who was a resident of one of the most dangerous public housing projects in Boston. Sandra wrote, "My world is full of people getting rape. People shooting on another. Kids and grownups fighting over girlsfriends. And people without jobs who can't afford to get a education so they can get a job ... winos on the streets raping and killing little girls." Her words poignantly express a growing Black feminist sensibility that she may be victimized by racism and poverty. They also reveal her awareness that she is vulnerable to rape as a gender-specific form of sexual violence. In spite of her feelings about her community, Sandra not only walked the streets daily but managed safely to deliver three younger siblings to school. In doing so she participated in a Black women's legacy of struggle.

This legacy of struggle constitutes one of several core themes of a Black women's standpoint. Efforts to reclaim the Black feminist intellectual tradition are revealing Black women's longstanding attention to a series of core themes first recorded by Maria W. Stewart (Richardson 1987). Stewart's treatment of the interlocking nature of race, gender, and class oppression, her call for replacing denigrated images of Black womanhood with self-defined images, her belief in Black women's activism as mothers, teachers, and Black community leaders, and her sensitivity to sexual politics are all core themes advanced by a variety of Black feminist intellectuals.

Variation of Responses to Core Themes

The existence of core themes does not mean that African-American women respond to these themes in the same way. Diversity among Black women produces different concrete experiences that in turn shape various reactions to the core themes. For example, when faced with stereotypical, controlling images of Black women, some women—such as Sojourner Truth—demand, "ain't I a woman?" By deconstructing the conceptual apparatus of the dominant group, they invoke a Black women's legacy of struggle. In contrast, other women internalize the controlling images and come to believe that they are the stereotypes (Brown-Collins and Sussewell 1986).

A variety of factors explain the diversity of responses. For example although all African-American women encounter racism, social class differences among African-American women influence how racism is experienced. ...

Sexual orientation provides another key factor. Black lesbians have identified homophobia in general and the issues they face living as Black lesbians in homophobic communities as being a major influent on their angle of vision on everyday events (Shockley 1974; Lorde 1982, 1984[b]; Clarke et al. 1983; Barbara Smith 1983). ...

Other factors such as ethnicity, region of the country, urbanization, and age combine to produce a web of experiences shaping diversity among African-American women. As a result, it is more accurate to discuss a Black *women's* standpoint than a Black *woman's* standpoint.

The Interdependence of Experience and Consciousness

Black women's work and family experiences and grounding in traditional African-American culture suggest that African-American women as a group experience a world different from that of those who are not Black and female. Moreover, these concrete experiences can stimulate a distinctive Black feminist consciousness concerning that material reality.[2] Being Black and female may expose African-American women to certain common experiences, which in turn may predispose us to a distinctive group consciousness, but it in no way guarantees that such a consciousness will develop among all women or that it will be articulated as such by the group.

Many African-American women have grasped this connection between what one does and how one thinks. Hannah Nelson, an elderly Black domestic worker, discusses how work shapes the perspectives of African-American and white women: "Since I have to work, I don't really have to worry about most of the things that most of the white women I have worked for are worrying about. And if these women did their own work, they would think just like I do—about this, anyway" (Gwaltney 1980, 4). Ruth Shays, a Black inner-city resident, points out how variations in men's and women's experiences lead to differences in perspective. "The mind of the man and the mind of the woman is the same" she notes, "but this business of living makes women use their minds in ways that men don' even have to think about" (Gwaltney 1980, 33).

This connection between experience and consciousness that shapes the everyday lives of all African-American women pervades the works of Black women activists and scholars. In her autobiography, Ida B. Wells describes how the lynching of her friends had such an impact on her worldview that she subsequently devoted much of her life to the antilynching cause (Duster 1970). Sociologist Joyce Ladner's (1972) *Tomorrow's Tomorrow,* a ground-breaking study of Black female adolescence, emerged from her discomfort with the disparity between the teachings of mainstream scholarship and her experiences as a young Black woman in the South. Similarly, the transformed consciousness experienced by Janie, the light-skinned heroine of Zora Neale Hurston's (1937) classic *Their Eyes Were Watching God,* from obedient granddaughter and wife to a self-defined African-American woman, can be directly traced to her experiences with each of her three husbands. In one scene Janie's second husband, angry because she served him a dinner of scorched rice, underdone fish, and soggy bread, hits her. That incident stimulates Janie to stand "where he left her for unmeasured time" and think. Her thinking leads to the recognition that "her image of Jody tumbled down and shattered … she had an inside and an outside now and suddenly she knew how not to mix them" (p. 63).

Consciousness and the Struggle for a Self-Defined Standpoint

African-American women as a group may have experiences that provide us with a unique angle of vision. But expressing a collective, self-defined Black feminist consciousness is problematic precisely because dominant groups have a vested interest in suppressing such thought.[3] As Hannah Nelson notes, "I have grown to womanhood in a world where the saner you are, the madder you are made to appear" (Gwaltney 1980, 7). Ms. Nelson realizes that those who control the schools, media, and other cultural institutions of society prevail in establishing their viewpoint as superior to others.

An oppressed group's experiences may put its members in a position to see things differently, but their lack of control over the ideological apparatuses of society makes expressing a self-defined standpoint more difficult. Elderly domestic worker Rosa Wakefield assesses how the standpoints of the powerful and those who serve them diverge:

> If you eats these dinners and don't cook 'em, if you wears these clothes and don't buy or iron them, then you might start thinking that the good fairy or some spirit did all that. …

Black folks don't have no time to be thinking like that. … But when you don't have anything else to do, you can think like that. It's bad for your mind, though. (Gwaltney 1980, 88)

Ms. Wakefield has a self-defined perspective growing from her experiences that enables her to reject the standpoint of more powerful groups. And yet ideas like hers are typically suppressed by dominant groups. Groups unequal in power are correspondingly unequal in their ability to make their standpoint known to themselves and others.

Individual African-American women have long displayed varying types of consciousness regarding our shared angle of vision. By aggregating and articulating these individual expressions of consciousness, a collective, focused group consciousness becomes possible. Black women's ability to forge these individual, unarticulated, yet potentially powerful expressions of everyday consciousness into an articulated, self-defined, collective standpoint is key to Black women's survival. As Audre Lorde points out, "it is axiomatic that if we do not define ourselves for ourselves, we will be defined by others—for their use and to our detriment" (1984, 45).

One fundamental feature of this struggle for a self-defined standpoint involves tapping sources of everyday, unarticulated consciousness that have traditionally been denigrated in white, male-controlled institutions. For Black women, the struggle involves embracing a consciousness that is simultaneously Afrocentric and feminist. What does this mean?

Research in African-American Studies suggests that an Afrocentric worldview exists which is distinct from and in many ways opposed to a Eurocentric worldview (Okanlawon 1972; Asante 1987; Myers 1988). Standard scholarly social constructions of blackness and race define these concepts as being either reflections of quantifiable, biological differences among humans or residual categories that emerged in response to institutionalized racism (Lyman 1972; Bash 1979; Gould 1981; Omi and Winant 1986). In contrast, even though it often relies on biological notions of the "race," Afrocentric scholarship suggests that "blackness" and Afrocentricity reflect longstanding belief systems among African peoples (Diop 1974; Richards 1980; Asante 1987). While Black people were forced to adapt these Afrocentric belief systems in the face of different institutional arrangements of white domination, the continuation of an Afrocentric worldview has been fundamental to African-Americans' resistance to racial oppression (Smitherman 1977; Webber 1978; Sobel 1979; Thompson 1983). In other words, being Black encompasses *both* experiencing white domination *and* individual and group valuation of an independent, long-standing Afrocentric consciousness.

African-American women draw on this Afrocentric worldview to cope with racial oppression. But far too often Black women's Afrocentric consciousness remains unarticulated and not fully developed into a self-defined standpoint. In societies that denigrate African ideas and peoples, the process of valuing an Afrocentric worldview is the result of self-conscious struggle.

Similar concerns can be raised about the issue of what constitutes feminist ideas (Eisenstein 1983; Jaggar 1983). Being a biological female does not mean that one's ideas are automatically feminist. Self-conscious struggle is needed in order to reject patriarchal perceptions of women and to value women's ideas and actions. The fact that more women than men identify themselves as feminists reflects women's greater experience with the negative consequences of gender oppression. Becoming a feminist is routinely described by women (and men) as a process of transformation, of struggling to develop new interpretations of familiar realities.

The struggles of women from different racial/ethnic groups and those of women and men within African-American communities to articulate self-defined standpoints represent similar yet distinct processes. While race and gender are both socially constructed categories, constructions of gender rest on clearer biological criteria than do constructions of race. Classifying African-Americans into specious racial categories is consider- ably more difficult than noting the clear biological differences distinguishing females from males (Patterson 1982). But though united by biological sex, women do not form the same type of group as do African-Americans, Jews, native Americans, Vietnamese, or other groups with distinct histories, geographic origins, cultures, and social institutions. The absence of an identifiable tradition uniting women does not mean that women are characterized more by differences than by similarities. Women do share common experiences, but the experiences are not generally the same type as those affecting racial and ethnic groups (King 1988). Thus while expressions of race and gender are both socially constructed, they are not constructed in the same way. The struggle for an Afrocentric feminist consciousness requires embracing both an Afrocentric worldview and a feminist sensibility and using both to forge a self-defined standpoint.[4]

The Interdependence of Thought and Action

One key reason that standpoints of oppressed groups are suppressed is that self-defined standpoints can stimulate resistance. Annie Adams, a Southern Black woman, describes how she became involved in civil rights activities:

> When I first went into the mill we had segregated water fountains … Same thing about the toilets. I had to clean the toilets for the inspection room and then, when I got ready to go to the bathroom, I had to go all the way to the bottom of the stairs to the cellar. So I asked my boss man, "what's the difference? If I can go in there and clean them toilets, why can't I use them?" Finally, I started to use that toilet. I decided I wasn't going to walk a mile to go to the bathroom. (Byerly 1986, 134).

In this case Ms. Adams found the standpoint of the "boss man" inadequate, developed one of her own, and acted on it. Her actions illustrate the connections among concrete experiences with oppression, developing a self-defined standpoint concerning those experiences, and the acts of resistance that can follow.

This interdependence of thought and action suggests that changes in thinking may be accompanied by changed actions and that altered experiences may in turn stimulate a changed consciousness. … The struggle for a self-defined Afrocentric feminist consciousness occurs through a merger of thought and action.

This dimension of a Black women's standpoint rejects either/or dichotomous thinking that claims that *either* thought *or* concrete action is desirable and that merging the two limits the efficacy of both. Such approaches generate deep divisions among theorists and activists which are more often fabricated than real. Instead, by espousing a both/and orientation that views thought and action as part of the same process, possibilities for new relationships between thought and action emerge. That Black women should embrace a both/and conceptual orientation grows from Black women's experiences living as both African-Americans and women and, in many cases, in poverty.

Very different kinds of "thought" and "theories" emerge when abstract thought is joined with concrete action. Denied positions as scholars and writers which allow us to emphasize purely theoretical concerns, the work of most Black women intellectuals is influenced by the merger of action and theory. The activities of nineteenth-century Black women intellectuals such as Anna J. Cooper, Frances Ellen Watkins Harper, Ida B. Wells, and Mary Church Terrell exemplify this tradition of merging intellectual work and activism. These women both produced analyses of Black women's oppression and worked to eliminate that oppression. The Black women's club movement they created was both an activist and an intellectual endeavor.

Contemporary Black women intellectuals continue to draw on this tradition of using everyday actions and experiences in our theoretical work.[5] bell hooks describes the impact working as an operator at the telephone company had on her efforts to write *Ain't I a Woman: Black Women and Feminism* (1981). The women she worked with wanted her to "write a book that would make our lives better, one that would make other people understand the hardships of being black and female" (1989, 152). To hooks, "it was different to be writing in a context where my ideas were not seen as separate from real people and real lives" (p. 152). Similarly, Black feminist historian Elsa Barkley Brown describes the importance her mother's ideas played in the scholarship she eventually produced on African-American washerwomen. Initially Brown used the lens provided by her training as a historian and assessed her sample group as devalued service workers. But over time she came to understand washerwomen as entrepreneurs. By taking the laundry to whoever had the largest kitchen, they created a community and a culture among themselves. In explaining the shift of vision that enabled her to reassess this portion of Black women's history, Brown notes, "it was my mother who taught me how to ask the right questions—and all of us who try to do this thing called scholarship on a regular basis are fully aware that asking the right questions is the most important part of the process" (1986, 14).

Rearticulating a Black Women's Standpoint

The existence of a Black women's standpoint does not mean that African- American women appreciate its content, see its significance, or recognize the potential that a fully articulated Afrocentric feminist standpoint has as a catalyst for social change. One key role for Black women intellectuals is to ask the right questions and investigate all dimensions of a Black women's standpoint with and for African-American women.[6] Black women intellectuals thus stand in a special relationship to the community of African-American women of which we are a part, and this special relationship frames the contours of Black feminist thought.

This special relationship of Black women intellectuals to the community of African-American women parallels the existence of two interrelated levels of knowledge (Berger and Luckmann 1966). The commonplace, taken-for-granted knowledge shared by African-American women growing from our everyday thoughts and actions constitutes a first and most fundamental level of knowledge. The ideas that Black women share with one another on an informal, daily basis about topics such as how to style our hair, characteristics of "good" Black men, strategies for dealing with white folks, and skills of how to "get over" provide the foundations for this taken-for-granted knowledge.

Experts or specialists who participate in and emerge from a group produce a second, more specialized type of knowledge. … [T]heir theories clarifying a Black women's standpoint form the specialized knowledge of Black feminist thought. The two types of knowledge are interdependent. While Black feminist thought articulates the taken-for-granted knowledge shared by African-American women as a group, the consciousness of Black women may be transformed by such thought. The actions of educated Black women within the Black women's club movement typify this special relationship between Black women intellectuals and the wider community of African-American women:

> It is important to recognize that black women like Frances Harper, Anna Julia Cooper, and Ida B. Wells were not isolated figures of intellectual genius; they were shaped by and helped to shape a wider movement of Afro-American women. This is not to claim that they were representative of all black women; they and their counterparts formed an educated, intellectual elite, but an elite that tried to develop a cultural and historical perspective that was organic to the wider condition of black womanhood. (Carby 1987, 115).

The work of these women is important because it illustrates a tradition of joining scholarship and activism, and thus it taps the both/and conceptual orientation of a Black women's standpoint.

The suppression of Black feminist thought in mainstream scholarship and within its Afrocentric and feminist critiques has meant that Black women intellectuals have traditionally relied on alternative institutional locations to produce specialized knowledge about a Black women's standpoint. Many Black women scholars, writers, and artists have worked either alone, as was the case with Maria W. Stewart, or within African-American community organizations, the case for Black women in the club movement. The emergence of Black women's studies in colleges and universities during the 1980s, and the creation of a community of African-American women writers such as Toni Morrison, Alice Walker, and Gloria Naylor, have created new institutional locations where Black women intellectuals can produce specialized thought. Black women's history and Black feminist literary criticism constitute two focal points of this renaissance in Black women's intellectual work (Carby 1987). These are parallel movements: the former aimed at documenting social structural influences on Black women's consciousness; the latter, at exploring Black women's consciousness (self-definitions) through the freedom that art provides.

One danger facing African-American women intellectuals working in these new locations concerns the potential isolation from the types of experiences that stimulate an Afrocentric feminist consciousness—lack of access to other Black women and to a Black women's community. Another is the pressure to separate thought from action—particularly political activism—that typically accompanies training in standard academic disciplines. In spite of these hazards, contemporary Afrocentric feminist thought represents the creative energy flowing between these two focal points of history and literature, an unresolved tension that both emerges from and informs the experiences of African-American women.

The potential significance of Black feminist thought as specialized thought goes far beyond demonstrating that African-American women can be theorists. Like the Black women's activist tradition from which it grows and which it seeks to foster, Black feminist thought can create collective identity among African-American women about the dimensions of a Black women's standpoint. Through the process of rearticulation, Black women intellectuals offer African-American women a different view of themselves and their world from that forwarded by the dominant group (Omi and Winant 1986, 93). By taking the core themes of a Black women's standpoint and infusing them with new meaning, Black women intellectuals can stimulate a new consciousness that utilizes Black women's everyday, taken-for-granted knowledge. Rather than raising consciousness, Black feminist thought affirms and rearticulates a consciousness that already exists. More important, this rearticulated consciousness empowers African-American women and stimulates resistance.

… Thus Black feminist thought aims to develop a theory that is emancipatory and reflective and which can aid African-American women's struggles against oppression.

The earlier definition of Black feminist thought can now be reformulated to encompass the expanded definition of standpoint, the relationship between everyday and specialized thought, and the importance of rearticulation as one key dimension of Black feminist thought. Restated, Black feminist thought consists of theories or specialized thought produced by African-American women intellectuals designed to express a Black women's standpoint. The dimensions of this standpoint include the presence of characteristic core themes, the diversity of Black women's experiences in encountering these core themes, the varying expressions of Black women's Afrocentric feminist consciousness regarding the core themes and their experiences with them, and the interdependence of Black women's experiences, consciousness, and actions. This specialized thought should aim to infuse Black women's experiences and everyday thought with new meaning by rearticulating the interdependence of Black women's experiences and consciousness. Black feminist thought is *of* African-American women in that it taps the multiple relationships among Black women needed to produce a self-defined Black women's standpoint. Black feminist thought is *for* Black women in that it empowers Black women for political activism.

At first glance, this expanded definition could be read to mean that only African-American women can participate in the production of Black feminist thought and that only Black women's experiences can form the content of that thought. But this model of Black feminism is undermined as a critical perspective by being dependent on those who are biologically Black and female. Given that I reject exclusionary definitions of Black feminism which confine "black feminist criticism to black women critics of black women artists depicting black women" (Carby 1987, 9), how does the expanded definition of Black feminist thought address the two original definitional tensions?

Who Can Be a Black Feminist? : The Centrality of Black Women Intellectuals to the Production of Black Feminist Thought

I aim to develop a definition of Black feminist thought that relies exclusively neither on a materialist analysis—one whereby all African-American women by virtue of biology become automatically registered as "authentic Black feminists"—nor on an idealist analysis whereby the background, worldview, and interests of the thinker are deemed irrelevant in assessing his or her ideas. Resolving the tension between these two extremes involves reassessing the centrality Black women intellectuals assume in producing Black feminist thought. It also requires examining the importance of coalitions with Black men, white women, people of color, and other groups with distinctive standpoints. Such coalitions are essential in order to foster other groups' contributions as critics, teachers, advocates, and disseminators of a self-defined Afrocentric feminist standpoint.

Black women's concrete experiences as members of specific race, class, and gender groups as well as our concrete historical situations necessarily play significant roles in our perspectives on the world. No standpoint is neutral because no individual or group exists unembedded in the world. Knowledge is gained not by solitary individuals but by Black women as socially constituted members of a group (Narayan 1989). These factors all frame the definitional tensions in Black feminist thought.

Black women intellectuals are central to Black feminist thought for several reasons. First, our experiences as African-American women provide us with a unique standpoint on Black womanhood unavailable to other groups. It is more likely for Black women as members of an oppressed group to have critical insights into the condition of our own oppression than it is for those who live outside those structures. One of the characters in Frances Ellen Watkins Harper's 1892 novel, *Iola Leroy*, expresses this belief in the special vision of those who have experienced oppression:

> Miss Leroy, out of the race must come its own thinkers and writers. Authors belonging to the white race have written good books, for which I am deeply grateful, but it seems to be almost impossible for a white man to put himself completely in our place. No man can feel the iron which enters another man's soul. (Carby 1987, 62)

Only African-American women occupy this center and can "feel the iron" that enters Black women's souls, because we are the only group that has experienced race, gender, and class oppression as Black women experience them. The importance of Black women's leadership in producing Black feminist thought does not mean that others cannot participate. It does mean that the primary responsibility for defining one's own reality lies with the people who live that reality, who actually have those experiences.

Second, Black women intellectuals provide unique leadership for Black women's empowerment and resistance. In discussing Black women's involvement in the feminist movement, Sheila Radford-Hill points out the connections among self-definition, empowerment, and taking actions in one's own behalf. ... Black feminist thought cannot challenge race, gender, and class oppression without empowering African-American women. "Oppressed people resist by identifying themselves as subjects, by defining their reality, shaping their new identity, naming their history, telling their story," notes bell hooks (1989, 43). Because self-definition is key to individual and group empowerment, using an epistemology that cedes the power of self-definition to other groups, no matter how well-meaning, in essence perpetuates Black women's subordination. As Black feminist sociologist Deborah K. King succinctly states, "Black feminism asserts self-determination as essential" (1988, 72).

Stressing the importance of Black women's centrality to Black feminist thought does not mean that all African-American women exert this leadership. While being an African-American woman generally provides the experiential base for an Afrocentric feminist consciousness, these same conditions suppress its articulation. It is not acquired as a finished product but must continually develop in relation to changing conditions.

... As Patrice L. Dickerson contends, "a person comes into being and knows herself by her achievements, and through her efforts to become and know herself, she achieves" (personal correspondence 1988). Here is the heart of the matter. An Afrocentric feminist consciousness constantly emerges and is part of a self-conscious struggle to merge thought and action.

Third, Black women intellectuals are central in the production of Black feminist thought because we alone can create the group autonomy that must precede effective coalitions with other groups. This autonomy is quite distinct from separatist positions whereby Black women withdraw from other groups and engage in exclusionary politics. In her introduction to *Home Girls, A Black Feminist Anthology,* Barbara Smith describes this difference: "Autonomy and separatism are fundamentally different. Whereas autonomy comes from a position of strength, separatism comes from a position of fear. When we're truly autonomous we can deal with other kinds of people, a multiplicity of issues, and with difference, because we have formed a solid base of strength" (1983, xi). Black women intellectuals who articulate an autonomous, self-defined standpoint are in a position to examine the usefulness of coalitions with other groups, both scholarly and activist, in order to develop new models for social change. However, autonomy to develop a self-defined, independent analysis does not mean that Black feminist thought has relevance only for African-American women or that we must confine ourselves to analyzing our own experiences. As Sonia Sanchez points out, "I've always known that if you write from a black experience, you're writing from a universal experience as well. ... I know you don't have to whitewash yourself to be universal" (in Tate 1983, 142).

While Black feminist thought may originate with Black feminist intellectuals, it cannot flourish isolated from the experiences and ideas of other groups. The dilemma is that Black women intellectuals must place our own experiences and consciousness at the center of any serious efforts to develop Black feminist thought yet not have that thought become separatist and exclusionary. bell hooks offers a solution to this problem by suggesting that we shift from statements such as "I am a feminist" to those such as "I advocate feminism." Such an approach could "serve as a way women who are concerned about feminism as well as other political movements could express their support while avoiding linguistic structures that give primacy to one particular group" (1984, 30).

By advocating, refining, and disseminating Black feminist thought, other groups—such as Black men, white women, white men, and other people of color—further its development. Black women can produce an attenuated version of Black feminist thought separated from other groups. Other groups cannot produce Black feminist thought without African-American women. Such groups can, however, develop self-defined knowledge reflecting their own standpoints. But the full actualization of Black feminist thought requires a collaborative enterprise with Black women at the center of a community based on coalitions among autonomous groups.

Coalitions such as these require dialogues among Black women intellectuals and within the larger African-American women's community. Exploring the common themes of a Black women's standpoint is an important first step. Moreover, finding ways of handling internal dissent is especially important for the Black women's intellectual community. Evelynn Hammond describes how maintaining a united front for whites stifles her thinking: "What I need to do is challenge my thinking, to grow. On white publications sometimes I feel like I'm holding up the banner of black womanhood. And that doesn't allow me to be as critical as I would like to be" (in Clarke et al. 1983, 104). Cheryl Clarke observes that she has two dialogues: one with the public and the private ones in which she feels free to criticize the work of other Black women. Clarke states that the private dialogues are the ones that "have changed my life, have shaped the way I feel … have mattered to me" (p. 103).

Coalitions also require dialogues with other groups. Rather than rejecting our marginality, Black women intellectuals can use our outsider-within stance as a position of strength in building effective coalitions and stimulating dialogue. Barbara Smith suggests that Black women develop dialogues based on a "commitment to principled coalitions, based not upon expediency, but upon our actual need for each other" (1983, xxxiii). Dialogues among and coalitions with a range of groups, each with its own distinctive set of experiences and specialized thought embedded in those experiences, form the larger, more general terrain of intellectual and political discourse necessary for furthering Black feminism. Through dialogues exploring how relations of domination and subordination are maintained and changed, parallels between Black women's experiences and those of other groups become the focus of investigation.

Dialogue and principled coalition create possibilities for new versions of truth. Alice Walker's answer to the question of what she felt were the major differences between the literature of African-Americans and whites offers a provocative glimpse of the types of truths that might emerge through an epistemology based on dialogue and coalition. Walker did not spend much time considering this question, since it was not the difference between them that interested her, but, rather, the way Black writers and white writers seemed to be writing one immense story, with different parts of the story coming from a multitude of different perspectives. In a conversation with her mother, Walker refines this epistemological vision: "I believe that the truth about any subject only comes when all sides of the story are put together, and all their different meanings make one new one. Each writer writes the missing parts to the other writer's story. And the whole story is what I'm after" (1983, 49). Her mother's response to Walker's vision of the possibilities of dialogues and coalitions hints at the difficulty of sustaining such dialogues under oppressive conditions: "'Well, I doubt if you can ever get the *true* missing parts of anything away from the white folks,' my mother says softly, so as not to offend the waitress who is mopping up a nearby table; 'they've sat on the truth so long by now they've mashed the life out of it'" (1983, 49).

What Constitutes Black Feminism? The Recurring Humanist Vision

A wide range of African-American women intellectuals have advanced the view that Black women's struggles are part of a wider struggle for human dignity and empowerment. In an 1893 speech to women, Anna Julia Cooper cogently expressed this alternative worldview:

> We take our stand on the solidarity of humanity, the oneness of life, and the unnaturalness and injustice of all special favoritisms, whether of sex, race, country, or condition. …The colored woman feels that woman's cause is one and universal; and that … not till race, color, sex, and condition are seen as accidents, and not the substance of life; not till the universal title of humanity to life, liberty, and the pursuit of happiness is conceded to be inalienable to all; not till then is woman's lesson taught and woman's cause won—not the white woman's nor the black woman's, not the red woman's but the cause of every man and of every woman who has writhed silently under a mighty wrong. (Loewenberg and Bogin 1976, 330–31)

Like Cooper, many African-American women intellectuals embrace this perspective regardless of particular political solutions we propose, our fields of study, or our historical periods. Whether we advocate working through separate Black women's organizations, becoming part of women's organizations, working within existing political structures, or supporting Black community institutions, African-American women intellectuals repeatedly identify political actions such as these as a *means* for human empowerment rather than ends in and of themselves. Thus the primary guiding principle of Black feminism is a recurring humanist vision (Steady 1981, 1987).[7]

Alice Walker's preference for the term *womanist,* a term she describes as "womanist is to feminist as purple is to lavender," addresses this notion of the solidarity of humanity. To Walker, one is "womanist" when one is "committed to the survival and wholeness of entire people, male and female." A womanist is "not a separatist, except periodically for health" and is "traditionally universalist, as is 'Mama, why are we brown, pink, and yellow, and our cousins are white, beige, and black?' Ans.: 'Well, you know the colored race is just like a flower garden, with every color flower represented'" (1983, xi). By redefining all people as "people of color," Walker universalizes what are typically seen as individual struggles while simultaneously allowing space for autonomous movements of self-determination.

In assessing the sexism of the Black nationalist movement of the 1960s, Black feminist lawyer Pauli Murray identifies the dangers inherent in separatism as opposed to autonomy, and also echoes Cooper's concern with the solidarity of humanity:

> The lesson of history that all human rights are indivisible and that the failure to adhere to this principle jeopardizes the rights of all is particularly applicable here. A built-in hazard of an aggressive ethnocentric movement which disregards the interests of other disadvantaged groups is that it will become parochial and ultimately self-defeating in the face of hostile reactions, dwindling allies, and mounting frustrations. … Only a broad movement for human rights can prevent the Black Revolution from becoming isolated and can insure ultimate success. (Murray 1970, 102)

Without a commitment to human solidarity, suggests Murray, any political movement—whether nationalist, feminist or antielitist—may be doomed to ultimate failure.

bell hook's analysis of feminism adds another critical dimension that must be considered: namely, the necessity of self-conscious struggle against a more generalized ideology of domination:

> To me feminism is not simply a struggle to end male chauvinism or a movement to ensure that women will have equal rights with men; it is a commitment to eradicating the ideology of domination that permeates Western culture on various levels—sex, race, and class, to name a few—and a commitment to reorganizing U.S. society so that the self-development of people can take precedence over imperialism, economic expansion, and material desires. (hooks 1981, 194)

Former assemblywoman Shirley Chisholm also points to the need for self-conscious struggle against the stereotypes buttressing ideologies of domination. In "working toward our own freedom, we can help others work free from the traps of their stereotypes," she notes. "In the end, antiblack, antifemale, and all forms of discrimination are equivalent to the same thing—antihumanism. … We must reject not only the stereotypes that others have of us but also those we have of ourselves and others" (1970, 181).

This humanist vision is also reflected in the growing prominence of international issues and global concerns in the works of contemporary African-American women intellectuals (Lindsay 1980; Steady 1981, 1987). …

The words and actions of Black women intellectuals from different historical times and addressing markedly different audiences resonate with a strikingly similar theme of the oneness of all human life. Perhaps the most succinct version of the humanist vision in Black feminist thought is offered by Fannie Lou Hamer, the daughter of sharecroppers, and a Mississippi civil rights activist. While sitting on her porch, Ms. Hamer observed, "Ain' no such thing as I can hate anybody and hope to see God's face" (Jordan 1981, xi).

Taken together, the ideas of Anna Julia Cooper, Pauli Murray, bell hooks, Alice Walker, Fannie Lou Hamer, and other Black women intellectuals too numerous to mention suggest a powerful answer to the question "What is Black feminism?" Inherent in their words and deeds is a definition of Black feminism as a process of self-conscious struggle that empowers women and men to actualize a humanist vision of community.

Notes

1. For discussions of the concept of standpoint, see Hartsock (1983a, 1983b), Jaggar (1983), and Smith (1987). Even though I use standpoint epistemologies as an organizing concept in this volume, they remain controversial. For a helpful critique of standpoint epistemologies, see Harding (1986). Haraway's (1988) reformulation of standpoint epistemologies approximates my use here.

2. Scott (1985) defines consciousness as the symbols, norms, and ideological forms people create to give meaning to their acts. For de Lauretis (1986), consciousness is a process, a "particular configuration of subjectivity ... produced at the intersection of meaning with experience. ... Consciousness is grounded in personal history, and self and identity are understood within particular cultural contexts. Consciousness ... is never fixed, never attained once and for all, because discursive boundaries change with historical conditions" (p. 8).

3. The presence of a Black women's culture of resistance (Terborg-Penn 1986; Dodson and Gilkes 1987) that is both Afrocentric and feminist challenges two prevailing interpretations of the consciousness of oppressed groups. One approach claims that subordinate groups identify with the powerful and have no valid independent interpretation of their own oppression. The second assumes the oppressed are less human than their rulers and are therefore less capable of interpreting their own experiences (Rollins 1985; Scott 1985). Both approaches see any independent consciousness expressed by oppressed groups as being either not of their own making or inferior to that of the dominant group. More important, both explanations suggest that the alleged lack of political activism on the part of oppressed groups stems from their flawed consciousness of their own subordination.

4. Even though I will continue to use the term *Afrocentric feminist* thought interchangeably with the phrase *Black feminist thought*, I think they are conceptually distinct.

5. Canadian sociologist Dorothy Smith (1987) also views women's concrete, everyday world as stimulating theory. But the everyday she examines is individual, a situation reflecting in part the isolation of white, middle-class women. In contrast, I contend that the collective values in Afrocentric communities, when combined with the working-class experiences of the majority of Black women, provide a collective as well as an individual concrete.

6. See Harold Cruse's (1967) analysis of the Black intellectual tradition and John Child's (1984) discussion of the desired relationship of Black intellectuals to African-American culture. ... Like Childs, I suggest that the role of Black women intellectuals is to "illuminate the very intricacy and strength of the peoples' thought" (p. 87).

7. My use of the term *humanist* grows from an Afrocentric historical context distinct from that criticized by Western feminists. I use the term to tap an Afrocentric humanism as cited by West (1977–78), Asante (1987) and Turner (1984) and as part of the Black theological tradition (Mitchell and Lewter 1986; Cannon 1988). See Harris (1981) for a discussion of the humanist tradition in the works of three Black women writers. See Richards (1990) for a discussion of African-American spirituality, a key dimension of Afrocentric humanism. Novelist Margaret Walker offers one of the clearest discussions of Black humanism. Walker claims: "I think it is more important now to emphasize humanism in a technological age than ever before, because it is only in terms of humanism that society can redeem itself. I believe that mankind is only one race—the human race. There are many strands in the family of man—many races. The world has yet to learn to appreciate the deep reservoirs of humanism in all races, and particularly in the Black race" (Rowell 1975, 12).

38.
SEPARATING LESBIAN THEORY FROM FEMINIST THEORY
Cheshire Calhoun
(1994)

Heidi Hartmann once said of the marriage of Marxism and feminism that it "has been like the marriage of husband and wife depicted in English common law: marxism and feminism are one, and that one is marxism."[1] Lesbian theory and feminism, I want to suggest, are at risk of falling into a similar unhappy marriage in which "the one" is feminism.

Although lesbian feminist theorizing has significantly contributed to feminist thought, it has also generally treated lesbianism as a kind of applied issue. Feminist theories developed outside of the context of lesbianism are brought to bear on lesbianism in order to illuminate the nature of lesbian oppression and women's relation to women within lesbianism. So, for example, early radical lesbians played off the feminist claim that all male–female relationships are dominance relationships. They argued either that the lesbian is *the* paradigm case of patriarchal resister because she refuses to be heterosexual or that she fits on a continuum of types of patriarchal resisters.[2] In taking this line, lesbian theorists made a space for lesbianism by focusing on what they took to be the inherently feminist and antipatriarchal nature of lesbian existence. Contemporary lesbian theorists are less inclined to read lesbianism as feminist resistance to male dominance.[3] Instead, following the trend that feminist theory has itself taken, the focus has largely shifted to women's relation to women: the presence of ageism, racism, and anti-Semitism among lesbians, the problem of avoiding a totalizing discourse that speaks for all lesbians without being sensitive to differences, the difficulty of creating community in the face of political differences (e.g., on the issue of sadomasochism [s/m]), and the need to construct new conceptions of female agency and female friendship.[4] All of these are issues that have their birthplace in feminist theory. They become lesbian issues only because the general concern with women's relation to women is narrowed to lesbians' relation to fellow lesbians. Once again, lesbian thought becomes applied feminist thought.

Now, there is nothing wrong with using feminist tools to analyze lesbianism. Indeed, something would be wrong with feminist theory if it could not be usefully applied to lesbianism in a way that both illuminates lesbianism and extends feminist theory itself. And there would surely be something lacking in lesbian thought if it did not make use of feminist insights. My worry is that if this is all that lesbian feminism amounts to then there is no lesbian *theory*. Lesbian theory and feminist theory are one, and that one is feminist theory. What more could one want?

When Hartmann complained that Marxism had swallowed feminism, her point was that because traditional Marxism lacks a notion of sex-class, and thus of patriarchy as a political system distinct from capitalism, it must treat women's oppression as a special case of class oppression. Marxism is of necessity blind to the irreducibly gendered nature of women's lives. A parallel complaint might be raised about feminist theory. To the extent that feminist theory lacks a concept of heterosexuals and nonheterosexuals as members of different sexuality classes and thus of heterosexuality as a political structure separable from patriarchy, feminist theory must treat lesbian oppression as a special case of patriarchal oppression and remain blind to the irreducibly lesbian nature of lesbian lives.

Lesbian feminism is for several reasons at high risk of doing just that. First, the most extensive analyses of heterosexuality available to feminists are those developed in the late 1970s and early 1980s by Charlotte Bunch, Gayle Rubin, Adrienne Rich, Monique Wittig, and Kate Millett.[5] Heterosexuality, on this account, is both product and essential support of patriarchy. Women's heterosexual orientation perpetuates their social, economic, emotional, and sexual dependence on and accessibility by men. Heterosexuality is thus a system of male ownership of women, participation in which is compulsory for men and especially for women. The lesbian's and heterosexual woman's relation to heterosexuality on this account is fundamentally the same. Both experience it as the demand that women be dependent on and accessible by men. Both are vulnerable to penalties if they resist that demand. Thus heterosexuality is equally compulsory for heterosexual women and lesbians; and compulsory heterosexuality means the same thing for both. There is no specifically lesbian relation to heterosexuality.

Second, lesbian feminists have had to assert their differences from gay men and thus their distance from both the political aims and the self-understanding of the gay movement. The gay rights movement has suffered from at least two defects. On the one hand, in focusing on lesbians' and gays' shared status as sexual deviants, the gay rights movement was unable to address the connection between lesbian oppression and women's oppression. On the other hand, it tended to equate gay with gay male and failed to address the patriarchal attitudes embedded in the gay movement itself.[6] Making clear the difference between lesbians and gay men meant that lesbian feminists' focus had to be on the experience of lesbians in a patriarchal culture, not on their experience as deviants in a heterosexist culture.

Third, the fact that to be lesbian is to live out of intimate relation with men and in intimate relation with women encourages the reduction of "lesbian" to "feminist".[7] Early radical feminists were quite explicit about this, claiming that lesbians are the truly woman-identified women. Contemporary lesbian feminists, recognizing that lesbians may share patriarchal attitudes toward women, resist such grand claims. But even if lesbian feminism is no longer at risk of equating being lesbian with being a "true" feminist, the danger remains that it may equate "lesbian issues" with "feminist issues". If what counts as lesbian issues are only those visible through a feminist lens, then lesbian issues will simply be a special class of feminist ones.

Finally, the historical circumstances that gave birth to lesbian feminism had a decided impact on the direction that lesbian feminism took. The first major lesbian feminist statement, "The Woman Identified Woman," was a direct response to Betty Friedan's charge that lesbians posed a "lavender menace" to the women's movement.[8] In Friedan's and many National Organization for Women (NOW) members' view, the association of feminism with lesbianism, and thus with deviancy, undermined the credibility of women's rights claims. Threatened with ostracism from the women's movement, the Radicalesbians argued in "The Woman Identified Woman" that lesbians, because they love women and refuse to live with or devote their energies to the oppressor, are the paradigm feminists.[9] The political climate of the 1970s women's movement thus required lesbian feminists to assert their allegiance to feminist aims and values rather than calling attention to lesbians' differences from their heterosexual sisters. It was neither the time nor the place for lesbians to entertain the possibility that heterosexuality might itself be a political system and that heterosexual women and men, as a consolidated and powerful class, might have strong interests in maintaining a system of heterosexual privileges. In affirming their commitment to opposing patriarchy, lesbian feminists instead committed themselves to a specifically feminist account of the interests motivating the maintenance of a heterosexual system: men have patriarchal interests in securing sexual/emotional access to women, and heterosexual women have complicitous interests in securing access to a system of male privileges. This move effectively barred lesbian feminists from asking whether heterosexual women and men have, as heterosexuals, a class interest in constructing heterosexual sex as the only real, nonimitative sex, in eliminating historical, literary, and media representations of lesbians and gay men, in reserving jobs, public accommodations, and private housing for heterosexuals only, in barring lesbians and gay men from access to children in the educational system, children's service organizations, and adoption and artificial insemination agencies, in reducing lesbianism and homosexuality to biologically or psychodevelopmentally rooted urges while propagating the myth of a magical heterosexual romantic love, and in securing for the married heterosexual couple exclusive pride of place in the social world. Nor could or did lesbian feminists ask whether these privileges taken as a set could provide a sufficient motivating interest for maintaining a heterosexual system even in the absence of patriarchy.

For all four reasons, treating sexual orientation on a par with gender, race, and economic class—that is, as a distinct and irreducible dimension of one's political identity—may not come naturally to lesbian feminist thinking. But separating sexuality politics from gender politics is exactly what must happen if there is to be a specifically *lesbian* feminist theory rather than simply feminist theory applied to lesbians. A lesbian feminist theory would need, among other things, to focus on what is distinctive about the lesbian's relation to heterosexuality, to the category "woman', and to other women. That is, it would need to put into clear view the difference between being a lesbian who resists heterosexuality, being a woman, and loving men rather than women and being a feminist who resists the same things.

In what follows, I will be arguing that, like patriarchy and capitalism, or white imperialism, patriarchy and heterosexual dominance are two, in principle, separable systems. Even where they work together, it is possible conceptually to pull the patriarchal aspect of male–female relationships apart from their heterosexual dimensions. …

The Lesbian Not-Woman

Monique Wittig ends "The Straight Mind" with this sentence: "Lesbians are not women."[10] Wittig denies that "man" and "woman" are natural categories, arguing instead that the two sex-classes—men, women—are the product of heterosexual social relations in which "men appropriate for themselves the reproduction and production of women and also their physical persons by means of a contract called the marriage contract."[11] Thus, "it is oppression that creates sex and not the contrary."[12] Lesbians, however, refuse to participate in heterosexual social relations. … Thus Wittig observes, "Lesbianism is the only concept know of which is beyond the categories of sex (woman and man), because the designated subject (lesbian) is not a woman, either economically, or politically, or ideologically. For what makes a woman is a specific social relation to a man, a relation that we have previously called servitude, a relation which implies personal and physical obligation as well as economic obligation ('forced residence,' domestic corvée, conjugal duties, unlimited production of children, etc.), a relation which lesbians escape by refusing to become or to stay heterosexual."[13] What I want to highlight in Wittig's explanation of what bars lesbians from the category "woman" is that it claims both too much and too little for lesbians as well as reads lesbianism from a peculiarly heterosexual viewpoint. To say that only lesbians exist beyond sex categories … claims too much for lesbians. If to be a woman just means living in a relation of servitude to men, there will be other ways short of lesbianism of evading the category "woman". The heterosexual celibate, virgin, single-parent head of household, marriage resister, or the married woman who insists on an egalitarian marriage contract all apparently qualify as escapees from the category "woman".[14]

Although Wittig does remark that runaway wives are also escaping their sex class, she clearly thought that lesbians are in some special sense *not women*. But her own analysis does not capture lesbians' special deviancy from the category "woman". There is indeed no conceptual space in Wittig's framework for pursuing the question of how a heterosexual woman's refusal to be a woman differs from a lesbian's refusal to be a woman. It is in that failure that she claims too little for lesbians. Because lesbians and heterosexual resisters must have, on her account, the same relation to the category "woman", there can be no interesting differences between the two. This, I think, is a mistake, and I will argue in a moment that lesbians are in a quite special sense not-women.

Finally, to equate lesbians' escape from heterosexuality and the category "woman" with escape from male control is to adopt a peculiarly heterosexual viewpoint on lesbianism. The fact that heterosexuality enables men to control women's domestic labor is something that would be salient only to a *heterosexual* woman. Only heterosexual women do housework for men, raise children for men, have their domiciles determined by men, and so on. Thus, from a heterosexual standpoint lesbianism may indeed appear to offer a liberating escape from male control. But from the standpoint of a woman unaccustomed to living with men, that is, from a lesbian standpoint, lesbianism is not about a refusal to labor for men. Nor is heterosexuality experienced primarily as a form of male dominance over women, but instead as heterosexual dominance over lesbians and gay men. Nor is the daily experience of lesbianism one of liberation but, instead, one of acute oppression.

Because Wittig looks at lesbianism from a (heterosexual) feminist perspective, asking how lesbians escape the kinds of male control to which paradigmatically heterosexual women are subject, she misses the penalties attached to lesbians' exit from heterosexuality. Indeed, contrary to Wittig's claim, the lesbian may as a rule have *less* control over her productive and reproductive labor than her married heterosexual sister. Although the lesbian escapes whatever control *individual* men may exercise over their wives within marriage, she does not thereby escape control of her productive and reproductive labor either in her personal life with another woman or in her public life. To refuse to be heterosexual is simply to leap out of the frying pan of individual patriarchal control into the fire of institutionalized heterosexual control. Wittig's claim that "lesbianism provides for the moment the only social form in which we can live freely" vastly underestimates the coercive forces brought to bear on the lesbian for her lesbianism.[15] She may be unable to adopt children or be denied custody of and visiting privileges to her children. In order to retain her job, she will most likely have to hide her lesbianism and pretend to be heterosexual. She will likely be punished for public displays of affection. She may be denied the housing of her choice or be forced to move from her home as a result of harassment by neighbors. If she is "out," she will find herself alternately abused and subjected to lascivious interest by heterosexual men. Even if she is no longer at risk of being burned at the stake or subjected to clitoridectomy or electroshock, she may still be subjected to "therapies" that insist that she cannot be both lesbian and a healthy, mature adult. She will be labeled a dyke and scrutinized for symptoms of mannishness in her anatomy, dress, behavior, and interests. She will not see her lesbian sexuality or romantic love for another woman reflected in the public media. And both because there are no publicly accessible models of lesbian relationships and because such coercive pressure is brought to bear against lesbian relationships, sustaining a stable personal life will be very difficult. The lesbian may be free from an individual man in her personal life, but she is not free.

What these criticisms suggest is, first, that the political structure that oppresses heterosexual women is patriarchy; but the political structure that most acutely oppresses lesbians is more plausibly taken to be heterosexuality. Second, these criticisms suggest that heterosexual women's (especially heterosexual feminists') and lesbians' relation to the category "woman" are not the same.

From a feminist point of view, the problem with the category "woman" is not so much that there is one. The problem lies in its specific construction within patriarchal society. "Woman" has been constructed as the Other and the deficient in relation to "man". To "woman" have been assigned all those traits that would both rationalize and perpetuate women's lack of power in relation to men. Women are weak, passive, dependent, emotional, irrational, nurturant, closer to nature, maternal, and so on. This is to say that, from a feminist point of view, the problem with the category "woman" is that "woman" has been equated with subordination to men. The feminist task, then, is to rupture that equation. With the exception of early liberal feminists' recommendation of androgyny and possibly contemporary French feminists' deconstruction of "woman", the feminist project has not been the elimination of the category "woman". Instead, the project has been one of reconstructing that category. ...

The feminist experience of her relation to the category "woman", thus, has been the experience of *being* a woman in a male dominant, as well as racist and classist, society, which imposes on her a conception of what it means to be a woman that she rejects. Her refusal to be a woman has extended only to refusal to be the kind of woman that a patriarchal, racist, and classist society demands that she be. And that refusal has gone hand in hand with claiming the category "woman" (or categories of "women") for herself and insisting on a woman-identified construction of that category.

This is not the lesbian relation to the category "woman". Although partly mistaken, I think, in her reasons, Wittig was correct to say that to be lesbian is to exit the category "woman" altogether. It is to be ungendered, unsexed, neither woman nor man. This is because (here following Wittig) sex/gender is the result of institutionalized heterosexuality.[16] Heterosexual systems are ones that organize reproduction via hetero*sexual* practice. That practice requires the production of two sex/genders so that sexual desire can be heterosexualized. It also requires that sex/gender map onto reproductive differences. Thus, within heterosexual systems, "'intelligible' genders are those which in some sense institute and maintain relations of coherence and continuity among sex, gender, sexual practice, and desire."[17] Individuals who violate the unity of reproductive anatomy, heterosexual desire, and gender behavior fall out of the domain of intelligible gender identity. At best, lesbians are not-women. That is, for them the closest available category of sex/gender identity is one that does not fit. Neither anatomy nor desire nor gender can link her securely to the category "woman". Within heterosexist ideology her anatomy itself is suspect. Much was made, for example, in the sexologists' literature of physical masculinity in the lesbian, including reports of an enlarged clitoris. The postulate of a biological basis of homosexuality and lesbianism continues to guide research today. And many lesbians' insistence on having been born lesbian reinforces such suspicions about anatomical differences from heterosexual women. In addition, her anatomy cannot link her to "woman" because what lesbianism reveals is the fundamental lie that differences in male and female anatomy destine a difference in males' and females' sexual and social relation to females, that is, destine one to be functionally a man or a woman. The lesbian's female body in no way bars her from functioning as a man in relation to women. She shares with members of the category "man" a sexual desire for and love of women. Also, the very traits that Wittig took to be definitive of "man"—the enactment of masculine dominance over women, physically, psychologically, socially, and economically—are an option for her in a way that they are not an option for heterosexual women. The lesbian thus exits the category of "woman", though without thereby entering the category "man".

Gender-deviant heterosexual women (i.e., women who resist patriarchal understandings of what it means to be a woman) do not similarly exit the category "woman".

Gender deviance would result in not-woman status only if the content of the category "woman" were fully exhausted by a description, such as Wittig's, of what it means to be a woman. I have been suggesting, on the contrary, that heterosexuality is a critical component of the category "woman". Heterosexuality secures one's status as a "natural" woman, which is to say, as having a body whose sex as female is above suspicion. Heterosexuality also guarantees a significant nonidentity between one's own and men's relation to women. The heterosexual woman will not have a sexual, romantic, marital, coparenting relation to other women; she will have instead a *woman's* relation to women. Thus even in her gender deviance, the heterosexual resister of patriarchally defined gender remains unambiguously a woman.

Because the lesbian stands outside the category "woman", her experience of womanliness and its oppressive nature is not identical to that of the heterosexual feminist, who stands within the category "woman", even if resistantly. Womanliness is not something the lesbian has the option of refusing or reconstructing for a better fit. It is a fundamental impossibility for her. To be a not-woman is to be incapable of *being* a woman within heterosexual society. The lesbian can thus be womanly only in the modes of being in drag and of passing. And if she experiences womanliness—the demand that she look like a woman, act like a woman—as oppressive, it is not because womanliness requires subordination to men (although this may also be her experience). It is instead because the demand that she be womanly is the demand that she pretend that the sex/gender "woman" is a natural possibility for her and that she pass as a woman. It is thus also a demand that she not reveal the nonexhaustiveness and, potentially, the nonnaturalness of the binary categories "woman" and "man".

The lesbian experience of her relation to the category "woman", thus, is the experience of being a not-woman in a heterosexual society that compels everyone to be either a woman or a man and requires that she be a woman.[18] It is also the experience of being oppressed by a womanliness that denies her desire for women, and of being deviantly outside of sex/gender categories. That deviancy is harshly punished. In an attempt to compel her back into the category "woman", her lesbian desire and unwomanly relation to women are punished or treated. At the same time, she is denied the heterosexual privileges to which "real" women have access.

From a lesbian perspective, the category "woman" is oppressive because, within heterosexual societies, that category is compulsory for all anatomically female individuals. Feminist reconstructions of "woman" do not typically challenge compulsory sex/gender. They implicitly assume that "woman" and "man" exhaust the field of possible sorts of persons to be (even if it takes multiple categories of each to exhaust the taxonomy). … The lesbian objection to being a woman is not met by admissions that the category "woman" as well as what it means to be anatomically female are open to social construction and reconstruction. Nor is it met by the suggestion that there is no single category "woman" but instead multiple categories of women. From a lesbian perspective, what has to be challenged is heterosexual society's demand that females be women. For that demand denies the lesbian option. The lesbian option is to be a not-woman, where being a not-woman is played out by insisting on being neither identifiably woman nor man, or by enacting femininity as drag, or by insisting on switching gender categories and thus being a man, which within patriarchy means being dominant in relation to women and potentially also misogynistic.

Failure to see the difference between feminist and lesbian relations to the category "woman" may well result in mislocating lesbian politics and failing to see the potential friction between feminist and lesbian politics. I take the feminist critique of butch and femme lesbianism as a case in point. On that critique, both the lesbian appropriation of femininity by femmes (and more recently by lipstick lesbians) and the lesbian appropriation of masculinity through butch sexual-social dominance repeat between women the power politics and misogyny that typifies male–female relations in a patriarchal society. Julia Penelope, for instance, argues that "those aspects of behavior and appearance labeled "femininity" in HP [heteropatriarchy] are dangerous for us. We still live *in* a heteropatriarchy and Lesbians who incorporate male ideas of appropriate female behaviors into their lives signal their acceptance of the HP version of reality."[19] In particular, the feminine lesbian confirms heteropatriarchy's acceptance of the feminine woman and rejection of any trace of mannishness in women.

From a feminist point of view there is no way of rendering politically harmless the appropriation of a role that requires sexual-social passivity and subordination, … Here the argument against femininity in lesbians directly parallels the argument against the masochist role in lesbian s/m. … Both femininity and female masochism acquire their meaning from what Penelope calls "heteropatriarchal semantics" as well as from the historical and material conditions of women's oppression. Those meanings cannot be dissolved at will. … To adopt either femininity or female masochism for oneself is to make use of a set of meanings produced through and sustained by men's oppression of women. It is thus to reveal one's personal failure to come to critical grips with the politics of women's position within patriarchy. Even if the femme's or masochist's personal choices are not political in the sense that they also publicly endorse femininity or masochism in women, they are still political in the sense that they make use of public meanings which are tied to gender politics.

Nor, the feminist critic might add, can the appropriation of masculine dominance, aggression, and misogyny be rendered politically harmless. What the butch (as well as the sadist in lesbian s/m) confirms is the patriarchal equation of power with sexual dominance and superiority with masculinity. Janice Raymond's caustic remarks about lesbian s/m might equally express the feminist critique of butch-femme roles: "It is difficult to see what is so advanced or progressive about a position that locates 'desire,' and that imprisons female sexual dynamism, vitality, and vigor, in old forms of sexual objectification, subordination, and violence, this time initiated by women and done with women's consent. The libertarians offer a supposed sexuality stripped naked of feminine taboo, but only able to dress itself in masculine garb. It is a male-constructed sexuality in drag."[20]

I have no intention of disagreeing with the claim that butch-femme role-playing runs contrary to feminist politics. What I do intend to take issue with is the assumption that feminist politics are necessarily lesbian politics. Judith Butler gives a quite different reading of the multiple appropriations of femininity and masculinity within the lesbian/gay community by butches, femmes, queens, dykes, and gay male girls. It is a reading that I take to be closer to a lesbian perspective, even if farther from a feminist one.

What the feminist critique omits is the fact that "Within lesbian contexts, the 'identification' with masculinity that appears as butch identity is not a simple assimilation of lesbianism back into the terms of heterosexuality. As one lesbian femme explained, she likes her boys to be girls. ... As a result, that masculinity, ... is always brought into relief against a culturally intelligible 'female body'. It is precisely this dissonant juxtaposition and the sexual tension that its transgression generates that constitute the object of desire."[21] It is also precisely this dissonant juxtaposition of masculinity and female body that enables the butch to enact a comedic parody of masculinity that denaturalizes the category "man". Heterosexual society assumes that masculinity is naturally united to the male body and desire for women. Similarly, it assumes that femininity is naturally united to the female body and desire for men. Butler argues, however, that gender identity is not natural but the result of continuous gender performances. One can be a man, for example, only by continuously performing masculinity and desire for women through a male body. Heterosexual society sustains the illusion of natural gender identities—"heterosexual man", "heterosexual woman"—by outlawing alternative performances. The butch lesbian gives an outlawed performance. She performs masculinity and desire for women through a female body. The butch gay man similarly gives an outlawed performance by performing masculinity in tandem with desire for men through a male body. Such multiple locations of masculinity—on the heterosexual male body, the lesbian body, the gay man's body—help create a condition in which "after a while, everyone starts to look like a drag queen."[22] The categories "woman" and "man" cease to appear natural. Without such clearly natural or original gender identities, lesbians' subordinate status cannot be rationalized on the grounds that lesbians are unnatural, imitative beings. And, one might add, the exclusively heterosexual organization of sexuality, romantic love, marriage, and the family begin to appear arbitrary. ...

... A feminist might well raise the following objection: butch and femme lesbianism may indeed undermine heterosexual society. It does not follow, however, that butch-femme lesbianism undermines patriarchy. The original objection still stands: butch lesbianism leaves in place the patriarchal equation of masculinity with power and dominance, while femme lesbianism leaves in place the patriarchal equation of femininity with weakness and subordination. Butler's ... political program would at best simply replace heterosexuality-based patriarchy (male power), with masculinity-based patriarchy (masculine power). Under masculinity-based patriarchy, anatomical females and males would have an equal opportunity to appropriate masculine power over feminine individuals, who themselves could be either anatomically male or female.

What the disagreement between Butler and many feminists reveals is the fact that challenging heterosexual society and challenging patriarchy are not the same thing. The feminist political opposition to patriarchal power relations disables lesbians from effectively challenging heterosexual society. The lesbian political opposition to compulsory heterosexual gender performances disables feminists from effectively challenging patriarchal society. But neither Butler nor feminists who critique butch and femme lesbians see this. Both assume the *identity* of feminist politics and lesbian politics. This is simply a mistake. Heterosexuality and patriarchy are analytically distinct social systems, just as capitalism and patriarchy are distinct. Patriarchy can survive just as easily in a nonheterosexual society as it can in a noncapitalist society. Butch-femme culture is a case in point. On the flip side, heterosexuality can survive in a nonpatriarchal society. Heterosexual societies simply require that masculinity be united with a male body and desire for women and that femininity be united with a female body and desire for men. Heterosexual systems do *not* depend on femininity and masculinity being defined and valued the way they are in patriarchal societies. Matriarchies are heterosexual systems.[23]

Given this, one should expect that feminist politics and lesbian politics, though typically overlapping, may sometimes part company. Moreover, when those politics do conflict, there is no reason to expect that feminist lesbians will or should give priority to feminist politics. Being a woman (or better, being mistaken for a woman) and being oppressed as a woman are often not the most important facts in a lesbian's life. Being a lesbian and being oppressed as a lesbian often matter more.

Which Heterosexuality?

... I intend to begin this section by expanding on the argument against reducing the institution of heterosexuality to (a part of) the institution of male dominance. ... I will conclude with a quite different reading of heterosexuality, one that I take to be closer to a lesbian view, if farther from a feminist one.

Heterosexuality as Male Dominance

Heterosexuality, in Wittig's view, is a political and economic system of male dominance. The heterosexual social contract (to which only men have consented) stipulates that women belong to men. ... It is thus heterosexuality that enables men to appropriate women's labor and that supports a system of male dominance. ... Wittig's equation of lesbian resistance with feminist resistance is both obvious and explicit. She claims that to be a feminist is to fight for the disappearance of the sex-class "woman" by refusing to participate in the heterosexual relations that created the sex-class "woman" in the first place.[24] To be a feminist just *is* to be a lesbian.

In "Lesbians in Revolt," Charlotte Bunch similarly equates heterosexuality with male control over women's labor; and like Wittig, she regards lesbianism as a political revolt against a system in which neither a woman nor her labor belong to herself. "The lesbian ... refuses to be a man's property, to submit to the unpaid labor system of housework and childcare. She rejects the nuclear family as the basic unit of production and consumption in capitalist society."[25] In Bunch's view, commitment to heterosexuality is necessarily a commitment to supporting a male world, and thus a barrier to struggle against women's oppression. "Being a lesbian means ending identification with, allegiance to, dependence on, and support of heterosexuality. It means ending your personal stake in the male world so that you join women individually and collectively in the struggle to end oppression."[26]

At least two different objections might be raised to Wittig's and Bunch's implicit claim that one must be a lesbian to be a feminist. First, lesbianism only challenges male control of women in the family. But women's labor power is also extensively control-led in the public sphere through male bosses, absence of maternity leave, sexual har-assment, the job requirement of an "appropriately" feminine appearance, insufficient availability of day care, sex segregation of women into lower paid jobs, and so on. As Ann Ferguson observes, enforced heterosexuality "may be one of the mechanisms [of male dominance], but it surely is not the single or sufficient one. Others, such as the control of female biological reproduction, male control of state and political power, and economic systems involving discrimination based on class and race, seem analytically distinct from coercive heterosexuality, yet are causes which support and perpetuate male dominance."[27] Moreover, given both the decline of male power within the nuclear family and of the nuclear family itself, one might well claim that the public control of women's productive and reproductive labor is far more critical to the maintenance of patriarchy than the private control of women's labor within the nuclear family.

… [A] second objection focuses on the fact that … there are any number of ways of evading the terms of this contract without ceasing to be heterosexual. Thus the claim that heterosexual relations are male dominant ones is insufficient to support the claim that only lesbians are genuine resisters. Indeed, the heterosexual feminist who insists on a more equal partnership may resist patriarchy more effectively than many lesbians. …

Heterosexualism versus Heterosexuality

Both [Janice] Raymond and [Sarah] Hoagland avoid equating "lesbian" with "femi-nist" by distinguishing heterosexuality from "hetero-relations" (Raymond) and "heter-osexualism" (Hoagland).[28] Within their writing, "heterosexuality" retains its custom-ary referent to sexual object choice. "Hetero relations" and "heterosexualism" refer to the patriarchal nature of male–female relations in both the private and public spheres. … It is, in their view, hetero-relationalism, not heterosexuality, per se, that subordi-nates women to men.

By distinguishing hetero-relations and heterosexualism from heterosexuality Ray-mond and Hoagland avoid exaggerating the feminist element in lesbianism. … Both recognize the potential failure of lesbians to disengage from heterosexualism. Lesbians themselves may be misogynistic and may engage in the same dominance-subordinance relations that typify heterosexualism. Thus lesbian resistance to heterosexuality is not automatically a resistance to patriarchy. … In addition, by recognizing that heterosex-ual women can redefine their relations to men in such a way that they both leave space for gyn-affectionate relations with women and refuse to participate in hetero-relations with men, Raymond avoids pitting lesbians against heterosexual women within the feminist community in a battle over who counts as a "true" feminist.

Their attempt, however, to avoid claiming too much for lesbianism comes at the cost of ultimately claiming too little for it. By putting the concept of hetero-relations or heterosexualism at the center of their lesbian feminism, both effectively eliminate space for a *lesbian* theory. Within their work, lesbian resistance to heterosexuality does not, in itself, have either political or conceptual significance. Whatever political significance lesbian personal lives may have is due entirely to the presence of or resistance to hetero-relations within those lives. The reduction of lesbian politics to feminist politics is quite obvious in Raymond's "Putting the Politics Back into Lesbianism."[29] There, Raymond sharply criticizes lesbian lifestylers and sexual libertarians for failure to see that in advocating an anything-goes sexuality (including lesbian pornography and s/m) as the path to liberation, they are simply repeating the patriarchal image of woman as essentially sexual being. Moreover, as I mentioned earlier, insofar as lesbian lifestylers advocate aggressive and violent forms of sexuality, they are simply putting a "male-constructed sexuality in drag."[30] What I want to underscore in Raymond's critique is that putting politics into lesbianism means putting *feminist* politics into lesbianism. She does not demand that lesbians put resistance to heterosexuality and to lesbian oppression at the center of their lives. Thus she does not ask whether or not lesbian s/m promotes *lesbian* politics.

One important consequence of equating lesbian with feminist politics in this way is that lesbians who have suffered the worst oppression, for example, the 1950s butches and femmes who risked repeated arrest and police harassment, often turn out to be the least politically interesting from a feminist point of view. Shane Phelan's criticism of Adrienne Rich for marginalizing "real" lesbians who resisted heterosexuality and for giving nonlesbians who resisted dependency on men pride of place on her lesbian continuum applies generally to those who equate lesbian politics with feminist politics. ...

From a feminist point of view whose political yardstick measures only distance from patriarchal practices and institutions, butches and femmes, lesbian sex radicals who promote pornography and s/m, lesbian mothers, and married lesbians all fail to measure up. All are vulnerable to the charge of appropriating for women and between women the very practices and institutions that have served so well to oppress women. Yet it is precisely these women, who insist on the reality and value of romance, sexuality, parenting, and marriage between women, who resist most strongly heterosexual society's reservation of the private sphere for male–female couples only. From a lesbian point of view whose political yardstick measures resistance to heterosexuality and heterosexual privilege, they are neither politically uninteresting nor assimilationist.

Not only does this focus on heterosexualism rather than heterosexuality leave no space for understanding the inherently political nature of lesbianism, it also leaves no space for understanding the significance of specifically lesbian love. ... Specifically lesbian sexual and romantic attraction to women is left without any politically or conceptually interesting place to be. Raymond is by no means the first or only lesbian feminist to marginalize lesbian love in favor of a form of love between women that is more directly tied to feminist solidarity. Bunch, for example, claims that "the lesbian, woman-identified-woman commits herself to women not only as an alternative to oppressive male–female relationships but primarily because she *loves* women."[31] That this is not a particularized conception of love but rather feminist "love" of women as a class becomes clear in the way she connects lesbian love with class solidarity: "When women do give primary energies to other women, then it is possible to concentrate fully on building a movement for our liberation."[32] In a more recent piece, Nett Hart similarly equates lesbian love with love of women as a class: "We love women as a class and we love specific women. We embrace the concept that women can be loved, that women are inherently worthy of love."[33] In both Bunch and Hart, there is a conceptual slide from "love" in the sense of a sexual-romantic love of a particular woman to "love" in the sense of valuing and respecting members of the category "woman". Although Raymond differs in being much more careful to keep the two sorts of love conceptually separated, all three prioritize love of women as a class. From a feminist point of view it is indeed the capacity to value members of the category "woman" and to form strong primary bonds of friendship with many women that matters politically. But this is not lesbian love. Lesbians fall in love with, want to make love to, decide to set up a household with a particular other woman, not a class of women. It is for this particularized, sexualized love that lesbians are penalized in heterosexual society. Because of this, lesbian theory needs to move specifically lesbian love to the center of its political stage.

None of these remarks are intended either to undercut the value for feminists of work being done by lesbians or the need to subject lesbian practice to feminist critique. They are meant to suggest that a full-blown lesbian feminism cannot afford to reduce the political institution of heterosexuality to an institution of male dominance.

Heterosexuality as a Political System

I have been arguing so far that reading heterosexuality and lesbianism solely in relation to patriarchal gender politics fails to yield an adequate picture of lesbians' political position. I turn now to an exploration of the thesis that heterosexuality is itself a political system that shapes our social structure as systematically as do patriarchal, racial imperialist, and class systems.

I do not mean to deny that in patriarchal societies heterosexuality enables what Gayle Rubin called the "traffic in women." I *do* mean to deny that heterosexual systems' only function is to support a system of male privilege. I suggest instead that heterosexual systems, whether patriarchal or not, function to insure reproduction by making the male–female unit fundamental to social structure, particularly, though not exclusively, to the structure of what might broadly be called the private sphere. That is, heterosexual systems assign the heterosexual couple-based family a privileged social status as the only legitimate site of sexuality, child bearing, child rearing, the care of individuals' physical and emotional needs, the maintenance of a household, and the creation of kinship bonds. It is because the purpose of heterosexual systems is to sustain reproduction that threats to that system—for example, the education of women, or homosexuality—inevitably evoke in Anglo-American history some version of the race suicide argument.

Heterosexuality then is not just a matter of the orientation of individual sexual desire. It is a method of socially organizing a broad spectrum of reproductive activities. Accordingly, the taboo on homosexuality does not simply outlaw same-sex desire. More basically it outlaws the female–female or male–male couple as the site of any reproductive activities.[34] Thus, if one wants a complete set of the regulations that constitute the taboo on lesbianism and homosexuality, one needs to look at all of the practices that directly or indirectly insure that the family will be built around a male–female pair. The social and legal prohibition of same-sex sex is only the tip of the iceberg of the systematic heterosexualization of social life.

This socially foundational status of the male–female couple gets ideologically expressed and reinforced through the language of naturalness: the individuals who make up society are taken to be naturally gendered as men or women, naturally heterosexual, and naturally inclined to establish a family based around the male–female reproductive unit. The alleged natural inevitability of gender differences, heterosexual desire, and heterosexually reproductive families enables heterosexual societies to take it for granted that "of course" the social, economic, and legal structure of any society will, and ought to, reflect these basic facts.

Social practices, norms, and institutions are designed to meet heterosexual systems' need to produce sex/gender dimorphism—masculine males and feminine females—so that desire can then be heterosexualized. Gendered behavioral norms; gendered rites of passage, a sexual division of labor, and the like produce differently gendered persons out of differently sexed persons. Prohibitions against gender crossing (e.g., against cross-dressing, effeminacy in men, mannishness in women) also help sustain the dimorphism necessary to heterosexualize desire.

Children and especially adolescents are carefully prepared for heterosexual interaction. They are given heterosexual sex education, advice for attracting the opposite sex, norms for heterosexual behavior, and appropriate social occasions (such as dances or dating rituals) for enacting desire. Adult heterosexuality is further sustained through erotica and pornography, heterosexualized humor, heterosexualized dress, romance novels, and so on.

Heterosexual societies take it for granted that men and women will bond in an intimate relationship, ultimately founding a family. As a result, social conventions, economic arrangements, and the legal structure treat the heterosexual couple as a single, and singularly important, social unit. The couple is represented linguistically (boyfriend–girlfriend, husband–wife) and is treated socially as a single unit (e.g., in joint invitations or in receiving joint gifts). It is legally licensed and legally supported through such entitlements as communal property, joint custody or adoption of children, and the power to give proxy consent within the couple. The couple is also recognized in the occupational structure via such provisions as spousal health care benefits and restrictions on nepotism. Multiple practices and institutions help heterosexual individuals to couple and create families and support the continuation of those couples and couple-based families. These include dating services, matchmakers, introductions to eligible partners, premarital counseling, marriage counseling, marriage and divorce law, adoption services, reproductive technologies, family rates, family health care benefits, tax deductions for married couples, and so on.

The sum total of all the social, economic, and legal arrangements that support the sexual and relational coupling of men with women constitutes heterosexual privilege. And it is privilege of a peculiar sort. Heterosexuals do not simply claim *greater* socio-politico legal standing than nonheterosexuals. They claim as natural and normal an arrangement where *only* heterosexuals have socio-politico-legal standing. Lesbians and gay men are not recognized as social beings because they cannot enter into the most basic social unit, the male–female couple. Within heterosexual systems the only social arrangements that apply to nonheterosexuals are eliminative in nature. The coercive force of the criminal law, institutionalized discrimination, "therapeutic" treatment, and individual prejudice and violence is marshaled against the existence of lesbians and gay men. At best, lesbians and gay men have negative social reality. Lesbians are not-women engaged in nonsex within nonrelationships that may constitute a nonfamily.

It would be a mistake to think that legal prohibition of discrimination on the basis of sexual orientation or legal recognition of domestic partnerships would give lesbians and gay men any genuine sociopolitico-legal standing. The legal reduction of lesbianism to mere sexuality which is implicit in "sexual orientation" legislation only reconfirms the heterosexual assumption that lesbianism cannot itself provide the site for the broad spectrum of reproductive activities. Only heterosexuality, which "everyone knows" is more than mere sexual desire, can provide this site in the form of the heterosexual couple. Because lesbianism is supposedly mere sex and not a mode of sociality, no fundamental alteration needs to be made in the social practices and institutions that constitute the private sphere. Domestic partnership laws fall in the same boat. They set up what amount to separate but allegedly equal spheres for heterosexuals and nonheterosexuals. Heterosexuals retain coverage by marriage laws. All other possible private arrangements are covered under domestic partnerships. The point of excluding lesbian and gay marriages from marriage law itself is, of course, to reaffirm heterosexual society's most basic belief that only the male–female couple constitutes a natural, basic social unit.

In short, unlike the heterosexual woman, including the heterosexual feminist, the lesbian experience of the institution of heterosexuality is of a system that makes her sexual, affectional, domestic, and reproductive life unreal. Within heterosexual society, the experience between women of sexual fulfillment, of falling in love, of marrying, of creating a home, of starting a family have no social reality. Unlike the heterosexual feminist, the lesbian has no socially supported private sphere, not even an oppressive one.

Failure to see the difference between the heterosexual feminist's and the lesbian's relation to the institution of heterosexuality may well result in mislocating lesbian politics. From a feminist point of view, sexual interaction, romantic love, marriage, and the family are all danger zones because all have been distorted to serve male interests. It thus does not behoove feminist politics to begin by championing the importance of sexual interaction, romantic love, marriage, and the (couple-based) family. But it does behoove lesbian politics to start in precisely these places. Her recognition as a social being, and thus as an individual with socio-politico-legal standing, depends upon the female-female couple being recognized as a primary social unit. That in turn cannot be done without directly challenging the reservation of the primary structures of the private sphere for heterosexuals. Just as the heart of male privilege lies in the "right" of access to women, so the heart of heterosexual privilege lies in the "right" of access to sexual-romantic-marital-familial relationships.

Notes

1. Heidi Hartmann, [Reading 19].
2. On the former, see, e.g., Charlotte Bunch, "Lesbians in Revolt," in her *Passionate Politics, Essays 1968–1986* (New York: St. Martin's, 1987); and Monique Wittig, *The Straight Mind and Other Essays* (Boston: Beacon, 1992). Regarding the latter, see Adrienne Rich, "Compulsory Heterosexuality and the Lesbian Continuum," in *The Signs Reader: Women, Gender, and Scholarship*, ed Elizabeth Abel and Emily K. Abel (Chicago: University of Chicago Press, 1983).
3. For instance, … Jeffner Allen, *Lesbian Philosophies and Cultures*, (Albany, N.Y.: SUNY Press, 1990), …
4. See, e.g., [ibid.], as well as Sarah Lucia Hoagland's *Lesbian Ethics* (Palo Alto, Calif.: Institute of Lesbian Studies, 1990 and Janice G. Raymond's *A Passion for Friends* (Boston: Boston, 1986).
5. Charlotte Bunch, "Lesbians in Revolt," "Learning from Lesbian Separatism," and "Lesbian-Feminist Theory," all in her *Passionate Politics*; Gayle Rubin, "The Traffic in Women," in *Toward an Anthropology of Women*, ed. Rayna Reiter (New York: Monthly Review, 1975); Kate Millett, *Sexual Politics* (New York: Doubleday, 1969); Rich; Wittig, *The Straight Mind*.
6. See, e.g., Marilyn Frye's critical assessment of the gay rights movement in … *The Politics of Reality* (Freedom, Calif.: Crossing, 1983) …
7. Charlotte Bunch, e.g., observes that "lesbianism and feminism are both about women loving and supporting women and women revolting against the so-called supremacy of men and the patriarchal institutions that control us." ("Lesbian-Feminist Theory," p. 196).
8. For brief historical discussions of this event, see Shane Phelan, *Identity Politics: Lesbian Feminism and the Limits of Community* (Philadelphia: Temple University Press, 1989); and Terralee Bensinger, "Lesbian Pornography: The Re/Making of (a) Community," *Discourse* 15 (1992): 69–93.
9. Radicalesbians, "The Woman Identified Woman," in *Radical Feminism*, ed. Anne Koedt et al. (New York: Quandrangle, 1973).
10. Monique Wittig, … *The Straight Mind and Other Essays*, p. 32.
11. Monique Wittig, "The Category of Sex," p. 6.
12. Ibid., p. 2.
13. Monique Wittig, "One Is Not Born a Woman."
14. This point has been made by a number of authors, including Marilyn Frye, … *The Politics of Reality*, and Kathryn Pyne Addelson ("Words and Lives," *Signs* 7 [1981]: 187–99).
15. Wittig, "One Is Not Born a Woman."
16. I use "sex/gender" rather than "gender" throughout the argument that lesbians are not-women in order to avoid implying that what makes lesbians not-women is simply their gender deviance (e.g., their butchness or refusal to be subordinate to men). I want to stress instead that lesbians are not clearly female. It is sex deviance combined with gender deviance that I think results in lesbians' exit from the category "woman".
17. Judith Butler, *Gender Trouble: Feminism and the Subversion of Identity* (New York: Routledge, 1990), p. 17.
18. Frye [1983] quite vividly describes the phenomenon of compulsory sex/gender …
19. Julia Penelope, *Call Me Lesbian: Lesbian Lives, Lesbian Theory* (Freedom, Calif.: Crossing, 1992).
20. Janice G. Raymond, "Putting the Politics Back into Lesbianism," *Women's Studies International Forum* 12 (1989): 149–56.
21. Butler, *Gender Trouble*, p. 123 …
22. Quote of the week from Allan Berubé in *City on a Hill* 26, no. 30 (1992): 10 … Frye [1983] similarly comments that "heterosexual critics of queers' 'role-playing' ought to look at themselves in the mirror on their way out for a night on the town to see who's in drag. The answer is, everybody is" (p. 29).
23. Wittig makes this point in "One Is Not Born a Woman," p. 10.
24. Ibid., p. 14.
25. Bunch, "Lesbians in Revolt," p. 165.

26. Ibid., p. 166.

27. Ann Ferguson, "Patriarchy, Sexual Identity, and the Sexual Revolution," in Ann Ferguson, Jacquelyn N. Zita, and Kathryn Pyne Addelson, "Viewpoint: On "Compulsory Heterosexuality and Lesbian Existence': Defining the Issues," *Signs* 7 (1981): 147–88, p. 159.

28. [See Sarah Lucia Hoagland's *Lesbian Ethics: Toward New Value* (Palo Alto, Calif.: Institute of Lesbian Studies, 1990); and Janice G. Raymond's *A Passion for Friends* (Boston: Beacon, 1986).]

29. Raymond, "Putting the Politics Back into Lesbianism." See also her criticisms of lesbian s/m in ... *A Passion for Friends.*

30. [Ibid] p. 150.

31. Bunch, "Lesbians in Revolt," p. 162.

32. Ibid.

33. Nett Hart, "Lesbian Desire as Social Action," in Allen, ed., p. 297.

34. This helps to explain why it is relatively easy to garner toleration of lesbianism and homosexuality as private bedroom practices, while attempts to sanction lesbian and gay parenting and marriages meet with intense resistance. I thank Mary Going for bringing me to see the critical importance of challenging the heterosexual couple-based family.

39.
SITUATED KNOWLEDGES: THE SCIENCE QUESTION IN FEMINISM AND THE PRIVILEGE OF PARTIAL PERSPECTIVE

Donna Haraway
(1988)

Academic and activist feminist inquiry has repeatedly tried to come to terms with the question of what *we* might mean by the curious and inescapable term "objectivity." We have used a lot of toxic ink and trees processed into paper decrying what *they* have meant and how it hurts *us*. The imagined "they" constitute a kind of invisible conspiracy of masculinist scientists and philosophers replete with grants and laboratories. The imagined "we" are the embodied others, who are not allowed *not* to have a body, a finite point of view, and so an inevitably disqualifying and polluting bias in any discussion of consequence. …

It has seemed to me that feminists have both selectively and flexibly used and been trapped by two poles of a tempting dichotomy on the question of objectivity. Certainly I speak for myself here, and I offer the speculation that there is a collective discourse on these matters. Recent social studies of science and technology, for example, have made available a very strong social constructionist argument for *all* forms of knowledge claims, most certainly and especially scientific ones.[1] According to these tempting views, no insider's perspective is privileged, because all drawings of inside–outside boundaries in knowledge are theorized as power moves not moves toward truth. … Social constructionists make clear that official ideologies about objectivity and scientific method are particularly bad guides to how scientific knowledge is actually *made*. Just as for the rest of us, what scientists believe or say they do and what they really do have a very loose fit. …

In any case, social constructionists might maintain that the ideological doctrine of scientific method and all the philosophical verbiage about epistemology were cooked up to distract our attention from getting to know the world *effectively* by practicing the sciences. From this point of view, science—the real game in town—is rhetoric, a series of efforts to persuade relevant social actors that one's manufactured knowledge is a route to a desired form of very objective power. Such persuasions must take account of the structure of facts and artifacts, as well as of language-mediated actors in the knowledge game. Here, artifacts and facts are parts of the powerful art of rhetoric. Practice is persuasion, and the focus is very much on practice. All knowledge is a condensed node in an agonistic power field. The strong program in the sociology of knowledge joins with the lovely and nasty tools of semiology and deconstruction to insist on the rhetorical nature of truth, including scientific truth. History is a story Western culture buffs tell each other; science is a contestable text and a power field; the content is the form.[2] Period.

So much for those of us who would still like to talk about *reality* with more confidence than we allow to the Christian Right when they discuss the Second Coming and their being raptured out of the final destruction of the world. We would like to think our appeals to real worlds are more than a desperate lurch away from cynicism and an act of faith like any other cult's, no matter how much space we generously give to all the rich and always historically specific mediations through which we and everybody else must know the world. But the further I get in describing the radical social constructionist program and a particular version of postmodernism, coupled with the acid tools of critical discourse in the human sciences, the more nervous I get. The imagery of force fields, of moves in a fully textualized and coded world, which is the working metaphor in many arguments about socially negotiated reality for the postmodern subject, is, just for starters, an imagery of high-tech military fields, of automated academic battlefields, where blips of light called players disintegrate (what a metaphor!) each other in order to stay in the knowledge and power game. Technoscience and science fiction collapse into the sun of their radiant (ir)reality-war.[3] It shouldn't take decades of feminist theory to sense the enemy here. Nancy Hartsock got all this crystal clear in her concept of abstract masculinity.[4]

I, and others, started out wanting a strong tool for deconstructing the truth claims of hostile science by showing the radical historical specificity, and so contestability, of *every* layer of the onion of scientific and technological constructions, and we end up with a kind of epistemological electroshock therapy. … We wanted a way to go beyond showing bias in science (that proved too easy anyhow) and beyond separating the good scientific sheep from the bad goats of bias and misuse. It seemed promising to do this by the strongest possible constructionist argument that left no cracks for reducing the issues to bias versus objectivity, use versus misuse, science versus pseudoscience. We unmasked the doctrines of objectivity because they threatened our budding sense of collective historical subjectivity and agency and our "embodied" accounts of the truth, and we ended up with one more excuse for not learning any post-Newtonian physics and one more reason to drop the old feminist self-help practices of repairing our own cars. They're just texts anyway, so let the boys have them back.

Some of us tried to stay sane in these disassembled and dissembling tunes by holding out for a feminist version of objectivity. Here, motivated by many of the same political desires, is the other seductive end of the objectivity problem. Humanistic Marxism was polluted at the source by its structuring theory about the domination of nature in the self-construction of man and by its closely related impotence in relation to historicizing anything women did that didn't qualify for a wage. But Marxism was still a promising resource as a kind of epistemological feminist mental hygiene that sought our own doctrines of objective vision. Marxist starting points offered a way to get to our

own versions of standpoint theories, insistent embodiment, a rich tradition of critiquing hegemony without disempowering positivisms and relativisms and a way to get to
nuanced theories of mediation.[5] ...

Another approach, "feminist empiricism," also converges with feminist uses of
Marxian resources to get a theory of science which continues to insist on legitimate
meanings of objectivity and which remains leery of a radical constructivism conjugated
with semiology and narratology.[6] Feminists have to insist on a better account of the
world; it is not enough to show radical historical contingency and modes of construction for everything. Here, we, as feminists, find ourselves perversely conjoined with the
discourse of many practicing scientists, who, when all is said and done, mostly believe
they are describing and discovering things *by means of* all their constructing and arguing. Evelyn Fox Keller has been particularly insistent on this fundamental matter, and
Sandra Harding calls the goal of these approaches a "successor science." Feminists have
stakes in a successor science project that offers a more adequate, richer, better account
of a world, in order to live in it well and in critical, reflexive relation to our own as well
as others' practices of domination and the unequal parts of privilege and oppression
that make up all positions. In traditional philosophical categories, the issue is ethics and
politics perhaps more than epistemology.

So, I think my problem, and "our" problem, is how to have *simultaneously* an
account of radical historical contingency for all knowledge claims and knowing subjects, a critical practice for recognizing our own "semiotic technologies" for making
meanings, *and* a no-nonsense commitment to faithful accounts of a "real" world,
one that can be partially shared and that is friendly to earthwide projects of finite freedom, adequate material abundance, modest meaning in suffering, and limited happiness. ...

The Persistence of Vision

I would like to proceed by placing metaphorical reliance on a much maligned sensor
system in feminist discourse: vision.[7] Vision can be good for avoiding binary oppositions. I would like to insist on the embodied nature of all vision and so reclaim the
sensory system that has been used to signify a leap out of the marked body and into a
conquering gaze from nowhere. ... I would like a doctrine of embodied objectivity that
accommodates paradoxical and critical feminist science projects: Feminist objectivity
means quite simply *situated knowledges*.

The eyes have been used to signify a perverse capacity—honed to perfection in the
history of science tied to militarism, capitalism, colonialism, and male supremacy—to
distance the knowing subject from everybody and everything in the interests of unfettered power. The instruments of visualization in multinationalist, postmodernist culture have compounded these meanings of disembodiment. The visualizing technologies are without apparent limit. ...

But, of course, that view of infinite vision is an illusion, a god trick. I would like
to suggest how our insisting metaphorically on the particularity and embodiment of
all visions (although not necessarily organic embodiment and including technological

mediation), and not giving in to the tempting myths of vision as a route to disembodiment and ... a usable, but not an innocent, doctrine of objectivity. I want a feminist writing of the body that metaphorically emphasizes vision again, because we need to reclaim that sense to find our way through all the visualizing tricks and powers of modern sciences and technologies that have transformed the objectivity debates. We need to learn in our bodies, endowed with primate color and stereoscopic vision, how to attach the objective to our theoretical and political scanners in order to name where we are and are, in dimensions of mental and physical space we hardly know how to name. So, not so perversely, objectivity turns out to be about particular and specific embodiment and definitely not about the false vision promising transcendence of all limits and responsibility. The moral is simple: only partial perspectives promise objective vision. All Western cultural narratives about objectivity are allegories of the ideologies governing the relations of what we call mind and body, distance and responsibility. Feminist objectivity is about limited location and situated knowledge, not about transcendence and splitting of subject and object. It allows us to become answerable for what we learn how to see.

There are lessons that I learned in part walking with my dogs and wondering how the world looks without a fovea and very few retinal cells for color vision but with a huge neural processing and sensory area for smells. It is a lesson available from photographs of how the world looks to the compound eyes of a insect or even from the camera eye of a spy satellite or the digitally transmitted signals of space probe-perceived differences "near" Jupiter that have been transformed into coffee table color photographs. The "eyes" made available in modern technological sciences shatter any idea of passive vision; these prosthetic devices show us that tall eyes, including our organic ones, are active perceptual systems, building on translations and specific *ways* of seeing, that is, ways of life. There is no unmediated photograph or passive camera obscura in scientific accounts of bodies and machines; there are only highly specific visual possibilities, each with a wonderfully detailed, active, partial way of organizing worlds. All these pictures of the world should not be allegories of infinite mobility and interchangeability but of elaborate specificity and difference and the loving care people might take to learn how to see faithfully from another's point of view, even when the other is our own machine. That's not alienating distance; that's a *possible* allegory for feminist versions of objectivity. Understanding how these visual systems work, technically, socially, and psychically, ought to be a way of embodying feminist objectivity.

Many currents in feminism attempt to theorize grounds for trusting especially the vantage points of the subjugated; there is good reason to believe vision is better from below the brilliant space platforms of the powerful.[8] Building on that suspicion, this essay is an argument for situated and embodied knowledges and an argument against various forms of unlocatable, and so irresponsible, knowledge claims. Irresponsible means unable to be called into account. There is a premium on establishing the capacity to see from the peripheries and the depths. But here there also lies serious danger of romanticizing and/or appropriating the vision of the less powerful while claiming to see from their positions. To see from below is neither easily learned nor unproblematic, even if "we" "naturally" inhabit the great underground terrain of subjugated knowledges. The positionings of the subjugated are not exempt from critical reexamination, decoding, deconstruction, and interpretation; that is, from both semiological and hermeneutic modes of critical inquiry. The standpoints of the subjugated are not "innocent" positions. On the contrary, they are preferred because in principle they are least likely to allow denial of the critical and interpretive core of all knowledge. They are knowledgeable of modes of denial through repression, forgetting, and disappearing acts—ways of being nowhere while claiming to see comprehensively. The subjugated have a decent chance to be on to the god trick and all its dazzling—and, therefore, blinding—illuminations. "Subjugated" standpoints are preferred because they seem to promise more adequate, sustained, objective, transforming accounts of the world. But *how* to see from below is a problem requiring at least as much skill with bodies and language, with the mediations of vision, as the "highest" technoscientific visualizations.

Such preferred positionings is a hostile to various forms of relativism as to the most explicitly totalizing versions of claims to scientific authority. But the alternative to relativism is not totalization and single vision, which is always finally the unmarked category whose power depends on systematic narrowing and obscuring. The alternative to relativism is partial, locatable, critical knowledges sustaining the possibility of webs of connections called solidarity in politics and shared conversations in epistemology. Relativism is a way of being nowhere while claiming to be everywhere equally. The "equality" of positioning is a denial of responsibility and critical inquiry. Relativism is the perfect mirror twin of totalization in the ideologies of objectivity; both deny the stakes in location, embodiment, and partial perspective; both make it impossible to see well. Relativism and totalization are both "god tricks" promising vision from everywhere and nowhere equally and fully, common myths in rhetorics surrounding Science. But it is precisely in the politics and epistemology of partial perspectives that the possibility of sustained, rational, objective inquiry rests.

So, with many other feminists, I want to argue for a doctrine and practice of objectivity that privileges contestations, deconstruction, passionate construction, webbed connections, and hope for transformation of systems of knowledge and ways of seeing. But no just any partial perspective will do; we must be hostile to easy relativisms and holisms built out of summing and subsuming parts. "Passionate detachment"[9] requires more than acknowledged and self-critical partiality. We are also bound to seek perspective from those points of view, which can never be known in advance, that promise something quite extraordinary, that is, knowledge potent for constructing worlds less organized by axes of domination. ...

A commitment to mobile positioning and to passionate detachment is dependent on the impossibility of entertaining innocent "identity" politics and epistemologies as strategies for seeing from the standpoints of the subjugated in order to see well. One cannot "be" either a cell or molecule—or a woman, colonized person, laborer, and so on—if one intends to see and see from these positions critically. "Being" is much more problematic and contingent. Also, one cannot relocate in any possible vantage point without being accountable for that movement. Vision is *always* a question of the power to see—and perhaps of the violence implicit in our visualizing practices. With whose blood were my eyes crafted? These points also apply to testimony from the position of "oneself." We are not immediately present to ourselves. Self-knowledge requires a semiotic-material technology to link meaning and bodies. ... The Western eye has fundamentally been a wandering eye, a traveling lens. These peregrinations have often been violent and insistent on having mirrors for a conquering self—but not always. Western feminists also *inherit* some skill in learning to participate in revisualizing worlds turned upside down in earth-transforming challenges to the views of the masters. All is not to be done from scratch.

The split and contradictory self is the one who can interrogate positionings and be accountable, the one who can construct and join rational conversations and fantastic imaginings that change history.[10] Splitting, not being, is the privileged image for feminist epistemologies of scientific knowledge. ... This geometry pertains within and among subjects. Subjectivity is multidimensional; so, therefore, is vision. The knowing self is partial in all its guises, never finished, whole, simply there and original; it is always constructed and stitched together imperfectly, and *therefore* able to join with another, to see together without claiming to be another. Here is the promise of objectivity: a scientific knower seeks the subject position, not of identity, but of objectivity, that is, partial connection. There is no way to "be" simultaneously in all, or wholly in any, of the privileged (i.e., subjugated) positions structured by gender, race, nation, and class. And that is a short list of critical positions. The search for such a "full" and total position is the search for the fetishized perfect subject of oppositional history, sometimes appearing in feminist theory as the essentialized Third Word Woman.[11] Subjugation is not ground for an ontology; it might be a visual clue. Vision requires instruments of vision; an optics is a politics of positioning. Instruments of vision mediate standpoints; there is no immediate vision from the standpoints of the subjugated. Identity, including self-identity, does not produce science; critical positioning does, that is, objectivity. Only those occupying the positions of the dominators are self-identical, unmarked, disembodied, unmediated, transcendent, born again. It is unfortunately possible for the subjugated to lust for and even scramble into that subject position—and then disappear from view. Knowledge from the point of view of the unmarked is truly fantastic, distorted, and irrational. The only position from which objectivity could not possibly be practiced and honored is the standpoint of the master, the Man, the One God, whose Eye produces, appropriates, and orders all difference. No one ever accused the God of monotheism of objectivity, only of indifference. The god trick is self-identical, and we have mistaken that for creativity and knowledge, omniscience even.

Positioning is, therefore, the key practice in grounding knowledge organized around the imagery of vision, and much Western scientific and philosophic discourse is organized in this way. Positioning implies responsibility for our enabling practices. It follows that politics and ethics ground struggles for and contests over what may count as rational knowledge. That is, admitted or not, politics and ethics ground struggles over knowledge projects in the exact, natural, social, and human sciences. Otherwise, rationality is simply impossible, an optical illusion projected from nowhere comprehensively. Histories of science may be powerfully told as histories of the technologies. These technologies are skilled practices. How to see? Where to see from? What limits to vision? What to see for? Whom to see with? Who gets to have more than one point of view? Who gets blinded? Who wears blinders? Who interprets the visual field? What other sensory powers do we wish to cultivate besides vision? Moral and political discourse should be the paradigm for rational discourse about the imagery and technologies of vision. ... Struggles over what will count as rational accounts of the world are struggles over *how* to see. ...

The issue in politically engaged attacks on various empiricism, reductionisms, or other versions of scientific authority should not be relativism—but location. ... For example, local knowledges have to be in tension with the productive structurings that force unequal translations and exchanges—material and semiotic—within the webs of knowledge and power. Webs *can* have the property of being systematic, even of being centrally structured global systems with deep filaments and tenacious tendrils into time, space, and consciousness, which are the dimensions of world history. Feminist accountability requires a knowledge tuned to resonance, not to dichotomy. Gender is a field of structured and structuring difference, in which the tones of extreme localization, of the intimately personal and individualized body, vibrate in the same field with global high-tension emissions. Feminist embodiment, then, is not about fixed location in a reified body, female or other wise, but about nodes in fields, inflections in orientations, and responsibility for difference in material-semiotic fields of meaning. Embodiment is significant prosthesis; objectivity cannot be about fixed vision when what counts as an object is precisely what world history turns out to be about.

How should one be positioned in order to see, in this situation of tensions, reasonances, transformations, resistances, and complicities? Here, primate vision is not immediately a very powerful metaphor or technology for feminist political-epistemological clarification, because it seems to present to consciousness already processed and objectified fields; things seem already fixed and distanced. But the visual metaphor allows one to go beyond the fixed appearances, which are only the end products. The metaphor invites us to investigate the varied apparatuses of visual production, including the prosthetic technologies interfaced with our biological eyes and brains. And here we find highly particular machineries for processing regions of the electromagnetic spectrum into our pictures of the world. It is in the intricacies of these visualization technologies in which we are embedded that we will find metaphors and means for understanding and intervening in the patters of objectification in the world—that is, the patterns of reality for which we must be accountable. In these metaphors, we find means for appreciating simultaneously *both* the concrete, "real" aspect and the aspect of semiosis and production in what we call scientific knowledge.

I am arguing for politics and epistemologies of location, positioning, and situating, where partiality and not universality is the condition of being heard do make rational knowledge claims. These are claims on people's lives. I am arguing for the view from a body, always a complex, contradictory, structuring, and structured body, versus the view from above, from nowhere, from simplicity. Only the god trick is forbidden. ...

Feminism loves another science: the sciences and politics of interpretation, translation, stuttering, and the partly understood. Feminism is about the sciences of the multiple subject with (at least) double vision. Feminism is about a critical vision consequent upon a critical positioning in unhomogeneous gendered social space.[12] Translation is always interpretive, critical, and partial. Here is a ground for conversation, rationality, and objectivity—which is power-sensitive, not pluralist, "conversation." … There is no single feminist standpoint because our maps require too many dimensions for that metaphor to ground our visions. But the feminist standpoint theorists' goal of an epistemology and politics of engaged, accountable positioning remains eminently potent. The goal is better accounts of the world, that is, "science."

Above all, rational knowledge does not pretend to disengagement: to be from everywhere and so nowhere, to be free from interpretation, from being represented, to by fully self-contained or fully formalizable. Rational knowledge is a process of ongoing critical interpretation among "fields" of interpreters and decoders. Rational knowledge is power-sensitive conversation.[13] Decoding and transcoding plus translation and criticism; all are necessary. So science becomes the paradigmatic model, not of closure, but of that which is contestable and contested. Science becomes the myth, not of what escapes human agency and responsibility in a realm above the fray, but rather, of accountability and responsibility for translations and solidarities linking the cacophonous visions and visionary voices that characterize the knowledges of the subjugated. A splitting of senses, a confusion of voice and sight, rather than clear and distinct ideas, becomes the metaphor for the ground of the rational. We seek not the knowledges ruled by phallogocentrism (nostalgia for the presence of the one true Word) and disembodied vision. We seek those ruled by partial sight and limited voice—not partiality for its own sake but, rather, for the sake of the connections and unexpected openings situated knowledges make possible. Situated knowledges are about communities, not about isolated individuals. The only way to find a larger vision is to be somewhere in particular. The science question in feminism is about objectivity as positioned rationality. Its images are not the products of escape and transcendence of limits (the view from above) but the joining of partial views and halting voices into a collective subject position that promises a vision of the means of ongoing finite embodiment, of living within limits and contradictions—of views from somewhere.

Objects as Actors: The Apparatus of Bodily Production

Throughout this reflection on "objectivity," I have refused to resolve the ambiguities built into referring to science without differentiating its extraordinary range of contexts. Through the insistent ambiguity, I have foregrounded a field of commonalities binding exact, physical, natural, social, political, biological, and human sciences; and I have tied this whole heterogeneous field academically (and industrially, e.g., in publishing, the weapons trade, and pharmaceuticals) institutionalized knowledge production to a meaning a science that insists on is potency in ideological struggles. But, partly in order to give play to both the specificities and the highly permeable boundaries of meanings in discourse on science, I would like to suggest a resolution to one ambiguity. Throughout the field of meanings constituting science, one of the commonalities concerns the status of any object of knowledge and of related claims about the faithfulness of our accounts to a "real world," no matter how mediated for us and no matter how complex and contradictory these worlds may be. Feminists, and others who have been most active as critics of the sciences and their claims or associated ideologies, have shied away from doctrines of scientific objectivity in part because of the suspicion that an "object" of knowledge is a passive and inert thing. Accounts of such objects can seem to be either appropriations of a fixed and determined world reduced to resource for instrumentalist projects of destructive Western societies, or they can be seen as masks for interests, usually dominating interests.

For example, "sex" as an object of biological knowledge appears regularly in the guise of biological determinism, threatening the fragile space for social construction-ism and critical theory, with their attendant possibilities for active and transformative intervention, which were called into being by feminist concepts of gender as socially, historically, and semiotically positioned difference. And yet, to lose authoritative bio-logical accounts of sex, which set up productive tensions with gender seems to be to lose too much; it seems to be to lose not just analytic power within a particular Western tradition but also the body itself as anything but a blank page for social inscription, including those of biological discourse. The same problem of loss attends the radical "reduction" of the objects of physics or of any science to the ephemera of discursive production and social construction.[14]

But the difficulty and loss are not necessary. They derive partly from the analytic tradition, deeply indebted to Aristotle to the transformative history of "White Capi-talist Patriarchy" (how may we name this scandalous Thing?) that turns everything into a resource for appropriation, in which an object of knowledge is finally itself only matter for the seminal power, the act, of the knower. Here, the object both guarantees and refreshes the power of the knower, but any status as *agent* in the productions of knowledge must be denied the object. It—the world—must, in short, be objectified as a thing, not as an agent; it must be matter for the self-formation of the only social being in the productions of knowledge, the human knower. ... Nature is only the raw mate-rial culture, appropriated, preserved, enslaved, exalted, or other wise made flexible for disposal by culture in the logic of capitalist colonialism. Similarly, sex is only matter to the act of gender; the productionist logic seems inescapable in traditions of Western binary oppositions. This analytical and historical narrative logic accounts for my nerv-ousness about the sex/gender distinction in the recent history of feminist theory. Sex is "resourced" for its representation as gender, which "we" can control. It has seemed all but impossible to avoid the trap of an appropriationist logic of domination built into the nature/culture opposition and its generative lineage, including the sex/gender distinction.

It seems clear that feminist accounts of objectivity and embodiment—that is, of a world—of the kind sketched in this essay require a deceptively simple maneuver within inherited Western analytical traditions, a maneuver begun in dialectics but stopping short of the needed revisions. Situated knowledges require that the object of knowledge be pictured as an actor and agent, not as a screen or a ground or a resource, never finally as slave to the master that closes off the dialectic in his unique agency and his authorship of "objective" knowledge. The point is paradigmatically clear in critical approaches to the social and human sciences, where the agency of people studied itself transforms the entire project of producing social theory. Indeed, coming to terms with the agency of the "objects" studied is the only way to avoid gross error and false knowledge of many kinds in these sciences. But the same point must apply to the other knowledge projects called sciences. ... Accounts of a "real" world do not, then, depend on a logic of "discovery" but on a power-charged social relation of "conversation." The world neither speaks itself nor disappears in favor of a master decoder. The codes of the world are not still, waiting only to be read. ...

My simple, perhaps simple-minded, maneuver is obviously not new in Western philosophy, but it has a special feminist edge to it in relation to the science question in feminist and to the linked question of gender as situated difference and the question of female embodiment. Ecofeminists have perhaps been most insistent on some version of the world as active subject, not as resource to be mapped and appropriated in bourgeois, Marxist, or masculinist projects. Acknowledging the agency of the world in knowledge makes room for some unsettling possibilities, including a sense of the world's independent sense of humor. Such a sense of humor is not comfortable for humanists and others committed to the world as resource. There are, however, richly evocative figures to promote feminist visualization of the world as witty agent. We need not lapse into appeals to a primal mother resisting her translation into resource. The Coyote or Trickster, as embodied in Southwest native American accounts, suggests the situation we are in when we give up mastery but keep searching for fidelity, knowing all the while that we will be hoodwinked. I think these are useful myths for scientists who might be our allies. Feminist objectivity makes room for surprises and ironies at the heart of all knowledge production; we are not in charge of the world. We just live here and try to strike up noninnocent conversations by means of our prosthetic devices, including our visualization technologies. No wonder science fiction has been such a rich writing practice in recent feminist theory. I like to see feminist theory as a reinvented coyote discourse obligated to its sources in many heterogeneous accounts of the world.

Another rich feminist practice in science in the last couple of decades illustrates particularly well the "activation" of the previously passive categories of objects of knowledge. This activation permanently problematizes binary distinctions like sex and gender, without eliminating their strategic utility. I refer to the reconstructions in primatology (especially, but not only, in women's practice as primatologists, evolutionary biologists, and behavioral ecologists) of what may count as sex, especially as female sex, in scientific accounts.[15] The *body*, the object of biological discourse, becomes a most engaging being. Claims of biological determinism can never be the same again. When female "sex" has been so thoroughly retheorized and revisualized that it emerges as practically indistinguishable from "mind," something basic has happened to the categories of biology. The biological female peopling current biological behavioral accounts has almost no passive properties left. She is structuring and active in every respect; the "body" is an agent, not a resource. Difference is theorized *biologically* as situational, not intrinsic, at every level from gene to foraging pattern, thereby fundamentally changing the biological politics of the body. The relations between sex and gender need to be categorically reworked within these frames of knowledge. I would like to suggest that this trend in explanatory strategies in biology is an allegory for interventions faithful to projects of feminist objectivity. The point is not that these new pictures of the biological female are simply true or not open to contestation and conversation—quite the opposite. But these pictures foreground knowledge as situated conversation at every level of its articulation. The boundary between animal and human is one of the stakes in this allegory, as is the boundary between machine and organism. ...

Objectivity is not about disengagement but about mutual *and* usually unequal structuring, about taking risks in a world where "we" are permanently mortal, that is, not in "final" control. ... Feminist embodiment, feminist hopes for partiality, objectivity, and situated knowledges, turn on conversations and codes at this potent node in fields of possible bodies and meanings. Here is where science, science fantasy and science fiction converge in the objectivity question in feminism. Perhaps our hopes for accountability, for politics, for ecofeminism, turn on revisioning the world as coding trickster with whom we must learn to converse.

Notes

1. For example, see Karin Knorr-Cetina and Michael Mulkay, eds., *Science Observed* (London: Sage, 1983); Wiebe E. Bijker, Thomas P. Hughes, and Trevor Pinch, eds., *The Social Construction of Technological Systems* (Cambridge: MIT Press, 1987); and esp. Bruno Latour's *Les microbes, guerre et paix, suivi de irréductions* (Paris: Métailié, 1984) and *The Pastuerization of France, Followed by Irreductions* (Cambridge: Harvard University Press, 1988). Borrowing from Michel Tournier's *Vendredi* (Paris: Gallimard, 1967), *Les microbes* (p. 171). ...

2. For an elegant and very helpful elucidation of a noncartoon version of this argument, see Hayden White, *The Content of the Form* (Baltimore: Johns Hopkins University Press, 1987). ...

3. In "Through the Lumen " (Ph.D. diss. University of California at Santa Cruz, 1988), Zoe Sofoulis has produced a dazzling (she will forgive me the metaphor) theoretical treatment of technoscience, the psychoanalysis of science fiction culture, and the metaphorics of extraterrestrialism, including a wonderful focus on the ideologies and philosophies of light, illumination, and discovery in Western mythics of science and technology. My essay was revised in dialogue with Sofoulis's arguments and metaphors in her dissertation.

4. Nancy Hartsock, *Money, Sex, and Power* (Boston: Northeastern University Press, 1984).

5. Crucial to this discussion are Sandra Harding, *The Science Question in Feminism* (Ithaca: Cornell University Press, 1987); Evelyn Fox Keller, *Reflections on Gender and Science* (New Haven: Yale University Press, 1984); Nancy Hartsock, "The Feminist Standpoint," in *Discovering Reality*, eds. Sandra Harding and Merrill B. Hintikka (Dordrecht, The Netherlands: Reidel, 1983): 283–310; Jane Flax's "Political Philosophy and the Patriarchal Unconscious," in *Discovering Reality*, 245–81; and "Postmodernism and Gender Relations in Feminist Theory," *Signs* 12 (Summer 1987): 621–43; Evelyn Fox Keller and Christine Grontkowski, "The Mind's Eye," in *Discovering Reality*, 207–24; Hilary Rose, "Women's Work, Women's Knowledge," in *What Is Feminism? A Re-Examination*, eds. Juliet Mitchell and Ann Oakley (New York: Pantheon, 1986), 161–83; Donna Haraway, "A Manifesto for Cyborgs," *Socialist Review*, no. 80 (March-April 1985): 65–107; and Rosalind Pollack Petchesky, "Fetal Images," Feminist Studies 13 (Summer 1987): 263–92. ...

6. Harding, 24–26, 161–62.

7. John Varley's science fiction short story, "The Persistence of Vision," in *The Persistence of Vision* (New York: Dell, 1978), 263–316, is part of the inspiration for this section. ...

8. See Hartsock, "The Feminist Standpoint"; and Chela Sandoval, *Yours in Struggle Women Respond to Racism* (Oakland: Center for Third World Organizing, n.d.); Harding; and Gloria Anzaldua, *Borderlands/La Frontera* (San Francisco: Spinsters/Aunt Lute, 1987).

9. Annette Kuhn, *Women's Pictures* (London: Routledge & Kegan Paul, 1982), 3–18.

10. ... See Theresa de Lauretis, "Feminist Studies/Critical Studies," in her *Feminist Studies/Critical Studies* (Bloomington: Indiana University Press, 1986), 14–15.

11. Chandra Mohanty, "Under Western Eyes," *Boundary* 2 and 3 (1984): 333–58.

12. In *The Science Question in Feminism* (p. 181), Harding suggests that gender has three dimensions, each historically specific: gender symbolism, the social-sexual division of labor, and processes of constructing individual gendered identity. I would enlarge her point to note that there is no reason to expect the three dimensions to covary or codetermine each other, at least not directly. That is, extremely steep gradients between contrasting terms in gender symbolism may very well not correlate with sharp social-sexual divisions of labor or social power, but they may be closely related to sharp racial stratification or something else. Similarly, the processes of gendered subject formation may not be directly illuminated by knowledge of the sexual division of labor or the gender symbolism in the particular historical situation under examination. ...

13. Katie King, "Canons without Innocence" (Ph.D. diss., University of California at Santa Cruz, 1987).

14. Evelyn Fox Keller, in "The Gender/Science System" (*Hypatia* 2 [Fall 1987]): 37–49), has insisted on the important possibilities opened up by the construction of the intersection of the distinction between sex and gender, on the one hand, and nature and science, on the other. She also insists on the need to hold to some nondiscursive grounding in "sex" and "nature," perhaps what I am calling the "body" and "world."

15. Donna Haraway, *Primate Visions* (New York: Routledge & Kegan Paul), forthcoming Spring 1989.

POSTSTRUCTURALIST
EPISTEMOLOGIES

40.
THIS SEX WHICH IS NOT ONE[1]
Luce Irigaray
(1977)

Female sexuality has always been theorized within masculine parameters. Thus, the opposition "virile" clitoral activity/"feminine" vaginal passivity which Freud—and many others—claims are alternative behaviors or steps in the process of becoming a sexually normal woman, seems prescribed more by the practice of masculine sexuality than by anything else. For the clitoris is thought of as a little penis which is pleasurable to masturbate, as long as the anxiety of castration does not exist (for the little boy), while the vagina derives its value from the "home" it offers the male penis when the now forbidden hand must find a substitute to take its place in giving pleasure.

According to these theorists, woman's erogenous zones are no more than a clitoris-sex, which cannot stand up in comparison with the valued phallic organ; or a hole-envelope, a sheath which surrounds and rubs the penis during coition; a nonsex organ or a masculine sex organ turned inside out in order to caress itself.

Woman and her pleasure are not mentioned in this conception of the sexual relationship. Her fate is one of "lack," "atrophy" (of her genitals), and "penis envy," since the penis is the only recognized sex organ of any worth. Therefore she tries to appropriate it for herself, by all the means at her disposal by her somewhat servile love of the father-husband capable of giving it to her; by her desire of a penis-child, preferably male; by gaining access to those cultural values which are still "by right" reserved for males alone and are therefore always masculine, etc. Woman lives her desire only as an attempt to possess at long last the equivalent of the male sex organ.

All of that seems rather foreign to her pleasure however, unless she remains within the dominant phallic economy. Thus, for example, woman's autoeroticism is very different from man's. He needs an instrument in order to touch himself: his hand, woman's genitals, language—and this self-stimulation requires a minimum of activity. But a woman touches herself by and within herself directly, without mediation, and before any distinction between activity and passivity is possible. A woman "touches herself" constantly without anyone being able to forbid her to do so, for her sex is composed of two lips which embrace continually. Thus, within herself she is already two—but not divisible into ones—who stimulate each other.

This autoeroticism, which she needs in order not to risk the disappearance of her pleasure in the sex act, is interrupted by a violent intrusion: the brutal spreading of these two lips by a violating penis. If, in order to assure an articulation between autoeroticism and heteroeroticism in coition (the encounter with the absolute other which always signifies death), the vagina must also, but not only, substitute for the little boy's hand, how can woman's autoeroticism possibly be perpetuated in the classic representation of sexuality? Will she not indeed be left the impossible choice between defensive virginity, fiercely turned back upon itself, or a body open for penetration, which no longer recognizes in its "hole" of a sex organ the pleasure of retouching itself? The almost exclusive, and ever so anxious, attention accorded the erection in Occidental sexuality proves to what extent the imaginary that commands it is foreign to everything female. For the most part, one finds in Occidental sexuality nothing more than imperatives dictated by rivalry among males: the "strongest" being the one who "gets it up the most," who has the longest, thickest, hardest penis or indeed the one who "pisses the farthest" (cf. little boys' games). These imperatives can also be dictated by sadomasochist fantasies, which in turn are ordered by the relationship between man and mother: his desire to force open, to penetrate, to appropriate for himself the mystery of the stomach in which he was conceived, the secret of his conception, of his "origin." Desire-need, also, once again, to make blood flow in order to revive a very ancient—intrauterine, undoubtedly, but also prehistoric—relation to the maternal.

Woman, in this sexual imaginary, is only a more or less complacent facilitator for the working out of man's fantasies, It is possible, and even certain, that she experiences vicarious pleasure there, but this pleasure is above all a masochistic prostitution of her body to a desire that is not her own and that leaves her in her well-known state of dependency. Not knowing what she wants, ready for anything, even asking for more, if only he will "take" her as the "object" of *his* pleasure, she will not say what *she* wants. Moreover, she does not know, or no longer knows, what she wants. As Freud admits, the beginnings of the sexual life of the little girl are so "obscure," so "faded by the years," that one would have to dig very deep in order to find, behind the traces of this civilization, this history, the vestiges of a more archaic civilization which could give some indication as to what woman's sexuality is all about. This very ancient civilization undoubtedly would not have the same language, the same alphabet—Woman's desire most likely does not speak the same language as man's desire, and it probably has been covered over by the logic that has dominated the West since the Greeks.

In this logic, the prevalence of the gaze, discrimination of form, and individualization of form is particularly foreign to female eroticism. Woman finds pleasure more in touch than in sight and her entrance into a dominant scopic economy signifies, once again, her relegation to passivity: she will be the beautiful object. Although her body is in this way eroticized and solicited to a double movement between exhibition and pudic retreat in order to excite the instincts of the "subject," her sex organ represents the honor of having nothing to see. In this system of representation and desire, the vagina is a flaw, a hole in the representation's scoptophilic objective. It was admitted already in Greek statuary that this "nothing to be seen" must be excluded, rejected, from such a scene of representation. Woman's sexual organs are simply absent from this scene: they are masked and her "slit" is sewn up.

In addition, this sex organ which offers nothing to the view has no distinctive form of its own. Although woman finds pleasure precisely in this incompleteness of the form of her sex organ, which is why it retouches itself indefinitely, her pleasure is denied by a civilization that privileges phallomorphism. The value accorded to the only definable form excludes the form involved in female autoeroticism. The *one* of form, the individual sex, proper name, literal meaning—supersedes, by spreading apart and dividing, this touching of *at least two* (lips) which keeps woman in contact with herself, although it would be impossible to distinguish exactly what "parts" are touching each other.

Whence the mystery that she represents in a culture that claims to enumerate everything, cipher everything by units, inventory everything by individualities. *She is neither one nor two.* She cannot, strictly speaking, be determined either as one person or as two. She renders any definition inadequate. Moreover she has no "proper" name. And her sex organ, which is not *a* sex organ, is counted as *no* sex organ. It is the negative, the opposite, the reverse, the counterpart, of the only visible and morphologically designatable sex organ (even if it does pose a few problems in its passage from erection to detumescence): the penis.

But woman holds the secret of the "thickness" of this "form," its many-layered volume, its metamorphosis from smaller to larger and vice versa, and even the intervals at which this change takes place. Without even knowing it. When she is asked to maintain, to revive, man's desire, what this means in terms of the value of her own desire is neglected. Moreover, she is not aware of her desire, at least not explicitly. But the force and continuity of her desire are capable of nurturing all the "feminine" masquerades that are expected of her for a long time.

It is true that she still has the child, with whom her appetite for touching, for contact, is given free reign, unless this appetite is already lost, or alienated by the taboo placed upon touching in a largely obsessional civilization. In her relation to the child she finds compensatory pleasure (or the frustrations she encounters all too often in sexual relations proper. Thus maternity supplants the deficiencies of repressed female sexuality. Is it possible that man and woman no longer even caress each other except indirectly through the mediation between them represented by the child? Preferably male. Man, identified with his son, rediscovers the pleasure of maternal coddling; woman retouches herself in fondling that part of her body: her baby-penis-clitoris.

What that entails for the amorous trio has been clearly spelled out. The Oedipal interdict seems, however, a rather artificial and imprecise law—even though it is the very means of perpetuating the authoritarian discourse of fathers—when it is decreed in a culture where sexual relations are impracticable, since the desire of man and the desire of woman are so foreign to each other. Each of them is forced to search for some common meeting ground by indirect means: either an archaic, sensory relation to the mother's body, or a current, active or passive prolongation of the law of the father. Their attempts are characterized by regressive emotional behavior and the exchange of words so far from the realm of the sexual that they are completely exiled from it. "Mother" and "father" dominate the couple's functioning, but only as social roles. The division of labor prevents them from making love. They produce or reproduce. Not knowing too well how to use their leisure. If indeed they have any, if moreover they want to have any leisure. For what can be done with leisure? What substitute for amorous invention can be created?

We could go on and on—but perhaps we should return to the repressed female imaginary? Thus woman does not have a sex. She has at least two of them, but they cannot be identified as ones. Indeed she has many more of them than that. Her sexuality, always at least double, is in fact *plural*. Plural as culture now wishes to be plural? Plural as the manner in which current texts are written, with very little knowledge of the censorship from which they arise? Indeed, woman's pleasure does not have to choose between clitoral activity and vaginal passivity, for example. The pleasure of the vaginal caress does not have to substitute itself for the pleasure of the clitoral caress. Both contribute irreplaceably to woman's pleasure but they are only two caresses among many to do so. Caressing the breasts, touching the vulva, opening the lips, gently stroking the posterior wall of the vagina, lightly massaging the cervix, etc., evoke a few of the most specifically female pleasures. They remain rather unfamiliar pleasures in the sexual difference as it is currently imagined, or rather as it is currently ignored: the other sex being only the indispensable complement of the only sex.

But *woman has sex organs just about everywhere.* She experiences pleasure almost everywhere. Even without speaking of the hysterization of her entire body, one can say that the geography of her pleasure is much more diversified, more multiple in its differences, more complex, more subtle, than is imagined—in an imaginary centered a bit too much on one and the same.

"She" is indefinitely other in herself. That is undoubtedly the reason she is called temperamental, incomprehensible, perturbed, capricious—not to mention her language in which "she" goes off in all directions and in which "he" is unable to discern the coherence of any meaning. Contradictory words seem a little crazy to the logic of reason, and inaudible for him who listens with ready-made grids, a code prepared in advance. In her statements—at least when she dares to speak out—woman retouches herself constantly. She just barely separates from herself some chatter, an exclamation, a half-secret, a sentence left in suspense—When she returns to it, it is only to set out again from another point of pleasure or pain. One must listen to her differently in order to hear an *"other meaning" which is constantly in the process of weaving itself, at the same time ceaselessly embracing words and yet casting them off to avoid becoming fixed, immobilized.* For when "she" says something, it is already no longer identical to what she means. Moreover, her statements are never identical to anything. Their distinguishing feature is one of contiguity. They touch (*upon*). And when they wander too far from this nearness, she stops and begins again from "zero": her body-sex organ.

It is therefore useless to trap women into giving an exact definition of what they mean, to make them repeat (themselves) so the meaning will be clear. They are already elsewhere than in this discursive machinery where you claim to take them by surprise. They have turned back within themselves, which does not mean the same thing as "within yourself." They do not experience the same interiority that you do and which perhaps you mistakenly presume they share. "Within themselves" means *in the privacy of this silent, multiple, diffuse tact.* If you ask them insistently what they are thinking about, they can only reply: nothing. Everything.

Thus they desire at the same time nothing and everything. It is always more and other than this *one*—of sex, for example—that you give them, that you attribute to them and which is often interpreted, and feared, as a sort of insatiable hunger, a voracity which will engulf you entirely. While in fact it is really a question of another economy which diverts the linearity of a project, undermines the target-object of a desire, explodes the polarization of desire on only one pleasure, and disconcerts fidelity to only one discourse–

Must the multiple nature of female desire and language be understood as the fragmentary, scattered remains of a raped or denied sexuality? This is not an easy question to answer. The rejection, the exclusion of a female imaginary undoubtedly places woman in a position where she can experience herself only fragmentarily as waste or as excess in the little structured margins of a dominant ideology, this mirror entrusted by the (masculine) "subject" with the task of reflecting and redoubling himself. The role of "femininity" is prescribed moreover by this masculine specula(riza)tion and corresponds only slightly to woman's desire, which is recuperated only secretly, in hiding, and in a disturbing and unpardonable manner.

But if the female imaginary happened to unfold, if it happened to come into play other than as pieces, scraps, deprived of their assemblage, would it present itself for all that as *a* universe? Would it indeed be volume rather than surface? No. Unless female imaginary is taken to mean, once again, the prerogative of the maternal over the female. This maternal would be phallic in nature however, closed in upon the jealous possession of its valuable product, and competing with man in his esteem for surplus. In this race for power, woman loses the uniqueness of her pleasure. By diminishing herself in volume, she renounces the pleasure derived from the nonsuture of her lips: she is a mother certainly, but she is a virgin mother. Mythology long ago assigned this role to her in which she is allowed a certain social power as long as she is reduced, with her own complicity, to sexual impotence.

Thus a woman's (re)discovery of herself can only signify the possibility of not sacrificing any of her pleasures to another, of not identifying with anyone in particular, of never being simply one. It is a sort of universe in expansion for which no limits could be fixed and which, for all that, would not be incoherency. Nor would it be the polymorphic perversion of the infant during which its erogenous zones await their consolidation under the primacy of the phallus.

Woman would always remain multiple, but she would be protected from dispersion because the other is a part of her, and is autoerotically familiar to her. That does not mean that she would appropriate the other for herself, that she would make it her property. Property and propriety are undoubtedly rather foreign to all that is female. At least sexually. *Nearness*, however, is not foreign to woman, a nearness so close that any identification of one or the other, and therefore any form of property, is impossible. Woman enjoys a closeness with the other that is *so near she cannot possess it, any more than she can possess herself.* She constantly trades herself for the other without any possible identification of either one of them. Woman's pleasure, which grows indefinitely from its passage in/through the other, poses a problem for any current economy in that all computations that attempt to account for woman's incalculable pleasure are irremediably destined to fail.

However, in order for woman to arrive at the point where she can enjoy her pleasure as a woman, a long detour by the analysis of the various systems of oppression which affect her is certainly necessary. By claiming to resort to pleasure alone as the solution to her problem, she runs the risk of missing the reconsideration of a social practice upon which *her* pleasure depends.

For woman is traditionally use-value for man, exchange-value among men. Merchandise, then. This makes her the guardian of matter whose price will be determined by "subjects": workers, tradesmen, consumers, according to the standard of their work and their need-desire. Women are marked phallically by their fathers, husbands, procurers. This stamp-(ing) determines their value in sexual commerce. Woman is never anything more than the scene of more or less rival exchange between two men, even when they are competing for the possession of mother-earth.

How can this object of transaction assert a right to pleasure without extricating itself from the established commercial system? How can this merchandise relate to other goods on the market other than with aggressive jealousy? How can raw materials possess themselves without provoking in the consumer fear of the disappearance of his nourishing soil? How can this exchange in nothingness that can be defined in "proper" terms of woman's desire not seem to be pure enticement, folly, all too quickly covered over by a more sensible discourse and an apparently more tangible system of values?

A woman's evolution, however radial it might seek to be, would not suffice then to liberate woman's desire. Neither political theory nor political practice have yet resolved nor sufficiently taken into account this historical problem, although Marxism has announced its importance. But women are not, strictly speaking, a class and their dispersion in several classes makes their political struggle complex and their demands sometimes contradictory.

Their underdeveloped condition stemming from their submission by/to a culture which oppresses them, uses them, cashes in on them, still remains. Women reap no advantage from this situation except that of their quasi-monopoly of masochistic pleasure, housework, and reproduction. The power of slaves? It is considerable since the master is not necessarily well served in matters of pleasure. Therefore, the inversion of the relationship, especially in sexual economy, does not seem to be an enviable objective.

But if women are to preserve their auto-eroticism, their homo-sexuality, and let it flourish, would not the renunciation of heterosexual pleasure simply be another form of this amputation of power that is traditionally associated with women? Would this renunciation not be a new incarceration, a new cloister that women would willingly build? Let women tacitly go on strike, avoid men long enough to learn to defend their desire notably by their speech, let them discover the love of other women protected from that imperious choice of men which puts them in a position of rival goods, let them forge a social status which demands recognition, let them earn their living in order to leave behind their condition of prostitute—These are certainly indispensable steps in their effort to escape their proletarization on the trade market. But, if their goal is to reverse the existing order—even if that were possible—history would simply repeat itself and return to phallocratism, where neither women's sex, their imaginary, nor their language can exist.

Translated by Claudia Reeder

Note

1 …. This title is, of course a pun: woman's sex is not a sex within the Freudian paradigm and within Irigaray's paradigm it is not one but multiple, plural.

41.

MULTIPLE MEDIATIONS: FEMINIST SCHOLARSHIP IN THE AGE OF MULTINATIONAL RECEPTION
Lata Mani
(1990)

"unusual knowing", a cognitive practice, a form of consciousness that is not primordial, universal, or coextensive with human thought. [...] but historically determined and yet subjectively and politically assumed' (de Lauretis, March 1990).

On the acupuncturist's table, Berkeley, California, July 1988.

I am lying in wait for the complex verbal negotiation that attends each visit to my acupuncturist. I want a diagnosis—a definable illness, a definite cure. He is disdainful of this desire for clarity and resolution and insists on treating my body as a zone in which energies rise and fall, sometimes rebelliously, at other times gracefully and once even, as he put it, 'stroppily'. As I ponder the frustrating untranslatability of his idiom, he asks the dreaded question: 'Well, what is your Ph.D. thesis about?'

I stare at the infra-red lamp and wonder which version to present. The various responses I have elicited over the years race through my mind like a film running at high speed. My usual strategy is to assess the cultural politics of those addressing me (such as I can discern them), the tenor of the question (is this a serious inquiry or merely a polite one?) and my frame of mind at the time (do I want to educate, be patronized or try to avoid both by being vague, but thereby risking the impression that I know not what I am doing?). I did not, however, have time for such musings. I was trapped under the beady eye of my white American doctor of needles who, having taken my pulse, was awaiting a reply. So I blurted out what I consider my minimalist 'no-nonsense' description: 'I am working on the debate between colonial officials, missionaries and the indigenous male elite on sati *(widow burning) in colonial India.'*

I felt weak, as though it had been a confession extorted from me after intense cross-examination. I sighed inwardly. Meanwhile, my declaration had provoked what turned out to be a half-hour lecture on the dilemmas of cross-cultural understanding. He said that such practices would always be difficult for Westerners to comprehend, hastily adding that it was important none the less not to impose alien values and that sati *probably had a particular significance within Indian culture which it would be enlightening to know. At this point he turned away from my foot, into which he had just finished inserting needles, and asked, 'So how do you understand widow burning?'*

I felt myself stiffen. He had thrown me a challenge that would require a command performance in colonial and post-colonial history and discourse, one that I did not feel equal to at the time. So I said evasively, 'It's a long story and I'm trying to sort it out.'

'Good', said the genial man in the white coat tapping my arm. Not waiting for a response, he continued. 'Of course, you are Westernized and your ideas have probably changed from living here. I wonder what women in India feel about it?' So saying, he left the room.

I was furious. I had not interrupted his liberal, relativist, patronizing discourse, and was as a result caught in its pincer movement: an apparent but ultimately repressive tolerance, a desire for 'true' knowledge, and a demand for authenticity that was impossible for me to meet, given that any agreement between us, however fragile and superficial, would immediately make me 'Westernized': not like 'them' but like 'him'. I wished for the millionth time that I had been working on a less contentious topic, one that, unlike sati, *had not served as metonym for Indian society itself … or had had the panache to wag my finger like him and say, 'Read my book and you'll find out'.*

The Emergence of a Politics of Location

This paper explores questions of positionality and location and their relation to the production of knowledge as well as its reception. These issues have animated feminism from its inception. Here they are approached through a set of interconnected reflections, on the processes that shaped my study of debates on *sati* under British colonialism, and on the different ways in which this analysis has been received in Britain and in India. Such alternative readings thematize the politics of intellectual work in neo/postcolonial contexts, and the difficulties of achieving an international feminism sensitive to the complex and diverse articulations of the local and the global.

Contemporary theory in feminism and in the humanities has brought a critical self-consciousness to bear both on the place and mode of enunciation (who speaks and how) and that of its reception (how it is interpreted and why). As claims to universality and objectivity have been shown to be the alibis of a largely masculinist, heterosexist and white Western subject, both readers and writers have had to confront their particularity and history. Gender, race, class, sexuality and historical experience specify hitherto unmarked bodies, deeply compromising the fictions of unified subjects and disinterested knowledges.

Such developments, or should I say acknowledgements, require attentiveness to the theoretical and political impulses that shape our projects, and an openness to the inevitable fact that different agendas may govern their reception. Needless to say, there have always been multiple investments and diverse audiences. Our accounting of these phenomena today simply attests to the successful struggles for discursive spaces of those overlapping and hitherto marginalized groups, women, Third World people, gays and lesbians. Institutional concessions to the heterogeneity of the social landscape has prompted the emergence of new fields of study within US universities, for instance ethnic studies and women's studies. It has also given new momentum to interdisciplinary work. The current mobilization of talents and energies around culture studies is a case in point.[1]

The revolt of the particular against that masquerading as the general, of what Donna Haraway has called 'situated' as against 'disembodied knowledges' (Haraway, 1988), has brought to the fore theoretical and political questions regarding positionality and identity. This issue has probably been most fully developed within feminism, in part in debates about the relationship between experience and knowledge. One locus of such discussion in the Euro-American context has been the related struggles over racism and white centredness of dominant feminism (Moraga and Anzaldua, 1981; hooks, 1981; Amos *et al.*, 1984; Bhavnani anti Coulson, 1986, among others) and its replication of elements of colonial discourse (Spivak, 1981; Mohanty, 1984; Minh-ha 1986/7; Lazreg, 1988). Feminists have called for a revised politics of location—'revised' because, unlike its initial articulation, the relation between experience and knowledge is now seen to be one not of correspondence, but fraught with history, contingency and struggle (In addition to the authors already cited, see Bulkin *et al.*, 1984; Segrest, 1985; Rich, 1986; de Lauretis, 1986; Kaplan, 1987.)[2] These terms powerfully suggest some of the problems of positionality as they confront me: a post-colonial Third World feminist working on India in the United States.

Chandra Talpade Mohanty argues that developing a politics of location requires exploration of 'the historical, geographic, cultural, psychic and imaginative boundaries which provide the ground for political definition and self-definition' (Mohanty, 1987: 31). Location, in her terms, is not a fixed point but a 'temporality of struggle', (p. 40) characterized by multiple locations and nonsynchronous processes of movement 'between cultures, languages, and complex configurations of meaning and power' (p. 42). These processes, in Mohanty's view, enable 'a paradoxical continuity of self, mapping and ... political location ... [M]y location forces and enables specific modes of reading and knowing the dominant. The struggles I choose to engage in are then the intensification of these modes of knowing' (p. 42). This definition of the space of politics very nicely illuminates the dynamics of how my conception of a project on the debate on *sati* in colonial India bears the traces of movement between cultures and configurations of meaning, multiple locations and specific modes of knowing.

My research examines colonial official, missionary and indigenous elite discourses on *sati* in Britain and India in the late eighteenth- and early-nineteenth centuries. I investigate the conditions of production and the burden of each of these discourses, the intersections, differences and tensions between them, and the competing and overlapping ways in which they were deployed. Among other things, I argue that a specifically colonial discourse on India framed the debate on *sati* producing troubling consequences for how 'the woman's question' in India was to be posed thereafter, whether by Indian nationalists, or Western feminists (Mani, 1989).

One of the things that has prompted and sustained my energy through hours of plodding through archival documents and reels of dizzying microfilm has been a conviction of the importance of the contemporary ideological and political legacy of such debates about women and culture. I have always been aware that this legacy has had a differential trajectory in India and in, for example, the US or Britain: that the relation of this earlier discourse to contemporary knowledges, popular and specialist, about India in the West, was different from its relation to the contemporary self-knowledge of Indians. It is the contours of this difference that this paper will now explore.

The following section reflects on the experience of presenting my work (Mani, 1987) to groups in the US, Britain and India and discovering that the audiences in these places seized on entirely different aspects of my work as politically significant. These responses in turn have caused me to reflect on how moving between different 'configurations of meaning and power' can prompt different 'modes of knowing'. The experience has also required me squarely to confront a problem not adequately theorized in discussions of positionality or of the function of theory and criticism: the politics of simultaneously negotiating not multiple but discrepant audiences, different 'temporalities of struggle'.[3]

Back to the Future: The After-Lives of Colonial Discourses

'Colonial' or Eurocentric discourses on India, and on the Third World more generally, have an abiding presence in the USA and Britain, the two Western countries with which I am most familiar. Television documentaries, scholarly writing and popular wisdom circulate such notions as the centrality of religion—whether framed as the essential 'spirituality' of the East or as the dominance of caste (Inden, 1986; Appadurai, 1988)—the antiquity of Indian 'culture', and the victimization of women. These ideas 'hail' those of us living here with a systematicity that, over time, makes them truly oppressive. As a Marxist-feminist who had come to feminism in India, I initially responded to the predominance of culturalist understandings of Indian society with surprise and bemusement at the ignorance they betrayed. I assumed that such ignorance must also account for my having so often to explain the supposed anomaly of being an Indian feminist.

The repetition of such incidents as my encounter with the acupuncturist, the dynamics of which I would barely have been able to fathom when I first arrived in the US, compelled me to think seriously about the prehistory of such knowledges about India and Indian women. I brought this new sensibility to bear on reading the debate on *sati*. It has been, I believe, by and large productive. For although I have read many of the same documents as other historians, Indian and non-Indian, an alertness to how British colonialism may have shaped knowledge about colonized society has turned up unexpected disjunctures, contests and determinations, for instance, over what constitutes 'tradition'. Given a context in which elements of this nineteenth-century discourse continue to circulate, on occasion virtually unreconstructed, in the service of British racism and US cultural imperialism, I consider excavation of the colonial prehistory of such ideas to be a political gesture.

By and large, most discussions that followed presentations of my work in the US or Britain tended to focus on the contemporary replications, resonances or rearticulations of what I had sketched. In Britain, for instance, we explored how the British state manipulates women's 'oppression' in Indian and Pakistani 'culture' to legitimate virginity tests, immigration controls and policing of Asian marriages and family life. This 'civilizing' racist British state has placed black feminists in Britain in a position analogous to that of nineteenth-century Indian male social reformers, who defended 'culture' and 'women' in a similarly overdetermined context (Parmar, 1982; Amos *et al.*, 1984; Grewal *et al.*, 1988). The significant difference between then and now is that black feminists (unlike many male nationalists) have insisted on keeping women at the centre of the struggle, refusing to let themselves become mere pawns in a contest between the state and community. They have charted a complex strategy. On the one hand, they have challenged the self-serving appropriation of 'women's issues' by a racist British state. Simultaneously, they have resisted both the 'protection' of men in the black community when it has come with a defence of practices oppressive to women, and white feminist attempts to rescue them from patriarchy. In short, black feminists in Britain have refused 'salvation', whether by the state in the name of civilized modernity, by black men on behalf of tradition and community integrity, or by white feminists in the interest of ethnocentric versions of women's liberation. In this context, discussions after my presentations explored, among other things, questions of rhetoric and strategy: how to argue for women's rights in ways that were not complicit in any way with patriarchal, racist or ethnocentric formulations of the issues. Thus, given that the British state draws on key elements of nineteenth-century discourses on India to further its own current projects, my delineation of the colonial dimension of these discourses was seen to have an explicitly political character.

In India, however, this dimension of my project was interpreted quite differently, primarily as an academic and historical argument. To some extent this is not surprising. Notions of 'timeless textual traditions' or the essential spirituality of Indian society have a different afterlife in the Indian public domain. Quite simply, they are not, as in Britain, critical to the elaboration of hegemony. Certainly, development policies explicitly embrace the logic of modernity, brahmanical texts have come to represent quintessential Hinduism, and the colonial legacy of making religious scriptures the basis of civil law has enormously complicated feminist projects of legal reform. However, notions like 'timeless traditions' function most often to inspire literature from the Indian Tourist Development Corporation or to feed the fantasy life of petit-bourgeois middle- and high-caste Indians regarding the glory of ancient India (read, 'of their own lineage'). Except in the case of Government of India documentaries on tribal peoples, or sometimes in relation to remote rural areas, there does not exist a serious convention of representing Indian citizens as lacking agency, inhabiting a timeless zone, and immobilized by 'tradition'. Indeed, this kind of analysis would be difficult to sustain, given that the authority of the Indian state has been continually challenged since independence, and is bolstered today not by a democratic consensus but through a brutal and increasingly unashamed use of violence.

The Indian context thus presents a sharp contrast to the West; naming something 'colonial' in India has, accordingly, a different import. It becomes a question of periodization, rather than a crucial move in developing an oppositional, anti-imperialist critical practice. Such a reading is further comprehensible because, in a palpable, existential sense, when one is in India, colonialism does indeed seem like a thing long past. Despite India's economically dependent status in the world economy and its willful exploitation by multinationals and agencies like the World Bank, 'the West' as ideological and political presence articulates with such a density of indigenous institutions, discourses, histories and practices that its identity as 'Western' is refracted and not always salient. This is not to say that Indians are naive about the impact of the West. (There was, for example, little confusion about the ultimate culpability of the US-based corporation Union Carbide, in the Bhopal industrial disaster.) What I am suggesting is that, unlike, for example, many nations in the Caribbean or in Central America, in India it is not the boot of imperialism that is felt as an identifiable weight upon one's neck. The pressure one feels compelled to resist is rather that of the nation state, dominant social and political institutions, and religious 'fundamentalisms' of various kinds. No doubt, the activities of the nation state are themselves related in complex ways to regional and global geopolitical trends, but it is the local face of this international phenomenon against which one is moved to struggle.

It comes as no surprise, then, that in India, the 'political' dimension of my work is seen to be expressed primarily in my engagement with nationalism, the limited parameters within which nationalists posed the question of women's status, the marginality of women to nineteenth-century discussions supposedly about them, and the legacy of colonialism in contemporary discussion of women's issues. This last point was made in my presentation in relation to the recent controversy over reform of Islamic law provoked by the 'Shahbano case'. The case was one in which the Supreme Court had upheld the application of a Muslim woman, Shahbano, for lifelong maintenance from her ex-husband. The Supreme Court's verdict became a rallying point for many Muslims who felt that the court had (contrary to its claims) violated Islamic law and thus undermined the only legal protection Indian Muslims enjoyed as a religious minority (Punwani, 1985; Kishwar, 1986; Engineer, 1987; Pathak and Sunder Rajan, 1989). In analyzing the case, it was possible to point out how, in this as in many instances in the nineteenth century, contests over women's rights were being debated as contests over scriptural interpretation, and as struggles over a community's autonomy and right to self-determination. While these terms do not exhaust the arguments made in relation to the case, they point to significant parallels between nineteenth- and twentieth-century debates on women (Mani, 1987: 153–6). My interest in such continuities was in the ways in which they constrained the form and content of contemporary discussions. I did not assume that the persistence of certain discursive elements implied unchanged significance, meanings or effects; ideas are potentially available for different kinds of appropriation by different social forces. Suffice it to say that the case, more than any theoretical argument about 'colonial discourse', served to convey some of the political impulses of my project. Even here, however, the 'colonial' dimension was of academic interest. The burden of the discussion, not inappropriately, fell to the practical problems of building coalitions between Hindu and Muslim women in the wake of the divisiveness produced by the Shahbano case and the growth of communalism in Indian politics.

Situating Our Interventions

These differing receptions of my work in Britain and India raise questions regarding the relationship between 'experience' and 'theory', one's geographical location and the formulation of one's projects. It seems to me that travelling to the US and living under its regimes of truth regarding India and the Third World more generally have intensified for me certain 'modes of knowing'. The disjunctions between how I saw myself and the kinds of knowledge about me that I kept bumping into in the West, opened up new questions for social and political inquiry.

Reading Edward Said's *Orientalism* in this context was enormously productive and energizing (Said, 1979). It contextualized the phenomena, discourses and attitudes I was encountering and helped me in the task of situating personal experiences within a historical problematic. It quickened my impulse to take more seriously than I had previously been inclined to, colonial official and missionary discourses on India. My interest in these was not merely that of a historian of ideas, but of someone curious about the history of the present. I can only wonder at how my project might have been fashioned in the absence of this experience of travel to a different economy of power and knowledge. In this regard, I find it significant that an Indian friend of mine once remarked that the full force of Said's argument in *Orientalism* had come home to her only after spending time in Europe. Prior to this she had believed, and this is a fairly common perception in India, that Said was perhaps overstating his case, stretching a point.[4]

It seems to me that the politics and epistemology of differing readings such as these dramatizes the dilemma of post-colonial intellectuals working on the Third World in the West. One diagnosis of this situation accuses such intellectuals of inauthenticity or ideological contamination by the West. This charge may be levelled by First World intellectuals demanding a spurious authenticity of their Third World colleagues. It often works to challenge the latter groups' credibility, by implying that their politics are exceptional and ungeneralizable. This analysis may, however, also be shared by Third World intellectuals working in the Third World. The criticism in this instance may be rooted in the assumption, not always unwarranted, that intellectuals abroad are, so to speak, 'selling out'. It is, however, ultimately simplistic because it overgeneralizes, and one does not, of course, have to leave home to sell out. Alternatively, assertions about ideological contamination are often shorthand allusions to genuine issues, such as asymmetries in the material conditions of scholarship in metropolitan and Third World contexts. Such problems are, however, not clarified by a moralistic formulation of the issue in terms of purity or pollution.

In the face of this discourse of authenticity, some Third World intellectuals working in the First World have reterritorialized themselves as hybrid. This strategy is compelling when such a demonstration of hybridity becomes, as in Gloria Anzaldua's *Borderlands* (1987) an enabling moment for the possibility of a collective politics attentive to difference and contradiction. When, however, the elaboration of hybridity becomes an end in itself, serving only to undo binary oppositions, it runs the risk of dodging entirely the question of location. To this one must say, 'necessary but insufficient'.

Finally, for those intellectuals from the geographical Third World who have an elsewhere to return to, there is the possibility of adopting a tactic which would separate projects into what is deemed appropriate or inappropriate to do 'while one is in the West'. Here again we have a prescription which may make sense in specific instances, for political and practical reasons. On the other hand this strategy also has the potential for side-stepping the issue. It implicitly conceives of the West and non-West as autonomous spaces and thereby evades the thorny issue of their intersections and mutual implications (Mohanty, 1989).

How, then, would I proceed to delineate, in my own case, the potential and limits of my location, working on the Third World in the belly of the First? For one thing, it seems to me that the mode of knowing enabled by the experience of existing between discursive systems makes it difficult for me to isolate colonialism as a distinct historical period with little claim on the present. Consequently, I have tried to train myself to look for discontinuities in apparently smooth surfaces, and continuities across the dominant and oppositional. Secondly, the deadening essentialism of much historical and contemporary Western representation of the Third World has confirmed for me, albeit in a different way, a lesson learnt earlier from Marxism: an abiding suspicion of primarily cultural explanations of social phenomena. At the same time, perhaps not paradoxically, experiences of such a persistent privileging of 'culture' have in turn compelled me to take very seriously the domain designated by it. What counts as 'culture'? How is it conceived and represented? With what consequences? In short, I have been persuaded of the need to open to critical reflection the vexed and complex issue of the relationship between colonialism and questions of culture.

This is a problem that is, to my mind, yet to be adequately thematized in the literature on colonialism in India. Historiography on nineteenth-century India, for instance, has produced sophisticated analysis of the impact of colonialism on India's economy and politics, but has paid comparatively little attention to its impact on culture or on conceptions of it. Perhaps the ways in which I may be tempted to frame the problem will be marked by the fact that it became an issue for me as a result of my experience of Britain and the US. It may be that I accent the colonial rather more heavily than my imagined counterpart, the feminist writing in India. But as I reflect on what moves me, I also need to be aware that I now inescapably participate in multiple conversations, not all of which overlap. As for the gains of being situated in the interstices, only time will tell. In the meantime, it seems to me that my attempt to specify location might also be fruitfully undertaken in dialogue with feminists in India. After all, the dangers of reading the local as global are potentially present both in India and in the West: in the former through minimizing colonialism, in the latter through aggrandizing it.

Priorities Redetermined: The Aftermath of Roop Kanwar's Burning

The difficulties of straddling different temporalities of struggle cannot, however, always be resolved through listening for and talking about our specificities. There are political moments which pose limits to the possibility of conceiving of international feminist exchanges (whether between First and Third World women in the West or between

Third World women cross-nationally) as negotiated dialogues which, while they may alternately diverge and intersect, are ultimately benign and noncontradictory.

On 22 September 1987, Roop Kanwar died on the funeral pyre of her husband in Deorala, Rajasthan. The incident has sparked off a nationwide controversy on *sati* in India, unearthed the information that there have been at least thirty-eight widow immolations in Rajasthan since independence, and dragged out of the closet vociferous supporters of the practice. In this recent case, the government of India vacillated in taking action against family members found to have coerced Roop. State officials were present along with an estimated 300,000 others at an event 'honouring' the episode thirteen days after the burning, and when the state finally banned glorification of *sati,* the response was too little, too late.

Meanwhile, a massive debate on *sati* had been set in motion, with opponents and defenders staking out their claims in terms that were in many ways remarkably reminiscent of the nineteenth-century controversy which is the subject of my own research. As in the colonial period, issues of scriptural interpretation, the so-called 'traditional' nature of *sati,* its barbarity, the role of the state, women's social conditioning and the question of the widow's consent, all emerged as key items in the debate.

Four positions were discernible in the discussions that followed upon Roop Kanwar's death. Each of these is more elaborate than my characterization of it suggests, but my purpose here is merely to sketch in broad strokes the discursive space that was constituted, referring readers to others who have analyzed them more thoroughly (Patel and Kumar, 1988; Sangari, 1988, among others). There was firstly, a 'liberal' position, critical of *sati* as 'traditional', 'religious' and barbaric and arguing that the incident represented the failure of the project of modernization. Secondly, and opposed to this, was the conservative, pro-*sati* lobby. This valorized *sati's* 'traditional' and 'religious' status and argued that the rationality of the practice was necessarily inaccessible to Westernized, urban Indians.

Ostensibly critical of both these positions, although reserving the burden of its critique for the former and ultimately aligning itself with the latter, was a third stance (Nandy, 1987, 1988a, 1988b). Ashis Nandy, a trenchant critic of the philosophies of modernization and development, castigated liberal condemnation of *sati* as the response of a rootless, decultured urban bourgeoisie, unable, if not unwilling, to comprehend the masses. We may agree with Nandy that the incomprehension of *sati* expressed by the liberal media required examination and critique: after all, *sati* is only one among many practices exploitative of women. In a sense, contemporary liberal incomprehension parallels nineteenth-century colonial horror. Both cast *sati* simultaneously as an exceptional practice and one that is emblematic of society as a whole. The sense of its exceptionalism emerges in analyses of *sati* which treat it in isolation from women's subordination in general, while its emblematic status is dramatized in the way in which the incident has provoked anxiety about the nature and extent of India's social progress.

This, however, is not the direction in which Nandy develops his argument. Nandy's ire is directed mainly at what he perceives as the 'Western' modes of denouncing *sati* reproduced by 'modernists'. Nandy's stand on *sati* has drawn sharp criticism from feminists (Qadeer and Hasan, 1987; Patel and Kumar, 1988; Sangari, 1988; Philipose and Setalvad, 1988) whom he scorns as modernist, overlooking thereby important distinctions between feminist and liberal critiques of the practice (Nandy, 1988b). What is even more curious, however, is that Nandy's critique of the colonial mentality of these modernists itself reproduces three key moves of colonial discourse. He reaffirms the 'tradition'/'modernity' dichotomy in analyzing the practice, and replicates the colonial oppositions, 'glorious past/degraded present' and 'authentic/inauthentic *sati*'. The latter two are brought together in his positive evaluation of the original, mythological *sati*, said to express women's sacred and magical powers, as against his negative description of contemporary widow burning which, he claims, is merely the product of a dehumanized market morality.

The fourth, and to my mind, genuinely anti-imperialist position (even though, unlike Nandy's it was not articulated as such) was that taken by feminists. Not surprisingly, concern for women's lives was very much at the centre of feminist discourse. Feminists insisted that Roop Kanwar's death should be understood in the context of the general subordination of women in Indian society, challenged attempts to frame the issue as one of tradition or religion and located the Deorala incident within post-independent political and economic developments in Rajasthan (Kishwar and Vanita, 1987; Bhasin and Menon, 1988; Vaid, 1988, among others). Feminists also pointed to the modernity of the incident and to the character of the pro-*sati* lobby, whose members were urban, educated men in their twenties and thirties. For example, Madhu Kishwar and Ruth Vanita argued that Deorala was not a rural backwater, but rather a prosperous town with electricity, tap water and a 70 per cent literacy rate (Kishwar and Vanita, 1987). Further, they pointed out that Roop Kanwar was a city-educated woman while her husband had a degree in science and her father-in-law, one of the abettors, was employed as a school teacher. In addition to the insufficiency of derisively analyzing *sati* as 'traditional', feminists argued that such a ploy would play into the hands of pro-*sati* 'traditionalists'. Religious arguments were similarly exposed as serving to legitimate the oppression of women. Again, Kishwar and Vanita described how the daily rituals around the spot where the burning had taken place resembled victory celebrations, not religious devotion. In arguing that cries of 'religion' could not absolve anyone of murder, Indira Jaising put it thus: 'just as the personal is political, the religious is secular where women are concerned' (Jaising, 1987).

Finally, feminists warned against the danger of demanding more stringent laws and greater state intervention, the recurring pleas of liberal opponents of *sati*. They highlighted the appalling lack of will demonstrated by the state in prosecuting Roop's in-laws, and the possibility that the state would merely abuse the greater powers that would accrue to it. These fears have largely been realized. Local police have used their powers to harass journalists and others investigating the case and, despite the law against abetting and glorifying *sati*, an estimated 8,000 people gathered at Deorala in September 1988 to 'celebrate' the one year anniversary of the burning of Roop Kanwar (Pachauri, 1988). And perhaps worst of all, one of the provisions of the legislative act on *sati* makes its victims liable to punishment: women who attempt *sati* are hereafter to be subject to fine or imprisonment!

The events that have followed Roop Kanwar's burning have radically changed the Indian context for my work. Widow burning is no longer, as it had been when I began, a 'historical' problem, but very much a charged and explosive contemporary issue. Although my own discussion here has focused most on feminist arguments, they are, alas, marginal to the current debate. The discursive space is principally being defined by conservatives and liberals. The former are more active in mobilizing a constituency and have had the support of political parties more wedded to securing votes than to fundamental rights of any kind. This context has made it imperative to contextualize and frame in particular ways some of the arguments I develop in my thesis.

How, for instance, might my critique of the civilizing mission be appropriated in the current situation? Part of my argument has been to show, in some detail, what is occluded in the following statement which represents a dominant story about colonialism and the question of woman: 'we came, we saw, we were horrified, we intervened'. Taking the instance of *sati*, whose abolition by the British in 1829 supposedly illuminates, *par excellence*, the legitimacy of this account, I have tried to suggest that the story is much more complicated. Among other things, I point out that legislative prohibition of *sati* was preceded by its legalization, a procedure that involved British officials in determining and enforcing a colonial version of the practice deemed traditional and authentic; that intervention in *sati* provided grounds for intervention in civil society; and that a fundamental ambivalence to *sati* structured colonial attitudes to the practice (Mani, 1987). I argue that missionary involvement in *sati* was similarly complex and ambivalent, with horror being reserved primarily for fundraising material produced for a British public. My point is that ultimately, for both officials and missionaries, women were not really at issue. Women rather provided ground for the development of other agendas.

I make a related argument about nineteenth-century indigenous discourses on *sati*. I argue that these developed within the constraints of a discourse on Indian society privileged by the British, that ambivalence to the practice is discernible even among those passionately opposed to *sati*, and that here too, concern for women seems secondary to concern for 'tradition' or for the general good of society. Women thus appear as obstacles to societal reform, and as individuals who must be trained to take up the duties of modern life with its own requirements of good wife and mother. My argument, then, has called into question the overly positive evaluation of the civilizing impulses of colonialism and the modernizing desires of proto-nationalism and nationalism: not because women did not gain from them, but because neither seemed to me to be selfless and benign in their espousal of women's rights, nor even centrally concerned with them.

How will such a critique of colonialist and nationalist arguments against *sati* resonate in India today? Is there any danger that my critique of the *terms* of these arguments will be read reductively as support for *sati*? Authorial intention, it is generally conceded, guarantees nothing. Considerable care will be necessary in framing my discussion in such a way that only a deliberate misreading can appropriate my arguments to reactionary ends. In addition, perhaps in my discussion of the nineteenth-century debate on *sati* I should also explicitly engage the contemporary moment so as to clarify how once again, with the signal exception of feminists and some progressives, arguments about women's rights have provided the basis for a further entrenchment of patriarchy in the name of 'tradition' (a point made by many Indian feminists) and for the arrogation of greater powers to the; state in the name of 'modernity'.

I was lucky to be in India in the aftermath of Deorala. Lucky, because, in and of themselves, newspaper clippings and magazine articles could not have conveyed to me the political temperature there. Grasping the situation required the cumulative experience of countless conversations with friends, family members and neighbours, chance encounters on buses and trains, reports from feminists and civil libertarians who had travelled to Deorala, public meetings, and accounts of group discussions held in schools, colleges, political and community organizations. Much of this would obviously have been unavailable in print. My combined impressions strongly suggest that great care will have to be exercised in making arguments such as a critique of the Western civilizing mission.

The possible implications of other issues, such as exploration of the question of women's agency, appear to be even more treacherous. The problem of women's agency occupies a paradoxical position in feminist thinking in that, despite being a central concern, it remains poorly theorized. This is equally true of post-structuralist theory which, while being critical of the bourgeois conception of agency as the free will of an autonomous self, has yet to produce an adequate alternative formulation.

The widow's will has been a recurring theme in both the nineteenth- and twentieth-century debates on *sati*. Here, discussion of agency is framed around the limited and analytically unhelpful binary terms, coercion and consent. Those defending *sati* have, then as now, made claims about the 'voluntary' nature of the act. Against this, opponents of *sati* have emphasized coercion, and questioned the meaning of consent. In the earlier debate, consent was sometimes conceived as impossible by definition: women were simply deemed incapable of it. At other times, the issue was formulated more broadly in terms of women's social position and of the meagre alternatives available to them. For instance, it was pointed out that one could hardly speak of consent when widowhood imposed its own regimes of misery. By and large, those against *sati* today have developed this latter argument, feminists far more consistently than liberals. In the colonial situation, this dualistic conception of agency led to legislation requiring women to be cross-examined at the pyre and being permitted to burn if their action was declared to be voluntary. A static conception of agency intersected with he assumption of religious hegemony to marginalize the ways in which women actively negotiated and struggled against the social and familial constraints upon them. Nowhere is this more evident than in colonial eyewitness accounts of *sati*, which consistently effaced signs of women's agency in struggle, resistance and coercion (Mani, 1989).

I have long felt anxious about how a broader consideration of women's agency is foreclosed by its reductive translation into an issue of whether or not the widow went willingly. Limiting discussion of women's agency in this way makes it difficult to engage simultaneously women's systematic subordination *and* the ways in which they negotiate oppressive, even determining, social conditions (Ong, 1987 and Gordon, 1989 develop such complex analyses of women's agency). I know that part of my own concern with these questions comes from a sense of the extent to which Third World peoples are consistently represented in Eurocentric discourses as lacking agency. I also know that it comes from a conviction that structures of domination are best understood if we can grasp how we remain agents even in the moments in which we are being intimately, viciously oppressed.

The discourse of woman as victim has been invaluable to feminism in pointing to the systematic character of gender domination. But if it is not employed with care, or in conjunction with a dynamic conception of agency, it leaves us with reductive representations of women as primarily beings who are passive and acted upon. In other words we are left with that common figure of Eurocentric feminist discourse: the Third World woman as 'always, already victim' (Mohanty, 1984). What is forsaken here is the notion of women's oppression as a multifaceted and contradictory social process. It is crucial to stress in this regard, however, that when Indian feminists speak of woman as victim it is in a complex material sense. It is also important to note than in emphasizing women's systematic subordination rather than debating questions of agency, Indian feminists are specifically attempting to counter right-wing discourse that falsely proposes women's total freedom.[5]

Questions of agency provoke issues at the heart of feminism. But in raising them in the current Indian context, one walks a tightrope. Firstly, given the dominant discourse on *sati*, to claim that women are agents even in their coercion is to court the possibility of misappropriation by the right wing. Secondly, current legislation on *sati*, by making women attempting *sati* liable to punishment, implicitly conceives of them as 'free agents'. The law states that any such punishment must take account of the circumstances in which the woman's decision was taken. But given that legal and political institutions routinely punish victims instead of perpetrators, why should we trust that this proviso will not work against women? In the short term, then, it seems safest to counter the notion of woman as free agent by emphasizing her victimization. However, unless we include in this a complex sense of agency, we run the risk of producing a discourse which sets women up to be saved. This would situate women within feminist analysis in ways that are similar to their positioning within colonialist or nationalist discourse.

The example of women's agency is a particularly good instance of the dilemmas confronted in simultaneously attempting to speak within different historical moments and to discrepant audiences. What might be a valuable pushing of the limits of current rethinking of agency in Anglo-American feminism, may, if not done with extreme care, be an unhelpful, if not disastrous move in the Indian context. If criticism is to be 'worldly' (Said, 1983: 1–30) or 'situated' (Haraway, 1988), or engaged, it must take account of the worlds in which it speaks. Perhaps to Bruce Robbins' suggestion that theory is a 'when' not a 'what' (Robbins, 1987/8: 5) we should also add the notion of a 'where'.

Notes

Lata Mani received her Ph.D. from the University of California, Santa Cruz in 1989. She has been active in feminist struggles in India and in feminist and antiracist work in the US.

Kum-Kum Bhavnani, Vivek Dhareshwar, Ruth Frankenberg, Mary John and Kamala Visweswaran have left the imprint of their critical readings on the final version of this paper. I am also indebted to Indian feminists and progressives whose political insight and imaginative interventions in the contemporary debate on widow burning have been inspiring and instructive. An earlier version of this paper appeared in *Inscriptions*, no. 5, University of California, Santa Cruz, 1989.

1. The relative rapidity with which the concept of 'culture studies' has found institutional support in the US academy compared to ethnic or women's studies should give us pause. bell hooks (Gloria Watkins) and Gayatri C. Spivak have recently mapped out what is at stake intellectually and politically in the kinds of theoretical and curricular agendas being privileged and excluded in the institutionalization of 'Third World' or 'culture studies': bell hooks, 'Critical integration: talking race, resisting racism', Conference on Feminisms and Cultural Imperialism: The Politics of Difference, Cornell University, 1989 April 22–3; Gayatri C. Spivak, 'Post-coloniality and the field of value', Conference on Feminisms and Cultural Imperialism, Cornell University, 1989, April 22–3.

2. As a whole, however, as Norma Alarcon (forthcoming), Aida Hurtado (1989) and Chela Sandoval (forthcoming) have recently argued, the critique of US white feminism has been taken up very unevenly and has failed fundamentally to transform dominant feminist thinking.

3. Edward Said (1986) raises the problem of discrepant experiences and constituencies but develops instead a case for foregrounding the *shared* intellectual and political terrain produced by colonialism. See also, Said, 1983: 226–47.

4. There may be many reasons for a critique of Said's *Orientalism*, some more persuasive than others (Mani and Frankenberg, 1985). There is firstly the theoretical resistance of those working within an objectivist paradigm to his social constructionist approach. Then there is the question of the scope of his argument. Many Indian readers, for example, felt that the book's value for them was seriously limited by its primary focus on the West and its lack of analysis of internal class and power relations in colonized territories. My point here, then, is not that there are no grounds to criticize *Orientalism*: rather that, in India, the political and ideological impetus of Said's project has generally not been apprehended as compelling, a response tied to both geographical location and historical experience.

5. Rajeswari Sunder Rajan is approaching the problem of the widow's subjectivity in *sati* from a different perspective. She argues that the 'methodological impasse' generated by the 'coercion-consent' framework can be avoided if the question of the widow's subjectivity is engaged via an exploration of 'both the phenomenology of pain and a politics that recognizes pain as constitutive of the subject' [1990].

42.
FOUCAULT, FEMININITY, AND THE MODERNIZATION OF PATRIARCHAL POWER
Sandra Lee Bartky
(1990)

I.

In a striking critique of modern society, Michel Foucault has argued that the rise of parliamentary institutions and of new conceptions of political liberty was accompanied by a darker counter-movement, by the emergence of a new and unprecedented discipline directed against the body. More is required of the body now than mere political allegiance or the appropriation of the products of its labor: the new discipline invades the body and seeks to regulate its very forces and operations, the economy and efficiency of its movements.

The disciplinary practices Foucault describes are tied to peculiarly modern forms of the army, the school, the hospital, the prison, and the manufactory; the aim of these disciplines is to increase the utility of the body, to augment its forces:

> What was then being formed was a policy of coercions that act upon the body, a calculated manipulation of its elements, its gestures, its behaviour. The human body was entering a machinery of power that explores it, breaks it down and rearranges it. A "political anatomy", which was also a "mechanics of power", was being born: it defined how one may have a hold over others' bodies, not only so that they may do what one wishes, but so that they may operate as one wishes, with the techniques, the speed and the efficiency that one determines. Thus, discipline produces subjected and practiced bodies, "docile" bodies.[1]

The production of "docile bodies" requires that an uninterrupted coercion be directed to the very processes of bodily activity, nor just their result; this "micro-physics of power" fragments and partitions the body's time, its space, and its movements.[2]

The student, then, is enclosed within a classroom and assigned to a desk he cannot leave; his ranking in the class can be read off the position of his desk in the serially ordered and segmented space of the classroom itself. Foucault tells us that "Jean-Baptiste de la Salle dreamt of a classroom in which the spatial distribution might provide a whole series of distinctions at once, according to the pupil's progress, worth, character, application, cleanliness and parents' fortune."[3] The student must sit upright, feet upon the floor, head erect; he may not slouch or fidget his animate body is brought into a fixed correlation with the inanimate desk.

The minute breakdown of gestures and movements required of soldiers at drill is far more relentless[.] ... These "body-object articulations" of the soldier and his weapon, the student and his desk effect a "coercive link with the apparatus of production." We are far indeed from older forms of control that "demanded of the body only signs or products, forms of expression or the result of labour."[4]

The body's time, in these regimes of power, is as rigidly controlled as its space: the factory whistle and the school bell mark a division of time into discrete and segmented units that regulate the various activities of the day. ... Control this rigid and precise cannot be maintained without a minute and relentless surveillance.

Jeremy Bentham's design for the Panopticon, a model prison, captures for Foucault the essence of the disciplinary society. At the periphery of the Panopticon, a circular structure; at the center, a tower with wide windows that opens onto the inner side of the ring. The structure on the periphery is divided into cells, each with two windows, one facing the windows of the tower, the other facing the outside allowing an effect of backlighting to make any figure visible within the cell. "All that is needed, then, is to place a supervisor in a central tower and to shut up in each cell a madman, a patient, a condemned man, a worker or a schoolboy."[5] Each inmate is alone, shut off from effective communication with his fellows, but constantly visible from the tower. The effect of this is "to induce in the inmate a state of conscious and permanent visibility that assures the automatic functioning of power"; each becomes to himself his own jailer.[6] This "state of conscious and permanent visibility" is a sign that the tight, disciplinary control of the body has gotten a hold on the mind as well. In the perpetual self-surveillance of the inmate lies the genesis of the celebrated "individualism" and heightened self-consciousness that are hallmarks of modern times. For Foucault, the structure and effects of the Panopticon resonate throughout society: Is it surprising that "prisons resemble factories, schools, barracks, hospitals, which all resemble prisons"?[7]

Foucault's account in *Discipline and Punish* of the disciplinary practices that produce the "docile bodies" of modernity is a genuine *tour de force*, incorporating a rich theoretical account of the ways in which instrumental reason takes hold of the body with a mass of historical detail, But Foucault treats the body throughout as if it were one, as if the bodily experiences of men and women did not differ and as if men and women bore the same relationship to the characteristic institutions of modern life. Where is the account of the disciplinary practices that engender the "docile bodies" of women, bodies more docile than the bodies of men? Women, like men, are subject to many of the same disciplinary practices Foucault describes. But he is blind to those disciplines that produce a modality of embodiment that is peculiarly feminine. To overlook the forms of subjection that engender the feminine body is to perpetuate the silence and powerlessness of those upon whom these disciplines have been imposed. Hence, even though a liberatory note is sounded in Foucault's critique of power, his analysis as a whole reproduces that sexism which is endemic throughout Western political theory.

We are born male or female, but not masculine or feminine. Femininity is an artifice, an achievement, "a mode of enacting and reenacting received gender norms which surface as so many styles of the flesh."[8] In what follows, I shall examine those disciplinary practices that produce a body which in gesture and appearance is recognizably feminine. I consider three categories of such practices: those that aim to produce a body of a certain size and general configuration; those that bring forth from this body a specific repertoire of gestures, postures, and movements; and those that are directed toward the display of this body as an ornamented surface. I shall examine the nature of these disciplines, how they are imposed and by whom. I shall probe the effects of the imposition of such discipline on female identity and subjectivity. In the final section I shall argue that these disciplinary practices must be understood in the light of the modernization of patriarchal domination, a modernization that unfolds historically according to the general pattern described by Foucault.

II.

Styles of the female figure vary over time and across cultures; they reflect cultural obsessions and preoccupations in ways that are still poorly understood. Today, massiveness, power, or abundance in a woman's body is met with distaste. The current body of fashion is taut, small-breasted, narrow-hipped, and of a slimness bordering on emaciation; it is a silhouette that seems more appropriate to an adolescent boy or a newly pubescent girl than to an adult woman. Since ordinary women have normally quite different dimensions, they must of course diet.

Mass-circulation women's magazines run articles on dieting in virtually every issue. ... After the diet-busting Christmas holidays and, later, before summer bikini season, the titles of these features become shriller and more arresting. The reader is now addressed in the imperative mode: Jump into shape for summer! ... More women than men visit diet doctors, while women greatly outnumber men in such self-help groups as Weight Watchers and Overeaters Anonymous—in the case of the latter, by well over 90 percent.[9]

Dieting disciplines the body's hungers: appetite must be monitored at all times and governed by an iron will. Since the innocent need of the organism for food will not be denied, the body becomes one's enemy, an alien being bent on thwarting the disciplinary project. Anorexia nervosa, which has now assumed epidemic proportions, is to women of the late twentieth century what hysteria was to women of an earlier day: the crystallization in a pathological mode of a widespread cultural obsession.[10] ...

Dieting is one discipline imposed upon a body subject to the "tyranny of slenderness"; exercise is another.[11] Since men as well as women exercise, it is not always easy in the case of women to distinguish what is done for the sake of physical fitness from what is done in obedience to the requirements of femininity. Men as well as women lift weights and do yoga, calisthenics, and aerobics, though "jazzercise" is a largely female pursuit. Men and women alike engage themselves with a variety of machines, each designed to call forth from the body a different exertion ... However, given the widespread female obsession with weight, one suspects that many women are working out ... with an aim in mind and in a spirit quite different from men's.

... [T]here are classes of exercises meant for women alone, these designed not to firm or to reduce the body's size overall, but to resculpture its various pans on the current model. ... There are exercises to build the breasts and exercises to banish "cellulite," said by "figure consultants" to be a special type of female fat. There is "spot-reducing," an umbrella term that covers dozens of punishing exercises designed to reduce "problem areas" like thick ankles or "saddlebag" thighs. The very idea of "spot-reducing" is both scientifically unsound and cruel, for it raises expectations in women that can never be realized—the pattern in which fat is deposited or removed is known to be genetically determined.

It is not only her natural appetite or unreconstructed contours that pose a danger to woman: the very expressions of her face can subvert the disciplinary project of bodily perfection. An expressive face lines and creases more readily than an inexpressive one. Hence, if women are unable to suppress strong emotions, they can at least learn to inhibit the tendency of the face to register them. Sophia Loren recommends a unique solution to this problem: a piece of tape applied to the forehead or between the brows will tug at the skin when one frowns and act as a reminder to relax the face.[12] The tape is to be worn whenever a woman is home alone.

III.

There are significant gender differences in gesture, posture, movement, and general bodily comportment: women are far more restricted than men in their manner of movement and in their spatiality. In her classic paper on the subject, Iris Young observes that a space seems to surround women in imagination that they are hesitant to move beyond: this manifests itself both in a reluctance to reach, stretch, and extend the body to meet resistances of matter in motion—as in sport or in the performance of physical tasks—and in a typically constricted posture and general style of movement. Woman's space is not a field in which her bodily intentionality can be freely realized but an enclosure in which she feels herself positioned and by which she is confined.[13] The "loose woman" violates these norms: her looseness is manifest not only in her morals, but in her manner of speech and quite literally in the free and easy way she moves.

In an extraordinary series of over two thousand photographs, many candid shots taken in the street, the German photographer Marianne Wex has documented differences in typical masculine and feminine body posture. Women sit waiting for trains with arms close to the body, hands folded together in their laps, toes pointing straight ahead or turned inward, and legs pressed together.[14] The women in these photographs make themselves small and narrow, harmless; they seem tense; they take up little space. Men, on the other hand, expand into the available space; they sit with legs far apart and arms flung out at some distance from the body. Most common in these sitting male figures is what Wex calls the "proffering position": the men sit with legs thrown wide apart, crotch visible, feet pointing outward, often with an arm and a casually dangling hand resting comfortably on an open, spread thigh.

In proportion to total body size, a man's stride is longer than a woman's. The man has more spring and rhythm to his step; he walks with toes pointed outward, holds his arms at a greater distance from his body and swings them farther; he tends to point the whole hand in the direction he is moving. The woman holds her arms closer to her body, palms against her sides: her walk is circumspect. If she has subjected herself to the additional constraint of high-heeled shoes, her body is thrown forward and off balance: the struggle to walk under these conditions shortens her stride still more.

But women's movement is subjected to a still finer discipline. Feminine faces, as well as bodies are trained to the expression of deference. Under male scrutiny, women will avert their eyes or cast them downward; the female gaze is trained to abandon its claim to the sovereign status of seer. The "nice" girl learns to avoid the bold and unfettered staring of the "loose" woman who looks at whatever and whomever she pleases. Women are trained to smile more than men, too. In the economy of smiles, as elsewhere, there is evidence that women are exploited, for they give more than they receive in return; in a smile elicitation study, one researcher found that the rate of smile return by women was 93 percent, by men only 67 percent.[15] In many typical women's jobs, graciousness, deference and the readiness to serve are part of the work; this requires the worker to fix a smile on her face for a good part of the working day, whatever her inner state.[16] The economy of touching is out of balance, too: men touch women more often and on more parts of the body than women touch men: female secretaries, factory workers, and waitresses report that such liberties are taken routinely with their bodies.[17]

Feminine movement, gesture, and posture must exhibit not only constriction, but grace and a certain eroticism restrained by modesty: all three. Here is field for the operation for a whole new training: a woman must stand with stomach pulled in, shoulders thrown slightly back and chest out, this to display her bosom to maximum advantage. While she must walk in the confined fashion appropriate to women, her movements must, at the same time, be combined with a subtle but provocative hip-roll. But too much display is taboo: women in short, low-cut dresses are told to avoid bending over at all, but if they must, great care must be taken to avoid an unseemly display of breast or rump. ...

All the movements we have described so far are self-movements; they arise from within the woman's own body. But in a way that normally goes unnoticed, males in couples may literally steer a woman everywhere she goes: down the street, around corners, into elevators, through doorways, into her chair at the dinner table, around the dance floor. The man's movement "is not necessarily heavy and pushy or physical in an ugly way; it is light and gentle but firm in the way of the most confident equestrians with the best trained horses."[18]

IV.

We have examined some of the disciplinary practices a woman must master in pursuit of a body of the right size and shape that also displays the proper styles of feminine motility. But woman's body is an ornamented surface too, and there is much discipline involved in this production as well. Here, especially in the application of makeup and the selection of clothes, art and discipline converge, though, as I shall argue, there is less art involved than one might suppose.

A woman's skin must be soft, supple, hairless, and smooth; ideally, it should betray no sign of wear, experience, age, or deep thought. Hair must be removed not only from the face but from large surfaces of the body as well, from legs and thighs … With the new high-leg bathing suits and leotards, a substantial amount of pubic hair must be removed too. The removal of facial hair can be more specialized. Eyebrows are plucked out by the roots with a tweezer. Hot wax is sometimes poured onto the mustache and cheeks and then ripped away when it cools. The woman who wants a more permanent result may try electrolysis: this involves the killing of a hair root by the passage of an electric current down a needle that has been inserted into its base. The procedure is painful and expensive.

The development of what one "beauty expert" calls "good skincare habits" requires not only attention to health, the avoidance of strong facial expressions, and the perform-ance of facial exercises, but the regular use of skincare preparations, many to be applied more often than once a day: cleansing lotions (ordinary soap and water "upsets the skin's acid and alkaline balance"), wash-off cleansers (milder than cleansing lotions), astringents, toners, makeup removers, night creams, nourishing creams, eye creams, moisturizers, skin balancers, body lotions, hand creams, lip pomades, suntan lotions, sunscreens, and facial masks. … Black women may wish to use "fade creams" to "even skin tone." Skincare preparations are never just sloshed onto the skin, but applied according to precise rules: eye cream is dabbed on gently in movements toward, never away from, the nose; cleansing cream is applied in outward directions only, straight across the forehead, the upper lip, and the chin, never up but straight down the nose and up and out on the cheeks.[19] …

The ordinary circumstances of life as well as a wide variety of activities cause a crisis in skincare and require a stepping-up of the regimen as well as an additional laying-on of preparations. Skincare discipline requires a specialized knowledge: a woman must know what to do if she has been skiing, taking medication, doing vigorous exercise, boating, or swimming in chlorinated pools; or if she has been exposed to pollution, heated rooms, cold, sun, harsh weather, the pressurized cabins on airplanes, saunas or steam rooms, fatigue, or stress. Like the schoolchild or prisoner, the woman mastering good skincare habits is put on a timetable: Georgette Klinger requires that a shorter or longer period of attention be paid to the complexion at least four times a day.[20] Hair-care, like skincare, requires a similar investment of time, the use of a wide variety of preparations, the mastery of a set of techniques, and, again, the acquisition of a special-ized knowledge.

The crown and pinnacle of good haircare and skincare is, of course, the arrange-ment of the hair and the application of cosmetics. Here the regimen of haircare, skin-care, manicure, and pedicure is recapitulated in another mode. A woman must learn the proper manipulation of a large number of devices—the blow dryer, styling brush, curling iron, hot curlers, wire curlers, eye-liner, lipliner, lipstick brush, eyelash curler, mascara brush—and the correct manner of application of a wide variety of products— foundation, toner, covering stick, mascara, eyeshadow, eyegloss, blusher, lipstick, rouge, lip gloss, hair dye, hair rinse, hair lightener, hair "relaxer," etc.

In the language of fashion magazines and cosmetic ads, making-up is typically portrayed as an aesthetic activity in which a woman can express her individuality. In reality, while cosmetic styles change every decade or so, and while some variation in makeup is permitted depending on the occasion, making-up the face is, in fact, a highly stylized activity that gives little rein to self-expression. Painting the face is not like painting a picture; at best, it might be described as painting the same picture over and over again with minor variations. Little latitude is permitted in what is considered appropriate makeup for the office and for most social occasions; indeed, the woman who uses cosmetics in a genuinely novel and imaginative way is liable to he seen not as an artist but as an eccentric. Furthermore, since a properly made-up face is, if not a card of entree, at least a badge of acceptability in most social and professional contexts, the woman who chooses not to wear cosmetics at all faces sanctions of a sort that will never be applied to someone who chooses not to paint a watercolor.

V.

Are we dealing in all this merely with sexual *difference*? Scarcely. The disciplinary practices I have described are part of the process by which the ideal body of femininity—and hence the feminine body-subject—is constructed; in doing this, they produce a "practiced and subjected" body, that is, a body on which an inferior status has been inscribed. A woman's face must be made-up, that is to say, made-over, and so must her body: she is ten pounds overweight; her lips must be made more kissable, her complexion dewier; her eyes more mysterious. The "art" of makeup is the art of disguise, but this presupposes that a woman's face, unpainted, is defective. Soap and water, a shave, and routine attention to hygiene may he enough for *him*; for *her* they are not. The strategy of much beauty-related advertising is to suggest to women that their bodies are deficient; but even without such more or less explicit teaching, the media images of perfect female beauty that bombard us daily leave no doubt in the minds of most women that they fail to measure up. The technologies of femininity are taken up and practiced by women against the background of a pervasive sense of bodily deficiency: this accounts for what is often their compulsive or even ritualistic character.

The disciplinary project of femininity is a "setup": it requires such radical and extensive measures of bodily transformation that virtually every woman who gives herself to it is destined in some degree to fail. Thus, a measure of shame is added to a woman's sense that the body she inhabits is deficient: she ought to take better care of herself; she might after all have jogged that last mile. Many women are without the time or resources to provide themselves with even the minimum of what such a regimen requires, for example, a decent diet. Here is an additional source of shame for poor women, who must hear what our society regards as the more general shame of poverty. The burdens poor women bear in this regard are not merely psychological, since conformity to the prevailing standards of bodily acceptability is a known factor in economic mobility.

The larger disciplines that construct a "feminine" body out of a female one are by no means race- or class-specific. There is little evidence that women of color or working-class women are in general less committed to the incarnation of an ideal femininity than their more privileged sisters: this is not to deny the many ways in which factors of race, class, locality, ethnicity, or personal taste can be expressed within the kinds of practices I have described. The rising young corporate executive may buy her cosmetics at Bergdorf-Goodman, while the counter-server at McDonald's gets hers at the K-Mart … Both are aiming at the same general result.

In the regime of institutionalized heterosexuality, woman must make herself "object and prey" for the man: it is for him that these eyes are limpid pools, this cheek baby-smooth.[21] In contemporary patriarchal culture, a panoptical male connoisseur resides within the consciousness of most women: they stand perpetually before his gaze and under his judgment. Woman lives her body as seen by another, by an anonymous patriarchal Other. We are often told that "women dress for other women." There is some truth in this: who but someone engaged in a project similar to my own can appreciate the panache with which I bring it off? But women know for whom this game is played: they know that a pretty young woman is likelier to become a flight attendant than a plain one, and that a well-preserved older woman has a better chance of holding onto her husband than one who has "let herself go."

Here it might be objected that performance for another in no way signals the inferiority of the performer to the one for whom the performance is intended: the actor, for example, depends on his audience but is in no way inferior to it; he is not demeaned by his dependency. While femininity is surely something enacted, the analogy to theater breaks down in a number of ways. First, as I argued earlier, the self-determination we think of as requisite to an artistic career is lacking here: femininity as spectacle is something in which virtually every woman is required to participate. Second, the precise nature of the criteria by which women are judged, not only the inescapability of judgment itself, reflects gross imbalances in the social power of the sexes that do not mark the relationship of artists and their audiences. An aesthetic of femininity, for example, that mandates fragility and a lack of muscular strength produces female bodies that can offer little resistance to physical abuse, and the physical abuse of women by men, as we know, is widespread. It is true that the current fitness movement has permitted women to develop more muscular strength and endurance than was heretofore allowed indeed, images of women have begun to appear in the mass media that seem to eroticize this new muscularity. But a woman may by no means develop more muscular strength than her partner; the bride who would tenderly carry her groom across the threshold is a figure of comedy, not romance.[22]

Under the current "tyranny of slenderness" women are forbidden to become large or massive; they must take up as little space as possible. The very contours a woman's body takes on as she matures—the fuller breasts and rounded hips—have become distasteful. The body by which a woman feels herself judged and which by rigorous discipline she must try to assume is the body of early adolescence, slight and unformed, a body lacking flesh or substance, a body in whose very contours the image of immaturity has been inscribed. The requirement that a woman maintain a smooth and hairless skin carries further the theme of inexperience, for an infantilized face must accompany her infantilized body, a face that never ages or furrows its brow in thought. The face of the ideally feminine woman must never display the marks of character, wisdom, and experience that we so admire in men.

To succeed in the provision of a beautiful or sexy body gains a woman attention and some admiration but little real respect and rarely any social power. A woman's effort to master feminine body discipline will lack importance just because she does it: her activity partakes of the general depreciation of everything female. In spite of unrelenting pressure to "make the most of what she has," women are ridiculed and dismissed for their interest in such "trivial" things as clothes and makeup. Further, the narrow identification of woman with sexuality and the body in a society that has for centuries displayed profound suspicion toward both does little to raise her status. ...

But it is perhaps in their more restricted motility and comportment that the inferiorization of women's bodies is most evident: women's typical body language, a language of relative tension and constriction, is understood to be a language of subordination when it is enacted by men in male status hierarchies. In groups of men, those with higher status typically assume looser and more relaxed postures: the boss lounges comfortably behind the desk, while the applicant sits tense and rigid on the edge of his seat. Higher status individuals may touch their subordinates more than they themselves get touched; they initiate more eye contact and are smiled at by their inferiors more than they are observed to smile in return.[23] What is announced in the comportment of superiors is confidence and ease, especially ease of access to the Other. Female constraint in posture and movement is no doubt over-determined: the fact that women tend to sit and stand with legs, feet, and knees close or touching may well be a coded declaration of sexual circumspection in a society that still maintains a double standard, or an effort, albeit unconscious, to guard the genital area—in the latter case, a woman's tight and constricted posture must be seen as the expression of her need to ward off real or symbolic sexual attack. Whatever proportions must be assigned in the final display to fear or deference, one thing is clear: woman's body language speaks eloquently, though silently, of her subordinate status in a hierarchy of gender.

VI.

If what we have described is a genuine discipline—a system of "micropower" that is "essentially non-egalitarian and asymmetrical"—who then are the disciplinarians?[24] Who is the top sergeant in the disciplinary regime of femininity? Historically, the law has had some responsibility for enforcement: in times gone by, for example individuals who appeared in public in the clothes of the other sex could be arrested. While crossdressers are still liable to some harassment, the kind of discipline we are considering is not the business of the police or the courts, Parents and teachers, of course, have extensive influence, admonishing girls to be demure and ladylike, to "smile pretty," to sit with their legs together. The influence of the media is pervasive, too, constructing as it does an image of the female body as spectacle ...

But none of these individuals—the skincare consultant, the parent, the policeman—does in fact wield the kind of authority that is typically invested in those who manage more straightforward disciplinary institutions. The disciplinary power that inscribes femininity in the female body is everywhere and it is nowhere; the disciplinarian is everyone and yet no one in particular. Women regarded as overweight, for example, report that they are regularly admonished to diet, sometimes by people they scarcely know. These intrusions are often softened by reference to the natural prettiness just waiting to emerge: "People have always said that I had a beautiful face and 'if you'd only lose weight you'd be really beautiful.'"[25] Here, "people"—friends and casual acquaintances alike—act to enforce prevailing standards of body size.

Foucault tends to identify the imposition of discipline upon the body with the operation of specific institutions, for example, the school, the factory, the prison. To do this, however, is to overlook the extent to which discipline can be institutionally *unbound* as well as institutionally bound.[26] The anonymity of disciplinary power and its wide dispersion have consequences that are crucial to a proper understanding of the subordination of women. The absence of a formal institutional structure and of authorities invested with the power to carry out institutional directives creates the impression that the production of femininity is either entirely voluntary or natural. The several senses of "discipline" are instructive here. On the one hand, discipline is something imposed on subjects of an "essentially non-egalitarian and asymmetrical" system of authority. Schoolchildren, convicts, and draftees are subject to discipline in this sense. But discipline can be sought voluntarily as well—for example, when an individual seeks initiation into the spiritual discipline of Zen Buddhism. Discipline can, of course, be both at once: the volunteer may seek the physical and occupational training offered by the army without the army's ceasing in any way to be the instrument by which he and other members of his class are kept in disciplined subjection. Feminine bodily discipline has this dual character: on the one hand, no one is marched off for electrolysis at gunpoint, nor can we fail to appreciate the initiative and ingenuity displayed by countless women in an attempt to master the rituals of beauty. Nevertheless, insofar as the disciplinary practices of femininity produce a "subjected and practiced," an inferiorized, body, they must be understood as aspects of a far larger discipline, an oppressive and inegalitarian system of sexual subordination. This system aims at turning women into the docile and compliant companions of men just as surely as the army aims to turn its raw recruits into soldiers.

Now the transformation of oneself into a properly feminine body may be any or all of the following: a rite of passage into adulthood, the adoption and celebration of a particular aesthetic, a way of announcing one's economic level and social status, a way to triumph over other women in the competition for men or jobs, or an opportunity for massive narcissistic indulgence. The social construction of the feminine body is all these things, but at its base it is discipline, too, and discipline of the inegalitarian sort. The absence of formally identifiable disciplinarians and of a public schedule of sanctions only disguises the extent to which the imperative to be "feminine" serves the interest of domination. This is a lie in which all concur: making-up is merely artful play; one's first pair of high-heeled shoes is an innocent part of growing up, not the modern equivalent of foot-binding.

Why aren't all women feminists? In modern industrial societies, women are not kept in line by fear of retaliatory male violence; their victimization is not that of the

South African black. Nor will it suffice to say that a false consciousness engendered in women by patriarchal ideology is at the basis of female subordination. This is not to deny that women are often subject to gross male violence or that women and men alike are ideologically mystified by the dominant gender arrangements. What I wish to suggest instead is that an adequate understanding of women's oppression will require an appreciation of the extent to which not only women's lives but their very subjectivities are structured within an ensemble of systematically duplicitous practices. The feminine discipline of the body is a case in point: the practices that construct this body have an overt aim and character far removed, indeed, radically distinct, from their covert function. In this regard, the system of gender subordination, like the wage-bargain under capitalism, illustrates in its own way the ancient tension between what-is and what-appears: the phenomenal forms in which it is manifested are often quite different from the real relations that form its deeper structure.

VII.

… Whatever its ultimate effect, discipline can provide the individual upon whom it is imposed with a sense of mastery as well as a secure sense of identity. There is a certain contradiction here: while its imposition may promote a larger disempowerment, discipline may bring with it a certain development of a person's powers. Women, then, like other skilled individuals, have a stake in the perpetuation of their skills, whatever it may have cost to acquire them and quite apart from the question whether, as a gender, they would have been better off had they never had to acquire them in the first place. Hence, feminism, especially a genuinely radical feminism that questions the patriarchal construction of the female body, threatens women with a certain de-skilling, something people normally resist: beyond this, it calls into question that aspect of personal identity that is tied to the development of a sense of competence.

Resistance from this source may be joined by a reluctance to part with the rewards of compliance; further, many women will resist the abandonment of an aesthetic that defines what they take to be beautiful. But there is still another source of resistance, one more subtle, perhaps, but tied once again to questions of identity and internalization. To have a body felt to be "feminine"—a body socially constructed through the appropriate practices—is in most cases crucial to a woman's sense of herself as female and, since persons currently can *be* only as male or female, to her sense of herself as an existing individual. To possess such a body may also be essential to her sense of herself as a sexually desiring and desirable subject. Hence, any political project that aims to dismantle the machinery that turns a female body into a feminine one may well be apprehended by a woman as something that threatens her with desexualization, if not outright annihilation.

The categories of masculinity and femininity do more than assist in the construction of personal identities; they are critical elements in our informal social ontology. This may account to some degree for the otherwise puzzling phenomenon of homophobia and for the revulsion felt by many at the sight of female bodybuilders; neither the homosexual nor the muscular woman can be assimilated easily into the categories that structure everyday life. The radical feminist critique of femininity, then, may pose a threat not only to a woman's sense of her own identity and desirability but to the very structure of her social universe.

... Foucault has argued that modern bourgeois democracy is deeply flawed in that it seeks political rights for individuals constituted as unfree by a variety of disciplinary micropowers that lie beyond the realm of what is ordinarily defined as the "political." "The man described for us whom we are invited to free," he says, "is already in himself the effect of a subjection much more profound than himself."[27] If, as I have argued, female subjectivity is constituted in any significant measure in and through the disciplinary practices that construct the feminine body, what Foucault says here of "man" is perhaps even truer of "woman." ... Femininity as a certain "style of the flesh" will have to be surpassed in the direction of something quite different, not masculinity, which is in many ways only its mirror opposite, but a radical and as yet unimagined transformation of the female body.

VII.

Foucault has argued that the transition from traditional to modern societies has been characterized by a profound transformation in the exercise of power by what he calls "a reversal of the political axis of individualization."[28] In older authoritarian systems, power was embodied in the person of the monarch and exercised upon a largely anonymous body of subjects; violation of the law was seen as an insult to the royal individual. While the methods employed to enforce compliance in the past were often quite brutal, involving gross assaults against the body, power in such a system operated in a haphazard and discontinuous fashion; much in the social totality lay beyond its reach.

By contrast, modern society has seen the emergence of increasingly invasive apparatuses of power: these exercise a far more restrictive social and psychological control than was heretofore possible. In modern societies, effects of power "circulate through progressively finer channels, gaining access to individuals themselves, to their bodies, their gestures and all their daily actions."[29] Power now seeks to transform the minds of those individuals who might be tempted to resist it, not merely to punish or imprison their bodies. This requires two things: a finer control of the body's time and of its movements—a control that cannot be achieved without ceaseless surveillance and a better understanding of the specific person, of the genesis and nature of his "case." The power these new apparatuses seek to exercise requires a new knowledge of the individual; modern psychology and sociology are born. Whether the new modes of control have charge of correction, production, education, or the provision of welfare, they resemble one another; they exercise power in a bureaucratic mode—faceless, centralized, and pervasive. A reversal has occurred: Power has now become anonymous, while the project of control has brought into being a new individuality. In fact, Foucault believes that the operation of power constitutes the very subjectivity of the subject. Here, the image of the Panopticon returns: knowing that he may be observed from the tower at any time, the inmate takes over the job of policing himself. The gaze that is inscribed in the very structure of the disciplinary institution is internalized by the inmate: modern technologies of behavior are thus oriented toward the production of isolated and self-policing subjects.[30]

Women have their own experience of the modernization of power. One that begins later but follows in many respects the course outlined by Foucault. In important ways, a woman's behavior is less regulated now then it was in the past. She has more mobility and is less confined to domestic space. She enjoys what to previous generations would have been an unimaginable sexual liberty. Divorce, access to paid work outside the home, and the increasing secularization of modern life have loosened the hold over her of the traditional family and, in spite of the current fundamentalist revival, of the church. Power in these institutions was wielded by individuals known to her. Husbands and fathers enforced patriarchal authority in the family. As in the *ancien régime*, a woman's body was subject to sanctions if she disobeyed. ...

By contrast, the disciplinary power that is increasingly charged with the production of a properly embodied femininity is dispersed and anonymous; there are no individuals formally empowered to wield it; it is, as we have seen, invested in everyone and in no one in particular. This disciplinary power is peculiarly modern: it does not rely upon violent or public sanctions, nor does it seek to restrain the freedom of the female both to move from place to place. For all that, its invasion of the body is well-nigh total: The female body enters "a machinery of power that explores it, breaks it down and re-arranges it."[31] The disciplinary techniques through which the "docile bodies" of women are constructed aim at a regulation that is perpetual and exhaustive—a regulation of the body's size and contours, its appetite, posture, gestures and general comportment in space, and the appearance of each of its visible parts.

As modern industrial societies change and as women themselves offer resistance to patriarchy, older forms of domination are eroded. But new forms arise, spread, and become consolidated. ... Normative femininity is coming more and more to be centered on woman's body—not its duties and obligations or even us capacity to bear children, but its sexuality, more precisely, its presumed heterosexuality and its appearance. There is, of course, nothing new in women's preoccupation with youth and beauty. What is new is the growing power of the image in a society increasingly oriented toward the visual media. Images of normative femininity, it might be ventured, have replaced the religiously oriented tracts of the past. New too is the spread of this discipline to all classes of women and its deployment throughout the life cycle. What was formerly the specialty of the aristocrat or courtesan is now the routine obligation of every woman, he she a grandmother or a barely pubescent girl.

To subject oneself to the new disciplinary power is to be up-to-date, to be "with-it"; as I have argued, it is presented to us in ways that are regularly disguised. It is fully compatible with the current need for women's wage labor, the cult of youth and fitness, and the need of advanced capitalism to maintain high levels of consumption. Further, it represents a saving in the economy of enforcement: since it is women themselves who practice this discipline on and against their own bodies, men get off scot-free.

The woman who checks her makeup half a dozen times a day to see if her foundation has caked or her mascara has run, who worries that the wind or the rain may spoil her hairdo, who looks frequently to see if her stockings have bagged at the ankle or who, feeling fat, monitors everything she eats, has become, just as surely as the inmate of the Panopticon, a self-policing subject, a self committed to a relentless self-surveillance. This self-surveillance is a form of obedience to patriarchy. It is also the reflection in woman's consciousness of the fact that *she* is under surveillance in ways that *he* is not, that whatever else she may become, she is importantly a body designed to please or to excite. There has been induced in many women, then, in Foucault's words, "a state of conscious and permanent visibility that assures the automatic functioning of power."[32] Since the standards of female bodily acceptability are impossible fully to realize, requiring as they do a virtual transcendence of nature, a woman may live much of her life with a pervasive feeling of bodily deficiency. Hence a tighter control of the body has gained a new kind of hold over the mind.

Foucault often writes as if power constitutes the very individuals upon whom it operates[.] … Nevertheless, if individuals were wholly constituted by the power-knowledge regime Foucault describes, it would make no sense to speak of resistance to discipline at all. Foucault seems sometimes on the verge of depriving us of a vocabulary in which to conceptualize the nature and meaning of those periodic refusals of control that, just as much as the imposition of control, mark the course of human history.

… Historically, the forms and occasions of resistance are manifold. Sometimes, instances of resistance appear to spring from the introduction of new and conflicting factors into the lives of the dominated: the juxtaposition of old and new and the resulting incoherence or "contradiction" may make submission to the old ways seem increasingly unnecessary. In the present instance, what may be a major factor in the relentless and escalating objectification of women's bodies—namely, women's growing independence—produces in many women a sense of incoherence that calls into question the meaning and necessity of the current discipline. As women (albeit a small minority of women) begin to realize an unprecedented political, economic, and sexual self-determination, they fall ever more completely under the dominating gaze of patriarchy. It is this paradox … that produces, here and there, pockets of resistance.

… We women cannot begin the re-vision of our own bodies until we learn to read the cultural messages we inscribe upon them daily and until we come to see that even when the mastery of the disciplines of femininity produces a triumphant result we are still only women.

Notes

1. Michel Foucault, *Discipline and Punish*, trans. Alan Sheridan (New York: Vintage Books, 1979), p. 138.
2. Ibid., p. 28.
3. Ibid., p. 147.
4. Ibid., p. 153.
5. Ibid., p. 200.
6. Ibid., p. 201.
7. Ibid., p. 228.
8. Judith Butler, "Embodied Identity in de Beauvoir's *The Second Sex*" (unpublished manuscript presented to American Philosophical Association, Pacific Division, March 22, 1985), p. 11.

9. Marcia Millman, *Such a Pretty Face: Being Fat in America* (New York: W.W. Norton, 1980), p. 46.

10. Susan Bordo, "Anorexia Nervosa," *Philosophical Forum* 17, no. 2 (Winter 1985–86): 73–104. …

11. Phrase taken from the title of Kim Chernin's *The Obsession: Reflections on the Tyranny of Slenderness* (New York: Harper and Row, 1981) …

12. Sophia Loren, *Women and Beauty* (New York: William Morrow, 1984), p. 57.

13. Iris Young, "Throwing Like a Girl," *Human Studies* 3 (1980): 137–56.

14. Marianne Wex, *Let's Take Back Our Space* (Berlin: Frauenliteraturverlag Hermine Fees. 1979.) Wex claims (p. 23) that Japanese women are still taught to position their feet so that the toes point inward, a traditional sign of submissiveness.

15. Nancy Henley, *Body Politics* (Englewood Cliffs, N.J.: Prentice-Hall, 1977). p. 176.

16. … see Arlie Hochschild, *The Managed Heart* (Berkeley, Calif.: University of California Press, 1983).

17. Henley, *Body Politics*, p. 108.

18. Ibid., p. 149.

19. Georgette Klinger and Barbara Rowes, *Georgette Klinger's Skincare* (New York: William Morrow, 1978), pp. 102, 105, 151, 188, and passim.

20. Ibid., pp. 137–40.

21. "It is required of woman that in order to realize her femininity she must make herself object and prey, which is to say that she must renounce her claims as sovereign subject." Simone de Beauvoir, *The Second Sex* (New York: Bantam Books, 1968), p. 642.

22. The film *Pumping Iron II* portrays very clearly the tension for female bodybuilders (a tension that enters into formal judging in the sport) between muscular development and a properly feminine appearance.

23. Henley, *Body Politics*, pp. 101, 153, and passim.

24. Foucault, *Discipline and Punish*, p. 222.

25. Millman, *Such a Pretty Face*, p. 80. These sorts of remarks are made so commonly to heavy women that sociologist Millman takes the most clichéd as title of her study of the lives of the overweight.

26. I am indebted to Nancy Fraser for the formulation of this point.

27. Foucault, *Discipline and Punish*, p. 30.

28. Ibid., p. 44.

29. Michel Foucault, *Power/Knowledge*, ed. Colin Gordon (Brighton, U.K.: 1980), p. 151. Quoted in Peter Dews, "Power and Subjectivity in Foucault," *New Left Review*, No. 144, March–April 1984, p. 17.

30. Ibid., p. 77.

31. Foucault, *Discipline and Punish*, p. 138.

32. Ibid., p. 201.

43.
PERFORMATIVE ACTS AND GENDER CONSTITUTION: AN ESSAY IN PHENOMENOLOGY AND FEMINIST THEORY
Judith Butler
(1997)

Philosophers rarely think about acting in the theatrical sense, but they do have a discourse of "acts" that maintains associative semantic meanings with theories of performance and acting. For example, ... the phenomenological theory of "acts," espoused by Edmund Husserl, Maurice Merleau-Ponty, and George Herbert Mead, among others, seeks to explain the mundane way in which social agents *constitute* social reality through language, gesture, and all manner of symbolic social sign. Though phenomenology sometimes appears to assume the existence of a choosing and constituting agent prior to language (who poses as the sole source of its constituting acts), there is also a more radical use of the doctrine of constitution that takes the social agent as an *object* rather than the subject of constitutive acts.

When Simone de Beauvoir claims, "one is not born, but, rather, *becomes* a woman," she is appropriating and reinterpreting this doctrine of constituting acts from the phenomenological tradition.[1] In this sense, gender is in no way a stable identity of locus of agency from which various acts proceed; rather, it is an identity tenuously constituted in time—an identity instituted through a *stylized repetition of acts*. Further, gender is instituted through the stylization of the body and, hence, must be understood as the mundane way in which bodily gestures, movements, and enactments of various kinds constitute the illusion of an abiding gendered self. This formulation moves the conception of gender off the ground of a substantial model of identity to one that requires a conception of a constituted *social temporality*. Significantly, if gender is instituted through acts which are internally discontinuous, then the *appearance of substance* is precisely that, a constructed identity, a performative accomplishment which the mundane social audience, including the actors themselves, come to believe and to perform in the mode of belief. If the ground of gender identity is the stylized repetition of acts through time, and not a seemingly seamless identity, then the possibilities of gender transformation are to be found in the arbitrary relation, between such acts, in the possibility of a different sort of repeating, in the breaking or subversive repetition of that style.

Through the conception of gender acts sketched above, I will try to show some ways in which reified and naturalized conceptions of gender might be understood as constituted and, hence, capable of being constituted differently. In opposition to theatrical or phenomenological models which take the gendered self to be prior to its acts, I will understand constituting acts not only as constituting the identity of the actor, but constituting that identity as a compelling illusion, an object of *belief*. In the course of making my argument, I will draw from theatrical, anthropological, and philosophical discourses, but mainly phenomenology, to show that what is called gender identity is a performative accomplishment compelled by social sanction and taboo. In its very character as performative resides the possibility of contesting its reified status.

I. Sex/Gender: Feminist and Phenomenological Views

Feminist theory has often been critical of naturalistic explanations of sex and sexuality that assume that the meaning of women's social existence can be derived from some fact of their physiology. In distinguishing sex from gender, feminist theorists have disputed causal explanations that assume that sex dictates or necessitates certain social meanings for women's experience. Phenomenological theories of human embodiment have also been concerned to distinguish between the various physiological and biological causalities that structure bodily existence and the *meanings* that embodied existence assumes in the context of lived experience. In Merleau-Ponty's reflections in *The Phenomenology of Perception* on "the body in its sexual being," he takes issue with such accounts of bodily experience and claims that the body is "an historical idea" rather than "a natural species."[2] Significantly, it is this claim that Simone de Beauvoir cites in *The Second Sex* when she sets the stage for her claim that "woman," and by extension, any gender, is an historical situation rather than a natural fact.[3]

In both contexts, the existence and facticity of the material or natural dimensions of the body are not denied, but reconceived as distinct from the process by which the body comes to bear cultural meanings. For both Beauvoir and Merleau-Ponty, the body is understood to be an active process of embodying certain cultural and historical possibilities, a complicated process of appropriation which any phenomenological theory of constitution needs to describe. In order to describe the gendered body, a phenomenological theory of constitution requires an expansion of the conventional view of acts to mean both that which constitutes meaning and through which meaning is performed or enacted. In other words, the acts by which gender is constituted bear similarities to performative acts within theatrical contexts, My task, then, is to examine in what ways gender is constructed through specific corporeal acts, and what possibilities exist for the cultural transformation of gender through such acts.

Merleau-Ponty maintains not only that the body is an historical idea but a set of possibilities to be continually realized. In claiming that the body is an historical idea, Merleau-Ponty means that it gains its meaning through a concrete and historically mediated expression in the world. That the body is a set of possibilities signifies (a) that its appearance in the world, for perception, is not predetermined by some manner of interior essence, and (b) that its concrete expression in the world must be understood as the taking up and rendering specific of a set of historical possibilities. Hence, there is an agency which is understood as the process of rendering such possibilities determinate. These possibilities are necessarily constrained by available historical conventions. The body is not a self-identical or merely factic materiality; it is a materiality that bears meaning, if nothing else, and the manner of this bearing is fundamentally dramatic. By dramatic I mean only that the body is not merely matter but a continual and incessant *materializing* of possibilities. One is not simply a body, but, in some very key sense, one does one's body and, indeed, one does one's body differently from one's contemporaries and from one's embodied predecessors and successors as well.

It is, however, clearly unfortunate grammar to claim that there is a "we" or an "I" that does its body, as if a disembodied agency preceded and directed an embodied exterior. More appropriate, I suggest, would be a vocabulary that resists the substance metaphysics of subject-verb formations and relies instead on an ontology of present participles. The "I" that is its body is, of necessity, a mode of embodying, and the "what" that it embodies is possibilities. But here again the grammar of the formulation misleads, for the possibilities that are embodied are not fundamentally exterior or antecedent to the process of embodying itself. As an intentionally organized materiality, the body is always an embodying *of* possibilities both conditioned and circumscribed by historical convention. In other words, the body *is* a historical situation, as Beauvoir has claimed, and is a manner of doing, dramatizing, and *reproducing* a historical situation.

To do, to dramatize, to reproduce, these seem to be some of the elementary structures of embodiment. This doing of gender is not merely a way in which embodied agents are exterior, surfaced, open to the perception of others. Embodiment clearly manifests a set of strategies or what Sartre would perhaps have called a style of being or Foucault, "a stylistics of existence." This style is never fully self-styled, for living styles have a history, and that history conditions and limits possibilities. Consider gender, for instance, as *a corporeal style*, an "act," as it were, which is both intentional and performative, where "performative" itself carries the double-meaning of "dramatic" and "non-referential."

When Beauvoir claims that "woman" is a historical idea and not a natural, fact, she clearly underscores the distinction between sex, as biological facticity, and gender, as the cultural interpretation or signification of that facticity. To be female is, according to that distinction, a facticity which has no meaning, but to be a woman is to have *become* a woman, to compel the body to conform to an historical idea of "woman," to induce the body to become a cultural sign, to materialize oneself in obedience to an historically delimited possibility, and to do this as a sustained and repeated corporeal project. The notion of a "project," however, suggests the originating force of a radical will, and because gender is a project which has cultural survival as its end, the term *"strategy"* better suggests the situation of duress under which gender performance always and variously occurs. Hence, as a strategy of survival, gender is a performance with clearly punitive consequences. Discrete genders are part of what "humanizes" individuals within contemporary culture; indeed, those who fail to do their gender right are regularly punished. Because there is neither an "essence" that gender expresses or externalizes nor an objective ideal to which gender aspires; because gender is not a fact, the various acts of gender, and without those acts would be no gender at all. Gender is, thus, a construction that regularly conceals its genesis. The tacit collective agreement to perform, produce, and sustain discrete and polar genders as cultural fictions is obscured by the credibility of its own production. The authors of gender become entranced by their own fictions whereby the construction compels one's belief in its necessity and naturalness. The historical possibilities materialized through various corporeal styles are nothing other than those punitively regulated cultural fictions that are alternately embodied and disguised under duress.

How useful is a phenomenological point of departure for a feminist description of gender? On the surface it appears that phenomenology shares with feminist analysis a commitment to grounding theory in lived experience, and in revealing the way in which the world is produced through the constituting acts of subjective experience. Clearly, not all feminist theory would privilege the point of view of the subject (Kristeva once objected to feminist theory as "too existentialist")[4] and yet, the feminist claim that the personal is political suggests, in part, that subjective experience is not only structured by existing political arrangements, but effects and structures those arrangements in turn. Feminist theory has sought to understand the way in which systemic or pervasive political and cultural structures are enacted and reproduced through individual acts and practices, and how the analysis of ostensibly personal situations is clarified through situating the issues in a broader and shared cultural context. Indeed, the feminist impulse, and I am sure there is more than one, has often emerged in the recognition that my pain or my silence or my anger or my perception is finally not mine alone, and that it delimits me in a shared cultural situation which in turn enables and empowers me in certain unanticipated ways. The personal is thus implicitly political inasmuch as it is conditioned by shared social structures, but the personal has also been immunized against political challenge to the extent that public/private distinctions endure. For feminist theory, then, the personal becomes an expansive category, one which accommodates, if only implicitly, political structures usually viewed as public. Indeed, the very meaning of the political expands as well. At its best, feminist theory involves a dialectical expansion of both of these categories. My situation does not cease to be mine just because it is the situation of someone else, and my acts, individual as they are, nevertheless reproduce the situation of my gender, and do that in various ways. In other words, there is, latent in the personal is political formulation of feminist theory, a supposition that the life-world of gender relations is constituted, at least partially, through the concrete and historically mediated *acts* of individuals. Considering that "the" body is invariably transformed into his body or her body, the body is only known through its gendered appearance. It would seem imperative to consider the way in which this gendering of the body occurs. My suggestion is that the body becomes its gender through a series of acts which are renewed, revised, and consolidated through time. From a feminist point of view, one might try to reconceive the gendered body as the legacy of sedimented acts rather than a predetermined or foreclosed structure, essence or fact, whether natural, cultural, or linguistic.

The feminist appropriation of the phenomenological theory of constitution might employ the notion of an *act* in a richly ambiguous sense. If the personal is a category which expands to include the wider political and social structures, then the *acts* of the gendered subject would be similarly expansive. Clearly, there are political acts which are deliberate and instrumental actions of political organizing, resistance, and collective intervention with the broad aim of instating a more just set of social and political relations. There are thus acts which are done in the name of women, and then there are acts in and of themselves, apart from any instrumental consequence, that challenge the category of women itself. Indeed, one ought to consider the futility of a political program which seeks radically to transform the social situation of women without first determining whether the category of woman is socially constructed in such a way that to be a woman is, by definition, to be in an oppressed situation. In an understandable desire to forge bonds of solidarity, feminist discourse has often relied upon the category of woman as a universal presupposition of cultural experience which, in its universal status, provides a false ontological promise of eventual political solidarity. In a culture in which the false universal of "man" has for the most part been presupposed as coextensive with humanness itself, feminist theory has sought with success to bring female specificity into visibility and to rewrite the history of culture in terms which acknowledge the presence, the influence, and the oppression of women. Yet, in this effort to combat the invisibility of women as a category feminists run the risk of rendering visible a category which mayor may not be representative of the concrete lives of women. As feminists, we have been less eager, I think, to consider the status of the category itself and, indeed, to discern the conditions of oppression which issue from an unexamined reproduction of gender identities which sustain discrete and binary categories of man and woman.

When Beauvoir claims that woman is an "historical situation," she emphasizes that the body suffers a certain cultural construction, not only through conventions that sanction and proscribe how one acts one's body, the "act" or performance that one's body is, but also in the tacit conventions that structure the way the body is culturally perceived. Indeed, if gender is the cultural significance that the sexed body assumes, and if that significance is codetermined through various acts and their cultural perception, then it would appear that from within the terms of culture it is not possible to know sex as distinct from gender. The reproduction of the category of gender is enacted on a large political scale, as when women first enter a profession or gain certain rights, or are reconceived in legal or political discourse in significantly new ways. But the more mundane reproduction of gendered identity takes place through the various ways in which bodies are acted in relation to the deeply entrenched or sedimented expectations of gendered existence. Consider that there is a sedimentation of gender norms that produces the peculiar phenomenon of a natural sex, or a real woman, or any number of prevalent and compelling social fictions, and that this is a sedimentation that over time has produced a set of corporeal styles which, in reified form, appear as the natural configuration of bodies into sexes which exist in a binary relation to one another.

II. Binary Genders and the Heterosexual Contract

To guarantee the reproduction of a given culture, various requirements, well-established in the anthropological literature of kinship, have instated sexual reproduction within the confines of a heterosexually-based system of marriage which requires the reproduction of human beings in certain gendered modes which, in effect, guarantee the eventual reproduction of that kinship system. As Foucault and others have pointed out, the association of a natural sex with a discrete gender and with an ostensibly natural "attraction" to the opposing sex/gender is an unnatural conjunction of cultural constructs in the service of reproductive interests.[5] Feminist cultural anthropology and kinship studies have shown how cultures are governed by conventions that not only regulate and guarantee the production, exchange, and consumption of material goods, but also reproduce the bonds of kinship itself, which require taboos and a punitive regulation or reproduction to effect that end. Levi-Strauss has shown how the incest taboo works to guarantee the channelling of sexuality into various modes of heterosexual marriage,[6] Gayle Rubin has argued convincingly that the incest taboo produces certain kinds of discrete gendered identities and sexualities.[7] My point is simply that one way in which this system of compulsory heterosexuality is reproduced and concealed is through the cultivation of bodies into discrete sexes with "natural" appearances an "natural" heterosexual dispositions. Although the enthnocentric conceit suggests a progression beyond the mandatory structures of kinship relations as described by Levi-Strauss, I would suggest, along with Rubin, that contemporary gender identities are so many marks or "traces" of residual kinship. The contention that sex, gender, and heterosexuality are historical products which have become conjoined and reified as natural over time has received a good deal of critical attention not only from Michel Foucault, but Monique Wittig, gay historians, and various cultural anthropologists and social psychologists in recent years.[8] These theories, however, still lack the critical resources for thinking radically about the historical sedimentation of sexuality and sex-related constructs if they do not delimit and describe the mundane manner in which these constructs are produced, reproduced, and maintained within the field of bodies.

Can phenomenology assist a feminist reconstruction of the sedimented character of sex, gender, and sexuality at the level of the body? In the first place, the phenomenological focus on the various acts by which cultural identity is constituted and assumed provides a felicitous starting point for the feminist effort to understand the mundane manner in which bodies get crafted into genders. The formulation of the body as a mode of dramatizing or enacting possibilities offers a way to understand how a cultural convention is embodied and enacted. But it seems difficult, if not impossible, to imagine a way to conceptualize the scale and systemic character of women's oppression from a theoretical position which takes constituting acts to be its point of departure. Although individual acts do work to maintain and reproduce systems of oppression, and, indeed, any theory of personal political responsibility presupposes such a view, it doesn't follow that oppression is a sole consequence of such acts. One might argue that without human beings whose various acts, largely construed produce and maintain oppressive conditions, those conditions would fall away, but note that the relation between acts and conditions is neither unilateral nor unmediated. There are social contexts and conventions within which certain acts not only become possible but become conceivable as acts at all. The transformation of social relations becomes a matter, then, of transforming hegemonic social conditions rather than the individual acts that are spawned by those conditions. Indeed, one runs the risk of addressing the merely indirect, if not epiphenomenal, reflection of those conditions if one remains restricted to a politics of acts.

But the theatrical sense of an "act" forces a revision of the individualist assumptions underlying the more restricted view of constituting acts within phenomenological discourse. As a given temporal duration within the entire performance, "acts" are a shared experience and "collective action." Just as within feminist theory the very category of the personal is expanded to include political structures, so is there a theatrically-based and, indeed, less individually-oriented view of acts that goes some of the way in defusing the criticism of act theory as "too existentialist." The act that gender is, the act that embodied agents *are* inasmuch as they dramatically and actively embody and, indeed, *wear* certain cultural significations, is clearly not one's act alone. Surely, there are nuanced and individual ways of *doing* one's gender, but *that* one does it, and that one does it in *accord with* certain sanctions and proscriptions, is clearly not a fully individual matter. Here again, I don't mean to minimize the effect of certain gender norms which originate within the family and are enforced through certain familial modes of punishment and reward and which, as a consequence, might be construed as highly individual, for even there family relations recapitulate, individualize, and specify preexisting cultural relations; they are rarely, if ever, radically original. The act that one does, the act that one performs, is, in a sense, an act that has been going on before one arrived on the scene, Hence, gender is an act which has been rehearsed, much as a script survives the particular actors who make use of it, but which requires individual actors in order to be actualized and reproduced as reality once again. The complex components that go into an act must be distinguished in order to understand the kind of acting in concert and acting in accord which acting one's gender invariably is.

In what senses, then, is gender an act? As anthropologist Victor Turner suggests in his studies of ritual social drama, social action requires a performance which is *repeated*. This repetition is at once a reenactment and reexperiencing of a set of meanings already socially established; it is the mundane and ritualized form of their legitimation.[9] When this conception of social performance is applied to gender, it is clear that although there are individual bodies that enact these significations by becoming stylized into gendered modes, this "action" is immediately public as well. There are temporal and collective dimensions to these actions, and their public nature is not inconsequential; indeed, the performance is effected with the strategic aim of maintaining gender within its binary frame. Understood in pedagogical terms, the performance renders social laws explicit.

As a public action and performative act, gender is not a radical choice or project that reflects a merely individual choice, but neither is it imposed or inscribed upon the individual, as some post-structuralist displacements of the subject would contend. The body is not passively scripted with cultural codes, as if it were a lifeless recipient of wholly pregiven cultural relations. But neither do embodied selves preexist the cultural conventions which essentially signify bodies. Actors are always already on the stage, within the terms of the performance. Just as a script may be enacted in various ways, and just as the play requires both text and interpretation, so the gendered body acts its part in a culturally restricted corporeal space and enacts interpretations within the confines of already existing directives.

Although the links between a theatrical and a social role are complex and the distinctions not easily drawn (Bruce Wilshire points out the limits of the comparison in *Role-Playing and Identity: The Limits of Theatre as Metaphor*),[10] it seems clear that, although theatrical performances can meet with political censorship and scathing criticism, gender performances in nontheatrical contexts are governed by more clearly punitive and regulatory social conventions. Indeed, the sight of a transvestite onstage can compel pleasure and applause while the sight of the same transvestite on the seat next to us on the bus can compel fear, rage, even violence. The conventions which mediate proximity and identification in these two instances are clearly quite different. I want to make two different kinds of claims regarding this tentative distinction. In the theatre, one can say, "this is just an act," and de-realize the act, make acting into something quite distinct from what is real. Because of this distinction, one can maintain one's sense of reality in the face of this temporary challenge to our existing ontological assumptions about gender arrangements; the various conventions which announce that "this is only a play" allows strict lines to be drawn between the performance and life. On the street or in the bus, the act becomes dangerous, if it does, precisely because there are no theatrical conventions to delimit the purely imaginary character of the act, indeed, on the street or in the bus, there is no presumption that the act is distinct from a reality; the disquieting effect of the act is that there are no conventions that facilitate making this separation. Clearly, there is theatre which attempts to contest or, indeed, break down those conventions that demarcate the imaginary from the real (Richard Schechner brings this out quite clearly in *Between Theatre and Anthropology*).[11] Yet in those cases one confronts the same phenomenon, namely, that the act is not contrasted with the real, but *constitutes* a reality that is in some sense new, a modality of gender that cannot readily be assimilated into the preexisting categories that regulate gender reality. From the point of view of those established categories, one may want to claim, but oh, this is *really* a girl or a woman, or this is *really* a boy or a man, and further that the *appearance* contradicts the *reality* of the gender, that the discrete and familiar reality must be there, nascent, temporarily unrealized, perhaps realized at other times or other places. The transvestite, however, can do more than simply express the distinction between sex and gender, but challenges, at least implicitly, the distinction between appearance and reality that structures a good deal of popular thinking about gender identity. If the "reality" of gender is constituted by the performance itself, then there is no recourse to an essential and unrealized "sex" or "gender" which gender performances ostensibly express. Indeed, the transvestite's gender is as fully real as anyone whose performance complies with social expectations.

Gender reality is performative which means, quite simply, that it is real only to the extent that it is performed. It seems fair to say that certain kinds of acts are usually interpreted as expressive of a gender core or identity, and that these acts either conform to an expected gender identity or contest that expectation in some way. That expectation, in turn, is based upon the perception of sex, where sex is understood to be the discrete and factic datum of primary sexual characteristics. This implicit and popular theory of acts and gestures as *expressive* of gender suggests that gender itself is something prior to the various acts, postures, and gestures by which it is dramatized and known; indeed, gender appears to the popular imagination as a substantial core which might well be understood as the spiritual or psychological correlate of biological sex.[12] If gender attributes, however, are not expressive but performative, then these attributes effectively constitute the identity they are said to express or reveal. The distinction between expression and performativeness is quite crucial, for if gender attributes and acts, the various ways in which a body shows or produces its cultural signification, are performative, then there is no preexisting identity by which an act or attribute might be measured; there would be no true or false, real or distorted acts of gender, and the postulation of a true gender identity would be revealed as a regulatory fiction. That gender reality is created through sustained social performances means that the very notions of an essential sex, a true or abiding masculinity or femininity, are also constituted as part of the strategy by which the performative aspect of gender is concealed.

As a consequence, gender cannot be understood as a *role* which either expresses or disguises an interior "self," whether that "self" is conceived as sexed or not. As performance which is performative, gender is an "act," broadly construed, which constructs the social fiction of its own psychological interiority. As opposed to a view such as Erving Goffman's which posits a self which assumes and exchanges various "roles" within the complex social expectations of the "game" of modern life,[13] I am suggesting that this self is not only irretrievably "outside," constituted in social discourse, but that the ascription of interiority is itself a publicly regulated and sanctioned form of essence fabrication. Genders, then, can be neither true nor false, neither real nor apparent. And yet, one is compelled to live in a world in which genders constitute univocal signifiers, in which gender is stabilized, polarized, rendered discrete and intractable. In effect, gender is made to comply with a model of truth and falsity which not only contradicts its own performative fluidity, but serves a social policy of gender regulation and control. Performing one's gender wrong initiates a set of punishments both obvious and indirect, and performing it well provides the reassurance that there is an essentialism of gender identity after all. That this reassurance is so easily displaced by anxiety, that culture so readily punishes or marginalizes those who fail to perform the illusion of gender essentialism should be sign enough that on some level there is social knowledge that the truth or falsity of gender is only socially compelled and in no sense ontologically necessitated.[14]

III. Feminist Theory: Beyond an Expressive Model of Gender

This view of gender does not pose as a comprehensive theory about what gender is or the manner of its construction, and neither does it prescribe an explicit feminist political program. Indeed, I can imagine this view of gender being used for a number of discrepant political strategies. Some of my friends may fault me for this and insist that any theory of gender constitution has political presuppositions and implications, and that it is impossible to separate a theory of gender from a political philosophy of feminism. In fact, I would agree, and argue that it is primarily political interests which create the social phenomena of gender itself, and that without a radical critique of gender constitution feminist theory fails to take stock of the way in which oppression structures the ontological categories through which gender is conceived. Gayatri Spivak has argued that feminists need to rely on an operational essentialism, a false ontology of women as a universal in order to advance a feminist political program.[15] She knows that the category of "women" is not fully expressive, that the multiplicity and discontinuity of the referent mocks and rebels against the univocity of the sign, but suggests it could be used for strategic purposes. Kristeva suggests something similar, I think, when she prescribes that feminists use the category of women as a political tool without attributing ontological integrity to the term, and adds that, strictly speaking, women cannot be said to exist.[16] Feminists might well worry about the political implications of claiming that women do not exist, especially in light of the persuasive arguments advanced by Mary Anne Warren in her book, *Gendercide.*[17] She argues that social policies regarding population control and reproductive technology are designed to limit and, at times, eradicate the existence of women altogether. In light of such a claim, what good does it do to quarrel about the metaphysical status of the term, and perhaps, for clearly political reasons, feminists ought to silence the quarrel altogether.

But it is one thing to use the term and know its ontological insufficiency and quite another to articulate a normative vision for feminist theory which celebrates or emancipates an essence, a nature, or a shared reality which cannot be found. The option I am defending is not to redescribe the world from the point of view of women. I don't know what that point of view is, but whatever it is, it is not singular, and not mine to espouse. It would only be half-right to claim that I am interested in how the phenomenon of a men's or women's point of view gets constituted, for while I do think that those points of views are, indeed, socially constituted, and that a reflexive genealogy of those points of view is important to do, it is not primarily the gender episteme that I am interested in exposing, deconstructing, or reconstructing. Indeed, it is the presupposition of the category of "woman" itself that requires a critical genealogy of the complex institutional and discursive means by which it is constituted. Although some feminist literary critics suggest that the presupposition of sexual difference is necessary for all discourse, that position reifies sexual difference as the founding moment of culture and precludes an analysis not only of how sexual difference is constituted to begin with but how it is continuously constituted, both by the masculine tradition that preempts the universal point of view, and by those feminist positions that construct the univocal category of "women" in the name of expressing or, indeed, liberating a subjected class. As Foucault claimed about those humanist efforts to liberate the criminalized subject, the subject that is freed is even more deeply shackled than originally thought.[18]

Clearly, though, I envision the critical genealogy of gender to rely on a phenomenological set of presuppositions, most important among them the expanded conception of an "act" which is both socially shared and historically constituted, and which is performative in the sense I previously described. But a critical genealogy needs to be supplemented by a politics of performative gender acts, one which both redescribes existing gender identities and offers a prescriptive view about the kind of gender reality there ought to be. The redescription needs to expose the reifications that tacitly serve as substantial gender cores or identities, and to elucidate both the act and the strategy of disavowal which at once constitute and conceal gender as we live it. The prescription is invariably more difficult, if only because we need to think a world in which acts, gestures, the visual body, the clothed body, the various physical attributes usually associated with gender, *express nothing*. In a sense, the prescription is not utopian, but consists in an imperative to acknowledge the existing complexity of gender which our vocabulary invariably disguises and to bring that complexity into a dramatic cultural interplay without punitive consequences.

Certainly, it remains politically important to represent women, but to do that in a way that does not distort and reify the very collectivity the theory is supposed to emancipate. Feminist theory which presupposes sexual difference as the necessary and invariant theoretical point of departure clearly improves upon those humanist discourses which conflate the universal with the masculine and appropriate all of culture as masculine property. Clearly, it is necessary to reread the texts of western philosophy from the various points of view that have been excluded, not only to reveal the particular perspective and set of interests informing those ostensibly transparent descriptions of the real, but to offer alternative descriptions and prescriptions; indeed, to establish philosophy as a cultural practice, and to criticize its tenets from marginalized cultural locations. I have no quarrel with this procedure, and have clearly benefited from those analyses. My only concern is that sexual difference not become a reification which unwittingly preserves a binary restriction on gender identity and an implicitly heterosexual framework for the description of gender, gender identity, and sexuality. There is, in my view, nothing about femaleness that is waiting to be expressed; there is, on the other hand, a good deal about the diverse experiences of women that is being expressed and still needs to be expressed, but caution is needed with respect to that theoretical language, for it does not simply report a pre-linguistic experience, but constructs that experience as well as the limits of its analysis. Regardless of the pervasive character of patriarchy and the prevalence of sexual difference as an operative cultural distinction, there is nothing about a binary gender system that is given. As a corporeal field of cultural play, gender is a basically innovative affair, although it is quite clear that there are strict punishments for contesting the script by performing out of turn or through unwarranted improvisation. Gender is not passively scripted on the body, and neither is it determined by nature, language, the symbolic, or the overwhelming history of patriarchy. Gender is what is put on, invariably, under constraint, daily and incessantly, with anxiety and pleasure, but if this continuous act is mistaken for a natural or linguistic given, power is relinquished to expand the cultural field bodily through subversive performances of various kinds.

Notes

1. For a further discussion of Beauvoir's feminist contribution to phenomenological theory, see my "Variations on Sex and Gender: *Beauvoir's The Second Sex,*" *Yale French Studies* 172 (1986).

2. Maurice Merleau-Ponty, "The Body in Its Sexual Being," in *The Phenomenology of Perception*, trans. Colin Smith (Boston: Routledge and Kegan Paul, 1962).

3. Simone de Beauvoir, *The Second Sex*, trans. H. M. Parshley (New York: Vintage, 1974), p. 38.

4. Julia Kristeva, *Histoire d'amour* (Paris: Editions Denoel, 1983), p. 242.

5. See Michel Foucault, *The History of Sexuality*, trans. Robert Hurley (New York: Random House, 1980), p. 154: "the notion of 'sex' made it possible to group together, in an artificial unity, anatomical elements, biological functions, conducts, sensations, and pleasures, and it enabled one to make use of this fictitious unity as a causal principle."

6. See Claude Levi-Strauss, *The Elementary Structures of Kinship* (Boston: Beacon, 1965).

7. Gayle Rubin, "The Traffic in Women: Notes on the "Political Economy" of Sex," in *Toward an Anthropology of Women*, ed. Rayna R. Reiter (New York: Monthly Review Press, 1975), 178–85.

8. See my "Variations on Sex and Gender: Beauvoir, Wittig, and Foucault," in *Feminism as Critique*, ed. Seyla Benhabib and Drucila Cornell (London: Basil Blackwell, 1987 [distributed by the University of Minnesota Press]).

9. See Victor Turner, *Dramas, Fields, and Metaphors* (Ithaca: Cornell University Press, 1974). Clifford Geertz suggests in "Blurred Genres: The Refiguration of Thought," in *Local Knowledge* (New York: Basic, 1983), that the theatrical metaphor is used by recent social theory in two, often opposing, ways. Ritual theorists like Victor Turner focus on a notion of social drama of various kinds as a means for settling internal conflicts within a culture and regenerating social cohesion. On the other hand, symbolic action approaches, influenced by figures as diverse as Emile Durkheim, Kenneth Burke, and Michel Foucault, focus on the way in which political authority and questions of legitimation are thematized and settled within the terms of performed meaning. Geertz himself suggests that the tension might be viewed dialectically; his study of political organization in Bali as a "theatre-state" is a case in point. In terms of an explicitly feminist account of gender as performative, it seems clear to me that an account of gender as ritualized, public performance must be combined with an analysis of the political sanctions and taboos under which that performance may and may not occur within the public sphere free of punitive consequence.

10. Bruce Wilshire, *Role-Playing and Identity: The Limits of Theatre as Metaphor* (Boston: Routledge and Kegan Paul, 1981).

11. Richard Schechner, *Between Theatre and Anthropology* (Philadelphia: University of Pennsylvania Press, 1985). See especially, "News, Sex, and Performance," pp. 295–324.

12. In *Mother Camp: Female Impersonators in America* (Englewood Cliffs, N.J.: Prentice-Hall, 1972), Anthropologist Esther Newton gives an urban ethnography of drag queens in which she suggests that all gender might be understood on the model of drag. In *Gender: An Ethnomethodological Approach* (Chicago: University of Chicago Press, 1978), Suzanne J. Kessler and Wendy McKenna argue that gender is an "accomplishment" which requires the skills of constructing the body into a socially legitimate artifice.

13. See Erving Goffmann, *The Presentation of Self in Everyday Life* (Garden City, N.Y.: Doubleday, 1959).

14. See Michel Foucault's edition of *Herculine Barbin: The Journals of a Nineteenth Century French Hermaphrodite*, trans. Richard McDougall (New York: Pantheon, 1984), for an interesting display of the horror evoked by intersexed bodies. Foucault's introduction makes clear that the medical delimitation of univocal sex is yet another wayward application of the discourse on truth-as-identity. See also the work of Robert Edgerton in *American Anthropologist* on the cross-cultural variations of response to hermaphroditic bodies.

15. Remarks at the Center for Humanities, Wesleyan University, Spring, 1985.

16. Julia Kristeva, "Woman Can Never Be Defined," trans. Marilyn A. August, in *New French Feminisms*, ed. Elaine Marks and Isabelle de Courtivron (New York: Schocken, 1981).

17. Mary Anne Warren, Gendercide: *The Implications of Sex Selection* (New Jersey: Rowman and Allanheld. 1985).

18. Ibid.; Michel Foucault, *Discipline and Punish* trans. Alan Sheridan (New York: Vintage, 1978).

SECTION IV

IMAGINE OTHERWISE

INTRODUCTION

Section IV includes readings that build on the insights of both postmodern and standpoint theories to construct new knowledge about the recurring questions of feminist theory. The readings address the topics of bodies, emotions, identity, difference, connection, location, and transnational social justice. We borrow the term, "Imagine Otherwise," from the works of two feminist scholars: Avery Gordon's *Ghostly Matters: Haunting and the Sociological Imagination* (1997) and Kandice Chuh's *Imagine Otherwise: On Asian Americanist Critique* (2003). In *Ghostly Matters*, Gordon critiques both "traditional" positivist modes of inquiry and the postmodern turn in the field of sociology. She proposes a new methodology and a new epistemology to take into account "ghosts and haunting" as part of a sociological imagination.[1] Ghosts, according to Gordon, are those on the periphery who have been marginalized by social power relations, and, she argues, transformation in knowledge production can occur only through our confronting these ghosts: "To study social life one must confront the ghostly aspects of it. This confrontation requires (or produces) a fundamental change in the way we know and make knowledge" (1997: 7).

For Gordon, a methodology of following ghosts changes knowledge-building because "being haunted draws affectively, sometimes against our will and always a bit magically, into the structure of feeling of a reality we come to experience, not as cold knowledge, but as a transformative recognition" (8).[2] Through this alternative mode of knowledge production, Gordon offers to bridge the gaps in sociology regarding truth, meaning, knowledge, language, and affect.[3] In so doing, she endeavors to bring back "affect" and "feeling" into the domain of social criticism. In the same vein, Gordon cautions us that "following the ghosts is about making a contact that changes you and refashions the social relations in which you are located" (22). Thus, Gordon emphasizes that the location of the haunted is as important as the ghosts are; the types of narratives that are possible from one haunted social position may not be possible from another. Further she contends that the accounting for and reckoning with these ghosts is motivated "out of a concern for justice" (60). This prompts us to ask, in our own quest for justice, have we created some of our own ghosts that we must now go in search of? In this way, Gordon concurs with Caren Kaplan, another feminist scholar writing about the politics of location, who notes, "Examining the politics of location in the production and reception of theory can turn the terms of inquiry from desiring, inviting, and granting space to others to becoming accountable for one's own investments in cultural metaphors and values" (1994: 139). Following ghosts allows us to reposition knowledge production to take account of the margins. Following ghosts allows us to begin to re-imagine the grounds of transnational feminist social justice movements.

While Gordon urges us to search for a new methodology that can lead us into an alternative space where justice is possible for powerless ghosts, Kandice Chuh takes another approach to building knowledge for social justice. In *Imagine Otherwise*, Chuh rejects fixed, essentialized, identity politics as characterizing the Asian American subject, and seeks to move from cultural or national identity discourses to focus on economic and social justice. She starts by asking: "what happens when we radically query the stability of unitary identity in imagining the Asian American?" Analyzing the term Asian American as an "impossible subject" and mapping the contours of its varied history, Chuh not only recognizes multiplicity and difference but tries to account for difference as interfaced with other differences, rather than collapsed, foreclosed, and resolved into identity and sameness with the U.S. nation (Lim et al. 2006: 4).[4] She proposes transnationalism as a critical tool for Asian American Studies, and shows "… [h]ow each of the various subgroupings of the Asian American has been produced by different transnational dynamics and specific laws and state actions against those groups in the United States" (Lim et al. 2006: 522). Her analysis of Filipino/a American, Japanese American, and Korean American literature shows that the multiple spaces and temporalities of transnationality do not add up to a composite Asian American subject. Chuh deploys transnational as "a cognitive analytic that traces the incapacity of the nation-state to contain and represent fully the subjectivities and ways of life that circulate within the nation-space" (2003: 62).

Arguing against a conceptualization of Asian Americans as identifiable and knowable subjects, Chuh contends that Asian American Studies needs to be re-theorized as a "subjectless discourse." This move will open "the conceptual space to prioritize difference by foregrounding the discursive constructedness of subjectivity. In other words, it points attention to the constraints on the liberatory potential of … subjectivity by reminding us that a 'subject' only becomes recognizable and can act as such by conforming to certain regulatory matrices." In that sense, political subjectivity is always configured within specific historical conditions of agency, recognition, and regulatory constraint, which can be analyzed to inform social justice movements. Chuh argues that as an analytic lens the transnational provides "a critical frame that deliberately recognizes the circumstantiality of knowledge" (63).

We point to Chuh and Gordon to reemphasize that Women's Studies relies on and builds circumstantial knowledge. The metaphors of ghosts, haunting, impossible subjects, and circumstantial knowledge prompt feminist theorists to assume an intellectual attitude of openness to possibility and methodological flexibility. It reminds us that to build effective knowledge for social justice in a world of asymmetrical relational differences, we must develop tools that investigate the "whereabouts unknown," to "ask the other question," and to "ask what else is going on here." It reminds us again, as Chelá Sandoval notes "the meaning of our sisterhood will change. If society's powers are ever mobile and in flux, as they are, then our oppositional moves must not be ideologically limited to one, single, frozen, 'correct' response" (Sandoval 1990: 66). This intellectual stance allows us to imagine otherwise and through that imagination to reconsider the possible bases for transnational feminist solidarity.

Bodies and Emotions

The readings in the Bodies and Emotions subsection explore "the affective turn" that occurred in the mid-1990s when renewed interest in bodies and emotions emerged in a number of disciplinary sites (cf. Clough and Halley 2007). In the humanities, affect theory surfaced first in sites concerned with psychoanalysis, performance theory, and cultural studies as a way out of the impasses of the structural-poststructuralist debates.[5] Attention to the affective components of living—visceral responses, emotional states, and the mood of the room—provide a fruitful vector for connecting the discursive and the material. That is, attending to affect allows theorists to address the "how" of discursive effects on/in bodies without resorting to identity, essentialism, or individualist subjectivities. Texts matter through the affect ("feelings") they archive within them and the affect (impact) they have in the world. At the same time, it provides a way to get beneath the surface of performances to questions of how bodies are moved to act. Affect theory is thus concerned with "the doings of bodies." However, "bodily capacity is never defined by a body alone but is always aided and abetted by and dovetails with the field or context of its force-relations." Bodies are "conjured" by the "regimes of discourse that constitute the ways in which we live our lives," that regulate, discipline, and structure feeling (Gregg and Seigworth 2010: 9, 313). In this sense, bodies and worlds are co-configured; they come into being in complex and messy relationality. However, not only bodies are affected. Gut responses, emotions, public moods, inhere in, and adhere to things as well as people. It is what makes some things fashionable, a favorite, revered and others feared and reviled. Following the affects that haunt people, places, and things, as Gordon recommends, allows us to trace how affects "circulate" and "stick" (Ahmed Reading 46).

The first reading offers an early foray into feminist theorizing about emotions. Alison Jaggar (Reading 44) offers a critique of the "Dumb View" of emotions, with which positivist science dismisses emotions as "an impediment to knowledge" (Narayan Reading 36). Jaggar argues instead that the contrast between objective reason and subjective emotion is gendered, raced, and classed because emotionality is not "equally" attributed to everyone. "[R]eason has been associated with members of the dominant political, social, and cultural groups and emotions with members of subordinated groups" (Reading 44). The contrast between reason and emotion thus serves ideologically to enhance the epistemic authority of the dominant group, which claims objectivity and impartiality for itself. The contrast simultaneously discredits the "observations and claims" of subordinated social groups as subjective, biased, or special interests. So then, "what are emotions," how do/should they shape knowledge?

Jaggar regards emotions as historically specific, socially constructed "habitual responses" to people and events, as well as the expression of those feelings. While emotions are experienced and expressed in and through individual human bodies, they occur within social contexts from which they get their meaning. An "emotional hegemony," normalizes "appropriate" emotions that "serve the interests of the dominant group," such as who can cry and when, who should smile and when. Thus, she argues, often what makes us happy or sad, what we observe as fair or unfair, follows social prescription. Moreover, she observes, emotions are not separable from values. "Emotions and values are closely related." That is, "emotions presuppose values" because they "provide the experiential basis" for interpreting what is good or bad, right or wrong, just or unjust, happiness making, or saddening. The emotional hegemony and its underlying values shape knowledge-building by suggesting what research questions are important, which approaches are reliable, and what findings might be significant. So, for instance, in the United States, many more resources are devoted to research on gender difference rather than gender sameness. However, she notes, individuals do not always respond or express normative emotions as prescribed. These "outlaw emotions" are a vital resource for feminist theorizing (Reading 44). Drawing on standpoint theories, she concludes that the anger, sadness, and related emotions that members of subordinated social groups may feel in the face of contradictions between dominant ideology and their lived experiences can become the source of political theorizing and activism when shared. However, she cautions against uncritical acceptance of the evidence of outlaw emotions. Feminist theorizing is most valuable, she argues, when it pursues self-reflexivity, when it focuses attention on the emotional or affective components of investigation, observation, and evaluation in building knowledge.

In an essay that argues for the value of the feminist classic, *Our Bodies Ourselves (OBOS)*, Kathy Davis (Reading 45) provides a narrative of the key turns in feminist body theory. In particular, she takes issue with the conclusion by feminists theorists that *OBOS* is a "naïve" effort to "recover" "authentic knowledge" of women's bodily experiences. To the contrary, Davis argues that *OBOS* is a "feminist epistemological project" because it "has taken the materiality of the female body as a starting point for understanding the condition of being a woman in a social order hierarchically organized by gender and other intersecting categories of inequality" (Reading 45). It can contribute to the debates and conversations about the three recurring problems in feminist theory. The first is the body problem—theorizing embodiment without essentialism. By treating the body as multilayered, anatomical, physiological, experiential, and culturally embedded, *OBOS* provides accounts of differently situated female bodies that are both non-essentialist and defined by bodily materiality. The second problem is whether and how to value women's experiential knowledge. Davis argues that through the multivocal narrative of experiences offered by women in different kinds of bodies and life circumstances, the book gives authority and encouragement to readers for critical engagement with their lived experiences of health and illness. The third problem, which follows from the second, is that of agency. Here Davis suggests that the coalitional work that produced the various editions and translations of *OBOS* offers a robust model of empowerment and feminist agency.

Davis's analysis draws from both poststructuralist feminist theory and standpoint theory claims. She concludes that poststructuralist feminist theories of the body have provided valuable and necessary correctives to the feminist tendency to essentialize sexed bodies and to take experience as self-explanatory. Yet at the same time, she concludes, *OBOS* can provide an invaluable corrective to poststructuralist tendencies toward excessive abstraction and disembodied theory. *OBOS,* she concludes, provides a "theory in the flesh," [6] through a sentient, situated knowledge of women's condition (Reading 45). Taking poststructural correctives seriously, she calls for a methodology for theory in the flesh that would require careful analysis of the discursive ideological mediation of embodied observations and knowledge-claims.

While Kathy Davis critiques the wordplay central to some poststructuralist feminist theorizing as distracting from thoroughgoing analyses of women's condition, the essay by Sara Ahmed clearly demonstrates that the tools of poststructuralist wordplay can also be used to produce meticulous accounts of how discourse shapes our experiences and emotions. The essay by Sara Ahmed (Reading 46) is a prime example of the generative work being done by feminist theorists in the emergent field of affect theory.

Nominally a commentary on British race relations, Ahmed's essay deploys her concept of affective economies to analyze how the uneven distribution of emotion that Jaggar described functions. Concerned with theorizing the "messiness of the experiential," she locates affect in "the contingent gap between the impression we have of others and the impression we make on others." In this sense, affect inheres in that space between inside and outside, public and private, body and world. Using "happiness to think with," she investigates the cultural politics of emotion, producing an insightful analysis of the ideological processes by which affects stick to (human and non-human) objects as they circulate in social and cultural spaces/expressions and configure gender, race, queer, and immigrant others. Deftly deploying the tools of discursive analysis, the essay intervenes in the smooth ideological functioning of the words and images that convey promises of happiness, sadness, threat, comfort, and/or discomfort. Her discussion develops through a critical reading the "public fantasy" of "the promise of happiness" as it functions in the popular film, *Bend It Like Beckham* (Ahmed Reading 46). She shows how individuals are called into alignment with dominant culture through affective figurations. In the process, she interrogates affective figurations such as the happy housewife (the pretty smiling woman), the feminist killjoy (s/he always "brings us down" by pointing out sexism), the melancholy immigrant and angry black woman (why can't "they" just let go of past slights and injuries), the could be lesbian (short-haired girls playing soccer/football) and the real queer (the single gay man).

In each of these figurations, the promise of happiness resides in proximity to the handsome heterosexual white man. The film's happy ending, the resolution of conflict, comes through choosing him, and all that he represents (the national game). She also illuminates what is concealed, kept from view, in and through those objects. In this regard, she notes, bodies are construed as the origin of bad feelings because they disturb the promise of happiness. The feminist killjoy, angry black woman, and melancholy immigrant cause bad feelings because they do not go along to get along. They insist on pointing out the sexism, racism, homophobia, that reveals the circulating normative objects of happiness (the good life—marriage, kids, joining the national game) as less than promising. Thus Ahmed's essay brings new tools to old questions important to feminist theory, questions about how difference is valued, about non/belonging, and about how to bring head and heart to bear on these questions.

We end the section with a poem by Lucille Clifton, Poet Laureate of the State of Maryland. "lumpectomy eve" (Reading 47) appeared in Clifton's first book of poems published after her first breast cancer diagnosis at age 58 in 1994. Her poetry "grew out of the totality of her life experiences, the obstacles she faced, her perceptions, and her understanding of evolving human conditions. Her poems about cancer were written amid her other poetry, as part of the tapestry of her creative life" (Sulik 2010). In the poem, Clifton narrates a dream from the night before her surgery, as she recalled her breast's role in her life and imagined her other breast comforting it in the face of its impending loss. Presented without any punctuation and with unconventional line breaks and gaps left between the words, Clifton directs our attention to the importance of bodily experience as a site of feminist knowledge production. As such, "lumpectomy eve" epitomizes what Kathy Davis calls theory in the flesh.

Solidarity Reconsidered

The readings in the Solidarity Reconsidered sub-section take up not only questions of how to locate one's self and negotiate differences among various locations but also how feminist political activism, expanded beyond a narrow focus on gender, might be pursued. These readings reposition women's lives and everyday experiences as a central focus of feminist theorizing, and reassert the social group "women," however unstable, as the agent of feminist politics. We also bring the readers' attention to the notion of "common differences" (Mohanty Reading 48) that emphasizes the possibility of building future solidarity while acknowledging the difference among women.

Suzanna Walters (Reading 49) and Paula Moya (Reading 50) focus on the ab/uses of postmodernism in feminist knowledge building. In particular, they criticize the totalizing tendencies of postmodern theorizing. The complete destabilization of identity that results from its otherwise perceptive analysis of categorization and normalization, in their view, undermines the grounds for feminist agency. Postmodernism's "critique of identity … seems to place feminist activism in a straitjacket, unable to move" (Walters Reading 49). They argue that feminists must be able to make knowledge claims as women in order to fight against structural oppressions.

Suzanna Walters's essay specifically engages the tensions between postmodern queer theories of heteronormativity and feminist theories of gender. She argues that queer theory often elides lesbian feminism in claiming to "transcend" the gender binary. She notes that "feminism has taught us" that such a claim represents "a move of gender domination," and she argues that all too often queer "erases lesbian specificity" in favor of "gay maleness" (Walters Reading 49). Beginning with the assertion that "effective progressive political movements" are the goal of feminist theorizing, Paula Moya argues that through postmodernism, feminism becomes a depoliticized academic exercise rather than a radical challenge to the status quo. In her view, postmodernism limits feminist activism and visions of a progressive future. Through a review of postmodern Chicana feminist theory, Moya reasserts the claims of earlier Chicana feminist theorists, such as Gloria Anzaldúa and Chela Sandoval, that Chicana feminism provides an exemplary model for all feminist theorizing. She argues that "la facultad," the oppositional consciousness, made possible by the intersectional experiences of oppression in Chicanas' daily lives, provides a more solid ground for feminist theory and politics than the "contingent" and "strategic" agent of postmodernism (Moya Reading 50).

Neither author, however, relies uncritically on a modernist subjectivity. Both find great value in the postmodern challenges to the fixity and clarity of identity, but they also warn of the risk of renewed essentialism that may result from rigid theorizing from any binary. Walters concludes that queer theory has demonstrated that "sexuality is not reducible to gender," which is an important insight. Yet, similarly, queer theory cannot be effective when it ignores feminist insights about gender processes (Walters Reading 49). In Moya's postpositivist realist perspective, "la facultad" is not built on a naive view of experience as a certain source of knowledge that is unmediated by ideology. In her view, experience is a socially and intellectually mediated, approximate, and revisable basis of knowledge and action.

In Reading 48, Chandra Talpade Mohanty reconsiders the arguments she made in her tremendously influential essay, "Under Western Eyes." In 1986, this essay intervened and changed U.S. feminist conversations about Third World feminisms. Mohanty rejects the frequently offered interpretation that the essay should be read as a postmodern critique of Western feminist discourse. The essay did analyze the power relationships underlying Western feminist thinking about Third World women. However, Mohanty finds the relativism and contingency of postmodern theories to be of limited use for understanding the complex workings of power in global capitalism, which is now her central concern. She also rethinks the terms of her earlier critique, arguing that she "downplayed the commonalities between the two positions" of "Western" and "Third World" feminist practices (Mohanty Reading 48). In the current essay, she employs a postpositivist realism to theorize the grounds for solidarity and organizing against globalization. Postpositivist realism, also advocated by Moya (Reading 50), mediates between modernist constructions of truth and absolute objectivity and postmodernist tendencies toward extreme relativism. By building from "common differences"—that is acknowledging that differences among women do matter but that they should not stop us from forming alliances—Mohanty finds another way to conceptualize feminism without essentializing it. Calling her method feminist comparative analysis, she contrasts it to the other pedagogical approaches she has found in U.S. women's studies classrooms. The contrast offers useful guidance on how to weigh differences and commonalities across historically specific locations, and points to ways in which effective transnational feminist activism, expanded beyond a narrow focus on gender, can be pursued.

Written for the 2003 opening of the "Voicing the Abstract" exhibition featuring young black South African women artists, the South African poet Malika Ndlovu writes in "Out of Now-here" (Reading 51) about the obstacles that the black woman artist faces. Through imagery of fire and river, she conveys women's determined struggles for recognition in the midst of subjective and institutional oppression. In so doing, she demands the reader to recognize that her identity—"Black, Woman, Artist"—is an intersecting rather than fragmented one. As a form of art activism, Ndlovu uses her poem to raise consciousness of black women in South Africa. As a form of feminist writing, it resonates with the voice of poet and activist Yosano Akiko (Reading 1), who seeks to celebrate the creative power of women to challenge the injustices they confront. As can be heard through the voices of the two poets whose words bracket almost a century of feminist activism, these tasks are and always will be complex, conditioned by time and place, and full of possibility. The essays in this final section, remind us that our answers are never final and the ongoing feminist epistemological project is important to build our capacity to think carefully again and again as we endeavor to change the world and are changed ourselves.

Notes

1. The sociological imagination, which grasps the relationship between history and biography, is attributed to C. W. Mills's highly influential book, *The Sociological Imagination* (1959).
2. Raymond Williams' "structure of feelings," is a different methodology that Gordon urges us to appreciate. Structure of feelings acknowledges the "affective elements of consciousness," conceives social experience as "still in progress"…" and enables 'sensuous knowledge, a historical materialism characterized constitutively by the tangle of the subjective and the objective, experience and belief, feeling and thought, the immediate and the general, the personal and the social'" (Williams 129, quoted in Gordon 200).
3. Ann Cvetkovich (2003) focuses on the ephemeral elements of everyday life that build identities. Similar to Avery Gordon, Cvetkovich argues for the place of "affect" in theorizing and knowledge production (249).
4. Along the same vein, Chuh's question, "What does it mean to be a practitioner of Asian American studies when the anchoring terms—'Asian' and 'American'—seem so fatally unstable?" (2003: 4), forces us to rethink beyond the identity-based knowledge production.
5. One strain of affect theory in the social and biological sciences renaturalizes feelings and emotions as hardwired and evolutionarily important. See Gregg and Seigworth (2010).
6. Davis borrows the concept from Cherrie Moraga and Gloria Anzaldúa (1981).

BODIES AND EMOTIONS

44.
LOVE AND KNOWLEDGE: EMOTION IN FEMINIST EPISTEMOLOGY
Alison M. Jaggar
(1989)

I. Introduction: Emotion in Western Epistemology

Within the Western philosophical tradition, emotions have usually been considered potentially or actually subversive of knowledge.[1] From Plato until the present, with a few notable exceptions, reason rather than emotion has been regarded as the indispensable faculty for acquiring knowledge.[2]

Typically, although again not invariably, the rational has been contrasted with the emotional, and this contrasted pair then often linked with other dichotomies. Not only has reason been contrasted with emotion, but it has also been associated with the mental, the cultural, the universal, the public and the male, whereas emotion has been associated with the irrational, the physical, the natural, the particular, the private and, of course, the female.

Although Western epistemology has tended to give pride of place to reason rather than emotion, it has not always excluded emotion completely from the realm of reason. In the *Phaedrus*, Plato portrayed emotions, such as anger or curiosity, as irrational urges (horses) that must always be controlled by reason (the charioteer). On this model, the emotions were not seen as needing to be totally suppressed, but rather as needing direction by reason: for example, in a genuinely threatening situation, it was thought not only irrational but foolhardy not to be afraid.[3] The split between reason and emotion was not absolute, therefore, for the Greeks. Instead, the emotions were thought of as providing indispensable motive power that needed to be channelled appropriately. Without horses, after all, the skill of the charioteer would be worthless.

The contrast between reason and emotion was sharpened in the seventeenth century by redefining reason as a purely instrumental faculty. ... With the rise of modern science, ... the realms of nature and value were separated: nature was stripped of value and reconceptualized as an inanimate mechanism of no intrinsic worth. Values were relocated in human beings, rooted in their preferences and emotional responses. The separation of supposedly natural fact from human value meant that reason, if it were to provide trustworthy insight into reality, had to be uncontaminated by or abstracted from value. ... The validity of logical inferences was thought independent of human attitudes and preferences; this was now the sense in which reason was taken to be objective and universal.

The modern redefinition of rationality required a corresponding reconceptualization of emotion. This was achieved by portraying emotions as non-rational and often irrational urges that regularly swept the body, rather as a storm sweeps over the land. The common way of referring to the emotions as the 'passions' emphasized that emotions happened to or were imposed upon an individual, something she suffered rather than something she did.

… British empiricism, succeeded in the nineteenth century by positivism, took its epistemological task to be the formulation of rules of inference that would guarantee the derivation of certain knowledge from the 'raw data' supposedly given directly to the senses. Empirical testability became accepted as the hallmark of natural science; this, in turn, was viewed as the paradigm of genuine knowledge. Often epistemology was equated with the philosophy of science, and the dominant methodology of positivism prescribed that truly scientific knowledge must be capable of intersubjective verification. Because values and emotions had been defined as variable and idiosyncratic, positivism stipulated that trustworthy knowledge could be established only by methods that neutralized the values and emotions of individual scientists.

Recent approaches to epistemology have challenged some fundamental assumptions of the positivist epistemological model. … However, few challenges have been raised thus far to the purported gap between emotion and knowledge. In this paper, I wish to begin bridging this gap through the suggestion that emotions may be helpful and even necessary rather than inimical to the construction of knowledge. My account is exploratory in nature and leaves many questions unanswered. It is not supported by irrefutable arguments or conclusive proofs; instead, it should be viewed as a preliminary sketch for an epistemological model that will require much further development before its workability can be established.

PART ONE: EMOTION

II. What Are Emotions?

The philosophical question, 'What are emotions?' requires both explicating the ways in which people ordinarily speak about emotion and evaluating the adequacy of those ways for expressing and illuminating experience and activity. Several problems confront someone trying to answer this deceptively simple question. One set of difficulties results from the variety, complexity, and even inconsistency of the ways in which emotions are viewed, both in daily life and in scientific contexts. It is in part this variety that makes emotions into a 'question' at the same time that it precludes answering that question by simple appeal to ordinary usage. A second difficulty is the wide range of phenomena covered by the term 'emotion': these extend from apparently instantaneous 'knee-jerk' responses of fright to lifelong dedication to an individual or a cause; from highly civilized aesthetic responses to undifferentiated feelings of hunger and thirst; … from background moods such as contentment or depression to intense and focused involvement in an immediate situation. It may well be impossible to construct a manageable account of emotion to cover such apparently diverse phenomena.

A further problem concerns the criteria for preferring one account of emotion to another. The more one learns about the ways in which other cultures conceptualize human faculties, the less plausible it becomes that emotions constitute what philosophers call a 'natural kind'. Not only do some cultures identify emotions unrecognized in the West, but there is reason to believe that the concept of emotion itself is a historical invention, like the concept of intelligence (Lewontin [1982]) or even the concept of mind (Rorty [1979]). For instance, anthropologist Catherine Lutz argues that the 'dichotomous categories of "cognition" and "affect" are themselves Euroamerican cultural constructions, master symbols that participate in the fundamental organization of our ways of looking at ourselves and others [1985, 1986], both in and outside of social science' (1987, p. 308). If this is true, then we have even more reason to wonder about the adequacy of ordinary Western ways of talking about emotion. Yet we have no access either to our own emotions or to those of others independent of or unmediated by the discourse of our culture.

In the face of these difficulties, I shall sketch an account of emotion with the following limitations. First, it will operate within the context of Western discussions of emotion: I shall not question, for instance, whether it would be possible or desirable to dispense entirely with anything resembling our concept of emotion. Second, although this account attempts to be consistent with as much as possible of Western understandings of emotion, it is intended to cover only a limited domain, not every phenomenon that may be called an emotion. On the contrary, it excludes as genuine emotions both automatic physical responses and non-intentional sensations, such as hunger pangs. Third, I do not pretend to offer a complete theory of emotion; instead, I focus on a few specific aspects of emotion that I take to have been neglected or misrepresented, especially in positivist and neopositivist accounts. Finally, I would defend my approach not only on the ground that it illuminates aspects of our experience and activity that are obscured by positivist and neopositivist construals, but also on the ground that it is less open than these to ideological abuse. In particular, I believe that recognizing certain neglected aspects of emotion makes possible a better and less ideologically biased account of how knowledge is, and so ought to be, constructed.

III. Emotions as Intentional

Early positivist approaches to understanding emotions assumed that an adequate account required analytically separating emotion from other human faculties. ... [S]o positivist accounts of emotion tried to separate emotion conceptually from both reason and sense perception. As part of their sharpening of these distinctions, positivist construals of emotion tended to identify emotions with the physical feelings or involuntary bodily movements that typically accompany them, such as pangs or qualms, flushes or tremors; emotions were also assimilated to the subduing of physiological function or movement, as in the case of sadness, depression or boredom The continuing influence of such supposedly scientific conceptions of emotion can be seen in the fact that 'feeling' is often used colloquially as a synonym for emotion, even though the more central meaning of 'feeling' is physiological sensation. On such accounts, emotions were not seen a being *about* anything: instead, they were contrasted with and seen as potential disruptions of other phenomena that *are* about some thing, phenomena such as rational judgments, thoughts, and observations. The positivist approach to under-standing emotion has been called the Dumb View (Spelman [1982]).

The Dumb View of emotion is quite untenable. For one thing, the same feeling or physiological response is likely to be interpreted as various emotions, depending on the context of experience. This point often is illustrated by reference to a famous experi-ment; excited feelings were induced in research subjects by the injection of adrenalin, and the subjects then attributed to themselves appropriate emotions depending on their context (Schachter and Singer (1969]). Another problem with the Dumb View is that identifying emotions with feelings would make it impossible to postulate that a person might not be aware of her emotional state, because feelings by definition are a matter of conscious awareness. Finally, emotions differ from feelings, sensations or physiologi-cal responses in that they are dispositional rather than episodic. For instance, we may assert truthfully that we are outraged by, proud of or saddened by certain events, even if at that moment we are neither agitated nor tearful.

In recent years, contemporary philosophers have tended to reject the Dumb View of emotion and have substituted more intentional or cognitivist understandings. These newer conceptions emphasize that intentional judgments as well as physiological dis-turbances are integral elements in emotion.[4] They define or identify emotions not by the quality or character of the physiological sensation that may be associated with them, but rather by their intentional aspect, the associated judgment. Thus, it is the content of my associated thought or judgment that determines whether my physical agitation and restlessness are defined as 'anxiety about my daughter's lateness' rather than as 'anticipation of tonight's performance'.

Cognitivist accounts of emotion have been criticized as overly rationalist, inappli-cable to allegedly spontaneous, automatic or global emotions, such as general feelings of nervousness, contentedness, *Angst*, ecstasy or terror. Certainly, these accounts entail that infants and animals experience emotions, if at all, in only a primitive, rudimentary form. Far from being unacceptable, however, this entailment is desirable because it suggests that humans develop and mature in emotions as well as in other dimensions, increasing the range, variety and subtlety of their emotional responses in accordance with their life experiences and their reflections on these.

Cognitivist accounts of emotion are not without their own problems. A serious difficulty with many is that they end up replicating within the structure of emotion the very problem they are trying to solve—namely, that of an artificial split between emotion and thought—because most cognitivist accounts explain emotion as having two 'components': an affective or feeling component and a cognition that supposedly interprets or identifies the feelings. Such accounts, therefore, unwittingly perpetuate the positivist distinction between the shared, public, objective world of verifiable cal-culations, observations, and facts and the individual, private, subjective world of idi-osyncratic feelings, and sensations. This sharp distinction breaks any conceptual links between our feelings and the 'external' world: if feelings are still conceived as blind or raw or undifferentiated, then we can give no sense to the notion of feelings fitting or failing to fit our perceptual judgments, that is, being appropriate or inappropriate. When intentionality is viewed as intellectual cognition and moved to the center of our picture of emotion, the affective elements are pushed to the periphery and become shadowy conceptual danglers whose relevance to emotion is obscure or even negligible. An adequate cognitive account of emotion must overcome this problem.

Most cognitivist accounts of emotion thus remain problematic in so far as they fail to explain the relation between the cognitive and the affective aspects of emotion. Moreover, in so far as they prioritize the intellectual over the feeling aspects, they reinforce the traditional Western preference for mind over body.[5] Nevertheless, they do identify a vital feature of emotion overlooked by the Dumb View, namely, its intentionality.

IV. Emotions as Social Constructs

We tend to experience our emotions as involuntary individual responses to situations, responses that are often (though, significantly, not always) private in the sense that they are not perceived as directly and immediately by other people as they are by the subject of the experience. The apparently individual and involuntary character of our emotional experience is often taken as evidence that emotions are presocial, instinctive responses, determined by our biological constitution. This inference, however, is quite mistaken. Although it is probably true that the physiological disturbances characterizing emotions (facial grimaces, changes in the metabolic rate, sweating, trembling, tears, and so on) are continuous with the instinctive responses of our prehuman ancestors and also that the ontogeny of emotions to some extent recapitulates their phylogeny, mature human emotions can be seen neither as instinctive nor as biologically determined. Instead, they are socially constructed on several levels.

The most obvious way in which emotions are socially constructed is that children are taught deliberately what their culture defines as appropriate responses to certain situations: to fear strangers, to enjoy spicy food or to like swimming in cold water. On a less conscious level, children also learn what their culture defines as the appropriate ways to express the emotions that it recognizes. Although there may be crosscultural similarities in the expression of some apparently universal emotions, there are also wide divergences in what are recognized as expressions of grief, respect, contempt or anger. On an even deeper level, cultures construct divergent understandings of what emotions are. For instance, English metaphors and metonymies are said to reveal a 'folk' theory of anger as a hot fluid contained in a private space within an individual and liable to dangerous public explosion (Lakoff and Kovecses [1987]). By contrast, the Ilongot, a people of the Philippines, apparently do not understand the self in terms of a public/private distinction and consequently do not experience anger as an explosive internal force: for them, rather, it is an interpersonal phenomenon for which an individual may, for instance, be paid (Rosaldo [1984]).

Further aspects of the social construction of emotion are revealed through reflection on emotion's intentional structure. If emotions necessarily involve judgments, then obviously they require concepts, which may be seen as socially constructed ways of organizing and making sense of the world. For this reason, emotions are simultaneously made possible and limited by the conceptual and linguistic resources of a society. This philosophical claim is borne out by empirical observation of the cultural variability of emotion. ... Even apparently universal emotions, such as anger or love, may vary crossculturally. We have just seen that the Ilongot experience of anger is apparently quite different from the contemporary Western experience. Romantic love was invented in the Middle Ages in Europe and since that time has been modified considerably; for instance, it is no longer confined to the nobility, and it no longer needs to be extramarital or unconsummated. In some cultures, romantic love does not exist at all. ...

Thus there are complex linguistic and other social preconditions for the experience, that is, for the existence of human emotions. The emotions that we experience reflect prevailing forms of social life. ... This is not to say that group emotions historically precede or are logically prior to the emotions of individuals; it is to say that individual experience is simultaneously social experience. ... In later sections, I shall explore the epistemological and political implications of this social rather than individual understanding of emotion.

V. Emotions as Active Engagements

We often interpret our emotions as experiences that overwhelm us rather than as responses we consciously choose: that emotions are to some extent involuntary is part of the ordinary meaning of the term 'emotion'. Even in daily life, however, we recognize that emotions are not entirely involuntary and we try to gain control over them in various ways. ...

... Perhaps it is more helpful to think of emotions as habitual responses that we may have more or less difficulty in breaking. We claim or disclaim responsibility for these responses depending on our purposes in a particular context. We could never experience our emotions entirely as deliberate actions, for then they would appear nongenuine and inauthentic, but neither should emotions be seen as nonintentional, primal or physical forces with which our rational selves are forever at war. As they have been socially constructed, so may they be reconstructed, although describing how this might happen would have to be a long and complicated story.

Emotions, then, are wrongly seen as necessarily passive or involuntary responses to the world. Rather, they are ways in which we engage actively and even construct the world. They have both 'mental' and 'physical' aspects, each of which conditions the other; in some respects they are chosen but in others they are involuntary; they presuppose language and a social order. Thus, they can be attributed only to what are sometimes called 'whole persons', engaged in the on-going activity of social life.

VI. Emotion, Evaluation, and Observation

Emotions and values are closely related. ... [T]he grain of important truth in emotivism is its recognition that values presuppose emotions to the extent that emotions provide the experiential basis for values. If we had no emotional responses to the world, it is inconceivable that we should ever come to value one state of affairs more highly than another.

Just as values presuppose emotions, so emotions presuppose values. The object of an emotion—that is, the object of fear, grief, pride, and so on—is a complex state of affairs that is appraised or evaluated by the individual. For instance, my pride in a friend's achievement necessarily incorporates the value judgment that my friend has done something worthy of admiration.

Emotions and evaluations, then, are logically or conceptually connected. …

… Without characteristically human perceptions of and engagements in the world, there would be no characteristically human emotions.

Just as observation directs, shapes, and partially defines emotion, so too emotion directs, shapes, and even partially defines observation. Observation is not simply a passive process of absorbing impressions or recording stimuli; instead, it is an activity of selection and interpretation. What is selected and how it is interpreted are influenced by emotional attitudes. On the level of individual observation, this influence has always been apparent to common sense, which notes that we remark very different features of the world when we are happy, depressed, fearful, or confident. …

The most obvious significance of this sort of example is in illustrating how the individual experience of emotion focuses our attention selectively, directing, shaping, and even partially defining our observations, just as our observations direct, shape, and partially define our emotions. In addition, the example has been taken further in an argument for the social construction of what are taken in any situation to be undisputed facts, showing how these rest on intersubjective agreements that consist partly in shared assumptions about 'normal' or appropriate emotional responses to situations (McLaughlin [1985]). Thus these examples suggest that certain emotional attitudes are involved on a deep level in all observation, in the intersubjectively verified and so supposedly dispassionate observations of science as well as in the common perceptions of daily life. In the next section, I shall elaborate this claim.

PART TWO: EPISTEMOLOGY

VII. The Myth of Dispassionate Investigation

As we have already seen, Western epistemology has tended to view emotion with suspicion and even hostility. … This derogatory Western attitude toward emotion … fails to recognize that emotion … is necessary to human survival. Emotions prompt us to act appropriately, to approach some people and situations and to avoid others, to caress or cuddle, fight or flee. Without emotion, human life would be unthinkable. Moreover, emotions have an intrinsic as well as an instrumental value. Although not all emotions are enjoyable or even justifiable, as we shall see, life without any emotion would be life without any meaning.

Within the context of Western culture, however, people have often been encouraged to control or even suppress their emotions. Consequently, it is not unusual for people to be unaware of their emotional state or to deny it to themselves and others.

This lack of awareness, especially combined with a neopositivist understanding of emotion that construes it as just a feeling of which one is aware, lends plausibility to the myth of dispassionate investigation. But lack of awareness of emotions certainly does not mean that emotions are not present subconsciously or unconsciously, or that subterranean emotions do not exert a continuing influence on people's articulated values and observations, thoughts, and actions. ...

Within the positivist tradition, the influence of emotion is usually seen only as distorting or impeding observation or knowledge. Certainly it is true that contempt, disgust, shame, revulsion or fear may inhibit investigation of certain situations or phenomena. Furiously angry or extremely sad people often seem quite unaware of their surroundings or even of their own conditions; they may fail to hear or may systematically misinterpret what other people say. People in love are notoriously oblivious to many aspects of the situation around them.

In spite of these examples, however, positivist epistemology recognizes that the role of emotion in the construction of knowledge is not invariably deleterious and that emotions may make a valuable contribution to knowledge. But the positivist tradition will allow emotion to play only the role of suggesting hypotheses for investigation. Emotions are allowed this because the so-called logic of discovery sets no limits on the idiosyncratic methods that investigators may use for generating hypotheses.

When hypotheses are to be tested, however, positivist epistemology imposes the much stricter logic of justification. The core of this logic is replicability, a criterion believed capable of eliminating or cancelling out what are conceptualized as emotional as well as evaluative biases on the part of individual investigators. The conclusions of Western science thus are presumed 'objective', precisely in the sense that they are uncontaminated by the supposedly 'subjective' values and emotions that might bias individual investigators (Nagel [1968, pp. 33–34]).

But if, as has been argued, the positivist distinction between discovery and justification is not viable, then such a distinction is incapable of filtering out values in science. For example, although such a split, when built into the Western scientific method, is generally successful in neutralizing the idiosyncratic or unconventional values of individual investigators, it has been argued that it does not, indeed, cannot, eliminate generally accepted social values. These values are implicit in the identification of the problems that are considered worthy of investigation, in the selection of the hypotheses that are considered worthy of testing and in the solutions to the problems that are considered worthy of acceptance. The science of past centuries provides ample evidence of the influence of prevailing social values, whether seventeenth-century atomistic physics (Merchant [1980]) or nineteenth-century competitive interpretations of natural selection (Young [1985]).

Of course, only hindsight allows us to identify clearly the values that shaped the science of the past and thus to reveal the formative influence on science of pervasive emotional attitudes, attitudes that typically went unremarked at the time because they were shared so generally. For instance, it is now glaringly evident that contempt for (and perhaps fear of) people of color is implicit in nineteenth-century anthropology's interpretations and even constructions of anthropological facts. ...

Values and emotions enter into the science of the past and the present not only at the level of scientific practice but also at the metascientific level, as answers to various questions: What is science? How should it be practiced? And what is the status of scientific investigation versus nonscientific modes of inquiry? For instance, it is claimed with increasing frequency that the modern Western conception of science, which identifies knowledge with power and views it as a weapon for dominating nature, reflects the imperialism, racism, and misogyny of the societies that created it. ...

Positivism views values and emotions as alien invaders that must be repelled by a stricter application of the scientific method. If the foregoing claims are correct, however, the scientific method and even its positivist construals themselves incorporate values and emotions. Moreover, such an incorporation seems a necessary feature of all knowledge and conceptions of knowledge. Therefore, rather than repressing emotion in epistemology it is necessary to rethink the relation between knowledge and emotion and construct conceptual models that demonstrate the mutually constitutive rather than oppositional relation between reason and emotion. Far from precluding the possibility of reliable knowledge, emotion as well as value must be shown as necessary to such knowledge. Despite its classical antecedents and as in the ideal of disinterested inquiry, the ideal of dispassionate inquiry is an impossible dream, but a dream none the less or perhaps a myth that has exerted enormous influence on Western epistemology. Like all myths, it is a form of ideology that fulfils certain social and political functions.

VIII. The Ideological Function of the Myth

So far, I have spoken very generally of people and their emotions, as though everyone experienced similar emotions and dealt with them in similar ways. It is an axiom of feminist theory, however, that all generalizations about 'people' are suspect. The divisions in our society are so deep, particularly the divisions of race, class, and gender, that many feminist theorists would claim that talk about people in general is ideologically dangerous because such talk obscures the fact that no one is simply a person but instead is constituted fundamentally by race, class, and gender. Race, class, and gender shape every aspect of our lives, and our emotional constitution is not excluded. Recognizing this helps us to see more clearly the political functions of the myth of the dispassionate investigator.

Feminist theorists have pointed out that the Western tradition has not seen everyone as equally emotional. Instead, reason has been associated with members of dominant political, social, and cultural groups and emotion with members of subordinate groups. Prominent among those subordinate groups in our society are people of color, except for supposedly 'inscrutable orientals', and women.[6]

Although the emotionality of women is a familiar cultural stereotype, its grounding is quite shaky. Women appear to be more emotional than men because they, along with some groups of people of color, are permitted and even required to express emotion more openly. In contemporary Western culture, emotionally inexpressive women are suspect as not being real women,[7] whereas men who express their emotions freely are suspected of being homosexual or in some other way deviant from the masculine ideal.

Modern Western men, in contrast with Shakespeare's heroes, for instance, are required to present a façade of coolness, lack of excitement, even boredom, to express emotion only rarely and then for relatively trivial events, such as sporting occasions, where the emotions expressed are acknowledged to be dramatized and so are not taken entirely seriously. Thus, women in our society form the main group allowed or even expected to express emotion. A woman may cry in the face of disaster, and a man of color may gesticulate, but a white man merely sets his jaw.[8]

White men's control of their emotional expression may go to the extremes of repressing their emotions, failing to develop emotionally or even losing the capacity to experience many emotions. Not uncommonly, these men are unable to identify what they are feeling, and even they may be surprised, on occasion, by their own apparent lack of emotional response to a situation, such as a death, where emotional reaction is perceived to be appropriate. In some married couples, the wife is implicitly assigned the job of feeling emotion for both of them. White, college-educated men increasingly enter therapy in order to learn how to 'get in touch with' their emotions, a project other men may ridicule as weakness. In therapeutic situations, men may learn that they are just as emotional as women but less adept at identifying their own or others' emotions. In consequence, their emotional development may be relatively rudimentary; this may lead to moral rigidity or insensitivity. Paradoxically, men's lacking awareness of their own emotional responses frequently results in their being more influenced by emotion rather than less.

Although there is no reason to suppose that the thoughts and actions of women are any more influenced by emotion than the thoughts and actions of men, the stereotypes of cool men and emotional women continue to flourish because they are confirmed by an uncritical daily experience. In these circumstances, where there is a differential assignment of reason and emotion, it is easy to see the ideological function of the myth of the dispassionate investigator. It functions, obviously, to bolster the epistemic authority of the currently dominant groups, composed largely of white men, and to discredit the observations and claims of the currently subordinate groups including, of course, the observations and claims of many people of color and women. The more forcefully and vehemently the latter groups express their observations and claims, the more emotional they appear and so the more easily they are discredited. The alleged epistemic authority of the dominant groups then justifies their political authority.

The previous section of this paper argued that dispassionate inquiry was a myth. This section has shown that the myth promotes a conception of epistemological justification vindicating the silencing of those, especially women, who are defined culturally as the bearers of emotion and so are perceived as more 'subjective', biased and irrational. In our present social context, therefore, the ideal of the dispassionate investigator is a classist, racist, and especially masculinist myth. …

IX. Emotional Hegemony and Emotional Subversion

As we have seen already, mature human emotions are neither instinctive nor biologically determined, although they may have developed out of presocial, instinctive responses. Like everything else that is human, emotions in part are socially constructed;

like all social constructs, they are historical products, bearing the marks of the society that constructed them. Within the very language of emotion, in our basic definitions and explanations of what it is to feel pride or embarrassment, resentment or contempt, cultural norms and expectations are embedded. Simply describing ourselves as angry, for instance, presupposes that we view ourselves as having been wronged, victimized by the violation of some social norm. Thus, we absorb the standards and values of our society in the very process of learning the language of emotion, and those standards and values are built into the foundation of our emotional constitution.

Within a hierarchical society, the norms and values that predominate tend to serve the interests of the dominant groups. Within a capitalist, white suprematist, and male-dominant society, the predominant values will tend to be those that serve the interests of rich white men. Consequently, we are all likely to develop an emotional constitution that is quite inappropriate for feminism. Whatever our color, we are likely to feel what Irving Thalberg has called 'visceral racism'; whatever our sexual orientation, we are likely to be homophobic; whatever our class, we are likely to be at least somewhat ambitious and competitive; whatever our sex, we are likely to feel contempt for women. Such emotional responses may be rooted in us so deeply that they are relatively impervious to intellectual argument and may recur even when we pay lip service to changed intellectual convictions. ...

By forming our emotional constitution in particular ways, our society helps to ensure its own perpetuation. The dominant values are implicit in responses taken to be precultural or acultural, our so-called gut responses. Not only do these conservative responses hamper and disrupt our attempts to live in or prefigure alternative social forms but also, and in so far as we take them to be natural responses, they blinker us theoretically. For instance, they limit our capacity for outrage; they either prevent us from despising or encourage us to despise; they lend plausibility to the belief that greed and domination are inevitable human motivations; in sum, they blind us to the possibility of alternative ways of living.

... The picture, however, is not complete; it ignores the fact that people do not always experience the conventionally acceptable emotions. They may feel satisfaction rather than embarrassment when their leaders make fools of themselves. They may feel resentment rather than gratitude for welfare payments and hand-me-downs. They may be attracted to forbidden modes of sexual expression. They may feel revulsion for socially sanctioned ways of treating children or animals. In other words, the hegemony that our society exercises over people's emotional constitution is not total.

People who experience conventionally unacceptable, or what I call 'outlaw' emotions often are subordinated individuals who pay a disproportionately high price for maintaining the *status quo*. The social situation of such people makes them unable to experience the conventionally prescribed emotions: for instance, people of color are more likely to experience anger than amusement when a racist joke is recounted, and women subjected to male sexual banter are less likely to be flattered than uncomfortable or even afraid.

When unconventional emotional responses are experienced by isolated individuals, those concerned may be confused, unable to name their experience; they may even doubt their own sanity. Women may come to believe that they are 'emotionally disturbed' and that the embarrassment or fear aroused in them by male sexual innuendo is prudery or paranoia. When certain emotions are shared or validated by others, however, the basis exists for forming a subculture defined by perceptions, norms, and values that systematically oppose the prevailing perceptions, norms, and values. By constituting the basis for such a subculture, outlaw emotions may be politically because epistemologically subversive.

Outlaw emotions are distinguished by their incompatibility with the dominant perceptions and values, and some, though certainly not all, of these outlaw emotions are potentially or actually feminist emotions. Emotions become feminist when they incorporate feminist perceptions and values, just as emotions are sexist or racist when they incorporate sexist or racist perceptions and values. For example, anger becomes feminist anger when it involves the perception that the persistent importuning endured by one woman is a single instance of a widespread pattern of sexual harassment, and pride becomes feminist pride when it is evoked by realizing that a certain person's achievement was possible only because that individual overcame specifically gendered obstacles to success. …

Outlaw emotions stand in a dialectical relation to critical social theory: at least some are necessary for developing a critical perspective on the world, but they also presuppose at least the beginnings of such a perspective. Feminists need to be aware of how we can draw on some of our outlaw emotions in constructing feminist theory, and also of how the increasing sophistication of feminist theory can contribute to the re-education, refinement, and eventual reconstruction of our emotional constitution.

X. Outlaw Emotions and Feminist Theory

The most obvious way in which feminist and other outlaw emotions can help in developing alternatives to prevailing conceptions of reality is by motivating new investigations. … As we have seen already, theoretical investigation is always purposeful, and observation always selective. Feminist emotions provide a political motivation for investigation and so help to determine the selection of problems as well as the method by which they are investigated. Susan Griffin makes the same point when she characterizes feminist theory as following 'a direction determined by pain, and trauma, and compassion and outrage' (Griffin [1979, p. 31]).

As well as motivating critical research, outlaw emotions may also enable us to perceive the world differently from its portrayal in conventional descriptions. They may provide the first indications that something is wrong with the way alleged facts have been constructed, with accepted understandings of how things are. Conventionally unexpected or inappropriate emotions may precede our conscious recognition that accepted descriptions and justifications often conceal as much as reveal the prevailing state of affairs. Only when we reflect on our initially puzzling irritability, revulsion, anger or fear may we bring to consciousness our 'gut-level' awareness that we are in a situation of coercion, cruelty, injustice or danger. Thus, conventionally inexplicable emotions, particularly though not exclusively those experienced by women, may lead us to make subversive observations that challenge dominant conceptions of the *status quo*. They may help us to realize that what are taken generally to be facts have been constructed in a way that obscures the reality of subordinated people, especially women's reality.

But why should we trust the emotional responses of women and other subordinated groups? How can we determine which outlaw emotions are to be endorsed or encouraged and which rejected? In what sense can we say that some emotional responses are more appropriate than others? What reason is there for supposing that certain alternative perceptions of the world, perceptions informed by outlaw emotions, are to be preferred to perceptions informed by conventional emotions? Here I can indicate only the general direction of an answer, whose full elaboration must await another occasion.[9] ...

... Here I appeal to a claim for which I have argued elsewhere: the perspective on reality that is available from the standpoint of the subordinated, which in part at least is the standpoint of women, is a perspective that offers a less partial and distorted and therefore more reliable view (Jaggar [1983, ch. 11]). Subordinated people have a kind of epistemological privilege in so far as they have easier access to this standpoint and therefore a better chance of ascertaining the possible beginnings of a society in which all could thrive. For this reason, I would claim that the emotional responses of subordinated people in general, and often of women in particular, are more likely to be appropriate than the emotional responses of the dominant class. That is, they are more likely to incorporate reliable appraisals of situations. ...

XI. Some Implications of Recognizing the Epistemic Potential of Emotion

Accepting that appropriate emotions are indispensable to reliable knowledge does not mean, of course, that uncritical feeling may be substituted for supposedly dispassionate investigation. Nor does it mean that the emotional responses of women and other members of the underclass are to be trusted without question. Although our emotions are epistemologically indispensable, they are not epistemologically indisputable. Like all our faculties, they may be misleading, and their data, like all data, are always subject to reinterpretation and revision. Because emotions are not presocial, physiological responses to unequivocal situations, they are open to challenge on various grounds. They may be dishonest or self-deceptive, they may incorporate inaccurate or partial perceptions, or they may be constituted by oppressive values. Accepting the indispensability of appropriate emotions to knowledge means no more (and no less) than that discordant emotions should be attended to seriously and respectfully rather than condemned, ignored, discounted or suppressed.

Just as appropriate emotions may contribute to the development of knowledge, so the growth of knowledge may contribute to the development of appropriate emotions. For instance, the powerful insights of feminist theory often stimulate new emotional responses to past and present situations. Inevitably, our emotions are affected by the knowledge that the women on our faculty are paid systematically less than the men, that one girl in four is subjected to sexual abuse from heterosexual men in her own family, and that few women reach orgasm in heterosexual intercourse. We are likely to feel different emotions toward older women or people of color as we re-evaluate our standards of sexual attractiveness or acknowledge that black is beautiful. The new emotions evoked by feminist insights are likely in turn to stimulate further feminist observations and insights, and these may generate new directions in both theory and political practice. There is a continuous feedback loop between our emotional constitution and our theorizing such that each continually modifies the other and is in principle inseparable from it. …

The alternative epistemological models that I suggest would display the continuous interaction between how we understand the world and who we are as people. They would show how our emotional responses to the world change as we conceptualize it differently and how our changing emotional responses then stimulate us to new insights. They would demonstrate the need for theory to be self-reflexive, to focus not only on the outer world but also on ourselves and our relation to that world, to examine critically our social location, our actions, our values, our perceptions, and our emotions. The models would also show how feminist and other critical social theories are indispensable psychotherapeutic tools because they provide some insights necessary to a full understanding of our emotional constitution. Thus, the models would explain how the reconstruction of knowledge is inseparable from the reconstruction of ourselves.

A corollary of the reflexivity of feminist and other critical theory is that it requires a much broader construal than positivism accepts of the process of theoretical investigation. In particular, it requires acknowledging that a necessary part of theoretical process is critical self-examination. Time spent in analyzing emotions and uncovering their sources should be viewed, therefore, neither as irrelevant to theoretical investigation nor even as a prerequisite for it; it is not a kind of clearing of the emotional decks, 'dealing with' our emotions so that they will not influence our thinking. Instead, we must recognize that our efforts to reinterpret and refine our emotions are necessary to our theoretical investigation, just as our efforts to re-educate our emotions are necessary to our political activity. Critical reflection on emotion is not a self-indulgent substitute for political analysis and political action. It is itself a kind of political theory and political practice, indispensable for an adequate social theory and social transformation.

Finally, the recognition that emotions play a vital part in developing knowledge enlarges our understanding of women's claimed epistemic advantage. We can now see that women's subversive insights owe much to women's outlaw emotions, themselves appropriate responses to the situations of women's subordination. In addition to their propensity to experience outlaw emotions, at least on some level, women are relatively adept at identifying such emotions, in themselves and others, in part because of their social responsibility for caretaking, including emotional nurturance. It is true that women, like all subordinated peoples, especially those who must live in close proximity with their masters, often engage in emotional deception and even self-deception as the price of their survival. Even so, women may be less likely than other subordinated groups to engage in denial or suppression of outlaw emotions. Women's work of emotional nurturance has required them to develop a special acuity in recognizing hidden emotions and in understanding the genesis of those emotions. This emotional acumen can now be recognized as a skill in political analysis and validated as giving women a special advantage both in understanding the mechanisms of domination and in envisioning freer ways to live.

XII. Conclusion

The claim that emotion is vital to systematic knowledge is only the most obvious contrast between the conception of theoretical investigation that I have sketched here and the conception provided by positivism. For instance, the alternative approach emphasizes that what we identify as emotion is a conceptual abstraction from a complex process of human activity that also involves acting, sensing, and evaluating. This proposed account of theoretical construction demonstrates the simultaneous necessity for and interdependence of faculties that our culture has abstracted and separated from each other: emotion and reason, evaluation and perception, observation and action. The model of knowing suggested here is nonhierarchical and antifoundationalist; instead, it is appropriately symbolized by the radical feminist metaphor of the upward spiral. Emotions are neither more basic than observation, reason or action in building theory, nor secondary to them. Each of these human faculties reflects an aspect of human knowing inseparable from the other aspects. Thus, to borrow a famous phrase from a Marxian context, the development of each of these faculties is a necessary condition for the development of all.

In conclusion, it is interesting to note that acknowledging the importance of emotion for knowledge is not an entirely novel suggestion within the Western epistemological tradition. That archrationalist, Plato himself, came to accept in the end that knowledge required a (very purified form of) love. It may be no accident that in the *Symposium* Socrates learns this lesson from Diotima, the wise woman!

Notes

1. Philosophers who do not conform to this generalization and constitute part of what Susan Bordo calls a 'recessive' tradition in Western philosophy include Hume and Nietzsche, Dewey and James (Bordo [1987, pp. 114–18]).

2. The Western tradition as a whole has been profoundly rationalist, and much of its history may be viewed as a continuous redrawing of the boundaries of the rational. For a survey of this history from a feminist perspective, see Lloyd (1984).

3. Thus, fear or other emotions were seen as rational in some circumstances. To illustrate this point, Vicky Spelman quotes Aristotle as saying (in the *Nicomachean Ethics*, Bk. IV, ch. 5): '[Anyone] who does not get angry when there is reason to be angry, or who does not get angry in the right way at the right time and with the right people, is a dolt' (Spelman [1982, p. 1]).

4. Even adherents of the Dumb View recognize, of course, that emotions are not entirely random or unrelated to an individual's judgments and beliefs; in other words, they note that people are angry or excited *about* something, afraid or proud *of* something. On the Dumb View, however, the judgments or beliefs associated with an emotion are seen as its causes and thus as related to it only externally.

5. Cheshire Calhoun pointed this out to me in private correspondence.

6. E. V. Spelman (1982) illustrates this point with a quotation from the well known contemporary philosopher, R. S. Peters, who wrote 'we speak of emotional outbursts, reactions, upheavals and women' (*Proceedings of the Aristotelian Society*, New Series, vol. 62).

7. It seems likely that the conspicuous absence of emotion shown by Mrs. Thatcher is a deliberate strategy she finds necessary to counter the public perception of women as too emotional for political leadership. The strategy results in her being perceived as a formidable leader, but as an Iron Lady rather than a real woman. …

8. On the rare occasions when a white man cries, he is embarrassed and feels constrained to apologize. The one exception to the rule that men should be emotionless is that they are allowed and often even expected to experience anger. Spelman (1982) points out that men's cultural permission to be angry bolsters their claim to authority.

9. I owe this suggestion to Marcia Lind.

45.
RECLAIMING WOMEN'S BODIES: COLONIALIST TROPE OR CRITICAL EPISTEMOLOGY?
Kathy Davis
(2007)

… While the historical significance of *OBOS* [*Our Bodies, Ourselves*] as a catalyst for feminist health activism and its role in inspiring research on women's health are recognized by feminist scholars (Clarke and Olesen 1999a, 14), it is rarely viewed as having anything of relevance to offer feminist theory. This is especially surprising given the amount of attention that the topic of the body has received within contemporary feminist theory. With the plethora of recent publications devoted to feminist theoretical perspectives on the body, not a single one does more than mention *OBOS* in passing and none of the anthologies concerned with women's bodies and embodiment has included a chapter or even an excerpt from it.[1] Thus, it is safe to conclude that while *OBOS* has played a formative role in feminist (health) politics it has had little effect on the direction taken by current feminist body theory.

In a recent article, Kuhlmann and Babitsch (2002) have explored the reasons for what they call the "dissociation process" between contemporary feminist body theory and research and activism on women's health. In their view, postmodern feminist theory is the culprit. Its concepts and theories have become so esoteric, so ethereal, so divorced from women's everyday experiences with their bodies that they have been of little use to feminist health activists. This kind of abstract theorizing has not only prevented feminist health activists from profiting from the insights of feminist body theory, but it also signals an even more fundamental problem in the theory itself—specifically, a neglect of the materiality of the (sexed) body and the concrete processes of health and illness (433).

In order to better understand this dissociation process, let us take a brief look at an example in the form of a well-known and oft-cited essay by Donna Haraway called "The Virtual Speculum in the New World Order" (1999). Haraway is one of the most important contemporary feminist theorists on the body and, more generally, on the feminist politics of knowledge. She is generally given credit for raising—and, indeed, even answering—the questions that are most crucial for a feminist understanding of the body in the context of proliferating information and biotechnologies and the relationship of the body to the issues of women's subjectivity and agency. In this particular essay, which has been lauded as no less than an attempt to bring feminist theory into the new millennium by "opening up the New World Order for our collective examination and consideration" (Clarke and Olesen 1999, 25), Haraway addresses the politics of the women's health movement and takes a critical look at the role *OBOS* has played in shaping the direction these politics have taken.

Haraway provocatively couples *OBOS* (the book and the slogan) to feminist self-help, which was popular in the U.S. women's health movement in the early seventies. Initially developed by primarily white, middle-class, U.S. women, feminist self-help involved women meeting in small groups, sharing information and stories, educating themselves about their bodies and the medical establishment, and looking for remedies to minor bodily problems. ...

Although *OBOS* and self-help were never identical,[2] *OBOS* did draw on many of the insights of self-help. For example, it encouraged its readers to explore their own bodies—sometimes with mirror in hand. ... However, it is the emphasis of *OBOS* on women "discovering" their bodies and "recovering" ownership of their sexuality and reproduction through knowledge of their bodies that is the particular object of Haraway's critique.

> Armed with a gynecological speculum, a mirror, a flashlight, and—most of all—each other in a consciousness-raising group, women ritually opened their bodies to their own literal view. ... More than a little amnesiac about how colonial travel narratives work, we peered inside our vaginas toward the distant cervix and said something like, "Land ho!" We have discovered ourselves and claim the new territory for women. In the context of the history of Western sexual politics—that is, in the context of the whole orthodox history of Western philosophy and technology—visually self-possessed sexual and generative organs made potent tropes for the reclaimed feminist self. We thought we had our eyes on the prize. I am caricaturing, of course, but with a purpose. *Our Bodies, Ourselves* was both a popular slogan and the title of a landmark publication in women's health movements. (Haraway 1999, 67)

According to Haraway, when women look at their bodies through a speculum they unwittingly adopt the same objectifying medical "gaze" that historically has been central to the medical appropriation of women's bodies. By separating the feminist subject (who can "discover" and "recover") and the female body (as passive object), feminist health activists are merely reproducing medical discourse, thereby imitating masculinist dualisms about women's embodiment. ... For Haraway, the belief that women's privileged access to their bodies provides them with authentic knowledge beyond the purview of science and culture is mistaken. Feminist knowledge cannot exist outside dominant forms of knowledge. In Haraway's view, these would-be feminist "explorers" are no different than the male doctors they are attacking, and, indeed, they may even be considerably worse. Haraway employs the trope of "colonial travel" to compare feminist health activists to white European male colonizers who were also engaged in a discovery project—this time the project of conquering indigenous peoples in faraway places. The implication is that the "speculum" employed by white, well-educated, feminist health activists in the seventies represents a practice that is just as power laden as the colonial project and is, therefore, just as likely to be disempowering for nonwhite, non-Western women because it obscures dramatic differences in morbidity, mortality, and access in health care among U.S. women (72).

Haraway admits, of course, that she is providing something of a "caricature" by comparing feminist self-help to the "whole orthodox history of Western philosophy and technology," not to mention the nefarious masculinist colonial project of conquering land (nature) and peoples (natives). However, she defends her strategy as an important, and indeed necessary, intervention in U.S. feminist health politics. Her concern is the development of a critical and reflexive politics of knowledge—what she calls "the right speculum for the job" which will acknowledge differences in women's health and create structures of accountability between differently located women within the United States and worldwide. As Haraway puts it, it is only then that a "truly comprehensive" feminist politics of health can emerge (84).

While I believe that Haraway's claims are both important and in need of some critical attention,[3] it is not my intention here to criticize this particular essay. I have referred to Haraway's essay at some length because it is exemplary of a much broader and far-reaching phenomenon with feminist body theory—namely, the tendency to treat health activism as theoretically naive and methodologically flawed—and therefore has little of relevance to offer feminist body theory.

In this chapter, I will provide a more careful (and less caricatural) consideration of *OBOS* and, by implication, feminist health activism. To this end, I will not be treating *OBOS* as "just" a popular book on women's health but rather as an epistemological project.

OBOS as Epistemological Project

By epistemological project, I mean any project that centers on knowledge and knowledge practices. Traditionally, epistemology has dealt with questions such as the nature of knowledge, justification, objectivity, and epistemic agency. Feminist epistemologists have dealt with these questions and introduced new problems; including the politics of knowledge and the impact of the social position and the sexed body of the knower on the production and reception of knowledge (Alcoff and Potter 1993, 1–2). By these standards, *OBOS* is an epistemological project par excellence because it focuses on knowledge about the female body, on what counts as authoritative knowledge, on how this knowledge is justified, and on women's status as epistemic agents.[4]

As an epistemological project, *OBOS* has taken the female body as a starting point for understanding the condition of being a woman in a social order hierarchically organized by gender and other intersecting categories of inequality. The female body in *OBOS* is a complex, dynamic, multilayered entity, however. It is an *anatomical* body with breasts, clitoris, vagina, and uterus. It is also a *physiological* body, which may menstruate and have the capacity to become pregnant and which may or may not bear children.[5] It may become ill or disabled, will inevitably grow older, and will eventually die. It is an *experiential* body, which is lived and given meaning by the subject as she moves about in the world around her. And, finally, it is a body that is embedded in a *culture* that, to a greater or lesser degree, devalues femininity. In this culture, women's bodies are stereotyped, subjected to violence, exploited in the workplace, marginalized or excluded from the public domain, and subjected to the insults of racism and class inequities. Thus, in *OBOS* the female body in all its complexity is presented as the site from which women engage with the world, making it a potential locus for resistance and political action.

Second, *OBOS* has attributed authority to women's embodied experiences. Women are encouraged to take their bodily experiences seriously as a valuable source of knowledge. These experiences cover a broad spectrum, from sexuality and relationships, raising children, health problems, and finding one's way through the health care system to living in a society structured by poverty, racism, and gender inequalities. Women are invited to use these experiences to think critically about medical procedures and remedies and to develop strategies for staying healthy. Experiences are also treated as a necessary resource for interrogating cultural understandings that deny, distort, or misrepresent women's bodies and the circumstances and conditions of their embodied lives. Knowledge without experience is cast as the dividing line between the powerful and the marginalized whereby experiential knowledge provides women with the critical tools necessary for their survival.[6]

Third, *OBOS* treats women as active knowers rather than passive objects of the knowledge practices of others. By gaining knowledge about their bodies, it shows how women can gain control over their lives. This notion of agency is not the same as the "Just do it!" philosophy that pervades contemporary Western culture and is popular within self-help culture (Bordo 1997). In *OBOS*, the act of becoming knowledgeable, of understanding one's own experiences and using them to engage critically with dominant forms of knowledge, is treated as both individually and collectively empowering for women. By sharing the process of producing and disseminating alternative forms of knowledge about women's bodies and by finding ways to form coalitions with differently situated women across multiple locations, *OBOS* offers a vision of a collective feminist politics of knowledge that has shaped contemporary feminist health activism (Murphy 2004, 141–42).

… In order to pave the way for a more productive and mutually beneficial exchange between feminist body theory and feminist health activism, I will now turn to three highly publicized debates within contemporary feminist body theory. The first debate concerns the female body and the uses (and abuses) of biology in justifying gendered inequalities as "natural." The second debate concerns the validity of women's experiential knowledge as an arbiter of the "truth." And, finally, the third debate concerns how to conceptualize women's agency with regard to the production of subversive or empowering forms of knowledge. I will show how the confrontation with *OBOS* as an epistemological project can contribute to these debates, thereby making feminist body theory more amenable to the concerns of feminist health activism.

The Biological Body

Beginning with Simone de Beauvoir's (1953) famous adage that "a woman is not born, but rather becomes a woman," feminist theory in the West has been preoccupied with shifting attention away from biology as an explanation for inequalities between the sexes to the social and cultural conditions that produce femininity and masculinity.

One of the central tasks of feminist body theory has been, then, to avoid biological determinism by finding ways to conceptualize the body without reducing gendered inequalities to biologically based differences between women and men.

This has been a long-standing theoretical project with a wide diversity of perspectives and strategies. It began with the conceptual distinction between sex and gender, which became the cornerstone of modernist feminist body theory (Fraser and Greco 2005). The concept of sex was relegated to the realm of biology, implicitly specified in terms of anatomy, chromosomes, and hormones, while gender, in contrast, was used to refer to "all other socially constructed characteristics attributed to women and men" (Oudshoorn 1994, 2). Distinguishing between sex and gender got rid of the problem of biological determinism—at least for the time being. However, it did not resolve the problem of essentialism—that is, the assumption of an a priori, ontological, or biological "essence" for sexual difference. Under the influence of postmodernism, it became clear that the separation of biological sex from cultural gender was no longer regarded as an adequate solution to the problem of essentialism as it left the biological body as a kind of implicit "coat rack" for gender (Nicholson 1994). Feminist body theory, therefore, began to look for ways to theorize the body that would avoid biological determinism without running the risk of essentialism. For many, the solution to this problem seemed to reside in treating the body as a "text" on which culture inscribes its meanings (Bordo 1993) or as an "imaginary" site, an effect not of genetics but of relations of power. In this way, the entire notion of an anatomical or biological body could be viewed as little more than a discourse produced by a specific culture. ... Judith Butler (1989, 1993) took an even more radical approach to the problem of essentialism by questioning the entire distinction between biological sex and cultural gender. She rejected any notion of a physical substrate or even a surface on which culture imposes its meanings, arguing instead that bodies are best viewed as "performances" whereby sex—analogous to gender—is a contingent, fluctuating series of performative constructions. Although Butler claimed that her conception allowed space for the "materiality" of the body, it was a relentlessly discursive materiality, divorced from women's flesh and blood bodies.

Another strategy for avoiding both biological determinism and essentialism entailed dismantling the dualisms in Western thought that associated women with their bodies to begin with while allowing men the masculinist fantasy that they could transcend their bodies as "disembodied minds" (Bordo 1987). These dualisms trap women in the constraints of the flesh, making them prisoners of their bodies, while men are presumably able to "leap out of the marked body into a conquering gaze from nowhere" (Haraway 1991b, 188). Women are not alone in being reduced to their bodies. People of color, the elderly, the homosexual, the fat, and the disabled are also defined through their bodes as the "other" to white, Western, bourgeois men (Young 1990a). ... Feminist body theorists such as Bordo, Haraway, and many others have devoted considerable attention to exposing the gendered character of Western dualistic thinking, showing how binaries, which hierarchically privilege mind over body, rationality over emotions, culture over nature, and human over animal, are implicated in hierarchical relations of power. As a theoretical solution to the problem of dualistic conceptions of the body, Haraway (1991) introduced the metaphor of the cyborg, which imaginatively disrupted all conventional attempts to classify bodies in terms of conventional binaries. This metaphor enabled a conceptualization of the body as an endless process of morphing into new and uncategorizable forms (part human, part animal, part machine, both masculine and feminine, etc.). While the cyborg body seemed particularly suited to a postmodern information society, with its "codes, dispersal, and networks" (211), it was a decidedly ethereal body, farther removed from the material body than even Butler's conception. ...

Notwithstanding the differences between these perspectives and strategies, they share a common concern with deterministic, essentialist, dualistic, and static ways of thinking about women's bodies. Each theorist in her own particular way has been successful in pulling the rug out from under biological determinism and, more generally, criticizing the role that biology has played in justifying inequalities between the sexes as "natural." While theoretically this has been extremely important, as a focus for feminist body theory it is not without its drawbacks. As Kuhlman and Babitsch (2002) have noted, "We must face the question of what price we are willing to pay in exchange for the delimitation of naturalized categories" (436). By making the body central to the theoretical projects of dismantling biological determinism and essentialism, deconstructing dualisms, and emphasizing fluidity and transformation, the price may be—ironically—a disembodied body. As Spelman (1988) puts it, feminist body theory seems to have fallen prey to a kind of "somatophobia" whereby women's flesh and blood bodies have vanished from sight and we are left with the body as a mere metaphor for other, more pressing philosophical concerns. Even theorists who explicitly attend to the "materiality" of the body (like Butler) ... hardly pay any attention to the sensual physicality of the body. Feminist body theory seems to specialize in the surface of the body, a "body without organs" (Braidotti 1999) or, for that matter, bones, muscles, glands, or capillaries. The fragmented, fluid, and performed body that appears in feminist body theory bears little resemblance to the bodies that most women would be able to recognize as their own. Moreover, feminist body theory implies a transformability that belies the bodily constraints with which most women must live at different periods in their lives. While theoretical constructions such as the cyborg are useful for imagining the body in new ways in an increasingly technologized world, it has little to offer when it comes to understanding the vulnerabilities and limitations of the body that accompany illness, disease, disability, or the vicissitudes of growing older. The ubiquitous feminist theoretical rebuttal of biological determinism and essentialism has led to theories that deny the entire realm of the biological as having significance for feminist body theory. As the feminist biologist, Linda Birke (1999) warns, this failure to engage with biology—except to criticize it—"serves us ill, not least, because it is through the biological body that we live in and engage with the world at all" (175).

In contrast to feminist body theory, which has tended to subordinate the flesh and blood body to its theoretical projects, *OBOS* places the physical body on center stage. It offers a way of thinking about the anatomy, physiology, and organicity of women's bodies while avoiding the pitfalls of biological determinism, essentialism, and dualistic thinking. At the same time, *OBOS* seriously takes up the feminist critique of biological determinism, dualistic thinking, and essentialism but without completely rejecting biology. Highly critical of masculinist medicine's obsession with "wombs on legs" (Birke 1999, 12), *OBOS* questions any discourse that reduces women to their biology. However, biology is also regarded as a potential helpmeet when it comes to providing a complex and multilayered conception of the body as essential to a feminist epistemological project. As *OBOS* demonstrates, knowledge about women's biological bodies and how they work can be an integral part of a feminist body theory.

While *OBOS* rests on the assumption that most women have a body that is coded female, it firmly rejects any notion of an "essentially female" body by problematizing the automatic connection between the biological female body and gender identity. The subject of variations in gender identity was taken up in *OBOS* and the assumption that gender identity requires a specific kind of sexed body was problematized. *OBOS* focused on the varieties of gender identity, including transgender, transsexuality, and other "gender outlaws." Thus, while *OBOS* attends to anatomical specificities and physiological processes that are shared by many women, it also emphasizes the diversity and variety in women's (material, anatomical, and physiological) bodies.

Like feminist body theory, *OBOS* does not treat bodies as static entities, hermetically sealed off from the world. However, unlike feminist body theory, it adopts a holistic perspective toward the body whereby bodies are viewed as self-organizing, dynamic systems. Thus, *OBOS* both takes up and expands the notion of the body as "cultural text" (Bordo), as an assemblage of "performances" (Butler), and as "imaginary" (Grosz, Gatens) by including a body that is more than "skin deep." It shows that understanding women's bodies requires engaging with what goes on "under the surface" of the body, as well as with how the "inside" of the body interacts with and shapes women's interactions as embodied subjects with the world "outside" their bodies. This perspective treats bodies as both capable of change in interaction with the life circumstances of individual women and the cultural conditions under which they live and yet are also endowed with an organismic integrity that provides each body with its own idiosyncratic developmental history.[7] Rather than subordinating the body to a theoretical project, *OBOS* takes the body as a starting point for exploring how women actually negotiate deterministic or essentialist understandings of women's bodies or exploit dualisms in the context of their everyday lives.[8] While feminist body theory seems to prefer a discourse of fluidity, fracturing, and lack of fixed boundaries in order to show how the body's capacities can be enhanced through technology, *OBOS* reminds us that it is ultimately the physical body that calls a halt to the endless manipulation of the body through technological intervention.[9]

... It elaborates the consequences of the body's vulnerabilities for how our social environment should be organized in order to take differences in embodiment into account.[10]

Experiential Knowledge

Feminist theory has always entailed a critical engagement with science and, in particular, with its spurious claims to objectivity and value neutrality. Initially, women's experience was taken as an essential ingredient of this critical endeavor. Theorists such as Dorothy Smith (1990a, 1990b, 1987), Lorraine Code (1991), Sandra Harding (1991, 1986), Liz Stanley and Sue Wise (1993), Patricia Hill Collins (2000), and many others put forth women's experiential knowledge as an important epistemological resource for unmasking the objective and value-neutral pretensions of masculinist science. They argued that experience provided a basis for an alternative, critical feminist epistemology grounded in the material, social, and cultural realities of women's lives. ...

The ascendancy of postmodernism made this project considerably more complicated, however. In a seminal essay with the telling title "Experience" (1992), Joan Scott challenged the appeal to women's authentic experience as a basis for feminist epistemology. She argued that the general assumption that experience could provide an "originary point of explanation," let alone "incontestable evidence," rested on theoretical quicksand (24). In her view, experience was strictly a "linguistic event," which had no independent existence outside the language and discourses that constructed it (34). Scott's use of the "linguistic turn" to critically interrogate the centrality of experience for feminist epistemology has been highly influential. It has been taken up by many contemporary feminist theorists as a call to uncover the cultural biases and ideological commitments that inevitably mediate the experiences of individual women. As a result, feminist projects dedicated to recovering women's authentic experiences (or "voices") came to be viewed as hopelessly naive and ill-conceived.

Donna Haraway (1991b) elaborated this theoretical critique of experience by arguing that feminist theory itself could not aspire to a more "truthful" view of the world by drawing on women's experiences. In her view, all knowledge—including feminist knowledge—remained partial and would always be dependent on the social, cultural, and geopolitical location of the knower. Haraway's concept of "situated knowledges" provided a more sophisticated way of conceptually linking experience to the knower's location. Theoretically, it also offered a theoretical (and methodological) model for feminist inquiry into women's experiences, which would be both critical and self-reflexive. Unfortunately, however, Haraway's notion of "situated knowledges" stayed within the confines of her theoretical project of deconstructing the modernist discourses of science. This project, like Scott's, took precedence over, and at times—as we have seen—got in the way of, exploring women's experiences as situated knowledge and of assessing the possibilities this particular form of situated knowledge might have for feminist epistemology.

Without a doubt, Scott, Haraway, and many others have issued an important warning against treating "experience" as self-explanatory. Their reminder that experience is always ideologically mediated by cultural discourses and institutional arrangements is well taken. They have made a strong case for developing a feminist epistemology that can account for how all domains of knowledge, including feminist knowledge, are ideologically constituted and, therefore, cannot be drawn on as an unproblematic source of the "truth."

However, as many feminist scholars have already noted with growing concern, discrediting women's experiences altogether may risk "throwing the baby out with the bathwater" (Varikas 1995, 99). It leaves feminist theorists empty-handed when it comes to understanding how individual women give meaning to their lived experiences and, in particular, how they negotiate the tensions between these experiences and the cultural and institutionalized discourses in which they are embedded. It ignores how women's subjective accounts of their experiences can provide starting points for the critical interrogation of the social, cultural, and political contexts in which these accounts are embedded and from which they derive their meaning (Mediatore 2003). … In short, postmodern feminist theory produces more problems than it resolves when it discredits women's experiences as an important source of knowledge.

The very notion that feminist scholars should have to choose between treating experience unreflectively as an authentic source of knowledge or rejecting it as ideologically contaminated is itself a "false dilemma" (Alcoff 2000, 45). There is no reason why the postmodern claim that experience is "never epistemologically self-sufficient" cannot be reconciled with a stance that regards experience as "epistemologically indispensable" for feminist theory (45). … Feminist theorists don't have to draw on women's experiences in a naively empiricist way, that is, in order to "pin down the truth." Instead they can treat these experiences as an object for further analysis, thereby showing how women in their everyday lives "endure as well as react against discursive practices on multiple bodily, emotional and intellectual levels" (Mediatore 2003, 120). … Individual women's subjective accounts of their experiences and how they affect their everyday practices need to be linked to a critical interrogation of the cultural discourses, institutional arrangements, and geopolitical contexts in which these accounts are invariably embedded and which give meaning to them. In other words, rather than discarding experience as a "suspect" concept, feminist scholars should be devoting their energies to finding ways to *theorize* it (131).

As an epistemological project, *OBOS* resonates with these critiques. It amply demonstrates how women's experiences can be retrieved as a form of sentient, situated knowledge and can be used as a resource for feminist critiques of science and medicine. This knowledge is produced when individual women connect the physical, cognitive, and cultural dimensions of their embodied lives at the site of their bodies.

First, by showing what it feels like to have a particular bodily sensation (from menstrual cramps to labor pains) or to experience specific embodied events (childbirth, breast cancer, or bereavement), *OBOS* constructs women's experiential accounts as sentient knowledge. It draws on the experiences of differently embodied women in order to elaborate what it might be like to live in a specific kind of body—a disabled body, a lesbian body, the body of a woman of color. It does not treat this sentient knowledge as an unproblematic source of the "truth" about all women or even all women in a particular group. Instead women's perceptions, feelings, and understandings are validated as a useful resource in the ongoing, contradictory, and open-ended process of becoming knowledgeable about their bodies. The epistemological use of sentient knowledge produces a kind of "theory in the flesh" (Moya 1997), a theory that explores the physical realities of women's lives, including "our skin color; the land we grew up in, our sexual longings" (135). As theory in the flesh, *OBOS* helps to explain how these physical realities produce the conditions under which women can become knowledgeable and profoundly inform the contours their knowledge can take.

Second, by assembling the experiences of differently located women, *OBOS* explores the material effects of class, "race," and sexuality on women's embodied experiences. These different experiences are contextualized, enabling them to become a situated knowledge about how women's embodied lives are shaped by their living in a specific place at a particular moment in history.[11] While *OBOS* does not deny that women's experiences are shaped by cultural discourses and institutional structures, it does not treat these experiences as merely "discursive constructions" but rather as creative, multilayered, socially situated responses that are only partly ideologically constituted" (Mediatore 2003, 123). Thus, *OBOS* does not take women's experiences at face value, as—in Scott's terms—"revealing" the truth about women's lives but rather makes them discursively available. In this way, women's experiences can become accessible for further interpretation and debate.

Third, *OBOS* employs accounts of women's embodied and embedded experiences more specifically as an essential resource for developing a critical response to the discourses and practices of medicine. By juxtaposing women's experiences with medical knowledge, *OBOS* provides an occasion for a critical encounter between medicine and the embodied particulars of women's lives. It allows women to use their experiences to critically access and, when necessary, question the validity of medical knowledge for their particular health needs and within the specific circumstances of their lives. It counteracts the exclusion of women in the production of knowledge and produces alternative, and often oppositional, interpretations of women's health and health care needs. By drawing attention to the ways in which medicine historically has marginalized, distorted, or pathologized women's bodies, *OBOS* attempts to make it plausible that the use of women's sentient, situated knowledge can help make medicine more reliable, more responsible, and ultimately more responsive to women's health needs.

Women as Epistemic Agents

Contemporary feminist theory has struggled with the problem of how to theorize the relation between power and knowledge and, more specifically, the issue of women's agency. Many feminist theorists have drawn on the work of Michel Foucault, whose conception of power lends itself to exploring how cultural discourses construct femininity, shaping women's identities and embodied experiences, as well as their bodily practices (McNay 1992). Within this perspective, agency is brought about through the interplay between multiple and contradictory discursive systems. This notion of discursive agency has been taken up by feminist body theory to show how gender is continually "performed" through the body (Butler 1989) or to delineate the active participation of women in oppressive regimes of body surveillance and maintenance such as dieting, exercise, or cosmetic surgery (Bartky 1990; Bordo 1993; Davis 1995).

While Foucauldian feminist perspectives acknowledge that women's agency is integral to how discursive power works, they rest on a somewhat uneasy footing when it comes to women's epistemic agency—that is, the actions of embodied subjects capable of rational reflection and able to make experientially based evaluations of existing discourses. For example, Susan Bordo (1993), one of the leading feminist theorists of the body, … situates women's agency primarily in their active participation in disciplinary cultural discourses and body practices. From this perspective, women's agency is not necessarily empowering and subversive; it can also be disempowering and compliant. Even when women believe that they are exercising their individual freedoms—for example, when they refuse to eat or "choose" to embark on rigorous regimes of body maintenance—their agency is, in actual fact, merely a discursive by-product of the pernicious discourses of choice that pervade Western culture and channel women's energies into the hopeless quest for the perfect body.

While this strand of feminist theory has been influential in deconstructing the notion of an autonomous female subject, as well as severing the automatic link between women's agency and their empowerment, it is not without its problems.[12] Feminist scholars such as Smith (1990a, 1990b, 1999), Kruks (2001), Mohanty (2003), and others have argued that the focus on agency as an artifact of discourse can obstruct our ability to understand how women actively gain, evaluate, and critically interpret knowledge about themselves, their lives, and the world around them. By exaggerating the pervasive power of cultural discourses to shape women's bodily experiences and body practices, the notion of a female epistemic agent—that is, an agent capable of reflection and intentionality and able to envision a course of action that could (conceivably) empower her—is discredited. The conflation of agency with choice as a cultural discourse allows its dismissal as an erroneous belief in absolute freedom or the ability to act completely in accordance with one's personal wishes. It discounts the messy, ambivalent choices that individuals make in their everyday lives—choices that are neither free nor entirely in accordance with their wishes (Davis 2003). This strand of feminist theory fails to imagine how women might ever mobilize knowledge, embedded as it is in oppressive cultural discourses and institutional arrangements, for their personal empowerment let alone for collective feminist projects aimed at the empowerment of women more generally.

It is here that *OBOS* can be useful for bringing into relief what is missing in postmodern feminist body theory: a conception of epistemic agency that links women's knowledge practices to their possibilities and opportunities for individual and collective empowerment. First, instead of relegating women's agency to a discursive effect, *OBOS* conceives of agency as the outcome of the practical and—to some extent—intentional activities of situated knowers, who continually perceive, interpret, reflect on, and rework their experiences. This conception of agency assumes that women are "practical subjects" who are engaged in projects that "transform something into a further possibility" (Kruks 2001, 120). Women's experiences are not only the product of discourses converging at the site of the female body, but they are also integral to women's practical projects of empowerment. These projects can be anything from becoming more informed to getting support from friends to finding the right kind of professional help. They may also involve accepting the limitations of one's body or acknowledging the limits of medical knowledge. In this way, *OBOS* celebrates the subtle and variegated ways that women act, not in the sense of making clear-cut choices between an array of desirable and less than desirable options but in the sense of how women routinely engage in small acts of resistance and subversion in the context of their "trying to survive" (Lugones 2003).

Second, while *OBOS* proposes a notion of epistemic agency that invariably involves some degree of intentionality, it does not ignore the socially structured relations of power under which women's actions take place. In other words, it does not adopt what Maria Lugones (2003) has criticized as the "highly attenuated understandings of agency in late modernity," which abound in much of contemporary feminist body theory (6). Rather, *OBOS* clearly shows how poverty, poor housing, unemployment, and racism constrain women's possibilities for staying healthy or taking care of themselves and their families. While considerable attention is paid to the ideological effects of cultural discourses—for example, by representing women's bodies as inferior or blaming women for their own health problems rather than, say, environmental pollution or poor nutrition—women are not treated as "cultural dopes" who have had the ideological wool pulled over their eyes.[13] The book draws on a more sociological understanding of agency whereby the individual women are regarded as competent actors with a wide-ranging, intimate, and subtle knowledge of the circumstances in which they live (McNay 2000; Davis 2003, 1988). More specifically, *OBOS* explores the conditions of constraint and enablement under which women can become critical feminist subjects capable of drawing on their sentient, situated knowledge as a resource for generating empowering courses of action with regard to their lives, bodies, and health.

Third, *OBOS* provides a glimpse of how epistemic agency might be linked to resistance and empowerment—a problem that has been the source of some concern among feminist theorists. It shows that resistance to hegemonic discourses and the development of subversive alternatives requires more than a "recycling of existing metaphors and rhetorical strategies" (Mediatore 1998, 121). It requires an ongoing process involving interpretation and critical reflection, as well as the rearticulation of available cultural discourses into alternative forms of knowledge. By delineating the process by which differently situated women come to favor specific concepts or strategies over others and how these decisions are shaped by situational, biographical, and sociopolitical circumstances, *OBOS* contributes to a more comprehensive understanding of the relation between power, knowledge, and agency.[14] It demonstrates that even those who have been marginalized in the production of knowledge can be situated as epistemic agents capable of generating alternative and even oppositional forms of knowledge.

While *OBOS* treats epistemic agency as the sine qua non for the empowerment of women individually and collectively, it is not simply aimed at empowering individual women to become more knowledgeable about their own health. It also allows them an imaginative entry into the experiences of different women and, along with it, the understanding that each woman has her own specific project, depending on the circumstances of her embodiment and the social, cultural, and political context in which she lives. The recognition that others—however differently located—are also involved in intentional projects is what ultimately allows for reciprocity and the possibility of collective action (Kruks 2001, 124–25).[15]

In conclusion, while postmodern feminist theory has focused on the power of discourse to shape women's practices, it has tended to adopt a discursive concept of agency. Viewing agency as a discursive effect, however, makes it difficult to account for how individual women might resist dominant forms of knowledge or produce alternative, oppositional knowledge. In contrast, *OBOS* demonstrates that the recognition of the power of discourse does not automatically have to result in the abandonment of women's epistemic agency. It shows that women are capable of deliberately and strategically interpreting their lives and actively pursuing potentially empowering courses of action. And it provides ample proof of how women can become epistemic agents who are able to critically and reflexively think about medical discourses. Its approach toward agency is not abstract but based on the practical activities of differently located women. As such, it can offer contemporary feminist body theory valuable insights into how, why, and under what circumstances women might actively employ knowledge in the pursuit of an oppositional feminist politics of health.

Bridging the Gap

… By considering *OBOS* as an epistemological project, I have shown how it might contribute to some of the theoretical problems that have concerned feminist body theorists, especially the problems of how to conceptualize the biological female body, women's embodied experience, and women's epistemic agency. While *OBOS* obviously does not completely resolve these problems, it does provide useful ways of thinking about them. It can help "ground" feminist theoretical discussions more firmly in women's sentient and situated knowledge. More specifically, it provides avenues for the development of feminist body theories that are *less* disembodied, less disembedded, and *more* relevant to women's health concerns (Kuhlmann and Babitsch 2002, 433). By joining forces, feminist body theory and feminist health activism could develop a more effective critique of medicine and cultural discourses about women's bodies, as well as a more reflexive and potentially subversive feminist politics of health.

In this chapter, I have focused on the contribution *OBOS* as an epistemological project might make toward bridging the gap between feminist body theory and feminist health activism. However, there are other reasons for taking a closer look at its politics of knowledge. One of the most exciting aspects of *OBOS* as an epistemological project is its capacity to travel across borders of class, race, and sexuality, as well as national and cultural borders. It has invited differently embodied women across the globe to use their specific experiences to engage critically with the authoritative voice of medicine and situate their health concerns in the broader social, cultural, and political context of their lives. It has not only been more than a popular book on women's health; it has also been more than a typically U.S. feminist epistemological project. In the course of being taken up and adapted by different women's groups across the globe, *OBOS* has proved to be a "traveling theory" (Said 1983)—that is, a theory that, through its circulation across borders within and outside the United States, has been able to shape and transform knowledge about women's bodies and health in many other parts of the world. For feminist theorists who have been concerned about the hegemony of First World feminist scholarship, it may well be time to stop focusing on those theories that are most firmly embedded in the context being criticized (Western philosophy, modern medicine, the U.S. academy) and begin considering theories that have demonstrated that they are capable of movement and transformation. It seems to me that for anyone interested in the possibilities of a critical, nonimperialistic, feminist theory, *OBOS* deserves our most serious attention. ...

Notes

1. This is not to say that *OBOS* is not used in women's studies courses. It often appears on required reading lists for undergraduates. However, it tends to be presented as a useful handbook on women's health rather than a book of scholarly interest.

2. See Kapsalis 1997; Morgen 2002; Murphy 2004; Bell and Reverby 2005 for discussions on the conflicting perspectives on self help within the U.S. women's health movement.

3. This has been done at much greater length by others and goes beyond the scope of the present inquiry. ... [See Moore and Clarke (1995), Kapsalis (1997), Scudson (1997), Moya (1997).]

4. Like any feminist epistemology, *OBOS* is also a political project. However, for the purposes of this chapter I will be focusing on its epistemological features. The consequences for feminist politics of the body, particularly in a transcultural, transnational context, will be the subject of the subsequent chapters.

5. Even women who do not menstruate, have vaginas, or bear children will be influenced by societal expectations of what it means to have a female body. See, for example, Hall (2005) who, drawing on insights from queer theory, criticizes the taken for granted linkage of vaginas with feminine embodiment, which excludes disabled or differently embodied women.

6. In her experientially based epistemology, Patricia Hill Collins (2000) calls this the "wisdom to know how to deal with educated fools," something that is often the key to their survival (257). While her epistemology is based specifically on the experiences of U.S. American black women as a framework for black feminist thought, the centrality she gives to women's embodied experience as source of critical knowledge is very similar to that of *OBOS*.

7. The lack of attention to bodily integrity in contemporary feminist body theory has been a source of concern for feminist biologists like Birke 1999 and Fausto-Sterling 2005. See also Bordo 1993, 71–98.

8. This resonates with feminist phenomenological approaches to the body that explore the contradictions in women's embodiment (see, e.g., Bartky 1990; Young 1990b; Marshall 1996; Lindemann 1997; and Alcoff 2000).

9. This perspective resonates with the concern expressed by feminist biologists, who worry that the emphasis on the transformability of the body without a concomitant sense of the body's integrity can open the floodgates for a total manipulation of human and nonhuman nature. As Birke (1999) puts it, the literal dismemberment of bodies in modern medicine in organ transplantations, hysterectomies, and plastic surgery has already reduced the body to "a set of bits" that can be removed or manipulated (171). It is important that feminist body theory does not replicate this.

10. This perspective is very much in tune with critical disability studies (Breckenridge and Vogler 2001). ...

11. Moya (1997) refers to this as the "cognitive component" and uses this to frame her call for a more "realist" feminist epistemology, one that will be more relevant to the material concerns of Chicana women. ... See Mohanty 2003. ...

12. I do not wish to imply that Foucauldian feminist theorists employ identical conceptions of agency, and, indeed, there have been many debates concerning the problem of agency in feminist theory. ...

13. The term cultural dope is borrowed from sociology, where it was developed as a critique against deterministic and functionalist perspectives on human agency in which human actors have so completely internalized the norms and values of the society in which they live that their activities become limited to acting out a predetermined script. See Giddens 1976 and Davis 1995.

14. This approach to epistemic agency resonates with recent U.S. and Third World feminist critiques of poststructuralist feminist theory. Lugones (2003), Mohanty (2003), Moya (1997), and others have been skeptical of the abandonment of epistemic agency in favor of a more discursive notion of agency. They have argued that U.S. and Third World women have been constantly engaged in reflecting on and renaming their experiences—a process ultimately leading to the development of alternative forms of knowledge.
15. See Bartky 2002 for a similar argument.

46.

MULTICULTURALISM AND THE PROMISE OF HAPPINESS
Sara Ahmed
(2007/2008)

Betty Friedan in *The Feminine Mystique* identifies a problem that has no name by evoking what lies behind the image of the happy American housewife. What lies behind this image bursts through, like a boil, exposing an infection underneath her beaming smile. Friedan proceeds by exposing the limits of this public fantasy of happiness. The happy housewife is a fantasy figure that erases the signs of labour under the sign of happiness. The claim that women are happy, and that this happiness is behind the work they do, functions to justify gendered forms of labour not as products of nature, law or duty, but as an expression of a collective wish and desire. How better to justify an unequal distribution of labour, than to say that such labour makes people happy? How better to secure consent to unpaid or poorly paid labour than to describe such consent as the origin of good feeling?

You could say that images of happy housewives have been replaced by rather more desperate ones. I would argue that there is a diversification of affects tied to this figure, which gives her a more complex affective life, but that this does not necessarily dislodge the happiness that is presumed to reside in 'what' she does, even in descriptions of relative unhappiness. After all, explanations of relative unhappiness can also function to restore the power of an image of the good life. As Friedan shows, the unhappiness of the housewife is attributed to what is around her (such as the incompetent repair men), rather than the position she occupies. Unhappiness would here function as a sign of frustration, of being 'held back' or 'held up' from doing what makes her happy.

It is hence far from surprising that a recent study on happiness in the US suggested that feminist women are less happy than 'traditional housewives', as the American journalist Meghan O'Rourke explores in her aptly name article, 'Desperate Feminist Wives'.[1] Unhappiness is used as a way of signalling the need to return to something that has been lost: as if what we have lost in losing this or that is the very capacity to be happy. Happiness becomes in other words a defence of 'this and that'. As Simone de Beauvoir argued in *The Second Sex*: 'it is always easy to describe as happy the situation in which one wishes to place them'.[2] Happiness functions as a displacement of a social wish, and a defence against an imagined future of loss.

It is important to note here that the political question of what makes people happy has acquired some urgency. Commentators have described a 'crisis' in happiness, where the crisis is announced through a narrative of disappointment: the accumulation of wealth has not meant the accumulation of happiness. ...[3] What makes this crisis 'a crisis' in the first place is of course the regulatory effect of a social belief: that more wealth 'should' have made people happier. ... The new science of happiness might uncouple happiness from the accumulation of wealth, but it still locates happiness in certain places, especially marriage, widely regarded as the primary 'happiness indicator'.[4] ...

What is striking is that the crisis in happiness has not put social ideals into question, and if anything has reinvigorated their hold over both psychic and political life. The demand for happiness is increasingly articulated as a demand to return to social ideals, as if what explains the crisis of happiness is not the failure of these ideals, but our failure to follow them. What organises the 'crisis of happiness' is the belief that happiness should be an effect of following social ideals, almost as if happiness is the reward for a certain loyalty.

Unsurprisingly, then, when we consider how the new science of happiness might relate to recent debates about the future of multiculturalism we find the use of a nostalgic narrative: happiness is identified with ways of life that have been eroded by the mobility of populations within and between nation states. Take the BBC programme, 'The Happiness Formula' aired in 2006. In the third episode in this series, the question of community is posed as central to happiness. Having a good, close, safe and trusting community is treated as one of the primary happiness indicators alongside marriage, entailing the following simple belief: if you live in such a community you are more likely to be happy. The narrator of this episode argues that the social project 'to make people happier' thus means to 'make societies more cohesive,' or to 'put glue back into communities'. Clearly, this involves a nostalgic narrative: the mission to put glue back into communities not only suggests that communities lack such glue, but also that they once had it. Happiness becomes what we have lost in losing glue. Or we could say that happiness is understood here as glue; we need to glue the world back together through happiness. The programme imagines a world where people are less physically and socially mobile as a happier world, offering a romantic image of a French village, where people stay put over generations, as if happiness itself resides in staying put.

The programme argues not only that happy communities are communities that have a strong social bond, but also that the bond of such communities is based on 'being alike'; communities are happier if they are alike. Trevor Phillips, Chair of the Commission for Equality and Human Rights in the UK, is interviewed during this episode. Phillips claims that 'multicultural communities tend to be less trusting and less happy', and that 'people frankly, when there are other pressures, like to live in a comfort zone which is defined by racial sameness', and even that 'people feel happy if they are with people like themselves'. The argument is simple at one level: being amongst people with whom you are alike will cause happiness, and being amongst people from whom you differ will cause unhappiness. As such, this argument appears to withdraw social hope from the very idea of diversity—or indeed, multiculturalism as an imagined community of diverse peoples.

The programme does not simply give up on multiculturalism but suggests that we have an obligation to make multicultural communities happy, premised on the model of 'building bridges'. Trevor Phillips evokes unhappy instances of community conflict or violence between communities by claiming: '*this* is exactly what happens when people who look very different, and think they are very different, never touch and interact'. The 'this' stands for all that is unhappy, sliding into forms of violence that are evoked without being named (from personal distrust, to inter-group conflict, to international terrorism). Unhappiness is here read as caused not simply by diversity, but by the failure of people who are different to interact. Phillips then recommends that communities integrate by sharing 'an activity' such as football, 'that takes us out of our ethnicity and connects us with people of different ethnicities if only for hours a week, then I think we can crack the problem'.

We can see here that the shift from unhappy to happy diversity involves the demand for interaction. The image of happy diversity is projected into the future: when we have 'cracked the problem' through interaction, we will be happy with diversity. That football becomes a technique for generating happy diversity is no accident: after all, football is proximate to the ego ideal of the nation, as being a level playing field, where aspiration and talent is enough to get you there, providing the basis for a common ground.[5] Diversity becomes happy when it involves loyalty to what has already been given as a national ideal. Or we could say that happiness is promised as a return for loyalty to the nation, where loyalty is expressed as 'giving' diversity to the nation through playing its game.

In this essay, I will consider how happiness functions as promise, which directs us towards certain objects, which then circulate as social goods. My primary example will be the film, *Bend It Like Beckham*. I have chosen this film not only given that it is a 'happy film' but also as it is one of the most successful British films at the box office. The film is marketed as a 'delightful, feel good comedy'. It is also a film that projects a happy image of British multiculturalism, whereby football becomes a way of re-imagining the national ground as 'happily diverse'. My reading of the film will explore how multiculturalism is attributed a positive value through the alignment of a story of individual happiness with the social good.

Happy Objects

Happiness, one might assume, is an emotion, or an inner feeling state. One feels happy. One is happy. In everyday life, it would be common to use happiness as a way of describing how one feels. However, although some psychological models do describe happiness as a private or interior feeling state, most writing on happiness does not. Indeed, the association of happiness with feeling good is a modern one: in circulation from the eighteenth century onwards, as Darren McMahon shows in his monumental history of happiness.[6] In psychology, happiness is usually described as more than about 'feeling good', as involving cognition and evaluation. … [H]appiness involves affect and cognition insofar as it includes both joy and satisfaction.[7] Happiness is good to think with given how it mediates between individual and social, private and public, affective and evaluative, mind and body, as well as norms, rules and ideals and ways of being in the world. Happiness will allow us to consider how 'feeling good' becomes attached to other kinds of social good.

My starting point is always not to assume there is something called affect (or for that matter, emotion), that stands apart or has autonomy, as if it corresponds to an object in the world, but to consider the messiness of the experiential, the unfolding of bodies into worlds, and the drama of contingency, how we are touched by what comes near. It is useful to recall the etymology of 'happiness' relates precisely to this question of contingency: it is from the Middle English 'hap', suggesting chance. Happiness would be about whatever happens. Only later does 'the what' signal something good. Happiness becomes not only about chance, but evokes the idea of being lucky, being favoured by fortune, or being fortunate. Even this meaning may now seem archaic: we may be more used to thinking of happiness as an effect of what you do, say as a reward for hard work, rather than as what happens to you. But I find this original meaning useful, as it focuses our attention on the 'worldly' question of happenings.

What is the relation between the 'what' in 'what happens' and the 'what' that makes us happy? Empiricism provides us with a useful way of addressing this question, given its concern with 'what's what'. Take the work of John Locke. He argues that what is good is what is '*apt to cause or increase pleasure, or diminish pain in us*'.[8] So we judge something to be good or bad according to how it affects us, whether it gives us a pleasure or pain. Locke suggests that 'he loves grapes it is no more, but that the taste of grapes delights him'.[9] Locke describes happiness as the highest form of pleasure. So we could say that an object becomes happy if it affects us in a good way. Note the doubling of positive affect in Locke's example: we love what tastes delightful. To be affected by an object in a good way is also to have an orientation towards an object as being good.

Whilst happiness might be shaped by contact with objects, we could also say that happiness is intentional: it is directed towards objects. Happiness involves a specific kind of intentionality, which we can describe as 'end orientated'. After all, happiness is often described as 'what' we aim for: as a self-evident good, or an end-in-itself. In Aristotle's ethics, happiness is the name for *the end of all ends*, as what all human action is aiming towards. He says: 'Every rational activity aims at some end or good ... The end is no doubt happiness, but views of happiness differ ... What is the good for man? It must be the ultimate end or object of human life: something that is in itself completely satisfying. Happiness fits this description'.[10] In pursuing happiness one is pursuing what is good; indeed, happiness shows the purposeful nature of human action.

We don't have to agree with the argument that happiness is always an end-in-itself or the good of all goods to register the implications of what it means for happiness to be understood in these terms. Happiness is directed towards certain objects, which function as a means to what is not yet present. If objects provide a 'means' for making us happy, then in directing ourselves towards this or that object, we are aiming somewhere else: towards a happiness that is presumed to follow. The temporality of this following does matter. Happiness is what would come after. Happiness does not reside in objects; it is promised through proximity to certain objects.

So the promise of happiness—if you do this, then happiness is what follows—is what makes things seem 'promising', which means that the promise of happiness is not in the thing itself. Consider that a promise comes from Latin *promissum* 'send forth, foretell' from *pro*- 'before' and *mittere* 'to put, send'. The promise of happiness is what sends happiness forth; it is what allows happiness to be public in the sense of being out. Objects that embody the feeling are passed around: they are 'out and about'. Happiness involves the sociality of passing things around.

Does happiness itself get passed around or transmitted through such objects? If we were to say yes to this question, then we might also suggest that happiness is contagious (see also Blackman, this issue). A number of scholars have recently taken up the idea of affects as contagious, primarily drawing on the work of psychologist Silvan Tomkins.[11] As Anna Gibbs describes: 'Bodies can catch feelings as easily as catch fire: affect leaps from one body to another'.[12] Thinking of affects as contagious does help us to challenge what I have called the 'inside out' model of affect by showing how affects pass between bodies, affecting bodily surfaces or how bodies surface.[13] However, I think the concept of affective contagion tends to underestimate the extent to which affects are contingent (involving the hap of a happening): to be affected by another does not mean that an affect simply passes or 'leaps' from one body to another. The affect becomes an object only given the contingency of how we are affected.

Consider the opening sentence of Teresa Brennan's *The Transmission of Affect*: 'Is there anyone who has not, at least once, walked into a room and "felt the atmosphere"'.[14] Brennan writes very beautifully about the atmosphere 'getting into the individual', using what I have called an 'outside in' model, also very much part of the intellectual history of crowd psychology and also the sociology of emotion.[15] However, later in the introduction she makes an observation which involves a quite different model. Brennan suggests here that, 'if I feel anxiety when I enter the room, then that will influence what I perceive or receive by way of an "impression"'.[16] I agree. Anxiety is sticky: rather like Velcro, it tends to pick up whatever comes near. Or we could say that anxiety gives us a certain kind of angle on what comes near. Anxiety is, of course, one feeling state amongst others. If bodies do not arrive in neutral, if we are always in someway or another moody, then what we will receive as an impression will depend on our affective situation. This second argument challenges for me Brennan's first argument about the atmosphere being what is 'out there' getting 'in': it suggests that how we arrive, how we enter this room or that room, will affect what impressions we receive. After all, to receive is to act. To receive an impression is to make an impression.

So we may walk into the room and 'feel the atmosphere', but what we may feel depends on the angle of our arrival. Or we might say that the atmosphere is already angled; it is always felt from a specific point. The pedagogic encounter is full of angles. How many times have I read students as interested or bored, such that the atmosphere seemed one of interest or boredom (and even felt myself to be interesting or boring) only to find students recall the event quite differently! Having read the atmosphere in a certain way, one can become tense: which in turn affects what happens, how things move along. The moods we arrive with do affect what happens: which is not to say we always keep our moods. Sometimes I arrive feeling heavy with anxiety, and everything that happens makes me feel more anxious, whilst at other times, things happen which ease the anxiety, making the space itself seem light and energetic. We do not know in advance what will happen given this contingency, given the hap of what happens; we do not know 'exactly' what makes things happen in this way and that. Situations are affective given this gap between the impressions we have of others, which are lively, and the impressions we make on others.

Think too of experiences of alienation. I have suggested that happiness is attributed to certain objects that circulate as social goods. When we feel pleasure from such objects, we are aligned; we are facing the right way. We become alienated—out of line with an affective community—when we do not experience pleasure from proximity to objects that are attributed as being good. The gap between the affective value of an object and how we experience an object can involve a range of affects, which are directed by the modes of explanation we offer to fill this gap. If we are disappointed by something that we expected would make us happy, then we generate explanations of why that thing is disappointing. Such explanations can involve an anxious narrative of self-doubt (why I am not made happy by this, what is wrong with me?) or a narrative of rage, where the object that is 'supposed' to make us happy is attributed as the cause of disappointment, which can lead to a rage directed towards those that promised us happiness through the elevation of the object as being good. We become strangers, or affect aliens, in such moments.

So when happy objects are passed around, it is not necessarily the feeling that passes. To share such objects (or have a share in such objects) would simply mean you would *share an orientation towards those objects as being good*. The family for instance might be happy not because it causes happiness, but because of a shared orientation towards the family as being good. Happiness is precarious; it does not reside in subjects or objects, but is an effect of what gets passed around. What passes through the passing around of happy objects must remain an open question. Objects become sticky, saturated with affects, as sites of personal and social tension. After all, the word 'passing' can mean not only 'to send over' or 'to transmit', but also to transform objects by 'a sleight of hand'. Like the game Chinese whispers, what passes between proximate bodies, might be affective because it deviates and even perverts what was 'sent out'. What interests me is how affects involve perversion; and what we could describe as conversion points.

One of my key questions is how such conversions happen, and 'who' or 'what' gets seen as converting bad feeling into good feeling and good into bad. We need to attend to such points of conversion, and how they involve explanations of 'where' good and bad feelings reside. The sociality of affect involves 'tension' given the ways in which good and bad feelings are unevenly distributed in the social field. When I hear people say 'the bad feeling is coming from "this person" or "that person"' I am never convinced. I am sure a lot of my scepticism is shaped by childhood experiences of being a feminist daughter, at odds with the performance of good feeling in the family, always assumed to be bringing others down, for example, by pointing out sexism in other people's talk. Take the figure of the killjoy feminist. We can place her alongside the figure of the happy housewife. Does the feminist kill other people's joy by pointing out moments of sexism? Or does she expose the bad feelings that get hidden, displaced or negated under public signs of joy? Does bad feeling enter the room when somebody expresses anger about things, or could anger be the moment when the bad feelings that saturate objects get brought to the surface in a certain way? The feminist after all might kill joy precisely because she refuses to share an orientation towards certain things as being good, because she does not find the objects that promise happiness to be quite so promising. By not expressing happiness in response to proximity to such objects, the feminist becomes an affect alien; she 'brings things down'.

I have learnt most about the politics of affect and emotion from feminist writers such as Marilyn Frye and Andre Lorde who both point to how good and bad feelings are unevenly distributed in the social field. For Marilyn Frye, 'it is often a requirement upon oppressed people that we smile and be cheerful'. Indeed, she suggests that 'anything but the sunniest countenance exposes us to being perceived as mean, bitter, angry, or dangerous'.[17] So for an oppressed person not to smile or to show a sign of being happy is to be seen as negative: as the origin of bad feeling. Consider also the figure of the angry black woman. As Audre Lorde describes: 'When women of Color speak out of the anger that laces so many of our contacts with white women, we are often told that we are "creating a mood of helplessness," "preventing white women from getting past guilt", or "standing in the way of trusting communication and action"'.[18] The angry black woman could also be described as a killjoy; she may even kill feminist joy by pointing out forms of racism within feminist politics. The exposure of violence becomes the origin of violence. The black woman must let go of her anger for the white woman to move on.

These conversion points between good and bad feeling do matter; some bodies are presumed to be the origin of bad feeling insofar as they disturb the promise of happiness, which we can re-describe as the social pressure to maintain the signs of 'getting along'. This is why I do not describe the sociality of affect in terms of transmission or contagion, where feelings pass between proximate bodies, but in terms of the politics of attribution and conversion. There is a political struggle about how we attribute good and bad feelings, which hesitates around the apparently simple question of who affects whom, or who introduces what feelings to whom. Feelings can get stuck to certain bodies in the very way we describe spaces, situations, dramas. And bodies can get stuck depending on what feelings they get associated with.

Just Happiness

Some objects more than others embody the promise of happiness. In other words, happiness directs us to certain objects, as if they are the necessary ingredients for a good life. What makes this argument different to John Locke's account of loving grapes because they taste delightful is that the judgment about certain objects as being 'happy' is already made, before they are even encountered: certain objects are attributed as the conditions for happiness so that we arrive 'at' them with an expectation of how we will be affected by them, which affects how they affect us, even in the moment they fail to live up to our expectations. Happiness is an expectation of what follows, where the expectation differentiates between things, whether or not they exist in the present. For instance, the child might be asked to imagine happiness by imagining 'happy events' in the future, such as a wedding day, 'the happiest day of your life'. This is why happiness provides the emotional setting for disappointment, even if happiness is not given: we just have to expect happiness from 'this or that' for 'this and that' to be experienceable as objects of disappointment.

The apparent chanciness of happiness can be qualified: we do not just find happy objects anywhere. Happiness is not casual: certain objects are available to us because of lines that we have already taken. Our 'life courses' follow a certain sequence, which is also a matter of following a direction or of 'being directed' in a certain way (birth, child-hood, adolescence, marriage, reproduction, death), as Judith Halberstam has shown us in her reflections on the 'temporality' of the family and the expenditure of family time.[19] The promise of happiness directs life in some ways, rather than others. For a life to count as a good life, then it must return the debt of its life by taking on the direction promised as a social good, which means imagining one's futurity in terms of reaching certain points along a life course.

When we consider the cultural politics of happiness, we need to consider the rela-tionship between 'this' (an action, belief, a way of living) and 'that' (what is presumed to follow). Happiness is not only promised by certain objects, it is also what we promise to give to others as an expression of love. I am especially interested in the speech act, 'I just want you to be happy'. What does it mean to want 'just' happiness? What does it mean for a parent to say this to a child? In a way, the desire for the child's happiness seems to offer a certain kind of freedom, as if to say: 'I don't want you to be this, or to do that; I just want you to be or to do "whatever" makes you happy'. You could say that the 'whatever' seems to release us from the obligation of the 'what'. The desire for the child's happiness seems to offer the freedom of a certain indifference to the content of a future decision.

Take the psychic drama of the queer child. You could say that the queer child is an unhappy object for many parents. In some parental responses to the child coming out, this unhappiness is not so much expressed as being unhappy about the child being queer, but as being unhappy about the child being unhappy. Queer fiction is full of such moments. Take the following exchange that takes place in the lesbian novel, *Annie on My Mind* (1982) by Nancy Garden:

> 'Lisa', my father said, 'I told you I'd support you and I will ... But honey ... well, maybe it's just that I love your mother so much that I have to say to you I've never thought gay people can be very happy—no children for one thing, no real family life. Honey, you are probably going to be a very good architect—but I want you to be happy in other ways, too, as your mother is, to have a husband and children. I know you can do both ...' *I am happy*, I tried to tell him with my eyes. *I'm happy with Annie; she and my work are all I'll ever need; she's happy too—we both were until this happened.*[20]

The father makes an act of identification with an imagined future of necessary and inevitable unhappiness. Such an identification through grief about what the child will lose, reminds us that the queer life is already constructed as an unhappy life, as a life without the 'things' that make you happy (husband, children). The desire for the child's happiness is far from indifferent. The speech act 'I just want you to be happy' can be directive at the very point of its imagined indifference.

For the daughter, it is only the eyes that can speak; and they try to tell an alterna-tive story about happiness and unhappiness. In her response, she claims happiness, for sure. She is happy '*with* Annie'; which is to say, she is happy with *this* relationship and *this* life that it will commit her to. She says we were happy 'until' this happened, where the 'until' marks the moment that the father speaks his disapproval. The unhappy queer is here the queer who is judged to be unhappy. The father's speech act creates the very affective state of unhappiness that is imagined to be the inevitable consequence of the daughter's decision. When 'this' happens, unhappiness does follow.

One of the most striking aspects of the film *Bend It like Beckham* is how the conflict and obstacle of the film is resolved through this speech act, also addressed from father to daughter that takes the approximate form: 'I just want you to be happy'. How does this speech act direct the narrative? To answer this question, we need to describe the conflict of the film, or the obstacle to the happy ending. The film could be described as being about the generational conflict within a migrant Indian Sikh family living in Hounslow, London. Jess the daughter is good at football. Her idea of happiness would be to bend it like Beckham, which requires that she bends the rules about what Indian girls can do. The generational conflict between parents and daughter is represented as a conflict between the demands of cultures: as Jess says, 'anyone can cook Alo Gobi but who can bend the ball like Beckham'. This contrast sets up 'cooking Alo Gobi' as common place and customary, against an alternative world of celebrity, individualism and talent.

It is possible to read the film by putting this question of cultural difference to one side. We could read the story as being about the rebellion of the daughter, and an attempt to give validation to her re-scripting of what it means to have a good life. We might cheer for Jess, as she 'scores' and finds happiness somewhere other than where she is expected to find it. We would be happy about her freedom and her refusal of the demand to be a good girl, or even a happy housewife. We might applaud this film as showing the happiness that can follow leaving your parent's expectations behind and following less well trodden paths. Yet, of course such a reading would fall short. It would not offer a reading of the 'where' that the happiness of this image of freedom takes us.

We need to think more critically about how cultural differences are associated with different affects: we have a contrast between the open space of the football pitch, where there is movement, sound, and laughter, and the domestic interiors of Jess's home full of restrictions, demands and conflict. In other words, these two worlds are not given the same affective value. The happiness promised by football is over-determined. The desire to be like Beckham has a narrative function in the film. In the opening humorous shots, presented as Jess's fantasy (she stares at a poster of Beckham before the scene unfolds), Jess takes up a place beside Beckham on the football ground, and is the one who scores the goal. Football signifies not only the national game, but also the opportunity for new identifications, where you can embody hope for the nation by taking a place alongside its national hero. By implication, the world of football promises freedom allowing you not only to be happy, but to become a happy object, by bringing happiness to others, who cheer as you score. The inclusion of Jess in the national game might be framed as Jess's fantasy, but it also functions as a national fantasy about football, as the playing field which offers signs of inclusion and diversity, where 'whoever' scores will be cheered.

In her other world, Jess experiences frustration, pain and anxiety. The shots are all of domestic interiors: of dark and cramped spaces, where Jess has to do this or do that, where freedom is lost under the weight of duty. In her Indian home, she is the object of parental shame. Her mother says to her: 'I don't want shame on the family. That's it, no more football'. For Jess, playing football means having to play in secret, which in turn alienates her from her family. What makes her happy becomes a sign of shame, whilst her shame becomes an obstacle to happiness. In this secretive life she forms new bonds and intimacies: first with Jules who gets her on the girl's team, and then with Joe, the football coach, with whom she falls 'in love'. In other words, this other world, the world of freedom promised by football, puts her in intimate contact with a white girl and white man. In this narrative, freedom involves proximity to whiteness.

For Jess, the dilemma is: how can she be in both worlds at once? The final of the football tournament coincides with Pinkie's wedding. This coincidence matters: Jess cannot be at both events at once. Unhappiness is used to show how Jess is 'out of place' in the wedding: she is unhappy, as she is not where she wants to be: she wants to be at the football match. We want her to be there too, and are encouraged to identify with the injustice of being held back. At this point, the point of Jess's depression, her friend Tony intervenes and says she should go. Jess replies, 'I can't. Look how happy they are Tony. I don't want to ruin it for them'. In this moment, Jess accepts her own unhappiness by identifying with the happiness of her parents: she puts her own desire for happiness to one side. But her father overhears her, and says: 'Pinkie is so happy and you look like you have come to your father's funeral', and then, 'if this is the only way I am going to see you smiling on your sister's wedding day then go now. But when you come back, I want to see you happy on the video'. Jess's father lets her go because he wants to see her happy, which also means he wants to see others witness the family as being happy, as being what causes happiness.

Jess's father cannot be indifferent to his daughter's unhappiness: later he says to his wife, 'maybe you could handle her long face, I could not'. At one level, this desire for the daughter's happiness involves a form of indifference to the 'where' that she goes. From the point of view of the film, the desire for happiness is far from indifferent: indeed, the film works partly by 'directing' the apparent indifference of this gift of freedom. After all, this moment is when the father switches from a desire that is out of line with the happy object of the film (not wanting Jess to play) to being in line (letting her go), which in turn is what allows the film's happy ending. Importantly, the happy ending is about the co-incidence of happy objects. The daughters are happy (they are living the life they wish to lead), the parents are happy (as their daughters are happy), and we are happy (as they are happy). Good feeling involves these 'points' of alignment. We could say positive affect is what sutures the film, resolving the generational and cultural split: as soon as Jess is allowed to join the football game, the two worlds 'come together' in a shared moment of enjoyment. Whilst the happy objects are different from the point of view of the daughters (football, marriage) they allow us to arrive at the same point.

And yet, the film does not give equal value to the objects in which good feelings come to reside. Jess's happiness is contrasted to her sister Pinkie, who is ridiculed throughout the film as not only wanting less, but as being less in the direction of her want. Pinkie asks Jess why she does not want 'this'. Jess does not say that she wants something different; she says it is because she wants something 'more'. That word 'more' lingers, and frames the ending of the film, which gives us 'flashes' of an imagined future (pregnancy for Pinkie, photos of Jess on her sport's team, her love for her football coach Joe, her friendship with Jules). During the sequence of shots as Jess gets ready to join the football final, the camera pans up to show an airplane. Airplanes are everywhere in this film, as they often are in diasporic films. In *Bend It Like Beckham*, they matter as technologies of flight, signifying what goes up and away. Happiness in the film is promised by what goes 'up and away'. In an earlier scene, the song 'Moving on Up' is playing, as Jess and Jules run towards us. They overtake two Indian women wearing *Salwar Kameez*. I would suggest that the spatial promise of the 'up and away' is narrated as leaving Indian culture behind, even though Jess as a character articulates a fierce loyalty to her family and culture. The desire to play football, to join the national game, is read as leaving a certain world behind. Through the juxtaposition of the daughter's happy objects, the film suggests that this desire gives a better return.

In reading the 'directed' nature of narratives of freedom, we need in part to consider how the film relates to wider discourses of the public good. The film locates the 'pressure point' in the migrant family; who pressurises Jess to live a life she does not want to live. And yet, many migrant individuals and families are under pressure to integrate, where integration is a key term for what we now call in the UK 'good race relations'. Although integration is not defined as 'leaving your culture behind' (at least not officially), it is unevenly distributed, as a demand that new or would be citizens 'embrace' a common culture that is already given.[21] In this context, the immigrant daughter who identifies with the national game is a national ideal; the 'happy' daughter who deviates from family convention becomes a sign of the promise of integration. The unconventional daughter of the migrant family may even provide a conventional form of social hope.

Melancholic Migrants

The happiness of this film is partly that it imagines that multiculturalism can deliver its social promise by extending freedom to migrants on the condition that they embrace its game. Multiculturalism becomes in other words a happy object. I want to quote from one film critic, who identifies the film aptly as a 'happy smiling multiculturalism':

> Yet we need to turn to the U.K. for the exemplary commercial film about happy, smiling multiculturalism. *Bend It like Beckham* is the most profitable all-British film of all time, appealing to a multicultural Britain where Robin Cook, former Foreign Secretary, recently declared Chicken Tikka Massala the most popular national dish. White Brits tend to love *Bend It like Beckham* because it doesn't focus on race and racism—after all many are tired of feeling guilty.[22]

What makes this film 'happy' is in part what it conceals or keeps from view. What makes this film happy might precisely be the relief it offers from the negative affects surrounding racism. You might note that the negative affects are not attributed to the experience of racism, but to white guilt: the film might be appealing as it allows white guilt to be displaced by good feelings: you do not have to feel guilty about racism, as you can be 'uplifted' by the happiness of the story of migrant success. The film 'lifts you up'.

And yet of course to evoke 'happy multiculturalism' in the United Kingdom is to use a political language that is already dated. Multiculturalism is increasingly evoked as an unhappy object, as a sign of the failure of communities to 'happily integrate'. Multiculturalism has even been declared dead.[23] We do need to register this political shift as a shift. But we also need to register what stays in place through this shift.

I would argue that integration is what keeps its place as a place holder of national desire. …

… In his preface to the Commission for Racial Equality's Guide, *Good Race Relations*, Trevor Phillips suggests that: 'Multiculturalism no longer provides the right answer to the complex nature of today's race relations. Integration based on shared values and loyalties is the only way forward'.[24] Integration becomes what promises happiness (if only we mixed, we would be happy), by converting bad feelings (read unintegrated migrants) into good feelings (read integrated migrants). Integration is read not only as promising happiness, but also as a matter of life and death. The heading for Trevor Phillips's preface reads: 'Integration is not a dream: it is a matter of survival'. *Bend It Like Beckham* gives us a story of integration as being a dream and a form of survival. This film, released in 2001, could be read *simultaneously* as dated, insofar as it gives us an image of happy multiculturalism that has now been given up, and as anticipatory, insofar as happiness is promised as the reward for integration.

Although *Bend It Like Beckham* seems to be about the promise of happiness, I would argue that injury and bad feeling play an important narrative function in the film. As you know, I am interested in how bad feelings are converted into good feelings. What are the conversion points in this film? We can focus here on two speeches made by Jess's father: the first takes place early on in the film, and the second at the end of the film:

> When I was a teenager in Nairobi, I was the best fast bowler in our school. Our team even won the East African cup. But when I came to this country, nothing. And these bloody gora in the club house made fun of my turban and set me off packing … She will only end up disappointed like me.
>
> When those bloody English cricket players threw me out of their club like a dog, I never complained. On the contrary, I vowed that I would never play again. Who suffered? Me. But I don't want Jess to suffer. I don't want her to make the same mistakes her father made, accepting life, accepting situations. I want her to fight. And I want her to win.

In the first speech, the father says she *should not play* in order not to suffer like him. In the second, he says she *should play* in order not to suffer like him. The desire implicit in both speech acts is the avoidance of the daughter's suffering, which is expressed in terms of the desire not to repeat his own. I would argue that the father is represented in the first speech as melancholic:[25] as refusing to let go of his suffering, as incorporating the very object of own loss. His refusal to let Jess go is readable as a symptom of melancholia: as a stubborn attachment to his own injury, or as a form of self-harm (as he says: 'who suffered? Me'). I would argue that the second speech suggests that the refusal to play a national game is the 'truth' being the migrant's suffering: you suffer because you do not play the game, where not playing is read as a kind of self-exclusion. For Jess to be happy he lets her be included, narrated as a form of letting go. By implication, not only is he letting her go, he is also letting go of his own suffering, the unhappiness caused by accepting racism, as the 'point' of his exclusion.

The figure of the melancholic migrant is a familiar one in contemporary British race politics. The melancholic migrant holds onto the unhappy objects of differences, such as the turban, or at least the memory of being teased about the turban, which ties it to a history of racism. Such differences—one could think also of the burqa—become sore points or blockage points, where the smooth passage of communication stops. The melancholic migrant is the one who is not only stubbornly attached to difference, but who insists on speaking about racism, where such speech is heard as labouring over sore points. The duty of the migrant is to let go of the pain of racism by letting go of racism as a way of understanding that pain.

It is important to note that the melancholic migrant's fixation with injury is read not only as an obstacle to their own happiness, but also to the happiness of the generation-to-come, and even to national happiness. This figure may even quickly convert in the national imaginary to the 'could-be-terrorist'. His anger, pain, misery (all understood as forms of bad faith insofar as they won't let go of something that is presumed to be already gone) becomes 'our terror'.

To avoid such a terrifying end point, the duty of the migrant is to attach to a different happier object, one that can bring good fortune, such as the national game. The film ends with the fortune of this re-attachment. Jess goes to America to take up her dream of becoming a professional football player, a land which makes the pursuit of happiness an originary goal. This re-attachment is narrated as moving beyond the unhappy scripts of racism. We should note here that the father's experience of being excluded from the national game are repeated in Jess's own encounter with racism on the football pitch (she is called a 'Paki'), which leads to the injustice of her being sent off. In this case, however, Jess's anger and hurt does not stick. She lets go of her suffering. How does she let go? When she says to Joe, 'you don't know what it feels like', he replies, 'of course I know how it feels like, I'm Irish'. It is this act of identification with suffering that brings Jess back into the national game (as if to say, 'we all suffer, it is not just you'). The film suggests that whether racism 'hurts' depends upon individual choice and capacity: we can let go of racism as 'something' that happens, a capacity that is both attributed to skill (if you are good enough, you will get by), as well as the proximate gift of white empathy, where the hurt of racism is re-imagined as a common ground.

The love story between Jess and Joe offers another point of re-attachment. Heterosexuality becomes itself a form of happy return: promising to allow us to overcome injury. Heterosexual love is what heals. It is worth noting that the director of the film Gurinder Chadha originally planned to have the girls falling in love. This decision to drop the lesbian plot was of course to make the film more marketable.[26] We can see here the importance of 'appeal' as a form of capital, and how happiness can function as a moral economy: only some scripts can lead to happy endings given that happiness is both a good that circulates as well as a way of making things good. In *Bend It Like Beckham*, the heterosexual script involves proximity to queer. Not only does the film play with the possibility of female rebellion as lesbianism (girls with short hair who wear sports bras are presented as 'could be' lesbians rather than as 'being' lesbians), it also involves the use of a queer male character, Tony, in whom an alternative set of desires are deposited. As Gayatri Gopinath notes, the film 'ultimately reassures viewers that football-loving girls are indeed properly heterosexual by once again using the gay male figure as the "real" queer character in the film'.[27] Indeed, we could argue that the narrative of bending the rules of femininity involves a straightening device: you can bend, only insofar as you return to the straight line, which provides as it were our end point. So girls playing football leads to the male football coach. Narratives of rebellion can involve deviations from the straight line, if they return us to this point.

Heterosexuality also promises to overcome the injury or damage of racism. The acceptance of interracial heterosexual love is a conventional narrative of reconciliation as if love can overcome past antagonism and create what I would call 'hybrid familiality': *white with colour, white with another*. Such fantasies of proximity are premised on the following belief: *if only we could be closer, we would be as one*. Proximity becomes a promise: the happiness of the film is the promise of 'the one', as if giving love to the white man, as the ego ideal of the nation, would allow us to have a share in this promise.

The final scene is a cricket scene: the first of the film. As we know, cricket is an unhappy object in the film, associated with the suffering of racism. Jess's father is batting. Joe, in the foreground, is bowling. He smiles as he approaches us. He turns around, bowls, and gets the father out. In a playful scene, Joe then 'celebrates' and his body gestures mimic that of a plane, in a classic football gesture. As I have suggested, planes are happy objects in the film; associated with flight, with moving up and away. By mimicking the plane, Joe becomes the agent that converts bad feeling (unhappy racism) into good feeling (multicultural happiness). It is the white man who enables the father to let go of his injury about racism and to play cricket again. It is the white man who brings the suffering migrant back into the national fold. *His body is our conversion point.*

Such conversions function as displacements of injury from public view. We need to get beyond the appeal of happy surfaces. And yet, some critics suggest that we have paid too much attention to melancholia, suffering and injury and that we need to be more affirmative. Rosi Braidotti, for example, suggests that the focus on negativity has become a problem within feminism, and calls for a more affirmative feminism. She offers a bleak reading of bleakness: 'I actively yearn for a more joyful and empowering concept of desire and for a political economy that foregrounds positivity, not gloom'.[28] In her more recent book, the call for affirmation *rather* than negativity involves an explicit turn to happiness. Braidotti suggests that an affirmative feminism would make happiness a crucial political ideal. As she argues: 'I consider happiness a political issue, as are well-being, self-confidence and a sense of empowerment. These are fundamentally ethical concerns … The feminist movement has played the historical role of placing these items at the centre of the social and political agenda: happiness as a fundamental human right and hence a political question'.[29]

What concerns me is how much this turn to happiness actually depends on the very distinction between good and bad feelings that presume bad feelings are backward and conservative and good feelings are forward and progressive. Bad feelings are seen as orientated towards the past; as a kind of stubbornness that 'stops' the subject from embracing the future. Good feelings are associated here with moving up, and getting out. I would argue that it is the very assumption that good feelings are open and bad feelings are closed that allows historical forms of injustice to disappear. The demand for happiness is what makes those histories disappear or projects them onto others, by seeing them as a form of melancholia (you hold onto something that is already gone) or even as a paranoid fantasy. These histories have not gone: we would be letting go of that which persists in the present, a letting go which would keep those histories present.

I am not saying that feminist, anti-racist and queer politics do not have anything to say about happiness other than point to its unhappy effects. I think it is the very exposure of these unhappy effects that is affirmative, which gives us an alternative set of imaginings of what might count as a good or at least better life. If injustice does have unhappy effects, then the story does not end there. Unhappiness is not our end point. If anything, the experience of being outside the very ideals that are presumed to enable a good life still gets us somewhere. It is the resources we develop in sharing such experiences that might form the basis of alternative models of happiness. A concern with histories that hurt is not then a backward orientation: to move on, you must make this return. If anything we might want to reread the melancholic subject, the one who refuses to let go of suffering, and who is even prepared to kill some forms of joy, as offering an alternative social promise.

Notes

1. Meghan O'Rourke, 'Desperate Feminist Wives: Why Wanting Equality Makes Women Happy', 2006, available at: http://www.slate.com/id/2137537/. Last accessed on 27/06/07.
2. Simone de Beauvoir, *The Second Sex*, H.M. Parshley (trans), London, Vintage Books, 1997, p. 28.
3. Richard Layard, *Happiness: Lessons from a New Science*, London, Allen Lane, 2005, p. 1.
4. Michael Argyle, *The Psychology of Happiness*, London, Methuen and Co, 1987, p. 31.
5. I will not be considering the relation between football and multiculturalism beyond considering the symbolic function of football in the film *Bend It Like Beckham*. For an important analysis of football in relation to racism and national identity see Les Back, Tim Crabbe and John Solomos, *The Changing Face of Football: Racism, Identity and Multiculture in the English Game*, Oxford, Berg, 2001.
6. Darrin M. McMahon, *Happiness: A History*, New York, Atlantic Monthly Press, 2006.
7. Michael Argyle and Maryanne Martin, 'The Psychological Causes of Unhappiness' in Fritz Strack, Michael Argyle and Norbert Schwarz (eds), *Subjective Well-Being: An Interdisciplinary Perspective*, Oxford, Pergamon Press, 1991, p. 77.
8. John Locke, *An Essay Concerning Human Understanding*, London, Penguin Books, 1997, p. 216.
9. Ibid.

10. Aristotle, *The Nichomachean Ethics*, J.A.K. Thomson (trans), London, Penguin Books, 1976, p. 3, p. 6, p. 13.
11. See Anna Gibbs, 'Contagious Feelings: Pauline Hanson and the Epidemology of Affect', *Australian Humanities Review*, http:www.lib.latrobe.edu.au/AHR/archive/Issue-December-2001/gibbs.html; Eve Kosofsky Sedgwick, *Touching Feeling: Affect, Performativity, Pedagogy*, Durham, Duke University Press, 2003; Teresa Brennan, *The Transmission of Affect*, Ithaca, Cornell University Press, 2004; and Elspeth Probyn, *Blush: Faces of Shame*, Minneapolis, University of Minnesota Press, 2005.
12. Gibbs, 'Contagious Feelings', op. cit., p. 1.
13. Sara Ahmed, *The Cultural Politics of Emotion*, Edinburgh, Edinburgh University Press, 2004, p. 9.
14. Brennan, *Transmission*, op. cit., p. 1.
15. Ahmed, *The Cultural Politics*, op. cit., p. 9.
16. Brennan, *Transmission*, op. cit., p. 6.
17. Marilyn Frye, *The Politics of Reality: Essays in Feminist Theory*, Trumanburg, NY, The Crossing Press, 1983, p. 2.
18. Audre Lorde, *Sister Outsider: Essays and Speeches*, Trumanburg, NY, The Crossing Press, p. 131.
19. Judith Halberstam, *In a Queer Time and Place: Transgender Bodies, Subcultural Lives*, New York, New York University Press, 2005, pp. 152–3. See also my book *Queer Phenomenology: Orientations, Objects, Others*, Durham, Duke University Press, 2006, for an exploration of how bodies are directed by the time lines of inheritance and generation.
20. Nancy Garden, *Annie On My Mind*, Aerial Fiction, Farrar, Straus and Giroux, 1982, p. 191.
21. For an analysis of integration as 'the imperative to love difference' see chapter 5, 'In the Name of Love' in Ahmed, *Cultural Politics*, op. cit.
22. Daniel McNeil (2004), 'Dancing Across Borders', http://www.brightlightsfilm.com/44/pan.htm.
23. Multiculturalism has been associated with death, for instance, by being attributed as the cause of the London bombings in July 2005. As Paul Gilroy argues 'Multiculturalism was officially pronounced dead in July 2005', 'Multi-Culture in Times of War', Inaugural Lecture, London School of Economics, 10/05/06.
24. Commission for Racial Equality, *Good Race Relations Guide*, 2005: http://www.cre.gov.uk/duty/grr/index. html.
25. For excellent readings of racial melancholia see Anne Anlin Cheng, *The Melancholia of Race: Psychoanalysis, Assimilation and Hidden Grief*, Oxford, Oxford University Press, 2001; and David L. Eng and Shinhee Han, 'A Dialogue on Racial Melancholia', in David L. Eng and David Kazanjian (eds), *Loss: The Politics of Mourning*, Berkeley, University of California Press, 2003.
26. For a discussion of this decision see Sarah Warn, 'Dropping Lesbian Romance from Beckham the Right Decision', http://www.afterellen.com/Movies/beckham.html, last accessed 25/01/08.
27. Gayatri Gopinath, *Impossible Desires: Queer Diasporas and South Asian Public Cultures*, Durham, Duke University Press, 2005, p. 129.
28. Rosi Braidotti, *Metamorphoses: Towards a Materialist Theory of Becoming*, Cambridge, Polity, 2002, p. 57.
29. Rosi Braidotti, *Transpositions: On Nomadic Ethics*, Cambridge, Polity, 2006, p. 230.

47.
LUMPECTOMY EVE
Lucille Clifton
(1996)

all night i dream of lips
that nursed and nursed
and the lonely nipple

lost in loss and the need
to feed that turns at last
on itself   that will kill

its body for its hunger's sake
all night i hear the whispering
the soft

    love calls you to this knife
    for love   for love

all night it is the one breast
comforting the other

SOLIDARITY RECONSIDERED

48.

"UNDER WESTERN EYES" REVISITED: FEMINIST SOLIDARITY THROUGH ANTICAPITALIST STRUGGLES

Chandra Talpade Mohanty

(2003)

I write this chapter at the urging of a number of friends and with some trepidation, revisiting the themes and arguments of an essay written some sixteen years ago. This is a difficult chapter to write,[1] and I undertake it hesitantly and with humility—yet feeling that I must do so to take fuller responsibility for my ideas, and perhaps to explain whatever influence they have had on debates in feminist theory.

"Under Western Eyes" was not only my very first "feminist studies" publication, it remains the one that marks my presence in the international feminist community. I had barely completed my Ph.D. when I wrote this essay; I am now a professor of women's studies. The "under" of Western eyes is now much more an "inside" in terms of my own location in the U.S. academy.[2] The site from which I wrote the essay consisted of a very vibrant, transnational women's movement, while the site I write from today is quite different. With the increasing privatization and corporatization of public life, it has become much harder to discern such a women's movement from the United States (although women's movements are thriving around the world), and my site of access and struggle has increasingly come to be the U.S. academy. In the United States, women's movements have become increasingly conservative, and much radical, antiracist feminist activism occurs outside the rubric of such movements. Thus, much of what I say here is influenced by the primary site I occupy as an educator and scholar. It is time to revisit "Under Western Eyes," to clarify ideas that remained implicit and unstated in 1986 and to further redevelop and historicize the theoretical framework I outlined then. I also want to assess how this essay has been read and misread and to respond to the critiques and celebrations. And it is time for me to move explicitly from critique to reconstruction, to identify the urgent issues facing feminists at the beginning of the twenty-first century, to ask the question: How would "Under Western Eyes"—the Third World inside and outside the West—be explored and analyzed almost two decades later? What do I consider to be the urgent theoretical amid methodological questions facing a comparative feminist politics at this moment in history? …

… I wish to begin a dialogue between the intentions, effects, and political choices that underwrote "Under Western Eyes" in the mid-1980s and those I would make today. I hope it provokes others to ask similar questions about our individual and collective projects in feminist studies.

Revisiting "Under Western Eyes"

Decolonizing Feminist Scholarship: 1986

I wrote "Under Western Eyes" to discover and articulate a critique of "Western feminist" scholarship on Third World women via the discursive colonization of Third World women's lives and struggles. I also wanted to expose the power-knowledge nexus of feminist cross-cultural scholarship expressed through Eurocentric, falsely universalizing methodologies that serve the narrow self-interest of Western feminism. As well, I thought it crucial to highlight the connection between feminist scholarship and feminist political organizing while drawing attention to the need to examine the "political implications of our analytic strategies and principles." I also wanted to chart the location of feminist scholarship within a global political and economic framework dominated by the "First World."[3]

My most simple goal was to make clear that cross-cultural feminist work must be attentive to the micropolitics of context, subjectivity, and struggle, as well as to the macropolitics of global economic and political systems and processes. I discussed Maria Mies's study of the lacemakers of Narsapur as a demonstration of how to do this kind of multilayered, contextual analysis to reveal how the particular is often universally significant—without using the universal to erase the particular, or positing an unbridgeable gulf between the two terms. Implicit in this analysis was the use of historical materialism as a basic framework, and a definition of material reality in both its local and micro-, as well as global, systemic dimensions. I argued at that time for the definition and recognition of the Third World not just through oppression but in terms of historical complexities and the many struggles to change these oppressions. Thus I argued for grounded, particularized analyses linked with larger, even global, economic and political frameworks. I drew inspiration from a vision of feminist solidarity across borders, although it is this vision that has remained invisible to many readers. In a perceptive analysis of my argument of this politics of location, Sylvia Walby (2000) recognizes and refines the relation between difference and equality of which I speak. She draws further attention to the need for a shared frame of reference among Western, postcolonial, Third World feminists in order to decide what counts as difference. She asserts, quite insightfully, that

> Mohanty and other postcolonial feminists are often interpreted as arguing only for situated knowledges in popularisations of their work. In fact, Mohanty is claiming, via a complex and subtle argument, that she is right and that (much) white Western feminism is not merely different, but wrong. In doing this she assumes a common question, a common set of concepts and, ultimately the possibility of, a common political project with white feminism. She hopes to argue white feminism into agreeing with her. She is not content to leave white Western feminism as a situated knowledge, comfortable with its local and partial perspective. Not a bit of it. This is a claim to a more universal truth. And she hopes to accomplish this by the power of argument. (199)

Walby's reading of the essay challenges others to engage my notion of a common feminist political project, which critiques the effects of Western feminist scholarship on women in the Third World, but within a framework of solidarity and shared values. My insistence on the specificity of difference is based on a vision of equality attentive to power differences within and among the various communities of women. I did not argue against all forms of generalization, nor was I privileging the local over the systemic, difference over commonalities, or the discursive over the material. ...

Intellectually, I was writing in solidarity with the critics of Eurocentric humanism who drew attention to its false universalizing and masculinist assumptions. My project was anchored in a firm belief in the importance of the particular in relation to the universal—a belief in the local as specifying and illuminating the universal. My concerns drew attention to the dichotomies embraced and identified with this universalized framework, the critique of "white feminism" by women of color and the critique of "Western feminism" by Third World feminists working within a paradigm of decolonization. I was committed, both politically and personally, to building a noncolonizing feminist solidarity across borders. I believed in a larger feminist project than the colonizing, self-interested one I saw emerging in much influential feminist scholarship and in the mainstream women's movement. ...

I attribute some of the readings and misunderstandings of the essay to the triumphal rise of postmodernism in the U.S. academy in the past three decades. Although l have never called myself a "postmodernist," some reflection on why my ideas have been assimilated under this label is important.[4] In fact, one reason to revisit "Under Western Eyes" at this time is my desire to point to this postmodernist appropriation.[5] l am misread when l am interpreted as being against all forms of generalization and as arguing for difference over commonalities. This misreading occurs in the context of a hegemonic postmodernist discourse that labels as "totalizing" all systemic connections, and emphasizes only the mutability and constructedness of identities and social structures.

Yes, I did draw on Foucault to outline an analysis of power/knowledge, but I also drew on Anour Abdel Malek to show the directionality and material effects of a particular imperial power structure. I drew too on Maria Mies to argue for the need for a materialist analysis that linked everyday life and local gendered contexts and ideologies to the larger, transnational political and economic structures and ideologies of capitalism. What is interesting for me is to see how and why "difference" has been embraced over "commonality," and I realize that my writing leaves open this possibility. In 1986 I wrote mainly to challenge the false universality of Eurocentric discourses and was perhaps not sufficiently critical of the valorization of difference over commonality in postmodernist discourse.[6] Now I find myself wanting to reemphasize the connections between local and universal. In 1986 my priority was on difference, but now I want to recapture and reiterate its fuller meaning, which was always there, and that is its connection to the universal. In other words, this discussion allows me to reemphasize the way that differences are never just "differences." In knowing differences and particularities, we can better see the connections and commonalities because no border or boundary is ever complete or rigidly determining. The challenge is to see how differences allow us to explain the connections and border crossings better and more accurately, how specifying difference allows us to theorize universal concerns more fully. It is this intellectual move that allows for my concern for women of different communities and identities to build coalitions and solidarities across borders.

So what has changed and what remains the same for me? What are the urgent intellectual and political questions for feminist scholarship and organizing at this time in history? First, let me say that the terms "Western" and "Third World" retain a political and explanatory value in a world that appropriates and assimilates multiculturalism and "difference" through commodification and consumption. However, these are not the only terms I would choose to use now. With the United States, the European Community, and Japan as the nodes of capitalist power in the early twenty-first century, the increasing proliferation of Third and Fourth Worlds within the national borders of these very countries, as well as the rising visibility and struggles for sovereignty by First Nations/indigenous peoples around the world, "Western" and "Third World" explain much less than the categorizations "North/South" or "One-Third/Two-Thirds Worlds."

"North/South" is used to distinguish between affluent, privileged nations and communities, and economically and politically marginalized nations and communities, as is "Western/non-Western." While these terms are meant to loosely distinguish the northern and southern hemispheres, affluent and marginal nations and communities obviously do not line up neatly within this geographical frame. And yet, as a political designation that attempts to distinguish between the "haves" and the "have-nots," it does have a certain political value. An example of this is Arif Dirlik's formulation of North/South as a metaphorical rather than geographical distinction, where "North" refers to the pathways of transnational capital and "South" to the marginalized poor of the world regardless of geographical distinction.[7]

I find the language of "One-Third World" versus "Two-Thirds World" as elaborated by Gustavo Esteva and Madhu Sun Prakash (1998) particularly useful, especially in conjunction with "Third World/South" and "First World/North" These terms represent what Esteva and Prakash call social minorities and social majorities—categories based on the quality of life led by peoples and communities in both the North and the South.[8] The advantage of one-third/two-thirds world in relation to terms like "Western/Third World" and "North/South" is that they move away from misleading geographical and ideological binarisms.

By focusing on quality of life as the criteria for distinguishing between social minorities and majorities, "One-Third/Two-Thirds Worlds" draws attention to the continuities as well as the discontinuities between the haves and have-nots within the boundaries of nations and between nations and indigenous communities. This designation also highlights the fluidity and power of global forces that situate communities of people as social majorities/minorities in disparate form. "One-Third/Two-Thirds" is a nonessentialist categorization, but it incorporates an analysis of power and agency that is crucial. Yet what it misses is a history of colonization that the terms Western/Third World draw attention to.

As the above terminological discussion serves to illustrate, we are still working with a very imprecise and inadequate analytical language. All we can have access to at given moments is the analytical language that most clearly approximates the features of the world as we understand it. This distinction between One-Third/Two-Thirds World and, at times, First World/North and Third World/South is the language I choose to use now. Because in fact our language is imprecise, I hesitate to have any language become static. My own language in 1986 needs to be open to refinement and inquiry—but not to institutionalization.

Finally, I want to reflect on an important issue not addressed in "Under Western Eyes": the question of native or indigenous struggles. ...

... Native or indigenous women's struggles, which do not follow a postcolonial trajectory based on the inclusions and exclusions of processes of capitalist, racist, heterosexist, and nationalist domination, cannot be addressed easily under the purview of categories such as "Western" and "Third World."[9] But they become visible and even central to the definition of One-Third/Two-Thirds Worlds because indigenous claims for sovereignty, their lifeways and environmental and spiritual practices, situate them as central to the definition of "social majority" (Two-Thirds World). While a mere shift in conceptual terms is not a complete response ... I think it clarifies and addresses the limitations of my earlier use of "Western" and "Third World"—in all my complexities—in the context of "Under Western Eyes," in this new frame, I am clearly located within the One-Third World. Then again, now, as in my earlier writing, I straddle both categories. I am of the Two-Thirds World in the One-Third World. I am clearly a part of the social minority now, with all its privileges; however, my political choices, struggles, and vision for change place me alongside the Two-Thirds World. Thus, I am for the Two-Thirds World, but with the privileges of the One-Third World. I speak as a person situated in the One-Thirds World, but from the space and vision of, and in solidarity with, communities in struggle in the Two-Thirds World.

Under and (Inside) Western Eyes: At the Turn of the Century

There have been a number of shifts in the political and economic landscapes of nations and communities of people in the last two decades. ... [T]he hegemony of neoliberalism, alongside the naturalization of capitalist values, influences the ability to make choices on one's own behalf in the daily lives of economically marginalized as well as economically privileged communities around the globe.

The rise of religious fundamentalisms with their deeply masculinist and often racist rhetoric poses a huge challenge for feminist struggles around the world. Finally, the profoundly unequal "information highway" as well as the increasing militarization (and masculinization) of the globe, accompanied by the growth of the prison industrial complex in the United States, poses profound contradictions in the lives of communities of women and men in most parts of the world. I believe these political shifts to the right, accompanied by global capitalist hegemony privatization, and increased religious, ethnic, and racial hatreds, pose very concrete challenges for feminists. In this context, I ask what would it mean to be attentive to the micropolitics of everyday life as well as to the larger processes that recolonize the culture and identities of people across the globe. How we think of the local in/of the global and vice versa without falling into colonizing or cultural relativist platitudes about difference is crucial in this intellectual and political landscape. And for me, this kind of thinking is tied to a revised race-and-gender-conscious historical materialism.

The politics of feminist cross-cultural scholarship from the vantage point of Third World/South feminist struggles remains a compelling site of analysis for me.[10] Eurocentric analytic paradigms continue to flourish, and I remain committed to reengaging in the struggles to criticize openly the effects of discursive colonization on the lives and struggles of marginalized women. My central commitment is to build connections between feminist scholarship and political organizing. My own present-day analytic framework remains very similar to my earliest critique of Eurocentrism. However, I now see the politics and economics of capitalism as a far more urgent locus of struggle, I continue to hold to an analytic framework that is attentive to the micropolitics of everyday life as well as to the macropolitics of global economic and political processes. The link between political economy and culture remains crucial to any form of feminist theorizing—as it does for my work. It isn't the framework that has changed. It is just that global economic and political processes have become more brutal, exacerbating economic, racial, and gender inequalities, and thus they need to be demystified, reexamined, and theorized.

While my earlier focus was on the distinctions between "Western" and "Third World" feminist practices, and while I downplayed the commonalities between these two positions, my focus now ... is on what I have chosen to call an anticapitalist transnational feminist practice—and on the possibilities, indeed on the necessities, of cross-national feminist solidarity and organizing against capitalism. ...

"Under Western Eyes" sought to make the operations of discursive power visible, to draw attention to what was left out of feminist theorizing, namely, the material complexity, reality, and agency of Third World women's bodies and lives. This is in fact exactly the analytic strategy I now use to draw attention to what is unseen, undertheorized, and left out in the production of knowledge about globalization. While globalization has always been a part of capitalism and capitalism is not a new phenomenon, at this time I believe the theory, critique, and activism around antiglobalization has to be a key focus for feminists. This does not mean that the patriarchal and racist relations and structures that accompany capitalism are any less problematic at this time, or that antiglobalization is a singular phenomenon. Along with many other scholars and activists, I believe capital as it functions now depends on and exacerbates racist, patriarchal, and heterosexist relations of rule.

Feminist Methodologies: New Directions

What kinds of feminist methodology and analytic strategy are useful in making power (and women's lives) visible in overtly nongendered, nonracialized discourses? The strategy discussed here is an example of how capitalism and its various relations of rule can be analyzed through a transnational, anticapitalist feminist critique one that draws on historical materialism and centralizes racialized gender. This analysis begins from and is anchored in the place of the most marginalized communities of women—poor women of all colors in affluent and neocolonial nations; women of the Third World/ South or the Two-Thirds World.[11] I believe that this experiential and analytic anchor in the lives of marginalized communities of women provides the most inclusive paradigm for thinking about social justice. This particularized viewing allows for a more concrete and expansive vision of universal justice.

This is the very opposite of "special interest" thinking. If we pay attention to and think from the space of some of the most disenfranchised communities of women in the world, we are most likely to envision a just and democratic society capable of treating all its citizens fairly. Conversely, if we begin our analysis from, and limit it to, the space of privileged communities, our visions of justice are more likely to be exclusionary because privilege nurtures blindness to those without the same privileges. Beginning from the lives and interests of marginalized communities of women, I am able to access and make the workings of power visible—to read up the ladder of privilege. It is more necessary to look upward—colonized peoples must know themselves and the colonizer. This particular marginalized location makes the politics of knowledge and the power investments that go along with it visible so that we can then engage in work to transform the use and abuse of power. The analysis draws on the notion of epistemic privilege as it's developed by feminist standpoint theorists (with their roots in the historical materialism of Marx and Lukacs) as well as post positivist realists, who provide an analysis of experience, identity, and the epistemic effects of social location.[12] My view is thus a materialist and "realist" one and is antithetical to that of postmodernist relativism. I believe there are causal links between marginalized social locations and experiences and the ability of human agents to explain and analyze features of capitalist society. Methodologically, this analytic perspective is grounded in historical materialism. My claim is not that all marginalized locations yield crucial knowledge about power and inequity, but that within a tightly integrated capitalist system, the particular standpoint of poor indigenous and Third World/ South women provides the most inclusive viewing of systemic power. ... Herein lies a lesson for feminist analysis.

Feminist scientist Vandana Shiva, one of the most visible leaders of the antiglobalization movement, provides a similar and illuminating critique of the patents and intellectual property rights agreements sanctioned by the World Trade Organization (WTO) since 1995.[13] Along with others in the environmental and indigenous rights movements, she argues that the WTO sanctions biopiracy and engages in intellectual piracy by privileging the claims of corporate commercial interests, based on Western systems of knowledge in agriculture and medicine, to products and innovations derived from indigenous knowledge traditions. Thus, through the definition of Western scientific epistemologies as the only legitimate scientific system, the WTO is able to underwrite corporate patents to indigenous knowledge (as to the Neem tree in India) as their own intellectual property, protected through intellectual property rights agreements. As a result, the patenting of drugs derived from indigenous medicinal systems has now reached massive proportions. ... The contrast between Western scientific systems and indigenous epistemologies and systems of medicine is not the only issue here. It is the colonialist and corporate power to define Western science, and the reliance on capitalist values of private property and profit, as the only normative system that results in the exercise of immense power. Thus indigenous knowledges, which are often communally generated and shared among tribal and peasant women for domestic, local, and public use are subject to the ideologies of a corporate Western scientific paradigm where intellectual property rights can only be understood in possessive or privatized form. All innovations that happen to be collective, to have occurred over time in forests and farms, are appropriated or excluded. The idea of an intellectual commons where knowledge is collectively gathered and passed on for the benefit of all, not owned privately, is the very opposite of the notion of private property and ownership that is the basis for the WTO property rights agreements. Thus this idea of an intellectual commons among tribal and peasant women actually excludes them from ownership and facilitates corporate biopiracy.

Shiva's analysis of intellectual property rights, biopiracy, and globalization is made possible by its very location in the experiences and epistemologies of peasant and tribal women in India. Beginning from the practices and knowledges of indigenous women, she "reads up" the power structure, all the way to the policies and practices sanctioned by the WTO. This is a very clear example then of a transnational, anticapitalist feminist politics. …

An analysis that pays attention to the everyday experiences of tribal women and the micropolitics of their ultimately anticapitalist struggles illuminates the macropolitics of global restructuring. It suggests the thorough embeddedness of the local and particular with the global and universal, and it suggests the need to conceptualize questions of justice and equity in transborder terms. In other words, this mode of reading envisions a feminism without borders …

… Of course, if we were to attempt the same analysis from the epistemological space of Western, corporate interests, it would be impossible to generate an analysis that values indigenous knowledge anchored in communal relationships rather than profit-based hierarchies. Thus, poor tribal and peasant women, their knowledges and interests, would be invisible in this analytic frame because the very idea of an intellectual commons fails outside the purview of privatized property and profit that is a basis for corporate interests. The obvious issue for a transnational feminism pertains to the visions of profit and justice embodied in these opposing analytic perspectives. The focus on profit versus justice illustrates my earlier point about social location and analytically inclusive methodologies. It is the social location of the tribal women as explicated by Shiva that allows this broad and inclusive focus on justice. Similarly, it is the social location and narrow self-interest of corporations that privatizes intellectual property rights in the name of profit for elites.

… In fundamental ways, it is girls and women around the world, especially in the Third World/South, that bear the brunt of globalization. Poor women and girls are the hardest hit by the degradation of environmental conditions, wars, famines, privatization of services and deregulation of governments, the dismantling of welfare states, the restructuring of paid and unpaid work increasing surveillance and incarceration in prisons, and so on. And this is why a feminism without and beyond borders is necessary to address the injustices of global capitalism.

Women and girls are still 70 percent of the world's poor and the majority of the world's refugees. Girls and women comprise almost 80 percent of displaced persons of the Third World/South in Africa, Asia and Latin America. Women own less than one-hundredth of the world's property, while they are the hardest hit by the effects of war, domestic violence, and religious persecution. Feminist political theorist Zillah Eisenstein says that women do two-thirds of the worlds work and earn less than one-tenth of its income. ... (Eisenstein 1998b, esp. ch. 5).

... It is then the lives, experiences, and struggles of girls and women of the Two-Thirds World that demystify capitalism in its racial and sexual dimensions—and that provide productive and necessary avenues of theorizing and enacting anticapitalist resistance. ...

What does the above analysis suggest? That we—feminist scholars and teachers—must respond to the phenomenon of globalization as an urgent site for the recoloniza-tion of peoples, especially in the Two-Thirds World. Globalization colonizes women's as well as men's lives around the world, and we need an anti-imperialist, anticapitalist, and contextualized feminist project to expose and make visible the various, overlap-ping forms of subjugation of women's lives. Activists and scholars must also identify and reenvision forms of collective resistance that women, especially, in their different communities enact in their everyday lives. It is their particular exploitation at this time, their potential epistemic privilege, as well as their particular forms of solidarity that can be the basis for reimagining a liberatory politics for the start of this century.

Antiglobalization Struggles

... Given the complex interweaving of cultural forms, people of and from the Third World live not only under Western eyes but also within them. This shift in my focus from "Under Western eyes to under and inside" the hegemonic spaces of the One-Third World necessitates recrafting the project of decolonization.

My focus is thus no longer just the colonizing effects of Western feminist scholar-ship. This does not mean the problems I identified in the earlier essay do not occur now. But the phenomenon I addressed then has been more than adequately engaged by other feminist scholars. While feminists have been involved in the antiglobaliza-tion movement from the start, however, this has not been a major organizing locus for women's movements nationally in the West/North. It has, however, always been a locus of struggle for women of the Third World/South because of their location, Again, this contextual specificity should constitute the larger vision. Women of the Two-Thirds World have always organized against the devastations of globalized capital, just as they have always historically organized anticolonial and antiracist movements. In this sense they have always spoken for humanity as a whole. ...

What does it mean to make antiglobalization a key factor for feminist theorizing and struggle? To illustrate my thinking about antiglobalization, let me focus on ... [a] specific site where knowledge about globalization is produced. The ... site is a peda-gogical one and involves an analysis of the various strategies being used to internation-alize (or globalize)[14] the women's studies curriculum in U.S. colleges and universities.

I argue that this move to internationalize women's studies curricula and the attendant pedagogies that flow from this is one of the main ways we can track a discourse of global feminism in the United States. Other ways of tracking global feminist discourses include analyzing the documents and discussions flowing out of the Beijing United Nations conference on women, and of course popular television and print media discourses on women around the world. ...

Antiglobalization Pedagogies

Let me turn to the struggles over the dissemination of a feminist cross-cultural knowledge base through pedagogical strategies "internationalizing" the women's studies curriculum. The problem of "the (gendered) color line" remains, but is more easily seen today as developments of transnational and global capital. While I choose to focus on women's studies curricula, my arguments hold for curricula in any discipline or academic field that seeks to internationalize or globalize its curriculum. I argue that the challenge for "internationalizing" women's studies is no different from the one involved in "racializing" women's studies in the 1980s, for very similar politics of knowledge come into play here.[15]

So the question I want to foreground is the politics of knowledge in bridging the "local" and the "global" in women's studies. How we teach the "new" scholarship in women's studies is at least as important as the scholarship itself in the struggles over knowledge and citizenship in the U.S. academy. After all, the way we construct curricula and the pedagogies we use to put such curricula into practice tell a story—or tell many stories. It is the way we position historical narratives of experience in relation to each other, the way we theorize relationality as both historical and simultaneously singular and collective that determines how and what we learn when we cross cultural and experiential borders.

Drawing on my own work with U.S. feminist academic communities, I describe three pedagogical models used in "internationalizing" the women's studies curriculum and analyze the politics of knowledge at work. Each of these perspectives is grounded in particular conceptions of the local and the global, of women's agency, and of national identity, and each curricular model presents different stories and ways of crossing borders and building bridges. I suggest that a "comparative feminist studies" or "feminist solidarity" model is the most useful and productive pedagogical strategy for feminist cross-cultural work. It is this particular model that provides a way to theorize a complex relational understanding of experience, location, and history such that feminist cross-cultural work moves through the specific context to construct a real notion of universal and of democratization rather than colonization. It is through this model that we can put into practice the idea of "common differences" as the basis for deeper solidarity across differences and unequal power relations.

Feminist-as-Tourist Model

This curricular perspective could also be called the "feminist as international consumer" or, in less charitable terms, the "white women's burden or colonial discourse" model.[16] It involves a pedagogical strategy in which brief forays are made into non-Euro-American cultures, and particular sexist cultural practices addressed from an otherwise Eurocentric women's studies gaze. In other words, the "add women as global victims or powerful women and stir" perspective. This is a perspective in which the primary Euro-American narrative of the syllabus remains untouched, and examples from non-Western or Third World/South cultures are used to supplement and "add" to this narrative. The story here is quite old. The effects of this strategy are that students and teachers are left with a clear sense of the difference and distance between the local (defined as self, nation and Western) and the global (defined as other, non-Western, and transnational). Thus the local is always grounded in nationalist assumptions—the United States or western European nation-state provides a normative context. This strategy leaves power relations and hierarchies untouched since ideas about center and margin are reproduced along Eurocentric lines.

For example, in an introductory feminist studies course, one could include the obligatory day or week on dowry deaths in India, women workers in Nike factories in Indonesia, or precolonial matriarchies in west Africa while leaving the fundamental identity of the Euro-American feminist on her way to liberation untouched. Thus Indonesian workers in Nike factories or dowry deaths in India stand in for the totality of women in these cultures. These women are not seen in their everyday lives (as Euro-American women are)—just in these stereotypical terms. Difference in the case of non-Euro-American women is thus congealed, not seen contextually with all of its contradictions. This pedagogical strategy for crossing cultural and geographical borders is based on a modernist paradigm, and the bridge between the local and the global becomes in fact a predominantly self-interested chasm. This perspective confirms the sense of the "evolved U.S/Euro feminist." While there is now more consciousness about not using an "add and stir" method in teaching about race and U.S. women of color, this does not appear to be the case in "internationalizing" women's studies. Experience in this context is assumed to be static and frozen into U.S.- or Euro-centered categories. Since in this paradigm feminism is always/already constructed as Euro-American in origin and development, women's lives and struggles outside this geographical context only serve to confirm or contradict this originary feminist (master) narrative. This model is the pedagogical counterpart of the orientalizing and colonizing Western feminist scholarship of the past decades. In fact it may remain the predominant model at this time. Thus implicit in this pedagogical strategy is the crafting of the "Third World difference," the creation of monolithic images of Third World/South women. This contrasts with images of Euro-American women who are vital, changing, complex, and central subjects within such a curricular perspective.

Feminist-as-Explorer Model

This particular pedagogical perspective originates in area studies, where the "foreign" woman is the object and subject of knowledge and the larger intellectual project is entirely about countries other than the United States. Thus, here the local and the global are both defined as non-Euro-American. The focus on the international implies that it exists outside the U.S. nation-state. Women's, gender, and feminist issues are based on spatial/geographical and temporal/historical categories located elsewhere. Distance from "home" is fundamental to the definition of international in this framework. This strategy can result in students and teachers being left with a notion of difference and separateness, a sort of "us and them" attitude, but unlike the tourist model, the explorer perspective can provide a deeper, more contextual understanding of feminist issues in discretely defined geographical and cultural spaces. However, unless these discrete spaces are taught in relation to one another, the story told is usually a cultural relativist one, meaning that differences between cultures are discrete and relative with no real connection or common basis for evaluation. The local and the global are here collapsed into the international that by definition excludes the United States. If the dominant discourse is the discourse of cultural relativism, questions of power, agency, justice, and common criteria for critique and evaluation are silenced.[17]

In women's studies curricula this pedagogical strategy is often seen as the most culturally sensitive way to "internationalize" the curriculum. For instance, entire courses on "Women in Latin America" or "Third World Women's Literature" or "Postcolonial Feminism" ate added on to the predominantly U.S.-based curriculum as a way to "globalize" the feminist knowledge base. These courses can be quite sophisticated and complex studies, but they are viewed as entirely separate from the intellectual project of U.S. race and ethnic studies.[18] The United States is not seen as part of "area studies," as white is not a color when one speaks of people of color. This is probably related to the particular history of institutionalization of area studies in the U.S. academy and its ties to U.S. imperialism. Thus areas to be studied/conquered are "out there," never within the United States. The fact that area studies in U.S. academic settings were federally funded and conceived as having a political project in the service of U.S. geopolitical interests suggests the need to examine the contemporary interests of these fields, especially as they relate to the logic of global capitalism. In addition, as Ella Shohat argues, it is time to "reimagine the study of regions and cultures in a way that transcends the conceptual borders inherent in the global cartography of the cold war" (2001, 1271). The field of American studies is an interesting location to examine here, especially since its more recent focus on U.S. imperialism. However, American studies rarely falls under the purview of "area studies." ...

Separating area studies from race and ethnic studies thus leads to understanding or teaching about the global as a way of not addressing internal racism, capitalist hegemony, colonialism, and heterosexualization as central to processes of global domination, exploitation, and resistance. Global or international is thus understood apart from racism—as if racism were not central to processes of globalization and relations of rule at this time. An example of this pedagogical strategy in the context of the larger curriculum is the usual separation of "world cultures" courses from race and ethnic studies courses. Thus identifying the kinds of representations of (non-Euro-American) women mobilized by this pedagogical strategy, and the relation of these representations to implicit images of First World/North women are important foci for analysis. What kind of power is being exercised in this strategy? What kinds of ideas of agency and struggle are being consolidated? What are the potential effects of a kind of cultural relativism on our understandings of the differences and commonalities among communities of women around the world? Thus the feminist-as-explorer model has its own problems, and I believe this is an inadequate way of building a feminist cross-cultural knowledge base because in the context of an interwoven world with clear directionalities of power and domination, cultural relativism serves as an apology for the exercise of power.

The Feminist Solidarity or Comparative Feminist Studies Model

This curricular strategy is based on the premise that the local and the global are not defined in terms of physical geography or territory but exist simultaneously and constitute each other. It is then the links, the relationships, between the local and the global that are foregrounded, and these links are conceptual, material, temporal, contextual, and so on. This framework assumes a comparative focus and analysis of the directionality of power no matter what the subject of the women's studies course is—and it assumes both distance and proximity (specific/universal) as its analytic strategy.

Differences and commonalities thus exist in relation and tension with each other in all contexts. What is emphasized are relations of mutuality, co-responsibility, and common interests, anchoring the idea of feminist solidarity. For example, within this model, one would not teach a U.S. women of color course with additions on Third World/South or white women, but a comparative course that shows the interconnectedness of the histories, experiences, and struggles of U.S. women of color, white women, and women from the Third World/South. By doing this kind of comparative teaching that is attentive to power, each historical experience illuminates the experiences of the others. Thus, the focus is not just on the intersections of race, class, gender, nation, and sexuality in different communities of women but on mutuality and co-implication, which suggests attentiveness to the interweaving of the histories of these communities. In addition the focus is simultaneously on individual and collective experiences of oppression and exploitation and of struggle and resistance.

Students potentially move away from the "add and stir" and the relativist "separate but equal" (or different) perspective to the co-implication/solidarity one. This solidarity perspective requires understanding the historical and experiential specificities and differences of women's lives as well as the historical and experiential connections between women from different national, racial and cultural communities. Thus it suggests organizing syllabi around social and economic processes and histories of various communities of women in particular substantive areas like sex work, militarization, environmental justice, the prison/industrial complex, and human rights, and looking for points of contact and connection as well as disjunctures. It is important to always foreground not just the connections of domination but those of struggle and resistance as well.

In the feminist solidarity model the One-Third/Two-Thirds paradigm makes sense. Rather than Western/Third World, or North/South, or local/global seen as oppositional and incommensurate categories, the One-Third/Two-Thirds differentiation allows for teaching and learning about points of connection and distance among and between communities of women marginalized and privileged along numerous local and global dimensions. Thus the very notion of inside/outside necessary to the distance between local/global is transformed through the use of a One-Third/Two-Thirds paradigm, as both categories must be understood as containing difference/similarities, inside/outside, and distance/proximity. Thus sex work, militarization, human rights, and so on can be framed in their multiple local and global dimensions using the One-Third/Two-Thirds, social minority/social majority paradigm, I am suggesting then that we look at the women's studies curriculum in its entirety and that we attempt to use a comparative feminist studies model wherever possible.[19]

I refer to this model as the feminist solidarity model because, besides its focus on mutuality and common interests, it requires one to formulate questions about connection and disconnection between activist women's movements around the world. Rather than formulating activism and agency in terms of discrete and disconnected cultures and nations, it allows us to frame agency and resistance across the borders of nation and culture. I think feminist pedagogy should not simply expose students to a particularized academic scholarship but that it should also envision the possibility of activism and struggle outside the academy. Political education through feminist pedagogy should teach active citizenship in such struggles for justice.

My recurring question is how pedagogies can supplement, consolidate, or resist the dominant logic of globalization. How do students learn about the inequities among women and men around the world? … I look to create pedagogies that allow students to see the complexities, singularities, and interconnections between communities of women such that power, privilege, agency, and dissent can be made visible and engaged with.

… Feminist pedagogies of internationalization need an adequate response to globalization. Both Eurocentric and cultural relativist (postmodernist) models of scholarship and teaching are easily assimilated within the logic of late capitalism because this is fundamentally a logic of seeming decentralization and accumulation of differences. What I call the comparative feminist studies/feminist solidarity model on the other hand potentially counters this logic by setting up a paradigm of historically and culturally specific "common differences" as the basis for analysis and solidarity. Feminist pedagogies of antiglobalization can tell alternate stories of difference, culture, power, and agency. They can begin to theorize experience, agency, and justice from a more cross-cultural lens.

After almost two decades of teaching feminist studies in U.S. classrooms, it is clear to me that the way we theorize experience, culture, and subjectivity in relation to histories, institutional practice, and collective struggles determines the kind of stories we tell in the classroom. If these varied stories are to be taught such that students learn to democratize rather than colonize the experiences of different spatially and temporally located communities of women, neither a Eurocentric nor a cultural pluralist curricular practice will do. In fact narratives of historical experience are crucial to political thinking not because they present an unmediated version of the "truth" but because they can destabilize received truths and locate debate in the complexities and contradictions of historical life. It is in this context that postpositivist realist theorizations of experience, identity, and culture become useful in constructing curricular and pedagogical narratives that address as well as combat globalization.[20] These realist theorizations explicitly link a historical materialist understanding of social location to the theorization of epistemic privilege and the construction of social identity, thus suggesting the complexities of the narratives of marginalized peoples in terms of relationality rather than separation. These are the kinds of stories we need to weave into a feminist solidarity pedagogical model.

Antiglobalization Scholarship and Movements

... I return to an earlier question: What are the concrete effects of global restructuring on the "real" raced, classed, national, sexual bodies of women in the academy, in workplaces, streets, households, cyberspaces, neighborhoods, prisons, and in social movements? And how do we recognize these gendered effects in movements against globalization? Some of the most complex analyses of the centrality of gender in understanding economic globalization attempt to link questions of subjectivity, agency, and identity with those of political economy and the state. ... And it draws on a number of disciplinary paradigms and political perspectives in making the case for the centrality of gender in processes of global restructuring, arguing that the reorganization of gender is part of the global strategy of capitalism. ...

... [W]hile girls and women are central to the labor of global capital, antiglobalization work does not seem to draw on feminist analysis or strategies. Thus, while I have argued that feminists need to be anticapitalists, I would now argue that antiglobalization activists and theorists also need to be feminists. Gender is ignored as a category of analysis and a basis for organizing in most of the antiglobalization movements, and anti-globalization (and anticapitalist critique) does not appear to be central to feminist organizing projects, especially in the First World/North. ...

If we look carefully at the focus of the antiglobalization movements, it's the bodies and labor of women and girls that constitute the heart of these struggles. For instance, in the environmental and ecological movements such as Chipko in India and indigenous movements against uranium mining and breast-milk contamination in the United States, women are not only among the leadership; their gendered and racialized bodies are the key to demystifying and combating the processes of recolonization put in place by corporate control of the environment. ... Similarly, in the anticorporate consumer movements and in the small farmer movements against agribusiness and the antisweatshop movements, it is women's labor and their bodies that are most affected as workers, farmers, and consumers/household nurturers.

Women have been in leadership roles in some of the cross-border alliances against corporate injustice. Thus, making gender, and women's bodies and labor visible, and theorizing this visibility as a process of articulating a more inclusive politics are crucial aspects of feminist anticapitalist critique. ...

On the other hand, many of the democratic practices and process-oriented aspects of feminism appear to be institutionalized into the decision-making processes of some of these movements. Thus the principles of nonhierarchy, democratic participation, and the notion of the personal being political all emerge in various ways in this antiglobal politics. Making gender and feminist agendas and projects explicit in such antiglobalization movements thus is a way of tracing a more accurate genealogy, as well as providing potentially more fertile ground for organizing. And of course, to articulate feminism within the framework of antiglobalization work is also to begin to challenge the unstated masculinism of this work. The critique and resistance to global capitalism, and uncovering of the naturalization of its masculinist and racist values, begin to build a transnational feminist practice.

A transnational feminist practice depends on building feminist solidarities across the divisions of place, identity, class, work, belief, and so on. In these very fragmented times it is both very difficult to build these alliances and also never more important to do so. Global capitalism both destroys the possibilities and also offers up new ones.

Feminist activist teachers must struggle with themselves and each other to open the world with all its complexity to their students. Given the new multiethnic racial student bodies, teachers must also learn from their students. The differences and borders of each of our identities connect us to each other, more than they sever. So the enterprise here is to forge informed, self-reflexive solidarities among ourselves.

I no longer live simply under the gaze of Western eyes. I also live inside it and negotiate it every day. I make my home in Ithaca, New York, but always as from Mumbai, India. My cross-race and cross-class work takes me to inter-connected places and communities around the world—to a struggle contextualized by women of color and of the Third World, sometimes located in the Two-Thirds World, sometimes in the One-Third. So the borders here are not really fixed. Our minds must be as ready to move as capital is, to trace its paths and to imagine alternative destinations.

Notes

1. "Under Western Eyes" has enjoyed a remarkable life, being reprinted almost every year since 1986 when it first appeared in the left journal *Boundary* 2. The essay has been translated into German, Dutch, Chinese, Russian, Italian, Swedish, French and Spanish. It has appeared in feminist, postcolonial, Third World, and cultural studies journals and anthologies and maintains a presence in women's studies, cultural studies, anthropology, ethnic studies, political science, education and sociology curricula. It has been widely cited, sometimes seriously engaged with, sometimes misread, and sometimes used as an enabling framework for cross-cultural feminist projects.
2. Thanks to Zillah Eisenstein for this discussion.
3. Here is how I defined "Western feminist" then: "Clearly Western feminist discourse and political practice is neither singular or homogeneous in its goals, interests, or analyses. However, it is possible to trace a coherence of effects resulting from the implicit assumption of 'the West' (in all its complexities and contradictions) as the primary referent in theory and praxis. My reference to 'Western feminism' is by no means intended to imply that it is a monolith. Rather, I am attempting to draw attention to the similar effects of various textual strategies used by writers which codify Others as non-Western and hence themselves as (implicitly) Western." I suggested then that while terms such as "First" and "Third World" were problematic in suggesting oversimplified similarities as well as flattening internal differences, I continued to use them because this was the terminology available to us then. I used the terms with full knowledge of their limitations, suggesting a critical and heuristic rather than nonquestioning use of the terms. I come back to these terms later in this chapter.
4. See for instance the reprinting and discussion of my work in Nicholson and Seidman 1995, Phillips 1998, Warhol and Herndal 1997; and Phillips 1998.

5. I have written with Jacqui Alexander about some of the effects of hegemonic postmodernism on feminist studies; see the introduction to Alexander and Mohanty 1997.

6. To further clarify my position—I am not against all postmodern insights or analytic strategies. I have found many postmodernist texts useful in my work. I tend to use whatever methodologies, theories, and insights I find illuminating in relation to the questions I want to examine—Marxist, postmodernist, postpositivist realist, and so on. What I want to do here, however, is take responsibility for making explicit some of the political choices I made at that time—and to identify the discursive hegemony of postmodernist thinking in the U.S. academy, which I believe forms the primary institutional context in which "Under Western Eyes" is read.

7. Dirlik, "The Local in the Global," in Dirlik 1997.

8. Esteva and Prakash (1998, 16–17) define these categorizations thus:: The "social minorities" are those groups in both the North and the South that share homogeneous ways of modern (Western) life all over the world. Usually, they adopt as their own the basic paradigms of modernity. They are also usually classified as the upper classes of every society: the so-called formal sector. The "social majorities" have no regular access to most of the goods and services defining the average "standard of living" in the industrial countries. Their definitions of "a good life," shaped by their local traditions, reflect their capacities to flourish outside the "help" offered by "global forces." Implicitly or explicitly they neither "need" nor are dependent on the bundle of "goods" promised by these forces. They, therefore, share a common freedom in their rejection of "global forces."

9. I am not saying that native feminists consider capitalism irrelevant to their struggles. ... The work of Winona LaDuke, Haunani-Kay Trask, and Anna Marie James Guerrero offers very powerful critiques of capitalism and the effects of its structural violence in the lives of native communities. See Guerrero 197; LaDuke 1999; and Trask 1999.

10. See, for instance, the work of Ella Shohat, Lisa Lowe, Aihwa Ong, Uma Narayan, Inderpal Grewal and Caren Kaplan, Chela Sandoval, Avtar Brah, Lila Abu-Lughod, Jacqui Alexander, Kamala Kempadoo, and Saskia Sassen.

11. See the works of Maria Mies, Cynthia Enloe, Zillah Eisenstein, Saskia Sassen, and Dorothy Smith ... for similar methodological approaches. An early, pioneering example of this perspective can be found in the "Black Feminist" statement by the Combahee River Collective in the early 1980s.

12. See discussions of epistemic privilege in the essays by Mohanty, Moya, and Macdonald in Moya and Hames-Garcia 2000.

13. See Shiva, Jafri, Bedi, and Halla-Bhar 1997. For a provocative argument about indigenous knowledges, see Dei and Sefa 2000.

14. In what follows, I use the terms "global capitalism," "global restructuring," and "globalization" interchangeably to refer to a process of corporate global economic, ideological, and cultural reorganization across the borders of nation-states.

15. While the initial push for "internationalization" of the curriculum in U.S. higher education came from the federal government's funding of area studies programs during the cold war, in the post-cold war period it is private foundations like the MacArthur, Rockefeller, and Ford foundations that have been instrumental in this endeavor—especially in relation to the women's studies curriculum.

16. Ella Shohat refers to this as the "sponge/additive" approach that extends U.S.-centered paradigms to "others" and produces a "homogeneous feminist master narrative." See Shohat 2001, 1269–72.

17. For an incisive critique of cultural relativism and its epistemological underpinnings see Mohanty 1997, chapter 5.

18. It is also important to examine and be cautious about the latent nationalism of race and ethnic studies and of women's and gay and lesbian studies in the United States.

19. A new anthology contains some good examples of what I am referring to as a feminist solidarity or comparative feminist studies model. See Lay, Monk, and Rosenfelt 2002.

20. See especially the work of Satya Mohanty, Paula Moya, Linda Alcoff, and Shari Stone-Mediatore.

49.

FROM HERE TO QUEER: RADICAL FEMINISM, POSTMODERNISM, AND THE LESBIAN MENACE (OR, WHY CAN'T A WOMAN BE MORE LIKE A FAG?)

Suzanna Danuta Walters

(1996)

Queer Defined (NOT!)

Already, in this opening, I am treading on thin ice: how to define that which exclaims—with postmodern cool—its absolute undefinability? …

Queer is, in true postmodern fashion, a rather amorphous term and still emergent enough as to be vague and ill defined. …

It is not only "queer" theory and politics that are typified by shifting icons and activisms; feminism and feminist theory are themselves the subject of much critical ʻrevision and rethinking, particularly in light of both structural shifts (changes in family life, increasing numbers of women in the workforce) and ideological developments (renewed media attacks on feminism, the backlash phenomenon, the rise of right-wing Christian antifeminism and "family values"). In addition, the development of queer theory and politics (related but not identical phenomena) emerges in the context of changing definitions of feminist theory and politics. From challenges by women of color, working-class feminists, lesbians, and others, feminism has been undergoing profound changes. These changes are marked by increasingly frequent criticisms of feminist theory's refusal to reckon with the ways in which "other" differences (such as race or class) mark themselves on the body and insert themselves into constructions of oppositional identity. In other words, queer developments take place within a changing field of theory and practice; feminism (and gender theory and politics generally) is no longer the young upstart but, rather, has achieved a certain "stature" that now has produced a deeper and more thoroughgoing level of critical analysis and revision.

Keeping this in mind, I want to examine the relationship between new queer developments and feminism and feminist theory, with a specific focus on the displacements of radical and lesbian feminism by a queer theory that often posits itself as the antidote to a "retrograde" feminist theorizing. Let me begin by laying my cards on the table: I am wary of this phenomenon.[1] These new developments are not wholly propitious for the (shared, I hope) goals of ending homophobia, confronting compulsory heterosexuality, liberating sexuality. Nevertheless (and I would hope this goes without saying, but

I will say it anyway), this critique should be taken as an immanent one, from someone who lives within the gay and lesbian movement and who believes the new queer politics and theory to be largely well intentioned, however misguided and theoretically suspect.[2]

While my criticisms stand, I am also aware of the real strengths and possibilities embodied in the new queer designations. The full exploration of sexual desire in all its complexity is of course an important move, particularly as a neglected aspect of progressive discourse. And the queer challenge to the notion of sexual identity as monolithic, obvious, and dichotomous is a healthy corrective to our vexing inability to see beyond the limitations of the homo/hetero opposition. In addition, the openness of the term *queer* seems to many to provide the possibility of theorizing "beyond the hyphen," beyond the additive models (race, class, gender, sexual orientation = oppressed identity) that have so often seemed to set up new hierarchies or retreated instead into an empty recitation of "difference." Indeed, race critiques have consistently insisted on challenging binary models of identity in the development of concepts of positionality and intersectionality. Queer discourse is clearly not "the enemy,"[3] but neither is it unambiguously the new hope for a theory and/or politics to lead us into the next century. But enough of those provisos, let us continue with definitions.

There are many, often conflicting, ways of using this term *queer*. It can, of course, be used in the old-fashioned way, as nasty epithet. This raises a not insignificant question around the value of "reclaiming" the negative language that has been used to oppress us. I cannot help wondering if I would ever march with a group calling itself "Kike Nation." Perhaps the analogy does not hold, but "reclaiming" (or "resignifying") is never a simple and straightforward matter, and the use of the term *queer* needs to reckon with the arguments (made, for example, by older civil rights activists over the current trendiness among African-American youth of the term *nigger)* against recirculating a language constructed in hate and bigotry. Indeed, even Judith Butler, one of the theorists most associated with the new queer theory, questions the "reappropriation" of the term *queer*, wondering if the term can "overcome its constitutive history of injury" (1993a, 223).

That aside, the term *queer* can be used, loosely, as a synonym for (trendy) gay and lesbian studies and even for gay/lesbian identity. So *queer* can, on many occasions, be a rather undeliberate way of referencing *gay* or *lesbian*. But this is not the usage I will be examining, as it is merely a replacement term for *homosexual* or *gay* or *lesbian*.

Rather, more important for us here, *queer* is used as a signifier of a new kind of "in your face" confrontational gay/lesbian politics (Queer Nation, etc.), particularly a politics around AIDS that brings together gay men and lesbians in a direct and powerful attempt to change policies. So *queer* in this usage would signify a politics and theory with a difference, typically a generational difference but also a (asserted) difference of style, of strategy, of tactics, of ideology. As Rosemary Hennessy puts it, "By embracing the category used to shame and cast out sexual deviants, queer theory defiantly refuses the terms of the dominant discourse. Touting queerness is a gesture of rebellion against the pressure to be invisible or apologetically abnormal. It is an in-your-face rejection of the proper response to heteronormativity, a version of acting up" (1993, 967).

Queer discourse is often understood as nonreformist, in opposition to the "mainstream" gay/lesbian movement, or, as Michael Warner argues, "no longer content to carve out a buffer zone for a minoritized and protected subculture [that] has begun to challenge the pervasive and often invisible heteronormativity of modern societies" (1991, 3). …

… "[I]t rejects a minoritizing logic of toleration or simple political interest-representation in favor of a more thorough resistance to regimes of the normal" (1991, 16). This is a common theme of queer theory, the move against the idea of gays and lesbians as an interest group, an oppressed minority, and toward a more universalizing (and dispersed) conception of queer as anti- or nonnormal. While I applaud the radicalism here—and the explicit admonition against a desire for mere "toleration"—I fear that this definition of queer, as much as it wants to leap the bounds of binarism, finds itself defined against what it is not, "normal." Jeff Nunokawa wonders whether "queer means the opposite of not queer, just as homosexual meant the opposite of heterosexual. Queer is supposedly the agent for destabilizing that kind of binarism—but *when*, and for *whom*, and what exactly do we mean? Do we mean something more than a kind of academic effort?" (1992, 28; emphasis in original). I will come back to this concern later.

Many have embraced the term *queer* as a concept that traverses gender as it steers away from it as definitional: *queer* as a term of sexuality, not a term of gender identity. …

For queer *theory*, in particular, this has been a central tenet, exemplified in the work of Eve Sedgwick and, in a different and more cautious way, Butler (Butler 1990, 1993b; Sedgwick 1989, 1990, 1991). Queer theory in this sense positions itself as challenge to the "obvious categories (man, woman, latina, jew, butch, femme), oppositions (man vs. woman, heterosexual vs. homosexual), or equations (gender = sex) upon which conventional notions of sexuality and identity rely" (Hennessy 1993, 964). As Sedgwick writes:

> Part of what is interesting about queer … is that it suggests possibilities for organizing around a fracturing of identity. … What I hear when I hear the word *queer* is … the calling into question of certain assumptions: that once you know somebody's chromosomal sex, you are supposed to know a whole list of other things about them—including their gender, their self-perceived gender, the gender people perceive them to be, the gender of the people they are attracted to, whether they define themselves as heterosexual or homosexual, their fantasy life—which is supposed to be the same thing but a little more intense—whom they identify with and learn from, what their communities are. What I hear in queer is the question: What things in that list don't line up monolithically? (1993, 27)

Here, Sedgwick articulates a definition of queer that locates its power in a particularly postmodern (and deliberately nonessentialist) context of fractured identities and incommensurableness. Queer, for her and for many others, tears apart the seemingly obvious relationships between sex and gender, sexual desire and object choice, sexual practices and political identities, and renders subjectivities infinitely in determinant.

We might say that this presents a paradox as queers in this reading (say, Sedgwick) are not defined by their sexual choice but, rather, by what? Some vague identification with perversion? Some feeling of nonnormalcy? A political affiliation? A desire to listen to/be/watch Ru Paul? …

Like the separation of sexuality and gender, the criticism of identity politics (and the dualisms that identity politics are seen to impose) seems to be at the heart of queer theory, particularly in its more postmodern manifestations. …

Nevertheless, queer theory, like most theoretical enterprises, is by no means a monolithic and unified field of ideas and practices. The writers I discuss in this article do not, of course, all hold the same beliefs or adhere to the same political traditions and commitments. Indeed, many have engaged in substantive critiques of each other. … Nevertheless, … theorists such as Sedgwick, Butler, Warner, and Gayle Rubin … I would argue … all, to a certain extent, share a problematic perspective on feminism and the women's movement and have engaged, in different ways of course, with gay male identity as the site of privileged subjectivity. …

Of most concern to me here are these last definitions, the ways in which the term *queer* is thought to signify a new kind of politics as well as a new kind of theorizing, a theorizing marked by the very openness that allows so many definitional possibilities. Now, many would argue that this indeterminacy—this inability to ascertain a precise definition and framework for the term *queer*—is precisely what gives it its power: *queer* is many things to many people, irreducible, undefinable, enigmatic, winking at us as it flouts convention: the perfect postmodern trope, a term for the times, the epitome of knowing ambiguity. Good-bye simulacra, adios panopticon, arrivederci lack, adieu jouissance: hello *queer*! But what is lost in this fun deconstruction of the cohesion of identity? If queer becomes the new reigning subjectivity for hip activists and intellectuals alike, what kinds of politics and theories then become "transcended"; moved through and over in the construction of the queer hegemony? It is precisely my concern over the implicit and explicit marginalization and demonization of feminism and lesbian-feminism embedded in this "transcendence" that provoked this article.

Homo Politicus, Homo Academicus

The growth of queer theory and queer politics must be placed in a social and political context. The most important pieces of this are, of course, the AIDS crisis, the rise of postmodern/poststructural theory, the politics of academia, the sex debates,[4] and recent critiques of feminism. …

As many writers have noted, the AIDS crisis not only prompted a renewed and reinvigorated gay and lesbian movement but radically opened up (or re-created) new ways of doing politics. Although this was surely not the first time gay men and women had worked together, … [i]t encouraged a rethinking of gay politics … So, we would want to recognize the specificity of queer politics as emerging with the crisis of AIDS and the development of groups such as ACT-UP and Queer Nation … (Duggan 1992, 15). In addition, *queer* has developed as a way to broaden the definitions, so that the movement can be more inclusive (e.g., bisexual, transgendered, etc.). "…So, it seems to me that queer includes within it a necessarily expansive impulse that allows us to think about potential differences within that rubric" (Harper, White, and Cerullo 1993, 30).

This has prompted no small amount of debate, as one might imagine. On what basis are these different "identities" (practices?) joined together under the heading *queer?* ... To link politically and theoretically around a "difference" from normative hetero-sexuality imposes a (false) unity around disparate practices and communities. Politically, of course, these different groups/practices do not necessarily share a progressive political agenda on sexuality; nonnormativity is hardly a banner around which to rally. However, for many writers and activists alike (inspired, perhaps, by Michel Foucault's work) regulation itself is the problem; the creation of norms is the fundamental act of repression. With this logic, any unifying of the nonnormative raises the political stakes around regulation and thus opens the door to liberatory moves.

If, as bisexual writer Elisabeth Däumer writes, these new moves liberate "the queer in all of us" (1992, 92), then what happens to any conception of oppositional identity? Does this move of inclusivity (and the challenge to notions of authentic identity that it entails) run the risk of setting up another (albeit grander) opposition? And does it end up in a sort of meaningless pluralism motivated only by a vague sense of dissent, as Lisa Duggan suggests: "The notion of a 'queer community' ... is often used to construct a collectivity no longer defined solely by the gender of its members' sexual partners. This new community is unified only by a shared dissent from the dominant organization of sex and gender" (1992, 20).

The eighties and early nineties have also witnessed the rise of postmodernism and poststructuralism in social theory: the demise of the "grand narratives"; a new suspicion of "identity politics" as constructing a potential hegemony around the identity "gay" or "lesbian" as if that necessarily supposed a unified and coherent subjectivity: gay person. Identity is critiqued here as supposing a unity, squeezing out difference, perpetuating binarisms and dichotomous formations, and bordering on (if not instantiating) essentialism. So postmodern theory challenges the idea of gay identity as expressing "true"—not constructed—gay sexuality.

Many feminists have produced trenchant critiques of postmodernism,[5] and even more find themselves (ourselves) in an admittedly ambiguous relation to the challenges offered by postmodern theorizing. While this is not the place to delve into *that* whole debate, suffice it to say that many feminists have been wary of the quick dismissal of "the subject" and political agency just when it seemed that women were getting around to acquiring some. The critique of identity so central to postmodern theorizing seems to many to place feminist activism in a political straitjacket, unable to move (because moving requires reliance on identity concepts that are themselves suspect), yet needing desperately to organize women precisely around those newly suspect categories. ...

Queer theory's relation to the politics and theorizing of racialized identities is no less fraught than its relation to feminism and feminist identities. It seems to me ... that lesbian and gay writers of color are expressing both optimism with the new queer designations as well as trepidation. The optimism is located in the queer dethroning of gender and the (possible) opening up of queerness to articulations of "otherness" beyond the gender divide. In other words, if queer can be seen to challenge successfully gender hegemony, then it can make both theoretical and political space for more substantive notions of multiplicity and intersectionality. However, queer can "de-race" the homosexual of color in much the same way "old-time" gay studies often has, effectively erasing the specificity of "raced" gay existence under a queer rubric in which whiteness is not problematized. … Gloria Anzaldúa makes a somewhat different point; she feels more affinity with *queer* as a term of more working-class and "deviant" etymology than what she sees as the historically white and middle-class origins of the designations *lesbian* and *gay*. Cherríe Moraga and Amber Hollibaugh have made a similar argument in their use of the phrase *queer lesbian*, stressing their embrace of the term for its difference from middle-class lesbian feminist identities (1983). Yet Anzaldúa also accuses white academics of co-opting the term *queer* and using it to construct "a false unifying umbrella which all 'queers' of all races, ethnicities and classes are shoved under" (1991, 250). …

The Case of the Disappearing Lesbian (or, Where the Boys Are)

My main critique of the new popularity of "queer" (theory and, less so, politics) is that it often (and once again) erases lesbian specificity and the enormous difference that gender makes, evacuates the importance of feminism, and rewrites the history of lesbian feminism and feminism generally. Now this is not to say that strongly identified lesbians have not embraced queer theory and politics, or that those who do so are somehow acting in bad faith or are "antifeminist." Indeed, what makes queer theory so exciting in part is the way in which so many different kinds of theorists have been attracted to its promise. Many lesbians (including myself) have been attracted to queer theory out of frustration with a feminism that, they believe, either subsumes lesbianism under the generic category woman or poses gender as the transcendent category of difference, thus making cross-gender gay alliances problematic. To a certain extent, I, too, share this excitement and embrace the queer move that can complicate an often too-easy feminist take on sexual identity that links lesbianism (in the worst-case scenario) to an almost primordial and timeless mother-bond or a hazy woman-identification. At the same time, however, I fear that many lesbians' engagement with queer theory is informed itself by a rudimentary and circumscribed (revisionist) history of feminism and gender-based theory that paints an unfair picture of feminism as rigid, homophobic, and sexless. …

The story, alluded to above, goes something like this: once upon a time there was this group of really boring ugly women who never had sex, walked a lot in the woods, read bad poetry about goddesses, wore flannel shirts, and hated men (even their gay brothers). They called themselves lesbians. Then, thankfully, along came these guys named Foucault, Derrida, and Lacan dressed in girls' clothes riding some very large white horses. They told these silly women that they were politically correct, rigid, frigid, sex-hating prudes who just did not GET IT—it was all a game anyway, all about words and images, all about mimicry and imitation, all a cacophony of signs leading back to nowhere. To have a politics around gender was silly, they were told, because gender was just a performance anyway, a costume one put on and, in drag performance, wore backward. And everyone knew boys were better at dress up.

So, queerness is theorized as somehow beyond gender, a vision of a sort of transcendent polymorphous perversity deconstructing as it slips from one desiring/desired object to the other. But this forgets the very real and felt experience of gender that women, particularly, live with quite explicitly. Indeed, one could argue that this is really the dividing line around different notions of queer; to what extent do theorists argue *queer* as a term beyond (or through) gender? "Where de Lauretis retains the categories 'gay' and 'lesbian' and some notion of gender division as parts of her discussion of what 'queerness' is (or might be), Judith Butler and Sue-Ellen Case have argued that queerness is something that is ultimately beyond gender—it is an attitude, a way of responding, that begins in a place not concerned with, or limited by, notions of a binary opposition of male and female or the homo versus hetero paradigm usually articulated as an extension of this gender binarism" (Doty 1993, xv). But, again, this seems to assume that feminists (or gays and lesbians) have somehow created these binarisms.

Unlike the terms *gay* and *lesbian*, *queer* is not gender specific, and this of course has been one of its selling points, as it purports to speak to the diversity of the gay and lesbian community and to dethrone gender as the significant marker of sexual identity and sexual expression. ...

... But in a culture in which male is the default gender, in which *homosexual* (a term that also does not specify gender) is all too often imaged as male, and *gay* as both, to see queer as somehow gender *neutral* is ludicrous and willfully naive. Feminism has taught us that the idea of gender neutrality is not only fictitious but a move of gender domination. I applaud queer theory's expansion of the concept of difference but am concerned that, too often, gender is not *complicated* but merely ignored, dismissed, or "transcended." In contradistinction, I would argue that the critique of gender theory from the perspective of women of color has done precisely what the queer critique of gender is only partially and incompletely able to do. In other words, gender in black feminist writing is not "transcended" or somehow deemed an "enemy" concept. Rather, the concept of gender—and feminist theory more generally—is complicated, expanded, deepened both to challenge its "privileged" status and to render it susceptible to theories of intersectionality and multiplicity. The queer critique of the feminist mantra of the separation of sex and gender (sex being the biological "raw material" and gender the socially constructed edifice that creates masculinity and femininity) is helpful in complicating what has become a somewhat rote recitation of social constructionist argument, an argument that too often leaves the body and its various constructions unexamined. But in the light of recently resurgent theories of biological determinism, ... the insistence on a righteous social constructionism (women are made, not born; we are not simply an expression of our biological makeup, etc.) might be important strategically and politically. Too often in these queer challenges to this dichotomy, sex becomes the grand force of excess that can offer more possibilities for liberatory culture, and gender the constraint on that which would (naturally?) flow freely and polymorphously if left to its own devices. Biddy Martin has made the argument that, for Sedgwick and others, race and gender often assume a fixity, a stability, a ground, whereas sexuality (typically thematized as male) becomes the "means of crossing" and the figure of mobility. In the process of making the female body the "drag" on the (male) play of sexuality, "the female body appears to become its own trap, and the operations of misogyny disappear from view" (Martin 1994, 104, 109–10).

But it is also not clear to me that this vision of a genderless nonnormativity is a worthwhile goal. Is a degendered idea of sexual identity/sexual desire what we strive for? Is this just a postmodern version of a liberal pluralist "if it feels good, do it" ethos? Also, the images/signifiers for this transcendence (of gender) are suspiciously male (why can't a woman be more like a fag?). If the phallus has been replaced by the dildo as the prime signifier of sexual transgression, of queerness, how far have we really come, so to speak?

Queer discourse sets up a universal (male) subject, or at least a universal gay male subject, as its implicit referent. (It is interesting to note in this regard that the 1993 summer special "Queer Issue" of the *Village Voice* was called "Faith Hope & Sodomy.") We cannot deny the centrality of gay maleness to this reconstruction of queer as radical practice. For example, Sue-Ellen Case discusses her engagement with the word *queer* by saying that "I became queer through my readerly identification with a male homosexual author" (1991, 1). ...

Although lesbians are occasionally mentioned (usually when speaking of S/M), gay men most assuredly have become the model for lesbian radical sex (e.g., the celebration of pornography, the "reappropriation" of the phallus in the fascination with the dildo, the "daddy" fantasies, and reverence for public sex of Pat Califia, etc.).[6] This has entailed a denigration of lesbian attempts to rethink sexuality within a feminist framework. Granted (and we do not need to go through this one more time), lesbian sexuality has suffered from both a discursive neglect and an idealization on the part of lesbians themselves. The image of hand-holding, eye-gazing, woodsy eroticism, however, is not wholly the creation of lesbians but part of the devaluation and stereotyping of all women's sexuality by male-dominant culture. Even in that haven of supposedly uptight, separatist nonsex (Northampton, Massachusetts, in the late 1970s and early 1980s), I seem to remember we were all doing the nasty fairly well, and, for all the talk of the "lesbian sex police," no girl ever banged down my door and stymied my sexual expression. The straight gaybashers, however, did. We should never forget this difference as we glibly use words like *police*.

... Do we really want to relinquish a critique of male identification? After all, the feminist insight that a central impediment to women's liberation (yes, liberation) is an identification with and dependence on males and male approval, desire, status, and so on is so obvious as to be banal. Charges of male identification may have been spuriously made at times, but the *analysis* of male identification is central and important.

The construction of an old, bad, exclusive, policing lesbian feminism is necessary for the "bad girl" (dildo in tow) to emerge as the knight in leather armor, ready to make the world safe for sexual democracy...

Even further, not only are those repressed and repressive lesbians responsible for putting a major damper on our nascent sexuality, but feminism itself is responsible for that horror of all horrors: THE BINARY. Bensinger indicts "the binaries generated within feminist movement: feminism/patriarchy, inside/outside, and porn/erotica" (1992, 88). Certain strands of feminism might indeed have perpetuated some of these oppositions (and is feminism *not* opposed to patriarchy?), but, alas, they long predate second-wave feminism. Seventies feminism here becomes the ogre that haunts queer kids of today. "By the seventies feminism had sanitized lesbianism. Lesbophobia forced lesbians to cling to feminism in an attempt to retain respectability. However, in the eighties, discussions of sadomasochism permanently altered the relationship of many lesbians to feminism" (Morgan 1993, 39). I would have hoped most politically astute lesbians (and gay men, for that matter) were/are feminists; this should be a theory we embrace (not "cling to") and, of course, transform and challenge in that embrace.

Many queer activists and theorists seem to believe the media fiction that feminism is either (*a*) dead because we lost or (*b*) dead because we won: "1988. So feminism is dead, or it has changed, or it is still meaningful to some of us but its political currency in the world is weak, its radical heart excised, its plodding middle-class moderation now an acceptable way of life. Feminism has been absorbed by the same generation that so proudly claims to reject it, and instead of women's liberation I hear, 'Long live the Queer nation!'" (Maggenti 1993, 250). As Whisman notes, "Today's 'bad girls' rebel as much against their feminist predecessors as against male power" (1993, 48). In her review of the *differences* issue on queer theory, Hennessy challenges those writers who set up feminism as the enemy, "substitut[ing] feminism (the Symbolic Mother) for patriarchy as the most notable oppressive force that lesbian sexual politics and eroticism must contend with. For feminists this should seem a very disturbing perspective shift, especially when feminism, among young people in particular, is more than ever a bad word" (1993, 969).

This is not to deny the importance of the "sex debates" and the new discussions around lesbian sexuality that, I agree, are long overdue. The open and volatile discussion of sexuality permanently altered feminist praxis and allowed for a complex debate around the politics of passion and desire that recognized that the simplistic rendering of women's sexuality was in need of major revision. And this is not to say that some lesbians, and some feminists, do not "judge" and indeed condemn sexual practices that they have deemed antithetical to the project of constructing a postpatriarchal world. This censuring is to be heartily contested, as it has from numerous writers and activists. But I simply suggest that we apply our own theories consistently: the narrative of "sexless uptight dykes of the 1970s" is, after all, a narrative, and as we have been so adept at deconstructing narrative for the relations of power that inhere in the telling of history, we should be equally able to "read" this story with, well, a grain of salt at the very least.

Now gay male sex and *its* histories become the very model of radical chic: the backroom replaces the consciousness-raising session as site of transformation. Feminist critiques of objectification, concern with abuse of women, and desire to construct non-patriarchal forms of intimacy become belittled and denigrated as so much prudery and "political correctness," creating an ahistorical narrative that furthers the separation of feminism from queer politics and theory.

... I fear, here, we have a real failure of imagination. Are lesbians unable to construct, envision, imagine, enact radical sexualities without relying so fundamentally on male paradigms? Must we look to the boys in the backroom as our Sapphic saviors? ...

And why this (theoretical) obsession with the question of whether to call oneself a lesbian? In an article for the gay and lesbian anthology *Inside/Out*, Butler (1991) spends several pages pondering this puzzle, an analogous puzzle to that posed recently by feminists about whether there really are "women" and whether our use of that category reinscribes its ability to construct us in power relations. Sure, to a certain extent, all categories are, as Butler and others have put it, "regulatory regimes"; but so what? ... All categories have rules, to be sure, but not all follow the same rules. The historical conditions of growing up "gay" or "lesbian" in a homophobic culture may, in fact, produce categories of identity that are more fluid, more flexible than the categories of other identities, such as heterosexuality. Why must we assume that all identities form around the same structural binarisms and with the same inherent rigidities? Is *that* not essentialist?

And does this difference not make a difference in how we "think" identity? When Butler says that she is "not at ease with 'lesbian theories, gay theories,'" referring to the title of the anthology, because "identity categories tend to be instruments of regulatory regimes, whether as the normalizing categories of oppressive structures or as the rallying points for a liberatory contestation of that very oppression" (1991, 13–14), does she not want to stress the difference between these two moments—the moment of oppression and the moment of liberation? Are those different uses of identity categories just the surface that belies the "deep meaning" of identity as "really" about "oppressive structures"? Or can we see these different uses and meanings of identity as radically different, not just somehow superficially different? Indeed, does it not actually sound a bit strange to speak of heterosexual identity (or WASP identity, etc.) and should that not indicate something about the differences in these two usages/meanings? This is not simply to argue that we need to adopt the terms *woman* or *lesbian* as a sort of "strategic essentialism" as has been argued elsewhere, but rather to say let us think this concept *lesbian* through the historical developments of lesbian desires, bodies, passions, struggles, politics. ...

Shane Phelan, writing in the *Signs* special issue on lesbianism, joins others in critiquing the prominence of the "coming out" process for lesbian identity, asserting that the language of "coming out" implies "a process of discovery or admission rather than one of construction or choice" (1993, 773), thus producing an essentialist notion of a "real" lesbian identity that exists beneath the layers of denial or hiding. But I am not sure coming out is as unitary and simple a process as these theorists make it out to be. Granted, for many it can be that sort of a revelatory move, revealing that which was "really there" but hidden all along. But for others, coming out is, first, not a moment but rather a contradictory and complex process that involves (perhaps) self-revelation, construction, political strategy, choice, and so forth. Second, it seems ludicrous to pretend that internalized homophobia and the realities of heterosexism and heterosexual privilege are not operative in and around these "coming out" processes. Phelan and others seem to write as if we "come out" in a social and political vacuum. Phelan cites

Barbara Ponse and Mark Blasius as arguing for a conception of coming out as a sort of "becoming," learning the ways of being gay or lesbian (Phelan 1993, 774). But, again, I do not see these as mutually exclusive. Of course "coming out" implies a becoming, a construction of the self as gay, now not "hidden" within the fiction of heterosexuality. But this "becoming" is, for so many, also merged with a profound sense of "revealing" a "truth" that one had previously "hidden." That truth might indeed be a fiction …, but it is a fiction that many live through and in quite deeply. …

… And what of our responsibility to others? If one less young person feels alone and vulnerable, one less colleague isolated and marginalized, is that not something—at the very least—to consider? …

I Cross-Dress, Therefore I Am

I worry about the centrality of drag and camp to queer signification.[7] … From "Chicks with Dicks" to Ru Paul to butch/femme bravado, crossing has become the metaphor of choice and the privileged sign of the new queer sensibility. As much as lesbians may now be "playing" with these signifiers (and given the reality that there are women who cross-dress, etc.), these are, after all, historically primarily male activities, particularly in the mode of public performance. In addition, "playing gender" for male drag queens or cross-dressers cannot, in a world marked by the power of gender within patriarchy, be the same for women. As much as we might intellectually want to talk about a more fluid and shifting continuum of both gender and sexual desire (and the separation of the two) we cannot afford to slip into a theory of gender as simply play and performance, a theory that, albeit attired in postmodern garb, appears too much like the old "sex roles" framework or even an Erving Goffman-type "presentation of self" paradigm. …

The concept of "performance" has dominated recent feminist theory as well as gay/lesbian/queer theory. Butler is obviously key here, as her work has come to signify a radical move in both theoretical arenas, and the notions of gender play and performance that she elaborates have found themselves the starting points for any number of new works in feminist theory and queer theory. I want to be careful not to simplify her complex and compelling contributions to these discussions. I think she is much more careful about theorizing "performance" than many others who have constructed a less nuanced analysis. Indeed, in *Bodies That Matter*, Butler sets out to clarify what she sees as a misconstrual of her stance on performativity, particularly when it comes to the question of drag. Just as she is explicit that the performance of gender is never a simple voluntary act (like choosing the clothes one puts on in the morning) and is always already constituted by the rules and histories of gender, she reiterates that ambiguity of drag, arguing carefully that "drag is not unproblematically subversive … [and] there is no guarantee that exposing the naturalized status of heterosexuality will lead to its subversion" (1993a, 231). Yet, provisos (as in "performance is never simply voluntaristic action") do little when the performances remain removed from a social and cultural context that either enables or disenables their radical enactment.

Clearly, cross-dressing, passing, and assorted tropes of postmodern delight are sexier, more fun, more inventive than previous discourses of identity and politics. Indeed,

I think the performance motif the perfect trope for our funky times, producing a sense of enticing activity amid the depressing ruins of late capitalism. ... [Y]et this hand can, and has, been overplayed. In particular, this trope becomes vacuous when it is decontextualized, bandied about as the new hope for a confused world. Theories of gender as play and performance need to be intimately and systematically connected with the *power* of gender (really, the power of *male* power) to constrain, control, violate, and configure. Too often, mere lip service is given to the specific historical, social, and political configurations that make certain conditions possible and others constrained. ... Without substantive engagement with complex sociopolitical realities, those performance tropes appear as entertaining but ultimately depoliticized academic exercises.

There is great insight and merit in understanding gender and sexual identity as processes, acquisitions, enactments, creations, processes (and Butler is right to credit Simone de Beauvoir with this profound insight), and Butler and others have done us a great service in elaborating the dissimulating possibilities of simulation. But this insight gets lost if it is not theorized with a deep understanding of the limitations and constraints within which we "perform" gender. And without some elaborated social and cultural context, this theory of performance is deeply ahistorical and, therefore, ironically (because postmodernism fashions itself as particularism par excellence) universalistic, avoiding a discussion of the contexts (race, class, ethnicity, etc.) that make particular "performances" more or less likely to be possible in the first place. It is not enough to assert that all performance of gender takes place within complex and specific regimes of power and domination; those regimes must be explicitly part of the analytic structure of the performance trope, rather than asides to be tossed around and then ignored.[8]

I worry, too, about the romanticization of the margins and of the outlaw that this emphasis on "gender bending" often accompanies. Rearranging the signs of gender too often becomes a substitute for challenging gender inequity. Wearing a dildo will not stop me from being raped as a woman or being harassed as a lesbian. And while donning the accoutrements of masculinity might make me feel more powerful, it will not, short of "passing," keep me out of the ghettos of female employment. This deconstruction of signs—this exploration of the fictitious and constructed nature of gender encoding and gender itself—must be a part of any radical gay politics, but if it *becomes* radical gay politics, we are in trouble. ... So, I have a concern here about queer political activism (and theory) degenerating into a self-styled rebel stance. It can again become a simple inversion (we're here, we're queer, get used to it), a reveling in our otherness, embracing it, claiming a "dirty" identity. Ironically, the rebel queer has also been touted by mainstream media: "Meanwhile, deviant sexualities are in cultural fashion. From the unexpected response to *The Crying Game* to the popularity of Dame Edna and Ru Paul ('Queen for a Day'), from the seemingly endless parade of cross-dressers, transgenderists, and drag queens on daytime television to the spate of films about to emerge from Hollywood ... it appears the culture is slanting queerly" (Doty 1993, 8). Nevertheless, the recent public fascination with queerness in no way implies an anti-homophobic move; indeed, it is often quite the opposite.[9]

Reading these tales of modern queer life reveals the obsessive focus on the self, the relentless narcissism and individualism of narratives of queer theory: "I pack a dildo, therefore I am." It is sort of like, let us make a theory from our own sexual practices (e.g., "I'm a cross-dressing femme who likes to use a dildo while watching gay male porn videos with my fuck buddy who sometimes likes to do it with gay men. Hmm, what kind of a theory can I make from that?"). But, in my reading, the notion of the "personal is political" did not mean let us construct a theory from individual personal experiences. Rather, there was some notion of collective experience, shared experience. So that, in the early consciousness-raising sessions, developing theories out of, say, the inconsistency of male leftists not doing any housework or child care grew, not only out of an individual's experience with "her man," but out of a real sense that this was a significant social problem and social reality. Now, it might be that drag, cross-dressing, S/M, and other assorted practices might have a collective basis, but that is certainly not how it is being addressed in most literature. Indeed, I am astounded at the extent to which the distinction between the social and the individual is constantly elided, resulting all too often in either a naive social-psychological view of the world or a narcissistic obsession with oneself *as* the world.

Now, I would be the last to decry experience, to want to rope it off, out of the reach of theory. Indeed, one of the strongest and most lasting aspects of feminist theorizing has been an adamant refusal to isolate personal narratives out of the reach of theory making. But I fear that much of this work is taking "the personal is political" in an unintended direction: my life, my personal story is theory: I am the world. In addition, I think these are personal stories *designed* to be outrageous, to articulate the author as inheritor of the mantle of Sadean dissidence.

Susie Bright, self-styled maven of sexy hipness and hip sexiness, has been a central figure in this new queer sensibility.[10] ... In a grand (and simplistic) reversal, Bright champions porn as the final frontier of liberated sexuality. While the porn and sex debates within feminism, for all their divisiveness and tendency to hyperbolize, did open up significant theoretical and political discussion for feminists, this new (uncritical) embrace of porn seems somewhat empty. Porn was once reviled, now it is celebrated; dildos were once tarred with the brush of hetero imitation, now they are lauded as the grooviest addition to sexual pleasure since the clitoris was "found." Strippers, hookers, and other sex workers were once pitied for the abuse they received at the hands of the patriarchy, now they are applauded as the heroines for a sex radical future. Butch/femme was once "understood" as the debased detritus of the force of the closet, now it is the very epitome of radical sexual politics. Once there was a vision of mutual, tender, nonhierarchical sex as the model of liberation, now the model of liberation is premised on power and conflict, theorized as "essential" to sexual desire. This reversal, this pendulum-like movement, is both counterproductive and reductive, setting up a new hierarchy of the sexual sophisticate versus the old-fashioned prude. Is pornography now to be unproblematic ally celebrated? Is the prostitute the heroine? Is using a dildo and doing butch/femme where it's at (and only at)? This move "pits renegade sex 'radicals' against their bad 'feminist' mothers and, in the process, simplifies the complexity of lesbian history, which was never quite as sexless as they make it out to be" (Stein 1993, 19). ...

So, our identities, then, are wholly encompassed by particular sexual acts, appetites, tastes, positions, postures. And those acts themselves are conceived as separate from the genders of the actors who do them, paving the way for a construction of the queer person as someone who performs certain kinds of sexual practices or has certain sorts of desires, regardless of the gender of themselves or their various partners. What we have here is then a new sort of sexual essentialism. Now no longer "known" by some self-defined unitary identity that encompasses sexual acts but perhaps moves beyond and through them, we are now known only by what we do sexually (and not at all by whom we do it with). Again, personal transgression or predilection has metamorphosed into political and theoretical action. Sexual hobbies do not a theory make.

From Queer to Where? Murmurs of Dissent

Fortunately, many feminists and lesbians are beginning to challenge the new politics of "gender play" and express concern both with a new commodification of gay life and an evacuation of substantive political concern with changing actual social relations of power and domination. I would note, too, that much of this criticism is coming from within "queer studies" itself and that this process of self-criticism bodes well for the future. Many writers express ambivalence about the trashing of lesbian feminism and recognize that "those things that are real dangers—random, vicious violence against women and gay men and people of color, the decimation of a generation from AIDS and complacency, the slow, sure destruction of the air and water and land, the misery of urban poverty, and the latest wars—weren't created by lesbian feminists. Increasingly, I wonder whether we take each other on because we've lost faith in our ability to fight the big fights" (Whisman 1993, 55). Whisman also speaks of the alliance between gay women and men: "Some may play around with men, but lesbian queers see themselves as more like gay men than straight women. New lesbians make their chief political and cultural alliances with gay men, arguing that lesbians and gay men are two sides of the same coin" (56). I think this alliance has important political and intellectual potential and must continue to grow and expand. But all too often, this alliance is forged at the expense of a deepening of feminist commitment. ...

Many are wary of the easy dismissal of feminism, as if "gender" was now a done deal and we needed to move on to a new discourse of sexuality: "It would be premature to dismiss the insights of feminism—of a gender-based perspective—in favor of a queer discourse which sets up universal, that is, male, subjects as its implicit referent. Lesbians and gay men have every reason to be suspicious of 'queerness' and its promise of an instant identity" (Kader and Piontek 1992, 9). The universalizing move of "queerness" also has the potential to make a similar argument about race, thus evacuating the specificities of racialized identities in favor of a queer universalism that claims multiracial status without ever seriously developing a race-based critique of heteronormativity. ...

Many others are wary of the term *queer* itself, as feminist, lesbian performance artist Holly Hughes ... (and others) points out the possibility that queer will, in its eagerness to universalize, actually serve to ignore or erase the embodied power of gender even as it claims to move beyond it. I think she expresses quite accurately the ambivalence many lesbians and gay men feel toward the term—an embrace of its confrontational stance, a joy in its refusal of assimilationist liberalism, while at the same time a discomfort with its too-easy gloss over gender and the implications of sexism and sexual violence (1992, 29).

Queer may hold out some possibilities for a politics and a theory that challenge the fixity and clarity of identity, that speak to the fractured (non)self of postmodern subjectivity. In addition, the queer encouragement of new alliances between gay men and lesbians can offer both new knowledges and the development of innovative political formations. And we should embrace its recognition that much slips out of the rigid distinctions of hetero/homo, man/woman and that our theoretical and political engagements need to reckon creatively with the excess that dares not speak its name. The queer attempt to understand that sexuality and sexual desire is not reducible to gender and also not simply explicable by reference to it is important. But while sexuality is not reducible to gender, it is also not possible to "think" without it. For even the lionized drag queen, gender exerts a powerful force, one (perhaps) to be challenged or deconstructed. ...

The inclusive, universalizing move of queer theory and politics appears laudatory, but it can all too easily degenerate into a "we are the world" pluralism that refuses to see the lines of power as they mark themselves on the lives of gendered, raced, ethnic subjects. The inclusive move (queer as anything/everything not irredeemably heterosexual) seems at first glance like a model of coalition politics, but all too often is more like a melting pot, where substantive structural and experiential differences are erased in the battle against the het (really, the *normative* het) enemy. And what of other enemies? And other allies? Is it possible that race, for example, gets erased (or rather commodified to the point of invisibility) when whites appropriate working-class (or poor) African-American drag queens as cutting-edge metaphors?[11] What happens, then, to a sustained and systematic analysis of the workings of a racist economy?

... Have we learned nothing about process and the transformative nature of true coalition building? Barbara Smith criticizes the contemporary movement for its lack of political radicalism and its refusal to deal systematically and substantively with issues of race and class: "When the word 'radical' is used at all, it means confrontational, 'in your face' tactics, not strategic organizing aimed at the roots of oppression. Unlike the early lesbian and gay movement, which had both ideological and practical links to the left, black activism and feminism, today's 'queer' politicos seem to operate in an historical and ideological vacuum. 'Queer' activists focus on 'queer' issues, and racism, sexual oppression and economic exploitation do not qualify, despite the fact that the majority of 'queers' are people of color, female or working class" (1993, 13). In other words, queer here can become a new, all-embracing designation that falls into many of the traps it purportedly sets out to avoid in positing "queerness" as some sort of postmodern *uber*-identity. What is to keep queer from instantiating the same old exclusions of race and class? Why are so many of the purveyors of queerness white, male (or gay male identified), and economically privileged? The real and substantive issues of inclusion and coalitional politics cannot be addressed simply by a new rhetoric that names itself all embracing and expansive. As Zita writes, "To construct a new field of queer studies without addressing misogyny, gender, male supremacy, race, and class as these are differently experienced by a wide diversity of female and male queers, is to seal the happy marriage of gay and lesbian studies with a Hallmark card and a Falwellian blessing" (1994, 271).

The "answer," such as it is, is surely not to dismiss queer theory altogether, as I think I have made clear throughout the course of this article. But the part of "queer" that hinges on a separation from feminism (both theory and politics) seems to me misguided at best. A more profitable direction might be the constant and creative renegotiation of the relationship between feminism and queer theory and politics, with the "goal" not being a severance but rather more meaningful and substantive ties. ... I think it needs reiterating that there can be no radical theory and surely no radical politics without feminism, however much that feminism might be rendered plural and reconfigured. This is nowhere more true than in recent right-wing rhetoric regarding "the family" and the scary discourse of family values. Here, a nuanced and subtle understanding of the ways in which both patriarchy and heterosexism construct the discourse and produce the politics would be fruitful. For example, in analyzing the attacks on lesbian and gay parents ..., we might develop frameworks of knowledge that explicitly address the mutual "concatenation" of both gender discourses and sexuality discourses. ... A feminist queer theory might focus more on the material realities of lives lived under patriarchal, capitalist, racist regimes, not as background or aside, but as the very stuff of a political and politicized analysis. ...

Or the relation between queer and feminism can also proceed on queer's own turf. If queer theory insists on the separation of sex and gender (the study of sexuality as distinct from the study of gender), then I would be interested in studies that affirmatively and persuasively demonstrate this new analytic strategy. In studying any particular configuration of sexualities, is it possible to be fully outside of an analysis of gender? The regimes of sexuality and gender are not identical, either historically or theoretically, but I remain skeptical of their premature separation. A substantive demonstration of this new queer analytic would be helpful.

With all the righteous rage and empowering spectacle of queer performative politics, it is important to remember that "genderfuck" and kiss-ins are necessary but not sufficient aspects of a progressive politics and theory. As a cultural theorist and educator, and longtime activist, I am more than aware of the power of the semiotic and of the absolute necessity to engage on the level of the image, particularly in a culture that is so thoroughly infused with representation. And, god knows, progressive politics has long suffered from a failure of imagination; the new queer politics adds much needed panache and wit to the seemingly interminable struggles for basic equity. Yet this is not enough, or, rather, it must always be coupled with a recognition that playing with gender may engage in destabilizing it somewhat but will not, in itself, stop the power' of gender—a power that still sends too many women to the hospital, shelter, rape crisis center, despair. We must ask how images, representations, performance, gender scripts relate to "broader" structures, contexts, economies, histories. ... Sexism, homophobia, racism activate themselves in multiple realms, but too often queer theory operates as if our oppression is solely a matter of sexuality and its representation and regulation. As I have argued elsewhere, we cannot afford to lose sight of the materiality of oppression and its operation in structural and institutional spaces.[12] Hennessy's recent piece, "Queer Visibility in Commodity Culture" (1994), is an exemplary attempt to hold on to the insights of queer while forcing an examination of the class-based discourses that construct the new queer visibilities. Hennessy forcefully demands that queer theorists pay more attention to the processes of commodification and avoid valorizing a politics of the outrageous at the expense of attending to the realities of structured social relations, relations not reducible to the discursive or cultural, although certainly not determinative of them either.

Destabilizing gender (or rendering its artifice apparent) is not the same as overthrowing it; indeed, in a culture in which drag queens can become the hottest fashion, commodification of resistance is an omnipresent threat. Moreover, a queer theory that posits feminism (or lesbian theory) as the transcended enemy is a queer that will really be a drag.

Notes

1. Let me note here, too, that I am most assuredly not alone in my critique of "queer." Indeed, feminists have already initiated a substantial body of work that takes issue with the construction of "queer theory" as the "replacement" for feminist and lesbian and gay studies. Often, but not always, these critiques of "queer" dovetail with critiques of postmodernism, as will be brought out in the course of this article. See particularly Modleski 1991; and Bordo 1990. Biddy Martin's work (1993, 1994) has been particularly helpful. Wilson's 1992 critique of bisexuality and de Lauretis's 1991 thoughtful introduction to the *differences* issue on queer theory have also added to the growing discourse.
2. I should note here that queer theory and queer politics are not, of course, identical. ... Nevertheless, the two are, as are most theories and practices, intimately connected, albeit often in an implicit manner. ... While I do not mean to conflate the two, I *am* interested in discussing the connections between them and the implications for a radical politics given these newer developments. ...
3. Indeed, one of my chief concerns here is the danger of "queer" being used to construct an enemy of feminism.
4. Briefly, the term *sex debates* is shorthand for a reinvigorated discussion of sexuality, power, pornography, and fantasy that was, to a large extent, sparked by the events surrounding the 1982 Barnard Conference "The Scholar and the Feminist." At this conference, "sex radical" feminists came into often angry confrontation with antipornography activists who attempted to censor the speech of conference participants. Thus began a long and complicated series of debates about feminism and sexuality that has produced both acrimony and meaningful scholarship. See particularly Vance 1984.
5. See particularly Hartsock 1983; Bordo 1990; Nicholson 1990; and Modleski 1991.
6. See particularly Creet 1991; Reich 1992; Hall 1993; and Roy 1993.
7. I will forgo here any substantive discussion of the long and complicated history of drag and camp (themselves not synonymous, of course) within the lesbian and gay movement. ...
8. Again, I would note here that Butler's most recent work seems to address, rather successfully, many of my concerns. Nevertheless, I still am concerned that much of the discussion around drag, performance, crossing, etc., remains deeply decontextualized or that the context seems to be solely a textual and representational one.
9. I am currently working on a book that addresses precisely these questions: "The Gay 90s: Media, Politics, and the Paradox of Visibility."

10. I am by no means conflating the work of someone like Bright with theorists such as Butler, Sedgwick, or Rubin. Indeed, however much I disagree with them, these theorists are complicated and surely sophisticated in their various analyses of gender, sexuality, and the anatomy of desire. Bright, while often entertaining, is certainly not in the same category.
11. See particularly Reid-Pharr 1993.
12. See Walters 1995.

50.
CHICANA FEMINISM AND POSTMODERNIST THEORY
Paula M. L. Moya
(2001)

Over the past decade, a growing number of feminists have challenged the view that post-modernism is the most productive theoretical framework for feminist discourse. Barbara Christian, in her 1987 essay "The Race for Theory," and bell hooks, in her 1991 essay "Essentialism and Experience," were among the first to express reservations about the usefulness of a poststructuralist-influenced literary theory for their own critical projects.[1] Other feminists followed close behind: as early as 1992, Linda Singer sounded cautionary warnings about the "regulative effect" that postmodernism seemed to be having on femi-nist theorizing, and in an explanatory note preceding her 1994 essay "Purity, Impurity, Separation," Maria Lugones made the point of dissociating her theoretical account of multiplicity from postmodernist theorizing of the same. Both Judith Roof, in her 1994 essay "Lesbians and Lyotard: Legitimation and the Politics of the Name," and Linda Mar-tin Alcoff, in her 1997 essay "The Politics of Postmodern Feminism, Revisited," urged feminists to recognize the epistemological denial apparent in postmodernist projects that rely on unacknowledged legitimating metanarratives to establish the "truth value" of no truth. Jacqui Alexander and Chandra Talpade Mohanty, in their 1997 introduction to *Feminist Genealogies, Colonial Legacies, Democratic Futures,* suggested that "postmodern-ist theory … has generated a series of epistemological confusions regarding the intercon-nections between location, identity, and the construction of knowledge" (xvii). …

There have been, of course, a number of different reactions to the predicaments of postmodernism that these critics have identified … [E]ven among feminists who have engaged seriously with postmodernist theory and who remain wary of positivist or idealist conceptions of objectivity and knowledge, a call for a new kind of theoretical "pragmatism" that attempts to avoid the normative deficits of postmodernist theory has emerged. … Even Judith Butler—whose earlier work can be held accountable for authorizing the wholesale dismissal by a generation of young feminist scholars of any feminist project that betrays a concern for "truth," "identity," "experience," or "knowl-edge"—has recently acknowledged that "in order to set political goals, it is necessary to assert normative judgements" (1995, 141). Of course, … Butler is careful not to ground her normative judgments in metaphysical commitments, preferring to base her politics of subversive citation and redeployment instead on a contingent "'foundation' that moves, and which changes in the course of that movement" (141).

One of the questions I pose in this article is whether a purely "pragmatist" feminist theory is sufficient for a liberatory feminism. By a pragmatist feminist theory, I mean one that refuses to make any objective metaphysical claims—even limited ones—about the nature either of the world or of human beings and that, consequently, must justify its normative claims in purely conventional or strategic terms.[2] By way of an answer, I suggest that, insofar as it tacitly presupposes the same positivist conception of objectivity and knowledge that serves as a strawperson for postmodernist theory, the kind of pragmatist feminist theory that these critics propose is inadequate for theorizing and authorizing effective progressive political movements. As part of an ongoing effort to reconceptualize (within post-positivist realist terms) concepts such as identity, experience, knowledge, and truth, this essay argues for the necessity of revisiting the problem of justification. I maintain that progressive feminist theorists need to acknowledge that some of our ethical and political goals might indeed be based on reliable, objective knowledge of ourselves and our world. Rather than refusing to ground our politics, we need to ask what grounds might, in fact, be worth defending.

These are the larger theoretical concerns and questions that have informed my thinking as I have explored the influence of postmodernism on Chicana feminist theory. In my quest to find the best available language for theorizing feminist—and particularly Chicana feminist—subjectivity and identity, I have examined … influential Chicana theorists whose work has been significantly shaped by, and has contributed to the shaping of, the "postmodern turn" … I have found that … Chicana theorists demonstrate an ambivalent relationship to postmodernist theory even as they accept many of its presuppositions and claims. … They appreciate its dismantling of the transcendental subject of reason, for instance, while remaining committed to an account of subjectivity that allows some form of identity-based (i.e., "Chicana" or "women-of-color") agency. Over the course of this article, I show that their attempts to theorize the experience and agency of Chicanas and other women of color are not supported by the postmodernist presuppositions they employ. … I argue that an alternative theoretical framework postpositivist realist—would better serve … attempts to analyze and theorize the situation of Chicanas. My purpose in foregrounding this alternative framework is to contribute substantively to ongoing feminist theoretical discussions of the status of truth, knowledge, and experience, as well as the political and epistemic salience of the concept of identity.

When I speak of postpositivist realism in this article, I am referring to an epistemological position and political vision being articulated by a growing number of scholars in the United States and abroad who are developing an alternative to the reductionism and inadequacy of essentialist and postmodernist approaches to identity.[3] Broadly speaking, to be a realist in a given domain is to believe in a reality that is, at least in part, causally independent of humans' mental constructions of it. Thus, while humans' (better or worse) understandings of their world may provide their only access to "reality," their conceptual or linguistic constructions of the world do not constitute the totality of what can be considered "real." Clearly, then, when realists say that something is "real," they do not mean that it is *not* socially constructed; rather, their point is that it is *not only* socially constructed. Moreover, while realists typically acknowledge that ideologies have constitutive effects on the social world such that "the world" is what it is at least partially because of the way humans interact with and understand it, they insist that reality is not exhausted by how any given individual or group perceives it ideologically. This is so, realists argue, for two reasons: first, because there are processes of the natural world that operate independent of the human mind and that both shape and limit humans' ability to "construct" or "produce" the world; and, second, because the sheer variety of conflicting ideologies in a global society such as ours precludes anyone ideology from "producing" the entirety of the social world.

Underlying postpositivist realist epistemology is a conception of objectivity that avoids the aporias of essentialist and (ironically) postmodernist epistemologies by opposing error not to certainty but rather to objectivity as a theory-dependent, socially realizable goal. Because realists view experience (and the knowledge humans glean from that experience) as mediated from the start, they are able to avoid the sharp opposition that structures much postmodern thought: that experience must be self-evidently meaningful or else it will be epistemically unreliable. By seeing experience as theory-mediated, realists understand that it can be a source of genuine knowledge as well as of social mystification; by seeing experience as causally related to the (social and natural) world, realists provide a way to evaluate the reliability of the knowledge that humans gain from their experiences. They propose that the truth of different theories about the world can be evaluated comparatively by assessing how accurately they refer to real features of the world.[4] In this view, because of the presence of ideological distortion, "objective knowledge is the product not of disinterested theoretical inquiry so much as of particular kinds of social practice"; it is thus context-sensitive and empirically based, while remaining valid across social and cultural contexts (Mohanty 1997, 213). I draw on this postpositivist conception of objectivity throughout the article in order to suggest alternatives to the recognizably postmodernist positions ... For example, ... I suggest that when truth claims are understood in a realist way as fallible and subject to verification and revision, they can contribute dialectically to the development of reliable knowledge about the world. By rethinking, from an alternative theoretical perspective, notions of agency and truth, I hope to reinvigorate theoretical discussions among Chicana and other feminists about the relationship between theory and practice, between intellectual inquiry and our ongoing attempts to transform ourselves and our world.

I begin the article with a necessarily brief overview of the historical context from which Chicana feminism emerged. By situating historically the kinds of questions being asked and problems being addressed within Chicana feminist theory, I hope to make the point that just as Chicanas' political activism and struggles are often based on a certain theoretical knowledge, that knowledge is frequently produced from their experiences of political struggle. So, although the work I focus on in this article can be seen as formal expressions of Chicana feminist theory, they are not the only, or necessarily the most important, places where the theoretical insights arrived at by Chicanas and other women of color originate or are formulated and expressed. In refusing to draw a firm distinction between Chicana feminism and Chicana feminist theory, I am following Satya Mohanty, Sandra Harding, and Richard Boyd in making the more general Marxian theoretical point that knowledge is produced not in isolation from the world but through engagement with it.[5] My second purpose in invoking the contexts of Chicana feminism is to acknowledge the degree to which my thinking has been significantly shaped by my Chicana foremothers. I have inherited certain kinds of intellectual questions and issues that would not have been available to me without the important work of some of the same activists/theorists with whose theoretical approaches I now take issue.

... I then turn ... to Sandoval's oft-cited 1991 essay "U.S. Third World Feminism: The Theory and Method of Oppositional Consciousness in the Postmodern World" to show both that Sandoval's postmodernist presuppositions partially undermine her project of theorizing the experiences of women of color and also that her most cogent insights are compatible with a postpositivist realist theory of identity. In the last section, I return to the question of whether a purely pragmatist feminist theory is sufficient for a liberatory feminist politics. I look to the writings of Chicana authors Cherríe Moraga and Gloria Anzaldúa for a more appropriate theoretical trajectory for the cultural critic concerned with representing the cultural productions and experiences of women of color. In that section, I examine Chicana identity from within a postpositivist realist theoretical framework, positing Chicana identity not as a principle of abstract oppositionality but as a historically and materially grounded perspective from which feminists can work to disclose the complicated workings of oppression and resistance.

The Emergence of Chicana Feminism

As a distinct social movement, Chicana feminism emerged primarily in response to the sexism Chicanas experienced within the Chicano civil rights movement.[6] Together with their fathers, husbands, and brothers, Chicana civil rights workers of the 1960s and 1970s were engaged in a struggle against the various forms of oppression and discrimination that their Chicana/o communities had historically experienced. ... They struggled for better working conditions and attacked racial and sexual stereotypes, frequently articulating the connections between the discrimination they faced as women, as workers, and as members of a racial minority group.[7] Nevertheless, Chicanas in the Chicano movement were disturbed when the rights for which they were fighting continued to be unfairly distributed along gender lines within their own communities. Accordingly, throughout the 1970s Chicanas became increasingly vocal about their dissatisfaction at being expected to defer to and serve their Chicano brothers while being expected to perform a disproportionate share of the work required for successful political organizing.[8]

Despite their commitment to *la causa*, it became increasingly apparent to Chicana feminists that their interest in achieving gender equality within the Chicano community stood in opposition to a discourse of nationalism that emphasized the value of family loyalty in the project of cultural survival. In response to what they perceived as cultural genocide, Chicano cultural nationalists had self-consciously taken up a series of Mexican cultural icons in order to project an alternative, and more affirming, Mexicano/Chicano cultural reality. Among these were three female icons—La Virgen de Guadalupe, La Malinche, and La Llorona—which, taken together, shaped the boundaries of traditional Chicana womanhood. Partly because of the imagined links, symbolically conveyed by these three icons, between female sexual abnegation and cultural fidelity and between female sexual desire and cultural betrayal, attacks by Chicano nationalists on Chicanas who refused to toe the party line were often couched in terms of sexuality. … As the designated reproducers of culture, Chicanas in the movement were under greater pressure to conform to more traditional models of conduct than were men. Thus, Chicana feminists were trying to break out of traditional roles as biological and cultural reproducers at the exact moment that Chicano nationalists were attempting to reinscribe them into those roles. … As a result, the earliest expressions of what would come to constitute the origins of Chicana feminism were initially presented as intra-mural criticisms designed to strengthen *el movimiento.* Chicana critiques of "macho" attitudes were thus presented as contributions to an ideological self-critique, and Chicana struggles against gender oppression were undertaken in the service of destroying "a serious obstacle to women anxious to play a role in the struggle for Chicano liberation" (Vidal 1997, 23).[9]

Although most Chicanas placed their primary energies in the service of the Chicano movement, some began in the late 1970s to work within white women's liberation movements. But long-term coalitions never developed, largely because most white women could not or would not recognize the class and race biases inherent in the structures of their own organizations. Furthermore, white feminists often replicated, in another realm, the same kind of privileging of one form of oppression over another that had frustrated Chicanas in relation to movement Chicanos. … Consequently, in the 1980s, Chicana feminists, together with feminists of other nonwhite racial groups who had had similar experiences within their own ethnic nationalist movements, turned to their own experience as a ground for theorizing their multiple forms of oppression. In the process, a new political identity—women of color—emerged. Chicanas joined African American, Asian American, Latina, and other "third-world" feminists in a variety of efforts to challenge both the racism of Anglo American feminism and the sexism of ethnic nationalist movements. … The important development of a women-of-color identity and politics, which was seen as supplementing but not replacing a Chicana identity and politics, allowed Chicana feminists to engage in coalitional politics even as they retained at the center of their politics an analysis of the interrelationship of race, class, gender, and sexuality in explaining the particular conditions of their lives in the United States.[10] …

Epistemological Denial in Sandoval's Theory Of Differential Consciousness

In her essay "U.S. Third World Feminism: The Theory and Method of Oppositional Consciousness in the Postmodern World" (1991), Chela Sandoval draws on the work of writers such as Moraga, Lugones, Audre Lorde, Bernice Johnson Reagon, and Anzaldúa to describe what she sees as a previously unrecognized kind of postmodern consciousness and political practice employed by U.S. third-world feminists.[11] To lay the groundwork for her argument, Sandoval proposes a topography of "oppositional consciousness" onto which all forms of oppositional thought and activity can be mapped.

She identifies five general oppositional sites, each of which presupposes its own political program: equal rights, revolutionary, supremacist, separatist, and differential. Sandoval is careful to note that these sites of resistance are not temporally situated, and she suggests that each position is potentially as effective as any other. However, she privileges differential consciousness over the others because she locates it on another register altogether. Whereas equal rights, revolutionary, supremacist, and separatist modes of consciousness and resistance imply coherent ideologies with fixed political programs, differential consciousness involves switching among the other four sites as the conditions of oppression or the shape of power changes. Its value, according to Sandoval, lies in its practitioners' unique ability to respond to the rapidly changing conditions of the postmodern world.

Differential consciousness, Sandoval argues, implies a new kind of subjectivity developed under conditions of multiple oppression. This new subjectivity, kinetic and self-consciously mobile, manifests itself in the political practices of U.S. third-world feminists. ... As a result of having to continually privilege or de-emphasize different aspects of themselves in different situations, Sandoval says, U.S. third-world feminists have become practiced at shifting their ideologies and identities in response to different configurations of power.

> Differential consciousness requires grace, flexibility, and strength: enough strength to confidently commit to a well-defined structure of identity for one hour, day, week, month, year; enough flexibility to self-consciously transform that identity according to the requisites of another oppositional ideological tactic if readings of power's formation require it; enough grace to recognize alliance with others committed to egalitarian social relations and race, gender, and class justice, when their readings of power call for alternative oppositional stands. ... As the clutch of a car provides the driver the ability to shift gears, differential consciousness permits the practitioner to choose tactical positions, that is, to self-consciously break and reform ties to ideology, activities which are imperative for the psychological and political practices that permit the achievement of coalition across differences. (1991, 15)

... Sandoval suggests that, as a result of a shift in the cultural logic of contemporary capitalism, differential consciousness—which hitherto was enacted almost exclusively by U.S. third world feminists—is now available to "all first world citizens" (1991, 22, n. 50). She explains: "The praxis of U.S. third world feminism represented by the differential form of oppositional consciousness is threaded throughout the experience of social marginality. As such, it is also being woven into the fabric of experiences belonging to more and more citizens who are caught in the crisis of late capitalist conditions and expressed in the cultural angst most often referred to as the postmodern dilemma" (17). Sandoval thus sees U.S. third-world feminists as having generated a "common speech, a theoretical structure" that "provides access to a different way of conceptualizing not only U.S. feminist consciousness but oppositional activity in general" (1). Her theory demands a "new subjectivity, a political revision that denies anyone ideology as the final answer, while instead positing a *tactical subjectivity* with the capacity to recenter depending upon the kinds of oppression to be confronted" (14). ...

The beautiful audacity of Sandoval's project is precisely this: the heretofore lowly and despised U.S. third-world feminist is at the forefront political and theoretical—of present-day progressive politics.[12] All oppositional others must now follow the U.S. third-world feminist into the realm of differential consciousness, for its enactment is *"imperative* for the psychological and political practices that permit the achievement of coalition across difference" (1991, 15; emphasis added). ...

At this point, I want to step back from Sandoval's argument to highlight the elements of it that derive specifically from a postmodernist theoretical framework. Her work, I maintain, is a blend of realist insights and postmodernist assumptions. Her most cogent insights are compatible with the kind of realist framework I propose, but her postmodernist presuppositions unnecessarily limit her project of apprehending and representing the experiences of women of color.

Sandoval's first postmodernist assumption, that identities are radically unstable, predisposes her to see shifts in behavior, or changes in emphasis, as shifts in identity. A working-class mother of Mexican heritage who invests her sexual and erotic energy primarily in other women may present herself as a "Chicana" in one context, a "woman of color" in another, a "mother" in a third, a "lesbian" in a fourth, and a "worker" in a fifth. In each context, she highlights different aspects of her social identity, and, as a result, names herself differently. According to Sandoval's theory of differential consciousness, she undergoes several successive shifts in identity. A realist theory of identity, by contrast, would acknowledge that different aspects of the woman's social identity become more and less visible in different situations but would see that identity itself as more or less constant over the course of her movements.[13] It should be noted that throughout Sandoval's argument, U.S. third-world feminists remain U.S. third-world feminists. In the course of enacting differential consciousness, they do not become white men, or white women, or children, or non-feminists. They may privilege one or more aspects of their identity (gender, sexuality, race, class) over others at various times and in various situations, but they do not in fact "shift" their relatively stable social identities.[14] ...

Furthermore, I disagree with Sandoval's contention that practitioners of differential consciousness shift ideologies. The measure of self-consciousness that Sandoval attributes to U.S. third-world feminist political agents precludes that possibility. If, as she intimates, U.S. third-world feminists are perfectly self-conscious about what they are doing—if they know that their alliance with anyone group is strategic and temporary—then they are working from within an ideology of flux and cannot be said to be shifting ideologies. As Sandoval herself describes it, differential consciousness implies its own overriding ideology. Its practitioner participates in the activities implied by the other four oppositional sites, but she remains aloof to their ideologies, refusing to adopt their "fervid belief systems" because the overriding differential ideology denies any other ideology "as the final answer" (1991, 13–14). Thus, she remains committed to an ideology of flux and, by refusing "anyone ideology as the final answer," paradoxically participates in a denial of her own particular conception of truth.

Sandoval's own epistemological denial shows up in her statement that any "drive for truth ... can only end in producing its own brand of dominations" (1991, 14).[15]

With this statement, Sandoval exhibits a readiness characteristic of postmodernist theoretical projects—to attribute oppressive motivations or effects to any project associated with a quest for truth or the acquisition of knowledge. Postmodernist theorists typically deride epistemological projects by suggesting that anyone who wishes to avoid acting in an oppressive way will suspend judgment and refuse to decide among competing narratives about the world. Their logic proceeds something like this: everything we know about the world—including what can be considered true, beautiful, good, and right—comes to us through the distorting lens of ideology conditioned by the particular cultural and/or linguistic universe in which we exist. Because we have no unmediated access to the world, we will always be uncertain about whether or not our conception of truth, beauty, good, and right is true for everyone—particularly those cultural "others" who do not share our linguistic universe—and not just for us. Because we cannot know for sure that we are right, and because the difference between "us" and "them" appears to be "incommensurable;' we must refuse to impose "our" beliefs on "them" so as to avoid participating in colonizing, globalizing, and totalizing projects. The relativist stance I have just described appears to be an ethical one, but as many critics have pointed out, the logic on which it is based is fundamentally flawed. Judith Roof, for instance, notes that an analysis predicated on the "loss of metanarrative relies upon an unrecognized legitimating metanarrative that establishes the 'truth value' of no truth" (1994, 59). ... One metanarrative is thus replaced by another; one conception of truth is dismissed in favor of one that cannot be acknowledged.[16]

Sandoval, like every other theorist who makes an argument (postmodernist or not), draws on a specific conception of truth in order to criticize other accounts. ... I am not suggesting that Sandoval's claims and judgments arc wrong and should be abandoned, I am saying that they should be acknowledged for what they are—namely, truth claims and value judgments. Sandoval presents her claims and judgments in such a way as to suggest that they have the status of truth; her argument presumes that what she is saying is so not only for her, but for everyone. If it were not, Sandoval would have no grounds for her injunction that others (non-U.S. third-world feminists) *must* follow the U.S. third-world feminist into the realm of differential consciousness.

Despite her commitment to postmodernism, Sandoval offers some cogent insights that help reveal the theoretical and political value of U.S. third-world feminism. As Sandoval asserts, there is indeed a specific social movement—which she calls U.S. third-world feminism but which is more commonly thought of now as women-of-color feminism—whose characteristic feature is the capacity to form coalitions across difference. Moreover, she is perspicacious in her observation that the ability of women of color to work across difference (together with the underlying theoretical and political achievements implied by that ability) puts them at the forefront of present-day progressive politics. As the world's disparate economics become increasingly linked through the circuits of global capitalism, and as previously distant societies are brought closer together by rapidly developing technological advances in both communications and travel, the earth's citizens are more frequently confronted with their own and others' "otherness." As it becomes increasingly difficult for different kinds of people to remain separate, it becomes more and more important for everyone to learn the skills involved in acknowledging, negotiating, accommodating, celebrating, and, in some cases, transcending difference. As Sandoval demonstrates, women of color, for some time now, have been perfecting these very skills. And, as she proposes, they have generated knowledge out of the experiences they have had with forming coalitions across difference. It is this knowledge and these skills that women of color have to offer a world that is only now coming to grips with the fact that confronting difference entails changing the "self" as much as it involves colonizing the "other."

Theorizing Women-of-Color Identity: A Realist Reading of *La Facultad*

At this point I want to propose what I think is a more appropriate trajectory for the feminist critic concerned with theorizing the cultural productions and experiences of Chicanas and other women of color. Realists argue that a crucial task of the cultural critic is to attend to the links between social location and identity by theorizing the process of identity formation. … According to the realist theory of identity, identities are politically and epistemically significant because they can trace the links between individuals and groups and the central organizing principles of a society. Consequently, theorizing the process of identity formation can reveal the complicated workings of ideology and oppression. This task, however, requires a conception of identity that can account for the epistemic status—in terms of enlightenment *and* mystification—of identities. I approach this task by sketching out some basic premises of the postpositivist realist theory of identity before re-examining some of Sandoval's claims regarding the theoretical and political practices of women of color; I will end by providing a postpositivist realist account of those practices.

The most basic claim of the postpositivist realist theory of identity is that identities are both constructed and real: identities are constructed because they are based on interpreted experience and on theories that explain the social and natural world, but they are also real because they refer outward to causally significant features of the world. Identities are thus context-specific ideological constructs, even though they may refer in non-arbitrary ways to verifiable characteristics such as skin color, physiognomy, anatomical sex, and socioeconomic status. Because identities refer—sometimes in partial and inaccurate ways—to the changing but relatively stable contexts from which they emerge, they are neither self-evident, immutable, and essential nor are they radically unstable or arbitrary. Rather, they are socially significant constructs that become intelligible from within specific historical and material contexts.[17]

According to the realist theory, an individual's identity, experience, and knowledge are inextricably connected. This conclusion is based on the premises that an individual's social location (the particular nexus of race, class, gender, and sexuality in which she exists in the world) is causally relevant for the experiences she will have and that an individual's experiences will influence, although not determine, the formation of her social identity.[18] Because identities are, in part, theoretically mediated constructions that refer outward to the societies from which they emerge, they provide their bearers with particular perspectives on the world. As such, identities provide people with frameworks (the epistemic value of which varies widely) for interpreting their

experiences. In other words, a person's interpretation of an event will be at least partially dependent for its meaning on her self-conception—her understanding of her particular relation to the people and happenings surrounding that event.

A key postpositivist realist insight is that the epistemic status of different identities
can be evaluated by seeing how well they work as explanations or descriptions of the
social and natural world from which they emerge, by how well they "refer" to verifiable
aspects of the world they claim to describe. To the extent that identities do not work
well as explanations of the world—to the extent that they fail to "refer" adequately to
the societies from which they emerge—they can help to reveal the contradictions and
mystifications with which the members of those societies live.[19]

I turn back now to a consideration of Sandoval's arguments in order to show
how her postmodernist presuppositions partially undermine her realist insights. If we
look carefully, it is clear that the differential consciousness she describes is thoroughly
grounded in a specific type of consciousness that she understands as being common
to women of color. Quoting Moraga, she asserts that women of color have learned to
"measure and weigh what is to be said and when, what is to be done and how, and to
whom, … daily deciding/risking who it is we can call an ally, call a friend (whatever that
person's skin, sex, or sexuality)" (Sandoval 1991, 15; Moraga 1983c, xvii–xix). Here
Sandoval is referring to the experientially acquired knowledge that manifests itself
in the "survival tactic" described by Anzaldúa as *la facultad*, a skill that is developed
by marginalized people whose well-being is often dependent on the good will of others (Anzaldúa 1987, 38). Anzaldúa describes it variously as a "vestige of a proximity
sense," an "acute awareness mediated by the part of the psyche that does not speak,"
and a "shift in perception" honed by pain and developed most readily by "those who
do not feel psychologically or physically safe in the world" (38–39). As a survival skill,
la facultad allows such people to adjust quickly and gracefully to changing (and often
threatening) circumstances. With origins in experiences of pain and trauma, *la facultad*
involves a loss of innocence and an initiation into an awareness of discrimination, fear,
depression, illness, and death.

Perhaps in an effort to avoid charges of essentialism, Sandoval abstracts the experientially acquired knowledge and consciousness of women of color in order to make
it accessible to "all people" (1991, 23, n. 58). In order to do this, however, she must
weaken the links between social location, experiences of oppression, and the development of differential consciousness. … In the process, she covers over the pain involved
in Anzaldúa's account of the development of *la facultad* and presents an idealized por-
trait of the mobile subjectivity she sees as characteristic of differential consciousness:

> … In order for this survival skill to provide the basis for a differential and unifying method-
> ology, it must be remembered that la facultad is a process. Answers may be only temporarily
> effective, so that wedded to the process of la facultad is a flexibility that continually woos
> change. (Sandoval 1991, 22–23, n. 57)

Thus, Sandoval sees *la facultad* as the basis for the differential methodology she promotes. Moreover, she views the mode of behavior that characterizes *la facultad* as being

consistent with that of differential consciousness: both involve a "*tactical subjectivity with the capacity to recenter depending upon the kinds of oppression to be confronted*" (1991, 14).

Analyzing *la facultad* within a postpositivist realist framework rather than a postmodernist one allows us to acknowledge its non-essential nature and its epistemic significance without either severing the ties between social location, experience, and identity or idealizing *la facultad's* knowledge-generating potential. The postpositivist realist would readily agree that *la facultad* is not "determined by race, sex, or any other genetic status" and that there are marginalized individuals who do not develop *la facultad*. Similarly, she would concede that the skill does not "belong" to the "proletariat," the "feminist," or "*the oppressed, if the oppressed is considered a unitary category*" (Sandoval 1991, 23; emphasis added). Furthermore, the realist would agree with Sandoval that it would be a mistake to consider "the oppressed" as a unitary (and, by implication, essential) category. Her reasons for reaching this conclusion, however, would be different from Sandoval's. Unlike Sandoval, whose postmodernist presuppositions lead her to weaken the links among identity, experience, and social location so as to avoid the inference that they have any kind of essential connection, the realist would insist on the inextricable—but complex and variable—connections among them. The realist would point out that when we do not consider the oppressed as a unitary category—when we take into account the multiple determinations and the theory-mediated formation of social identity—we can still identify non-arbitrary experiential connections between being oppressed and developing *la facultad*. Furthermore, the realist would be wary of idealizing the knowledge-generating component of *la facultad*. Because an awareness of oppression or pain may lead to survival tactics that do not necessarily explain the world's social, political, and economic workings, the realist would be reluctant to use *la facultad* as the basis for a new feminist epistemology. As I will illustrate in an example taken from Moraga later in this essay, feelings of fear and alienation are not, in themselves, sufficient for an adequate understanding of one's social, political, and economic situation.

I should emphasize that, unlike the "ideal" postmodernist I am positing, Sandoval does not completely deny the connections among identity, experience, and social location. Nevertheless, she weakens them by minimizing the differences between the experiences of multiply oppressed people (such as nonwhite women) and "all first world citizens" caught in the crisis of late capitalism (see 17, 22, n. 50; 23, n. 58). Her refusal to take a firm stand regarding the role of multiple oppression in the development of *la facultad* makes her work susceptible to critiques such as mine. My point is that just as we want to avoid making the connections too secure, so we should avoid making them too elastic. Only by conducting a careful examination of how, when, and under what conditions *la facultad* develops—using the methodology and epistemology provided by a postpositivist realist theory of identity—will we be able to understand adequately the latent epistemic privilege of the oppressed.[20]

So, while I agree with Sandoval that women of color both develop and display the intuitive capabilities of the kind described by Moraga and named by Anzaldúa, I disagree with Sandoval's implication that the knowledge and skills acquired by women of color can be arrived at, in any sort of willful way, by people who do not share their social locations. Being multiply oppressed is a necessary—although not sufficient—condition for developing *la facultad*. Two realist premises are most relevant here: (1) as long as our world is hierarchically organized along enduring relations of domination, people occupying different social locations will tend to experience the world in systematically different ways; and (2) not everyone who has the same kind of experience will react in the same way or come to the same conclusions about that experience. Taken together, these two realist assumptions allow the claim that some people are better situated than others to develop *la facultad*, without falling into the essentialist trap of assuming a determinative relationship between social location and consciousness. ...

Within a realist framework, oppositional ideologies (and the identities they engender) are more than sites of political and theoretical resistance to be pragmatically or strategically occupied or abandoned. Rather, they are the ways individuals or groups perceive, interpret, and interact with the world around them. Thus, a change in ideology or identity can represent a movement toward a better (or worse) understanding of the social world. To the extent that the ideological framework through which a person views the world adequately explains that world's social, political, and economic workings, or to the extent that the identity she claims accurately describes the complex interactions between the multiple determinants of her particular social location, that ideology or identity will be epistemically (not just strategically) justified—it will constitute "objective" and reliable knowledge. Whether an identity has more (or less) epistemic value than a previous ideology or identity is not something that can be determined in advance; ideologies and identities must be compared with other (competing) ideologies and identities, evaluated for logical consistency, and tested empirically against the world they claim to describe. Thus, the realist claim is not that humans are always successful in their efforts to make successive approximations toward the truth but just that they *can* be.[21]

Let me illustrate the realist theoretical point I am making. As fallible human beings with no immediate access to the world, women of color have been as subject to mystification and error as anyone else. Consequently, ... some women who now identify as women of color may have participated in gender-based political movements without fully understanding that such organizations systematically neglected the race and class interests central to the lives of most nonwhite women. Cherríe Moraga is a case in point. During her participation in the women's movement of the 1970s and prior to her identification as a woman of color, she was not initially conscious that she was neglecting those interests. The realization came to her gradually, and manifested itself, at first, in discomfort—in the sense that something was missing, something was wrong. In the preface to *This Bridge Called My Back*, she recounts her coming to consciousness as a woman of color:

> A few days ago, an old friend said to me how when she first met me, I seemed so white to her. I said in honesty, I used to feel more white. You know, I really did. But at the meeting last night, dealing with white women here on this trip, I have felt so very dark: dark with anger, with silence, with the feeling of being walked over.

> I wrote in my journal: "My growing consciousness as a woman of color is surely seeming to transform my experience. How could it be that the more I feel with other women of color, the more I feel myself Chicana, the more susceptible I am to racist attack!" (Moraga 1983c, xv)

Here Moraga describes a growing awareness of her difference from white women. In the process of interacting with them, Moraga learns more about herself; she reconnects with the racialized aspect of her identity that she had previously denied. Her "transformation of experience" is thus a consequence of her reinterpretation of the things that happen/have happened to her in light of her new (and more accurate) perspective on the social world within which those experiences have meaning. Importantly, Moraga does not merely *choose* to be a woman of color, nor does she mentally *construct* the racialized aspect of her heritage (her Mexican ancestry) on the basis of which she identifies as a woman of color. Of course, inasmuch as the identity "woman of color" is a political construct and is only one among a range of identities defensible within a realist framework available to her, Moraga does have a choice. But her choice is not arbitrary or idealist; it is not unconnected to those social categories (race, class, gender, sexuality) that constitute her social location and influence her experience of the world. The realist argument is this: as a result of her expanded, more accurate understanding of the social world, Moraga's self-conception and her identity change. My claim here is that Moraga's new-found identity, "woman of color," is more epistemically and politically salient than her former identity, implicitly white "woman," insofar as it more accurately refers to the complexity and multiplicity of Moraga's social location. This is not to say that there could not be another identity that might also, or even more accurately, refer to the complex being she is. The realist claim I am making here is limited: not all identities a given individual can claim have equal political or epistemic salience.

Without diminishing the importance and relevance of *la facultad*, I would locate it at the level of quasi-self-consciousness … Within the realm of *la facultad*, theoretical understanding is preceded by fear, alienation, and pain. All too often, nonwhite women know that something is wrong: we feel it in our gut, in our spine, in our neck. But it takes time, sometimes distance, and occasionally education or a consciousness-raising group for us to figure out what is wrong or missing. Having her consciousness raised is, in effect, what Moraga describes in her essay "La Güera" (1983b) when she relates an incident that took place in an apple orchard in Sonoma. In an effort to help Moraga understand her "total alienation from and fear of [her] classmates," a friend said to her: "Cherríe, no wonder you felt like such a nut in school. Most of the people there were white and rich" (30–31). Before her friend's statement, Moraga had not fully realized that white and rich was something that she was not. More precisely, she had not yet come to acknowledge the salience of race or class in U.S. society—she had not come to understand how much difference those social categories make to an individual's experience of the world …

In hindsight, and from the perspective of a woman of color, Moraga embeds three realist insights regarding the theory-mediatedness of experience and the epistemic status of identity into her discussion of this event. First, she realizes that a person's social location is causally relevant to the experiences she will have. She reports that the source of her "total alienation" from her classmates was her lower socioeconomic status and her Mexican ancestry (30). Second, she recognizes that a person's interpretation of her experience is influenced by her identity. She notes that as long as she identified with her "white and rich" classmates—as long as she did not acknowledge the socially significant ways her position differed from theirs—she was unable to understand her feelings of alienation. Moraga's third realist insight follows from the second: if a person's self-conception (or identity) refers inaccurately or only partially to the social and natural world from which it emerges, her interpretations of her experiences will be epistemically impoverished. She explains that "all along [she] had felt the difference" between herself and her classmates, but it was not until she reinterpreted her college experience through a different theoretical framework one that incorporated the concepts of race and class as salient analytical categories—did her experience "make any sense" (31). When Moraga's identity more accurately referred to her social location, her perspective on the world became correspondingly more objective. So, while it is clear that Moraga's intuitions—her feelings of fear and alienation—were necessary to the development of her political and theoretical knowledge, it is also clear that they were not, in themselves, sufficient for an adequate understanding of her social, political, and economic situation. …

Viewing Moraga's coming-to-consciousness as a woman of color from a realist perspective shows that her changing political commitments are tied to her evolving conception of what her place in society is versus what it should be. At the end of "La Güera," Moraga articulates the desire to work through the fragmenting conditions she has faced in her own life. She writes, "I think: what is my responsibility to my roots—both white and brown, Spanish-speaking and English? I am a woman with a foot in both worlds; and *I refuse the split.* I feel the necessity for dialogue. Sometimes I feel it urgently" (1983b, 34; emphasis added). … Moraga and the other women of color whose work I draw on understand that instability is not a comfortable or desirable situation in which to exist; life on the margins or in the interstices, while exhilarating and potentially creative, also can be difficult and exhausting. As a result, they struggle to find a way to bring all of the disparate aspects of their social identities together into synthesized, if not completely homogenized, wholes. … Certainly, one of the major victories to date of women-of-color feminism is the ability some women of color now have to conceptualize themselves as nonfragmented beings constituted neither by lack nor by excess.

… Moraga … concludes "La Güera" by explaining her choice to practice women-of-color politics in terms that are recognizably realist. On the one hand, Moraga believes that a woman-of-color identity provides her with a better perspective from which to "recognize" and thus fight the oppressive effects of race and class "privilege." On the other, she hopes that coming together with other women of color who are similarly willing to confront their own ideological mystifications will enable her to participate in a dialogue that will help women of color to forge a truly liberatory feminist collective. Moraga's choice to identify as a woman of color is thus not "strategic" or "pragmatic"; it is based on her best estimation of what she must do to help create a nonoppressive world in which women of color, too, can have "joy in [their] lives" (l983b, 33–34). Women like Moraga, as individuals whose social location generally places them in a subordinate position within prevailing relations of domination, have a personal stake in knowing "what it would take to change [our world, and in] … identifying the central relations of power and privilege that sustain it and make the world what it is" (Mohanty 1997, 214). As a result, women of color like Moraga who work for social change generally do so with a great degree of seriousness, and with a steadfast commitment to discerning what is true from what is false for the purpose of perfecting their political practice.

Toward a Realist Feminist Theory

It seems to me that the call by some critics for a "pragmatist" feminist theory is at least partially motivated by the desire to avoid the positivist versions of truth and objectivity that postmodernists have long attributed to all epistemological projects. These feminists do not want to risk the possibility of making theoretically dogmatic truth claims that might turn out to have oppressive effects. So, in an effort to avoid being "wrong," they decide to avoid any overt commitment to what might be "right." They thus retain a positivist conception of truth and objectivity in their tendency to oppose the possibility of error to absolute certainty. From a postpositivist realist perspective, however, it would be a mistake to assume that a commitment to truth invariably leads to theoretical dogmatism. In the course of making a theoretical argument, I regularly make a number of truth claims. I understand them, however, to be fallible claims; they are open to contestation and revision. What makes them specifically *truth* claims is that I understand them to be true, and I cannot abandon them until I have an experience that causes me to rethink my position, or until someone, using argumentation and presenting evidence, persuades me that I have been partially or completely in error. At that point, I will acknowledge that the truth claims I have been making need to be abandoned or revised. I will then develop a new (and hopefully more accurate) conception of truth and continue to understand my (new) truth claims as being true.

The difference between saying that my truth claims are infallible versus saying that they are fallible is an important distinction and one that bears elaboration. The first stance, which corresponds to a positivist epistemology, presupposes that truth exists and that I have unmediated access to it. It leads to naiveté, inflexibility, and domination. The second stance, which corresponds to a postpositivist epistemology, assumes that truth exists and that I can make successive approximations toward it. … I acknowledge that I have no immediate access to truth and that, as a result, my ideas are subject to mystification and error. As such, I am required (if I care very much about truth at all) to consider alternative conceptions of what the truth is. I further realize that considering alternative versions of the truth may make me profoundly uncomfortable. I may—more precisely, *will*—have to question the very foundation of my being: my sense of my self, my understanding of what is or is not beautiful, what is or is not good. I will have to reevaluate all that I hold dear, everything that makes life meaningful. Indeed, I will have to ask whether human life has any meaning at all. The advantage of a postpositivist realist framework is, thus, that it incorporates the possibility of self-critique: insofar as the realist attempts to justify her normative judgments with reference to some acknowledged metaphysical claims about the nature of the world or of human beings, she is in a better position to question and revise those claims. ...

The radical and realist questioning of themselves and the world around them is what I see women of color doing and what I see as women of color feminism's genuine contribution to the project of progressive social change.[22] The women of color whose work I admire and teach understand both the contingency and the importance of cultural values; they understand that while anyone conception of truth may be culturally mediated, it cannot therefore be dismissed as a mental or discursive "construct" with no relevance to those beings located outside the culture within which it is true. As people who are frequently situated on the wrong side of dichotomous constructions of truth and beauty, such women have developed a deep suspicion toward hegemonic constructions of the same. However, I have not seen that they therefore have dismissed the concepts as in themselves hegemonic.

Indeed, women of color's commitment to a truth (however difficult to access) that transcends particular cultural constructions underlies their success in forming coalitions across difference. As committed as they are to the idea that they are right, women of color such as Bernice Johnson Reagon, Audre Lorde, Papusa Molina, Cherríe Moraga, Mitsuye Yamada, Chandra Talpade Mohanty, and Angela Davis have all allowed themselves, in one forum or another, to entertain the possibility that they may be (or may have been) wrong—they have admitted that their own culturally constructed conceptions of truth may need to be revised, complicated, or abandoned in order to make meaningful connections with women different from themselves. This willingness to question their own conceptions of truth in the service of negotiating difference is what occasions Reagon to say, "Most of the time you feel threatened to the core and if you don't, you're not really doing no coalescing" (1983, 356). It is what Lorde refers to when she says that difference must be seen as "a fund of necessary polarities between which our creativities spark like a dialectic" (1983, 99). And it is what Moraga means when she says that we have to look deep within ourselves and come to terms with our own suffering so that we can challenge, and if necessary, "change ourselves—even sometimes our most cherished block-hard convictions" (in Moraga and Anzaldúa 1983, i). These and other women of color have undertaken the task of asking and finding out the answers to the questions Why? When? What? Where? and How? In other words, they are committed to a "drive for truth." I contend, moreover, that it is precisely because they are *realists*, because they take truth so seriously—seriously enough to question their own truth-claims—that theirs is a process incapable of "freezing into a repressive order—or of disintegrating into relativism" (Sandoval 1991, 23, n. 58).

Within Chicana and Chicano studies, as in feminist and minority studies, scholars are currently facing what Linda Alcoff (1988) has called an "identity crisis." How we choose to accomplish the task of theorizing the identities of minority and female subjects will have decisive implications for the future of these fields. ... If we choose the realist approach, we will work to ground the complex and variable experiences of the women who take on the identity *Chicana* within the concrete historical and material conditions they inhabit. Rather than a figure for contradiction or opposition-ality, the Chicana would be a part of a believable and progressive social theory. I would like to suggest that only when we have a realist account of our identities, one that refers outward to the world we live in, will we be able to understand the social and political possibilities open to us for the purpose of working to build a better society than the one we currently live in.

Notes

1. See also Sánchez 1987, which, while not focusing on Chicana feminism, succinctly evaluates the implications of postmodernist theory for liberatory political practices.
2. Pragmatism as a solution to postmodernist predicaments, despite the impression created by these essays, is not new. … [See] Sánchez …1987 …
3. For more on the postpositivist realist theory of identity, see Mohanty 1997; Moya 1997; Moya and Hames-García 2000. …
4. For helpful discussions of the theory-mediatedness of experience, see Mohanty 1997, esp. 206–16; Wilkerson 2000.
5. See Boyd 1988, esp. 203–6; Harding 1991, esp. 123–27; Mohanty 1997, esp. 212–15.
6. I use the term *Chicana* in this essay to refer to a woman of Mexican ancestry who was born and/or raised in the United States and who possesses a radical political consciousness. Histori-cally, the term *Chicano* (of which *Chicana* is the feminine linguistic equivalent) was a pejora-tive name applied to working-class Mexican Americans. Like the term *black*, it was consciously appropriated and revalued (primarily) by students during the Chicano movement of the 1960s and 1970s. The term is generally understood to imply a politics of resistance to Anglo American domination.
7. For an excellent account of the continuity between Mexican American women's activism and feminism within Mexican American communities, see Ruíz 1998, esp. chaps. 4–6. See also Cotera 1997.
8. For more on the development of Chicana feminist thought, see [Alma] García [1989],1997, and Teresa Córdova, 1994. …
9. For more information about Chicanas in the Chicano movement, see Lopez 1977; Moraga 1983a, esp. 105–11; García 1989; Trujillo 1991; Gutiérrez 1993; Córdova 1994; Cotera 1997; Ruíz 1998.
10. For accounts of how women-of-color or third-world feminism emerged from Chicanas' and other nonwhite women's frustration with some white feminist organizations, see García1989; Sandoval 1990; Córdova 1994, esp. 186.
11. Sandoval uses the term *U.S. third world feminists* to refer to those nonwhite feminists living and working in the United States who came together in the late 1970s and early 1980s in an effort to complicate the gender- and race-based foci of white feminist and ethnic nationalist social move-ments. It is a term that is roughly synonymous and is often used interchangeably with *women of color*. In an effort to be faithful to Sandoval's text. I use her term when I am paraphrasing her argument and *women of color* in my own argument to refer to the same group of people.
12. In fact, I do not disagree with Sandoval's claim that women of color are at the forefront of pro-gressive politics; however, I do disagree with aspects of her explanation of how and why they are …
13. … [S]ee Hames-García 2000.
14. Of course, I do not mean to suggest that women of color never change the way they identify themselves. My point, though, is that the self-designations they discard and take up tend to remain within a range of identities defensible within a realist framework. …
15. I borrow the phrase from Linda Martín Alcoff, 1997. …
16. Satya Mohanty [1997] deepens the critique. …
17. See Mohanty 1997, esp. 202–34.
18. For six basic claims of the postpositivist realist theory of identity, see Moya 1997, esp. 136–41.

19. For an in-depth consideration of the consideration of the dialectical relation between error and objectivity, see chaps. 6–7 of Mohanty 1997, esp. 184–94, 206–16; Hau 2000, esp. 159–65; Wilkerson 2000.

20. As I use it, *epistemic privilege* refers to a special advantage with respect to possessing or acquiring knowledge about how fundamental aspects of our society (such as race, class, gender, and sexuality) operate to sustain matrices of power. ...

21. My claim is *not* that ideologies are mere lenses through which we view an already existing world but that some ideologies are better than others at describing the complex network of human interactions and natural phenomena that constitute the totality of our (constructed and discovered) reality.

22. I should *not* have to say this, but because of the potential for being misunderstood, I will. In saying that the radical questioning of themselves and the world around them constitutes the genuine contribution of women-of-color feminism to the project of progressive social change. I am *not* saying that this is all that women of color have to offer. Clearly, individual women of color have contributed and will continue to contribute to progressive social movements in variable and important ways. ...

51.
OUT OF NOW-HERE
Malika Ndlovu
(2003)

She is a fire borne of the same flame
She bears the same name
As any other
Burning her way
Through the baggage and bars
Of convention
Of domination
Of expectation

She is a river borne of the same source
Running the same human course
As any other
Claiming her right
To turn the other way
Dancing to the sacred melody
Of healing
Of self-discovery
Finding her own groove
She moves through her curves
Her shapes
Her circles
She spirals in and out of the darkness
Her own poison of self-doubt
Even more corrosive in this environment
This seemingly endless season of drought

Black
Woman
Artist

Artist
Woman
Black

Which part of this pyramid
Puzzles
Silences
Intimidates you most
Sets her on a distant or opposite pole
Predetermines her potential
Her outcome
Her role
Blinding your vision
Depriving her of recognition

Who knows how ancient her calling may be
Driving her to express that spirit
Shed her skin
Directing the force and flow
Of her artistry
That spirit she fights to liberate
She refuses to deny
The one she reincarnates
Makes vivid
On canvas
On paper
With metal and wood
How is it that she is so seldom seen
Even in her home
So rarely accepted or understood

Written for the opening of the "Voicing the Abstract" exhibition, featuring three young Black South African women artists, Trish Lovemore, Thembeka Qangule and Ernestine White and curated by Swedish PHD student Stina Edblom—19 May 2003.

WORKS CITED

The sources cited in parenthetical citations throughout the introductions and essays are listed below. Otherwise, footnoted materials are included within each essay.

Abu, K. 1983. The Separateness of Spouses. In *Female and Male in West Africa*, ed., C. Oppong, 156–168. London: George Alien & Unwin.

Acholonu, C. O. 1995. *Motherism: The Afrocentric Alternative to Feminism*. Owerri, Nigeria: Ma Publications.

Adams, A. and S. Castle. 1994. Gender Relations and Household Dynamics. In *Population Policies Reconsidered*, eds. G. Sen, A. Germain and L. C. Chen, 161–173. Cambridge: Harvard University Press.

Agarwal, B. 1987. Women and Land Rights in India. Unpublished manuscript.

——. Oct. 8, 1995. Beijing Women's Conference: From Mexico '75 to Beijing '95. *Mainstream*, 8–9.

Ahmed, L. 1992. *Women and Gender in Islam*. New Haven: Yale University Press.

Ahmed, S. 2000. *Strange Encounters*. London: Routledge.

Alarcón, N. 1990. The Theoretical Subject(s) of *This Bridge Called My Back* and Anglo-American Feminism. In *Making Face, Making Soul Haciendo Caras*, ed., G. Anzaldúa, 356–69. San Francisco: Aunt Lute Press.

Alcoff, L. 1988. Cultural Feminism versus Post-Structuralism. *Signs* 13: 405–435.

——. 1997. The Politics of Postmodern Feminism, Revisited. *Cultural Critique* 36 (Spring): 5–27.

——. 2000. Phenomenology, Post-structuralism, and Feminist Theory on the Concept of Experience. In *Feminist Phenomenology*, eds. L. Fisher and L. Embree, 39–56. Dordrecht: Kluwer.

Alcoff, L., and E. Potter. 1993. Introduction. In *Feminist Epistemologies*, eds. L. Alcoff and E. Potter, 1–14. New York: Routledge.

Alexander, J. M., and C. T. Mohanty. 1997. *Feminist Genealogies, Colonial Legacies, Democratic Futures*. New York: Routledge.

Althusser, L. and E. Balibar. 1968. *Reading Capital*, tr. B. Brewster. London: NLB.

Altman, D. 1972. *Homosexual*. Sydney: Angus & Robertson.

Alvarez, S. E. 1997. Even Fidel Can't Change That. Unpublished paper presented at the Department of Cultural Anthropology, Duke University.

——. 1998. Latin American Feminisms 'Go Global'. *Cultures of Politics/Politics of Cultures*. eds. S. E. Alvarez, E. Dagnino, and A. Escobar, 293–324. Boulder: Westview Press.

——. 2000. Translating the Global. *Meridians* 1(1) (Autumn): 29–67.

Amos, V. and P. Parmar. 1984. Challenging Imperial Feminism. *Feminist Review* no. 17: 3–19.

Amos, V., Lewis, G., Mama, A. and Parmar, P. eds. 1984. Many Voices, One Chant. *Feminist Review*, no. 17.

Andall, J. 1992. Women Migrant Workers in Italy. *Women's Studies International Forum* 15(1): 41–48.

Anderson, B. 1983. *Imagined Communities*. New York: Verso.

Anti-Discrimination Board, New South Wales. 1982. *Discrimination and Homosexuality*. Sydney: Anti-Discrimination Board.

Anzaldùa, G. 1987. La Conciencia de la Mestiza. In *Borderlands/La Frontera*, 77–98. San Francisco: Spinsters/Aunt Lute.

——. ed. 1990. *Making Face, Making Soul / Haciendo Caras*. San Francisco: Aunt Lute.

——. 1991. To(o) Queer the Writer – Loca, Escritora y Chicana. In *Inversions*, ed. B. Warland, 249–263. Vancouver: Press Gang Publishers.

——. 1999. *Borderlands La Frontera*. Second edition. San Francisco: Aunt Lute.

Appadurai, A. 1988. Putting Hierarchy in its Place. *Cultural Anthropology*, 3(1).

——. 1996. *Modernity at Large*. Minneapolis: University of Minnesota Press.

Armstrong, P. and H. Armstrong. 1990. *Theorizing Women's Work*. Toronto: Garamond Press.

Asante, M. K. 1987. *The Afrocentric Idea*. Philadelphia: Temple University Press.

Ashcroft, B., Griffiths, G., and Tiffin, H. 1998. *Keywords in Post-Colonial Studies*. London: Routledge.

Asian and Pacific Women's Resource Collection Network. 1990. *Asia and Pacific Women's Resource and Action Series*. Kuala Lumpur: Asia and Pacific Development Centre.

Asis, M. M. B. 1992. The Overseas Employment Program Policy. In *Philippine Labor Migration*, eds. Battistella and Paganoni, 68–112. Quezon City: Scalabrini Migration Center.

Azari, K. 1983. Islam's Appeal to Women in Iran. In *Women of Iran*, ed. F. Azari, 1–71. London: Ithaca Press.

Baca Zinn, M., and B.T. Dill, eds. 1994. *Women of Color in U.S. Society*. Philadelphia: Temple University Press.

Barkley Brown, E. 1992. What Happened Here. *Feminist Studies* 18(2): 295–308.

Baksh-Soodeen, R. 1998. Issues of Difference in Caribbean Feminism. *Feminist Review* 59: 74–85.

Barrett, M. 1980. *Woman's Oppression Today*. London: Verso.

Bartky, S. L. 2002. *"Sympathy and Solidarity" and Other Essays*. Lanham: Rowman and Littlefield.

——. 1990. *Femininity and Domination*. New York: Routledge.

Bash, H. H. 1979. *Sociology, Race and Ethnicity*. New York: Gordon and Breach.

Basch, L., N. Glick-Schiller, and C. Szanton Blanc. 1994. *Nations Unbound*. Langhorne, PA: Gordon and Breach Science.

Battistella, G., and A. Paganoni, eds. 1992. *Philippine Labor Migration*. Quezon City: Scalabrini Migration Center.

Baumgardner, J., and A. Richards, eds. 2000. *Manifesta*. New York: Farrar, Straus and Giroux.

Beal, F. 1970. Double Jeopardy. In *Liberation Now*, eds. D. Babcox and M. Belkin. New York: Dell.

Beale, F. 1970. Double Jeopardy. In *The Black Woman*, ed. T. Cade (Bambara), 90–100. New York: Signet.

Beechey, V. 1979. On Patriarchy. *Feminist Review* 3: 66–82.

Belenky, M., et. al. 1986. *Women's Ways of Knowing*. New York: Basic Books.

Bell, D. 2004. The Real Lessons of a "Magnificent Mirage." *Chronicle of Higher Education* (April 2).

Bell, S. E., and S. M. Reverby. 2005. Vaginal Politics. *Women's Studies International Forum* 28(5): 430–44.

Benmayor, R., R. M. Torruellas, and A. L. Juarbe. 1992. *Responses to Poverty Among Puerto Rican Women.* New York: Centro de Estudios Puertorriqueños, Hunter College.

Bensinger, T. 1992. Lesbian Pornography. *Discourse* 15(1): 69–93.

Berer, M. 1990. What Would a Feminist Population Policy Be Like? *Women's Health Journal* 18: 4–7.

——. 1993a. Population and Family Planning Policies. *Reproductive Health Matters* 1: 4–12.

Berger, P. L. and T. Luckmann. 1966. *The Social Construction of Reality.* New York: Doubleday.

Bhabha, H. 1990. *Nation and Narration.* New York: Routledge.

——. 1998. *The Location of Culture.* London: Routledge..

Bhasin, K., and N. Khan. 1986. *Some Questions on Feminism for Women in South Asia.* New Delhi: Kali.

Bhasin, K. and R. Menon. 1988. The Problem. *Seminar*, no. 342, Special Issue on Sati.

Bhavnani, K-K. 2001. *Feminism and Race.* New York: Oxford University Press.

Bhavnani, K-K. and Coulson, M. 1986. Transforming Socialist-Feminism. *Feminist Review*, no. 23.

Birke, L. 1999. *Feminism and the Biological Body.* New Brunswick: Rutgers University Press.

Bittman, M. 1991. *Juggling Time.* Canberra: Commonwealth of Australia, Office of the Status of Women.

Bloch, R. H. 1978. Untangling the Roots of Modern Sex Roles. *Signs* 4: 237–252.

Boland, R., S. Rao, and G. Zeidenstein. 1994. Honoring Human Rights in Population Policies. In *Population Policies Reconsidered*, eds. G. Sen, A. Germain and L. C. Chen, 89–105. Cambridge: Harvard University Press.

Bonilla Silva, E. 2006. *Racism without Racists.* Second Edition. Lanham: Rowman and Littlefield.

Bordo, S. 1986. The Cartesian Masculinization of Thought. *Signs* 11: 439–456.

——. 1987. *The Flight to Objectivity.* Albany: SUNY Press.

——. 1990. Feminism, Postmodernism, and Gender-Skepticism. In *Feminism/Postmodernism* ed. L. Nicholson, 133–156. New York: Routledge.

——. 1993. *Unbearable Weight.* Berkeley: University of California Press.

——. 1997. *Twilight Zones.* Berkeley: University of California Press.

——. 1998. Bringing Body to Theory. In *Body and Flesh*, ed. D. Welton, 84–98. Malden: Blackwell.

Boston Women's Health Book Collective. 1984. *The New Our Bodies, Ourselves.* New York: Simon and Schuster.

Boudhiba, A. 1985. *Sexuality in Islam.* London: Routledge & Kegan Paul.

——. 1985. The Social Space and the Genesis of Groups. *Social Science Information* 24(2): 195–220.

Boyd, R. N. 1988. How to Be a Moral Realist. In *Essays on Moral Realism*, ed. G. Sayre-McCord, 181–228. Ithaca: Cornell University Press.

Bozorgmehr, M., G. Sabagh, and I. Light. 1996. Los Angeles. In *Origins and Destinies*, eds. Pedraza and Rumbaut, 346–359. Belmont, CA: Wadsworth.

Braidotti, R. 1999. Signs of Wonder and Traces of Doubt. In *Feminist Theory and the Body*, eds. J. Price and M. Shildrick, 290–301. Edinburgh: Edinburgh University Press.

Braithwaite, A. 2004. 'Where We've Been' and 'Where We're Going.' In *Troubling Women's Studies, Pasts, Presents and Possibilities*, ed. A. Braithwaite et al., 93–146. Toronto: Sumach Press.

Breckenridge, C. A., and C. Vogler. 2001. The Critical Limits of Embodiment. *Public Culture* 13(3): 349–357.

Brennan, T., and C. Pateman. 1979. 'Mere Auxiliaries to the Commonwealth.' *Political Studies* 27(2): 183–200.

Brodkin, K. 1998. *How Jews Became White Folks and What That Says about Race in America.* New Brunswick: Rutgers University Press.

Brown, E. B. 1986. *Hearing Our Mothers' Lives.* Atlanta: Fifteenth Anniversary of African-American and African Studies, Emory University.

Brown, W. 1995. *States of Injury.* Princeton: Princeton University Press.

Brown-Collins, A., and D. R. Sussewell. 1986. The Afro-American Women's Emerging Selves. *Journal of Black Psychology* 13(1): 1–11.

Bruce, J. 1990. Fundamental Elements of the Quality of Care. *Studies in Family Planning* 21: 61–91.

Buchbinder, H., V. Burstyn, D. Forbes and M. Steedman. 1987. *Who's On Top? The Politics of Heterosexuality.* Toronto: Garamond Press.

Bulkin, E., Pratt, M. B. and Smith, B. 1984 *Yours in Struggle.* New York: Long Haul Press.

Bunch, C. 1979. Feminism and Education. *Quest* 1: 1–7.

——. 1990. Women's Rights as Human Rights. *Human Rights Quarterly* 12: 486–498.

——. 1995. *Paying the Price.* London: Zed.

Bunch, C., and Susana F. 1996. Beijing '95. *Signs* 22: 203.

Burris, B. 1971. The Fourth World Manifesto. In *Notes from the Third Year.* New York: Notes from the Second Year, Inc.

——. 1973. The Fourth World Manifesto. In *Radical Feminism*, eds. A. Koedt, E. Levine, and A. Rapone, 322–357. New York: Quadrangle.

Butler, Johnnella and John Walter. 1991. *Transforming the Curriculum.* Albany: SUNY Press, 1991.

Butler, J. 1989/1990. *Gender Trouble.* New York: Routledge.

——. 1990b. Gender Trouble, Feminist Theory, and Psychoanalytic Discourse. In *Feminism/ Postmodernism*, ed. L. Nicholson, 324–340. New York: Routledge.

——. 1991. Imitation and Gender Insubordination. In *Inside/Out*, ed. Fuss, 13–31. New York: Routledge.

——. 1992. Contingent Foundations. In *Feminists Theorize the Political*, eds. J. Butler and J. Scott, 3–21. New York: Routledge.

——. 1993a/1994. *Bodies That Matter.* New York: Routledge.

——.1993b. Critically Queer. *GLQ* 1(1): 17–32.

——. 1995. For a Careful Reading. In *Feminist Contentions*, eds. S. Benhabib, J. Butler, D. Cornell, and N. Fraser, 127–143. New York: Routledge.

——. 1997. *The Psychic Life of Power.* Stanford: Stanford University Press.

Byerly, V. 1986. *Hard Times.* Ithaca: Cornell University Press.

Cain, M., S. P. Khanan, and S. Nahar. 1979. Class, Patriarchy and Women's Work in Bangladesh. *Population and Development Review* 5: 408–416.

Caldwell, J. C. 1978. A Theory of Fertility. *Population and Development Review* 4: 553–577.

Cannon, K. O. 1985. The Emergence of a Black Feminist Consciousness. In *Feminist Interpretations of the Bible*, ed. L. M. Russell, 30–40. Philadelphia: Westminster Press.

——. 1988. *Black Womanist Ethics.* Atlanta: Scholars Press.

Carby, H. 1987. *Reconstructing Womanhood.* New York: Oxford.

Case, S. 1991. Tracking the Vampire. *Differences* 3(2): 1–20.

Castles, S., and M. J. Miller. 1998. *The Age of Migration.* 2nd ed. New York: Guilford Press.

Chafetz, J. S. and A. G. Dworkin. 1987. In Face of Threat. *Gender & Society* 1: 33–60.

Chen, K. 1996. Cultural Studies and the Politics of Internationalization. In *Stuart Hall*, eds. D. Morley and K. Chen, 392–408. London: Routledge.

Chesler, E. 1992. *Woman of Valor.* New York: Simon & Schuster.

Childs, J. B. 1984. Afro-American Intellectuals and the People's Culture. *Theory and Society* 13(1): 69–90.

Chin, M. H., and C.A. Humikowski. 2002. When is Risk Stratification by Race or Ethnicity Justified in Medical Care? *Academic Medicine* 77(3): 202–208.

Chincilla, N. 1997. Marxism, Feminism and the Struggle for Democracy in Latin America. In *Materialist Feminism*, eds. R. Hennessy and C. Ingraham, 214–226. New York: Routledge.

Chisholm, S. 1970. *Unbought and Unbossed.* New York: Avon.

Chodorow, N. 1978. *The Reproduction of Mothering.* Berkeley: University of California Press.

Chow, E. N. 1996. Making Waves, Moving Mountains. *Signs* 22: 187, 189.

Christian, B. 1987. The Race for Theory. *Cultural Critique* 6 (Spring): 51–63.

Chuh, K. 2003. *Imagine Otherwise.* Durham: Duke University Press.

Clarke, A. E., and V. L. Olesen. 1999a. Revising, Diffracting, Acting. In *Revisioning Women, Health, and Healing*, eds. A. E. Clarke and V. L. Olesen, 3–48. New York: Routledge.

Clarke, C., J., L. Gomez, E. Hammonds, B. Johnson, and L. Powell. 1983. Conversations and Questions. *Conditions: Nine* 3 (3): 88–137.

Clark, L.M. and L. Lange, eds. 1979. *The Sexism of Social and Political Theory.* Toronto: University of Toronto Press.

Clifford, J. 1997. *Routes.* Cambridge: Harvard University Press.

Clough, P. and J. Halley. 2007. *The Affective Turn.* Durham: Duke University Press.

Cobble, D. S. 2005. *The Other Women's Movement.* Princeton: Princeton University Press.

Code, L. 1991. *What Can She Know? Feminist Theory and the Construction of Knowledge.* Ithaca: Cornell University Press.

Cohen, R. 1992. Migration and the New International Division of Labour. *Ethnic Minorities and Industrial Change in Europe and North America*, ed. M. Cross. Cambridge: Cambridge University Press.

——. 1997. *Global Diasporas.* Seattle: University of Washington Press.

Cole, E. S., and K.S. Donley. 1990. History, Values, and Placement Policy Issues in Adoption. In *The Psychology of Adoption*, eds. D. M. Brodzinsky and M. Schechter, 273–294. New York: Oxford University Press.

The Combahee River Collective. 1982. A Black Feminist Statement. In *But Some of Us Are Brave*, eds. G. T. Hull, P. Bell Scott, and B. Smith, 13–22. Old Westbury: Feminist Press.

Cockburn, C. 1998. *The Space Between Us.* London: Zed.

Connell, R. W. 1985. Masculinity, Violence and War. In *War/Masculinity*, eds. P. Patton and R. Poole, 4–10. Sydney: Intervention.

——. 1987. *Gender and Power.* Cambridge: Polity Press.

Connell, R. W., M. Davis and G. W. Dowsett. 1993. A Bastard of a Life. *Australian and New Zealand Journal of Sociology* 29: 112–135.

Connell, R. W. and G. W. Dowsett, eds. 1992. *Rethinking Sex.* Melbourne: Melbourne University Press.

Conti, A. 1979. Capitalist Organization of Production Through Non-capitalist Relations. *Review of African Political Economy* 15/16: 75–91.

Cook, R. J. 1993a. International Human Rights and Women's Reproductive Health. *Studies in Family Planning* 24: 73–86.

——. 1993b. Women's International Human Rights Law. *Human Rights Quarterly* 15: 230–261.

Cooper, A. J. 1892. *A Voice from the South.* Xenia, OH: Aldine Printing House.

Copelon, R. 1994. Intimate Terror. In *International Women's Human Rights*, ed. R. J. Cook. Philadelphia: University of Pennsylvania.

Cordova, T. 1994. Roots and Resistance. In *Handbook of Hispanic Cultures in the United States*, ed. F. Padilla, 175–202. Houston: Arte Publico Press.

Correa, S. 1993. Sterilization in Brazil. Unpublished.

Cotera, M. 1997. Feminism. In *Chicana Feminist Thought*, ed. A. Garcia, 223–231. New York: Routledge

Cott, N. 1986a. Feminist Theory and Feminist Movements. In *What is Feminism*, eds. J. Mitchell and A. Oakley, 49–62. New York: Pantheon.

——. 1986b. *The Grounding of Modern Feminism.* New Haven: Yale University Press.

Creet, J. 1991. Daughter of the Movement. *Differences* 3(2): 135–159.

Crenshaw, K. 1991. Demarginalizing the Intersection of Race and Sex. In *Feminist Legal Theory*, eds. K. T. Bartlett and R. Kennedy, 81–94. Boulder: Westview Press.

——. 1993. Mapping the Margins. *Stanford Law Review* 43: 1241–1299.

——. 1993. Beyond Racism and Misogyny. In *Words That Wound*, eds. M. J. Matsuda, K. W. Crenshaw, R. Delgado, and C. R. Lawrence. Boulder: Westview Press.

Cruse, H. 1967. *The Crisis of the Negro Intellectual.* New York: William Morrow.

Cvetkovich, A. 2003. *An Archive of Feelings.* Durham: Duke University Press.

Daly, M. 1978. *Gyn/Ecology.* New York: Beacon Press.

Däumer, E. D. 1992. Queer Ethics. *Hypatia* 7(4): 91–105.

Davis, A. 1983. *Women, Race, and Class.* New York: Vintage Books.

Davis, A. 1996. Reaping Fruit and Throwing Seed. Paper presented at the Third Annual Undergraduate Women's Conference, State University of New York, Oneonta, April 20.

Davis, K. 1988. *Power under the Microscope.* Dordrecht: Faris.

——. 1995. *Reshaping the Female Body.* New York: Routledge.

——. 2003. *Dubious Equalities and Embodied Differences.* Lanham: Rowman and Littlefield.

Development Alternatives with Women for a New Era (DAWN). 1993. Population and Reproductive Rights Component. Unpublished.

Day, C. 1979. Access to Birth Records. *Adoption and Fostering* 98: 17–28.

de Beauvoir, S. 1953. *The Second Sex.* Trans. H. M. Parshley. New York: Knopf.

de Beauvoir, S. 2010. *The Second Sex.* Trans. C. Bode and S. Maloveany-Chevallier. New York Knopf.

The Declaration and Programme of Action, NGO Forum of the United Nations World Conference against Racism, September 3, 2001.

Dei, G., and J. Sefa. 2000. Rethinking the Role of Indigeneous Knowledges in the Academy. *International Journal of Inclusive Education* 4(2): 111–132.

de Lauretis, T. 1986. Feminist Studies/Critical Studies. In *Feminist Studies/Critical Studies*, ed. T. de Lauretis, 1–19. Bloomington: Indiana University Press.

——. 1990. Eccentric Subjects. *Feminist Studies.* 16 (Spring): 115–150.

——. 1991. Queer Theory. *Differences* 3(2): iii–xviii.

Delmar, R. 1986. What is Feminism? In *What is Feminism*, eds. J. Mitchell and A. Oakley, 8–33, New York: Pantheon.

Delphy, C. 1977/1980/1981. *The Main Enemy.* London: Women's Research and Resource Centre.

——. 1993. Rethinking Sex and Gender. *International Women's Studies Forum* 16(1): 1–9.

Denich, B. S. 1974. Sex and Power in the Balkans. In *Women, Culture and Society*, eds. M. Z. Rosaldo and L. Lamphere, 243–262. Palo Alto: Stanford University Press.

Desai, S. 1994. Women's Burdens. In *Population Policies Reconsidered*, eds. G. Sen, A. Germain and L. C. Chen, 139–150. Cambridge: Harvard University Press.

Dey, J. 1981. Gambian Women; Unequal Partner, in Rice Development Projects. In *African Women in the Development Process*, ed. N. Nelson, 109–122. London: Frank Cass.

Dill, B. T. 1983. Race, Class and Gender. *Feminist Studies* 9(1): 131–150.

——. 1994. *Across the Boundaries of Race and Class.* New York: Garland.

Dill, B. T., A. E. McLaughlin, and A. D. Nieves. 2007. Future Directions of Feminist Research. In *Handbook of Feminist Research*, ed. S. N. Hesse-Biber, 629–637. Thousand Oaks: Sage.

Dill, B.T., and M. B. Zinn. 1996. Theorizing Difference from Multiracial Feminisms. *Feminist Studies* 22(2): 321–331.

Dill, B. T., M. B. Zinn, and S. L. Patton. 1999. Race, Family Values and Welfare Reform. In *A New Introduction to Poverty*, eds. L. Kushnick and J. Jennings, 263–286. New York: New York University Press.

Dill, B. T., and T. Johnson. 2002. Between a Rock and a Hard Place. In *Sister Circle*, ed. S. Harley. New Brunswick, NJ: Rutgers University Press.

Diop, C. 1974. *The African Origin of Civilization.* New York: L. Hill.

Dirlik, A. 1996. The Global in the Local. In *Global/Local*, eds. R. Wilson and W. Dissanayake, 21–45. Durham: Duke University Press.

——. 1997. *The Postcolonial Aura.* Boulder: Westview Press.

Dixon-Mueller, R. 1993. *Population Policy and Women's Rights.* Westport: Praeger.

Dodson, J. E., and C. T. Gilkes. 1987. Something Within. In *Women and Religion in America*, Volume 3: 1900–1968, eds. R. Reuther and R. Keller, 80–130. New York: Harper and Row.

Donato, K. 1992. Understanding U.S. Immigration. In *Seeking Common Ground*, ed. D. Gabaccia, 159–184. Westport: Greenwood Press.

Doty, A. 1993. *Making Things Perfectly Queer.* Minneapolis: University of Minnesota Press.

DuBois, W. E. B. 1969. *The Souls of Black Folks.* New York: New American Library.

Duggan, L. 1992. Making It Perfectly Queer. *Socialist Review* 22(1): 11–31.

Duster, A. M., ed. 1970. *Crusade for Justice.* Chicago: University of Chicago Press.

Dyson. T. and M. Moore. 1983. On Kinship Structures. *Population and Development Review* 9: 35–60.

Ehrenreich, B. 1983. *The Hearts of Men.* London: Pluto Press.

Eisenstein, H. 1983. *Contemporary Feminist Thought.* Boston: G. K. Hall.

Eisenstein, H. and A. Jardine. 1980. *The Future of Difference.* Boston: G. K. Hall.

Eisenstein, Z., ed. 1978. *Capitalist Patriarchy and the Case for Socialist Feminism.* New York: Monthly Review Press.

——. 1981. *The Radical Future of Liberal Feminism.* New York: Longman; reprint 1986. Boston: Northeastern Univ. Press.

——. 1994. *The Color of Gender.* Berkeley: University of California Press.

——. 1998. *Global Obscenities.* New York: New York University Press.

Elias, C. 1991. *Sexually Transmitted Diseases and the Reproductive Health of Women in Developing Countries.* New York: Population Council.

Ellen, I. G., and M. A. Turner. 1997. Does Neighborhood Matter? *Housing Policy Debate* 8: 833–866.

Ellmann, R. 1987. *Oscar Wilde.* London: Hamish Hamilton.

Elshtain, J. 1981. *Public Man, Private Woman.* Princeton: Princeton University Press.

Engels, F. 1972. *The Origin of Family, Private Property, and The State*. E. Leacock, ed. New York: International Publishers.

Engineer, A. A. 1987. *The Shahbano Controversy*. Bombay: Orient Longman.

English, D. 1934. The Fear Thai Feminism Will Free Men First. In *Powers of Desire*, eds. A. Snitow, C. Stansell, and S. Thompson, 97–102. New York: Monthly Review Press.

Espiritu, Y. L. 1995. *Filipino American Lives*. Philadelphia: Temple University Press.

——. 1997. *Asian American Women and Men*. Thousand Oaks: Sage Publications.

Essed, P. 1991. *Understanding Everyday Racism*. Thousand Oaks: Sage.

Esteva, G., and M. S. Prakash. 1998. *Grassroots Post-Modernism*. London: Zed Press.

Etienne, M. and E. Leacock, eds. 1980. *Women and Colonization*. New York: Praeger.

Evans, D. T. 1993. *Sexual Citizenship*. New York: Routledge.

Ezeh, A. C. 1993. The Influence of Spouses Over Each Other's Contraceptive Attitudes in Ghana. *Studies in Family Planning* 24: 163–174.

Fabros, M. L. 1991. The WRRC's Institutional Framework and Strategies on Reproductive Rights. *Flights* 4. Women's Resource & Research Center, Quezon City, Philippines.

Fausto-Sterling, A. 2000. *Sexing the Body*. New York: Basic Books.

——. 2005. The Bare Bones of Sex, Part 1. *Signs* 30(2): 1491–1527.

Fischer, L. 1962. *The Essential Gandhi*. New York: Vintage.

Fisher, B. 1984. Guilt and Shame in the Women's Movement. *Feminist Studies* 10: 185–212.

Foster, F. S. 1983. The Struggle Continues. *Callaloo* 18: 132–134.

Foucault, M. 1977. *Discipline and Punish*. Harmondsworth: Peregrine.

——. 1978. *The History of Sexuality, Volume 1*. New York: Vintage Books.

——. 1980. *Power/Knowledge*. New York: Pantheon.

——. 1983. The Subject and Power. In *Michel Foucault*, eds. Dreyfus and Rabinow, 208–226. Chicago: University of Chicago Press.

Frankenberg, R. 1993. *White Women Race Matters*. Minneapolis: University of Minnesota Press.

Franzway, S., D. Court and R. W. Connell. 1989. *Staking a Claim*. Cambridge: Polity Press.

Fraser, N. 1992. Rethinking the Public Sphere, In *Habermas and the Public Sphere,* ed. C. Calhoun, 359–376. Cambridge: MIT Press.

Fraser, M., and M. Greco, eds. 2005. *The Body*. London: Routledge.

Freedman, L. P., and S. L. Isaacs. 1993. Human Rights and Reproductive Choice. *Studies in Family Planning* 24: 18–30.

Freire, P. 1970. *The Pedagogy of the Oppressed*. New York: Herder & Herder.

Friedman, M. 1992. Feminism and Modern Friendship. In *Communitarianism and Individualism*, eds. S. Avineri and A. de-Shalit, 101–119. New York: Oxford University Press.

Friedman-Kasaba, K. 1996. *Memories of Migration*. Albany, NY: SUNY Press.

Frye, M. 1983. *The Politics of Reality*. Trumansburg: Crossing Press.

Fuss, D. 1991a. *Inside/Out*. In Fuss 1991b, 1–12. New York: Routledge.

——. ed. 1991b. *Inside/Out*. New York: Routledge.

García, A. M. 1989. The Development of Chicana Feminist Discourse, 1970–1980. *Gender and Society* 3(2): 217–238.

——. ed. 1997. *Chicana Feminist Thought*. New York: Routledge.

Garcia-Moreno, C. and A. Claro. 1994. Challenges from the Women's Health Movement. In *Population Policies Reconsidered*, eds. G. Sen, A. Germain and L. C. Chen, 47–61. Cambridge: Harvard University Press.

Gardiner, J. K., ed. 2002. *Masculinity Studies and Feminist Theory*. New York: Columbia University Press.

Garrison, E. K. 2010. U.S. Feminism—Grrrl Style! In *No Permanent Waves*, ed. Nancy Hewitt, 379–402. New Brunswick: Rutgers University Press.

Gatens, M. 1999. Power, Bodies, and Difference. In *Feminist Theory and the Body*, eds. J. Price and M. Shildrick, 227–234. Edinburgh: Edinburgh University Press.

Geertz. C. 1973. *The Interpretation of Cultures*. New York: Basic Books.

Gibson, J. W. 1994. *Warrior Dreams*. New York: Hill & Wang.

Giddens, A. 1976. *New Rules of Sociological Method*. London: Hutchinson.

Giddings, P. 1984. *When and Where I Enter*. New York: William Morrow.

——. 1988. *In Search of Sisterhood*. New York: William Morrow.

Gilkes, C. T. 1985. Together and in Harness. *Signs* 10(4): 678–699.

Gilligan, C. 1982. *In a Different Voice*. Cambridge: Harvard University Press.

Ginsburg, F. 1984. The Body Politic. In *Pleasure and Danger*, ed. C. S. Vance, 173–188. London: Routledge.

Glenn, E. N. 1986. *Issei, Nisei, Warbride*. Philadelphia: Temple University Press.

Glick-Schiller, N., and G. Fouron. 1998. Transnational Lives and National Identities. In *Transnationalism from Below*, eds. Smith and Guarnizo, 130–161. New Brunswick: Transaction.

Glick-Schiller, N., L. Basch, and C. Szanton-Blanc. 1995. From Immigrant to Transmigrant. *Anthropological Quarterly* 68(1): 48–63.

Goldring, L. 1998. The Power of Status in Transnational Social Fields. In *Transnationalism from Below*, eds. Smith and Guarnizo, 165–195. New Brunswick: Transaction.

Gordon, A. 1997. *Ghostly Matters*. Minneapolis: University of Minnesota Press.

Gordon, L. 1976. *Woman's Body, Woman's Right*. New York: Penguin.

——. 1982. Why Nineteenth Canary Feminists Did Not Support (Birth Control) and Twentieth Century Feminists Do. In *Rethinking the Family*, eds. B. Thorne and M. Yalom, 40–53. New York: Longman.

——. 1989. *Heroes of their Own Lives*. New York: Penguin.

——. 1994. *Pitied but Not Entitled*. New York: Free Press.

Goreau, A. 1985. *The Whole Duty of a Woman*. New York: Dial Press.

Gould, S. J. 1981. *The Mismeasure of Man*. New York: W. W. Norton.

Grant, J. 1993. *Fundamental Feminism*. New York: Routledge.

Grant, J. and P. Tancred. 1992. A Feminist Perspective on State Bureaucracy. In *Gendering Organizational Analysis*, ed. A. J. Mills and P. Tancred, 112–128. Thousand Oaks: Sage.

Grasmuck, S., and P. Pessar. 1991. *Between Two Islands*. Berkeley and Los Angeles: University of California Press.

Gregg, M. and G. J. Seigworth. 2010. *The Affect Theory Reader*. Durham: Duke University Press.

Grewal, I. 1994. Autobiographic Subjects and Diasporic Locations. In *Scattered Hegemonies*, eds. I. Grewal and C. Kaplan, 231–254. Minneapolis: University of Minnesota Press.

Grewal, I. and C. Kaplan, editors. 1994. *Scattered Hegemonies*. Minneapolis: University of Minnesota Press.

Grewal, S., J. Kay, L. Landor, G. Lewis, and P. Parmar eds. 1988. *Charting the Journey*. London: Sheba.

Griffin, S. 1979. *Rape*. San Francisco: Harper & Row.

Gross, J. 1977 Feminist Ethics from a Marxist Perspective. *Radical Religion* 3(2): 52–56.

Grosz, E. 1994. *Volatile Bodies*. Bloomington: Indiana University Press.

Guarnizo, L. E., and M. P. Smith. 1998. The Locations of Transnationalism. In Smith and Guarnizo, *Transnationalism from Below*, 3–34. New Brunswick: Transaction.

Guerrero, M. A. J. 1997. Civil Rights versus Sovereignty. In *Feminist Genealogies, Colonial Legacies, Democratic Futures*, ed. M. Jacqui Alexander and C. T. Mohanty, 101–124. New York: Routledge.

Guinier, L. 2004. Top Colleges Take More Blacks, but Which Ones? *New York Times* (June 24) (Rimer & Arenson).

Gutiérrez, R. A. 1993. Community, Patriarchy, and Individualism. *American Quarterly* 45 (1): 44–72.

Guy-Sheftall, B. 1986. Remembering Sojourner Truth. *Catalyst* (Fall): 54–57.

Guyer, J. I. and P. E., Peters. 1987. Introduction to Conceptualizing the Household. *Development and Change* 18: 197–213.

Gwaltney, J. L. 1980. *Drylongso*. New York: Vintage.

Habermas, J. 1976. *Legitimation Crisis*. London: Heinemann.

Hagan, J. 1994. *Deciding to Be Legal*. Philadelphia: Temple University Press.

Hall, K. Q. 2005. Queerness, Disability, and *The Vagina Monologues*. *Hypatia* 20(1): 99–119.

Hall, L. K. C. 1993. Bitches in Solitude. In *Sisters, Sexperts, Queers*, ed. A. Stein, 218–229. New York: Plume Book/Penguin.

Hall, S. 1988. Minimal Selves. In *Identity, ICA Document* 6, 44–46. London: Institute of Contemporary Arts.

——. 1991a. Ethnicity, *Radical America* 23(4): 9–20.

——. 1991b. Old and New Identities, Old and New Ethnicities. In *Culture, Globalization, and the World-System*, ed. A. King, 41–68. London: Macmillan Education.

Hames-García, M. R. 2000. Who are Our Own People? In *Reclaiming Identity*, eds. P. M. L. Moya and M. R. Hames-García, 102–129. Berkeley: University of California Press.

Hanisch, C. 1970. The Personal is Political. In *Notes From the Second Year*, eds. S. Firestone and A., Koedt. New York: Radical Feminism.

Hanger, J. and J. Moris. 1973. Women and the Household Economy. In *Mwea*, eds. R. Chambers and J. Moris, 209–244. Munich: Weltforum Verlag.

Haraway, D. 1988. Situated Knowledges. *Feminist Studies* 14(3): 575–599.

——. 1991a. *Simians, Cyborgs, and Women*. London: Free Association Books.

——. 1991b. Situated Knowledges. In *Simians, Cyborgs, and Women*, 183–202. London: Free Association Books.

——. 1999. The Virtual Speculum in the New World Order. In *Revisioning Women, Health, and Healing*, eds. A. E. Clarke and V. L. Olesen, 49–96. New York: Routledge.

Harding, S. 1986. *The Science Question in Feminism*. Ithaca: Cornell University Press.

——. 1991. *Whose Science? Whose Knowledge?* Ithaca: Cornell University Press.

——. 1998. *Is Science Multicultural? Postcolonialisms, Feminisms, and Epistemologies*. Bloomington: Indiana University Press.

Harding, S., and M. Hintikka. 1983. *Discovering Reality*. Dordrecht: Reidel.

Harding, S., and J. O'Barr, eds. 1987. *Sex and Scientific Inquiry*. Chicago: University of Chicago Press.

Harper, P. B., E. F. White, and M. Cerullo. 1993. Multi/Queer/Culture. *Radical America* 24(4): 27–37.

Harris, T. 1981. Three Black Women Writers and Humanism. In *Black American Literature and Humanism*, ed. R. B. Miller, 50–74. Lexington: University of Kentucky Press.

Hartmann. H. 1981. The Unhappy Marriage of Marxism and Feminism. In *Women and Revolution*, ed. L. Sargent, 40–53. London: Pluto Press.

Hartsock, N. M. 1983a. The Feminist Standpoint. In *Discovering Reality*, eds. S. Harding and M.B. Hintikka, 283–310. Boston: D. Reidel.

——. 1983/b. *Money, Sex and Power*. Boston: Northeastern University Press & New York: Longman.

——. 1990. Foucault on Power. In F*eminism/Postmodernism*, ed. L. Nicholson, 157–175. New York: Routledge.

Harvey, D. 1989. *The Condition of Postmodernity*. New York: Basil Blackwell.

Hau, C. 2000. On Representing Others. In *Reclaiming Identity*, eds. P. Moya and M. Hames-García, 133–170. Berkeley: University of California Press.

Heise, L. 1992. Violence Against Women. In *Women's Health*, eds. M. A. Koblinsky, J. Timyan, and J. Gay, 171–195. Boulder: Westview Press.

Heller, A. 1992. Rights, Modernity, Democracy. In *Deconstruction and the Possibility of Justice*, eds. D. Cornell, M. Rosenfeld, and D. G. Carlson. New York: Routledge.

Hennessy, R. 1993. Queer Theory. *Signs* 18(4): 964–979.

——. 1994. Queer Visibility in Commodity Culture. *Cultural Critique*, 31–76.

Herrnstein, R. J., and C. A. Murray. 1994. *The Bell Curve*. New York: Free Press.

Hesford, W. S. and W. Kozol. 2001. *Haunting Violations*. Urbana: University of Illinois Press.

Higginbotham, E., M. Romero, eds. 1997. *Women and Work Exploring Race, Ethnicity, and Class*. Thousand Oaks: Sage.

Hill Collins, P. 1986. Learning from the Outsider Within. *Social Problems* 33 (6): 14–32.

——. 1990. *Black Feminist Thought*. Boston: Unwin Hyman.

——. 1998. *Fighting Words*. Minneapolis: University of Minnesota Press.

——. 2000. *Black Feminist Thought*, 2nd ed. New York: Routledge.

Hinman, L. 1986. Emotion, Morality and Understanding. Paper presented at Annual Meeting of the Central Division of the American Philosophical Association, St. Louis, Missouri, May 1986.

Hogeland, C., and K. Rosen. 1990. *Dreams Lost Dreams Found*. San Francisco: San Francisco Coalition for Immigrant Rights and Services.

Hogeland, L. 2001. Against Generational Thinking, or, Some Things That 'Third Wave' Feminism Isn't, *Women's Studies in Communication* 24: 107–121.

Hollway, W. 1984. Gender Difference and the Production of Subjectivity. In *Changing the Subject*, ed. J. Henriques et al., 227–263. London: Methuen.

Hondagneu-Sotelo, P. 1994. *Gendered Transitions*. Berkeley: University of California Press.

——. 1999. Introduction. *American Behavioral Scientist* 42(4): 565–576.

hooks, b. 1981. *Ain't I a Woman*. Boston: South End Press.

——. 1984. *From Margin to Center*. Boston: South End Press.

——. 1989. *Talking Back*. Boston: South End Press.

——. 1991. Essentialism and Experience. *American Literary History* 3(1): 172–183.

——. 1992. *Black Looks*. Boston: South End Press.

Hudson-Weems, C. 1993. *Africana Womanism*. Troy: Bedford Publishers.

——. 1998. African Womanism. In *Sisterhood, Feminisms, and Power*, ed. Obioma Nnaemeka. Trenton: Africa World Press

Hull, G. T., P. B. Scott, and B. Smith. 1982/2003. *But Some of Us are Brave*. New York: Feminist Press.

Hughes, H. 1992. Identity Crisis. Interview, A. Solomon. *Village Voice*, June 30.

Humphries, J. 1977. Class Struggle and the Persistence of the Working Class Family. *Cambridge Journal of Economics* 1: 241–258.

Hunt, P. 1980. *Gender and Class Consciousness*. London: Macmillan.

Hurston, Z. N. [1937] 1969. *Their Eyes Were Watching God*. Greenwich: Fawcett.

Hurtado, A. 1989. Relating to Privilege. *Signs*, 14 (4).

——. 1998. "*Sitios y Lenguas.*" *Hypatia* 13(2): 134–161.

Huston, P. 1992. *Motherhood by Choice.* New York: Feminist Press.

Inden, R. 1986. Orientalist Constructions of India. *Modern Asian Studies,* 20(3).

Jaggar, A. M. 1983. *Feminist Politics and Human Nature.* Totawa: Rowman & Allanheld.

——. 1989/1990. Love and Knowledge. In *Gender/Body/Knowledge,* eds. A. M. Jaggar and S. R. Bordo, 145–171. New Brunswick: Rutgers University Press.

Jain, A. and J. Bruce. 1994. A Reproductive Health Approach to the Objectives and Assessment of Family Planning Programs. In *Population Policies Reconsidered,* eds. G. Sen, A. Germain, and L. C. Chen, 193–209. Cambridge: Harvard University Press.

Jain, A., J. Bruce, and B. Mensch. 1992. Setting Standards of Quality in Family Planning Programs. *Studies in Family Planning* 23: 392–395.

Jaising, I. 1987. Women, Religion and the Law. *The Lawyers Collective,* 2(11).

Janeway, E. 1980. Who Is Sylvia? *Signs* 5: 573–589.

Jayawardena, K. 1993. *With a Different Voice.* London: Zed Books.

Jeffery, P., R. Jeffery, and A. Lyon. 1989. *Labour Pains and Labour Power.* London: Zed Books.

Johnson, K. A. 1983. *Women, the Family and Peasant Revolution in China.* Chicago: Chicago University Press.

Johnson-Odim, C. 1991. Common Themes, Different Contexts. In *Third World Women and the Politics of Feminism,* eds. C. Mohanty, A. Russo and L. Torres, 314–327. Bloomington: Indiana University Press.

Jones, M. S. 2010. Overthrowing the Monopoly of the Pulpit. In *No Permanent Waves.* ed. Nancy Hewitt, 121–143. New Brunswick: Rutgers University Press.

Jordan, J. 1981. *Civil Wars.* Boston: Beacon.

Kader, C., and T. Piontek. 1992. Introduction. *Discourse* 15(1): 5–10.

Kandiyoti, D. 1984. Rural Transformation in Turkey and Its Implications for Women's Studies. In *Women on the Move,* 17–29. Paris: UNESCO.

——. 1985. *Woman in Rural Production Systems.* Paris: UNESCO.

——. 1987a Emancipated but Unliberated? *Feminist Studies* 13: 317–338.

——. 1987b. The Problem of Subjectivity in Western Feminist Theory. Paper presented at the American Sociological Association Annual Meeting, Chicago.

Kaplan, C. 1987. Deterritorializations, *Cultural Critique,* no. 6.

——. 1994. The Politics of Location as Transnational Feminist Critical Practice. In *Scattered Hegemonies,* eds. I. Grewal and C. Kaplan. Minneapolis: University of Minnesota Press.

Kapsalis, T. 1997. *Public Privates.* Durham: Duke University Press.

Kearney, M. 1995. The Local and the Global. *Annual Review of Anthropology* 24: 547–565.

Keck, M., and K. Sikkink. 1998. *Activists Beyond Borders.* Ithaca: Cornell University Press.

Keller, E. F. 1985. *Reflections on Gender and Science.* New Haven: Yale University Press.

Kessler, S. 1998/2000. *Lessons from the Intersexed.* New Brunswick: Rutgers University Press.

Khandelwal, M. S. 1996. Indian Networks in the United States. In *Immigrants and Immigration Policy,* eds. H. O. Duleep and P. V. Wunnava, 115–131. Greenwich: JAI Press.

Khattab, H. 1992. *The Silent Endurance* Amman: UNICEF; and Cairo: Population Council.

Kibria, N. 1993. *Family Tightrope.* Princeton: Princeton University Press.

Kim, S. and C. McCann. 1998. Internationalizing Theories of Feminism. *Women's Studies Quarterly* 26 (Fall/Winter): 115–132.

Kimmel, M. S. 1987. Rethinking "Masculinity." In *Changing Men,* ed. M. S. Kimmel, 9–24. Newbury Park: Sage.

——. 2000. *The Gendered Society.* Oxford University Press.

King, D. 1988. Multiple Jeopardy, Multiple Consciousness. *Signs* 14(1): 42–72.

King, K. 1994. *Theory in Its Feminist Travels*. Bloomington: Indiana University Press.

King, R., and K. Rybaczuk. 1993. Southern Europe and the International Division of Labor. In *The New Geography of European Migrants*, ed. King, 175–206. London: Belhaven Press.

Kishwar, M. 1986. Pro-woman or anti-Muslim? The Shahbano controversy. *Manushi* 32: 4–13.

Kishwar, M. and R. Vanita 1987. The Burning of Roop Kanwar. *Manushi*, 42–43.

Kitzinger, C., and S. Wilkinson. 1994. Virgins and Queers: Rehabilitating Heterosexuality? *Gender & Society* 8(3): 444–463.

Knight, E. 1986. The Idea of Ancestry. In *The Essential Etheridge Knight*, 12–13. Pittsburgh: University of Pittsburgh Press.

Kolawale, M. M. 1997. *Womanism and African Consciousness*. Trenton: Africa World Press.

Kotz, L. 1992. The Body You Want. *Art-forum* 31: 82–89.

Kruks, S. 2001. *Retrieving Experience*. Ithaca: Cornell University Press.

Kuhlmann, E., and B. Babitsch. 2002. Bodies, Health, Gender. *Women's Studies International Forum* 25 (4): 433–442.

Kuhn, T. 1970. *The Structure of Scientific Revolutions* (2nd ed.). Chicago: Chicago University Press.

La Duke, W. 1999. *All Our Relations*. Boston: South End Press.

Ladner, J. 1972. *Tomorrow's Tomorrow*. Garden City: Doubleday.

Laguerre, M. 1994. Headquarters and Subsidiaries. In *Minority Families in the United States*, ed. R. Taylor, 47–61. Englewood Cliffs: Prentice Hall.

Lakoff, G. and Z. Kovecses. 1987. The Cognitive Model of Anger Inherent in American English. In *Cultural Models in Language and Thought*, eds. N. Quinn and D. Holland. New York: Cambridge University Press.

Laqueur, T. W. 1990. *Making Sex*. Cambridge: Harvard University Press.

LatCrit. 2006. Retrieved June 18, 2007, from www.arts.cornell.edu/latcrit/ PortfolioOf- Projects/ LCPortfolio9_29_2006.pdf.

Lavie, S., and T. Swedenburg. 1996. Introduction. In *Displacement, Diaspora and Geographies of Identity*, eds. S. Lavie and T. Swedenburg, 1–25. Durham: Duke University Press.

Lay, M. M., J. Monk, and D. Silverton Rosenfelt, eds. 2002. *Encompassing Gender*. New York: Feminist Press.

Lazreg, M. 1988. Feminism and Difference. *Feminist Studies*, 14(1).

Lewontin, R. C. 1982. Letter to the Editor. *New York Review of Books*, 4 February, 40–41.

Lim, S. et al. 2006 *Transnational Asian American Literature*. Philadelphia: Temple University Press.

Lindemann, G. 1997. The Body of Gender Difference. In *Embodied Practices*, ed. K. Davis, 73–92. London: Sage.

Lindsay, B., ed. 1980. *Comparative Perspectives of Third World Women*. New York: Praeger.

Lipsitz, G. 1998. *The Possessive Investment in Whiteness*. Philadelphia: Temple University Press.

Lipschutz, R. 1992. Reconstructing World Politics. *Millennium* 21(3): 389–420.

Lloyd, G. 1984. *The Man of Reason*. Minneapolis: University of Minnesota Press; London: Methuen.

Loewenberg, B. J., and R. Bogin, eds. 1976. *Black Women in Nineteenth-Century American Life*. University Park: Pennsylvania State University Press.

Lopez, I. 1993. *Constrained Choices* Unpublished manuscript.

Lopez, S. 1977. The Role of the Chicana within the Student Movement. In *Essays on La Mujer*, eds. R. Sanchez and R. Martinez Cruz. Los Angeles: University of California Press.

Lorber, J. 1994. *Paradoxes of Gender.* New Haven, CT: Yale University Press.

——. 1998. *Gender Inequality.* Los Angeles: Roxbury.

Lorde, A. 1981. An Open Letter to Mary Daly. In *This Bridge Called My Back*, eds. Cherrie Moraga and Gloria Anzaldúa, 94–97. New York: Kitchen Table Press.

——. 1982. *Zami.* Trumansberg: The Crossing Press.

——. 1983. The Master's Tools Will Never Dismantle the Master's House. In *This Bridge Called My Back*, eds. C. Moraga and G. Anzaldúa, 98–101. New York: Kitchen Table Press.

——. 1984a. Age, Race, Class, and Sex. In *Sister Outsider*, 114–123. Freedom: Crossing Press.

——. 1984b. *Sister Outsider.* Trumansberg: The Crossing Press.

Lowe, L. 1996. *Immigrant Acts.* Durham: Duke University Press.

Lugones, M. 1994. Purity, Impurity, and Separation. *Signs* 19(2): 458–479.

——. 2003. *Pilgimages/Peregrinajes.* Lanham: Rowman and Littlefield.

Lutz, C. 1985. Depression and the Translation of Emotional Worlds. In *Culture and Depression*, eds. A. Kleinman and B. Good, 63–100. Berkeley: University of California Press.

——. 1986. Emotion, Thought, and Estrangement. *Cultural Anthropology* 1: 287–309.

——. 1987. Goals, Events and Understanding in Ifaluck and Emotion Theory. In *Cultural Models in Language and Thought*, eds. N. Quinn and D. Holland. New York: Cambridge University Press.

Lyman, S. M. 1972. *The Black American in Sociological Thought.* New York: Capricorn.

Lynch, C. 1998. Social Movements and the Problem of Globalization, *Alternatives* 23: 149–173

MacKinnon, C. 1987. *Feminism Unmodified.* Cambridge: Harvard University Press.

Maggenti, M. 1993. Wandering through Herland. In *Sisters, Sexperts, Queers*, ed. A. Stein, 245–255. New York: Plume Book/Penguin.

Mahler, S. 1995. *American Dreaming.* Princeton: Princeton University Press.

——. 1998. Theoretical and Empirical Contributions Toward a Research Agenda for Transnationalism. In *Transnationalism from Below*, eds. Smith and Guarnizo, 64–100. New Brunswick: Transaction.

Majors, R. G. and J. U. Gordon. 1994. *The American Black Male.* Chicago: Nelson-Hall.

Mani, L. 1987. Contentious Traditions. *Cultural Critique*, 7.

——. 1989. Contentious Traditions. Dissertation, University of California, Santa Cruz.

Mani, L. and R. Frankenberg 1985. The Challenge of Orientalism. *Economy and Society*, 14(2).

Mann, K. 1985. *Marrying Well.* Cambridge: Cambridge University Press.

Marshall, H. 1996. Our Bodies, Ourselves: Why We Should Add Old Fashioned Empirical Phenomenology to the New Theories of the Body. *Women's Studies International Forum* 19(3): 253–265.

Martin, B. 1993. Lesbian Identity and Autobiographical Difference(s). In *The Lesbian and Gay Studies Reader*, ed. H. Abelove, M. A. Barale, and D. M. Halperin, 274–293. New York: Routledge.

——. 1994. Sexualities without Gender and Other Queer Utopias. *diacritics* 24(2–3): 104–121.

Marx, K.1977. The German Ideology. In *Karl Marx*, ed. David McLellan, 159–191. New York: Oxford University Press.

Massey, D., and N. Denton. 1993. *American Apartheid.* Cambridge: Harvard University Press.

Massey, D., R. Alarcon, J. Durand, and H. Gonzales. 1987. *Return to Aztlan.* Berkeley: University of California Press.

May, V. 2002. Disciplinary Desire and Undisciplined Daughters. *NWSA Journal* 14(1): 134–159.

Mbilinyi, M. J. 1982. Wife, Slave and Subject of the King. *Tanzania Notes and Records* 88/89: 1–13.

McCann, C. 1994. *Birth Control Politics in the United States, 1916–1945*. Ithaca: Cornell University Press.

McCarthy, J., and D. Maine. 1992. A Framework for Analyzing the Determinants of Maternal Mortality. *Studies in Family Planning* 23: 23–33.

McDermott, P. 1994. *Politics and Scholarship*. Urbana: University of Illinois Press.

——. 1998. Internationalizing the Core Curriculum. *Women's Studies Quarterly* 26 (Fall/Winter): 88–98.

McDonough, R. and R. Harrison. 1978. Patriarchy and Relations of Production. In *Feminism and Materialism*, eds. A. Kuhn and A. M. Wolpe, 11–41. London: Routledge & Kegan Paul.

McLaughlin, A. 1985. Images and Ethics of Nature. *Environmental Ethics* 7: 293–319.

McNay, L. 1992. *Foucault and Feminism*. Cambridge: Polity.

——. 2000. *Gender and Agency*. Cambridge: Polity.

Mediatore, S. S. 1998. Chandra Mohanty and the Revaluing of 'Experience'. *Hypatia* 13 (2): 116–133.

——. 2003. *Reading across Borders*. New York: Palgrave.

Merchant, C. M. 1980. *The Death of Nature*. New York: Harper & Row.

Mernissi, F. 1975. *Beyond the Veil*. New York: Wiley.

Messerschmidt, J. W. 1993. *Masculinity and Crime*. Lanham: Rowman & Littlefield.

Meyerowitz, J. 2002. *How Sex Changed*. Cambridge: Harvard University Press.

Midgley, M., and J. Hughes. 1983. *Women's Choices*. London: Weidenfeld & Nicolson.

Mies, M. 1986. *Patriarchy and Accumulation on a World Scale*. London: Zed.

Mill, J. S. 1980/1869/1883. *The Subjection of Women*. New York: Henry Holt and Co; Illinois: AHM Publishing.

Millet, K. 1970. *Sexual Politics*. New York: Avon.

Mills, C. W. 1959. *The Sociological Imagination*. Oxford: Oxford University Press.

Minh-Ha, T. T. ed. 1986/7. She the Inappropriate/d Other. *Discourse*, 8.

——. 1989. *Woman, Native, Other*. Indiana: Indiana University Press.

Mintzes, B., ed. 1992. *A Question of Control*. Amsterdam: WEMOS, Women & Pharmaceuticals Project.

Mitchell, H. H., and N. C. Lewter. 1986. *Soul Theology*. San Francisco: Harper & Row.

Mitchell, J. 1971/1973. *Woman's Estate*. Harmondsworth and New York: Penguin and Vintage.

——. 1986. Reflections on Twenty Years of Feminism. In *What is Feminism?* eds. J. Mitchell and A. Oakley, 34–48. Oxford: Basil Blackwell.

Mitchell, J. and O. Ann. 1986. Introduction. *What is Feminism?* 1–7. New York: Pantheon.

Modleski, T. 1991. *Feminism without Women*. New York: Routledge.

Moghadam, V. M. 1996a. Feminists Networks North and South. *Journal of International Communication* 3(1): 111–25.

——. 1996b. The Fourth World Conference on Women. *Bulletin of Concerned Asian Scholars* Jan–March: 28.

Mohanty, C. T. 1984. Under Western Eyes, *Boundary* 2, Spring/Fall, 12(3)/13(1).

——. 1987. Feminist Encounters, *Copyright*, 1(1).1.

——. 1991a. Cartographies of Struggle: Third World Women and the Politics of Feminism. In *Third World Women and the Politics of Feminism*, eds. C. T. Mohanty, A. Russo, and L. Torres, 1–47. Bloomington: University of Indiana Press.

——. 1991/1991b. Under Western Eyes. In *Third World Women and the Politics of Feminism*, eds. C. T. Mohanty, A. Russo, and L. Torres, 51–80. Bloomington: University of Indiana Press.

——. 1997. *Literary Theory and the Claims of History*. Ithaca: Cornell University Press.

——. 2003. *Feminism without Borders*. Durham: Duke University Press.

Mohanty, S. 1997. *Literary Theory and the Claims of History*. Ithaca: Cornell University Press.

Mohanty, S. P. 1989. Us and Them. *Yale Journal of Criticism*, 2(2).

Moller-Okin, S. 1979. *Woman in Western Political Thought*. Princeton: Princeton University Press.

——. 1984. Justice and Gender, paper presented at the Annual Meeting of the American Political Science Association, Washington, DC.

Molyneux, M. 1985. Mobilization Without Emancipation? Women's Interests, the State and Revolution in Nicaragua. *Feminist Studies*, 11: 227–254.

Moore, L. J., and A. E. Clarke. 1995. Clitoral Conventions and Transgressions: Graphic Representations in Anatomy Texts, c. 1900–1991. *Feminist Studies*, 21 (summer): 255–301.

Moraga, C. 1983a. *Loving in the War Years*. Boston: South End.

——. 1983b. La Güera. In *This Bridge Called My Back*, eds. C. Moraga and G. Anzaldúa, 27–34. New York: Kitchen Table Women of Color Press.

——. 1983c. Preface In *This Bridge Called My Back*, eds. C. Moraga and G. Anzaldúa, xiii–xix. New York Kitchen Table Women of Color Press.

Moraga, C., and A. Hollibaugh. 1983. What We're Rollin around in Bed With. In *Powers of Desire*, ed. A. Snitow, C. Stansell, and S. Thompson, 394–405. New York: Monthly Review Press.

Moraga, C., and G. Anzaldúa, eds. 1981/1983. *This Bridge Called My Back*. New York: Kitchen Table Press.

——. 2002. *This Bridge Called My Back*. Third edition. Berkeley: Third Woman Press.

Morgan, J. 1999. *When Chickenheads Come Home to Roost*. New York: Simon & Schuster.

Morgan, S. 2006. *The Feminist Theory Reader*. London: Routledge.

Morgan, T. 1993. Butch-Femme and the Politics of Identity. In *Sisters, Sexperts, Queers*, ed. A. Stein, 35–46. New York: Plume Book/Penguin.

Morgen, S. 2002. *Into Our Own Hands*. New Brunswick: Rutgers University Press.

Morsy, S. 1994. Maternal Mortality in Egypt. In *Conceiving the New World Order*, eds. F. Ginsburg and R. Rapp, 162–176. Berkeley: University of California Press.

Moses, C. 1998a. "What's in a Name? On Writing the History of Feminism," An unpublished paper presented to the International Academic Conference on Women' Studies and Development in the Twenty-First Century, Peking University, June.

——. 1998b. Made in America. *Feminist Studies*, 24 (Summer): 241–273.

Moya, P. M. L. 1997. Postmodernism, 'Realism,' and the Politics of Identity. In *Feminist Genealogies, Colonial Legacies, Democratic Futures*, eds. M. J. Alexander and C. T. Mohanty, 125–150, 379–384. New York: Routledge.

Moya, P. M. L., and M. R. Hames-Garcia, eds. 2000. *Reclaiming Identity*. Berkeley: University of California Press.

Mufti, A., and E. Shohat. 1997. Introduction, eds. A. McClintock, A. Mufti, and E. Shoha, 1–11. *Dangerous Liaisons*. Minneapolis: University of Minnesota Press.

Murphy, M. 2004. Immodest Witnessing. *Feminist Studies* 30(1): 115–147.

Murray, C. 1987. Class, Gender and the Household The Developmental Cycle in Southern Africa. *Development and Change* 18: 235–250.

Murray, P. 1970. The Liberation of Black Women. In *Voices of the New Feminism*, ed. M. L. Thompson, 87–102. Boston: Beacon.

Musallam, B. F. 1983. *Sex and Society in Islam.* Cambridge: Cambridge University Press.

Myers, K. A., C. D. Anderson, and B. J. Risman, eds. 1998. *Feminist Foundations.* Thousand Oaks, CA: Sage Publications.

Myers, L. J. 1988. *Understanding an Afrocentric World View.* Dubuque: Kendall/Hunt.

Nagel, E. 1968. The Subjective Nature of Social Subject Matter. In *Readings in the Philosophy of the Social Sciences,* ed. M. Brodbeck. New York: Macmillan.

Nandy, A. 1987. The Sociology of *Sati. Indian Express,* October 5.

———. 1988a. The Human Factor. *The Illustrated Weekly of India,* January 17, 1988.

———. 1988b. *Sati* in Kaliyuga. *Economic and Political Weekly,* September 17.

Narayan, U. 1989. The Project of Feminist Epistemology. In *Gender/ Body/ Knowledge,* eds. A. M. Jaggar and S. R. Bordo, 256–269. New Brunswick: Rutgers University Press.

Nash, J., and M. P. Fernandez Kelly, eds. 1983. *Women, Men and the International Division of Labor.* Albany: SUNY Press.

National Research Council. 1989. *Contraception and Reproduction.* Washington, D.C.: National Academy Press.

Nedelsky, J. 1989. Reconceiving Autonomy. *Yale Journal of Law and Feminism* 1: 7–36.

Nicholson, L, ed. 1990 *Feminism/Postmodernism.* New York: Routledge.

———. 1994. Interpreting Gender. *Signs* 20(1): 79–105.

———. 1997. *The Second Wave: A Reader in Feminist Theory.* New York: Routledge.

Nicholson, L., and S. Seidman, eds. 1995. *Social Postmodernism.* Cambridge: Cambridge University Press.

Njaka, E. N. 1974. *Igbo Political Culture.* Evanston: Northwestern University Press.

Nnaemeka, O. 1995. Feminism, Rebellious Women, and Cultural Boundaries. *Research in African Literatures* 26(2): 80–113.

———. 1998. Introduction. In *Sisterhood, Feminisms and Power,* ed. O. Nnaemeka. Trenton: Africa World Press

Nunokawa, J. 1992. Identity Crisis. Interview, A. Solomon. *Village Voice,* June 30.

Oakley, A. 1972. *Sex, Gender, and Society.* New York: Harper & Row.

O'Brien, M. 1981. *The Politics of Reproduction.* London: Routledge & Kegan Paul.

O'Connor, J. 1987. *The Meaning of Crisis.* Oxford: Blackwell. 1991.

Offen, K. 1985. Toward An Historical Definition of Feminism, Working Paper No. 22, Center for Research on Women, Stanford University.

O'Flaherty, W. D. 1980. *Women, Androgynes, and Other Mythical Beasts.* Chicago: University of Chicago Press.

Ogundipe-Leslie, M. 1994. *Re-Creating Ourselves.* Trenton: Africa World Press.

Ogunyemi, C. O. 1985/86. Womanism. *Signs* 11: 63–80.

———. 1996. *Africa Wo/Man Palava.* Chicago: The University of Chicago Press.

Okamura, J. 1998. *Imagining the Filipino American Diaspora.* New York: Garland.

Okanlawon, A. 1972. Africanism—A Synthesis of the African World-View. *Black World* 21(9): 40–44, 92–97.

Oliver, M., and T. M. Shapiro. 1995. *Black Wealth/White Wealth.* New York: Routledge Press.

Olsen, F. 1984. Statutory Rape. *Texas Law Review* 63: 387–432.

Omi, M., and H. Winant. 1986/1994. *Racial Formation in the United States.* New York: Routledge.

Ong, A. 1987. *Spirits of Resistance and Capitalist Discipline.* Albany: SUNY Press.

———. 1999. *Flexible Citizenship.* Durham: Duke University Press.

Ortner, S. 1978. The Virgin and the State. *Feminist Studies* 4: 19–36.

O'Sullivan, T., et al. 1994. *Key Concepts in Communication and Cultural Studies.* New York: Routledge.

Oudshoorn, N. 1994. *Beyond the Natural Body.* New York: Routledge.

Pachauri, P. 1988 Turning a Blind Eye. *India Today*, October 15.

Parmar, P. 1982. Gender, Race and Class. In *The Empire Strikes Back*, eds. Centre for Contemporary Cultural Studies, 1–11. London: Hutchinson.

Patel, S. and Kumar, K. 1988. Defenders of *Sati. Economic and Political Weekly*, January 23.

Pateman, C. 1980b. The Disorder of Women. *Ethics* 91: 20–34.

——. 1983b. Feminist Critiques of the Public/Private Dichotomy. In *Public and Private in Social Life*, eds. S. Benn and G. Gaus. Canberra and London: Croom Helm.

——. 1984. The Fraternal Social Contract: Some Observations on Patriarchy, paper presented at the Annual Meeting of the American Political Science Association Washington, DC.

Pathak, Z. and Sunder Rajan, R. 1989. Shahbano. *Signs*, 14(3).

Patterson, O. 1982. *Slavery and Social Death.* Cambridge: Harvard University Press.

Pearce, T. O. 1994. Women's Reproductive Practices and Biomedicine. In *Conceiving the New World Order*, eds. F. Ginsburg and R. Rapp, 195–208. Berkeley: University of California Press.

Pedraza, S. 1991. Women and Migration. *Annual Review of Sociology* 17: 303–325.

——. 1994. Introduction from the Special Issue Editor. *Social Problems* 41(1): 1–8.

Pedraza-Bailey, S. 1990. Immigration Research. *Social Science History* 14(1): 43–67.

Pessar, P. R. 1999. Engendering Migration Studies. *American Behavioral Scientist* 42(4): 577–600.

Petchesky, R. 1979. Reproductive Choice in the Contemporary United States. In *And the Poor Get Children*, ed. K. Michaelson. New York: Monthly Review Press.

——. 1990. *Abortion and Woman's Choice.* Revised ed. Boston: Northeastern University Press.

——. 1994. The Body as Property. In *Conceiving the New World*, eds. F. Ginsburg and R. Rapp, 387–405. Berkeley: University of California Press.

Petchesky, R. P., and J. Weiner. 1990. *Global Feminist Perspectives on Reproductive Rights and Reproductive Health.* New York: Reproductive Rights Education Project, Hunter College.

Phelan, S. 1993. (Be)Coming Out. *Signs* 18(4): 765–90.

Philipose, P. and Setalvad, T. 1988. Demystifying *sati. The Illustrated Weekly of India*, March 13.

Phillips, A. 1998. *Feminism and Politics.* Oxford: Oxford University Press.

Pies, C. n.d. *Creating Ethical Reproductive Health Care Policy.* San Francisco: Education Programs Associates, Inc.

Pitkin, H. F. 1984. *Fortune is a Women.* Berkeley: University of California Press.

Portes, A. 1997. Immigration Theory for a New Century. *International Migration Review* 31(4): 799–825.

——. 2000. The Resilient Significance of Class. *Political Power and Social Theory* 14: 249–284.

Portes, A., and J. Walton. 1981. *Labor, Class, and the International System.* New York: Academic Press.

Portes, A., and R. Rumbaut. 1996. *Immigrant America.* 2nd ed. Berkeley: University of California Press.

Pough, G. D. 2004. *Check It While I Wreck It.* Boston: Northeastern University Press.

Powers, S. 2002. *A Problem from Hell.* New York: Basic Books.

Ptacek, J. 1988. Why do Men Batter Their Wives? In *Feminist Perspectives on Wife Abuse*, eds. K. Yllö and M. Bograd, 133–157. Newbury Park: Sage.

Pugliese, E. 1996. Italy Between Emigration and Immigration and the Problems of Citizenship. In *Citizenship, Nationality and Migration in Europe*, eds. Cesarani and Fulbrook, 106–121. London: Routledge.

Punwani, J. 1985. The Strange Case of Shahbano. *The Sunday Observer*, November 24.

Qadeer, I. and Hasan, Z. 1987. Deadly Politics of the State and its Apologists. *Economic and Political Weekly*, November 14.

Ramusack, B. N. 1989. Embattled Advocates. *Journal of Women's History* 1: 34–64.

Rao, A. 1991. *Women's Studies International*. New York: Feminist Press.

Ravindran, T. K. S. 1993. Women and the Politics of Population and Development in India. *Reproductive Health Matters* 1: 26–38.

Reagon, B. J. 1983. Coalition Politics. In *Homegirls*, ed. B. Smith, 256–368. New York: Kitchen Table Women of Color Press.

Reich, J. L. 1992. Genderfuck. *Discourse* 15(1): 112–127.

Reich, R. 1991. *The Work of Nations*. New York: Vintage Books.

Reid-Pharr, R. 1993. The Spectacle of Blackness. *Radical America* 24(4): 57–65.

Repak, T. 1995. *Waiting on Washington*. Philadelphia: Temple University Press.

Rich, A. 1979. Disloyal to Civilization. In *On Lies, Secrets, and Silences*, 275–310. New York: Norton.

——. 1980. Compulsory Heterosexuality and Lesbian Existence. *Signs* 5 (Summer): 631–660.

——. 1986. Compulsory Heterosexuality. In *Blood Bread and Poetry*. New York: W. W. Norton.

Richards, D. 1980. European Mythology, In *Contemporary Black Thought*, eds. M. K. Asante and A. S. Vandi, 59–79. Beverly Hills, CA: Sage.

Richardson, M., ed. 1987. *Maria W. Stewart, America's First Black Woman Political Writer*. Bloomington: Indiana University Press.

Robbins, B. 1987/8. The Politics of Theory. *Social Text*, 18.

Rodriguez, C. E. 2000. *Changing Race*. New York: New York University Press.

Roediger, D. R. 1991. *The Wages of Whiteness*. New York: Verso Books.

Rollins, J. 1985. *Between Women*. Philadelphia: Temple University Press.

Romero, M. 1992. *Maid in the U.S.A.* New York and London: Routledge.

Roof, J. 1994. Lesbians and Lyotard. In *The Lesbian Postmodern*, ed. L. Doan, 47–66. New York: Columbia University Press.

Rorty, R. 1979. *Philosophy and the Mirror of Nature*. Princeton: Princeton University Press.

Rosaldo, M. Z. 1984. Towards an Anthropology of Self and Feeling. In *Culture Theory*, eds. R. A. Shweder and R. A. LeVine. Cambridge: Cambridge University Press.

Rosca, N. 1995. The Philippines' Shameful Export. *Nation* 260(15): 522–527.

Rose, S. O. 1992. *Limited Livelihoods*. Berkeley: University of California Press.

Rose, T. 1994. *Black Noise*. Hanover: University Press of New England.

Rosenfelt, D. 1998. Crossing Boundaries. *Women's Studies Quarterly* 26(Fall/Winter): 4–16.

Roth, B. 2004. *Separate Roads to Feminism: Black, Chicana and White Feminist Movements in America's Second Wave*. Cambridge: Cambridge University Press.

Rouse, R. 1991. Mexican Migration and the Social Space of Postmodernism. *Diaspora* 1(1): 8–23.

——. 1992. Making Sense of Settlement. *Towards a Transnational Perspective*. Annals of the New York Academy of Sciences, 645: 25–52

Rowell, C. H. 1975. An Interview with Margaret Walker. *Black World* 25(2): 4–17.

Rowley, M. 2007. Feminist Visions for Women in a New Era. *Feminist Studies* 33 (1): 64–87.

Roy, C. 1993. Speaking in Tongues. In *Sisters, Sexperts, Queers*, ed. A. Stein, 6–12. New York: Plume Book/Penguin.

Rubin, G. 1975. The Traffic in Women. In *Toward an Anthropology of Women*, ed. R. R. Reiter, 157–210. New York: Monthly Review Press.

Rubin, L. B. 1976. *Worlds of Pain.* New York: Basic Books.

Ruddick, S. 1982. Maternal Thinking. *Feminist Studies* 6(2): 342–369.

———. 1989. *Maternal Thinking.* Boston: Beacon Press.

Ruiz, V. L. 1998. *From Out of the Shadows.* New York: Oxford University Press.

Russell, D. E. H. 1982. *Rape in Marriage.* New York: Macmillan.

Ruthven, M. 1984. *Islam in the World.* New York: Oxford University Press.

Sabagh, G. 1993. Los Angeles, a World of New Immigrants, 97–126, in Luciani, *Migration Policies.*

Said, E. 1978/1979. *Orientalism.* New York: Pantheon Books & Vintage.

———. 1983. *The World, The Text and the Critic.* Cambridge: Harvard University Press.

———. 1986. Intellectuals in the Post-Colonial World. *Salmagundi*, 70–71.

Sánchez, R. 1987. Postmodernism and Chicano Literature. *Aztlán* 18(2): 1–14.

Sandoval, C. 1990. Feminism and Racism. In *Making Face, Making Soul / Haciendo Caras*, ed. G. Anzaldúa, 55–71. San Francisco: Aunt Lute.

———. 1991. U.S. Third World Feminism. *Genders* 10(Spring): 1–24.

Sangari, K. K. 1988. Perpetuating the Myth. *Seminar*, 342, Special Issue on *sati*.

Sangari, K.K. and Vaid, S. eds. 1989. *Recasting Women.* New Delhi: Kali.

Sanger, M. 1920. *Woman and The New Race.* New York: Brentano's.

Sartre, J. P. 1968 [1960]. *Search for a Method.* New York: Vintage.

Sassen, S. 1984. Notes on the Incorporation of Third World Women into Wage Labor through Immigration and Offshore Production. *International Migration Review* 18(4): 1144–1167.

———. 1988. *The Mobility of Labor and Capital.* New York: Cambridge University Press.

———. 1993. The Impact of Economic Internationalization on Immigration. *International Migration* 31(1): 73–99.

———. 1994. *Cities in a World Economy.* Thousand Oaks: Pine Forge Press.

———. 1996a. Analytic Borderlands. In *Re-Presenting the City*, ed. King, 183–202. New York: New York University Press.

———. 1996b. *Losing Control? Sovereignty in an Age of Globalization.* New York: Columbia University Press.

———. 1996c. New Employment Regimes in Cities. *New Community* 22(4): 579–594.

———. 1996d. Rebuilding the Global City. In *Re-Presenting the City*, ed. King, 23–42. New York: New York University Press.

———. 1998. Cracked Casings. Working paper. New York: Russell Sage Foundation and the Social Science Research Council Committee on Sovereignty.

Schachter, S., and J. B. Singer. 1969. Cognitive, Social and Psychological Determinants of Emotional State. *Psychological Review* 69: 379–399.

Schmitz, B., D. Rosenfelt, J. Butler, and B. Guy-Sheftall. 1995. Women's Studies and Curriculum Transformation. In *Handbook of Research on Multicultural Education*, ed. James A. Banks, 708–728. New York: Macmillan Publishing.

Schneider, E. M. 1991. The Dialectic of Rights and Politics. In *Feminist Legal Theory*, eds. K. T. Bartlett and R. Kennedy, 318–350. Boulder: Westview Press.

Scott, J. 1986. Gender: A Useful Category of Historical Analysis. *The American Historical Review* 91(5): 1053–1075.

———. 1992. Experience. In Feminists Theorize the Political eds. J. Butler and J. Scott, 22–40. New York: Routledge.

Scott, J. C. 1985. *Weapons of the Weak.* New Haven: Yale University Press.

Scudson, M. 1997. Cultural Studies and the Social Construction of 'Social Construction.' In *From Sociology to Cultural Studies*, ed. E. Long, 379–398. Oxford: Blackwell.

Sedgwick, E. K. 1989. Across Gender, Across Sexuality. *South Atlantic Quarterly* 88(1): 53–72.

———. 1990. *Epistemology of the Closet.* Berkeley: University of California Press.

———. 1991. How to Bring Your Kids up Gay. *Social Text* 29: 18–27.

———. 1993. *Tendencies.* Durham: Duke University Press.

Segrest, M. 1985. *My Mama's Dead Squirrel.* Ithaca: Firebrand Books.

Seidman, S. 1994. Queer Pedagogy/Queer-ing Sociology. *Critical Sociology* 20(3): 167–176.

Sen, G. 1980. The Sexual Division of Labor and the Working-Class Family. *Review of Radical Political Economics* 12(2): 76–86.

———. 1987. *Development, Crisis, and Alternative Visions.* New York: Monthly Review Press.

———. 1992. *Women, Poverty and Population.* Cambridge: Center for Population and Development Studies, Harvard University.

Sharma, U. 1980. *Women, Work and Property in Worth West India.* London: Tavistock.

Shiva, V., A. H. Jafri, G. Bedi, and R. Holla-Bhar. 1997. *The Enclosure and Recovery of the Commons.* New Delhi: Research Foundation for Science and Technology.

Shockley, A. A. 1974. *Loving Her.* Tallahassee: Naiad Press.

Shohat, E. 2001. Area Studies, Transnationalism, and the Feminist Production of Knowledge. *Signs* 26(4) (summer): 1269–1272.

Silliman, J., M. Gerber Fried, L. Ross, and R. Gutierrez. 2004. *Undivided Rights.* Boston: South End Press.

Singer, L. 1992. Feminism and Postmodernism. In *Feminists Theorize the Political*, ed. J. Butler and J. W. Scott, 464–475. New York: Routledge.

Smith, B. ed. 1983. *Home Girls.* New York: Kitchen Table Press.

———. 1993. Queer Politics. *Nation*, July 5, 12–16.

Smith, B., and B. Smith. 1981. Across the Kitchen Table. In *This Bridge Called My Back*, eds. C. Moraga and G. Anzaldua, 113–127. New York: Kitchen Table Press.

———. 1987. *The Everyday World as Problematic.* Boston: Northeastern University Press & Toronto: University of Toronto Press.

———. 1990/b. *Texts, Facts, and Femininity.* New York: Routledge.

———. 1990/a. *The Conceptual Practices of Power.* Boston: Northeastern Press.

———. 1999. *Writing the Social: Critique, Theory, and Investigations.* Toronto: University of Toronto Press.

Smith, J. 1989. *Misogynies.* London: Faber & Faber.

Smith, P. 1988. *Discerning the Subject.* Minneapolis: University of Minnesota Press.

Smith, R. C. 1998. Transnational Localities. In *Transnationalism from Below*, eds. Smith and Guarnizo, 196–238. New Brunswick: Transaction.

Smitherman, G. 1977. *Talkin and Testifyin.* Boston: Houghton Mifflin.

Sobel, M. 1979. *Trabelin' On.* Princeton: Princeton University Press.

Solinger, R. 1992. *Wake up Little Susie.* New York: Routledge Press.

Spelman, E. 1982. Anger and Insubordination. Manuscript; early version read to mid-western chapter of the Society for Women in Philosophy, spring.

———. 1988. *Inessential Woman.* New York: Beacon Press.

Spivak, G. 1981. French Feminism in an International Frame. *Yale French Studies*, 62.

———. 1988. Can the Subaltern Speak? In *Marxism and Interpretation*, eds. C. Nelson and Lawrence Grossberg, 271–313. Chicago: University of Illinois.

———. 1990. *The Post-Colonial Critic*. ed. S. Harasym. New York: Routledge.

Stacey, J. 1987. Sexism by a Subtler Name? Postindustrial Conditions and Postfeminist Consciousness in the Silicon Valley. *Socialist Review* (Nov): 7–28.

Stanley, L., and S. Wise. 1993. *Breaking Out*. London: Routledge.

Staples, R. 1982. *Black Masculinity*. San Francisco: Black Scholar Press.

Steady, F. C. 1981. The Black Woman Cross-Culturally. In *The Black Woman Cross-Culturally*, ed. F. C. Steady, 7–42. Cambridge: Schenkman.

———. 1987. African Feminism. In *Women in Africa and the African Diaspora*, eds. R. Terborg-Penn. S. Harley, and A. B. Rushing, 3–24. Washington, DC: Howard University Press.

Stein, A. 1993. The Year of the Lustful Lesbian. In *Sisters, Sexperts, Queers*, ed. A. Stein, 13–34. New York: Plume Book/Penguin.

Steinbugler, A., J. E. Press, and J. J. Dias. 2006. Gender, Race, and Affirmative Action. *Gender & Society* 20: 805–825.

Stern, A. 2005. *Eugenic Nation*. Berkeley: University of California Press.

Stoler, A. L. 2000. *Race and the Education of Desire*. Durham: Duke University Press.

Stone-Mediatore, S., 2000. Chandra Mohanty and the Revaluing of Experience. In *Decentering the Center*, eds. U. Narayan and S. Harding, 110–127. Bloomington: Indiana University Press.

Strathern, M. 1987. An Awkward Relationship: The Case of Feminism and Anthropology. *Signs* 12: 276–292.

Sulik, G. http://pinkribbonblues.org/2010. Accessed August 3, 2012.

Sunder Rajan, R. (forthcoming) The Subject of *Sati*. *Yale Journal of Criticism*.

Taylor, C. A. 1993. Positioning Subjects and Objects. *Hypatia* 8 (Winter 1993): 55–80.

Taylor, H. 1983. *Enfranchisement of Women*. London: Virago.

Tate, C., ed. 1983. *Black Women Writers at Work*. New York: Continuum Publishing.

Terborg-Penn, R. 1986. Black Women in Resistance. *In Resistance*, ed. G. Y. Okhiro, 188–209. Amherst: University of Massachusetts Press.

Theweleit, K. 1987. *Male Fantasies*. Cambridge: Polity Press.

Thompson, R. F. 1983. *Flash of the Spirit*. New York: Vintage.

Tolentino, R. 1996. Bodies, Letters, Catalogs. *Social Text* 48 (14:3): 49–76.

Toro-Morn, M. I. 1995. Gender, Class, Family and Migration. *Gender and Society* 9(6): 712–726.

Trask, H. 1999. *From a Native Daughter*. Honolulu: University of Hawaii Press.

Trinh T. M. 1989. *Woman Native Other*. Bloomington: University of Indiana Press.

Tronto, J. C. 1989/1990. Women and Caring. In *Gender/Body/Knowledge*, ed. A. M. Jaggar and S. R. Bordo, 172–187. New Brunswick: Rutgers University Press.

Trujillo, C. 1991. Chicana Lesbians. In *Chicana Lesbians*, ed. C. Trujillo, 186–194. Berkeley: Third Woman.

Turner, J. E. 1984. Foreword. In *The Next Decade*, ed. J. E. Turner, v–xxv. Ithaca: Cornell University Africana Studies and Research Center.

Tushnet, M. 1984. An Essay on Rights. *Texas Law Review* 62: 1363–1403.

Tyner, J. 1999. The Global Context of Gendered Labor Migration from the Philippines to the United States. *American Behavioral Scientist* 42(4): 671–689.

Unger, R. 1983. The Critical Legal Studies Movement. *Harvard Law Review* 96(3): 561–675.

United Nations Development Programme. 1992. *Human Development Report*. New York: Oxford University Press.

United States Bureau of the Census. 1993. *1990 Census of the Population, Asians and Pacific Islanders in the United States.* Washington, D.C.

Vaid, S. 1988. Politics of Widow Immolation. *Seminar,* 342, Special Issue on *sati.*

Valverde, M. 1985. *Sex, Power and Pleasure.* Toronto: Women's Press.

Vance, C., ed. 1984. *Pleasure and Danger.* New York: Routledge.

——. 1995. Gender, Experience, and Subjectivity: The Tilly-Scott Disagreement. *New Left Review* 211: 89–101.

Vasquez, C. Towards a Revolutionary Ethics. *Coming Up,* January 1983, 11.

Vidal, M. 1997. New Voice of La Raza. In *Chicana Feminist Thought.* ed. A. García, 21–24, New York: Routledge.

Village Voice. 1993. The Queer Issue. *Village Voice,* June 29.

Walby, S. 2000. Beyond the Politics of Location. *Feminist Theory* 1(2): 109–207.

Walker, A. 1983. *In Search of Our Mothers' Gardens.* New York: Harcourt Brace Jovanovich.

Walker, R. 1992. Becoming The Third Wave. *Ms. Magazine,* 39–41.

Wallerstein, I. 1974. *The Modern World System.* New York: Academic.

Walters, S. 1995. *Material Girls.* Berkeley: University of California Press.

Wapner, P. 1995. Politics Beyond the State. *World Politics* 47: 311–340.

Ward, K., ed. 1990. *Women Workers and Global Restructuring.* Ithaca: Cornell University Press.

Ware, C. 1970. *Woman Power.* New York: Tower Publications.

Warhol, R., and D. P. Herndl, eds. 1997. *Feminisms.* New York: Routledge.

Waring, M. 1988. *Counting for Nothing.* Wellington: Allen & Unwin and Port Nicholson Press.

Warner, M. 1991. Fear of a Queer Planet. *Social Text* 9(4): 3–17.

Wasserheit, J. 1993. The Costs of Reproductive Tract Infections in Women. In *Women and HIV/AIDS,* eds. M. Berer and S. Ray. London: Pandora.

Waters, M. C. 1990. *Ethnic Options.* Berkeley: University of California Press.

Webber, T. L. 1978. *Deep Like the Rivers.* New York: W. W. Norton.

Weber, L. 2001. *Understanding Race, Class, Gender, and Sexuality.* New York: McGraw-Hill Higher Education.

Weedon, C. 1997. *Feminist Practice and Poststructuralist Theory.* 2nd ed. Oxford and Cambridge: Blackwell.

Weeks, J. 1981. *Sex, Politics and Society* New York: Longman.

West, C. 1977–78. Philosophy and the Afro-American Experience. *Philosophical Forum* 9(2–3): 117–148.

Whisman, V. 1993. Identity Crises: Who Is a Lesbian, Anyway? In *Sisters, Sexperts, Queers,* ed. A. Stein, 47–60. New York: Plume Book/Penguin.

White, E. F. 1984. Listening to the Voices of Black Feminism. *Radical America* 18(2–3): 7–25.

Wilkerson, W. S. 2000. Is There Something You Need to Tell Me? In *Reclaiming Identity,* eds. P. Moya and M. Hames-García, 251–278. Berkeley: University of California Press.

Williams, D., and C. Collins. 1995. US Socioeconomic and Racial Differences in Health. *Annual Review of Sociology* 21: 349–386.

Williams, P. J. 1991. *The Alchemy of Race and Rights.* Cambridge: Harvard University Press.

Williams, R. 1980. *Problems in Materialism and Culture.* New York: Schocken.

Wilshire, D. 1989/1990. The Uses of Myth, Image, and the Female Body in Re-visioning Knowledge. In *Gender/Body/Knowledge,* ed. A. M. Jaggar and S. R. Bordo, 92–114. New Brunswick: Rutgers University Press.

Wilson, A. 1992. Searching for the Bisexual Politic. *Out/Look* 4(4): 22–28.

Wittig, M. 1992. *The Straight Mind.* Boston: Beacon Press.

Wolf, E. 1966. *Peasants.* Englewood Cliffs: Prentice-Hall.

———. 1982. *Europe and the People Without History.* Berkeley: University of California Press.

Wolf, M. 1972. *Women and the Family in Rural Taiwan.* Palo Alto: Stanford University Press.

———. 1975. Woman and Suicide in China? In *Women in Chinese Society,* eds. M. Wolf and R. Witke, 111–141. Palo Alto: Stanford University Press.

Wollstonecraft, M. 1975. *A Vindication of the Rights of Woman.* New York: Penguin.

Women's Global Network for Reproductive Rights. 1991. *Statement of Purpose.*

Wong, S. 1995. Denationalization Reconsidered. *Amerasia Journal* 21(1/2): 1–27.

Wotherspoon, G. 1991. *City of the Plain.* Sydney: Hale & Iremonger.

Young, I. 1980. Socialist Feminism and the Limits of Dual Systems Theory. *Socialist Review* 10(2/3): 169–188.

———. 1981. Beyond the Unhappy Marriage. In *Women and Revolution,* ed. L. Sargent, 43–69. London: Pluto Press.

Young, I. M. 1990a. *Justice and the Politics of Difference.* Princeton: Princeton University Press.

———. 1990b. *"Throwing Like a Girl" and Other Essays in Feminist Philosophy and Social Theory.* Bloomington: Indiana University Press.

Young, R. M. 1985. *Darwin's Metaphor.* Cambridge: Cambridge University Press.

Young. S. 1977. Fertility and Famine. In *The Roots of Rural Poverty in Central and Southern Africa,* eds. R. Palmer and N. Parsons, 66–81. London: Heinemann.

Zambrana, R. E., and B. T. Dill. 2006. Disparities in Latina Health. In *Gender, Race Class & Health,* eds. A. J. Schulz and L. Mullings. San Francisco: Jossey-Bass.

Zambrana, R. E, W. Mogel, and S.C.M. Scrimshaw. 1987. Gender and Level of Training Differences in Obstetricians' Attitudes towards Patients in Childbirth. *Women & Health* 12(1): 5–24.

Zimmerman, M., et al. 1990. Assessing the Acceptability of Norplant® Implants in Four Countries. *Studies in Family Planning* 21: 92–103.

Zita, J. N. 1992. The Male Lesbian and the Postmodernist Body. *Hypatia* 7(4): 106–127.

———. 1994. Gay and Lesbian Studies. In *Tilting the Tower,* ed. L. Garber, 258–276. New York: Routledge.

Zlotnick, H. 1990. International Migration Policies and the Status of Female Migrants. *International Migration Review* 24(2): 372–8:1.

Zolberg, A. R. 1983. International Migrations in Political Perspective. In *Global Trends in Migration,* eds. Kritz, Keely, and Tomasi, 3–27. Staten Island: Center for Migration Studies.

CREDITS

Akiko Yosano, "The Day the Mountains Move," translated by Laurel Rasplica Rodd, from *Recreating Japanese Women 1600–1945*, edited by Gail Lee Bernstein (Berkeley: University of California Press, 1991). Reprinted with the permission of the translator.

"Re-Rooting American Women's Activism: Global Perspectives on 1848" by Nancy Hewitt, from *Women's Rights and Human Rights: International Perspectives*, pp. 123–137. Copyright © 2001. Used by permission of Palgrave.

Simone De Beauvoir, "Introduction," from *The Second Sex*, translated by H.M. Parshley. Copyright 1952 and renewed © 1980 by Alfred A. Knopf, a division of Random House, Inc. Used by permission of Alfred A. Knopf, a division of Random House, Inc.

"Feminism in 'Waves': Useful Metaphor or Not?" by Linda Nicholson from *New Politics*, 201: 34–39/12(40): 48. Used by permission of the author.

"Multiracial Feminism: Recasting the Chronology of Second Wave Feminism" by Becky Thompson from *Feminist Studies*, 336–355/28(2). Copyright © 2002. Reprinted with permission.

'Are Waves Transatlantic?: Thinking Through How We Tell Feminist Stories" by Michelle Rowley (Revised Version) from *Feminist Studies*, 64–87/33(1). Copyright © 2007. Reprinted with permission.

Amrita Basu, "Globalization of the Local/Localization of the Global: Mapping Transnational Women's Movements" from *Meridians* 1, no. 1 (Autumn 2000): 68–109. Reprinted with the permission of Indiana University Press.

Muriel Rukeyser, "The Poem as Mask" from *A Muriel Rukeyser Reader*, edited by Jan Heller Levi. Copyright 1935, 1951, 1973 and renewed © 1963, 1979 by Muriel Rukeyser. Reprinted with the permission of International Creative Management, Inc.

T.V. Reed, "The Poetic Is the Political: Feminist Poetry and the Poetics of Women's Rights" from *The Art of Protest: Culture and Activism from the Civil Rights Movement to the Streets of Seattle*. Copyright © 2005 by T.V. Reed. Reprinted with the permission of University of Minnesota Press.

Deniz Kandiyoti, "Bargaining with Patriarchy," from *Gender & Society* 2.3 (1988): 274–290. Copyright © 1988 by Sociologists for Women in Society. Reprinted with the permission of Sage Publications, Inc.

"Introduction: The Theoretical Subversiveness of Feminism," from *Feminist Challenges: Social and Political Theory* by Carole Pateman and Elizabeth Gross. © University Press of New England, Lebanon, NH. Reprinted with permission.

Elizabeth Martinez, "La Chicana," from *Chicana Feminist Thought*, edited by Elizabeth Martinez. Originally from *Ideal* (September 5–20, 1972). Reprinted with permission.

"A Black Feminist Statement," from The Combahee River Collective. Reprinted by permission of Monthly Review Foundation.

"The Culture of Romance" by Shulamith Firestone from *The Dialectic of Sex: The Case for Feminist Revolution.* New York: William Morrow and Company, 1970.

Charlotte Bunch, "Lesbians in Revolt," in *Passionate Politics: Essays 1968–1986, Feminist Theory in Action,* by Charlotte Bunch, St. Martin's Press, 1987.

Rosalind Pollack Petchesky and Sonia Correa, "Reproductive and Sexual Rights: A Feminist Perspective," from *Population Policies Reconsidered,* edited by Gita Sen, Adrienne Germain, and Lincoln C. Chen. Copyright © 1994. Reprinted with the permission of Harvard University Center for Population and Development Studies, Harvard School of Public Health.

Leslie Feinberg, excerpt from *Transgender Liberation: A Movement Whose Time Has Come* (New York: World View, 1992). Reprinted with the permission of the author.

"Critical Thinking about Inequality: An Emerging Lens" by Bonnie Thornton Dill and Ruth Enid Zambrana from *Emerging Intersections: Race, Class, and Gender in Theory, Policy, and Practice.* Rutgers University Press, 2009.

Heidi Hartmann, "The Unhappy Marriage of Marxism and Feminism: Towards a More Progressive Union" from *Women and Revolution,* edited by Linda Sargent. Copyright © 1981. Reprinted with the permission of South End Press.

Rhacel Salazar Parrenas, excerpts from Chapters 1 and 2 from *Servants of Globalization: Women, Migration and Domestic Work.* Copyright © 2001 by The Board of Trustees of the Leland Stanford Junior University. Reprinted with the permission of Stanford University Press, www.sup.org.

Lila Abu Lughod, "Orientalism and Middle Eastern Feminist Studies," from *Feminist Studies* 21.1 (2001): 101–113. Copyright © 2001 by Feminist Studies, Inc. Reprinted with permission.

Mrinalini Sinha, excerpts from *Gender and Nation.* Copyright © 2006 by the American Historical Association. Reprinted by permission.

Raewyn Connell, "The Social Organization of Masculinity" from *Masculinities.* Copyright © 2005 by Raewyn Connell. Reprinted with the permission of University of California Press.

Monique Wittig, "One Is Not Born a Woman" from *The Straight Mind and Other Essays.* Originally in *Feminist Issues* 1, no. 2 (1981): 47–54. Copyright © 1981 by Transaction Publishers. Copyright © 1992 by Minique Wittig. Reprinted by permission of Beacon Press, Boston.

Donna Kate Rushin, "The Bridge Poem," from *The Black Back-Ups.* Copyright © 1993. Reprinted with the permission of Firebrand Books, www.firebrandbooks.com.

June Jordan, "Report from the Bahamas," from *On Call: Political Essays.* Copyright © 1985 by June Jordan. Reprinted with the permission of the author.

Gloria Anzaldúa, "The New Mestiza Nation: A Multicultural Movement, in Ana Louise Keating, *The Gloria Anzaldúa Reader,* 203–216 (Durham: Duke University Press, 2009).

Minnie Bruce Pratt, "Identity: Skin, Blood, Heart" from Elly Bulkin, Minnie Bruce Pratt, and Barbara Smith, *Yours in Struggle: Three Feminist Perspectives on Anti-Semitism and Racism.* Copyright © 1984, 1988, 2009 by Minnie Bruce Pratt. Reprinted by permission of the author.

Audre Lorde, "I Am Your Sister: Black Women Organizing Across Sexualities," from *A Burst of Light.* Copyright © 1988. Reprinted with the permission of Regula Noetzli, Literary Agent 2344

"The Veil Debate Again" by Leila Ahmed from *On Shifting Ground: Muslim Women in the Global Era.* The Feminist Press, © 2005.

Lionel Cantú with Eithne Luibhéid and Alexandra Minna Stern, "Well Founded Fear: Political Asylum and the Boundaries of Sexual Identity in the U.S. Mexico Borderlands," from *Queer Migrations: Sexuality, U.S. Citizenship, and Border Crossings,* edited by Eithne Luibhéid and

Lionel Cantú Jr. Copyright © 2005. Reprinted with the permission of University of Minnesota Press.

"Forward: Locating Feminisms/Feminists" by Obioma Nnaemeka from *The Dynamics of African Feminism* edited by Susan Arndt. Africa World Press, © 2002.

"Native American Feminism, Sovereignty, and Social Change" by Andrea Smith from *Feminist Studies*, 2005.

Mari J. Matsuda, "Beside My Sister, Facing the Enemy: Legal Theory Out of Coalition," from *Stanford Law Review* 43 (July 1991). Copyright © 1991 by Mari J. Matsuda. Reprinted with permission.

Nancy Hartsock, "The Feminist Standpoint: Toward a Specifically Feminist Historical Materialism," from *Money, Sex and Power*. Copyright © 1983. Reprinted with the permission of the author.

Uma Narayan, "The Project of Feminist Epistemology: Perspectives from a Nonwestern Feminist," from *Gender/Body/Knowledge*, edited by Alison Jagger and Susan R. Bordo. Copyright © 1989 by Rutgers, The State University. Reprinted with the permission of Rutgers University Press.

Patricia Hill Collins, "Defining Black Feminist Thought," from *Black Feminist Thought: Knowledge, Consciousness, and the Politics of Empowerment*, First Edition. Copyright © 1990 by Patricia Hill Collins. Reprinted with the permission of Routledge, via Copyright Clearance Center.

"Separating Lesbian Theory from Feminist Theory" by Cheshire Calhoun from *Ethics*, 558–581/104(3). Chicago: University of Chicago Press, 1994. Reprinted with permission.

Donna Haraway, "Situated Knowledges: The Science Question in Feminism and the Privilege of Partial Perspective," from *Feminist Studies* 14, no. 3 (Autumn 1988): 575–599. Reprinted with the permission of the publisher, Feminist Studies, Inc.

Luce Irigaray, "This Sex Which Is Not One," from *This Sex Which Is Not One*, translated by Catherine Porter and Carolyn Burke. Translation copyright © 1985 by Cornell University. Used by permission of the publisher, Cornell University Press

Lata Mani, "Multiple Mediations: Feminist Scholarship in the Age of Multinational Reception" from *Feminist Review* 35 (Summer 1990): 24–41. Reprinted with permission.

Sandra Bartky, "Foucault, Femininity, and the Modernization of Patriarchal Power," from *Feminism and Foucault: Paths of Resistance*, edited by Lee Quinby and Irene Diamond. © University Press of New England, Lebanon, NH. Reprinted with permission pages 61–85.

Judith Butler, "Performative Acts and Gender Constitution: An Essay in Phenomenology and Feminist Theory," *Theater Journal*, 1977, Columbia University Press.

"Love and Knowledge: Emotion in Feminist Epistemology" by Alison Jaggar from Inquiry, 151–176/32(2). New York: Routledge/Taylor & Francis, 1989. Reprinted with permission.

"Reclaiming Women's Bodies: Colonialist Trope or Critical Epistemology?," in *The Making Of Our Bodies, Ourselves*, Kathy Davis, pp. 120–141. Copyright, 2007, Duke University Press. All rights reserved. Reprinted by permission of the publisher, www.dukeupress.edu

Lucille Clifton, "lumpectomy eve" from *The Collected Poems Of Lucille Clifton*. Copyright © 1991 by Lucille Clifton. Reprinted with the permission of The Permissions Company, Inc. on behalf of BOA Editions Ltd., www.boaeditions.org.

"Multiculturalism and the Promise of Happiness" by Sara Ahmed from *New Formations* 63: 121–137. Published by Lawrence & Wishart (2008). Used by permission.

Chandra Talpade Mohanty, "Under Western Eyes Revisited: Feminist Solidarity through Anticapitalist Struggles," from *Signs: Journal of Women in Culture and Society* 28.2 (2003). Copyright © 2003 by The University of Chicago Press. Reprinted with permission.

Suzanna Walters, "From Here to Queer: Feminism, Postmodernism, and the Lesbian Menace (Or, Why Can't a Woman be More Like a Fag?)," from *Signs: Journal of Women in Culture and Society* 21.4 (Summer 1996): 830–869. Copyright © 1996 by The University of Chicago Press. Reprinted with permission.

Paula M. L. Moya, "Chicana Feminism and Postmodernist Theory," from *Signs: Journal of Women in Culture and Society* 26.2 (2001). Copyright © 2001 The University of Chicago Press. Reprinted with permission.

Malika Ndlovu, "Out of Now-here," from *Agenda* 57 (November 2003). Reprinted with the permission of the author.

INDEX